Way Beyond Bigness

The Need for a Watershed Architecture

Derek Hoeferlin

APPLIED RESEARCH +DESIGN

AR+D PUBLISHING
Published by Applied Research and Design Publishing, an imprint of ORO Editions.
Gordon Goff: Publisher

www.appliedresearchanddesign.com
info@appliedresearchanddesign.com

Graphic Design: Pablo Mandel, Silvina Synaj / CircularStudio
Text and Images: Derek Hoeferlin and contributors
AR+D managing Editor: Kirby Anderson
Layout concept: Derek Hoeferlin, portions inspired by his WashU College of Architecture ARCHIDAM 3.0 studio

10 9 8 7 6 5 4 3 2 1 First Edition

Library of Congress data available upon request. World Rights: Available

ISBN: 978-1-940743-59-2

Color Separations and Printing: ORO Group Ltd.
Printed in Singapore.

International Distribution: www.appliedresearchanddesign.com/distribution

ORO Editions makes a continuous effort to minimize the overall carbon footprint of its publications. As part of this goal, ORO Editions, in association with Global ReLeaf, arranges to plant trees to replace those used in the manufacturing of the paper produced for its books. Global ReLeaf is an international campaign run by American Forests, one of the world's oldest nonprofit conservation organizations. Global ReLeaf is American Forests' education and action program that helps individuals, organizations, agencies, and corporations improve the local and global environment by planting and caring for trees.

Cover image: Fort Peck Spillway, Missouri River, Montana, 2018 (image credit: Derek Hoeferlin)

for Max & Jake

What About Designers?

We are talking about a multifaceted global search that will require the cooperation of hydrologists, chemists, biologists, engineers, geologists, and environmentalists, as well as farmers, legislators, medical specialists, and an informed public.

— Augusta Goldin, "The First of Things is Water" in Water: Too Much, Too Little, Too Polluted, 1983

Fort Peck Spillway, Missouri River, Montana, 2018 (image credit: Derek Hoeferlin)

Cypress tree in high Mississippi River stage, St. Louis, Missouri, 2013 (image credit: Derek Hoeferlin)

Contents

Foreword (Margarita Jover) / 8

Acknowledgements / 12

Introduction Bigness, Katrina, Conflict, Hybridity & Audience / 18

Backstory "from Times Beach..." / 32

Definintions Watershed, Architecture & Way Beyond Bigness / 44

Appreciate + Analyze [A+A] / 53

Description (Anthony Acciavatti) / 55

Why the Mississippi, Mekong, & Rhine? / 62

Who Manages the River Basins? / 66

Mississippi, Mekong, and Rhine River Basin Atlas / 84
(with Jess Vanecek, Paul Wu, Chenyu Zhang)

Mississippi River Basin & the World / 86

Missouri River Basin / 96
Erasure (Kees Lokman) / 121
Scar (Meghan Kirkwood) / 132

Upper Mississippi, Ohio, & Tennessee River Basins / 144
Reconnection (Chuck Theiling) / 169
Depth (Jesse Vogler) / 183
Between (Jennifer Colten) / 196

Above (with Jess Vanecek) / 199

Lower Mississippi & Arkansas-White-Red River Basins / 202
Splitting (Forbes Lipschitz & Justine Holzman) / 227
Shifting (Alex Kolker) / 239

Mekong River Basin & the World / 250
Development (Dorothy Tang) / 260
Balance (Palakorn Chanbanyong & Simon Krohn) / 344
Adapt (Shelby Elizabeth Doyle) / 355
Monitor (Duong Van Ni) / 366

Rhine River Basin & the World / 378
Transform (Han Meyer) / 388
Revive (Robbert de Koning & Dale Morris) / 451

Speculate + Synthesize [S+S] /469

Context (Ian Caine) / 471

from the Big Six to the Birds Foot / 487
(with Jonathan Stitelman, Allison Méndez, L. Irene Compadre & Chad Fisk)

from the Third Pole to the Nine Dragons / 500
(with Jess Vanecek & Rob Birch)

from the Rheinquelle to the Leo Hollandicus / 518
(with Jess Vanecek, Paul Wu, & Han Meyer)

Collaborate + Catalyze [C+C] / 525

Advocacy (Neeraj Bhatia) / 527

Public Lab River Rat Pack / 539
(with Washington University in St. Louis)

Flood—Fight—Fail / 552

Territories—Watersheds—Infrastructures / 557
(with Washington University in St. Louis)

Tracing Our Mississippi / 584
(with Washington University in St. Louis)

Afterword "...to Quarantine Island" ("Big Muddy" Mike Clark) / 589

Foreword

Margarita Jover

Way Beyond Bigness: The Need for a Watershed Architecture is a book on an essential contemporary topic: large-scale urban thinking. It is part of a lineage of the awakening of architecture's discipline to the subject of large scale after five decades of progressive shrinking to smaller scales and the economically efficient production of buildings. In this sense, it is a book to celebrate. It offers a methodology for designers to urgently address the collective destiny of the built environment and its intertwined political, ecological, and social crises. In the United States, neoliberalism is hegemonic, which means it is an economic system and a cultural framework that implies suspicion of *collectivism* [1] and the public sphere while glorifying the market, the private sphere, and the individual. Added to this neoliberal hegemony is the citizen's distrust of large-scale national investments in the territory due to its historical tendency to favor the private interests of big companies and powerful individuals over the rest. This national investment's legacy makes it difficult to promote large-scale projects from the top, even if they genuinely seek the common good, without generating a societal distrust.

Before the advent of neoliberalism and the acceptance of the market as the main leading force for the design and construction of the city, large-scale territorial and urban design decisions were inscribed into a public-private legal practice called urbanism. The word *urbanism,*[2] coined during the mid-19th century in Europe, was the result of the search for new urban models and the construction of a new discipline to accommodate the transition from organic to *industrial societies*.[3] Reimagined urban models allowed the overcoming of the social and ecological crises of the crowded and polluted cities of emergent industrial societies, while facilitating their spiritual, physical, and economic flourishing. Successful deployment of urbanism occurred when collaboration between private actors looking after maximizing profit was in friction with strong public actors looking at increasing social welfare across all social classes while supporting ecological needs. However, this successful deployment of urbanism did not always take place.

Nineteenth-century urbanism emerged as a set of rules and methodologies similar to this book's spirit. Several architects, planners, landscape architects, and philanthropists advocating for reforms and new city models used different types of urbanism to respond to unregulated industrial cities and associated degradation. Thinkers such as Charles Fourier, William Morris, Otto Wagner, Patrick Geddes, Baron Haussman, Ildefons Cerda, Frederik Law Olmsted, Hendrik Petrus Berlage, Edwin Lutyens, and Tony Garnier, among many others, wrote about cities and designed parts of them. There were significant differences in each methodological approach and output, ranging from isolated utopian communities to the bulldozing of old cities or new cities' design. However, despite differences, the standard tread was the ambition to transform the medieval city model to accommodate population growth and industrialization.

This 19th-century lineage of urban thinkers on a large territorial and urban scale had its last cultural manifestations during the Modern Movement, when architectural culture organized the International Congresses of Modern Architecture (CIAM 1928–1959). Confident optimism in technology and sciences, mass production, and new aesthetic values characterized this period. Working-class upheavals and their increased societal influence and power allowed progressive universal suffrage, universal primary education, decent wages, and regulation of working hours. Social ambitions of equality in accessing resources for life and a more isotropic distribution of wealth in the urban context are often part of modernity's projects in Europe. Architectural projects, manifestoes, and regulations that came about in that period produced significant innovations and societal improvements. However, after this period of heroic modernity, the social and economic instability of the 1930s led to World War II, with more than 60 million deaths worldwide. Post–World War II reconstruction in Europe took time and used prewar modern principles that included societal ambitions of redistribution and new technologies and materials in the context of socialist democracies. Postwar United States took on modernity principles that were adapted and often cleansed of social ambitions. The *suburban model* of separated functions in the territory[4] took the lead, leaving behind the mixed-use city model with better social and ecological performances. The suburban model is predatory, with high levels of energy, land, and resource consumption, but it is successful for being a more efficient model of driving capital accumulation.

The giant American war industry—which saved Europe from tyranny and fascism—mutated and integrated into industrial societal dynamics creating new markets for its survival and subsequent growth. Today the *industry of war* is one of the major causes of climate change, but it runs unquestioned.[5] Consumerism, suburbanization, and a culture of abundant energy coincided with *postmodernity*[6] in architecture and planning, which meant skepticism towards grand narratives and a focus on building forms and their cultural meaning. During the 1980s, the discipline became an avoidable friction to capital accumulation and retreated into the building scale. In the meantime, market dynamics took on the logic of urbanization, increasingly faster and larger in scale, without social and ecological considerations, despite many American voices warning of ecological degradation while clamoring for social rights.[7] Rem Koolhaas, the last hero of modernity, surrenders to the seductive effects of unregulated globalization, and the homogenization of urbanization dynamics described in his text "Generic City" (1995).

The good news is that urbanism is coming back with renewed tools and objectives, and this book is part of this phenomenon. Forest urbanism, water urbanism, gender urbanism, and new urbanism are among the few emerging in the last decades. Each makes an emphasis on what seems to be missing in the way we develop cities today. Simultaneously, the sciences of ecology that studied ecosystems separated from humans have realized that everything on earth is affected by humans. Today, urban ecology is a new field wherein coevolutionary principles between humans and nonhumans, living and nonliving systems, are studied using system thinking theories. Recovering the social ambitions of early modernity and analyzing the cities as urban ecosystems can be the base for upgrading urbanism as a practice. Because the causes of climate change come down to urban models and lifestyles, the role of urban designers is paramount.

This book is the product of a long, vital journey led by the author and an ample network of collaborators. The account of experiences starts and ends at the Mississippi Rivers Watershed's geographical center in the midwestern region of St. Louis, Missouri, located just south of the confluence of the Mississippi and Missouri Rivers. With an eminent educational purpose, the book stands for a methodology for designers to embark on large-scale urban-territorial reforms to adapt and reverse climate change. The methodological content is divided into three parts: Appreciate + Analyze [A+A], Speculate + Synthesize [S+S], and Collaborate + Catalyze [C+C]—a clear and realistic three-step process that can be practiced with feedback loops when well used in design schools and the real world. First of the three parts [A+A] contains an atlas comparing three major global watersheds (more technically referred to as "river basins"): Mississippi, Mekong, and Rhine. Each river systematically covers four interdependent scales: continent, territory, region, and zone. Along with impressive and beautiful graphs and maps, reflections and potentials emerge when comparing watersheds' governance bodies, technologies, and cultural practices. Contemporary voices peppered within offer a kaleidoscopic understanding of the territories' complex realities cleverly framed within watersheds instead of countries or states. The second of the three parts [S+S] presents speculations on plausible futures within each watershed. Design speculations are conceived to engage the political scale and go beyond superficial philanthropy. The third of the three parts [C+C] accounts for advocacy which describes the difficulties for meaningful engagement in today's contemporary context marked by growing social inequalities and loose democracy. As polyhedric as it is, the book also offers a collection of breathtaking photographs of these watersheds and associated landscapes with historical photos that structure its narrative graphically.

The crises we face today demand plans and methodologies that will be ready when society is ready to use them. An organized counterculture with alternative methodologies and values is needed to enact alternative ways of inhabiting the planet. We cannot afford to fear the large-scale plans operating at the interface between top and down. Moreover, the counterculture should operate as a friction-force to capitalistic dynamics. It can present alternatives to unquestioned hegemonic urbanization dynamics, which operate today with predatory urban models, and whose only purpose is to produce capital for increasingly the few. This celebrated book seems to belong to this much-needed counterculture. Enjoy!

1. Odd Arne Westad, *The Global Cold War: Third World Interventions and the Making of Our Times* (Cambridge: Cambridge University Press, 2007).
2. Ildefons Cerda, *General Theory of Urbanization 1867* (Barcelona: ActarPublishers, 2017).
3. E. A. Wrigley, *The Path to Sustained Growth: England's Transition from an Organic Economy to an Industrial Revolution*, (Cambridge: Cambridge University Press, 2016).
4. *Athens Charter 1933*, Le Corbusier, the functional city of separated functions.
5. Christophe Bonneuil and Jean-Batiste Fressoz, *The Shock of the Anthropocene: The Earth, History and Us* (Brooklyn, London: Verso, 2016).
6. Jean-Francois Lyotard, *The Postmodern Condition: A Report on Knowledge* (Minneapolis: University of Minnesota Press, 1979).
7. Rachel Carson, *Silent Spring*, 1962; Ian McHarg, Baltimore and Washington Plans, 1963–65; Lewis Mumford, *The Myth of the Machine* 1968–70; Club of Rome, *The Limits to Growth Report*, 1972.

Singelgracht Canal, Amsterdam, Netherlands, 2012 (image credit: Derek Hoeferlin)

Acknowledgments

This project has taken quite some time to complete, too long really. The list of those to thank that encompasses intellectual, financial, structural, and maybe most importantly, emotional support, is humbling to say the least. My sincere apologies in advance if there are those of you who I have left out, particularly those who have helped me along the way on my several field-research trips in the Mississippi, Mekong, and Rhine River Basins.

First and foremost, I must give a big shout out to Washington University in St. Louis, my employer, and the institution that has primarily supported this effort, both financially and infrastructurally. More specifically, the Sam Fox School of Design & Visual Arts, where I have been afforded the opportunity to teach since 2005, has been incredible—especially since the leadership, my colleagues and my students have given me so much academic freedom, and dare I say, too long an academic leash, to both push the boundaries of what architecture can be, and to test out the ideas in this book. There are so many past and present colleagues to acknowledge at WashU. This of course begins with the leadership: Sam Fox School Dean Carmon Colangelo and Associate Dean Nicole Allen, particularly for awarding me multiple "Sam Fox School Creative Activity Research Grants" to support this research; and to Bruce Lindsey, the former Dean of the College of Architecture & Graduate School of Architecture & Urban Design, and to Heather Woofter, the current Director, for their consistent encouragement, patience, and support structure. Current and past WashU faculty I want to thank include: first and foremost, Ian Caine (now at University of Texas San Antonio)—for if it was not for my collaborative designs with Ian, I would not be able to present the "Speculate + Synthesize" portion of this book; to Jane Wolff (now at University of Toronto, as well as Elise Shelley at U of T) for our collaborative "Gutter to Gulf" advocacy efforts in New Orleans; to Eric Mumford for inviting me multiple times to present my research in his classes, and for his important critiques, especially for asking me "why does this matter for architecture?"; to John Hoal for our collaborative efforts in New Orleans and St. Louis, particularly our "MISI-ZIIBI" research for climate adaptation strategies; to Stephen Leet, Adrian Luchini, Phil Holden, and Sung Ho Him for comic relief; to Beth Martin, T. R. Kidder, Brent Williams, and Steve Braude for trusting me to present my design-based thoughts to "non-design" students in their climate change–based courses over the years; to Chandler Ahrens, Andrew Cruse, Paul Donnelly, Liane Hancock, Jen Maigret, Peter MacKeith, and Hongxi Yin for being patient past office mates. Although there are countless current and past WashU faculty to thank, I want to point out those who have either directly engaged my research, have provided important critiques of it, or just as importantly, have questioned and challenged its credibility. These include: Michael Allen, Rod Barnett, Matthew Bernstine, Elena Cánovas, Marcus Carter, Kristi Dykema Cheramie, Jennifer Colten, L. Irene Compadre, Gia Daskalakis, Eric Ellingsen, Ben Fehrmann, Matthew Fluharty, Patty Heyda, Dorothée Imbert, Carlos Jimenez, Meghan Kirkwood, Liz Kramer, Ersela Kripa, Gavin Kroeber, Erik L'Heureux, Kees Lokman, Emiliano Lopez, Gay Lorberbaum, Igor Marjanovic, Alexandra Mei, Allison Méndez, Robert McCarter, Stephen Mueller, Lynn Peemoeller, Mónica Rivera, David Ruy, Linda Samuels, Buzz Spector, Micah Stanek, Stan Strembicki, Jonathan Stitelman, Fred Stivers, Alex Wall, Michael Willis, Constance Vale, Jesse Vogler, Enrique Von Rohr, Kotchakorn Voraakhom, Natalie Yates, and Jennifer Yoos. I also want to give a special thanks to current and former staff at the Sam Fox School, including Ellen Bailey, Audrey Treece, Mandy Wortmann, Bobbe Winters, Karen Swiney, Katherine Welsch, Stephanie Schlaifer, Audrey Wescott, Kathleen O'Donnell, Leland Orvis, the late Sandy Brennen, Amanda Bowles, and Daphne Ellis; and, to Liam Otten, WashU Arts and Humanities News Director, for the many stories he has written about my research over the years. Additional support through grants has come from WashU's Provost Office COVID Faculty Support Initiative, and the International Center for Energy, Environment & Sustainability (InCEES), with particular thanks to David Fike, Chad Henry, and Himradi Pakrasi. Finally, and probably most importantly, I want to thank the hundreds of amazing students I have had the honor of teaching over the last 15-plus years (in case you don't know, WashU students are awesome!), and several research assistants, especially those who have gone on to collaborate with me on this project. These include: my primary research assistants Jess Vanecek and Paul Wu, who you will see have left indelible marks both graphically and textually throughout this book, as well as Chenyu Zhang, Lex Agnew, Caroline Amstutz, Rob Birch, Emily Chen, Christian Clerc, Lindsey Compeaux, Chad Fisk, Joel León, Brandon Hall, Michael Heller, Qingshan Hu, Weicong Huang, Andy Lee, John Monnat, Nathan Stanfield, Nate Smith, Wendy Stradley, and Tiffin Thompson. And although she did not contribute directly to this book, I want to specially recognize one of my very first WashU students, Jess Garz, for all of the early support during our challenging efforts in post-Katrina New Orleans, and all the great phone calls afterwards.

Outside of WashU, there are just as many to be grateful to for support. Above all, there is architect David Waggonner from New Orleans, my part former employer and part honorary big brother. The content of this book is in debt to David's "Dutch Dialogues" and water management advocacy efforts in New Orleans. I cannot thank David enough. Also to thank at Waggonner & Ball's office, past and present, for assistance with this research are Mac Ball, Aron Chang, Rami Diaz, as well as two of my former, and best, WashU students—John Kleinschmidt and Andy Sternad. Building upon David Waggonner's support, I want to thank all of the members of the "Dutch Dialogues" workshops, most importantly Dale Morris, who at the time of "DD" was the Senior Economist at the Royal Netherlands Embassy, Washington DC, and later went on to help facilitate my "NL-STL-NO" symposium and "MISI-ZIIBI" workshops, the latter two held at WashU. For years following the "Dutch Dialogues" efforts, I've remained in close contact with several "DD" members who have helped me on my research trips in the Netherlands, particularly my cool friend, Stijn Koole, for accompanying me on fieldwork research on the Rhine and for being a sharp critic, as well as Annebeth Loois, Robbert de Koning, Han Meyer, Steven Slabbers, and many others. Also in the Rhine River Basin, gratitude goes to Tabea Stötter and Laura Gangi at the International Commission for the Protection of the Rhine (ICPR) in Koblenz, Germany; Kai Kempmann at the Central Commission for the Navigation of the Rhine (CCNR) in Strasbourg, France; and, Marlene Willkomm in Cologne, Germany, all for taking the time to provide important information and tours about their efforts.

Back in New Orleans and Louisiana, special thanks go to my alma mater, Tulane School of Architecture, for always being a welcoming host to my students and me. This includes past and present faculty: especially Dan Etheridge and Byron Mouton, as well as Ila Berman, Richard Campanella, Margarita Jover, Judith Kinnard, John Klingman, Carol Reese, Emilie Taylor, Ann Yoachim, the current Dean Iñaki Alday, and former Dean Ken Schwartz. Appreciation goes to all of the community groups, stakeholders, and activists in New Orleans for being so gracious with their precious time. Special thanks to Shannon Dosemagen and Stevie Lewis from "Public Lab" and Scott Eustis from "Gulf Restoration Network" for introducing me to the magic that big red balloons (not drones) provide in field documentation; and to Dr. Jelagot Cheruiyot and her graduate assistants from Tulane's Department of Ecology & Evolutionary Biology. Also important to recognize, from when they were at Louisiana State University, are Elizabeth Mossop and Jeff Carney, as well as Clint Wilson and the team at the LSU Center for River Studies in Baton Rouge for giving my students and me multiple tours of the giant river model.

And then there's the indelible mark made on me by my professors at Yale School of Architecture, who, during my postprofessional studies there, broadened my perspective on what architecture can be, and this is especially the case with Keller Easterling and Mario Gooden.

Back in St. Louis, I want to point out two important partnerships: one with the river rats over at Big Muddy Adventures for all the amazing paddling trips on the Mississippi and Missouri Rivers, especially "Big Muddy" Mike Clark and Roo Yawitz. Just as important to acknowledge for crucial support, which included the granting of important access to critical infrastructure sites over the years, is the U.S. Army Corps of Engineers St. Louis District, including Eddie Brauer, Colonel Bryan K. Sizemore, Charlie Deutsch, Ben McGuire, and Lane Richter, among others. Additionally, at the USACE is Chuck Theiling, who I've gone on to become close friends with, and who's accompanied my students and me on multiple field trips and kayak tours on the Mississippi's backwaters.

For my multiple research trips to the Mekong, many thanks to Dr. Duong Van Ni from Can Tho University. If it were not for Dr. Ni and his trusty assistants, translators, and drivers, I would not have been able to pull off my most ambitious research trip throughout the Mekong Delta in 2011, a trip that eventually led me up to the border of Cambodia and Laos on the Mekong River. Also in the Mekong River Basin, I want to thank the Mekong River Commission and its assistants, both for offering me the opportunity to present my research in Vientiane, Laos, as well as in helping to facilitate access and a tour of the Xayaburi Dam construction site on the Mekong River in 2019.

Additional support over the years has come from invitations to test out my research through presentations and workshops at various venues. This includes: Haus der Kulturen der Welt's *Mississippi: An Anthropocene River and The Current* exhibition (Neli Wagner, Katrin Klingan, Fiona Shipwright, and others); Exhibit Columbus *New Middles* exhibition (Iker Gil, Mimi Zeiger, Anne Surak, Janice Shimizu, Richard McCoy, and many others); Pulitzer Arts Foundation's "Your Mississippi" event (Kristin Fleischmann Brewer, Joshua Stulen); Missouri Historical Society "Valuing the River" speaker series (David Lobbig, Lindsay Newton); Great River Passage Conservancy "Virtual Speaker Series" (Mary deLaittre, Angie Tillges); St. Louis Art Museum's *Navigating the River* film series; *Art + Landscape STL* exhibition (Gavin Kroeber); Chicago Humanities Festival "Speculative Infrastructure" symposium (Chicago Freshwater Lab, Rachel Havrelock); U.S. Green Building Council St. Louis Chapter "Water Justice" symposium (Hannah Roth, Hope Gribble, Nick Redding, Colin Wellenkamp); American Institute of Architects (AIA) St. Louis Chapter continuing education seminars; multiple Association of Collegiate Schools of Architecture (ACSA) conferences; St. Louis Earth Day keynote lecture, 2014; "Chicago Expander Shared Waters Panel" (Iker Gil, Joshua Stein); TU Delft's "New Urban Configurations" Conference; Environmental Design & Research Association (EDRA) conferences; Chulalongkorn University; University of Texas San Antonio; Harvard Graduate School of Design's "A Forum for Chasing the City"; Tulane School of Architecture's "River and Coastal Urbanism Dialogues"; Dredge Research Collective (Rob Holmes, Brett Milligan, Gena Wirth and team); USACE River Resources Action Team barge trips; "Water Futures" workshops in Rotterdam, Netherlands and Brisbane, Australia (James Davidson, Sam Bowstead, Piet Filet, and others); "Living Earth Collaborative" speaker series (Jonothan Losos/WashU, Iván Jiménez/Missouri Botanical Garden); "River Soundings" conference (Rachel Bartels); and "DELTAS 2013" conference in Ho Chi Minh City, Vietnam (America's Wetland Foundation).

I also need to recognize several publications that have acted as important peer-reviewed and editorial platforms foreshadowing the content of this book, including: *Chasing the*

City (Joshua Nason and Jeffrey Nesbit, editors); *Journal of Architectural Education* "H2O"-themed issue (Alpa Nawre and Carey Clouse, editors); *New Orleans Under Reconstruction: The Crisis of Planning* (Carol Reese, the late Michael Sorkin, Anthony Fontenot, editors); *Scenario Journal* (Stephanie Carlisle & Nicholas Pevzner, editors); *Labour Journal* (David Elashi, Micah Macaulay, Rory Thibault, editors); *MAS Context* (Iker Gil, editor) and *The Anthropocene Review* themed issue "The Mississippi" (Christoph Rosol, Thomas Turnbull, Jürgen Renn, editors).

It goes without saying that I am so appreciative for my publishers and the team at Applied Research + Design and ORO: Gordon Goff, Kirby Anderson, Jake Anderson, and others, as well the graphic design team at CircularStudio led by Pablo Mandel, especially for all of their patience with me getting them the work!

Lastly, and it again goes without saying, I am in debt to the amazing cast of contributors for this book, and to the much broader network spread across these incredible river basins. The people I have met along the way, many by chance, are foundational for what follows in this project.

And of course, if it weren't for family, none of this could be possible. To my Mom (Madonna), for the empathetic words of encouragement and optimism throughout the years. To my Dad (Jim), for being my first and consistent teacher about design for all. To my sister (Andrea), for showing me the importance of sticking to fierce belief systems. To my wife, Caron, for always being patient with me, for always being a reality check, and for forgiving me for dragging her on those trips to the dams on the Missouri and Tennessee Rivers, or that time when we attempted to drive up the "foothills of the Himalayas" along the Yangtze River during the onset of monsoon season, and almost got killed in a rockslide. That's a whole other story! To my two sons, Max and Jake, for teaching me to be young again and making me smile every day. And to my dogs along the way—Jack, Rocket, Saturn and Rhea—for barking at me to go on two walks a day to make sure I stretched my legs and cleared my head.

Thank you, Mississippi, Mekong, and Rhine.
Thank you, St. Louis and New Orleans.
And it goes without saying, thank you WATER, our collective gift.

—Derek Hoeferlin

Ascending the silos at Continental Cement Company, St. Louis, Missouri, 2019 (image credit: Derek Hoeferlin)

Confluence of the Mississippi and Ohio Rivers, Cairo, Illinois, 2018 (image credit: Derek Hoeferlin)

Introduction

Designers, Bigness, Katrina, Conflict, Hybridity, & Audience

All my daydreams are disasters
She's the one I think I love
Rivers burn and then run backwards
For her, that's enough.[1]

— Uncle Tupelo, "New Madrid" 1993

Bigness

Implies a web of umbilical cords to other disciplines whose performance is as critical as the architect's: like mountain climbers tied together by life-saving ropes, the makers of Bigness are a team… Beyond signature, Bigness surrenders to technologies; to engineers, contractors, manufacturers; to politics; to others. It promises architecture a kind of post-heroic status—a realignment with neutrality.(2)

- Rem Koolhaas, "Bigness, or the problem of Large," in S,M,L,XL, 1995

Katrina

Early in the morning on August 29, 2005, Hurricane Katrina struck the Gulf Coast of the United States. When the storm made landfall, it had a Category 3 rating on the Saffir-Simpson Hurricane Scale—it brought sustained winds of 100 to 140 miles per hour—and stretched some 400 miles across. The storm itself did a great deal of damage, but its aftermath was catastrophic. Levee breaches led to massive flooding, and many people charged that the federal government was slow to meet the needs of the people affected by the storm. Hundreds of thousands of people in Louisiana, Mississippi and Alabama were displaced from their homes, and experts estimate that Katrina caused more than $100 billion in damage.(3)

- https://www.history.com/topics/natural-disasters-and-environment/hurricane-katrina

New Orleans, Louisiana, 2005 (image credit: Derek Hoeferlin)

For context, two moments have led me to question my role as an architect in relation to larger, contemporary issues of the built environment, and by extension why architects, as well as other design disciplines, should be part of such efforts. At first glance, both may seem an odd couple, and a borderline, let alone superficial way to theoretically underpin a book about water-based design. But in all honesty, both are how I came to this body of work, so it's kind of personal, and please take it as it is.

1) The publication of *S,M,L,XL* in October 1995, featuring Rem Koolhaas's manifesto *Bigness, or the problem of Large*.

2) The landfall of Hurricane Katrina just outside of New Orleans in August 2005.

In "Bigness," Rem Koolhaas specifically targeted architects to surrender to complex modes of technologies, politics, and economics. When the essay was published in 1995, it was set within *emerging* issues of globalization in the 1990s, that is emerging at least to the architecture discipline. At the time, I was an architecture student and fascinated by Koolhaas's provocation, albeit with naïveté. As he states in the above quote, Koolhaas challenged "the makers of Bigness [to be] a team." But as time has passed and as I have moved through my academic and professional career, I now wonder if Koolhaas was actually charging architects to work outside of the scale of a building, or just to better work with consultants to design bigger and bigger buildings. And bigger buildings that ultimately could consume the notion of the city, or become the city? All the while, set within a globalized, neoliberal economic context? I argue that we (architects, landscape architects, urban designers) need to go "Way Beyond" what I believe can be regarded in our contemporary context as a myopic definition of "Bigness."

Rather, specific to the themes I present in this book, the contemporary question to ask is: Why should the term architecture, or any design discipline for that matter, be part of river basin–scale decision-making? And ones, particularly in the United States, that are designed both in policy and physicality through engineered forms?

In order to address the complex challenges impacting multiple scales set within river basin contexts, I believe a new synthetic notion of architecture, as well as landscape architecture, urban design, and other design disciplines needs to emerge and work far beyond an envelope of a building, or a definition of a landscape, or a boundary of a city, or a predominantly engineered system.

Designers need to be part of a new type of interdisciplinary, trans-boundary, decision-making design table. This table is a messy one for sure, and one rife with conflict. But designers possess a particularly unique toolset to negotiate possibilities within such a milieu.

Ten years later, in 2005, Hurricane Katrina catapulted the fields of design into an unprecedented human-altered "natural disaster," and as such, challenged designers to prove their relevance. Although still the costliest "natural disaster" in U.S. history, we would soon realize that Hurricane Katrina was not just a one-off, let alone a disaster specific to the Gulf Coast of the United States, or other coastal contexts for that matter. Since Katrina in 2005, and especially since 2008, frequent extreme weather events and water-related catastrophes in the United States—both coastal and inland—have repeated over and over and over again. Couple this with the accelerating realities of the effects of climate change and crises in the U.S. and elsewhere, and we can only assume that more events will continue relentlessly and with intensity. While Koolhaas does not refer to water in "Bigness," Hurricane Katrina was almost all about water. But both "Bigness" and Katrina are definitely what I define as "watershed," or tipping-point events for the design disciplines, and more selfishly for my research interests as an architect. To repeat, although Koolhaas targeted architecture in "Bigness," I extend this is not limited to the discipline of architecture.

Highlighting U.S. water-based catastrophes since 2005:[4]
(NOTE: these do not include other water-based catastrophes representing lack of water, such as droughts or fires.)

2005: Hurricane Katrina, Gulf Coast ($125 billion USD damage, tied for costliest in U.S. history, 1,833 fatalities)
Hurricane Rita, Gulf Coast ($18.5 billion USD damage, 120 fatalities)
Hurricane Wilma, Florida ($22.4 billion USD damage, 62 fatalities)

2008: Hurricane Gustav, Louisiana ($8 billion USD damage, 153 fatalities)
Hurricane Ike, Texas ($34.8 billion USD damage, 195 fatalities)
Mississippi river spring floods

2010: Deepwater Horizon/BP Oil Spill, Gulf of Mexico (11 fatalities, 1,300 miles of oil covered coastal Louisiana, estimated 800,000 bird fatalities)

2011: "Great" Mississippi River spring floods (largest floods since 1927, 1973, and 1993 floods)
Midwest tornadoes (553 fatalities, second-most since 1925)
Hurricane Irene, Eastern Seaboard ($15.8 billion USD damage, 49 fatalities)

2012: "Superstorm" Sandy, Eastern Seaboard ($62 billion USD damage, 285 fatalities)

2013: Mississippi River spring floods and winter storms

2014: Mississippi River spring floods and winter storms

2016: Mississippi River winter floods

2017: Mississippi River winter floods
Hurricane Irma, Florida ($50 billion USD damage, 134 fatalities)
Hurricane Maria, Puerto Rico ($100 billion USD damage; 3,057 fatalities, unconfirmed)
Hurricane Harvey, Texas ($125 billion USD damage, tied for costliest in U.S. history, 68 fatalities)
(These three hurricanes totaled the costliest cyclone season on record)

2018: Hurricane Florence, North Carolina ($22 billion USD damage, 53 fatalities)
Hurricane Michael, Florida ($25.5 billion USD damage, 59 fatalities)

2019: Mississippi/Missouri Rivers spring and summer floods (second-highest floods on record)

2020: Hurricane Laura (26 fatalities)

2021: Hurricane Ida (115 fatalities)

2022: St. Louis and Kentucky floods (42 fatalities)
Hurricane Ian, Florida (100+ fatalities as of 10/04/2022)

And on and on and on... By extension, these calamities have challenged design disciplines' roles in complicated community, political, and multiscale postdisaster contexts. We are now challenged as designers to step up, and to engage, and to finally get out of our bubbles, both academic and professional ones. But how to do so? Can the academic-professional divide truly remain intact to adequately address such challenges? I contend it cannot. Therefore, this is a dilemma that is "Way Beyond Bigness."

But maybe there's a clue. Can water-based design optimistically engage such "impossible problems," and in doing so, productively offer new possibilities?

Therefore, the following design-research project prioritizes WATER as a transformative agent for the design disciplines, and at multiple scales—what I define as **"Way Beyond Bigness: The Need for a Watershed Architecture."**

As architects, it is our responsibility to APPRECIATE, to SPECULATE and to COLLABORATE regarding the possibilities of how the engagement with water ultimately impacts, and potentially prioritizes, our design decisions. These global fundamentals must reinstate an understanding of the complicated built environments we and all other species share. These are ones we cannot continue to dominate with hard-line and static interventions, but rather ones we should begin to design with adaptive and dynamic negotiations. To do so, architects must become better aware of architecture's trans-scalar relationships—spatially, temporally, and geopolitically. This is not just for architecture's sake, but also, more importantly, for architecture's multiscaled integration with landscape architecture, engineering, infrastructure, urbanism, policy, economy, ecology, law, hydrology, public health, etc.; and ultimately, the larger distribution context of watersheds that all designs inhabit. In other words, the inevitable, and hopefully smarter, next step in the dynamic networking of human manipulated built environments.

Way Beyond Bigness prioritizes two approaches:

1) The understanding of the larger-scale effects of "watersheds" for design decisions. More specifically, how can designing with water and infrastructure integrate best with the built environment?

2) The inevitable, yet resilient, need to adapt to contemporary, tipping-point "watershed" events in time.

Way Beyond Bigness proposes a simple, adaptive framework that utilizes an integrative design-research methodology, structured in the book in three parts:

Appreciate	+	Analyze	[A+A]
Speculate	+	Synthesize	[S+S]
Collaborate	+	Catalyze	[C+C]

Woven throughout the three parts, Way Beyond Bigness attempts to realign watersheds and architecture across multiple:

Scales	(sites to river basins)
Disciplines	(ecologists to economists)
Narratives	(hyperboles to pragmatics)
Venues	(academics to professionals)

This necessary realignment is what I define as "Watershed Architecture [WA]." Given our complex contemporary challenges—specifically in relation to water—current design-research cannot be accomplished by one author, or for that matter, by one architect, landscape architect, or urban designer. Rather, it requires collaborations that oscillate inside and outside typical design disciplines' definitions, breaking down typical professional and academic dichotomies.

Conflict, Hybridity, & Audience

But for Watershed Architecture to succeed, first we need to return to the earlier-mentioned topic of "conflict." Conflicts are difficult positions for designers to comfortably engage. Primarily, what is the designer's role is such water-based problems and "conflict resolution?"

New Orleans, Louisiana, 2005 (image credit: Derek Hoeferlin)

If the architect, landscape architect, or urban designer does intervene, what are the rules of engagement, the appropriate interventions, the legible processes, and the ultimate impacts? The first answer I mention above: these problems cannot be addressed by a single decision-maker, aka, the authority.

This is especially the case when water-based challenges are inherently about conflicts, usually between multiple parties arguing over water resource allocations across geopolitical boundaries. Historically, such conflicts and their resolutions have fallen outside of the design disciplines' influence, which I contend is not productive, and hopefully will be evidenced by the notion of Watershed Architecture I present in this book.

In *Transboundary Water Conflict Resolutions: Substitutes or Complements*, Ahmed Tayia reviews various theories about the management of transboundary water resources "that are shared across political borders, which is henceforth referred to as transboundary water conflicts."[5] Tayia assesses multiple approaches to water conflict resolutions, specifically focused on the disciplines of engineering, economics, political science, and management—the "facilitation of the process of water management."[6] Although the author acknowledges that each of the disciplinary approaches offers specific mechanisms to water conflicts, including allocations, optimizations, the applications of game theory, and political constraints, they have not "resulted in tangible actual practice of transboundary water conflict resolution." [7] The author ends the essay by arguing for "hybrid mechanisms" to integrate multiple approaches, requiring "more collaboration and openness by practitioners to research and academic community."[8] But to be clear, the author (similar to Augusta Goldin's quote at the beginning of the book) never mentions any design disciplines as part of the components to the equation. However, I believe this "hybrid" space is *precisely where the design disciplines can intervene, and where we possess the agency for analyzing, synthesizing, and catalyzing multiple points of views, across multiple scales.* With the possibility of Watershed Architecture, designers can contribute their unique capabilities to offer the beginnings of comprehensive, graphically legible templates for multiple user-groups and stakeholders to debate, and to do so precisely in the space of conflict resolution.

The intended goal of this book advocates for design disciplines to possess new tools to engage a wider audience of river basin management projects, by gaining an objective and more technical perspective on issues with which they may not be familiar. I believe architects, landscape architects, urban designers, and practitioners of other design disciplines can contribute important ideas, both in terms of graphic legibility, as well as important ideas that directly impact the built environment at territorial scales beyond their typical disciplinary definitions and scales. But to do so, designers need to embrace a more technical grounding from other fields working in river basin management. And conversely, these other fields have much to gain from various, more generalist-oriented skill sets that design disciplines bring to promoting a healthier and more adaptive built environment.

Book Overview

The body of work presented in this book represents a selection of efforts, most of which are ongoing, that have been conducted with amazing professional colleagues, along with wonderful faculty, research assistants, and students from Washington University in St. Louis. It is important to note that this work at WashU has been deeply informed by additional institutional collaborations since 2005, including the University of Toronto Department of Landscape Architecture, Tulane University School of Architecture in New Orleans, and Massachusetts Institute of Technology Department of Urban Studies and Planning, as well as with Waggonner & Ball Architects in New Orleans. Current and past community collaborations represented in this book include unique efforts with the U.S. Army Corps of Engineers St. Louis District, Big Muddy Adventures (St. Louis), Public Lab (Louisiana), Continental Cement Company (St. Louis), Pulitzer Arts Foundation (St. Louis), Haus der Kulturen der Welt (Berlin), Exhibit Columbus (Columbus, Indiana), and Granite City Arts and Design District (G-CADD, Granite City, Illinois), among many others. Since my primary home and workplace is in St. Louis, along with prior and continuing work in New Orleans, the bulk of the work in the book ***begins, prioritizes, and ends, in the Mississippi River Basin***. But this work is critically understood comparatively with two other major river basins: the Mekong and the Rhine.

As mentioned above, I structure the book in three interrelated parts. And to be clear, although I present the three parts in order as the book form dictates, they are not meant to be linear. For instance, sometimes collaboration or speculation comes first,

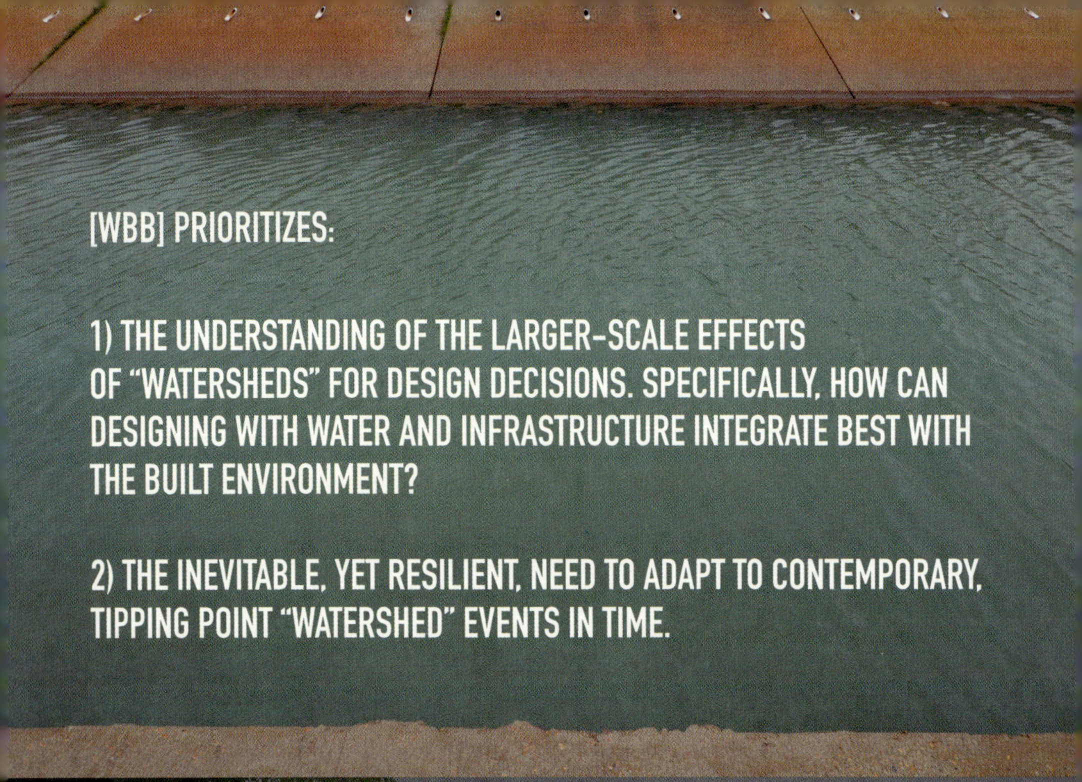

[WBB] PRIORITIZES:

1) THE UNDERSTANDING OF THE LARGER-SCALE EFFECTS OF "WATERSHEDS" FOR DESIGN DECISIONS. SPECIFICALLY, HOW CAN DESIGNING WITH WATER AND INFRASTRUCTURE INTEGRATE BEST WITH THE BUILT ENVIRONMENT?

2) THE INEVITABLE, YET RESILIENT, NEED TO ADAPT TO CONTEMPORARY, TIPPING POINT "WATERSHED" EVENTS IN TIME.

[WBB]
PROPOSES A SIMPLE, ADAPTIVE FRAMEWORK THAT UTILIZES AN INTEGRATIVE DESIGN-RESEARCH METHODOLOGY, STRUCTURED IN 3 PARTS:

APPRECIATE + ANALYZE [A+A]
SPECULATE + SYNTHESIZE [S+S]
COLLABORATE + CATALYZE [C+C]

Monticello drainage canal, Orleans and Jefferson Parish boundary, Louisiana, 2011
(BOTTOM) Sluice gate managing fresh and saline balances, Mekong Delta, Vietnam, 2011
(image credit: Derek Hoeferlin)

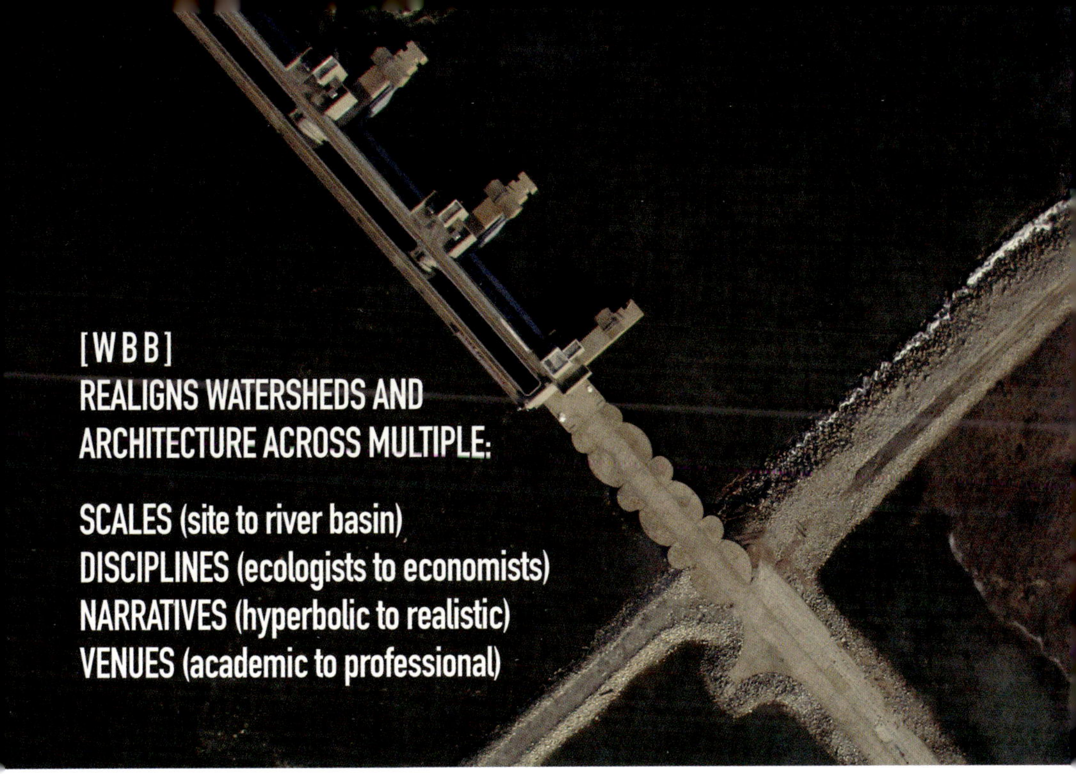

Melvin Price Locks & Dam, West Alton, Missouri, 2016 (image credit: Public Lab River Rat Pack)

leading towards addressing needed gaps in analyses. I first contextualize these three parts with my own personal backstory, as well as elaborating on the definitions and key themes addressed above. All of this is bracketed by a foreword from the architect/landscape architect/urbanist Margarita Jover, and an afterword by the educator/river rat guide "Big Muddy" Mike Clark.

My contributions are intentionally hybridized. I represent the work primarily as a mixture across orthographic analytical drawings, fieldwork photography, speculative designs, and alternative platforms and models for community-engaged efforts. While I support all of the work with explanatory texts, my textual contributions are purposely supplementary in scope. To be honest, my interests lie in the intersection between various modes of representation—particularly drawing, photography, and human-scaled installations. To provide more substantial textual support, I underpin and deeply inform my work with external contributions from several colleagues of mine whom I highly admire, and with most of whom I have directly collaborated. These experts represent an important interdisciplinary cross-section for contemporary water-based research and design, and their particular contributions far exceed my expertise on many matters. I do not say the following lightly: I regard their efforts as some of the most critical contributions to our water-based challenges at this time, and across the globe. And of course, there are many more that I wish I had the space to include in this book. However, since the scope of the book is spread across vast territories and millions and millions of acres, these contributions are in no way comprehensive. Rather, they are carefully curated snapshots. I am the first to admit that there are still many gaps I have neglected to address or to include. The thoughtful contributions range from critical essays, to experimental projects, to photographic journeys, and to interactive dialogues. They provide portals into very focused and particular interventions in each of the three river basins. And I selected them because I believe they are unconventional alternatives to the status quo of river management practices. They include architects, artists, cartographers, ecologists, economists, educators, engineers, historians, landscape architects, lawyers, lobbyists, photographers, scientists, urban designers, and of course … river rats. I wanted to be sure to include important, and sometimes contrarian, points of view that are outside of design disciplines too!

For the three sections of the book, I first provide a brief introduction to the content of each section and then for each section of the book I ask accomplished experts in their own right to introduce and theoretically frame each one. Appreciate + Analyze is introduced by the historian/cartographer/architect Anthony Acciavatti. Speculate + Synthesize is introduced by the architect/urban designer Ian Caine. And Collaborate + Catalyze is introduced by the architect/urban designer Neeraj Bhatia. After each introductory essay, sections purposely follow different content-driven paths.

In Part One, Appreciate + Analyze, after Anthony Acciavatti's introductory essay "Description," I introduce why I am studying the Mississippi, Mekong, and Rhine River Basins and hypothesize—simplistically—the current state of development for each river basin. Through flowcharts and diagrams, I untangle, or maybe retangle, the overall management structures of each basin and then diagram key metrics of each comparatively. These metrics include lengths, areas, populations, urbanizations, densities, territories, tributaries, volumes, and topographies for each river basin. Again, I need to emphasize that these metrics are in no way comprehensive. Rather, they lay the framework for the extensive atlases that follow. The atlases represent the bulk of my work highlighted in this first section, as well as the book. In the atlases, I present each river basin atlas at five scales: world, continent, territory, region, and zone. Each scale is drawn the same for each river basin. Obviously, it becomes clear that the Rhine is smaller than the Mekong, and the Mekong is smaller than the Mississippi. Interlaced throughout the atlases are the guest contributions from experts conducting particular efforts, depending on scales. Each essay has a single word title encompassing the overall theme for said piece. Each River Basin Atlas ends with a series of my photographs organized under key themes addressed in each of the scales in addition to the guest essays. These photographs, as well as the majority of others throughout the book, represent my multiple field documentation trips, too many to count in fact, to each of the river basins over the last 15 years.

In the Mississippi River Basin Atlas, the essays highlight efforts at multiple scales, including: 1) Missouri River Basin, 2) Upper Mississippi/Ohio/Tennessee River Basins and 3) Lower Mississippi/Arkansas-White-Red River Basins.

For the Missouri River Basin, which is by far the largest of the territory scales, contributors include photographer Meghan Kirkwood and landscape architect Kees Lokman. In Lokman's essay "Erasure," he examines the double stresses of climate change and climate justice, particularly on indigenous lands, as a result of the large-scale construction of dams along the Missouri River. In Kirkwood's essay "Scar," she documents the traces of the Dakota Access Pipeline and its impacts on various land uses and landscapes throughout the Missouri via text and revealing photographs.

For the Upper Mississippi/Ohio/Tennessee River Basins, contributors include ecologist Chuck Theiling, artist/designer Jesse Vogler, photographer Jennifer Colten, and a drone photograph piece by Jess Vanecek and me. Each of these focuses on particular zones in the Upper Mississippi River Basin portion of this territorial scale. In Theiling's essay "Reconnection," he explains various wetland restoration efforts he has been part of in coordination with the U.S. Army Corps of Engineers and local farmers and landowners in the "pooled" portions of the Upper Mississippi River. In Vogler's essay "Depth," he asks us to comprehend what is beneath the surface of the ground-plane, specifically of the American Bottom floodplain in Illinois, a sprawling, complex area stretching from just south of the confluence of the Mississippi and Missouri Rivers to the Kaskaskia River, with St. Louis, Missouri just across the river from the bottom. Building upon Vogler's piece, photographer Jennifer Colten contributes a photographic essay, "Between," of her longtime work in the same region of the American Bottom, oftentimes in collaboration with Vogler, where she presents a series of photographs depicting liminal spaces between the levees and the Mississippi River. Jess Vanecek and I contribute a photographic piece of our drone photographs above the 2019 flood in St. Louis.

For the Lower Mississippi/Arkansas–White–Red River Basin, contributions include landscape researchers Justine Holzman and Forbes Lipschitz, and ecologist Alex Kolker. Each of these focuses on the Lower Mississippi River Basin portion of this territorial scale. In the Holzman/Lipschitz essay "Splitting," through text and exquisite drawings, they speculate on future alternate practices for catfish farming in the Yazoo Delta portion of the Lower Mississippi River Basin. In Kolker's essay "Shifting" he points our attention downriver to the Mississippi River Delta and asks us to focus on alternate, unforeseen locations along the river's path to the Gulf of Mexico—locations that may change the river's course(s) in the future.

In the Mekong River Basin Atlas, one essay addresses developmental histories and challenges across the entire river basin at the continental scale. While three additional essays focus on issues within the Lower Mekong River Basin and its delta at the territory scale, all three are set within the context of the dynamic conditions across the entire basin.

For the continental scale of the entire Mekong River Basin, the contribution includes landscape architect/urban researcher Dorothy Tang. In her essay "Development," she frames an important understanding of the history of geopolitics, regionalism, and global investment in major infrastructure projects from countries including the United States, Japan, and China, among others.

For the Lower Mekong River Basin, contributors include sustainable hydropower specialists Palakorn Chanbanyong and Simon Krohn, architect Shelby Doyle and agricultural scientist Duong Van Ni. In the Chanbanyong/Krohn essay "Balance," they describe the delicate economic and environmental negotiation structures of the Mekong River Commission, the only entity in the Mekong to address transboundary challenges, specifically in regards to recent dam infrastructure projects and climate adaptation strategies within the basin. In Doyle's essay "Flood," she analyzes the unique phenomena of the Tonlé Sap River and Lake in Cambodia in relation to the urbanization of Phnom Penh and the Mekong River, which typically reverses its flow to backfill the lake in the wet season. But in recent years its seasonal pulses are inconsistent at best, particularly due to recent droughts and upriver dam constructions. In Ni's essay, he presents his impactful, on-the-ground work with local farmers in the Mekong Delta to monitor salinity levels with a low-cost toolkit, in turn educating and empowering farmers and community members and stakeholders to gather accurate data to determine and deploy adaptation practices.

In the Rhine River Basin Atlas, two essays cast a new light on the relationships between the Dutch Delta and larger influences of the Rhine River Basin.

For the continental scale of the Rhine River Basin, urbanist Han Meyer's essay "Transform" addresses multiple phases of historical transformations of the Rhine River Basin and begs the question of what will be the next phase of the Rhine Delta (and by extension the basin at-large). His essay helps frame the speculative Watershed Architecture proposal that follows in the "Speculate + Synthesize" portion of the book.

For the Lower Rhine River Basin, landscape architect Robbert de Koning and economist Dale Morris reflect on their particular contributions to the "Room for the River" program in the Netherlands and revisit the recently completed project with a fresh set of eyes, focusing on the de Koning and team's stunning Noordwaard project. They also ask how the work can move into the next phase given contemporary challenges, as well as assessing the work in relation to their experiences in advocating for similar integrated spatial designs and policy shifts in the United States.

In Part Two, Speculate + Synthesize, after Ian Caine's introductory essay "Context," I then propose transboundary speculative futures for the Mississippi, Mekong and Rhine River Basins. These build upon the Appreciate + Analyze section, but reciprocally, these speculations have informed content for the Appreciate + Analyze section as well. The Mississippi proposal, designed with Jonathan Stitelman, Allison Méndez, Irene Compadre and Chad Fisk, is titled "from the BIG SIX to the BIRDS FOOT." The Mekong proposal, designed with Jess Vanecek and Rob Birch, is titled "from the THIRD POLE to the NINE DRAGONS." The Rhine proposal, designed with Jess Vanecek, Paul Wu and Han Meyer, is titled "from the RHEINQUELLE to the LEO HOLLANDACUS."

In Part Three, Collaborate + Catalyze, after Neeraj Bhatia's introductory essay "Advocacy," I feature three specific efforts in the St. Louis, Missouri, region at the confluence of the Upper Mississippi and Missouri River Basins, in addition to an exhibition contribution in Columbus, Indiana, in the Ohio River Basin. Although I have conducted other collaborative efforts downriver in the New Orleans deltaic region, as well as interdisciplinary workshops and engagements in the Mekong and Rhine, I have made the decision to return to, and feature, where I grew up and currently live—St. Louis, and more broadly, the Midwest. The four projects constitute what I believe offer alternative forms of "engagement." "Public Lab River Rat Pack" highlights alternative modes of *field documentations*. Collaborating with the citizen-science nonprofit Public Lab, I led an interdisciplinary seminar at Washington University in St. Louis in the spring term of 2016. "FLOOD—FIGHT—FAIL" and "Tracing Our Mississippi" highlight alternative modes of *site interventions*. "FLOOD—FIGHT—FAIL" was part of *Art + Landscape STL*, curated by Gavin Kroeber, at the Granite City Arts and Design District (G-CADD) in Granite City, Illinois (within the American Bottom floodplain), and then re-presented later at the *Decoys and Depictions* symposium and exhibition at Washington University in St. Louis, curated by Constance Vale. "Tracing Our Mississippi" was part of the *New Middles: From Main Street to Megalopolis, What Is the Future of the Middle City?* exhibition at *Exhibit Columbus*, co-curated by Iker Gil and Mimi Zeiger. "Territories—Watersheds—Infrastructures" highlights alternate modes of *programmatic usages*. As part of the Haus der Kulteren der Welt (HKW) *Mississippi: An Anthropocene River* project, I led another interdisciplinary seminar at Washington University in St. Louis in the fall of 2019 that collaborated with Continental Cement Company, Big Muddy Adventures, and the Pulitzer Arts Foundation. At Continental Cement Company's industrial site along the Mississippi River, we took over its platform barge for a day, and reprogrammed it as a reconstituted and hybridized series of "platform zones of dialogues and exhibits."

In short, I do hope the following pages offer a template to interrogate such transboundary, multiscaled challenges, or at the very least, serve as a platform to debate the merits of designers' roles in such work.

1. Farrar-Tweedy, Uncle Tupelo, "New Madrid," track 6 on *Anodyne*, Sire Records, 1993, LP.

2. Rem Koolhaas, "Bigness, or the Problem of Large," in *S,M,L,XL: Office of Metropolitan Architecture*, ed. Jennifer Sigler (Rotterdam: 010 Publishers, 1995), 513–514.

3. History.com Editors, "Hurricane Katrina," HISTORY, accessed November 4, 2020, https://www.history.com/topics/natural-disasters-and-environment/hurricane-katrina (A&E Television Networks, original published date 2009, last updated 2019).

4. Data from *Google.com*, NOTE: statistics are not confirmed because they vary based on source and metrics and are meant only to provide generalized understandings.

5. Ahmed Tayia, "Transboundary Water Conflict Resolution Mechanisms: Substitutes and Complements," *Water* 11 (June 2019).

6. Ibid., 2.

7. Ibid.

8. Ibid., 33.

Backstory:

"From Times Beach…"

The Missouri is my right arm, Ohio is my left
But I'm livin' on the Mississippi River where
I like life the best

I don't mind the west coast, and I don't mind
the east coast

Oh, baby but I ain't gonna live on no coast
I'm just a plain ole Midwestern boy
Gettin' by on Central time.[1]

— Pokey LaFarge, "Central Time," 2013

An Impossible Problem and a Gordian Knot

When design is a primary driver in a form of research, it is difficult to separate the personal from the empirical, or to negotiate the intuitive with the scientific, and maybe even determine fact from fiction. Or at least I find it to be. In architecture school, we are taught to not let the personal cloud the clarity of the proposal, or at least not to present our work that way. How else could a "juror" review our work "empirically"? As an educator, I've always struggled with this pedagogical approach, and even more so as I've slogged along in what has become a complicated, more or less fifteen-year project, and by extension, the scope of this book. This is especially the case when the central character of this project is water, and when there have already been copious amounts of inspiring water-based design research conducted, particularly around the discipline of landscape architecture, its offshoots of landscape and ecological urbanism, and more recently the emerging field of delta urbanism.[2] Other than a handful of examples, I believe the majority of this work has not worked across multiple scales *of entire river basins*, and going a step further, done so comparatively. This book will attempt to fill a portion of what I consider to be an overlooked gap.

Water is seemingly such a simple molecule, yet one that is so intimately tied to the personal, and of course to the person, and to you, and to me, and to all of us, and to the collective enterprise *that is life*. In short, water embodies complexity. Especially when water, at the end of the day, is absolutely uncertain. In other words, and as hard as we try, ultimately, we cannot control water. To put it another way, does water really care about us, the user, even though we certainly care about using, and more often than not, misusing, water? And therein lies both the quandary and the beauty, for water-based design research. Water eludes both the quantitative and the qualitative, and by extension, water eludes all of us. I think my friend David Waggonner once told me, "water is an impossible problem." Or as another friend, Jane Wolff, puts it, a water-based challenge "is a Gordian knot."

So, I'll start with a little personal background, and as such, why water obsesses me. In short, St. Louis (Missouri), New Orleans (Louisiana), and the Mississippi River and its tributaries that connect the two regions are why I've made this book. So the following is a little more context.

St. Louis and the Mississippi River

I'm a Midwesterner. I grew up in the woods just outside of suburban St. Louis, up on a hill above the Meramec River and its floodplain. What was then just "unincorporated southwest St. Louis County," has since been rebranded as "Wildwood." Even though there are still lots of "woods," it's not really that "wild." But with incorporation come bigger homes and a bigger tax base and suburbanization and more elite schools, so there be it (and I'll leave that dynamic to other important discussions outside the scope of this book). St. Louis is landlocked, smack dab in the middle of the Mississippi watershed, where three great rivers—the Illinois, Mississippi, and Missouri—all join with uniquely different riverine forces just north of St. Louis. These rivers coalesce as the beginning of the free-flowing

Paddling through Melvin Price Locks & Dam, West Alton, Missouri, 2019 (image credit: Derek Hoeferlin)

portion of the Mississippi River to the south. Once the Mississippi connects with the Ohio River's massive flow further south in Cairo, Illinois, the Mississippi truly become "mighty." So basically around St. Louis, nothing stops the turbulent, and turbid, waters until the Gulf of Mexico. History tells us it's these rivers and St. Louis's location as to why President Thomas Jefferson dispatched Meriwether Lewis and William Clark from here to chart the unknown West. At least that's the story told by the colonizers. We even have a big, beautiful stainless-steel arch commemorating the event. Or rather, commemorating *leaving* St. Louis. St. Louisans believe their city's strategic location is why Jefferson purchased Louisiana from France, although New Orleanians certainly would be offended by that assertion. But in all seriousness, the colonizers waged a series of insidious campaigns of indigenous displacement in this region. As such, we must acknowledge that these are the ancestral lands of the Osage Nation, Missouria, Kickapoo, and Illini Confederacy. This is the land of Cahokia—North America's "First City." All of us must respect this fact, first and foremost.

Meramec River and Forest 44

But back to the Meramec River. The Meramec is a smaller, yet ecologically crucial tributary that joins the Mississippi River just to the south of St. Louis. The Meramec is especially important since its source is southwest of St. Louis near Mark Twain National Forest in the scenic foothills of the Ozark Mountains. Although I grew up close to the Meramec, I didn't actually spend much time floating the river ("floating" is what we do in the Midwest). Rather, like most car-dependent Midwesterners in the 1980s, my parents drove my sister and I over the Meramec on Interstate 44, not just once, but twice each way, commuting to school in suburban St. Louis. The fact that we crossed the river, and its floodplain, at least four times a day always mesmerized me as a kid. Something about its meandering path made me daydream about rivers not giving a damn about north, south, east, west, and especially interstates, for that matter. That stretch along Interstate 44 is both beautiful and hideous. Beautiful because between the floodplains, one passes through a contiguous set of hilly, institutionally protected forested areas, including Washington University in St. Louis's Tyson Research Center, parks including Castlewood, Lone Elk Park, and Antire Valley, and a zone referred to as Forest 44 Conservation Area. The latter is such a spatially ironic, yet truly American name—mashing up a forest with an interstate via the rulebook of conservation. Rumor has it that these zones comprise the largest area of protected stretch that is so close to an urbanized area in the U.S. Not sure that is true, or who made that up, maybe my mom or dad did on our way to school, but it sounds pretty good, and maybe it should stay that way. And hideous, because just down from the hills, in the towns of Fenton and Valley Park, I-44 cuts through a stretch of overdeveloped floodplain that is riddled with cheap, suburban, big-box development, and most notably the site of the demolished Chrysler Assembly Plant (which unsurprisingly is being redeveloped as a giant office park). Of course, this is not dissimilar from most floodplains in the U.S. that have evolved from natural systems to indigenously inhabited lands, to welcoming floods, to colonized lands, to agricultural or industrial land uses, to dewatered zones, to big-box developments protected by bigger and bigger levees, to catastrophic floods, to who knows what's next.

Flood of 1982 + Contaminations

But here's the rub. Ask anyone living in St. Louis in the 1980s and they will tell you we used to have very cold and wet winters, with lots of big snowstorms. We're talking like over-a-foot-or-two-or-so snowstorms. Today we're lucky to have a couple of dustings a season, and our winters are riddled mostly with torrential rains the last few years. Anyway, I vividly remember the winter of 1982 when I was eight years old. Most St. Louisans at that time remember the 1982 winter, not just because our beloved baseball Cardinals had won the World Series a few weeks earlier, but also because of the fierce winter and *what happened as a result.* We had a lot of snow—and rain—that winter. What I most remember was once tagging along with my dad in his Jeep Golden Eagle to help snow-plow parking lots in what was then a little-known river town called Times Beach, also along the Meramec, and in the floodplain. And I remember my dad and I grinding up that asphalt while we snowplowed, over and over and over. Then just a couple of weeks later, after receiving over 10 inches of rain over a short period, the Meramec crested and flooded Times Beach, a town originally formed in the 1920s as a weekend cottage retreat, then turned mobile home park decades later. My dad went back in his Jeep to help pull people out of the flood, and probably got himself stuck too. And then St. Louisans—and the world—found out that the road's toppings were contaminated with dioxin. And the rest is history. The federal government bought everyone out and the area is now "Route 66 State Park"—again, an American mash-up of environment and infrastructure. But as an eight-year-old, this chain of events, truly anthropogenic and bizarrely American, left a powerful imprint on me. Kind of like what happened to Captain Kurtz in *Apocalypse Now*. How could something go so sideways? How the hell could we do such things, in floodplains no less? We now know Times Beach's contamination is not a one-off in the St. Louis region. Environmental injustice has occurred all over our metropolitan landscape—Coldwater Creek, West Lake Landfill, Weldon Springs, Sauget, Illinois (formerly Monsanto Town), lead contaminations, radioactive dumping sites from the Manhattan Project, and the list goes on and on.

Great Flood of 1993 and Floodplain Strip Malls

Fast-forward to summer of 1993. At the time, I was in college in New Orleans, but home in St. Louis for the summer, working at an architecture firm designing McMansions for rich clients in suburban St. Louis. The Great Flood of 1993 still stands as the record crest for the Mississippi and Missouri Rivers in the St. Louis region, and one of the costliest, if not the costliest, floods in U.S. history. But who's counting? As with 1982, I distinctly remember the event. I headed out on Interstate 64 (known to locals as Highway 40) to witness the highway disappearing into the floodplain of the Missouri River in Chesterfield. At the time, and what was submerged underwater for weeks, was mostly vast farmland. I used to go with my family to get our Halloween pumpkins at Rombach Farms in what was then called the "Gumbo Flats." Of course, the flooding was disastrous for the farmers, but given time it could have proved beneficial due to all the sediment and nutrient depositions for the soil. However, since the land was cheap, after the floodwaters receded, bigger levees were built, and now the floodplain holds one of the longest—if not the longest—big-box developments in the entire United States. *The Great Flood of 1993 incentivized a massive strip mall—in a floodplain.* Again, as in 1982, I was baffled by the event and the aftermath of development. Naïve as it sounds, it still confounds me.

St. Louis Floods of 2011, 2013, 2014, 2016, 2017, 2019, 2022

We had a reprieve from serious flooding in the St. Louis region for almost 20 years, just enough to make us appropriately complacent. But during that time there was a serious drought in 1988 that devastated regional crops. Then came the summer 2011 floods, and quickly on the heels of that came the record 2012 drought, and then the summer 2013 floods, then summer 2014 floods, and most recently the record spring and summer 2019 floods (the second-highest on record behind 1993) and summer 2022 flash floods after. But between 2014 and 2019, something even stranger happened, and not since 1982. Massive winter deluges made the Meramec River rise again and flood Eureka and Valley Park in both 2016 and 2017—basically around the same area as Times Beach. But this time, the flooding was far worse than 1982. And many claim this is due to much more floodplain development since 1982. Others of course disagree. Regardless, 1982 haunted me.

New Orleans

And then there's New Orleans. During the middle of all of this, I lived, studied, and worked in the Crescent City from 1992 to 2003. New Orleans is a perfect place to spend college and your twenties, but that's another story. New Orleans was, and still is, a gift to me, maybe even a dream. As Bob Dylan muses, "There are a lot of places I like. But I like New Orleans better."[3] Some of my closest friends and most talented collaborators live and do amazing work there, and do so passionately, *for the city*. But looking back, during those years I really never attempted to appreciate the city's relationship with water—its good, bad, and ugly sides—other than occasionally watching the sublime freighters pass by along the levees on the Mississippi, or experiencing the flash flood of 1995, or taking the occasional swamp tour with guests from out of town. But water really began to obsess me, and certainly many others, on August 29, 2005, when the world woke up to the shock of Hurricane Katrina making landfall on Louisiana's Gulf Coast, just east of New Orleans.

And then the levees broke.

Hurricane Katrina

Katrina and its unjust aftermath marked a career shift for me for the following reasons:

1) Even though I was now residing upriver in my born-and-raised home of St. Louis, ironically enough I was instantly unemployed. At the time, I had been providing freelance work for the New Orleans firm Waggonner & Ball, but they were displaced far west of their submerged city.

2) Due to a fortunate last-minute request, I began teaching architecture at Washington University in St. Louis, just a couple of days after August 29. I was shell-shocked, but grateful I had a job.

3) And probably most importantly, as mentioned in the introduction, I immediately questioned my role as an architect set within such an unprecedented, human-altered "natural disaster," one that immediately cut across multiple scales and disciplines. And horribly timed, no less. Katrina was bookended by 9/11 and the 2008 recession. It happened in the middle of the Afghanistan and Iraq Wars. And, although maybe not as crazy as recent political divisions or the Covid pandemic, Katrina happened during another intractable American political climate. This was driven by the lack of coordinated leadership at all levels, the dysfunction of FEMA, especially since FEMA had been subsumed by the Department of Homeland Security after 9/11, just to name a few. In other words, at the given time, Hurricane Katrina undoubtedly was an unprecedented event for the U.S. But one could argue Hurricane Katrina was just the tipping point of more frequent calamities to come, and especially disastrous since these tend to target and affect mostly disadvantaged communities, and do so repetitively.

I asked myself, how would—*and why should*—the design disciplines respond? And more personally, how could my professional and teaching efforts respond at such a pivotal moment and potential tipping point for all design disciplines, especially architecture, landscape architecture and urban design? For me as a licensed architect, would it be just about the design and teaching of buildings in objectified isolation, or rather would it be about the design and teaching of architecture, landscape architecture, and urban design in a broader, cross-cultural, social, environmental, equitable and global context?

Reactionary Design

As such, the work in this book has resulted more out of self-critique, in response to my earlier years working and teaching within the milieu of the post–Hurricane Katrina disaster context of New Orleans, where I collaborated with a broad network of academics and professionals. Since the (then) unprecedented storm, many of us have come to agree that we always seemed to be operating in reactionary modes of design. We were just trying to catch up. And we were just trying to "get things done." I wrote about such work in my chapter contribution "Architectural Activism through Multiple Scales, Venues, Programs, and Collaborations," in *New Orleans Under Reconstruction: The Crisis of Planning*. I am thankful to the book's editors, including Carol Reese, the late Michael Sorkin, and Anthony Fontenot for the invitation to contribute to their important, and I would argue "ahead-of-its-time" project. My chapter chronicled my community-engaged professional and teaching design work in New Orleans from 2005 to 2011, responding to a specific set of crises—food, economic development, architecture, and water management. Collaborative projects ranged from a chicken coop for a community garden to adaptive reuse and business developments plans for New Orleans nonprofits, as well as the beginnings of water management advocacy efforts.[4] I am proud of the work, but to reiterate, it was reactionary in scope.

Absence of Water

The years right after Katrina soon became referred to as "plandemonium" by the distressed and exhausted residents, due to the plethora of actionless plans and the subsequent fatigue it caused locals. A sharp criticism of such can be found in Christine Boyer's powerful essay "New Orleans under Reconstruction: A Crisis in Planning and Human Security."[5] But something else was very frustrating. For many reasons, and mostly due to a lack of political will and of available funds, no one was publicly talking about the real big elephant that was ironically absent from New Orleans's sinking room, both rhetorically and functionally: WATER. Rhetorically, since water was frustratingly absent from the postdisaster planning efforts. (In 2009, after Hurricane Gustav narrowly missed New Orleans, I wrote an op-ed in the *St. Louis Post-Dispatch* discussing said absence and the need for a "Water Plan" for New Orleans.)[6] And functionally, since water had been drained from the urbanized areas of New Orleans for 20th-century development.[7] Other than the local residents' understandable fear of water due to the catastrophic levee failures that were partially enabled by the gross negligence of the U.S. Army Corps of Engineers, water was not prioritized, and actually was barely even being discussed, in the recovery and long-term rebuilding planning of New Orleans, for one simple, myopic reason. Many residents thought water planning was not about devoting areas of the city back to open space for equitable water management and access, but rather was a ruse for future development—aka, a land grab. Understandably, many disenfranchised residents had the right to fear this. American, Southern, and New Orleanian histories were not on their side. So there was no trust. There certainly was no leadership. And there was barely any post-Katrina funding flowing at the time. Environmental justice was absent, all the while a corrupt Mayor C. Ray Nagin was taking bribes, eventually landing him in jail as federal inmate No. 32751-034. And the city continued to sink, due to its lack of replenishing water. Again, a Gordian knot for sure.

Recovery Planning

From 2006 to 2007, while working with H3 Studio, Inc. of St. Louis, and assisted by Waggonner & Ball Architects, we helped lead the Unified New Orleans Plan (UNOP), which was the only formally city-adopted hurricane recovery plan for the city. H3 Studio was one of five teams selected as district planners. My role for H3 Studio was project manager, with John Hoal, the principal of H3 Studio, serving as project director. UNOP was a case-in-point example where water was conspicuously and politically absent from what ultimately became a top-down, city-adopted planning effort. However, in my opinion, our team succeeded in guiding these water-based conversations at the neighborhood level, from the bottom up, but frustratingly not "officially" endorsed by the city. To be clear, the planning teams were even discouraged from mentioning water and open space in meetings. Again baffled, I had several conversations with architect David Waggonner and landscape architecture professor Jane Wolff about how to develop innovative models of citizen-led and academic-based interdisciplinary research efforts that could bring, to the front-and-center of public consciousness, the critical importance of *living with water* in the delta urbanism of New Orleans—and ultimately beyond.

Water-Based Design Advocacy

In 2008, New Orleans architect David Waggonner, with assistance from the Royal Netherlands Embassy in Washington D.C. and the American Planning Association, began a series of multidisciplinary workshops titled "Dutch Dialogues." The workshops brought together Dutch and American experts to study integrated water management strategy scenarios in New Orleans. Representing Washington University, and given my longer history with Mr. Waggonner, I became a key design leader and facilitator during these workshops. This was my first exposure to the merits of the multidisciplinary design workshop methodology. The early "Dutch Dialogues" work is chronicled in the book Dutch Dialogues: *New Orleans/Netherlands, Common Challenges in Urbanized Deltas*, edited by David Waggonner with Han Meyer and Dale Morris.[8]

From the academic advocacy side, and also in 2008, I cofounded "Gutter to Gulf: Legible Water Infrastructure for New Orleans," a collaboration between myself at Washington University in St. Louis, along with Jane Wolff and Elise Shelley at the University of Toronto. Working both alongside—and independently of—"Dutch Dialogues," from 2008 to 2012 the "Gutter to Gulf" effort proposed multiscaled architecture, landscape architecture, and urban design integrated water management strategies, from the "scale of the gutter to the Gulf of Mexico." These were run as a series of collaborative Washington University in St. Louis graduate and undergraduate architecture and urban design studios and University of Toronto graduate landscape architecture studios.[9] At the time, "Dutch Dialogues" and "Gutter to Gulf" may have been the only efforts publicly advocating for comprehensive and integrated water management in the Greater New Orleans region. Both of these multi-year and complementary efforts helped lead to the "Greater New Orleans Urban Water Plan," commissioned in 2011 to an American-Dutch team led by Waggonner & Ball.[10]
I provided professional services to the Waggonner & Ball core team. As with "Dutch

Dialogues," I helped lead multidisciplinary design workshops; I worked very closely with the core Waggonner & Ball team; and I acted as a key liaison with Dutch team members, specifically Bosch-Slabbers Landscape Architects, helping to design priority demonstration projects for the plan, most notably the centerpiece project for the Lafitte Blueway. Although the project officially wrapped up in 2013, this is a very long-term project. At present, implemented projects are finally beginning to take shape, thanks mostly to the fearless leadership of David Waggonner, as well as Mac Ball, Aron Chang, Ramiro Diaz, Andy Sternad, and John Kleinschmidt, among others. Additionally, I am particularly proud that I helped enable several of my former Washington University students to contribute significantly to Waggonner & Ball's efforts: primarily John Kleinschmidt and Andy Sternad as mentioned above, as well as Lex Agnew, Francis Aguillard, Cari Alcombright, Jessica Garz, Zachary Gong, Annemarie Gray, John Monnat, Samantha Stein, and Tiffin Thompson.

In 2010, I further exposed this work at Washington University in St. Louis by organizing a one-day symposium, "NL-STL-NO: A Dialogue about Water's Implications for Design & Infrastructure." Supported by the then senior economist Dale Morris of the Royal Netherlands Embassy, Washington D.C., it featured Renée Jones-Bos, the Netherlands Ambassador to the United States. She spoke about the Dutch model of water-based design that attempts to marry policy and spatial quality, particularly the "Room for the River" program. Featuring a government official, and an ambassador no less, does not happen too often in architecture and design schools, so I felt this was the start of something fresh in terms of new forms of engagements. Other talks were delivered by David Waggonner and myself, with introductions from the then Dean of Architecture Bruce Lindsey, and responses from the then Dean of Art Buzz Spector and the then Chair of Landscape Architecture Dorothée Imbert. Further discussion on Room for the River will be included in the Rhine River Basin Atlas portion of this book, as well as in supplemental essays by Han Meyer, Robbert de Koning, and Dale Morris.

As already mentioned in the introduction, while my academic and professional research first focused on New Orleans and its regional environmental deltaic context of the Louisiana Gulf Coast, it has since scaled up to the Midwest and St. Louis region. While still engaging efforts in the Lower Mississippi River Basin and the New Orleans regions, including being a core member for the STUDIO MISI-ZIIBI team for the "Changing Course: Navigating the Future of the Lower Mississippi River Delta" design competition in 2015, the majority of my efforts with colleagues and students at Washington University have focused on the middle and upper portions of the river basin.

As an example, and as a result of my work on "Dutch Dialogues" and "NL-STL-NO," Dale Morris approached me regarding the organization of a workshop on floodplain management and climate change issues in the Midwest, in response to the 2011 floods and 2012 droughts. I felt this would be a perfect opportunity to both strike up a collaboration between myself and the Dutch Embassy here in St. Louis, and to collaborate with other faculty and students at Washington University. But for Dale Morris and me to really pull off the workshop in a timely manner and with strong community buy-in, I recommended to Dale that we include John Hoal as a co-organizer. At the time, John was the Chair of Urban Design. As a result, the three of us collaborated on a multi-year research effort to study issues of climate adaptation strategies in different fluvial zones along the great rivers in the Midwest, starting in St. Louis. Additional collaborative input from several other key partners included "American Rivers" (Eileen Shader), "Earth Economics" (Jennifer Harrison-Cox, Nora Wahlund, and others), HKV Consultants (Fredrik Huthoff), Southern Illinois University in Carbondale (Nicholas Pinter and others), and the U.S. Army Corps of Engineers (Chuck Theiling, Eddie Brauer, and others).

Our first "MISI-ZIIBI" (the Ojibwe/Algonquin native American name for Mississippi, meaning "Great River") workshop was held in March 2013 over the course of five days. It included well over 50 participants consisting of multiple disciplines from the U.S. and the Netherlands; my graduate option architecture studio students; Washington University faculty; and former students and Washington University alumni. We kicked off the workshop with a triple-billing keynote address delivered by Dale Morris and Dutch landscape architects Robbert de Koning and Steven Slabbers. The three presented the Netherlands Room for the River program. The workshop also included presentations from local and international experts and local stakeholders representing multiple interest groups. The final public presentation included a response from Rachel Jacobson, the then acting Assistant Director for U.S. Fish, Wildlife & Parks Services from the Department of the Interior. The majority of the support for the event came from the Dutch Embassy. Additional support came from Washington University's Graduate School of Architecture and Urban Design, the Gephardt Institute for Public Service Clinton Global Initiative University (CGIU) Programming Fund and the International Center for Advanced Renewable Energy and Sustainability (I-CARES). In fall 2013, we held a follow-up workshop at the Sam Fox School, cohosted by Earth Economics and the U.S. Army Corps of Engineers. We applied ecosystem service valuation metric scenarios to the outcomes from our March 2013 workshop. All in all, our main advocacy message from these workshops was "Climate Change Is Not Just Coastal."

Finally, I have run a series of architecture, landscape architecture, and urban design studios focused on the St. Louis and Midwest region, that have informed and built upon this research. The studios speculate on design's relationships to future understandings of water-related conditions; for instance, the futures of the agriculture, barge, and beer industries. All of this has led me to a clearer understanding of not necessarily cause-and-effect circumstances up and down the entire Mississippi River Basin, but rather dynamic and complex interrelationships and possibilities that need to be addressed, through design, in the future. And not just limited to coastal contexts. It is crucial to point out that the water-based work is to be comprehended at both the local and watershed scale, along with scales between. Then too, the Mississippi River Basin research situates itself within a comparative, collaborative, networked study of two other major global river basins—the Mekong and the Rhine.

"Gutter to Gulf hydrologic/hydraulic model of New Orleans," 2016
(image credit: Andy Sternad for Ripple Effect)

1. *LaFarge, Pokey*, "Central Time," track 1 on Pokey LaFarge, Third Man Records, 2013, LP.

2. Several publications have investigated design in relation to water. Examples include:
Three noteworthy publications by Anuradha Mathur and Dilip da Cunha: *Mississippi Floods: Designing a Shifting Landscape* (New Haven: Yale University Press, 2001); *Design in the Terrain of Water* (San Francisco: Applied Research + Design, 2014); SOAK: *Mumbai in an Estuary* (New Delhi: Rupa & Co., 2009). Others include, but are not limited to: Anthony Acciavatti, *Ganges Water Machine* (San Francisco: Applied Research + Design, 2015). Joan Busquets and Felipe Correa, *New Orleans: Strategies for a City in Soft Land* (Boston: Harvard University Press, 2005). Edward Burtynsky, *Water* (Gottingen, Germany: Steidl, 2013). Richard Campanella, *Delta Urbanism: New Orleans* (Chicago: American Planning Association Planners Press, 2010). Bruno De Meulder and Kelly Shannon, *Water Urbanisms* (Amsterdam: Uitgeverij SUN, 2008). Sarah Dunn and Martin Felsen, *Urban Bowling* (San Francisco: Applied Research and Design, 2017). Daniel Ibanez, Claire Lyster, Charles Waldheim, Mason White, *Third Coast Atlas: Prelude to a Plan* (New York: ACTAR, 2017). Margarita Jover and Alex Wall, *Ecologies of Prosperity: For the Living City* (San Francisco: Applied Research and Design, 2019). Erik G. L'Heureux, ed., *Probing Hydrological Urbanism: Cambodia/Singapore* (Singapore: Department of Architecture School of Design and Environment, National University of Singapore, 2010). Tracy Metz and Maartji van den Heuvel, *Sweet and Salt: Water and the Dutch* (Rotterdam: NAi Publishers, 2012). Han Meyer, Dale Morris, and David Waggonner, *Dutch Dialogues: New Orleans/Netherlands: Common Challenges in Urbanized Deltas* (Amsterdam: Uitgeverij SUN, 2008). Han Meyer, Inge Bobbink, and Steffan Nijus, *Delta Urbanism: The Netherlands* (Chicago: American Planning Association Planners Press, 2010). Mary Pat McGuire and Jessica Hensen, *Fresh Water: Design for Inland Water Territories* (San Francisco: Applied Research and Design, 2019). Richard Misrach and Kate Orff, *Petrochemical America* (New York: Aperture, 2013). Kate Orff, SCAPE, *Toward an Urban Ecology* (New York: Monacelli Press, 2016). Chris Reed and Nina Marie Lister, *Projective Ecologies* (New York: ACTAR, 2013).

3. Bob Dylan, *"Ghosts of New Orleans," in Chronicles, Volume One* (Simon & Schuster, 2004).

4. Derek Hoeferlin, *"Architectural Activism through Multiple Scales, Venues, Programs, and Collaborations," in New Orleans Under Reconstruction: The Crisis of Planning*, eds. C. Reese, M. Sorkin, and A. Fontenot (London: Verso, 2014).

5. For a thorough critique of the post-Katrina planning process, see: Christine Boyer, "New Orleans under Reconstruction: A Crisis in Planning and Human Security," in *New Orleans under Reconstruction: The Crisis of Planning*, ed. C. Reese, M. Sorkin, and A. Fontenot (London: Verso, 2014).

6. Derek Hoeferlin, *"New Orleans Needs a Water Plan," St. Louis Post-Dispatch* (August 30, 2009).

7. For more information on the manmade reasons why New Orleans is subsiding and now partially below sea level, see: Jane Wolff, Elise Shelley, and Derek Hoeferlin, "Why Is New Orleans Sinking?" Gutter to Gulf: Legible Water Infrastructure for New Orleans, accessed November 4, 2020, http://guttertogulf.com/Why-is-New-Orleans-sinking (University of Toronto and Washington University in St. Louis, original published date 2011, last updated 2020).

8. Han Meyer, Dale Morris, and David Waggonner, *Dutch Dialogues: New Orleans/Netherlands: Common Challenges in Urbanized Deltas* (Amsterdam: Uitgeverij SUN, 2008).

9. Jane Wolff, Elise Shelley, and Derek Hoeferlin, "Gutter to Gulf: Legible Water Infrastructure for New Orleans," accessed November 4, 2020, http://guttertogulf.com/ (University of Toronto and Washington University in St. Louis, original published date 2011, last updated 2020).

10. Waggonner & Ball Architects, "The Greater New Orleans Urban Water Plan," accessed November 4, 2020, https://livingwithwater.com/blog/urban_water_plan/about/.

Definitions

Watershed, Architecture Way Beyond Bigness

Water is the reason we can say its name.[1]

— Edward Burtynsky, Water, 2003

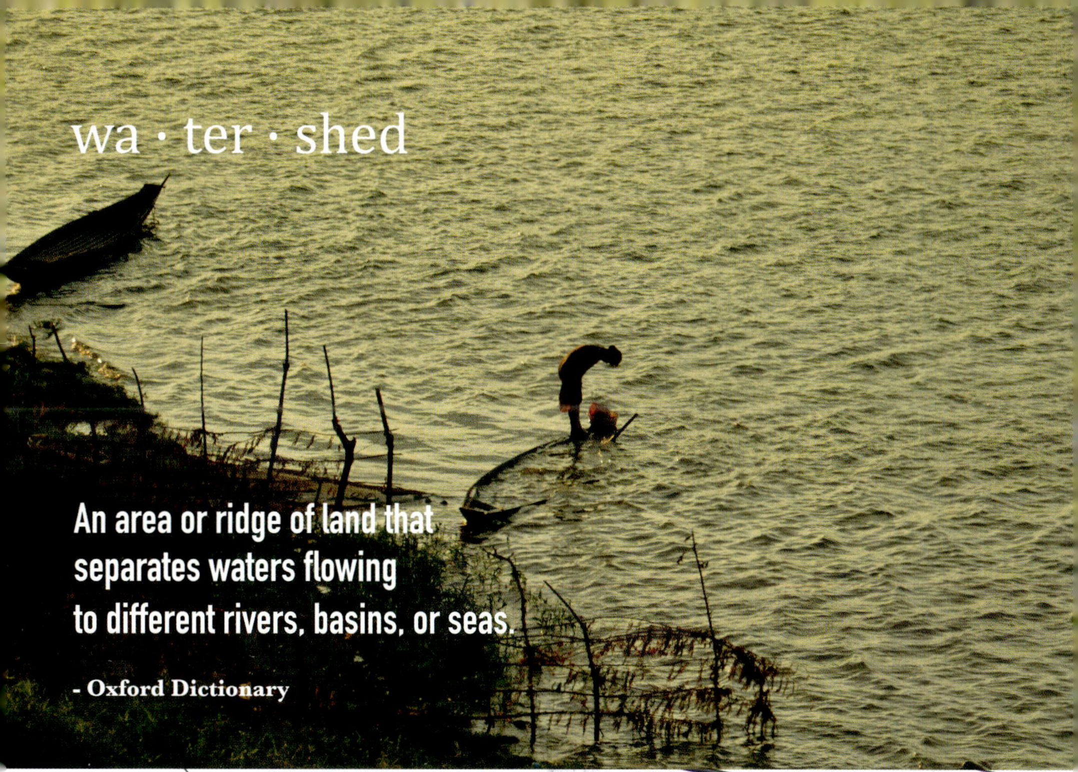

Tonle Sekong River, Stung Treng, Cambodia, 2011
(BOTTOM) Lower Ninth Ward neighborhood, New Orleans, Louisiana, 2005
(images credit: Derek Hoeferlin)

Watershed = Flows + Tipping Points

The tipping point is that magic moment when an idea, trend, or social behavior crosses a threshold, tips, and spreads like wildfire.[(2)]

—Malcolm Gladwell, The Tipping Point: How Little Things Can Make a Big Difference, 2000

[WBB] questions why a watershed's principle definition is "an area or ridge of land that separates waters flowing to different rivers, basins, or seas."[3] The scientist-geographer John Wesley Powell contextualized watersheds further, with his ubiquitously referenced view:

> *That area of land, a bounded hydrological system, within which all living things are inextricably linked by their common water course and where, as humans settled, simple logic demanded that they became part of a community.*[4]

Powell emphasizes a watershed's potential to prioritize a community's interaction—and I would add manipulation—within the hydrological boundary of a certain scaled watershed. In other words, what Shafiqul Islam and Lawrence E. Susskind, in *Water Diplomacy: A Negotiated Approach to Managing Complex Water Networks*, interpret as the coupling of the natural and societal domains.[5] But for designers, what skill sets can we contribute to better enable a watershed's integration within the realities of the built environment, many of which do not obey the logic of hydrological boundaries? And by extension, how can a better appreciation for watersheds make us better designers? These realities include the need for designers to engage contested issues such as architecture, infrastructure, landscape, urbanism, regimes of control, societies, politics, community advocacy, and climatic and/or geopolitical influences, all of which may reside within or outside of a watershed. The alternate, and possibly just as important definition for a watershed, is "an event or period marking a turning point in a situation in a course of action or state of affairs."[6] A definition not about water per se, but rather one having to do with major jolts, or minor glitches, in what seem to be ordinary states of affairs. Think major jolts like a hurricane, or minor glitches like a tweet. Either have consequence, be they positive or negative, visible or invisible, immediate or distant, fact or fiction, and they can be what

Sand pile full of oil, BP Oil Spill cleanup, Grand Isle, Louisiana, 2010 (image credit: Derek Hoeferlin).

Malcolm Gladwell refers to as a "tipping point … that magic moment when an idea, trend, or social behavior crosses a threshold, tips, and spreads like wildfire."[7]

[WBB] questions why architecture's principle definition is the "practice of designing and constructing buildings."[8] Although this disciplinary strength remains the priority for most architects, it also reinforces the discipline potentially operating in a silo, and dangerously out of touch. Maybe a more pertinent question is: what really constitutes a "building"?

The National Council of Architectural Registration Boards (NCARB) elaborates on what licensed architects are responsible for:

> *Licensed professionals trained in the art and science of the design and construction of buildings and structures that primarily provide shelter. An architect will create the overall aesthetic and look of buildings and structures, but the design of a building involves far more than its appearance. Buildings also must be functional, safe, and economical and must suit the specific needs of the people who use them. Most importantly, they must be built with the public's health, safety and welfare in mind.*[9]

The last sentence is crucial. Not only is it a legal mandate, at least in the United States, but it raises three important external influences—health, safety, and welfare. These are complexities that can be considered outside the realm—or enclosure—of a building. [WBB] argues that these can only be understood with a new appreciation for both watersheds and architecture. Water knows no boundaries. Buildings tend to want boundaries.

The alternate definition for architecture is "the complexity or carefully designed structure of something."[10] Albeit ridiculously vague, this idea of "something" is quite provocative for the discipline of architecture. Granted, it's considered heresy to those who believe that architecture can only be practiced by a licensed architect. In other words, only an architect can design buildings. This is primarily for legal reasons, but many perceive this liberal use of the term as a threat to the discipline. But let's face it, most of the built environment is not even stamped by a licensed architect. So if we suspend what can be argued to be an archaic view of the discipline, architecture no longer is about just designing buildings. Rather, architecture is more encompassing, broader, and is about designing complex, careful structures. So [WBB] contends that architecture does not need to be the creation from the authority of an architect. And more interestingly, the potential of this definition leads to the engagement of a more complex approach to architecture, and for the case of [WBB], the "something" is water. Authors Islam and Susskind argue for a diplomatic approach to "manage water networks" and contend that "water management problems are complex ... are not easily knowable and are usually unpredictable," and cannot be solved by "reductionism" or "systems engineering." Rather, "water resources might be more effectively managed if understood more about the interaction and feedback among components of the relevant natural, societal, and political systems."[11] This liberation of "unpredictability" may be what holds most potentiality for designers in relation to water. As an architect, just as I challenge my discipline to better engage watersheds and issues outside of the building envelope, in 2013, Rod Barnett challenged the landscape architecture discipline to better engage a theory of emergence. In his book *Emergence in Landscape Architecture*, Barnett builds upon the ideas of Bruno Latour, Gilles Deleuze, and Felix Guattari, explaining:

> *Emergence theory can help us understand the world not as an object or a process to be known, observed or represented, but as a dynamic, shifting assemblage in which humans, plants, animals, rivers, clouds, trees, suburbs, subways, heritage districts, and all manner of other things are embedded, shifting, and unfolding along with everything else.*[12]

I am not arguing for [WBB] to be a substitute for what the architecture or landscape architecture disciplines already accomplish so well, or a substitute for any specific design discipline, for that matter. Rather, I am arguing for [WBB] to be a flexible road map for various design disciplines to better engage water-based issues, and to do so by adding one's own disciplinary strength while productively learning from and contributing to other disciplines.

Shrimp drying, Tonle Sap Lake Region, Cambodia, 2010 (image credit: Derek Hoeferlin)

Way Beyond Bigness

Opportunities not Crises

Pessimistically, our collective 21st-century crisis in regards to the built environment is climate change, and more specifically, its relation to water-based disasters. If we couple these challenges with our globally failing physical and social infrastructures, the future is indeed grim. Optimistically, what if we disregard our archaic, reactive, crises-driven design approaches and reorient to *accommodate* climate change, and in doing so *adapt* to sea-level rise, to *transform* wastes to resources, to *live* with the water, and so forth? What if watersheds and architecture combine as a new and proactive design framework, potentially even as a new discipline, one that prioritizes contemporary water opportunities and tipping points in time that are way beyond our historically conventional understandings of such.

Proactive not Reactive

Life and society depend upon water. We often fail to appreciate that the molecular connection is so essential. Recent human-altered, water-based catastrophes in the U.S. alone, such as hurricanes, floods, droughts, dam failures, contaminations, and wildfires, place front-and-center that our technological supremacy over water can have unintended, and oftentimes disastrous, effects. We are repetitively reactive, rather than positively proactive. The status quo is economically, environmentally, and socially unacceptable.

Additionally, water may be the most politicized commodity on earth. But as my landscape architecture colleague Jane Wolff once mused, "water is apolitical." In other words, water ultimately flows where water wants to flow. *Water Always Wins.* Take the New Orleans region as an example. The city and surrounding Louisiana Delta have become ground zero for all things human-made water disasters— hurricanes, floods, oil spills, sinking lands, disappearing wetlands, rising seas, and yes, even droughts. However, it is important that New Orleans is not alone. Water is a continental issue and, of course, water is a global issue. Water, if not already so, will become *the* global crisis. But there is an alternate way. We need to anticipate (design as foresight), rather than wait (design as hindsight).

Downstream and Upstream

In the face of the uncertain issues of climate change, extreme weather, sea-level rise, water scarcities, and population fluctuations that are both exploding and depleting, significant attention has been brought to the comparative studies of deltas and their urbanized developments. Known as "delta urbanisms," these water-rich regions arguably are the economic lifeblood of most nations' economies. However, [WBB] argues that it is crucial to take a bigger step back and understand deltas and their urbanisms, not just within and compared among themselves, but also within their larger, cause-and-effect, distribution contexts of watersheds, or more technically, river basins. Upstream is the starting point, and downstream is the receiver. [WBB] argues for a shifting of priorities upstream set within a transboundary approach to design.

Pragmatism and Fundamentals

But since I am an optimist architect, I truly believe that deltas, their urbanisms, and their much larger-scale distributive river basin scale contexts must be the models for what my design collaborator Ian Caine and I define as 21st- and 22nd-century hydro-regions. But this optimism is not foolhardy idealism. Actually, it is rather pragmatic. In other words, hydro-regions, up and down entire river basins, must get their fundamentals straight. These fundamentals first begin with a return to basics: a foundational understanding that water is the primary component of the actual ground that is occupied.

1. Wade Davis and Marcus Schubert, eds., *Water* (Göttingen: Steidl, 2013).

2. Malcolm Gladwell, *The Tipping Point: How Little Things Can Make a Big Difference* (New York: Little, Brown, 2002).

3. Oxford Dictionary.

4. John Wesley Powell, *The Exploration of the Colorado and Its Canyons* (New York: Penguin Classics, 1875).

5. Shafiqul Islam and Lawrence E. Susskind, *Water Diplomacy: A Negotiated Approach to Managing Complex Water Networks* (New York: RFF Press/Routledge, 2013).

6. Oxford Dictionary.

7. Gladwell, *Tipping Point.*

8. Oxford Dictionary.

9. National Council of Architectural Registration Boards (NCARCB).

10. Oxford Dictionary.

11. Islam and Susskind, "Challenging the Conventional Wisdom about Water Management," in *Water Diplomacy: A Negotiated Approach to Managing Complex Water Networks* (New York: RFF Press/Routledge, 2013), 8–9.

12. Rod Barnett, "Introduction," in *Emergence in Landscape Architecture* (London and New York: Routledge, 2013), 5.

Amsterdam, Netherlands, 2011
(BOTTOM) Fish market along Ganh Hao River, Bac Lieu Province, Mekong Delta, Vietnam, 2011
(images credit: Derek Hoeferlin)

Salt Flat Farm, Mekong Delta, Vietnam, 2011 (image credit: Derek Hoeferlin)

[WBB] aspires for:

OPPORTUNITY, NOT CRISIS
PROACTIVE, NOT REACTIVE
DOWNSTREAM + UPSTREAM
PRAGMATISM + OPTIMISM

Appreciate + Analyze [A+A]

(or the need for transboundary understandings)

[A+A] includes field documentations and analytical drawings that highlight issues of living with, or living without, water in the Mississippi, Mekong, and Rhine River Basins. The primary method of documentation is photography, supplemented by short stationary videos, analytical animations, and geo-referenced, interactive online maps, all of which can be interactively engaged at www.waybeyondbigness.com. The multiscaled and multimedia analyses across these three river basins can serve as a platform for a clearer understanding of complex issues within and between the three basins, leading to additional analyses more particular to other global river basins.

In the following section of this book, and as part of my work with my research assistants Jess Vanecek, Paul Wu, Chenyu Zhang, and Caroline Amstutz, as well as building upon design studios at Washington University in St. Louis since 2010, we have created atlases for the Mississippi, Mekong, and Rhine. The structure and content are intentionally simple, and prioritize photographic documentations and orthographic two-dimensional mappings, along with other mapping techniques such as flowcharts and globe projections. These combine to legibly narrate very complicated themes and scales across the river basins, particularly in relation to dam infrastructure and methods of control across the three. The hope is for these to be used by people in both design and non-design-based disciplines, either academics or professionals, and to be shared with various communities and user groups for accessibility.

After an introductory essay by Anthony Acciavatti titled "Description," each basin's complicated management regimes are introduced—since trans-boundary negotiation structures underpin everything that follows. Second, metrics are organized around themes that include: lengths, areas, populations, urbanizations, densities, territories, tributaries, volumes, and topographies. Third, each river basin is individually understood and analyzed at multiple scales in orthographic plans and sections delineated at the same scales for comparative purposes: 1) World; 2) Continent (1 inch = 1,500,000 feet); 3) Territory (1 inch = 600,000 feet); 4) Region (1 inch = 30,000 feet; for example, reservoirs, lakes & pools), and 5) Zone (1 inch = 2,000 feet; for example, locks & dams, land uses, infrastructures).

To truly comprehend the enormous scale of trans-boundary challenges across the Mississippi, Mekong, and Rhine River Basins, particularly in regard to debating the impacts these have had on communities, ecologies, and industries, the atlases bluntly focus on the monumental methods of controlling the systems and how the methods layer on other sets of carefully curated information. To do so, the mappings are intentionally objective and fact-driven; orthographic and linework based; abstracted and stripped of extraneous information; delineated in only plan and section; and supplemented with my indicative photographs of each scale. Mappings prioritize black-and-white linework, with the exception of two colors: red, indicating forms of power (dams, levees, and transmission lines); and green, indicating large regions of production and growth (agriculture and forested areas). Subtle hatchings and gray tones indicate larger contested territories (indigenous lands, aquifers, urbanized areas, resource extraction landscapes, conservation areas, floodways, and spillways). The mappings intentionally riff on the orthographic tools of architectural and engineering projection methodologies, such as flowcharts and deploying the need for vertical exaggeration in section to abstract vast scales. They cast a critical light on these historically deployed "drawings of control" to be able to set the stage for the real impacts that "infrastructures of control" have had on communities and societal challenges.

Ultimately, the themes narrate complicated issues across each river basin that span multiple scales, and as such, act to highlight both similarities and differences between the river basins. But all three arguably emphasize one objective: the relentless control of each river basin's extractive landscapes for economic gain primarily via navigation, hydropower, and water supply regimes.

Within each river basin atlas, multiple contributions feature guests pursuing compelling scientific research, design efforts, and community engagements within each river basin. These contributions ground the analyses and expand the atlases with important site and community specificities.

Description

Drawn from Rivers

Anthony Acciavatti

Let us draw our attention to a river basin that is not specifically studied in this book but that occupies an important shelf in the history of stalking watersheds: the Ganges. I propose we look at a map and text, both drawn and written in the 18th century, by a swashbuckling figure of once notable repute named James Rennell.

In Rennell's 1786 *A Map… of the Ganges from Hurdwar to the Sea*, the floodgates are opening up—but you would never know it from the drawing. The river and its tributaries, drawn as single lines or double lines with crosshatching, slink across the sheet of paper and begin to multiply in number and girth before they meet the brackish waters of the earth's vastest delta: Bay of Bengal. Known as the "Herodotus of India" due to the accuracy of his maps, Rennell's work as the first surveyor general of Bengal for the East India Company rendered this mythical river basin visually legible as well as stable. **[Figure 1]**

Yet in 1781 the English naturalist, Sir Joseph Banks, read aloud before the Royal Society of London a description of the region written by Rennell that did not exactly square with his drawings. "The vast collection of vapours, wafted from the sea by the southerly or south-west monsoon, are suddenly stopped by the lofty ridge of mountains that runs from east to west through Thibet," he tells us. He then continues, "All the rivers that are situated within the limits of the monsoons, or shifting trade winds, are subject to overflowings at annually stated periods."[1] And yet, when drawing a map of the region, we see no sign of the wafted vapors stopped by the Tibetan plateau. Nor do we observe the way in which the precipitous vapors periodically cause rivers to overtake their banks. Not to mention, there is no record of the inordinate amounts of flotsam and jetsam that these vapors whip up. Indeed, how is it that the same person could develop such a thick description of the sectional qualities of the annual firewater cocktail known as the monsoons and then draw such an ossified map of this dynamic watershed? Answer: colonialism requires a flattening of space. Rennell, at least in the drawing, renders the routes of this territory legible for two tasks that were of great concern to the East India Company and many governments, namely guiding military campaigns and collecting taxes.

Flattening the space of this vast alluvial basin was no straightforward feat. Rennell, along with his assistants, made surveys using only a compass and chains along with Hadley's Quadrant to determine latitude. This practice of walking the land and taking measurements, known as a traverse survey or route survey, was the most popular method of topographic survey in the eighteenth century.[2] While Rennell spent a large portion of his time in a base office, compiling maps, his work also involved extensive fieldwork for surveying, which could sometimes be quite dangerous. While surveying near the frontier of Bhutan in 1776, Rennell was seriously wounded by a group of Sanyasi Fakirs and almost died from the loss of blood. The attack permanently weakened his constitution. By 1776, he had retired from the Company and returned to London, where along with becoming a member of the Royal Society in 1781 and an associate of the Institute of France in 1800, he would continue his work on cartography and oceanography for decades to come.

Rennell's impact on science in colonial India extended beyond his cartographic rendering of the subcontinent. Geologists cited his writings on how the Ganges Delta changes and moves for another eight decades. In *A Geological Manual* (1833), when English geologist Henry Thomas De La Bache detailed the "Delivery of Detritus into the Sea," he cited Major Rennell's observations on the modes by which the Ganges Delta changes over time as "always valuable" because they show the "mode in which they have been carried."[3] Sir Charles Lyell not only discusses Rennell's work on the Ganges in *Principles of Geology* (1865), but also cites his observations on ocean currents or "oceanic rivers" that came to be called "Rennell's Current."[4]

What Rennell achieved visually in terms of space, he achieved textually in terms of time. If the map renders the basin in a single snapshot, then the text describes change. Despite their different ends, both mediums and methods display a layering of geography, hydrography, and even meteorology. When we look at Rennell's map for the East India Company, it is easy to understand it as an object made for a particular purpose. However, when we draw our attention in and out of focus between his drawing and writing, there is a palpable sense of the river basin in a perpetual state of being made and unmade all at the same time.

•

What can we glean from a drawing and text from over two centuries ago? What can they tell us about the way we analyze and construct watersheds today?

First, the gulf between Rennell's drawing and writing marks two different states of attention. The foci of his attention could not be clearer. "Attention sorts out the world… It defines the tiny focus of what matters and the vast blurry remainder of what

[Figure 1] James Rennell, *A map of Bengal, Bahar, Oude & Allahabad: with part of Agra and Delhi, exhibiting the course of the Ganges from Hurdwar to the sea.* (image credit: London: Printed for W. Faden, Geog. to the King, Charing Cross, Jan. 1st, 1786)

doesn't," as historian Lorraine Daston reminds us in her 2012 essay "Attention."[5] It is this sorting out through a process of sustained attention that our language is enriched through description. These acts of description, as Daston rightly notes, define objects and processes ranging from a soffit to neap tides.

There is a range of scales and processes rendered and described in Rennell's work. This range in scale and experience is what the Catalan architect Manuel de Solà-Morales sets out to define in his 1989 essay "The Culture of Description."[6] Based on six drawings made over the course of a decade of Catalonia's urban territory for the *Laboratorio de Urbanismo de Barcelona* that he directed, the text and images foreground attention in action. What do I mean? The ways in which a territory is drawn say as much about the characteristics of the space being drawn as it does about the attention of the person doing the drawing. For de Solà-Morales, drawings are never literal but *literary*. They are not written but *calligraphic*. Even if there are affinities between writing and drawing, they remain distinct, if coeval, forms of description.

But where does the written description intersect with nonverbal description? Art historian and critic Caroline A. Jones's essay "Talking Pictures: Clement Greenberg's Pollock" is instructive. Published in 2004 in *Things That Talk: Object Lessons from Art and Science*, Jones argues for the important role that description played in defining the relationship between the work of the painter Jackson Pollock and the writings of the art critic Clement Greenberg. For Jones, the relationship between the writing and the object was the "thing" being authored. "A book and its reader resemble this kind of thing," too. Jones describes the relationship between artist and critic in order to address a pressing question about art, objects and things, asking, "If it is said, then is that what is historically available to be seen? If it is not said, then is it not seen at all?"[7] Whether describing a twentieth century painting or an eighteenth century map of a dynamic river basin, this question strikes me as a particularly poignant when we attend to *anything* with a past. Conversely, we do well to ask "if something is drawn, then is that what is historically available to be described?"

•

If we return our attention back to Rennell's written and drawn work, we can discern an attempt at "Building a Culture of Description." If it were understood grammatically as a tense, then it would be in the present continuous. It is always being built and rebuilt. This is not to suggest that Rennell deserves to be wreathed in laurels. Throughout his long career he displays laudable and condemnable aspects of building a culture of description. Rather, it is to plot the politics of attention coursing through cultures of description. To that end, these forms of description that we have encountered with Rennell, are simultaneously analytical and projective.

•

In the decades after the publication of Rennell's maps and written descriptions, a new actor comes on the scene: the engineer. The engineer of the nineteenth century does more than walk the land and mark it. Engineers reshape land and redirect rivers, creating an entirely new, artificial topography. The map proves the most important tool to do so.

Since their arrival on the global scene, there are few portions of the earth that have gone undrawn by the hand of engineers. Just as the Ganges has been an object of regard of the engineer, so too have the Mekong, Mississippi, and Rhine river basins.[8] Recent accounts by anthropologists and historians of these river basins describe the ways in which engineers render and re-route the flow of water and sediment through canals and dams.[9] A discipline long enamored with linear processes and achieving static equilibrium, the dynamism of river basins has long been forced to bend to the tools of the engineer.

The Mississippi River Basin in its current configuration is a menagerie of engineering tools to bend the dynamism of a river basin. And there are perhaps no more important maps that undergird the last seven decades of attempts at controlling the Muddy Mississippi than the visually arresting drawings of the meanderings of alluvium across the Lower Mississippi Valley than Harold Norman Fisk's "Ancient Courses: Mississippi River Meander Belt" (1944).[10] **[Figure 2]** Fisk, a geologist with a supposedly explosive personality and a penchant for reconstructing the choreography of riverbeds, overlaid cartographic maps dating from the eighteenth century with aerial photography and geological borings from the twentieth century to draw the convulsions of the Lower Mississippi River over the course of more than 12,000 years.[11] Fisk's dynamic map layers time chronologically to render spatially what many have since noted as the palimpsest nature of the Mississippi. Credited with drawing the behavior and "deep history" of the valley in three-dimensions, Fisk was hired as a consultant by the Mississippi River Commission (MRC) in Vicksburg, Mississippi, to plot out the stages of development and evolution of the valley. Founded in 1879 by the U.S. government to "prevent destructive floods" along with "promote commerce" throughout the basin, the MRC's mission, like that of the U.S. Army Corps of Engineers (USACE), was to control and manage the rhythms of water and alluvium. Not to accommodate it.[12]

If for Fisk his geological and cartographic investigations retrieved a story of what was controlling change over thousands of years across the valley, in the hands of the MRC and USACE these drawings exposed a road map for how to control the future of the river. Fisk's detailed maps guided engineering projects across the valley throughout the second half of the twentieth century and well into the twenty first century.[13] In the words of the writer John McPhee, these "engineers were intending to control it in space and arrest it in time."[14]

Today we recognize the limits of the engineer's "technological fix" to river management and their accompanying language of static description. Indeed, even engineers have grown wary of such approaches and have increasingly collaborated with landscape architects and architects along with ecologists and social scientists to holistically rethink watersheds.[15]

What then are we to make of Derek Hoeferlin's focus on engineering works and systems of management? What can it tell us about the architecture of watersheds as we witness a veritable watershed, and face a reality far different from the legible lines and poché drawn in maps?

First, one wants to inspect these engineering works. The architect cannot help but analyze how these dams and barrages shape space. We know, for instance from Hoeferlin's drawings and photographs, that these structures redirect the aleatory forces of nature in terms of water and soil to irrigate land and produce energy. Sluices and berms do not operate as autonomous entities. They are, as Hoeferlin shows us, not only managed by overlapping bureaucracies of engineers and politicians alongside maintenance crews, but they are also managed differently from one nation state to the next. Drawing the physical and political overlaps of these diverse constituencies draws our attention to how these systems of management align and clash with one another.

Following these points of confluence and opposition, Hoeferlin, who moves between cartographic and photographic modes of description, undertakes a recognizably formal analysis of the architecture of these watersheds. If for his formal forebearers these works were, in the words of Colin Rowe and Fred Koetter, "nostalgia producing instruments," then Hoeferlin attends to these instruments as they inscribe space and interface with political power.[16]

That is not all. The visual evidence collected for analysis in Hoeferlin's study must be understood in terms of the contentious relationship between watersheds and management itself. The "control" of "watersheds" is like trying to plow the sea. As we see across the three river basins profiled in this book, the fortifications needed to sustain and maintain the footings of a dam or weir draw into focus the mutability and dynamism of watersheds.

Rather than castigate the failures of these physical structures and the inability of their management teams to control river basins, we see a markedly different culture of description taking shape in Hoeferlin's study. Despite the intentions of engineers and governments to control the dynamic landscapes, there is an attention paid to how these riparian and estuarial spaces are the outcome of co-authorship. By drawing the ways in which these spaces change, which is to say by incorporating time, Hoeferlin achieves in maps what Rennell was only able to achieve through textual description.

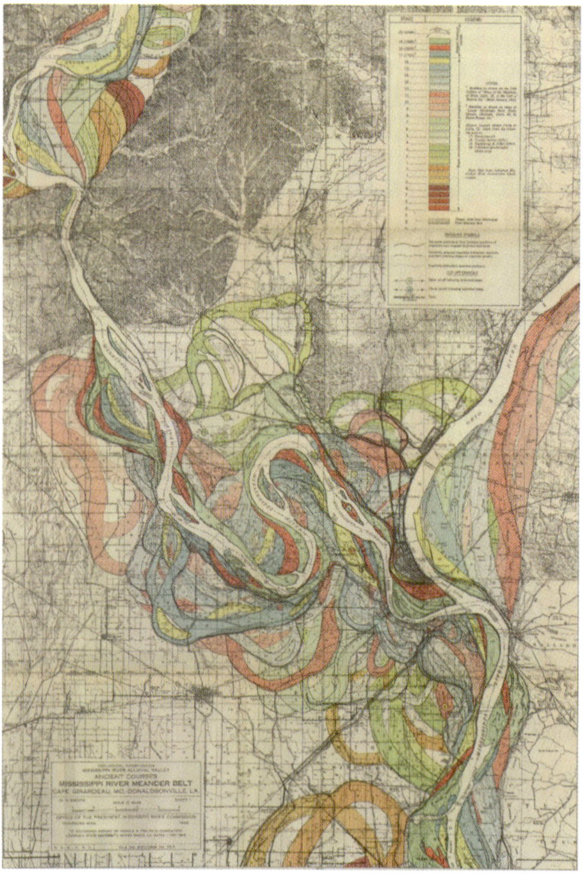

[Figure 2] Harold Norman Fisk, *Ancient Courses: Mississippi River Meander Belt, Plate 22, Sheet 1* (image credit: Vicksburg, Miss: Office of the President, Mississippi River Commission, 1944)

1. James Rennell, "An Account of the Ganges and Burrampooter *Rivers," Philosophical Transactions of the Royal Society of London* LXXI, Part I (1781): 103; also to be found in James Rennell, *Memoir of a Map of Hindoostan: or the Mogul Empire: With an Introduction, Illustrative of the Geography and Present Division of that Country: And a Map of the Countries Situated between the Head of the Indus, and the Caspian Sea* (London: M. Brown, 1788), 268.

2. For more on the history of the traverse or route survey, see Matthew Edney, *Mapping an Empire: The Geographical Construction of British India, 1765–1784* (Chicago: University of Chicago Press, 1997), 91–96.

3. Henry Thomas De La Bache, *A Geological Manual*, 3rd ed. (London: Charles Knight, 1833), 74–75.

4. Charles Lyell, *Principles of Geology; or, The Modern Changes of the Earth and Its Inhabitants Considered as Illustrative of Geology* (New York: D. Appleton & Co., 1865), 277–78, 293.

5. Lorraine Daston, ed., "Attention," in *Curiosity and Method: Ten Years of Cabinet Magazine* (Brooklyn: Cabinet, 2012), 467.

6. Manuel de Solà-Morales, "The Culture of Description," *Perspecta* 25 (1989): 16–25.

7. Caroline A. Jones, "Talking Pictures: Clement Greenberg's Pollock," in *Things That Talk: Object Lessons from Art and Science*, ed. Lorraine Daston (New York: Zone Books, 2004), 336.

8. For the work of engineers across the Ganges River basin, see Ian Stone, *Canal Irrigation in British India: Perspectives on Technological Change in a Peasant Economy* (London: Cambridge University Press, 1984); Anthony Acciavatti, *Ganges Water Machine: Designing New India's Ancient River* (San Francisco: Applied Research and Design, 2015).

9. On the Mekong River basin, see Andrew Johnson, *Mekong Dreaming: Life and Death along a Changing River* (Durham: Duke University Press, 2020) and Thongchai Winichakul, *Siam Mapped: A History of the Geo-body of a Nation* (Honolulu: University Of Hawai'i Press, 1997); on the Mississippi see Andy Horowitz, Katrina: A History, 1915–2015 (Cambridge: Harvard University Press, 2020); on the Rhine River basin see David Blackbourn, *The Conquest of Nature: Water, Landscape, and the Making of Modern Germany* (New York: W.W. Norton, 2007).

10. Harold N. Fisk, *Geological investigation of the alluvial valley of the lower Mississippi River* (Vicksburg: War Department, Corps of Engineers, 1944).

11. For more on Harold Norman Fisk's biography and work in geology, see Michael C. Robinson, "Harold N. Fisk: A Luminescent Man," Engineering Geology 45 (1996), 37–44; Ellis L. Krinitzsky, "The contributions of H. N. Fisk to engineering geology in the Lower Mississippi Valley," *Engineering Geology* 45 (1996): 45–58; For more on Fisk's interests in geology and cartography see Harold Norman Fisk et al., "Sedimentary framework of the modern Mississippi delta [Louisiana]," Journal of *Sedimentary Research* 24, no. 2 (1 June 1954), 76–99.

12. See *Mississippi River Commission Act of 1879*, 46th Congress, 1st Session, Ch. 43, Congressional Record (June 28, 1879), 37–38. Under the Act, the commission was composed of seven members appointed by the president of the United States with three members from the Engineer Corps of the Army, one member from the Coast and Geodetic Survey, and three from civil society (two of whom must be civil engineers). The commission reported directly to the secretary of war (Defense).

13. These projects epitomize what scholar Sofie Hellberg refers to as "hydromentalities," or assemblages for defining and governing water. See Sofie Hellberg, *The Biopolitics of Water: Governance, Scarcity and Populations* (New York: Routledge, 2018).

14. John McPhee, *The Control of Nature* (New York: Farrar, Straus and Giroux, 1989), 10.

15. A recent and multidisciplinary example is Catherine Seavitt Nordenson, Guy Nordenson, Julia Chapman, *Structures of Coastal Resilience* (Washington, DC: Island Press, 2018); Bruno de Meulder and Kelly Shannon, *Water Urbanisms East* 2 (Zurich: Park Books, 2013).

16. Colin Rowe and Fred Koetter, *Collage City* (Cambridge: MIT Press, 1978), 271.

Why the

Mississippi, Mekong, & Rhine?

People ask me, "Why these three river basins? Why not others?" The quick response is: "I *live* in the United States; I *love* Southeast Asia; and, I *learn* a lot from the Dutch about water." That's the personal answer. But in all seriousness, with running the risk of sounding overly simplistic, the Mississippi, Mekong, and Rhine River Basins, arguably, are remarkable examples at three different states of anthropogenic development. However, they share similar characteristics. In terms of physical control of the river systems, each enables large-scale industrial, agricultural systems to connect neoliberal economies, nation-states, and private industries across global trade networks. In the 19th and 20th centuries, the primary method of river control has been river basin–scale navigation projects of locks, dams, canals, and levee systems in the Mississippi and Rhine River Basins, and more recently in the 21st century, the Mekong has followed suit with similar methods of river control. Conflicting agendas result between industrialized and agrarian economies, conserved and polluted environments, and rural and urban communities.

Much can be learned from alternate understandings of these three river basins, specifically with the need for future trans-scalar, integrated design strategies. All three basins are at critical tipping points with each of their futures uncertain.

Stagnating?

Accelerating?

Adapting?

The Mississippi River Basin flows through two nations in North America, north to south from the southernmost portions of Canada to the Gulf of Mexico in United States. Although it is the largest of the three basins, it only flows through two countries, with the vast majority within the United States, and minimal portions in the southernmost parts of Alberta and Saskatchewan Provinces, Canada. I argue that the Mississippi currently represents *stagnating development.* The river system, and the United States, have relentless histories of acts of control, exemplified in the Mississippi River

Basin, first with colonialist conquests, which paved the way for infrastructural conquests throughout the 18th, 19th, and 20th centuries. Take for instance the construction of a series of massive dams along the Missouri River, several of which were strategically located within Native American reservations and which resulted in the dams' reservoirs flooding the tribes' agricultural lands. Many of the river basin's physical systems, particularly its locks, dams, and levees, suffer delayed maintenance in the 21st century; for example, the lock and dam navigation system up and down the Upper Mississippi River north of St. Louis.[1] The river management system has slowed down, if not outright degraded, in recent times. Left unchecked, stagnation and degradation affect us all. Without sufficient funds and political will to tackle contemporary infrastructure, ecological, and social issues, not just along the Mississippi main stem, but also along its tributaries and the terrestrial entirety of the watershed, the basin will continue to degrade. And if this is allowed to continue, the economy of the United States could also degrade, particularly in relation to its existing global economic reliance on large-scale monoculture food economies such as corn, soybeans, and grain that are enabled by large-scale petrochemical and transportation industries. Couple these infrastructural challenges with climate change stressors that include severe weather events which are increasing in intensity and duration and shattering flood and drought records on a yearly basis, especially in the last decade. Take for instance the 2019 floods which spread across 19 states in the basin, and were set off by a five-month period that was the wettest on record for the U.S. In March, 2020, the Mississippi River Cities and Towns Initiative released a report saying there were $20 billion in total direct losses due to the 2019 floods.[2] Also, despite historical efforts to control the river, there are indicators that the Mississippi River will continue to be a dynamic system and could very well change its course in certain locations, both as a result of human-induced measures such as channel shortening, as well as the river's natural process in which it alters its course every thousand years or so in an effort to seek out a shorter and steeper path to the Gulf of Mexico. We are very close to that "every thousand years or so." This is particularly true in the Mississippi River Delta. Within such a radical, and possibly imminent scenario, the obvious question then arises: Can the system, under these conditions that are both human and naturally induced, sustain itself in its currently managed form? Since the answer is likely not, can we optimistically and collectively take clues from the possibilities that the Mississippi River might indeed become more dynamic again—on its own?

The Mekong River Basin flows through six nations in Asia, north to south from the Tibetan Plateau in Qinhai Province, China, to the South China Sea in Vietnam.[3] I argue that the Mekong currently represents *accelerating development*. The effects of climate change, combined with ambitious campaigns of large-scale hydropower infrastructure projects, pose serious questions about the environmental and social resiliency for communities in the river basin, especially downstream and rural communities.[4] Lacking perceived transnational unity for successful water management, the Mekong represents a future with gains for wealthier nation-states and corporations, both Communist governments within the basin, but potentially more so outside the basin to energy conglomerates and urbanizations. However, with transboundary negotiation structures recently set up, several large-scale projects are being monitored and adapted for ecological purposes, including safe passages for fish and sediment, and alleged community benefits projects. However, given the sheer scale and scope of these projects, it remains uncertain whether adaptations will succeed.[5] Given the totalitarian nature of Mekong governments, will communities actually be accommodated in the face of large-scale change?

The Rhine River Basin flows through six nations in Europe, south to north from the Alps in Switzerland to the North Sea in the Netherlands. I argue that the Rhine currently represents *adaptive development*. The Rhine exhibits long-established successes in water management, particularly the Netherlands and its current Room for the River program.[6] Additional environmentally sensitive efforts are up-basin in Germany, France, and Switzerland. Not unlike other basins, many of these successes have only occurred due to major crises, including the Sandoz chemical spill in Basel, Switzerland in 1986, setting off considerable basin-wide environmental regulations including the Rhine Action Program (RAP) of 1987.[7] Relative political stability and nation-state agreements allow for greater cooperation when devising legislature to protect water and people within the river basin, especially in regards to the measures enabled by the navigation and environmental river commissions. Although the European Union in past decades has led to relative transboundary stability, recent environmental, sociopolitical, and public health threats including sustained droughts, hardening of borders, and the Covid-19 pandemic challenge future transboundary stability and negotiations.

1. For an explanation of the USACE's infrastructure costs for maintenance and improvements, see Jordan Golson, "It's Time to Fix America's Infrastructure: Here's Where to Start," *WIRED* (January 23, 2015), https://www.wired.com/2015/01/time-fix-americas-infrastructure-heres-start/.
2. In 2020, the Mississippi River Cities and Towns Initiative released a report saying there were $20 billion in total direct losses due to the 2019 floods, spread across 19 states. See: John Surrat, *Vicksburg Post*, https://www.vicksburgpost.com/2020/03/09/2019-flood-caused-negative-economic-impact-of-more-than-20-billion/.
3. It is important to recognize that there are different names for the "South China Sea," particularly in regards to historical and ongoing territorial disputes over the waters. China's name for it is "South Sea" and Vietnam's name for it is "East Sea." For the purpose of this book, it remains referred to by what the Western colonizers originally named it for trade route reasons.
4. Derek Hoeferlin, "The Watershed Architecture of the Mekong River Basin," *Journal of Architectural Education*, 74, no. 1, 70–82, 2020, https://www.tandfonline.com/doi/full/10.1080/10464883.2020.1693829.
5. Yukako Ono, "Mekong River Nations Face the Hidden Costs of China's Dams: Dozens of Projects Threaten Agriculture and Fishing in Southeast Asia," *Nikkei Asian Review*, May 9, 2018, https://asia.nikkei.com/Spotlight/Cover-Story/Mekong-River-nations-face-the-hidden-costs-of-China-s-dams.
6. https://www.dutchwatersector.com/news/room-for-the-river-programme.
7. https://www.iksr.org/fileadmin/user_upload/DKDM/Dokumente/Broschueren/EN/bro_En_2003_Upstream_Outcome_of_the_Rhine.pdf.

Who Manages the River Basins?

Each basin is managed by various governmental and nongovernmental agencies, with jurisdictions overlapping each other, and not always coordinated with watershed boundaries.

Mississippi → Mississippi River Commission *via* the United States Army Corps of Engineers

Mekong → Mekong River Commission for Sustainable Development

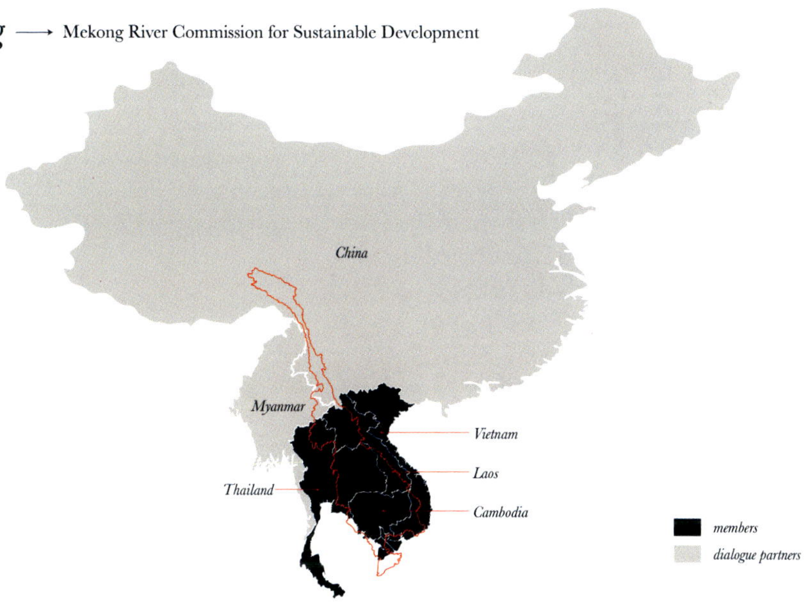

Rhine → Central Commission for the Navigation of the Rhine
→ International Commission for the Protection of the Rhine

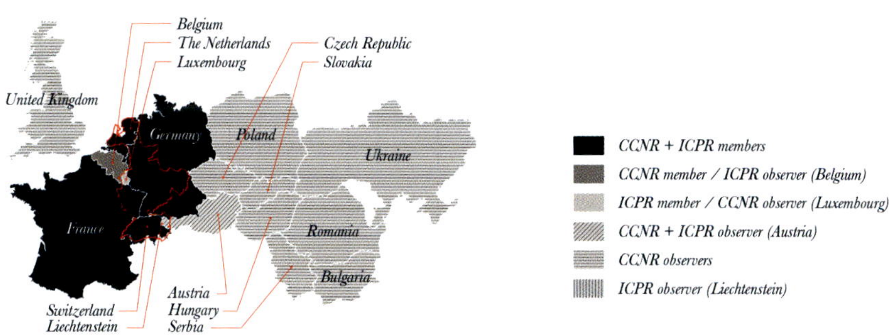

With the majority of the Mississippi River Basin (MRB) existing in one nation, the management functions under a single government jurisdiction. The Mississippi River Commission formed as a result of the 1879 Act of Congress that created legislature "to improve the condition of the river, foster navigation, promote commerce, and prevent destructive floods."[1] First established as an executive body reporting to the Secretary of War, the commission's goals are now carried out by the United States Army Corps of Engineers (USACE). The USACE funds the commission's major project, the Mississippi Rivers and Tributaries Project, headquartered in the Mississippi Valley Division in Vicksburg, Mississippi. The top-down structure allows for direct control over the river's activities, with USACE implementing all civil works projects along the river and throughout the basin. It is important to note that generally, and particularly along the Upper Mississippi mainstem, the priority mandated by Congress to the USACE is to properly maintain its navigation channel, the "9-foot Channel Project."[2] Further down river in the Lower Mississippi stretch, particularly in the delta reach of the river, the river is deeper and the USACE maintains a current draft depth up to 45 feet for oceangoing vessels. A recent agreement between the USACE and State of Louisiana will increase the draft depth to 50 feet from Baton Rouge to the Gulf of Mexico. Navigation projects are prioritized first to enable the status quo supply chain of freighters and barge fleets moving up and down the river, reinforcing different factors such as intensive mono-agriculture, resource extractivism, or petrochemical industries. Flood risk management, environmental regulations and other USACE missions receive lesser priority than navigation.[3] The recent closures to the locks and dams due to the MRB floods of 2019 exemplify the conflict between navigation prioritization and the need for new adaptive flood and riverine management.

Structured management of the Mekong is relatively recent. International development efforts date back to the 1950s with the establishment of the United Nations–sponsored Mekong Committee for infrastructure projects in the lower Mekong River Basin. More recently, the Mekong River Commission (MRC) was officially established in 1995. The MRC "is the only intergovernmental organization that works directly with the governments of Cambodia, Lao PDR, Thailand, and Vietnam to jointly manage the shared water resources and the sustainable development of the Mekong River."[4] But Myanmar and China exist as "dialogue partners" to the MRC. They do not contribute financially, are not committed legally to rulings, and contribute as much or as little information as they choose. The majority of the planned and built dams are upriver in China, and China controls the source of water. While the four member countries contribute financially to the operations of the MRC, it is largely funded by external development partners, including many European countries, the United States, Australia, Japan, and the World Bank. Most of the recent management, regardless of the MRC's recommendations, has been focused on large hydropower project deals made directly between governments inside the basin, such as Lao PDR, with governments and energy conglomerates outside the basin, such as portions of Thailand that are outside of the Mekong River Basin.

Under the European Union, the majority of the countries in the Rhine River Basin have established means of international communication and policy fabrication. Both the International Commission for the Protection of the Rhine (ICPR) and the

Central Commission for the Navigation of the Rhine (CCNR) operate under the EU departments of the Directorate-General for Environment and the Directorate-General for Mobility and Transport, respectively.[5] Structurally, both commissions operate similarly. However, key distinctions exist between their goals and stakeholders. The ICPR's primary mission is to protect the ecology of the river basin, with member and observer countries falling largely within the basin, drawing upon expertise of ecological groups. The CCNR is responsible for securing inland navigation of the river, coordinating with the United Nations Economic Commission for Europe (UNECE). The countries involved are those impacted by the economics of the river, as well as unionized and lobbying organizations such as the European Barge Union and the European Federation of Inland Ports, broader than those existing within the basin. Because of economic impact, the CCNR has an annual budget over double that of the ICPR.

1. https://www.mvs.usace.army.mil/Media/Fact-Sheets/Fact-Sheet-Article-View/Article/491918/mississippi-river-commission-history/.

2. https://www.mvr.usace.army.mil/Missions/Navigation/NESP/The-9-foot-Channel-Project/.

3. For a detailed explanation of the history of flood management of the Mississippi River Basin, in particular in the Lower Mississippi leading up to the Great Flood of 1927 with the "levees only" policy, and the massive efforts to control it afterwards until recent times, see: John M. Barry, *Rising Tide: The Great Mississippi Flood of 1927 and How It Changed America* (New York: Simon & Schuster, 1997).

4. http://www.mrcmekong.org/about-mrc/.

5. https://www.iksr.org/en/ (ICPR), https://www.ccr-zkr.org (CCPR) https://ec.europa.eu/dgs/environment/ (DG for Environment) https://ec.europa.eu/transport/home_en (DG for Mobility and Transport).

(TOP) Mississippi River, Minneapolis, Minnesota, 2014

(MIDDLE) Mekong River, Chiang Khong, Laos, 2019

(BOTTOM) Canal du Rhone au Rhin, at Grand Canal d'Alsace & Rhine River, Niffer, France, 2018

Mississippi River Basin Management Structures

Caernarvon Diversion, Louisiana, 2012
(image credit: Derek Hoeferlin)

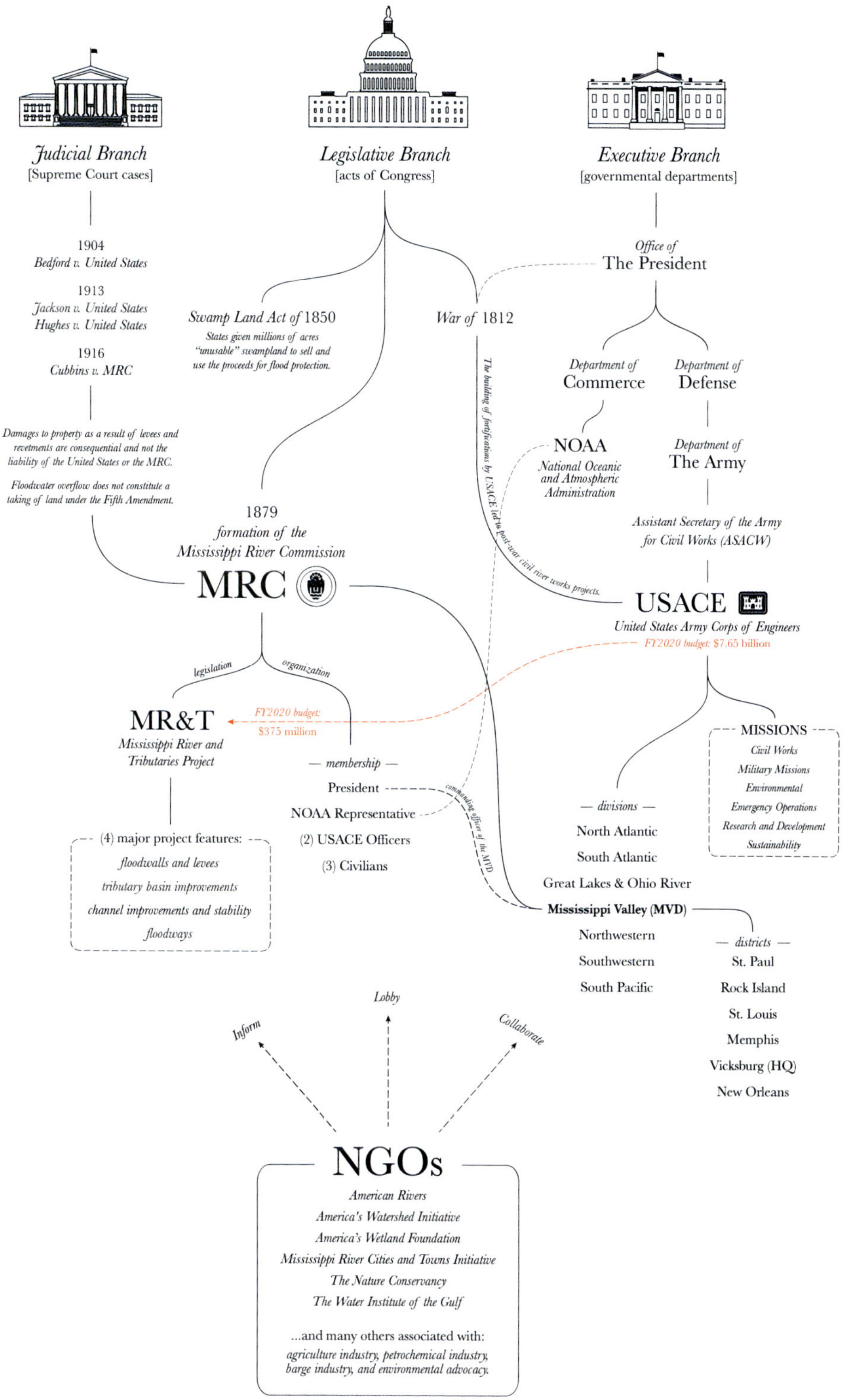

Judicial Branch
[Supreme Court cases]
1904
Bedford v. United States
1913
Jackson v. United States
Hughes v. United States
1916
Cubbins v. MRC
Damages to property as a result of levees and revetments are consequential and not the liability of the United States or the MRC.
Floodwater overflow does not constitute a taking of land under the Fifth Amendment.
Legislative Branch
[acts of Congress]
Swamp Land Act of 1850
States given millions of acres "unusable" swampland to sell and use the proceeds for flood protection.
War of 1812
The building of fortifications by USACE led to post-war civil river works projects.
1879
formation of the
Mississippi River Commission
MRC
legislation
organization
MR&T
Mississippi River and Tributaries Project
FY2020 budget:
$375 million
(4) major project features:
floodwalls and levees
tributary basin improvements
channel improvements and stability
floodways
— membership —
President
NOAA Representative
(2) USACE Officers
(3) Civilians
commanding officer of the MVD
Executive Branch
[governmental departments]
Office of
The President
Department of
Commerce
Department of
Defense
NOAA
National Oceanic and Atmospheric Administration
Department of
The Army
Assistant Secretary of the Army for Civil Works (ASACW)
USACE
United States Army Corps of Engineers
FY2020 budget: $7.65 billion
MISSIONS
Civil Works
Military Missions
Environmental
Emergency Operations
Research and Development
Sustainability
— divisions —
North Atlantic
South Atlantic
Great Lakes & Ohio River
Mississippi Valley (MVD)
Northwestern
Southwestern
South Pacific
— districts —
St. Paul
Rock Island
St. Louis
Memphis
Vicksburg (HQ)
New Orleans
Inform
Lobby
Collaborate
NGOs
American Rivers
America's Watershed Initiative
America's Wetland Foundation
Mississippi River Cities and Towns Initiative
The Nature Conservancy
The Water Institute of the Gulf
...and many others associated with:
agriculture industry, petrochemical industry, barge industry, and environmental advocacy.

United States Army Corps of Engineers (USACE) Boundaries & Divisions

U.S. Army Corps of Engineers (USACE) "Pathfinder" towboat, Mississippi River, 2017 (image credit: Derek Hoeferlin)

USACE

United States Army Corps of Engineers

DIVISIONS & DISTRICTS

Divisions → *Districts*

NORTH ATLANTIC

New England District
New York District
Philadelphia District
Baltimore District
Norfolk District

SOUTH ATLANTIC

Charleston District
Wilmington District
Savannah District
Mobile District
Jacksonville District

GREAT LAKES & OHIO RIVER

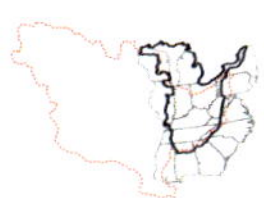

Detroit District
Chicago District
Buffalo District
Pittsburgh District
Huntington District
Louisville District
Nashville District

MISSISSIPPI VALLEY

St. Paul District
Rock Island District
St. Louis District
Memphis District
Vicksburg District (HQ)
New Orleans District

NORTHWESTERN

Seattle District
Portland District
Walla Walla District
Omaha District
Kansas City District

SOUTHWESTERN

Little Rock District
Tulsa District
Fort Worth District
Galveston District

SOUTH PACIFIC

San Francisco District
Sacramento District
Los Angeles District
Albuquerque District

MISSISSIPPI VALLEY DIVISION ⟷ MRC

Mississippi River Commission

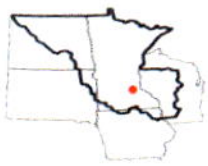

ST. PAUL DISTRICT
5 states
139,000 square land miles
243.6 miles of Mississippi River navigation channel
13 locks & dams (on the Mississippi)

ROCK ISLAND DISTRICT
5 states
78,000 square land miles
314 miles of Mississippi River navigation channel
12 locks & dams (on the Mississippi)

ST. LOUIS DISTRICT
2 states
28,000 square land miles
300 miles of Mississippi River navigation channel
4 locks & dams (on the Mississippi)

MEMPHIS DISTRICT
6 states
25,000 square land miles
355 miles of Mississippi River navigation channel
1 spillway (on the Mississippi)

VICKSBURG DISTRICT (HQ)
3 states
68,000 square land miles
278 miles of Mississippi River navigation channel

NEW ORLEANS DISTRICT
1 state
~20,000 square land miles (delta ever-changing)
400 miles of Mississippi River navigation channel
2 spillways (on the Mississippi)

Mekong River Basin Management Structures

Xayaburi Dam, Mekong River, Laos, 2019 (image credit: Derek Hoeferlin)

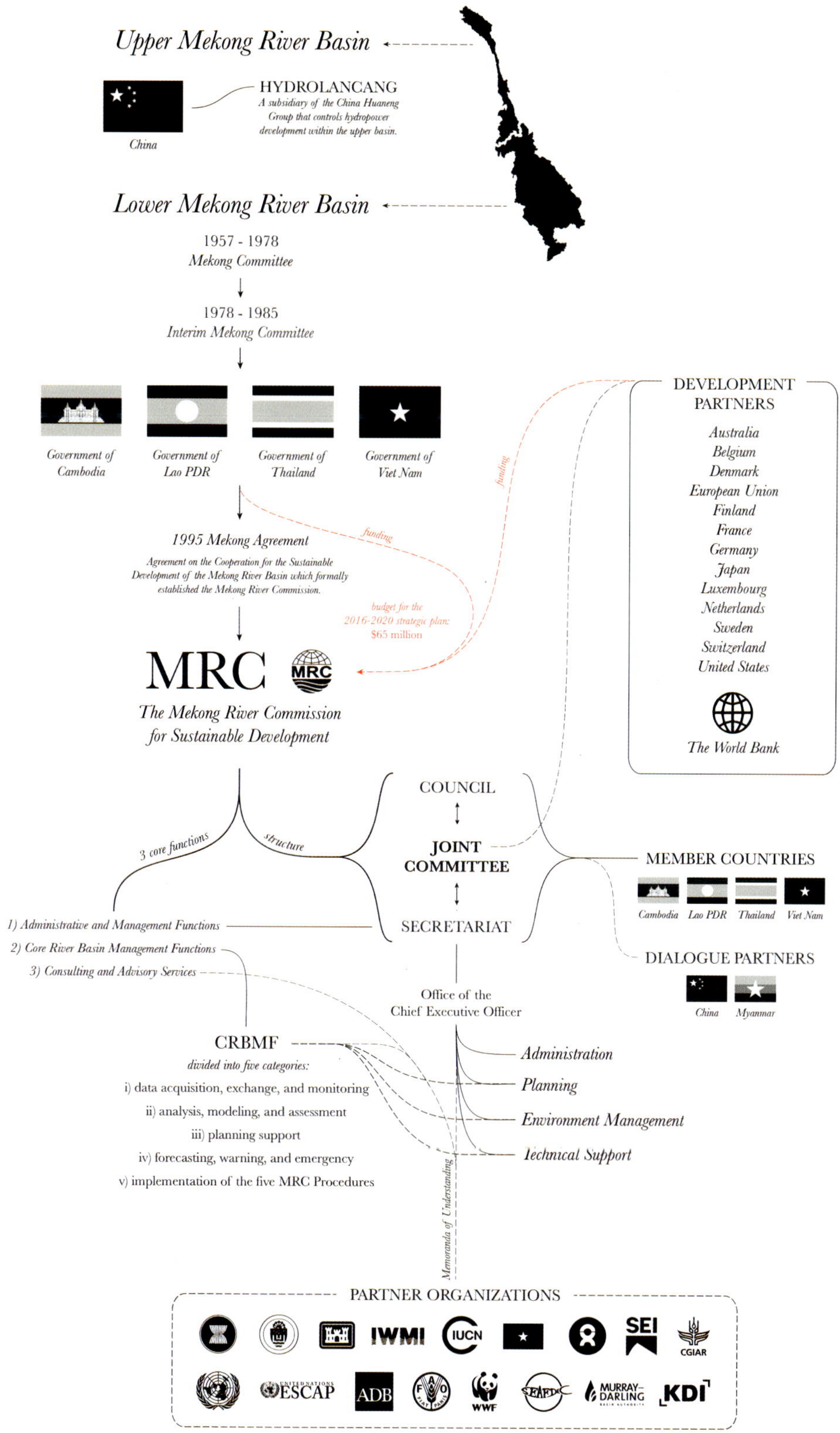
Upper Mekong River Basin
HYDROLANCANG
A subsidiary of the China Huaneng Group that controls hydropower development within the upper basin.
China
Lower Mekong River Basin
1957 - 1978
Mekong Committee
1978 - 1985
Interim Mekong Committee
Government of Cambodia
Government of Lao PDR
Government of Thailand
Government of Viet Nam
funding
funding
1995 Mekong Agreement
Agreement on the Cooperation for the Sustainable Development of the Mekong River Basin which formally established the Mekong River Commission.
budget for the 2016-2020 strategic plan: $65 million
MRC
MRC
The Mekong River Commission for Sustainable Development
DEVELOPMENT PARTNERS
Australia
Belgium
Denmark
European Union
Finland
France
Germany
Japan
Luxembourg
Netherlands
Sweden
Switzerland
United States
The World Bank
3 core functions
structure
COUNCIL
JOINT COMMITTEE
SECRETARIAT
MEMBER COUNTRIES
Cambodia
Lao PDR
Thailand
Viet Nam
DIALOGUE PARTNERS
China
Myanmar
1) Administrative and Management Functions
2) Core River Basin Management Functions
3) Consulting and Advisory Services
Office of the Chief Executive Officer
CRBMF
divided into five categories:
i) data acquisition, exchange, and monitoring
ii) analysis, modeling, and assessment
iii) planning support
iv) forecasting, warning, and emergency
v) implementation of the five MRC Procedures
Administration
Planning
Environment Management
Technical Support
Memoranda of Understanding
PARTNER ORGANIZATIONS
IWMI
IUCN
SEI
CGIAR
ESCAP
ADB
WWF
SEAFDEC
MURRAY–DARLING
KDI

Rhine River Basin Management Structures

Kembs Barrage, Grand Canal d'Alsace, France, 2018 (image credit: Derek Hoeferlin)

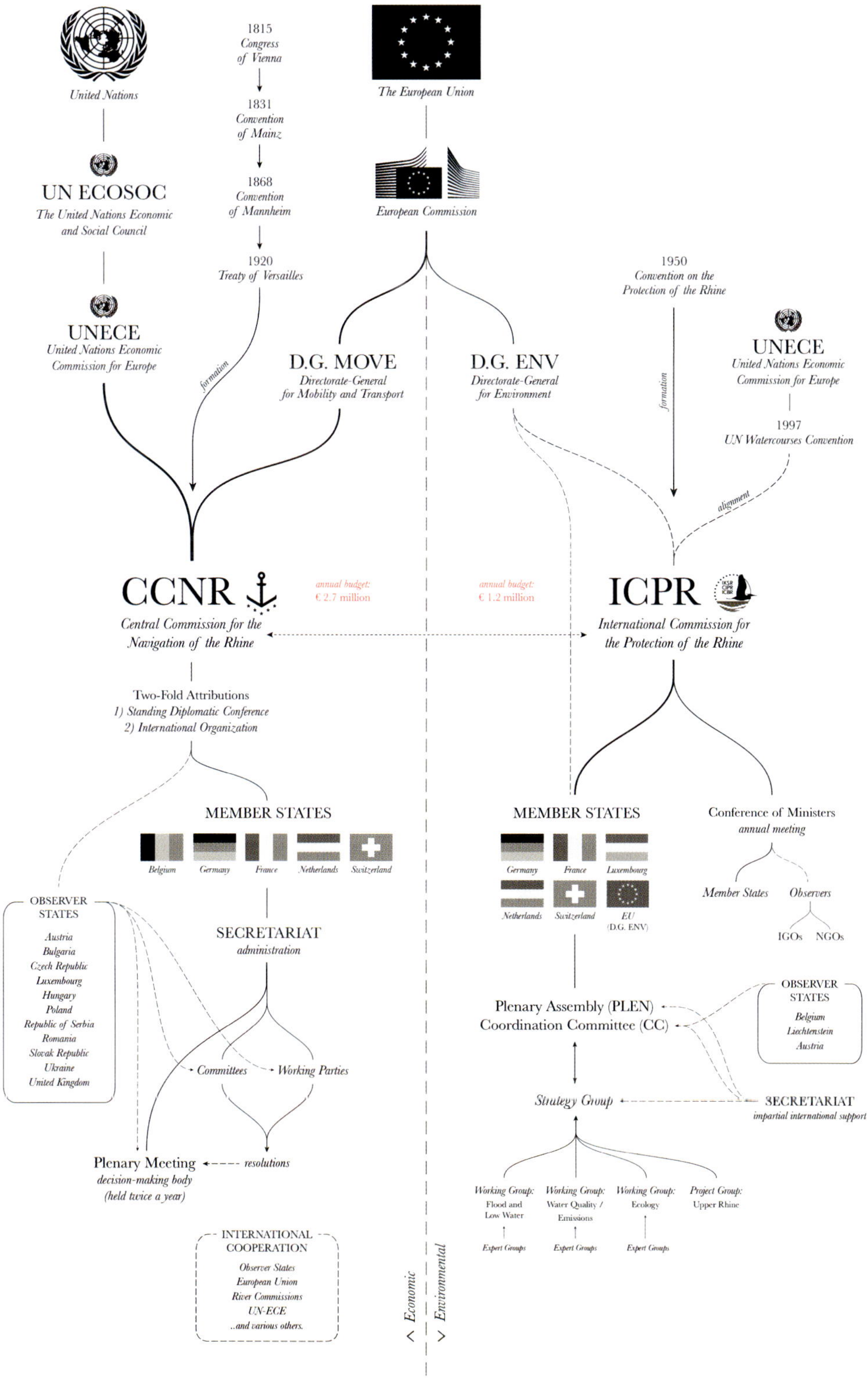

United Nations
UN ECOSOC
The United Nations Economic and Social Council
UNECE
United Nations Economic Commission for Europe
1815 Congress of Vienna
1831 Convention of Mainz
1868 Convention of Mannheim
1920 Treaty of Versailles
formation
The European Union
European Commission
D.G. MOVE
Directorate-General for Mobility and Transport
D.G. ENV
Directorate-General for Environment
1950 Convention on the Protection of the Rhine
formation
UNECE
United Nations Economic Commission for Europe
1997 UN Watercourses Convention
alignment
CCNR
Central Commission for the Navigation of the Rhine
annual budget: € 2.7 million
annual budget: € 1.2 million
ICPR
International Commission for the Protection of the Rhine
Two-Fold Attributions
1) Standing Diplomatic Conference
2) International Organization
MEMBER STATES
Belgium
Germany
France
Netherlands
Switzerland
OBSERVER STATES
Austria
Bulgaria
Czech Republic
Luxembourg
Hungary
Poland
Republic of Serbia
Romania
Slovak Republic
Ukraine
United Kingdom
SECRETARIAT
administration
Committees
Working Parties
Plenary Meeting
decision-making body
(held twice a year)
resolutions
INTERNATIONAL COOPERATION
Observer States
European Union
River Commissions
UN-ECE
..and various others.
Economic
Environmental
MEMBER STATES
Germany
France
Luxembourg
Netherlands
Switzerland
EU (D.G. ENV)
Conference of Ministers
annual meeting
Member States
Observers
IGOs
NGOs
Plenary Assembly (PLEN)
Coordination Committee (CC)
OBSERVER STATES
Belgium
Liechtenstein
Austria
Strategy Group
SECRETARIAT
impartial international support
Working Group: Flood and Low Water
Working Group: Water Quality / Emissions
Working Group: Ecology
Project Group: Upper Rhine
Expert Groups
Expert Groups
Expert Groups

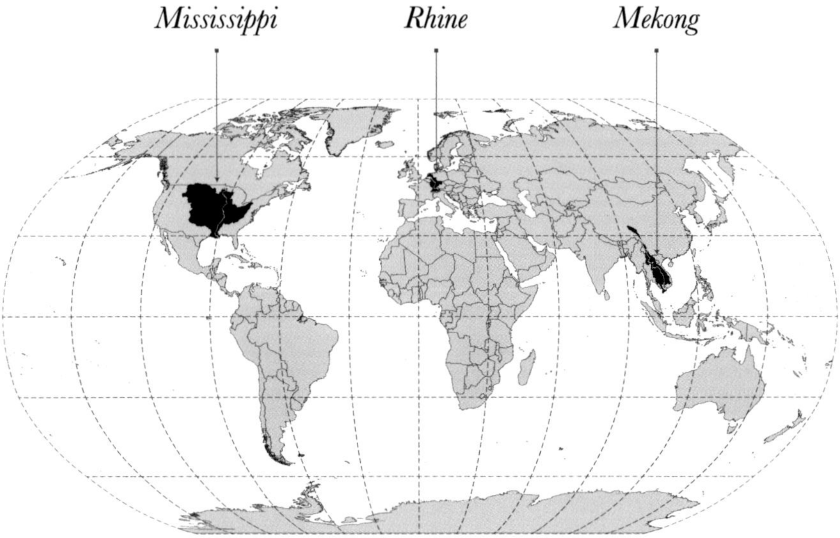

by LENGTH:

Mississippi River 2,350 mi

Mekong River 3,050 mi

Rhine River 765 mi

by AREA:

Mississippi Basin
1,200,000 mi²

Mekong Basin
307,000 mi²

Rhine Basin
85,000 mi²

population within the *Mississippi Basin*

78,173,975

via the Transboundary Waters Assessment Programme

major urban areas along the river:

data from metropolitan statiscal areas (MSAs) defined by The United States Office of Management and Budget as an urbanized area of 50,000 inhabitants or more; 2018 estimated populations.

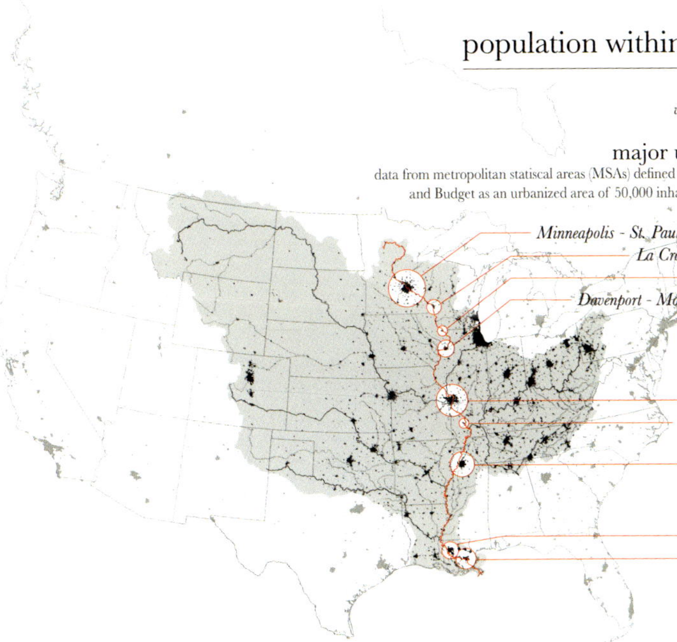

Minneapolis - St. Paul - Bloomington, MN-WI	3,629,190
La Crosse - Onalaska, MN-WI	136,808
Dubuque, IA-IL	96,854
Davenport - Moline - Rock Island, IA-IL	381,451
St. Louis, MO-IL	2,805,465
Cape Girardeau, MO-IL	96,982
Memphis, AR-TN-MS	1,350,620
Baton Rouge, LA	831,310
New Orleans, LA	1,270,399

population within the *Mekong Basin*

58,742,817

via the Transboundary Waters Assessment Programme

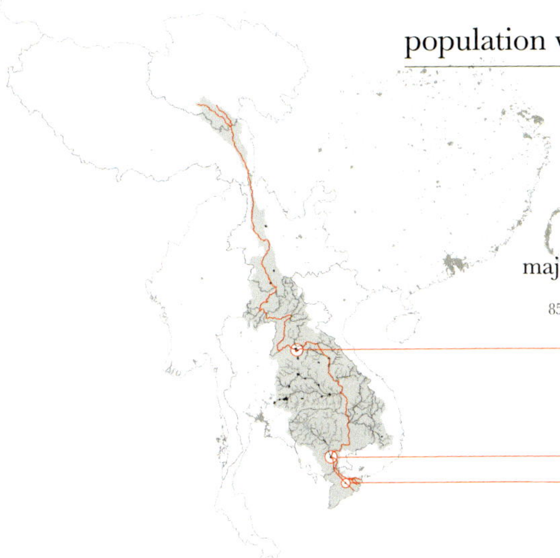

major urban areas along the river:

data from various country statiscal censuses; 85% of people live in rural agricultural communities

Vientiane, Laos	948,477
Phnom Penh, Cambodia	2,129,371
Can Tho, Vietnam	1,282,300

population within the *Rhine Basin*

48,831,090

via the Transboundary Waters Assessment Programme

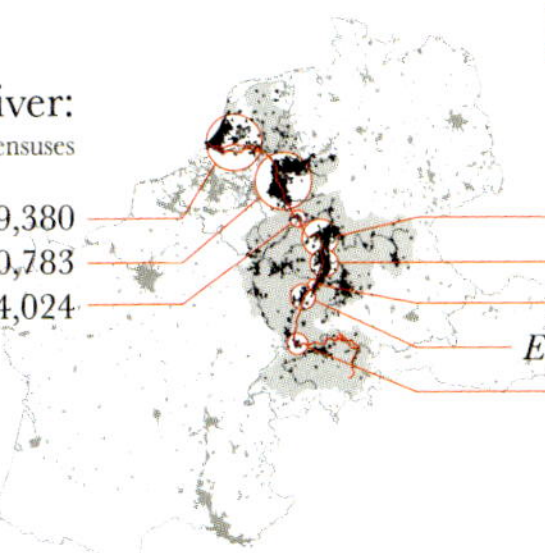

major urban areas along the river:

data from various country statiscal censuses

Randstad, Netherlands	8,219,380
Rhine-Rhur Region, Germany	10,680,783
Koblenz, Germany	114,024
Frankfurt Rhine-Main Region, Germany	5,821,523
Rhine-Neckar Region, Germany	2,362,000
Karlsruhe, Germany	313,092
Eurodistrict Strasbourg-Ortenau, France-Germany	958,421
Basel, Switzerland	177,595

territories within the *Mississippi Basin*

2 countries

2 Canadian provinces, 31 US states

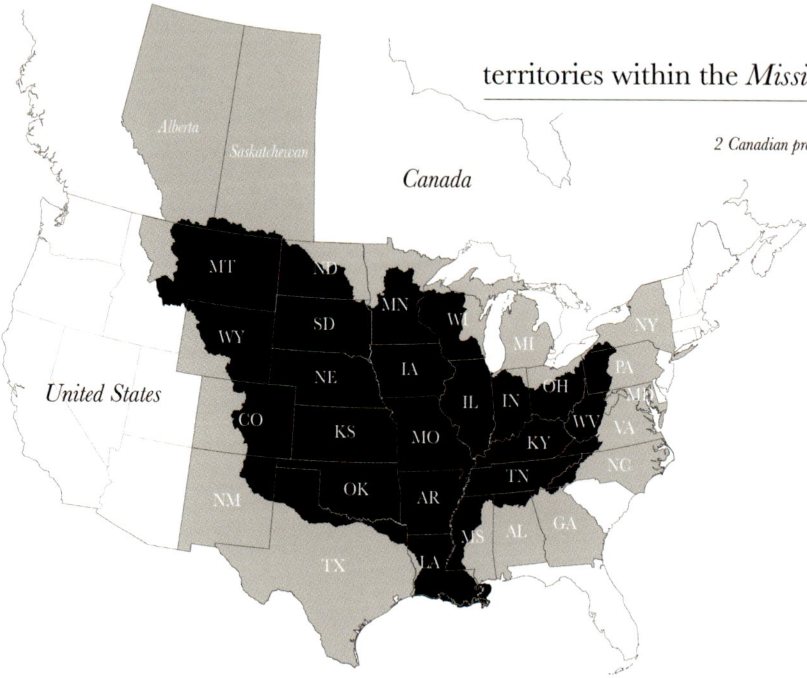

territories within the *Mekong Basin*

6 countries

3 Chinese provinces

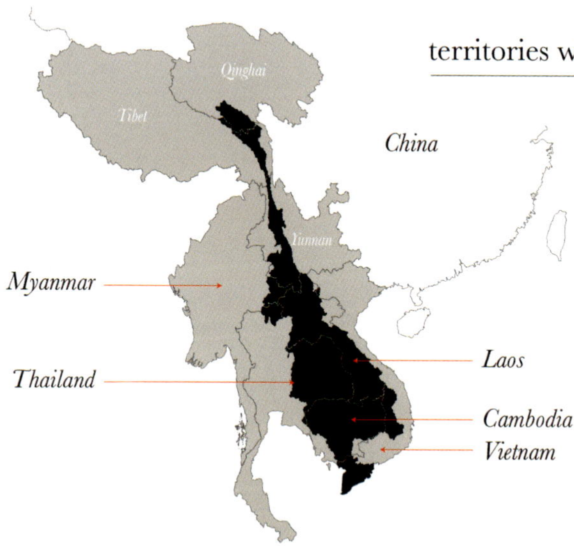

territories within the *Rhine Basin*

8 countries

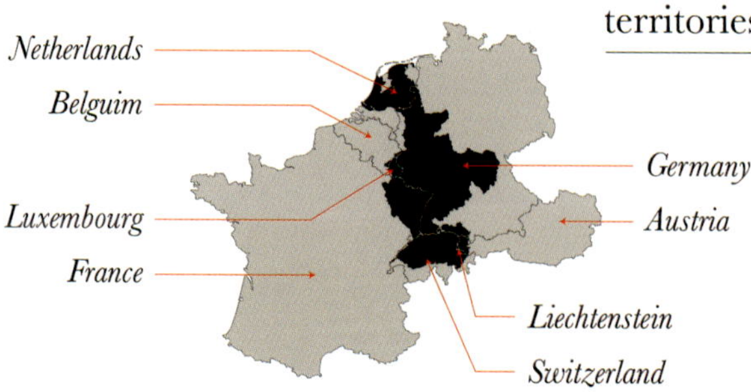

tributaries of the *Mississippi River*

6 major

combined length: 7,759 mi

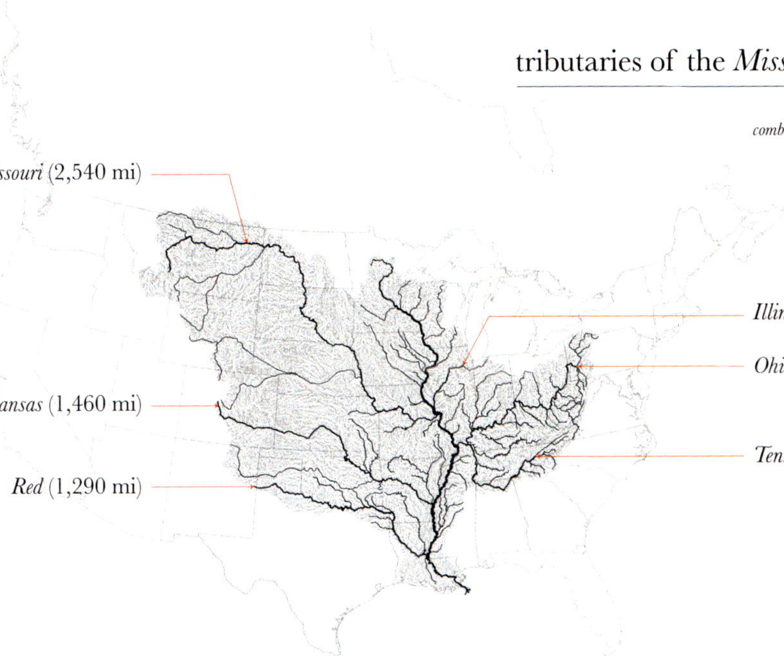

tributaries of the *Mekong River*

17 major

combined length: 3,839 mi

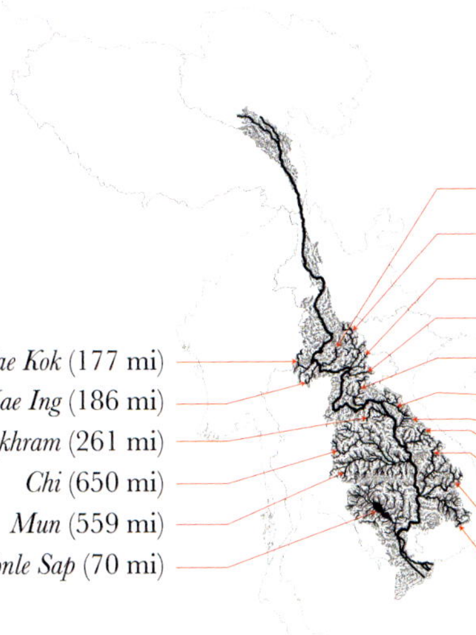

tributaries of the *Rhine River*

10 major

combined length: 1,825 mi

water volume within the *Mississippi Basin*

average annual mainstem discharge: 593,000 ft³/s

annual tributary discharge:

1	*Ohio River*	281,000 ft³/s
2	*Missouri River*	76,200 ft³/s
3	*Tennessee River*	68,000 ft³/s
4	*Red River*	56,000 ft³/s
5	*Arkansas River*	41,000 ft³/s
6	*Illinois River*	29,500 ft³/s

water volume within the *Mekong Basin*

average annual mainstem discharge: 531,900 ft³/s

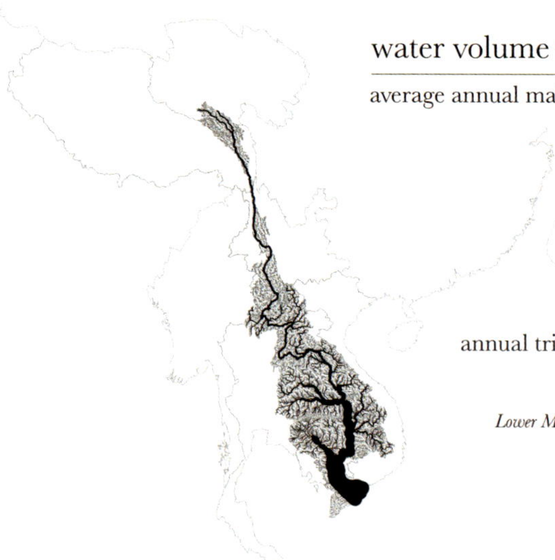

annual tributary discharge by region (%):

Upper Mekong (China)	16%
Lower Mekong, left bank (Chi, Mun, Tonle Sap)	55%
Lower Mekong, right bank	20%

water volume within the *Rhine Basin*

average mainstem discharge: 81,200 ft³/s

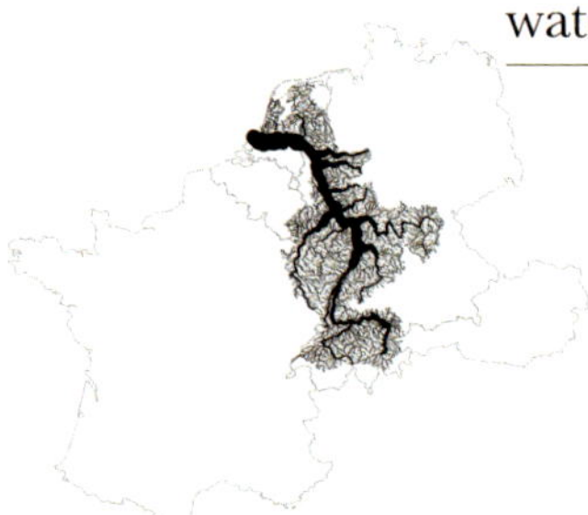

annual tributary discharge by region:

Alpine Rhine	8,200 ft³/s
High Rhine	37,400 ft³/s
Upper Rhine	56,000 ft³/s
Middle Rhine	72,100 ft³/s
Lower Rhine	81,000 ft³/s

topography of the *Mississippi Basin*

elevation gain: 1,475 ft

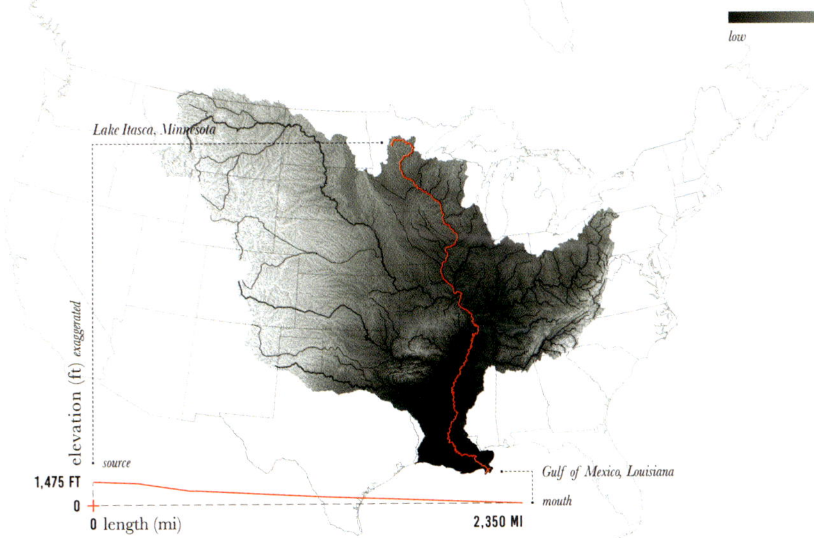

topography of the *Mekong Basin*

elevation gain: 14,800 ft

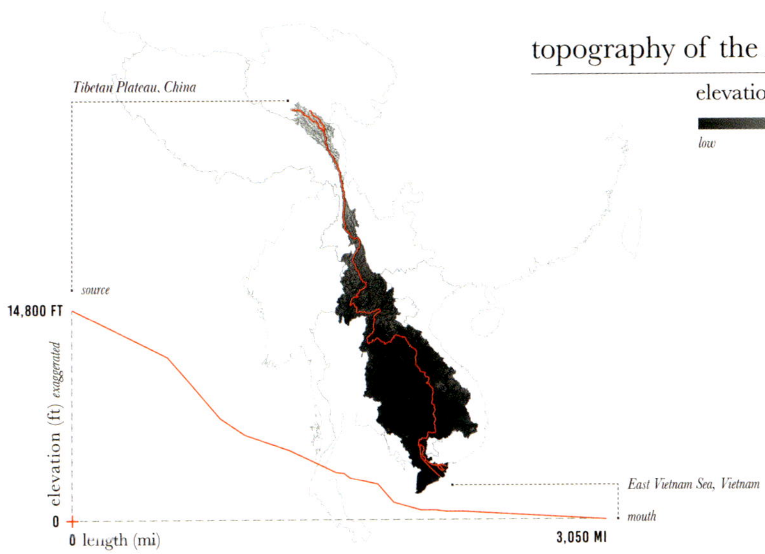

topography of the *Rhine Basin*

elevation gain: 7,695 ft

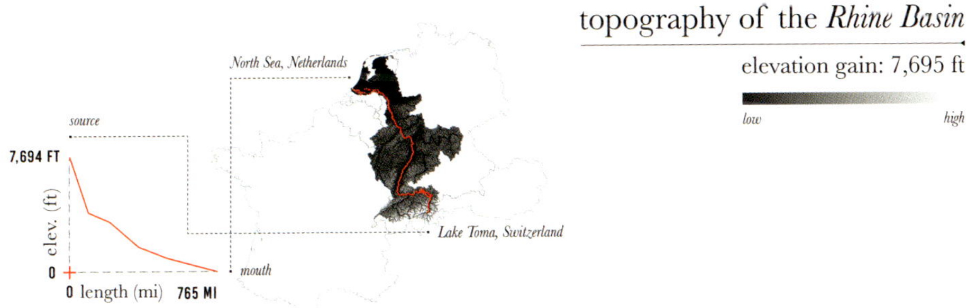

Mississippi, Mekong & Rhine River Basin Atlas

Derek Hoeferlin, with Jess Vanecek, Paul Wu, & Chenyu Zhang

World

Continent

Territory

Region

Zone

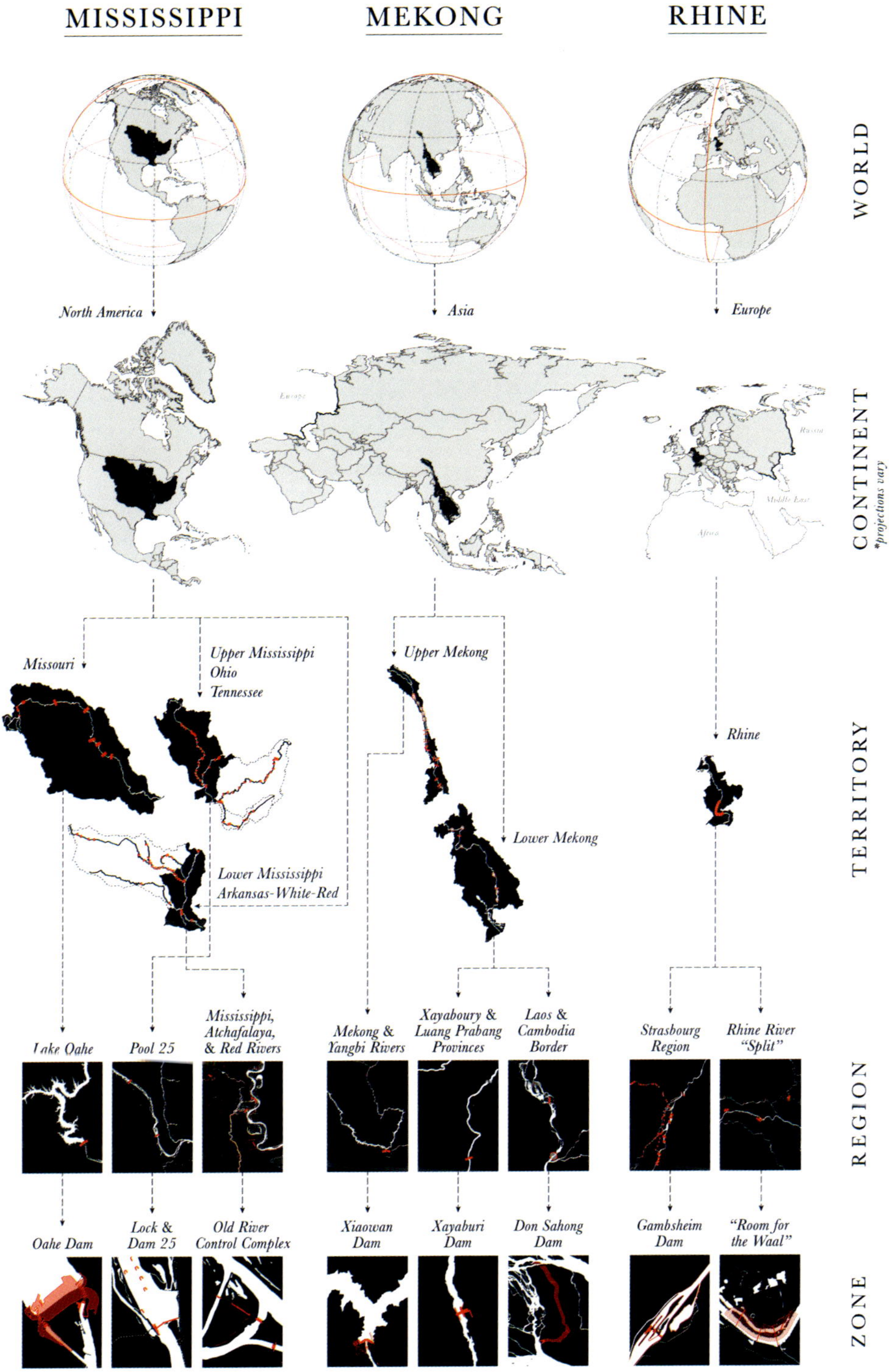
MISSISSIPPI
MEKONG
RHINE
WORLD
North America
Asia
Europe
CONTINENT
*projections vary
Missouri
Upper Mississippi
Ohio
Tennessee
Lower Mississippi
Arkansas-White-Red
Upper Mekong
Lower Mekong
Rhine
TERRITORY
Lake Oahe
Pool 25
Mississippi, Atchafalaya, & Red Rivers
Mekong & Yangbi Rivers
Xayaboury & Luang Prabang Provinces
Laos & Cambodia Border
Strasbourg Region
Rhine River "Split"
REGION
Oahe Dam
Lock & Dam 25
Old River Control Complex
Xiaowan Dam
Xayaburi Dam
Don Sahong Dam
Gambsheim Dam
"Room for the Waal"
ZONE

Mississippi River Basin & the World

Quoting Colin Wellenkamp, the executive director of the Mississippi River Cities and Towns Initiative:

"Forty percent of the world's food supply comes out of the Mississippi River Basin. An additional forty percent of all United States agricultural output from coast to coast moves up and down the river. One in every twelve human beings on Earth ingests commodities made in the Mississippi River Basin. Eighty percent of what is grown in the Mississippi River Basin goes overseas. If you wanted to destroy or otherwise compromise the globe's food web, shut down the Mississippi River and it could collapse."

Continent 01: Mississippi River Basin & North America

Continent 01 Plan

By all quantifiable measures, the Mississippi River is one of the largest river systems in the world. Its drainage basin has a total catchment area of 1,200,000 square miles, the largest watershed in North America and the fourth-largest in the world.[1] The Mississippi River and its tributaries are ecologically diverse, providing natural habitats for 260 fish species and 195 mammal and amphibian species, as well as a primary flyway for migratory birds.[2] Set almost entirely in the United States of America, the Mississippi River Basin (MRB) covers nearly 40 percent of the land in the continental U.S., across 31 states.[3] The main stem of the Mississippi River is the second-largest river in North America in terms of water volume and length. On average, it discharges 593,000 cubic feet per second into the Gulf of Mexico, which also makes the MRB the fifteenth-largest in the world when measured in volume of discharge.[4] The scale of this water volume is crucial in providing needed habitats for so many species to thrive. In the past, the volumes of water naturally flooded large swathes of land, creating fertile conditions for agriculture. The natural processes of flooding and sediment deposition also generated various wetland ecologies, and ones not just limited to the delta, but all across riparian zones up and down the main stems and tributaries. From source to mouth, the Mississippi River has a total length of 2,340 miles—only falling short to its own tributary, the Missouri River, by 200 miles.[5] While these physical measures begin to depict an impressive landscape, the manner and extent to which the MRB benefits the socioeconomic status of the U.S. has dictated its ongoing development and utilization. With its vast size and abundance of water, the MRB produces as much as 92 percent of all U.S. agricultural exports, which accounts for 78 percent of the world's grain and soybean trade.[6] Since the late 19th century, more than 100 dams and river-control structures have been developed on the Mississippi River and its major tributaries, taking

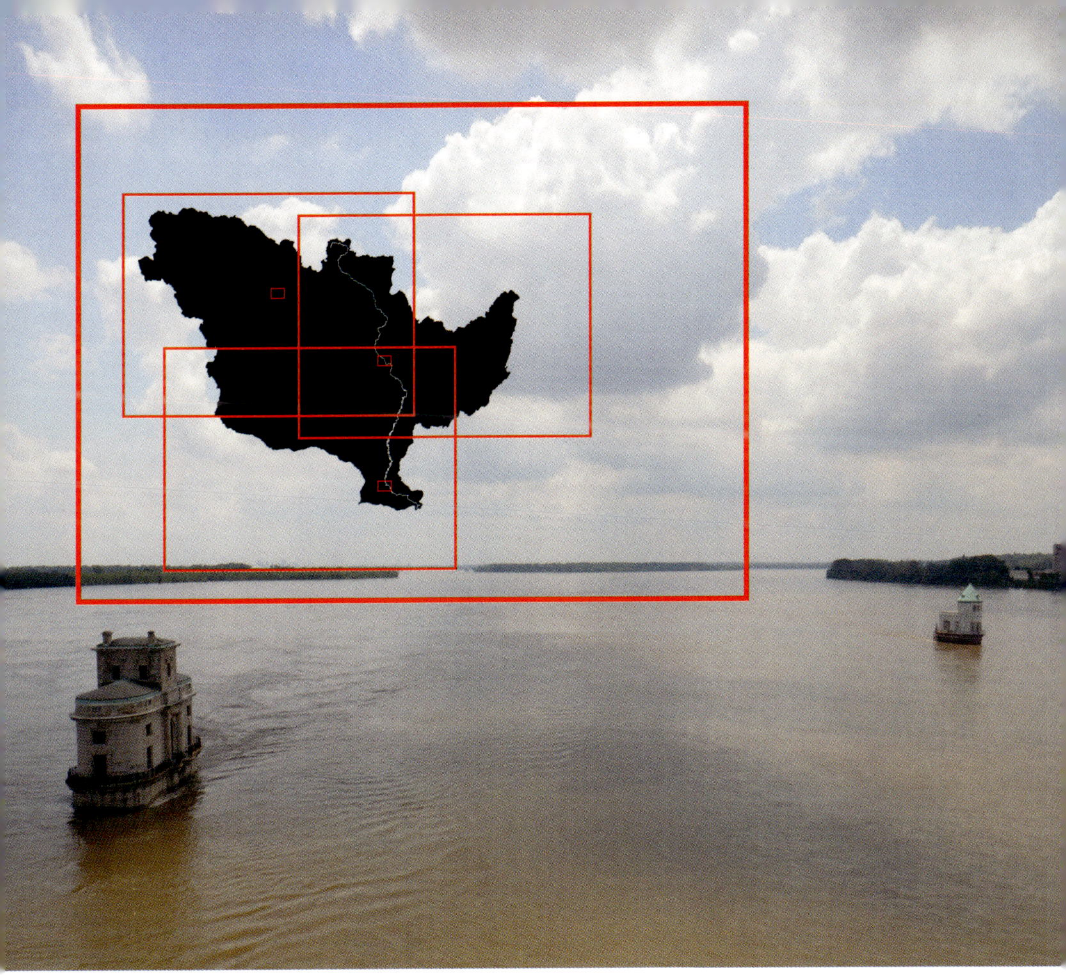

De-commissioned water intake towers, Mississippi River at flood stage at Chain of Rocks, St. Louis, Missouri, 2013 (image credit: Derek Hoeferlin)

advantage of the MRB's water resources.[7] These projects capitalize on the MRB's economic potential to generate hydroelectricity and to facilitate inland navigation from the delta to the upper reaches and create a link to the Great Lakes, the Erie Canal, and beyond.[8] A study conducted by the U.S. Department of Energy identified that nearly 40 percent of the country's hydroelectric capacity (estimated at 25,549MW out of a total 65,493MW) were attributed to the MRB.[9] Additionally, the MRB has become the country's most active waterway, and in 2007, 435 million tons of freight, worth $107 billion, were shipped through the basin.[10] Invaluable due to its scale and socioeconomic impact, the MRB is undoubtedly one of the most important river systems, not just in North America, but in the world.

Continent 01 Section A-A

The main stem of the Mississippi River begins in upper Minnesota and meanders to the south through the center of the United States, where it historically distributed its nutrient and sediment rich waters across the Mississippi River Delta in southeast

Louisiana. Similar in shape and function to a funnel, the Mississippi Watershed collects water from the central North American continent, and directs the waters towards the Gulf of Mexico, between a mostly human-altered, leveed landscape. While the Rocky and Appalachian Mountains are the source for many of North America's rivers, including the Mississippi's most significant tributaries, the main stem of the Mississippi River modestly begins in the relatively low-lying plains of the American upper Midwest at Lake Itasca, which has a surface elevation of 1,475 feet. For a modest-sized glacial lake that is fed by a stream only 18 feet wide and 18 inches deep, it is remarkable to contemplate how such a small headwater leads to such a big watershed across the North American continent. In total, the MRB includes six important "smaller" sub-basins, each of which are vast in their own right, exhibiting their own unique, riverine, infrastructural, and cultural characteristics. The main stem divides into the Upper and Lower Mississippi River Basins. The Ohio and Tennessee River Basins join the MRB from the east. The massive Arkansas-White-Red and Missouri River Basins join the MRB from the west. Almost every dam in the MRB provides basic functions including flood control, irrigation, recreation, and water supply. Whether they are equipped with the additional capacity to generate hydroelectricity or facilitate navigation depends on the physical qualities and pragmatic needs in each sub-basin. The large-scale demands from the United States' economic prowess of big agricultural and big industrial regimes have led to big engineered solutions as large-scale answers. Most of these were originally designed with little attention paid to adverse environmental impacts, which have led to "unintended consequences." On the more densely populated rivers of the Mississippi, Ohio, Illinois, Red, and lower Arkansas, the dams were built in part to enable year-round commercial shipping. Hydroelectric dams have been installed in the Missouri, Tennessee, and upper Arkansas Rivers partially because of suitable terrain and water volume as well as to meet the respective region's rising energy needs.[11] Being almost entirely an American watershed, the projects and management structure in the MRB has been primarily created through legislation passed by the U.S. Congress.[12] The U.S. Army Corps of Engineers (USACE) is the primary body that is responsible for the coordination, development, and maintenance of all federal projects in the MRB.[13] In its present state, the MRB is a highly engineered and controlled landscape. This type of monofunctional, engineered landscape directly impacts various land uses and communities' relationships to important places such as riverfronts, floodplains, wetlands, and public spaces.

Continental Divide, Montana

Three Forks, Montana

Pool 19, Illinois

TERRITORY 01
MISSOURI RIVER BASIN

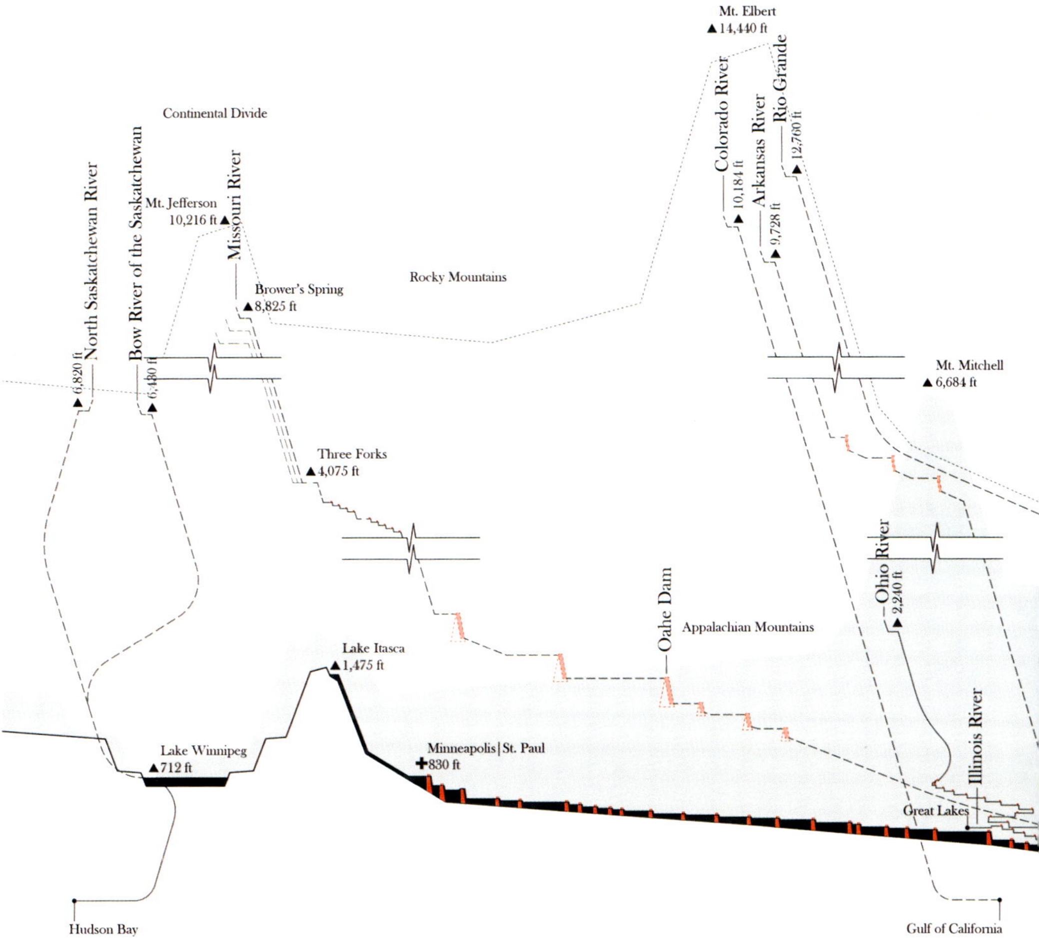

TERRITORY 02
UPPER MISSISSIPPI RIVER BASIN

SASKATCHEWAN RIVER BASIN

CAN

U

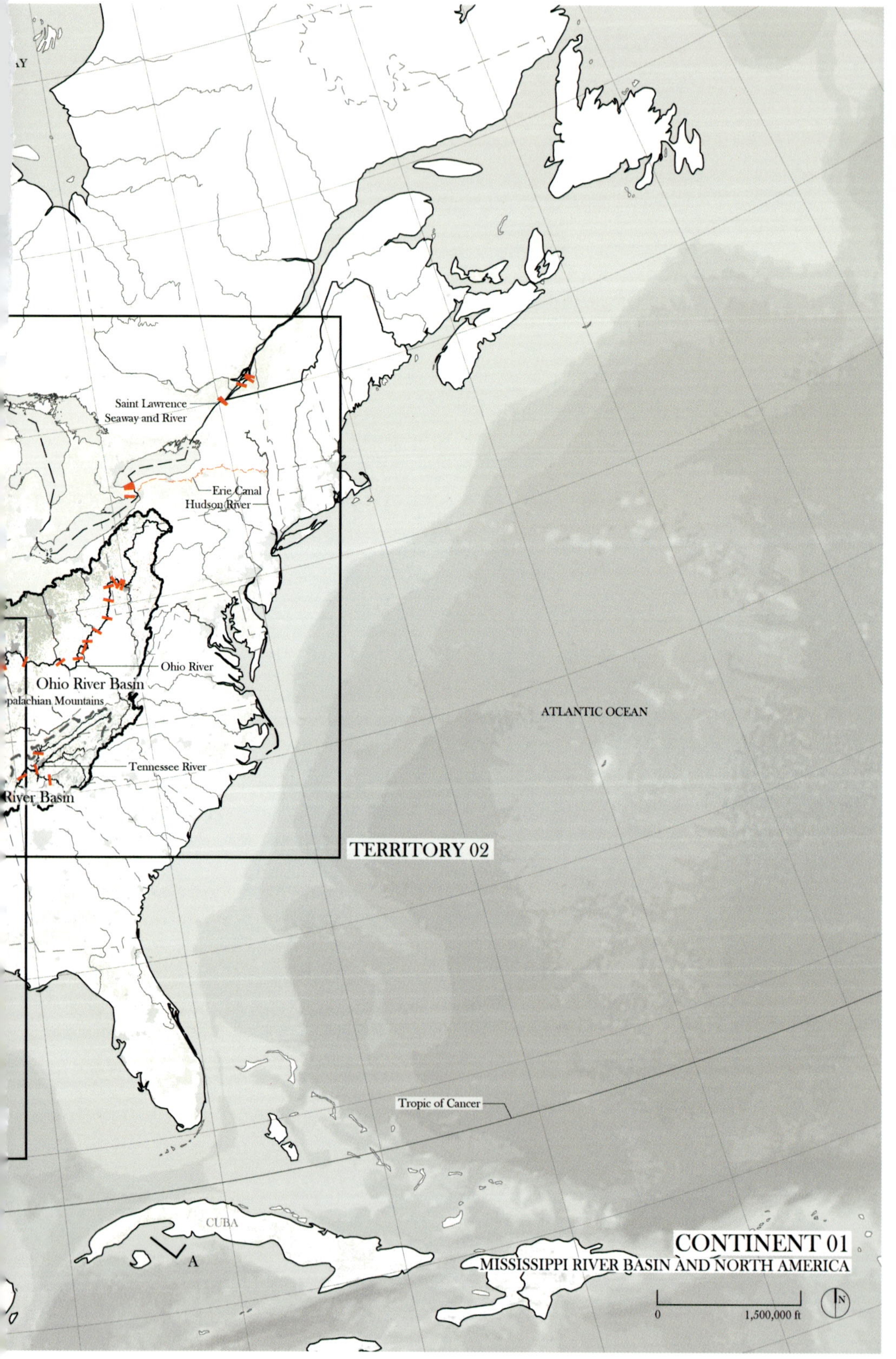

Saint Lawrence Seaway and River
Erie Canal
Hudson River
Ohio River
Ohio River Basin
palachian Mountains
Tennessee River
River Basin
TERRITORY 02
ATLANTIC OCEAN
Tropic of Cancer
CUBA
A
CONTINENT 01
MISSISSIPPI RIVER BASIN AND NORTH AMERICA
0
1,500,000 ft
N

HUDS
A
Saskatchewan River
Columbia River
TERRITORY 01
CANADA
Missouri River
Upper Mississippi River Basin
Great Lakes
REGION 01
Snake River
Upper Mississippi River
Rocky Mountains
Missouri River Basin
Illinois Rive
UNITED STATES OF AMERICA
REGION 0
Colorado River
Arkansas River
Arkansas-White-Red River Basin
White River
Colorado River Aqueduct
Tennessee
Rio Grande
Red River
Lower Mississippi River
Lower Mississippi River Basin
REGION 03
Atchafalaya River
Mississippi Delta
GULF OF CALIFORNIA
MEXICO
TERRITORY 03
GULF OF MEXICO

Fertilizer Plant, Missouri

New Madrid Floodway, Missouri

Saline Marsh, Louisiana

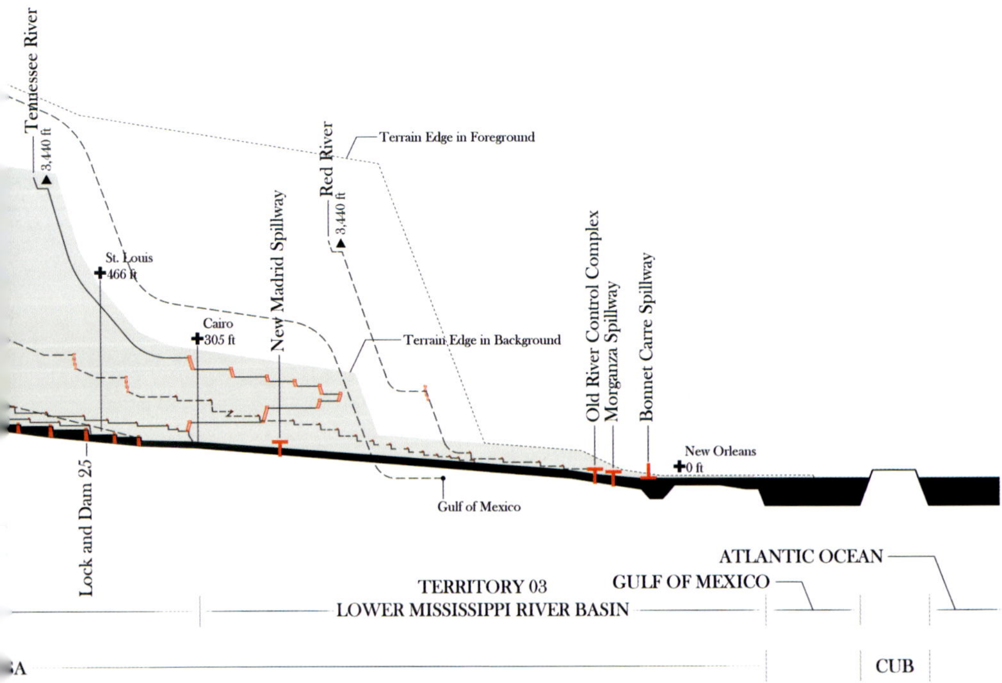

SECTION A-A
FOLLOWING THE PATH OF THE MISSISSIPPI RIVER

1. "Mississippi River Facts," Mississippi, National Park Service (November 24, 2018), https://www.nps.gov/miss/riverfacts.htm.

2. Ibid

3. Ibid.

4. Ibid.

5. *Lengths of Major Rivers*, U.S. Geological Survey, accessed May 6, 2021, https://web.archive.org/web/20090305045437/http://ga.water.usgs.gov/edu/riversofworld.html.

6. "Mississippi River Facts," Mississippi, National Park Service, November 24, 2018, https://www.nps.gov/miss/riverfacts.htm.

7. "Dams," Bureau of Transportation Statistics, United States Department of Transportation, 2019, https://data-usdot.opendata.arcgis.com/datasets/dams.

8. Jason S. Alexander, Richard C. Wilson, and W. Reed Green, *A Brief History and Summary of the Effects of River Engineering and Dams on the Mississippi River System and Delta* (Reston: U.S. Geological Survey, 2012), accessed January 4, 2021, https://pubs.usgs.gov/circ/1375/C1375.pdf, 1.

9. *Hydropower Vision: A New Chapter for America's 1st Renewable Energy Source* (Washington DC: U.S. Department of Energy, July 2016), accessed January 4, 2021, https://www.energy.gov/eere/water/downloads/hydropower-vision-report-full-report, 151.

10. Michael Margreta, Chester Ford, and M.A. Dipo, *U.S. Freight on the Move: Highlights from the 2007 Commodity Flow Survey Preliminary Data* (Washington DC: U.S. Department of Transportation Research and Innovative Technology Administration, September 2009), accessed January 4, 2021, https://www.bts.gov/archive/publications/special_reports_and_issue_briefs/special_report/2009_09_30/entire, 3.

11. Arthur E. Morgan, *The Making of the TVA* (Buffalo: Prometheus Books, 1974), 2; "Missouri River Mainstem Reservoir System: Master Water Control Manual" (Omaha: U.S. Army Corps of Engineers Northwestern Division, March 1, 2006), accessed December 7, 2020, https://digitalcommons.unl.edu/cgi/viewcontent.cgi?article=1070&context=usarmyceomaha, VII-1.

12. Alexander et al., *A Brief History and Summary*, 16.

13. Ibid., 17–18.

Territory 01: Missouri River Basin

Territory 01 Plan

The largest of the Mississippi River Basin's six sub-basins, the Missouri River Basin (MRB) is a vast and diverse territory with significant infrastructural development. The Missouri River begins in western Montana at the Three Forks, the tripartite confluence of three rivers. It runs in a southeast diagonal direction through the Great Plains and concludes in the Midwest, where it empties into the Mississippi River just north of St. Louis, Missouri. With a total length of 2,540 miles, the Missouri River is marginally longer than the Mississippi River.[1] On average, the Missouri River discharges 76,200 cubic feet of water per second into the Mississippi River, contributing roughly an eighth of the watershed's total flow. It drains an area of 529,350 square miles across ten states and two Canadian provinces.[2] Vast and diverse in territories, the MRB overlaps with unique natural formations like the Bakken Shale and Ogallala Aquifer. Many notable oil and natural gas pipelines cross through the basin, like the Dakota Access, Keystone, and the on-again, off-again Keystone XL (cancelled as of June, 2021), delivering resources extracted from southern Canada and northern U.S. to Midwest and southern states. This expanse of land, according to the U.S. Army Corps of Engineers' 2018 Master Manual, has a population of 15.5 million and is largely considered rural, with the exception of a few larger cities mostly scattered adjacent to the Missouri River.[3] Currently, there are 15 dams on the main stem of the Missouri River. Unlike the main stem of the Mississippi River, commercial navigation is only possible from Sioux City to St. Louis—downstream of the last main-stem dam.[4] The lower six projects, Fort Peck to Gavins Point, are a set of dams and reservoirs that were critically designed to operate as a coordinated system in order to optimize power generation and to provide maximum safety against floods.[5] Constructed and operated by the USACE, these six projects are the key structures and reservoirs that manage the Missouri River's water resources for irrigation, flood control,

Garrison Spillway, Missouri River, Coleharbor, North Dakota, 2018 (image credit: Derek Hoeferlin)

and generating hydroelectricity.[6] In the process of creating reservoirs, the six projects controversially destroyed millions of acres of Tribal Lands that are located along the Missouri River and its tributaries, displacing thousands of Native Americans who lived on the riparian landscape.[7] The program is also partially responsible for fomenting conflict between the economy, ecology, and politics in the region.[8] Recently, one reservation in particular, the Standing Rock Reservation located near the beginning of Oahe Dam's reservoir, was the site of the 2016 to 2017 protest against the construction of the Dakota Access Pipeline.[9] This event, in many ways, is the culmination of tensions, both environmental and social, that have been the result of land-use practices in the MRB.

Territory 01 Section B-B

The Missouri River has been altered from its natural state into a controlled water system by the main-stem infrastructural developments. While the Missouri River officially begins with the Three Forks, the three rivers that feed into the confluence start higher in the Continental Divide. The source of the Madison River, the tallest of the three and considered the main headwaters of the Missouri River, is marked by Brower's Spring, which has an elevation of 8,825 feet. From the Three Forks, nine dams quickly interrupt the natural flow of the Missouri River. After this, a series of six "system" dams, beginning with the Fort Peck Dam and concluding with the Gavins Point Dam, spanning a significant portion of the remainder of the river, ending just upriver from Sioux City, Iowa. Becoming operational in 1943, the Fort Peck hydroelectric dam was commissioned in 1933 at the height of the Great Depression and after sporadic years of droughts in the territory. The dam was an immediate solution to provide employment and long-term water resource security for the region.[10] After its completion, record precipitation levels in 1943 and 1944 led to consecutive years of flooding in the MRB.[11] There was a sense of urgency to create a large-scale project that could address the existing concerns, economic recovery, and flood control, through a cohesive water resource management plan in the MRB. Congress passed the Flood Control Act of 1944 which authorized the U.S. Army Corps of Engineers to enact the Pick-Sloan Missouri Basin Program. This comprehensive water management plan included the development of the remaining five main-stem hydroelectric dams, Garrison to Gavins Point, along with a hundred other tributary dams.[12] It was stressed that irrigation could provide stability to the region's economy while electricity could facilitate its growth.[13] In total, the Pick-Sloan Program is estimated to irrigate 5.3 million acres of farmland, and the six "system" dams have a combined energy generation capacity of 2,431 MW.[14] This monumental feat was accomplished by permanently impounding and inundating the river through the six dams to create reservoirs that have transformed the river into an artificial cascade. It has had numerous consequences on the ecosystem, chief among them being the unintended trapping of sediment. The Missouri River, nicknamed the "Big Muddy" due to its high sediment concentration, contributes an overwhelming majority of the sediment to the Mississippi River.[15] Since the completion of the Pick-Sloan Program, the amount of sediment exiting the Missouri River has decreased by half, causing a near 50 percent reduction in the total sediment load in the entire Mississippi River Basin.[16] Driven by socioeconomic progress, the main-stem damming of the Missouri River has irreversibly disrupted the natural environment.

Fort Peck Dam

Garrison Dam

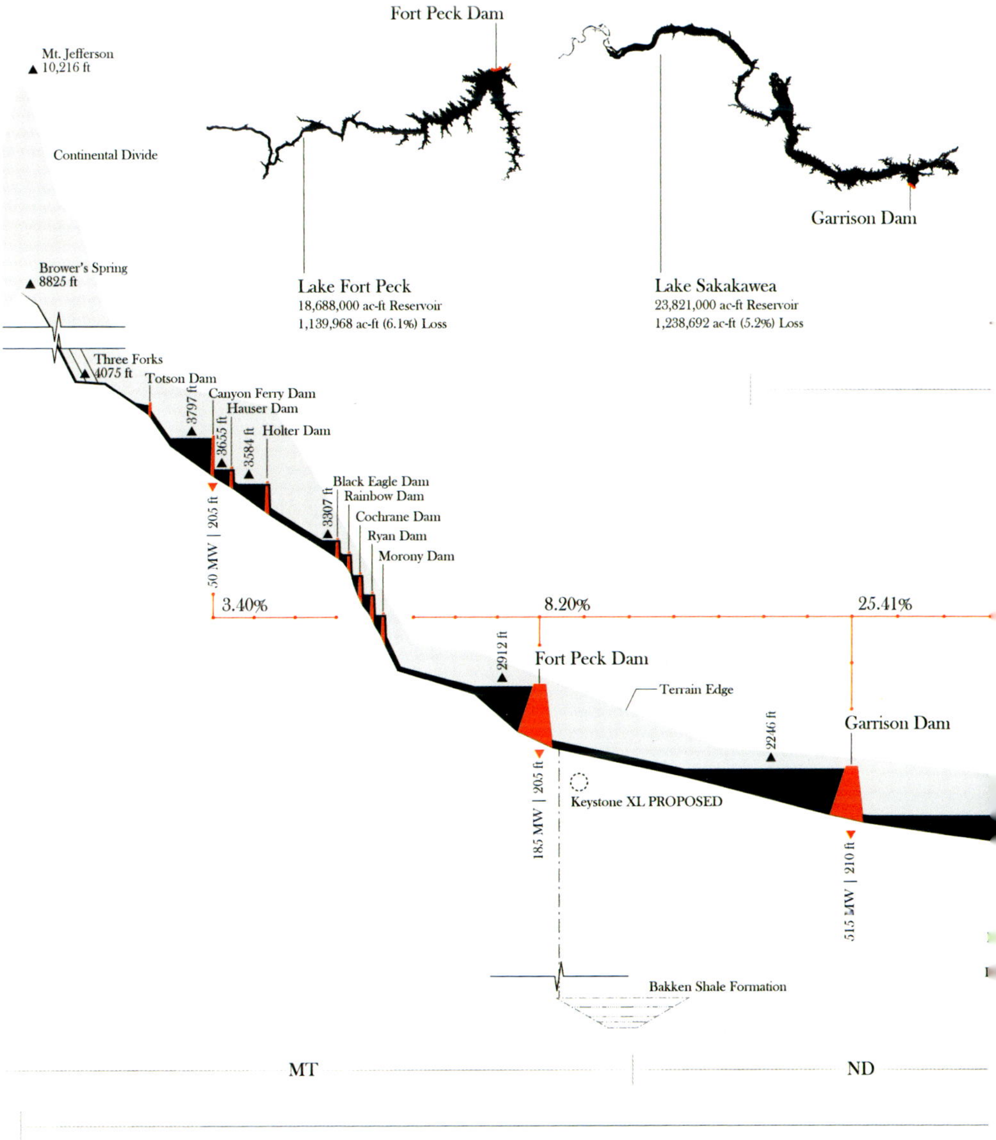
Fort Peck Dam
Mt. Jefferson
10,216 ft
Continental Divide
Garrison Dam
Brower's Spring
8825 ft
Lake Fort Peck
18,688,000 ac-ft Reservoir
1,139,968 ac-ft (6.1%) Loss
Lake Sakakawea
23,821,000 ac-ft Reservoir
1,238,692 ac-ft (5.2%) Loss
Three Forks
4075 ft
Totson Dam
3797 ft
Canyon Ferry Dam
Hauser Dam
3655 ft
3584 ft
Holter Dam
Black Eagle Dam
Rainbow Dam
3307 ft
Cochrane Dam
Ryan Dam
Morony Dam
50 MW | 205 ft
3.40%
8.20%
25.41%
2912 ft
Fort Peck Dam
Terrain Edge
2246 ft
Garrison Dam
185 MW | 205 ft
Keystone XL PROPOSED
515 MW | 210 ft
Bakken Shale Formation
MT
ND

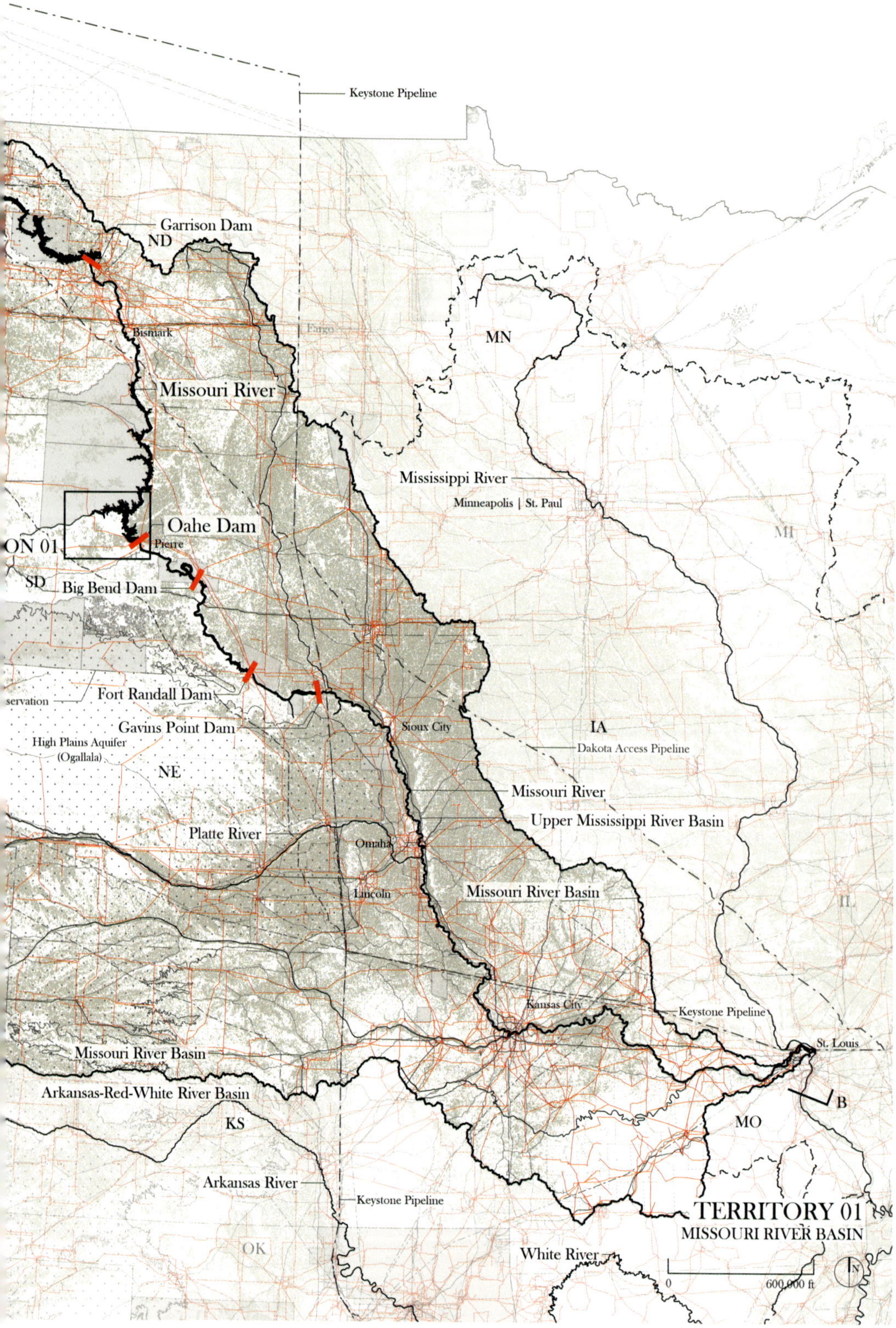
Keystone Pipeline
Garrison Dam
ND
Bismark
Fargo
Missouri River
MN
Mississippi River
Minneapolis | St. Paul
Oahe Dam
ON 01
Pierre
MI
SD
Big Bend Dam
servation
Fort Randall Dam
Gavins Point Dam
Sioux City
IA
Dakota Access Pipeline
High Plains Aquifer
(Ogallala)
NE
Missouri River
Upper Mississippi River Basin
Platte River
Omaha
Lincoln
Missouri River Basin
IL
Kansas City
Keystone Pipeline
St. Louis
Missouri River Basin
Arkansas-Red-White River Basin
B
KS
MO
Arkansas River
Keystone Pipeline
TERRITORY 01
MISSOURI RIVER BASIN
OK
White River
0
600,000 ft
N

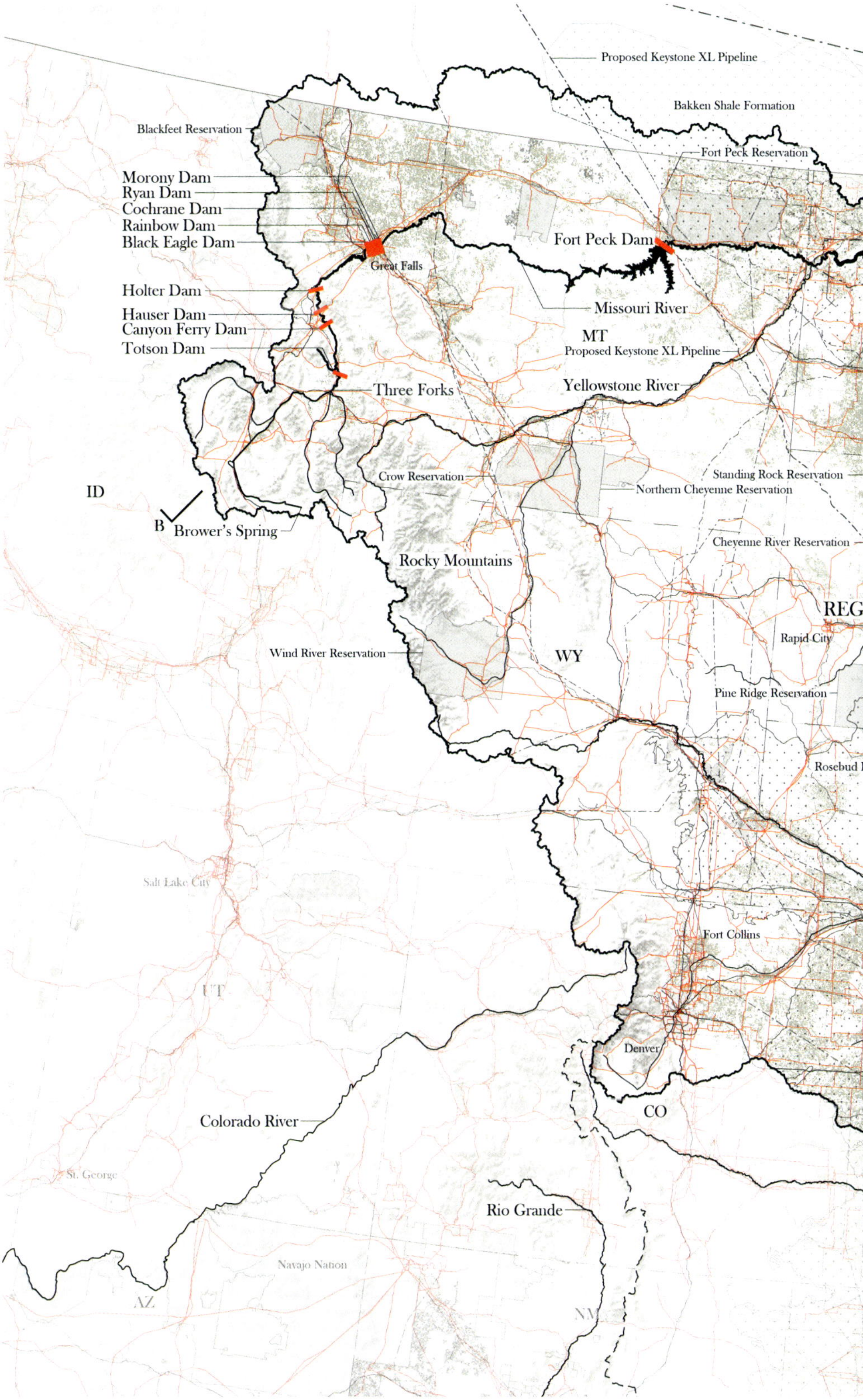

Proposed Keystone XL Pipeline
Bakken Shale Formation
Blackfeet Reservation
Fort Peck Reservation
Morony Dam
Ryan Dam
Cochrane Dam
Rainbow Dam
Black Eagle Dam
Fort Peck Dam
Great Falls
Holter Dam
Hauser Dam
Canyon Ferry Dam
Totson Dam
Missouri River
MT
Proposed Keystone XL Pipeline
Three Forks
Yellowstone River
Crow Reservation
Standing Rock Reservation
Northern Cheyenne Reservation
ID
B
Brower's Spring
Cheyenne River Reservation
Rocky Mountains
REG
Rapid City
Wind River Reservation
WY
Pine Ridge Reservation
Rosebud R
Salt Lake City
Fort Collins
UT
Denver
CO
Colorado River
St. George
Rio Grande
Navajo Nation
AZ
NM

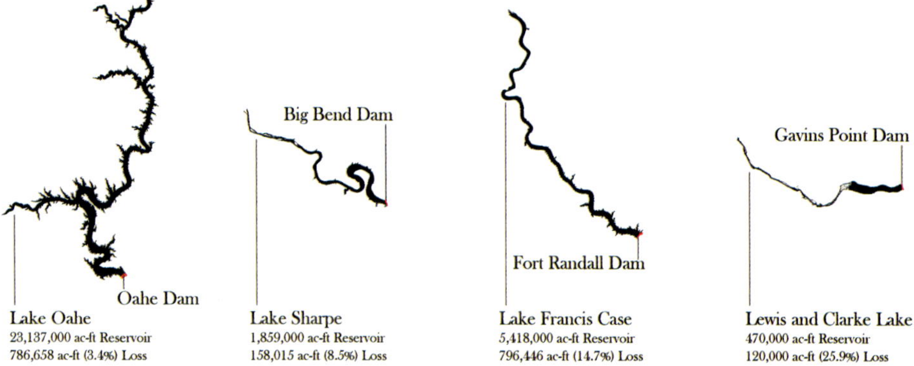

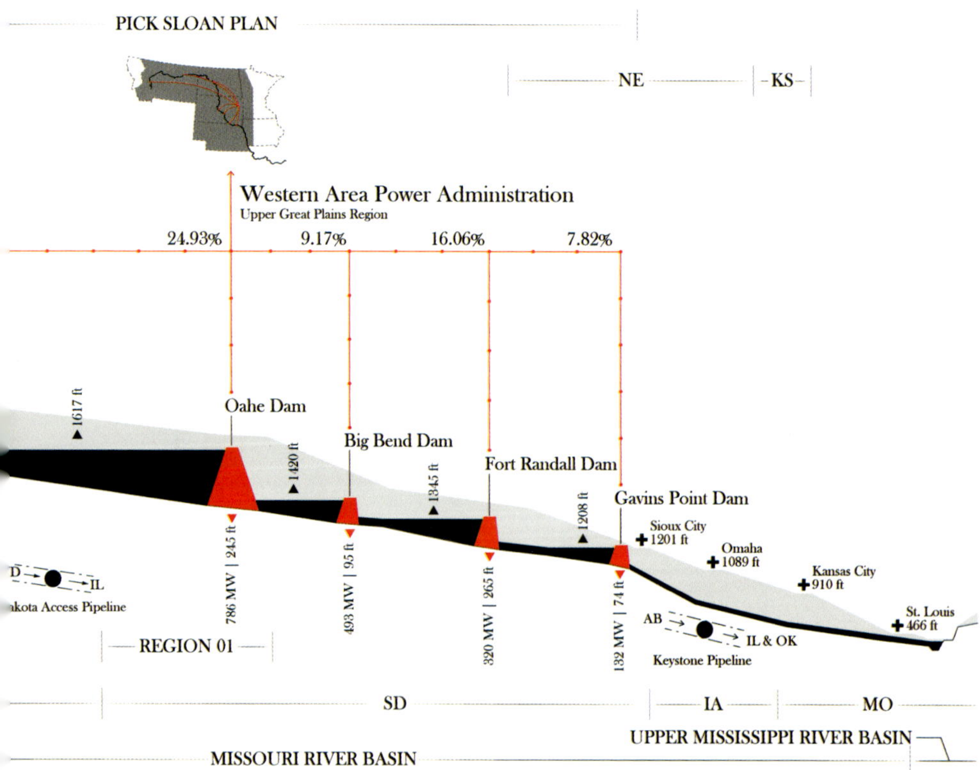

SECTION B-B

FOLLOWING THE PATH OF THE MISSOURI RIVER

Region 01: Lake Oahe

Region 01 Plan

The infrastructural development in the Missouri River took place during a period of significant growth in the United States. The six "system" dams in the Missouri River Basin are located in the Great Plains, a vast and largely flat landscape that is generally classified as semiarid, but quite varied in climate and annual weather patterns.[17] First populated by Native American Tribes, the United States claimed ownership of this territory, along with the entirety of the land that comprises the Missouri River Basin, in 1803, with the Louisiana Purchase. To chart its newly acquired land, the Lewis and Clark expedition traversed the entire length of the Missouri River to its source and eventually found a path through the Rocky Mountains to the Pacific Ocean. The land was surveyed through the Public Land Survey System—rationalized into a series of scalar grids—and repopulated by Americans, encouraged through federal programs like the Homestead Act of 1862. When the first settlers arrived, however, it quickly became clear that much of the basin would require significant infrastructural work to be arable. Founded in 1902, the Bureau of Reclamation helped secure water resources in the West, and by 1930, the upper reach of the Missouri River and almost all of its tributaries had at least one project to support nearby agriculture.[18] The Pick-Sloan Program was one of the largest and most significant acts of reclamation. While the United States was in a period of immense growth, much of it was at the expense of Native American Tribes. Removed from their traditional lands, the 1851 Indian Appropriations Act relocated and confined indigenous peoples to reservations.[19] Established in 1889, the Cheyenne River Reservation, located along the Missouri and Cheyenne Rivers, was one of five reservations, including the Standing Rock Reservation, that were dismantled from the Great Sioux Tribe in an effort led by American Senator Dawes

Lake Oahe and Power Intake Structure, South Dakota, 2018 (image credit: Derek Hoeferlin)

to erode tribal unity and assimilate both their lands and cultures into the growing country.[20] Already historically fraught, the reservations along the Missouri River would again be undermined, although arguably unintentionally, by the inundation of the river to create the six "system" dams. At the end of Lake Oahe, the width of the river has increased by magnitudes, and in the process, destroyed 55,000 and 100,000 acres in the Standing Rock and Cheyenne River Reservations respectively, displacing a total of 351 families.[21] The difference between the natural path of the river and its current state is both an index of the infrastructural development and its impact on the natural landscape.

Region 01 Section C-C

Lake Oahe is important for its individual impact on the region and its contributions to the water management system. Oahe Dam is located six miles upstream from the city of Pierre, the capital of South Dakota, near the confluence of the Missouri and Cheyenne Rivers. Its reservoir, Lake Oahe, extends 231 miles upstream and has a maximum storage capacity of 23,137,000 acre-feet—the largest reservoir in the MRB and the third-largest reservoir in the country.[22] As the reservoir approaches Oahe Dam, the river reaches a maximum depth of 200 feet, but it typically maintains an operating level of 197 feet with a surface elevation of 1,617 feet.[23] The Cheyenne River is a major source of sediment to the Missouri River, but the impoundment of the river by Oahe Dam has prevented it from continuing downstream.[24] Since 1958, the size of Lake Oahe has diminished by 613,985 acre-feet at a rate of 19,800 acre-feet per year, due to the trapping and accumulation of sediment.[25] Lake Oahe is estimated to supply irrigation to 130,000 acres of agricultural lands and municipal water facilities that serve 150,000 people.[26] The Oahe Dam generates nearly a quarter of all power in the main-stem Missouri River, and it is sold and distributed to states in the Upper Great Plains by the Western Area Power Administration. With its vast storage, the release of water from Lake Oahe is carried over for the dams downstream that would otherwise lack enough water resources to operate annually.[27] While undeniably important, the creation of Lake Oahe has had immense consequences on the natural environment. Among many physical changes to the river, the water temperature dropped—changing the biology of the river and causing the decline or proliferation of fish species depending on their acclimation to the new conditions.[28] Most devastating, many of the river's natural cycles and processes have been subverted and nearly all of its riparian landscape was inundated to facilitate the water management system. Before the Pick-Sloan Program, the riparian landscape consisted of floodplains that were highly fertile due to its steady supply of nutrient-rich sediment from annual water pulses.[29] They were vital habitats for plant and animal species, and without it, the Missouri River ecosystem has declined in productivity and biodiversity.[30] For the tribal reservations, the floodplain was invaluable for agriculture, grazing, hunting, and natural resources like timber.[31] More than just land was lost, it was another erasure of tribal livelihoods and culture. While the Oahe project has become a crucial infrastructural piece for the economic growth and stability of the region, it has had a significant impact on the environment, and disrupted natural systems that were important for the sustainability of the ecosystem and the cultural expression of indigenous populations.

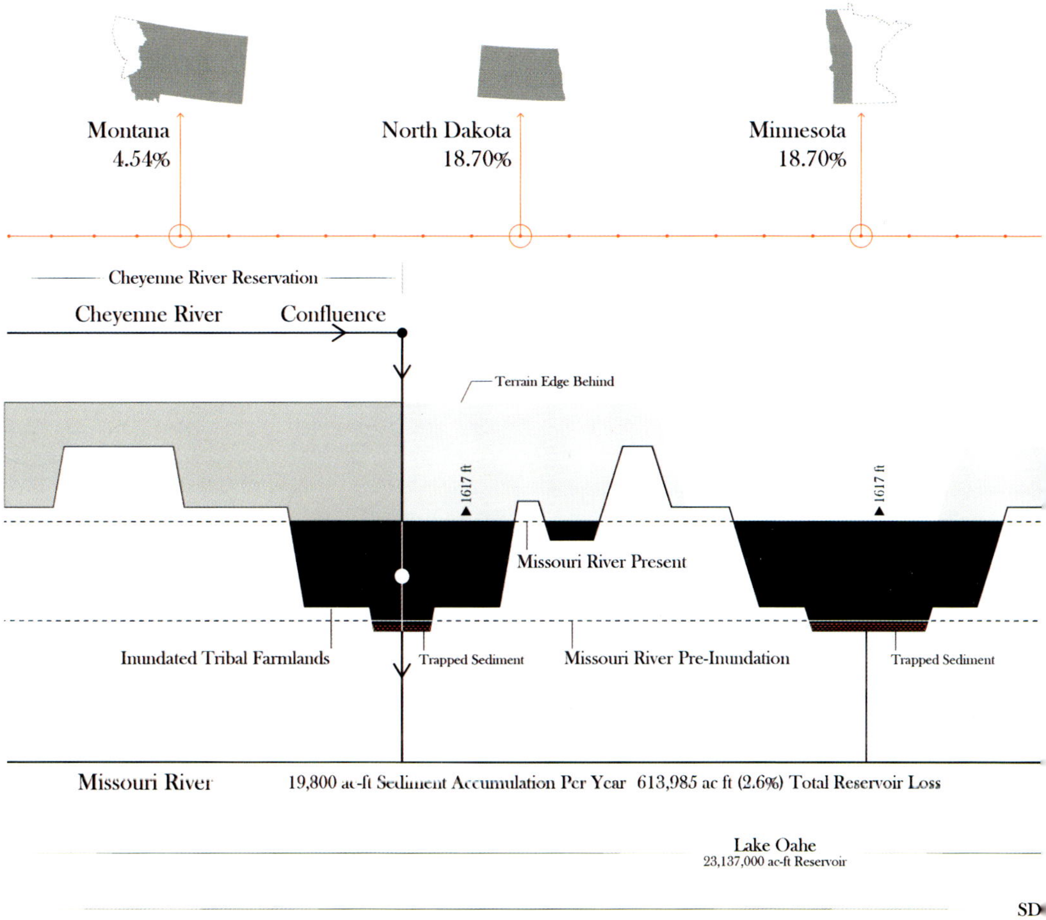

Montana
4.54%
North Dakota
18.70%
Minnesota
18.70%
Cheyenne River Reservation
Cheyenne River
Confluence
Terrain Edge Behind
1617 ft
1617 ft
Missouri River Present
Inundated Tribal Farmlands
Trapped Sediment
Missouri River Pre-Inundation
Trapped Sediment
Missouri River
19,800 ac-ft Sediment Accumulation Per Year
613,985 ac ft (2.6%) Total Reservoir Loss
Lake Oahe
23,137,000 ac-ft Reservoir
SD

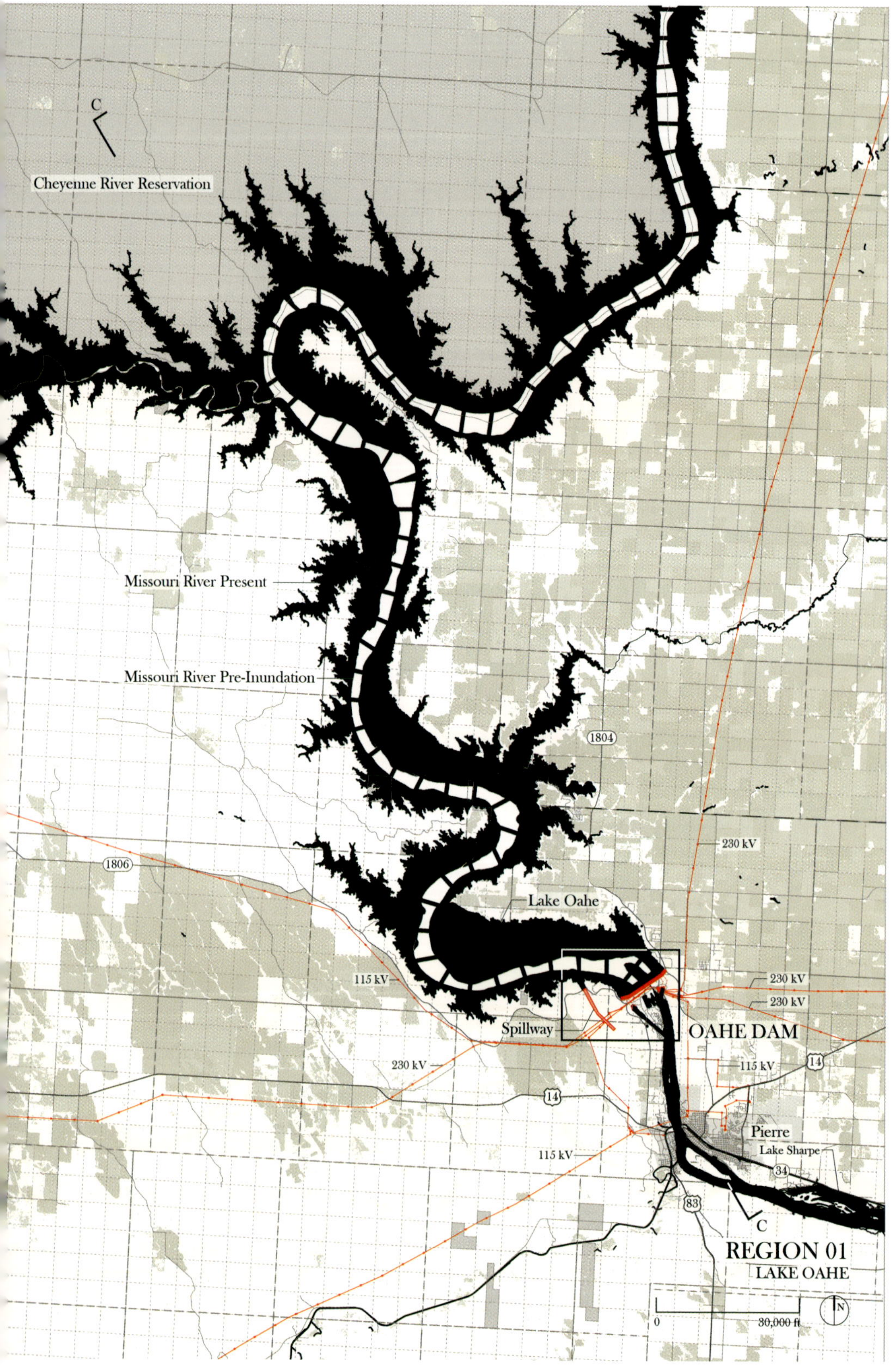
C
Cheyenne River Reservation
Missouri River Present
Missouri River Pre-Inundation
1804
230 kV
1806
Lake Oahe
230 kV
115 kV
230 kV
Spillway
OAHE DAM
230 kV
115 kV
14
14
Pierre
Lake Sharpe
115 kV
34
83
C
REGION 01
LAKE OAHE
0
30,000 ft
N

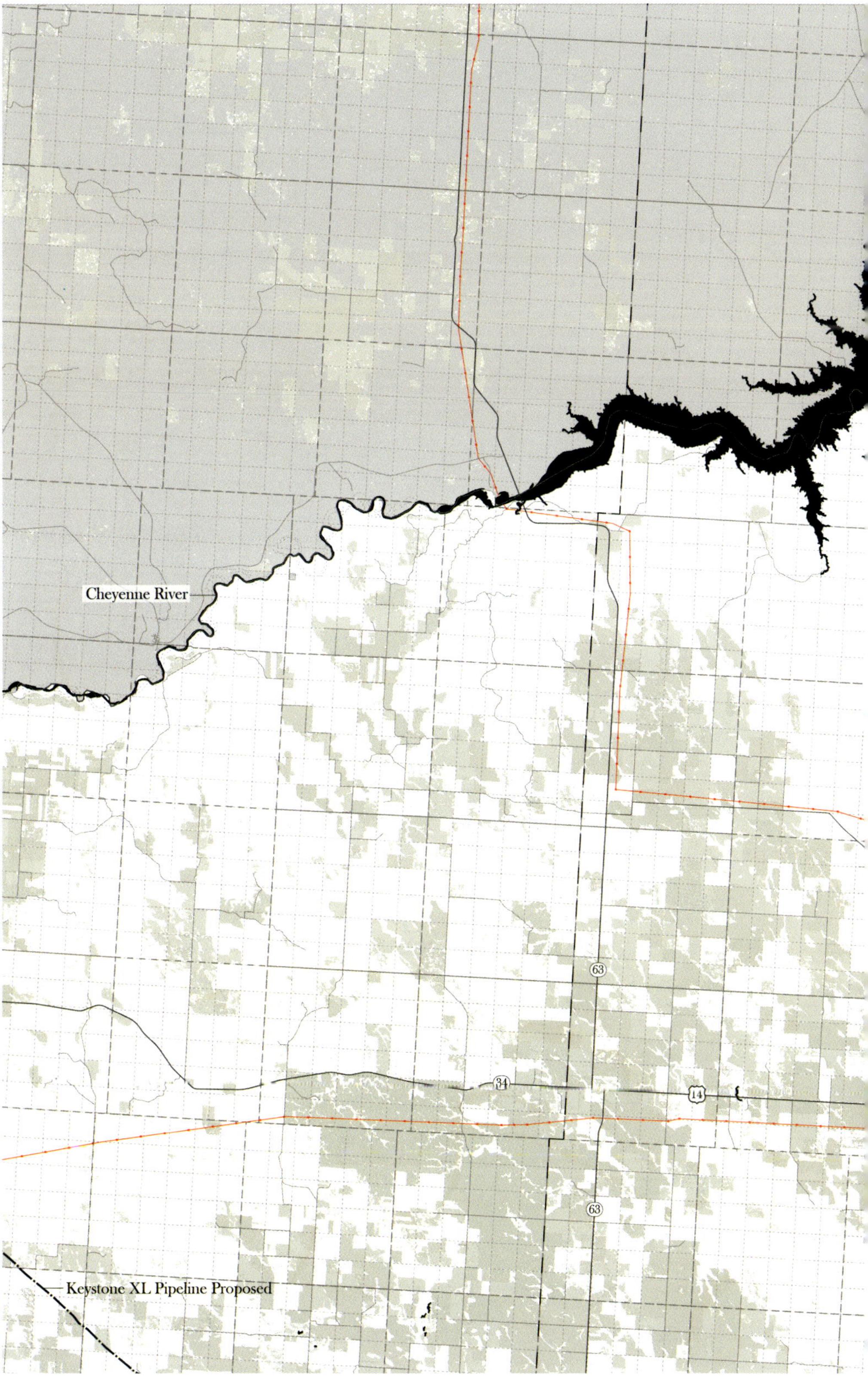

Cheyenne River
63
34
14
63
Keystone XL Pipeline Proposed

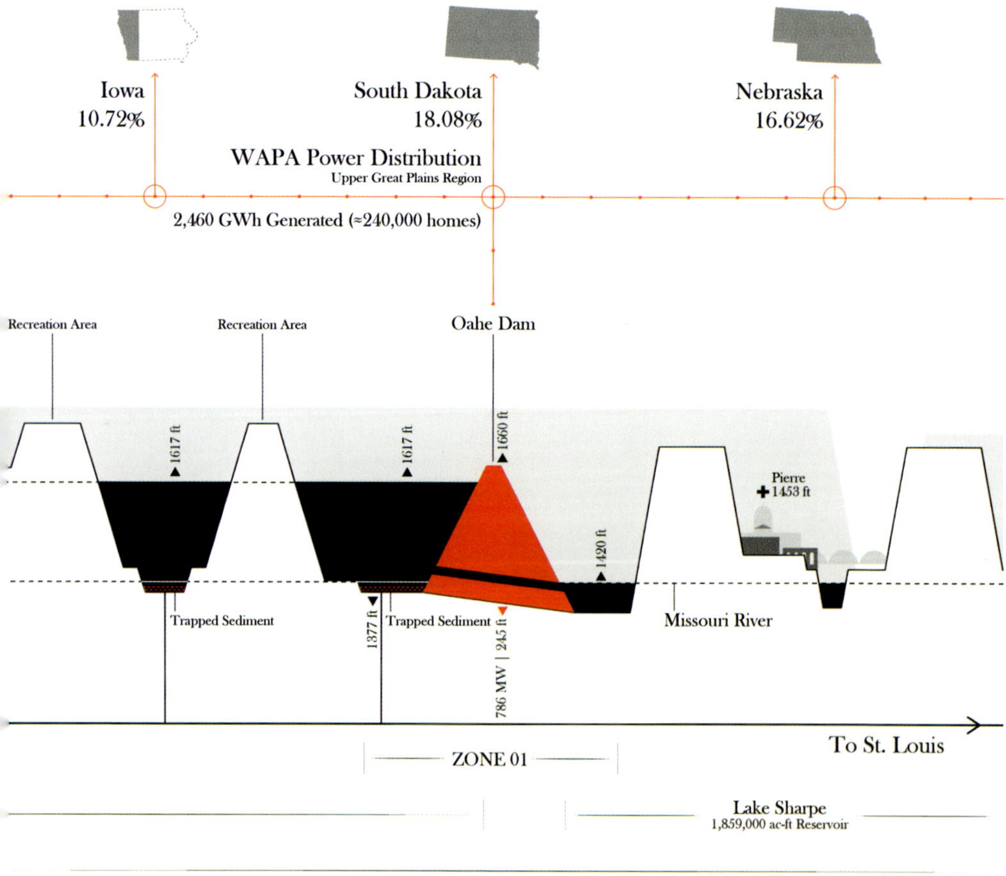

SECTION C-C

SECTION THROUGH LAKE OAHE

Zone 01: Oahe Dam

Zone 01 Plan

The importance of the Oahe Dam to the Pick-Sloan Program and its water regulation system is reflected in its impressive size. Located near the midpoint of the Missouri River and third in the cascade, Oahe Dam is typologically an earthen embankment structure. Its precise function is to manage the amount of water released from its reservoir, Lake Oahe, to ensure water security for the region and to produce hydroelectricity. The main structure consists of a flood control spillway and a powerhouse, and an emergency spillway constructed two miles west of the dam. The powerhouse embeds into the eastern flank of the dam, and transmission lines can be seen branching out from the switchyard nearby. Buried underneath the dam are two sets of tunnels that release water from the reservoir back into the main stem of the Missouri River. To the east, seven tunnels connect the powerhouse to the reservoir and the flood control spillway connects to the reservoir through six tunnels to the west. Typically, the powerhouse maintains a consistent flow of water for daily power generation, but the amount of water released from the reservoir through the flood control tunnels varies according to seasonal precipitation levels—peaking in the summer.[32] To construct the embankment dam, 92 million cubic yards of dirt were compacted across two miles with an average width of one mile.[33] Ostensibly a hill impounding the Missouri River, the main structure of the dam is impossible to discern from the natural landscape. The enormous footprint of the project is only revealed in the engineering schematics that rationalize the structure's gradual buildup. With its ease of access to Lake Oahe and the riverfront scenery, Oahe Dam has become a site for outdoor recreation. As originally envisioned by the Pick-Sloan Program, the dam has become a site for activities like camping, boating, swimming, hunting, and fishing.[34] Since the mid-1970s, the U.S. Army Corps of Engineers has been engaged in sporadic efforts to ameliorate harm to the environment by the main-stem dams.[35] Along with the South Dakota Department of Game, Fish, and Parks, fish are artificially spawned and stocked in Lake Oahe, sometimes up to millions of one species in a year.[36] Central to the Pick-Sloan Program, the systems of the water management plan and vision for the Missouri River Basin converge at the Oahe Dam.

Zone 01 Sections D-D, E-E, F-F

The Oahe Dam and the Pick-Sloan Program reflect a disposition for the Missouri River Basin that has persisted for over a century. They are projects that emerged to support the country's expansion by leveraging the Missouri River's immense water potential. In profile, the Oahe Dam is a seemingly naturalistic 245-foot hill whose artificiality is given away by its uncanny placement in the Missouri River and the water-regulating devices embedded throughout the structure. As valuable as it has been to develop and utilize the watershed's resources, the Pick-Sloan Program's resiliency and flood safety have been equally impactful. In 2011, record levels of water runoff in the first half of the year inundated the Missouri River for three months over the summer.[37] Compared to a normal year, six times the amount of water was being discharged through Oahe Dam's flood control tunnels at the height of the floods in June. But even as the reservoir neared maximum capacity, the emergency spillway remained unopened due to fears of the harm to the dam it could incur.[38] The U.S. Army Corps of Engineers estimated that the flood caused $1 billion in damages but that the system regulation in the Pick-Sloan Program prevented an additional $5.5 billion.[39] While the Pick-Sloan Program was largely successful in accomplishing many of its infrastructural goals, critics argue that the project did not meet its full vision for the development of the MRB in part because of changing economic conditions, and as a result, only the few urban centers in the watershed have grown in population while the population in rural areas has declined.[40] Steadily, public sentiment towards the environment has moved on from a definition of conservation that was realized in the early- and mid-20th century towards a new definition of conservation that aims to preserve and enjoy the natural environment.[41] Despite the diminishing health of the environment, the same critics believe there are too many political, economic, and societal factors that prefer to have the state of the MRB remain in a "status quo."[42] The future of the MRB, they state, must be adaptive.[43] The Pick-Sloan Program must be flexible to meet changing societal, economic, and cultural conditions and be able to accommodate uses both human and natural.

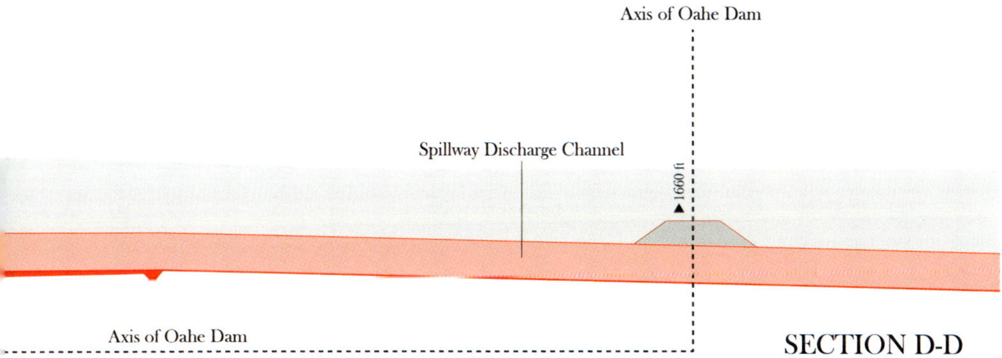

SECTION D-D

SECTION THROUGH THE OAHE DAM SPILLWAY

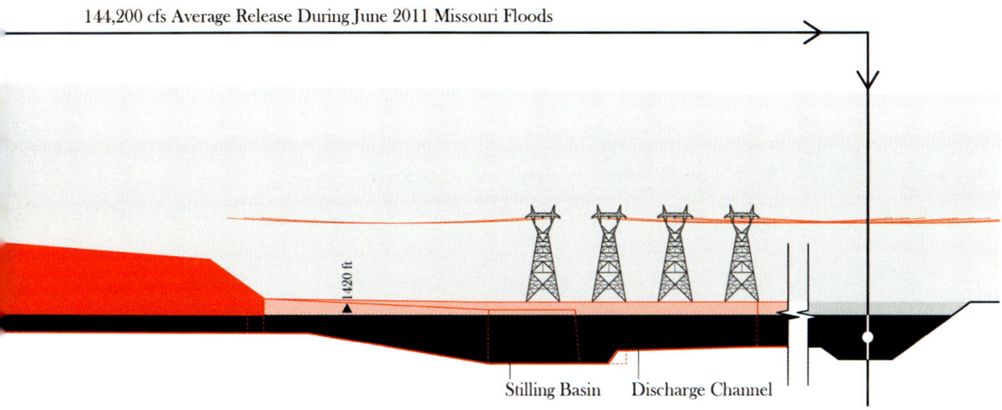

SECTION E-E

SECTION THROUGH THE OAHE DAM FLOOD CONTROL TUNNELS

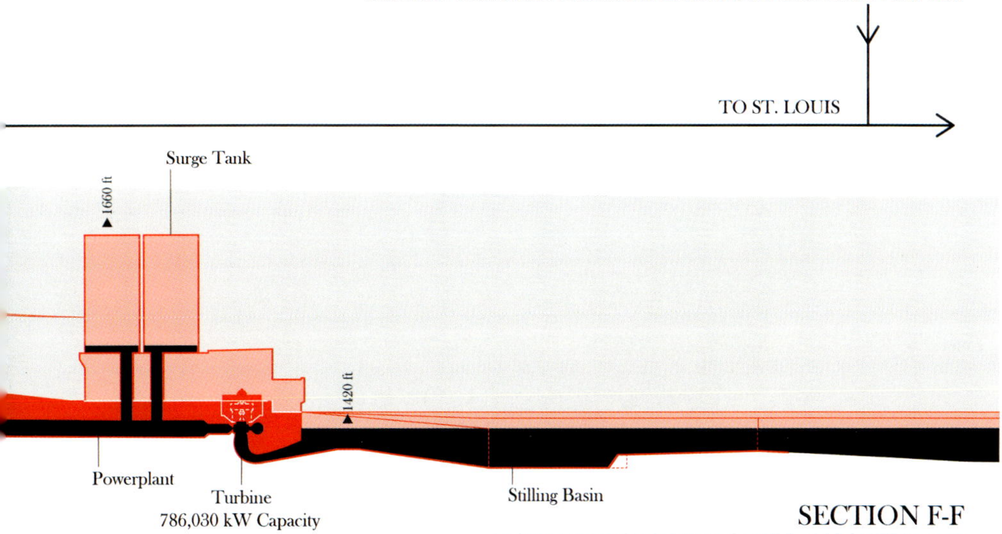

SECTION F-F

SECTION THROUGH THE OAHE DAM POWERPLANT

D
Lake
E
Approach Channel
Spillway
115
115
Spillway Discharge Channel
D

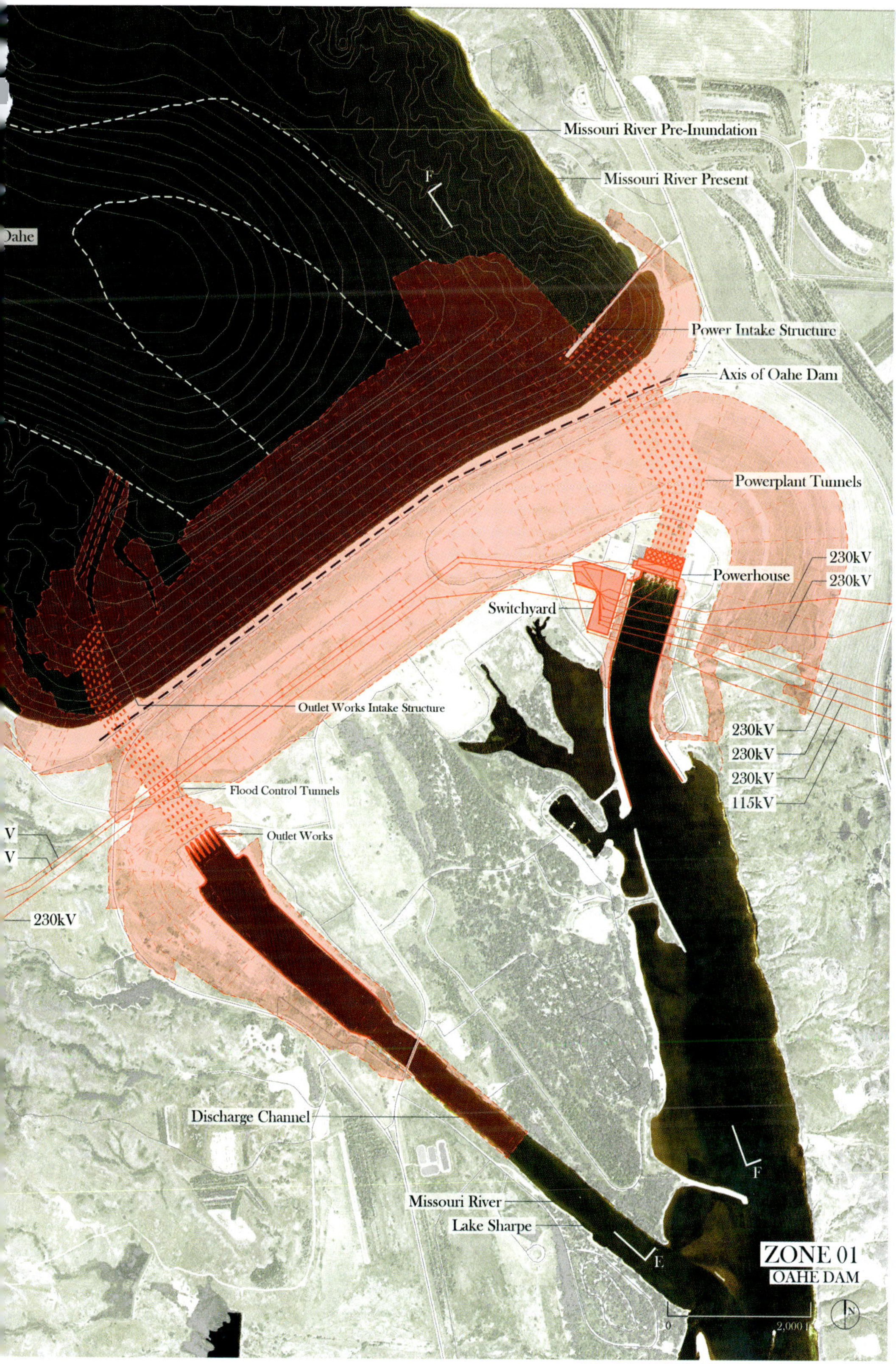

Missouri River Pre-Inundation
Missouri River Present
F
Dahe
Power Intake Structure
Axis of Oahe Dam
Powerplant Tunnels
230kV
230kV
Powerhouse
Switchyard
Outlet Works Intake Structure
230kV
230kV
230kV
115kV
Flood Control Tunnels
Outlet Works
V
V
230kV
Discharge Channel
F
Missouri River
Lake Sharpe
E
ZONE 01
OAHE DAM
0
2,000
N

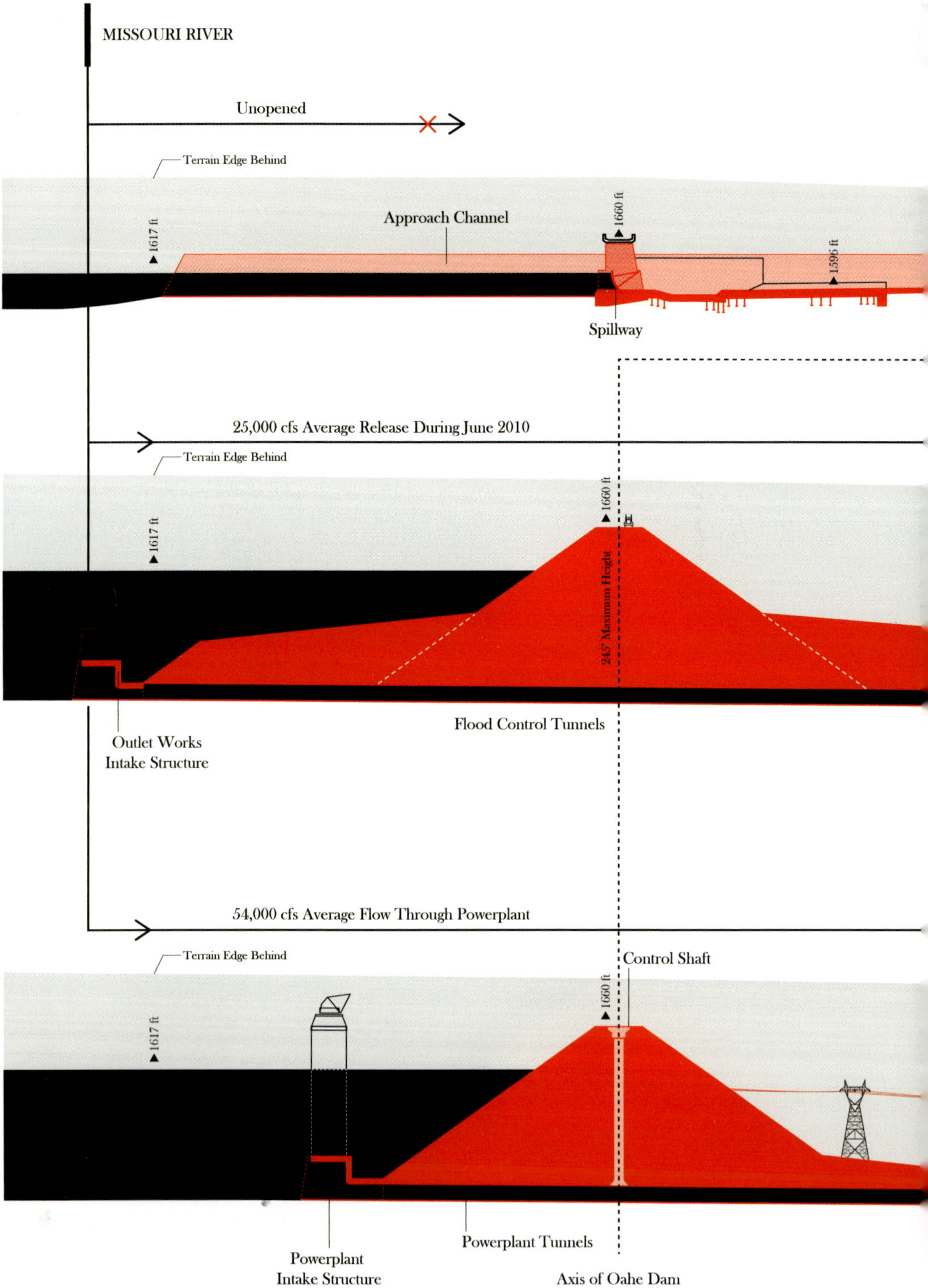
MISSOURI RIVER
Unopened
Terrain Edge Behind
Approach Channel
1617 ft
1660 ft
1596 ft
Spillway
25,000 cfs Average Release During June 2010
Terrain Edge Behind
1660 ft
1617 ft
245' Maximum Height
Outlet Works
Intake Structure
Flood Control Tunnels
54,000 cfs Average Flow Through Powerplant
Terrain Edge Behind
Control Shaft
1660 ft
1617 ft
Powerplant
Intake Structure
Powerplant Tunnels
Axis of Oahe Dam

Oahe Dam, South Dakota, 2018 (image credit: Derek Hoeferlin)

1. *Lengths of Major Rivers,* U.S. Geological Survey, accessed May 6, 2021, https://web.archive.org/web/20090305045437/http://ga.water.usgs.gov/edu/riversofworld.html.
2. *Master Water Control Manual: Missouri River Basin* (Omaha: U.S. Army Corps of Engineers Northwestern Division, November 2018), accessed January, 6, 2021, https://usace.contentdm.oclc.org/digital/collection/p266001coll1/id/8201/, III_1
3. Ibid., III_17.
4. Ibid., IV_28.
5. Ibid., VII_14, VII_51-51.
6. Ibid., I_1, IV_1.
7. Ibid., I_4.
8. Trymaine Lee, "No Man's Land: The Last Tribes of the Plains," MSNBC, Geography of Poverty (September 28, 2015), https://www.msnbc.com/msnbc/geography-of-poverty-northwest-msna686201.
9. "A timeline of the Dakota Access oil pipeline," Associated Press (October 12, 2017), https://apnews.com/article/1a00f95c83594dac931796a332540750.
10. *Water Control Manual: Fort Peck Dam–Fort Peck Lake*, (Omaha, U.S. Army Corps of Engineers Northwestern Division, December 2018), accessed January 8, 2021, https://www.nwd-mr.usace.army.mil/rcc/rcc_publications_reports.html, II_1, III_6.
11. *Master Water Control Manual*, A_4-5.
12. Ibid., II_3.

13. Ibid., II_6.

14. Ibid., II_6.

15. David C. Heimann, Lori A. Sprague, and Dale W. Blevins, *Trends in Suspended-Sediment Loads and Concentrations in the Mississippi River Basin, 1950-2009: Scientific Investigations Report 2011-5200* (Washington, DC: U.S. Geological Survey National Water-Quality Assessment Program, 2011), accessed January 12, 2021, https://pubs.usgs.gov/sir/2011/5200/, 1.

16. Ibid., 1.

17. Ibid., III_3.

18. *The Missouri River Ecosystem: Exploring the Prospects for Recovery* (Washington, DC: National Academies Press, 2002), accessed January 12, 2021, https://www.nap.edu/catalog/10277/the-missouri-river-ecosystem-exploring-the-prospects-for-recovery, 25–26.

19. Ibid., vii.

20. Frederick E. Hoxie, "From Prison to Homeland: The Cheyenne River Indian Reservation before WWI," *South Dakota History* 10, no. 1 (1979), accessed January 12, 2021, https://www.sdhspress.com/journal/south-dakota-history-10-1/from-prison-to-homeland-the-cheyenne-river-indian-reservation-before-wwi, 2.

21. U.S. Congress, Senate, Committee on Indian Affairs, *Impact of the Flood Control Act of 1944 on Indian Tribes Along the Missouri River*, 110th Cong., 1st sess., November 1, 2007; *The Missouri River Ecosystem*, 31.

22. *Final Oahe Dam/Lake Oahe Master Plan: Missouri River, South Dakota and North Dakota Design Memorandum MO-224*, (Omaha: U.S. Army Corps of Engineers Omaha District, September 2010), accessed January 12, 2021, https://usace.contentdm.oclc.org/digital/collection/p16021coll7/id/92, xiii.

23. Ibid.., xiii.

24. Ibid., 2_10.

25. Ibid., 2_10.

26. Ibid., 1_6.

27. *Master Water Control Manual*, VII–52.

28. *Final Oahe Dam/Lake Oahe Master Plan*, 2_38.

29. *The Missouri River Ecosystem*, 59.

30. Ibid., 67.

31. Ibid., 31.

32. *Final Oahe Dam/Lake Oahe Master Plan*, 2_23.

33. Ibid., xi.

34. Ibid., 2_5.

35. *The Missouri River Ecosystem*, 115.

36. *Final Oahe Dam/Lake Oahe Master Plan*, 2_39.

37. "Review of the Regulation of the Missouri River Mainstem Reservoir System During the Flood of 2011," (Portland: U.S. Army Corps of Engineers Northwestern Division, 2011), accessed January 19, 2021, https://www.nwd.usace.army.mil/MRWM/Reports/, 10.

38. Ibid., 70.

39. Ibid., 10; "Missouri River Mainstem Reservoir System: Summary of Actual 2011 Regulation" (Omaha: U.S. Army Corps of Engineers Northwestern Division, July 5, 2012), accessed December 7, 2020, https://www.nwd-mr.usace.army.mil/rcc/aop.html, 47.

40. *The Missouri River Ecosystem*, vii.

41. Ibid., 17–18.

42. Ibid., 111.

43. Ibid., 134.

Inundate Lands

(UPPER RIGHT) Cannonball River and view towards former site of Oceti Sakowin protest camp, North Dakota, 2018 (BACKGROUND) View towards Lake Oahe and Standing Rock Reservation, Mobridge, South Dakota, 2018 (image credit: Derek Hoeferlin)

Generate Powers

(UPPER RIGHT) Fort Peck Powerplant, Montana, 2018
(BACKGROUND) Garrison Powerplant, South Dakota, 2018 (image credit: Derek Hoeferlin)

Extract Resources

(UPPER RIGHT) Civeo Killdeer Lodge "pre-fabricated workforce accommodation facility," Killdeer, North Dakota, 2018 (BACKGROUND) Typical Bakken Shale Formation oil and natural gas drilling site, Killdeer, North Dakota, 2018 (image credit: Derek Hoeferlin)

Release Waters

(UPPER RIGHT AND BACKGROUND)
Garrison Spillway, North Dakota, 2018 (image credit: Derek Hoeferlin)

Erasure

Displacement, Decolonization, and Climate Justice

Kees Lokman

Large dams have had serious impacts on the lives, livelihoods, cultures, and spiritual existence of indigenous and tribal peoples. Due to neglect and lack of capacity to secure justice because of structural inequities, cultural dissonance, discrimination, and economic and political marginalization, indigenous and tribal peoples have suffered disproportionately from the negative impacts of large dams, while often being excluded from sharing in the benefits.(1)

—World Commission on Dams, 2000

Introduction

Dams express, par excellence, human control over nature.[2] Dams transform rivers from living, dynamic, and spiritual entities into "technological hydroscapes" that are highly controlled and play a key role in social power relations.[3] According to Hanna Werner, "As gigantic manifestations of state power, dams can be seen as visualising no less than a nation's dream of centralizing and controlling its resources—and demonstrating it to the rest of the world."[4] Serving at the nexus of complex social-ecological systems, dams, reservoirs, and associated infrastructure networks alter watersheds, displace human and nonhuman populations, and provide water and energy to urban areas, agriculture, and mining. In doing so, dams are central to shaping and sustaining "geographies of extractivism."[5] Extractivism describes the removal of large volumes of natural resources (such as oil, gas, wood, and water) as well as the sociopolitical and environmental contexts associated with these processes.[6] In practice, extractivism has been, and continues to be, a colonial mechanism to dispossess and appropriate natural resources from the environment and local (indigenous) communities in order to support capitalist economies, such as the United States, Australia, and Canada. As such, sites of extractivism become contested and politicized landscapes inherently tied to issues of social and environmental injustice.[7] **[Figure 1]** In the case of dams, seasonal pulses and fluctuations of free-flowing waters are reordered and programmed to supply electricity, irrigation, navigation, and recreation to specific interest groups. This requires the physical rearrangement of landscapes and hydrological processes at territorial scales. Floodplains, riparian areas, and farmlands are literally drowned and erased to allow for the construction of dams and reservoirs. Beyond severely uprooting human and more-than-human communities, impacts of dam construction include loss of land, food insecurity, and loss of grounded traditional knowledge, as well as health issues, aesthetic degradation, and biodiversity loss.[8]

Following a period in the 1990s and 2000s of greater awareness of the disruptive social and environmental impacts of dams—underscored by a "damming" report by the World Commission on Dams[9]—we are entering an era of renewed interest and investment in large-scale dams and hydropower developments.[10] "With the spectre of global warming," Marcus Nusser argues, "dam building has once again become en vogue as a climate-friendly technology … [and] large dams are now seen in a different light as mechanisms for mitigating against the adverse effects of climate change through their low emissions during power production."[11]

At the same time, dams constructed during the 1930s and 1960s are increasingly nearing the end of their lifespans. This has resulted in growing advocacy and support for the undamming of rivers and draining of reservoirs to advance Indigenous sovereignty, ecosystem regeneration, and the cultivation of sustainable land uses.[12] Already, over the past two decades, more than 850 dams have been removed in the United States alone. While most of these dams are relatively small, the removal of the 210-foot-high Glines Canyon Dam (1927–2014) in northwestern Washington State points to the real possibility of imagining more just and resilient social-ecological systems at regional scales.[13] **[Figure 2]** Consequently, as argued by Martin Doyle, "if we really want to start removing Western

[Figure 1] Fort Clark, ca. 1841. Lucas Weber after Karl Bodmer, 1833
(image credit: Detroit Institute of Arts)

dams, then we need an audacity to match that with which they went after building them."[14] In this context, I will discuss two trajectories of erasure in the Missouri River Basin (MRB). First, the historic and ongoing consequences of *erasure* of people and more-than-human communities due to the construction of dams and reservoirs. Second, the potential for decolonization and climate justice through the erasure of these dams and reservoirs. I will conclude by discussing ways in which designers and planners can aid in the revitalization of watersheds, particularly by supporting Indigenous communities, and by promoting different relationships to lands, waters, plants, and all living things.

Dams and Displacement

When the United States Congress passed the Flood Control Act of 1944—also known as the Pick-Sloan Plan—it authorized the construction and operation of an extensive system of dams and reservoirs in the MRB for the purposes of flood control, water supply, irrigation, energy developments, navigation, and recreation. Over a twenty-year period between 1946 and 1966, the United States Army Corps of Engineers (USACE) and the Bureau of Reclamation (BOR), implemented a substantial portion of this plan, including the construction of five of the world's largest earthen dams at the time, as well as a series of massive reservoirs that inundated more than one million acres of land and transformed

[Figure 2] The remains of the Glines Dam on the Elwha River (image credit: Alan Sandercock, CC by 2.0)

one-third of the Missouri River ecosystem into lake environments.[15] **[Figure 3]** While many towns and counties in the basin had advocated for localized irrigation and flood development measures in the century prior to 1944, none garnered enough political or financial support for implementation. However, when successive floods from April through June 1943 submerged part of Omaha and Kansas City, voices to develop comprehensive flood management throughout the MRB intensified. Spearheaded by the Missouri River States Committee (MRSC), public forums promoting the construction of dams, channelization works, and levees along the Missouri River were held across the basin, including in Williston, Bismarck, Pierre, Yankton, Sioux City, Omaha, and Kansas City.[16] Yet, glaringly absent were forums held in any of the Indigenous communities and reservations along the Missouri River.

Environmental historian Robert Kelley Schneiders offers a number of reasons as to why the MRSC neglected to engage Indigenous communities.[17] First, the hydroelectricity and irrigation water to be provided by the project was too expensive for Indigenous communities, and as such, any promotional meetings to these communities would be futile according to the MRSC. Second, developments would have to be cofinanced through tax revenues coming from cities and towns that would benefit from the project. Since Indigenous communities could not make any of these financial contributions and would essentially be receiving the project's benefits "for free," the MRSC deemed it unnecessary to consult them. Perhaps most concerning is the fact that the MRSC believed reservation lands were "underutilized" and of "low quality," and would therefore be much better served as part of a comprehensive project benefiting all of society.[18] In doing so, project planners and engineers not only systematically excluded Indigenous communities from the planning process, they also ignored the fact that the river, its tributaries, and floodplains were of irreplaceable value and critical importance for Indigenous ways of life. These landscapes serve(d) as a source of sustenance, a method of transport, and a living terrain for passing on grounded ecological knowledge. Instead, site selection for dams and reservoirs in the Pick-Sloan Plan were entirely driven by benefit-cost ratios. Purchasing prime agricultural land or urban real estate, and/or relocating infrastructures (bridges, railroads, utilities, etc.) would have significantly increased the overall cost of dam construction. Similarly, any reduction in reservoir storage capacity to respect reservation boundaries would reduce the economic efficiency of the project.

Despite the existence of the U.S Indian Law and the Treaty of Fort Laramie, which protected the rights of tribal nations to their land and water, USACE eventually seized 356,000 acres of Indigenous lands (one-third of the total project area) through eminent domain. This meant Indigenous peoples and other living beings were effectively erased from these lands. Forced to relocate to barren upland regions, the devastation caused by this illegal act of displacement continues to impact every aspect of Indigenous ways of life—from food sovereignty, economic development, and education to mental health, kin relations, and intergenerational knowledge-sharing. As argued by Nusser, "Once places are submerged and people relocated, cultural practices and local knowledge systems will necessarily undergo a change as well.... The loss of proximity that culminates in a feeling of alienation is probably the most significant aspect: the process of dislocation might actually be described as a shift from a place to a 'nonplace'; the transformation of landscape changes the experience of place itself."[19] Historian and activist Vine Deloria, Jr., a member of the Standing Rock Sioux Tribe, described the Pick-Sloan project as "the single most destructive act ever perpetuated on any tribe by the United States."[20]

Dam Futures

Over the past decade, a number of key events, including the Missouri River floods of 2011 and 2019, record droughts in 2012, the Bakken Formation fracking boom, and ongoing protests surrounding the Keystone XL and Dakota Access Pipelines, have underlined the need to reconsider relationships among water, energy, dams, Indigenous sovereignty, and the land. Furthermore, a 2012 report commissioned by BOR predicts average annual increases in both upper-basin and lower-basin by midcentury, signaling an increased annual exceedance probability for severe floods.[21] The destruction of Spencer Dam (located in a tributary of the Missouri River) in 2019 due to flooding, signals both the fragility of hydraulic infrastructure systems, and the need to rethink water management at the scale of the basin.

Other aspects that support a radical rethinking of water management in the MRB include longstanding issues surrounding navigation, irrigation, and sedimentation. At one percent of all waterborne commerce in the U.S., existing barge travel in the Lower Missouri River is pretty much nonexistent. [22] Yet, navigation flow support as well as river-channel dredging has major implications on seasonal flows, sediment dynamics, and

[Figure 3] President John F. Kennedy attends dedication ceremonies at the Oahe Dam and Reservoir near Pierre, South Dakota, August 17, 1962 (image credit: John F. Kennedy Presidential Library)

riverbed configurations in the Lower Missouri River. Similarly, most of the surface water irrigation methods planned in the upper Missouri River Basin were never developed. As a result, today nearly 90 percent of farmland in the basin is dependent on precipitation and/or groundwater irrigation. This puts into question the need for the upper-basin dams and reservoirs, which were primarily constructed to support irrigation, hydropower, and navigation on the river below Sioux City, Iowa. Finally, sedimentation has become a major issue. Since the dams were constructed, a total of 4,800,000 acre-feet of sediment has accumulated.[23] This is the equivalent of a lake 100 miles long, 10 miles wide, with an average depth of nearly 75 feet. This loss in water storage further exacerbates challenges related to flood storage and hydropower production as well as increased water treatment costs for municipal, rural, and industrial water systems. Moreover, nutrient loads and/or contaminants within the sediment is causing water quality issues and environmental degradation in the reservoirs and tributary streams.

Moving beyond gridlock and toward a socially and environmentally just recovery of the

MRB necessitates actions designed to be significant enough to enable the river's regime to be redirected to create new habitats, and to enable Indigenous communities to reclaim stolen land and sovereignty. This requires urgent and robust discussions around dam removal in the main stem of the Missouri River. "Removing the Missouri River dams," Schneiders says, "will rejuvenate the ecology of the Missouri Valley and represent the first step in the re-establishment of the species entourage that once thrived across the Northern Plains and Midwest. Dam removal will bring the Missouri back to life."[24]

Decisions around dam removal are inherently political and values-driven. Consequently, questions of decolonization and returning Indigenous land to Indigenous people—not unlike the seizing of Indigenous land as part of the implementation of the Pick-Sloan Plan—is not beyond the capacities of federal and state agencies.[25] It is fundamentally about political will, spatial justice, and embracing different value systems and world views. Michi Saagiig Nishnaabeg scholar, writer, and artist, Leanne Betasamosake Simpson pointedly remarks, "We can pit jobs in the economy versus the environment. We can perform superficial dances of reconciliation and dialogue and negotiate for the cheap gifts of economic and political inclusion … or we can imagine different worlds."[26]

Kate Orff powerfully writes that designing such alternative futures requires "new forms of architectural expression such as un-making, un-doing, subtracting, reversing, decarbonising, tearing out, ripping up, replanting, softening, and connecting."[27] As the removal of two dams in the Elwha River in northern Washington State has shown, the act of unmaking can dramatically transform watersheds. Since the removal of the dams, the delta has grown by at least 100 acres, creating valuable tidal marshland habitat for fish, birds, beavers, insects, and a variety of plant species. Threatened Chinook salmon populations, for example, have already doubled within the watershed.[28] With salmon able to return to the river to spawn and die, their bodies and nutrients will enrich riverine and terrestrial environments by nourishing plants, animals, and people along the riverbank.

Unmaking & Codesigning

Dams in the Missouri River Based have made powerful inscriptions, both into the landscape and the human psyche. As "temples of modernity"[29] and facilitators of "hydraulic capitalism,"[30] they continue to be used as instruments for nation-building, uneven geographic developments, and "control" over fluvial environments. As such, they actively silence other ways of knowing and being. Yet despite its many exploitations, the Missouri River continues to flow and permeate spatial relations and legal systems. Whether through periodic floods and droughts, or through contesting developments that threaten its ways of being, the river and its water protectors remind us of the complex web of colonial and decolonial relations shaped by its existence. More than simply confronting ourselves with (ongoing) violence enacted through colonial water infrastructures, more decisive action is needed to envision alternative futures where water—in its spiritual, material, and legal dimensions—becomes an agent of resistance that can shape new human and more-than-human relationships.[31]

As social movements to address the inequities and injustices done to Indigenous people and other marginalized communities intensify, it is critical to confront the legacies of colonial infrastructures and public works that continue to shape contemporary landscapes, ecologies, and social relations. As powerfully phrased by Indigenous historian Nick Estes: "If every struggle were made into a climate struggle, then every struggle in North America must be made into a struggle for decolonization."[32] Consequently, the design and evaluation of alternative visions should no longer be driven by those that violently reordered the territory in the first place. Instead, affected communities least responsible for climate change and the looting of earth's resources should be empowered to develop restorative practices according to their ways of life. Particularly Indigenous peoples, who through their distinct cultural practices and ways of relating to living systems, protect much of the world's biodiversity and waterways. Without recognizing and protecting Indigenous people's rights to territories, water, traditional knowledge, and self-determination, any measures to protect and enhance biodiversity will fail.[33]

A future for the MRB should therefore address the twin challenges of climate change and climate justice. This includes drastically rethinking our relationships to one another and to more-than human species in order to develop solutions that move far beyond the narrow techno-economic considerations that have driven water management policies and developments in the past. We need a revolution of values embedded in the way we relate to the land, water, air, and all living entities.

In her critically acclaimed book *Braiding Sweetgrass: Indigenous Wisdom, Scientific Knowledge and the Teaching of Plants*, Robin Wall Kimmerer speaks about Indigenous knowledge and embedded intelligence of all kinds of life.

> *In the indigenous worldview, a healthy landscape is understood to be whole and generous enough to be able to sustain its partners. It engages land not as a machine but as a community of respected non-human persons to whom we humans have a responsibility … reconnecting people and the landscape is as essential as reestablishing proper hydrology or cleaning up contaminants. It is medicine for the earth.*[34]

Academics, activists, and designers can foster and facilitate the coproduction of this knowledge to promote different visions and understandings of life, economy, and democracy.[35] This way of working is needed to produce new understandings of what water management, energy, sovereignty, and democracy mean to diverse communities. As such, designers need to become much more aware of the inherent power structures embedded in both design practices and the physical reordering of the built environment. This begins with renewed political engagement and a commitment to developing different models of community participation in planning, design, and engineering processes. Framed within larger "rights" based discourses, planners and designers need to challenge the hegemony of top-down, capitalist, and corporate-led practices that deplete natural resources and marginalize local and Indigenous communities.[36]

Moving forward, we must (re)imagine and (re)design dams no longer as blockades but as life-giving and generative elements that work with, instead of against, hydrological and ecological processes. We must learn from, and codesign with, the practices of more-than-humans, such as beavers, which have constructed dams that regenerate wetlands and create pools for fish, insects, birds, and mammals. We must envision interventions that continuously work with water, land, and all living things to bring about more life. In many cases, the most productive way to achieve this is through the unmaking of already designed interventions, such as dams, levees, and concretized channels. Let us embrace a future centered around practices of codesigning and unmaking.

1. World Commission on Dams, *Dams and Development: A New Framework for Decision-Making: The Report of the World Commission on Dams* (London; Sterling, VA: Earthscan, 2000).
2. Patrick McCully, *Silenced Rivers: The Ecology and Politics of Large Dams* (London; Atlantic Highlands, N.J.: Zed Books, 1996).
3. Marcus Nüsser, *Large Dams in Asia: Contested Environments between Technological Hydroscapes and Social Resistance* (Dordrecht: Springer, 2014).
4. Hanna Werner, "Rivers, Dams and Landscapes: Engaging with the Modern on Contested Grounds," in *Large Dams in Asia: Contested Environments between Technological Hydroscapes and Social Resistance* (Dordrecht: Springer, 2014), 124–127.
5. Daniela Del Bene, Armin Scheidel, and Leah Temper, "More Dams, More Violence? A Global Analysis on Resistances and Repression Around Conflictive Dams through Co-Produced Knowledge," *Sustainability Science* 13, no. 3 (2018): 617–633.
6. Alberto Acosta, "Post-Extractivism: From Discourse to Practice—Reflections for Action," *International Development Policy | Revue Internationale De Politique De Développement* 9, no. 9 (2017): 77–101.
7. Anna Willow, "Indigenous ExtrACTIVISM in Boreal Canada: Colonial Legacies, Contemporary Struggles and Sovereign Futures," *Humanities* 5, no. 3 (2016): 55.
8. Del Bene et al., "More Dams, More Violence?"
9. World Commission on Dams, *Dams and Development*.
10. Matthew A. Cole, Robert J.R. Elliott, and Eric Strobl, "Climate Change, Hydro-Dependency, and the African Dam Boom," *World Development* 60 (2014): 84–98.
11. Nüsser, *Large Dams*.
12. John Waldman, "Undamming Rivers: A Chance for New Clean Energy Source," *Yale Environment 360* (August 6, 2015), https://e360.yale.edu/features/undamming_rivers_a_chance_for_new_clean_energy_source.
13. Kees Lokman, "Dam[ned] Landscapes: Envisioning Fluid Geographies," *Journal of Architectural Education* 70, no. 01 (2016): 6–12.
14. Quoted from Anna Lieb, "The Undamming of America," *PBS Nova Next* (August 12, 2015), https://www.pbs.org/wgbh/nova/article/dam-removals/.
15. Peter Capossela, "Impacts of the Army Corps of Engineers' Pick-Sloan Program on the Indian Tribes of the Missouri River Basin," *Journal of Environmental Law and Litigation* 30, no. 1 (2015): 143–218.
16. Robert Kelley Schneiders, "Flooding the Missouri Valley: The Politics of Dam Site Selection and Design," *Great Plains Quarterly* 17, no. 3/4, (1997): 237–49.
17. Ibid, 237–49.

18. Department of the Army, U.S. Army Corps of Engineers, Omaha District, "Comprehensive Report on Missouri River Development, Appendix VIII, Plan of Improvement" (unpublished manuscript, Omaha: U.S. Army Corps of Engineers: 1944-1954). Quoted from Robert Kelley Schneiders, "Flooding the Missouri Valley: The Politics of Dam Site Selection and Design," *Great Plains Quarterly* 17, no. 3/4, (1997): 237-49.
19. Nüsser, *Large Dams in Asia*.
20. Quoted from Philip P. Frickey, "Domesticating Federal Indian Law," *Minnesota Law Review* (1996).
21. U.S. Department of the Interior, Bureau of Reclamation Technical Service Center, "Climate Change Analysis for the Missouri River Basin: Northwest Area Water Supply Project, North Dakota, *Reclamation: Managing Water in the West*, July, 2012, https://www.usbr.gov/gp/dkao/naws/FSEIS/climate_change_analysis_for_the_missouri_river_basin.pdf
22. Robert Schneiders, "Take down the dams," *Rapid City Journal*, December 7, 2020, https://rapidcityjournal.com/take-down-the-dams/article_ee2ba1c9-b6a5-57c1-8abd-e099ce47adc4.html#:~:text=Removing%20the%20Missouri%20River%20dams,the%20Missouri%20back%20to%20life.
23. U.S. Department of Agriculture—Natural Resources Conservation Service, "Phase II Sedimentation Assessment for the Upper Missouri River Basin," *Missouri Sedimentation Action Coalition* (June 2009), http://www.msaconline.com/Missouri%20River%20Phase%20II%20%20Report.pdf.
24. Robert Schneiders, "Take down the dams," *Rapid City Journal* (December 7, 2020), https://rapidcityjournal.com/take-down-the-dams/article_ee2ba1c9-b6a5-57c1-8abd-e099ce47adc4.html#:~:text=Removing%20the%20Missouri%20River%20dams,the%20Missouri%20back%20to%20life.
25. Nick Estes, "A Red Deal," *Jacobin Magazine* (August 6, 2019), https://www.jacobinmag.com/2019/08/red-deal-green-new-deal-ecosocialism-decolonization-indigenous-resistance-environment.
26. Leanne Betasamosake Simpson, "The Brilliance of Beavers: Learning from an Anishnaabe World," *CBC Radio-Canada* (April 16, 2020), https://www.cbc.ca/radio/ideas/the-brilliance-of-the-beaver-learning-from-an-anishnaabe-world-1.5534706.
27. Kate Orff, "What is Design Now? Unmaking the Landscape," *Architectural Design* 90, no. 1 (2020): 94–99.
28. Starre Vartan, "Beavers on the coast are helping salmon bounce back. Here's how," *National Geographic* (August 13, 2019), https://www.nationalgeographic.com/animals/2019/08/coastal-beavers-help-salmon-recovery-washington/#close.
29. Werner, "Rivers, Dams and Landscapes."
30. Rohan D'Souza, "Framing India's Hydraulic Crisis: The Politics of the Modern Large Dam," *Monthly Review* 60, no. 3 (2008): 112–124.
31. Kees Lokman, "The Missouri River Basin: Water, Power, Decolonization, and Design," *Scenario Journal 07: Power* (2019), https://scenariojournal.com/article/Missouri-River-Basin/.
32. Estes, "A Red Deal."
33. Krystyna Widerska, "Protecting indigenous cultures is crucial to saving the world's biodiversity," *The Conversation* (February 14, 2020), https://theconversation.com/protecting-indigenous-cultures-is-crucial-for-saving-the-worlds-biodiversity-123716.
34. Robin Wall Kimmerer, *Braiding Sweetgrass: Indigenous Wisdom, Scientific Knowledge and the Teachings of Plants* (Minneapolis: Milkweed Editions, 2013).
35. Arturo Escobar, *Territories of Difference: Place, Movements, Life, Redes* (Durham: Duke University Press, 2008).
36. Charlotte Coté, " 'Indigenizing' Food Sovereignty. Revitalizing Indigenous Food Practices and Ecological Knowledges in Canada and the United States," *Humanities* 5, no. 3 (2016).

Memorial commemorating Sitting Bull's possible resting place, Fort Yates, South Dakota, 2018 (image credit: Derek Hoeferlin)

Big Bend Spillway, Missouri River, Fort Thompson, South Dakota, 2018 (image credit: Derek Hoeferlin)

Scar

Dakota Access Pipeline through the Landscape

Meghan Kirkwood

Introduction

Comprehending the territorial scale of infrastructure projects is challenging for individual citizens. Most people only ever come into contact with portions of a system, if at all. Few are aware of where such systems begin or end. Further, many large infrastructure systems are designed to minimize their visibility and their impacts. For example, small markers are often the only signal that one is crossing a pipeline path. **[Figure. 1]** Taken together, individuals can be forgiven for not knowing the degree to which such systems divide and manage the spaces they inhabit. From the ground level, it can be hard to grasp just how far the engineered landscape extends.

Pipeline Ubiquity

Pipelines represent one type of infrastructure whose ubiquitous network remains something of a mystery to individuals. The United States has over 2.5 million miles of pipelines, which makes it home to the largest pipeline system in the world.[1] These systems of oil and natural gas transit lines are operated by more than 3,000 companies and are active in every single state.[2] Pipeline proponents and industry officials laud the safety, economic, and efficiency advantages of these networks. With respect to oil exports from the Bakken region in North Dakota, researchers estimate that greenhouse gas and air pollution costs are nearly twice as large for rail as for pipelines.[3] Bakken oil shipped by rail has caused deadly accidents in recent years, including a 2013 train derailment in Lac Megantic, Quebec, that killed 47 people, and another in Casselton, North Dakota, the same year.[4] Pipeline networks bring their own attendant risks, however, such as environmental damage from spills and other hazards to worker safety.[5]

Dakota Access Pipeline

However, apart from high-profile events such as a major spill or conflict over a pipeline route, most Americans have little engagement or knowledge of these underground transport systems. Few understand the avenues through which pipelines are developed, or the planning and approval process for determining where underground routes go. Indeed, by the time most Americans get involved in learning about a pipeline, it's already built or too far along in the process to lobby for significant changes. **[Figure 2]** The Dakota Access Pipeline offers one such example: by the time people around the country and world were marching in solidarity with the Standing Rock Sioux, nearly all construction on the nearly 1,200-mile pipeline had been completed. This can create a sense that the construction of such landscape-level projects is irreversible or that individuals are helpless to divert its course. Further, the conflict between the Standing Rock Sioux and the U.S. government echoed earlier incidents over land seizure and natural resource management: in constructing the Oahe Dam during the late 1950s and early 1960s, the U.S. Army Corps of Engineers dredged parts of the Cannonball River and flooded agricultural lands belonging to the Tribe.[6] According to Michael Lawson, the "Oahe Dam destroyed more Indian land than any other public-works project in America."[7] Historical precedents like those suffered by the Standing Rock Sioux may spur distrust about the motivation, intentions, and consequences of entities managing infrastructure development projects. Indeed, such misalignments between civic interest and infrastructure development procedures profoundly influence our continued relationship to large-scale resource management systems.

The 2016 protests over the Dakota Access Pipeline's route were the first time that I had ever seriously thought about infrastructure, pipelines, and their impacts at a local level. **[Figure 3]** At the time I was living outside Fargo, North Dakota, about two and a half hours from the Standing Rock Reservation and the pipeline's disputed river crossing. Before learning about the camp and the litigation over the pipeline crossing, I had no idea that a large-scale pipeline was being built or that there was any conflict over its path. North Dakota is a large state, and even the effects of the recent oil boom felt at a distance from me. Apart from the oil trains I could watch pass a few hundred feet from my office window, the extraction industry transforming the western part of the state felt like an abstraction.

Invisibility by Design

As noted, my own ignorance about this or any other pipeline wasn't unusual, but indicative of a broader pattern of how individuals engage with large-scale infrastructure projects: we rarely realize it's even there until we encounter some aspect of it firsthand. To be certain, this is part of its design. Pierre Bélanger observes that "often buried or overlooked as background to development, infrastructure is the unseen interface—urbanism's ghost—by which we influence and interact with the material, biological, and technological world."[8] Moreover, our relationship to infrastructure is also characterized by our lack of interest in its operations: the details of plans for large-scale projects like the Dakota Access Pipeline are highly technical, and, for many, boring. However, this perception and the inaccessibility of infrastructure systems such as pipeline networks obscures the power they yield. "Buried in its banal reputation," Bélanger writes, "infrastructure is instrumental as a 'tool and technique of power,' as Michel Foucault references, deployed as 'lines of control' and 'equipment of power' by institutions across vast territories from the City to the State."[9] Through our disengagement, we overlook the ways in which such systems exert a power reshaping force on the landscape.

Documenting the Route

After learning about the Standing Rock Protests in 2016, I committed to learning about pipelines—specifically the Dakota Access Pipeline and how it was impacting the four states it crossed. Through my work as a landscape photographer, I'd spent time in the Bakken region in the midst of the oil boom and witnessed some of the changes brought to the area: new roads, new housing, new well pads, construction of new transmission lines. These changes were considerable, and even as an irregular visitor over five years I felt the tenor of the environment alter. I saw open areas of grasslands transformed by the construction of new, temporary housing structures known as "man camps," which housed the influx of oil workers who descended on the sparsely populated Bakken region of northwestern North Dakota. **[Figure 4]** I waited in traffic behind (what felt like) miles of trucks, and had my car blanketed in dust from passing trucks on rural roads. **[Figure 5]**

[Figure 1] *Pipeline Marker*, 2018, Archival Inkjet Print, 16"x20"
Ubiquitous roadside markers found along the route of the Dakota Access Pipeline, here in North Dakota (image credit: Meghan Kirkwood)

[Figure 2] *Dakota Access Pipeline Construction*, 2016, Archival Inkjet Print, 16"x20"
This image shows a view of the construction of the pipeline in progress (image credit: Meghan Kirkwood)

But my questions extended beyond the epicenters of both the boom region and the protest areas: I wanted to know what the rest of the route looked like. What were the spaces alongside the Dakota Access route and how were they reshaped by the construction of the pipeline? What was visibly altered and what was not? And, similarly, my questions were generated from a position of self-responsibility. I grew up in New Hampshire in a small town surrounded by woods. I'd relied on resources from places like the Bakken my whole life, but I'd never seen or witnessed any part of what it took to get those resources to me.

In the fall of 2016, I began what would be a four-year journey to photograph the pipeline route in its entirety. At the pipeline's starting point in Stanley, North Dakota, a friend flew me over the first miles of the route. From this vantage point, the pattern of diagonal cuts through a landscape already carved up into a Jeffersonian grid was clear. **[Figure 6]** The remaining miles were traveled by car, which took me through hundreds of small towns and farms each linked by the underground transit line. **[Figure 7]** I watched the landscape shift from rolling grasslands to flatter plains of cash grain crops, and observed how the landscape absorbed the oil infrastructure differently. At some points along the tract, I witnessed the construction of the transport lines, and at others I photographed the shadows of the project still visible after four years. Most recently, I used a drone to document the scars still visible on the surface from the initial construction. **[Figure 8]**

Throughout this project I focused on documenting the landscape itself, and in doing so, tried to think about two questions. First, how could I use landscape imagery to examine the relationship between the footprint of the pipeline system and the aftermath of changes it set about onto the environments it crossed? So many infrastructure projects are presented in terms of their initial benefits—specifically jobs—and sold on their minimal costs: relatively limited scope, minimal environmental damages. But, as Pierre Bélanger reminds us, infrastructure is both a force and an impact, and it continues to exert changes long after its initial installation.[10] Second, I wanted to explore how landscape photography can help individuals address their own relationship to large-scale infrastructure systems such as the Dakota Access Pipeline. Could actually visualizing large portions of the route make these kinds of projects seem less like an abstraction? Could a better idea of what these things looked like help or inspire individuals to enter into the conversation before a spill happens or a landowner's home is forever reshaped?

To address the first question, I concentrated on photographing what seemed like small disruptions that sprang up along the pipeline route: disrupted plant communities, houses newly adjacent to pumping facilities, and the new lexicon on pipeline markers dotting the extensive route. **[Figures 9 and 10]** I was also interested in documenting traces of conflict and conversation about the pipeline, such as in *Stop Eminent Domain Abuse*. **[Figure 11]** Landscape-level projects such as the Dakota Access Pipeline do not impact environments evenly, and these impacts may linger or surface at a later time. Landscape images can focus our attention on these subtle changes, whether it's a selection of abandoned worker housing in North Dakota, or a reduced yield in a cornfield in Iowa. Too often, the documentation of pipeline areas only highlights the points of highest drama or media attention: construction, a spill and its aftermath, a site of conflict. But these incidents (and images) represent only a limited view of the long-term relationship citizens and landscapes have with infrastructure systems.

The second question was a key driver in the project design. By visiting and documenting the entirety of the route, I wanted to ask: what does it even look like to put a 1,172-mile pipeline into the ground? Landscape photographs allow us to consider spaces at different scales, from different vantage points, and to imagine ourselves in places very different from those we know. When we see a landscape photograph we look for patterns, evidence of action (current or past), and when we cannot quickly discern what is happening in an image, we often look harder. This process of sustained engagement, of quick glances that lead to questioning can invite engagement with spaces we might otherwise overlook. And in this case, looking harder helps the viewer to extract and build real detail around something that they can't see and may be challenged to fully comprehend.

For example, when we look closely at photographs such as *Pipeline Scar, Iowa,* we first observe an open expanse of agricultural land in late summer. **[Figure 12]** The square patches of green teem with color beneath the cloud-filled sky; the stretch of row crops in the foreground appears velvety and lush. The scene looks inviting, yet ordinary. But our eye also catches something that doesn't mesh with the patterned squares: a faint diagonal line tracing its way from the lower right corner of the frame up until the horizon. We can see it spill over from one crop to another and cut across the repetitive grid. It's not initially clear what caused this shadow line, but set within the context of the project, we know it's a surface marker of the pipeline path. The fact that we can see traces of something that lives underground prompts us to ask new questions, or, at the very least, to recognize that infrastructure never truly operates in the background; it's continually shaping the spaces in which we live.

Together, this seemingly simple landscape lets us experience and learn about one aspect of the pipeline's aftermath, something we couldn't do from the ground or even from reading about the development of or litigation over a pipeline.[11] In doing so, it offers a kind of data point with which we can break down what it means to create landscape-level change through infrastructure development. It lets us imagine what the effects are, not just in barrels per day transported, or to weigh the benefits of an underground transport system versus one using rails. Landscape photography can give us the space to consider literal impacts outside of the zoning assessment reports or opinion pages. It can break down the abstractions of infrastructure systems and allow us to experience its scale, even without having to choose a side.

1. Pipeline and Hazardous Materials Safety Administration, "General Pipeline FAQ," U.S. Department of Transportation (November 6, 2018), https://www.phmsa.dot.gov/faqs/general-pipeline-faqs.
2. Pipeline and Hazardous Materials Safety Administration, "Pipeline Basics," U.S. Department of Transportation, https://primis.phmsa.dot.gov/comm/PipelineBasics.htm, accessed September 13, 2020.
3. Karen Clay, Akshaya Jha, Nicholas Muller, and Randall Walsh, *The external costs of transporting petroleum products by pipelines and rail: evidence from shipments of crude oil from North Dakota*, no. w23852, National Bureau of Economic Research (2017).
4. Transportation Safety Board of Canada, "Lac-Mégantic runaway train and derailment investigation summary" (May 10, 2019), https://www.tsb.gc.ca/eng/rapports-reports/rail/2013/r13d0054/r13d0054-r-es.html; *Bismarck Tribune*, "Casselton train crash resulting in massive fire prompts call for evacuation" (December 30, 2013), https://bismarcktribune.com/news/state-and-regional/casselton-train-crash-resulting-in-massive-fire-prompts-call-for-evacuation/article_d57c4ba4-f401-11e4-b9fd-0f4c1a06422a.html.
5. Mike Soraghan, "Oil and Gas Industry Leads in Severe Injuries," E&E News (May 2, 2017), https://www.eenews.net/stories/1060053892; Amy Mall, "Pipeline Incident Statistics Reveal Significant Dangers," National Resource Defense Council (January 2, 2019), https://www.nrdc.org/experts/amy-mall/pipeline-incident-statistics-reveal-significant-dangers#:~:text=There%20are%20hundreds%20of%20thousands,a%20fatality%20every%2026%20days.; National Institute for Occupational Safety and Health (NIOSH), "Fatalities in the Oil and Gas Extraction Industry (FOG)," Centers for Disease Control and Prevention (March 20, 2020), https://www.cdc.gov/niosh/topics/fog/about.html.
6. Samantha L. Varsalona, "Pipelines, Protests and General Permits," Environmental Law Review Syndicate, accessed September 14, 2020, http://vjel.vermontlaw.edu/pipelines-protests-general-permits/.
7. Michael L. Lawson, *Dammed Indians: The Pick-Sloan Plan and the Missouri River Sioux, 1944–1980* (Norman: University of Oklahoma Press, 1994), 50.
8. Pierre Bélanger, "Is Landscape Infrastructure," in *Is landscape...?: Essays on the identity of landscape*, eds. Gareth Doherty and Charles Waldheim (London: Routledge, 2015), 191.
9. Ibid, 195.
10. Ibid, 191.
11. The Dakota Access Pipeline has undergone a number of legal challenges, many of which have been chronicled by mainstream media outlets in the U.S. In July 2020, the U.S. District Court for the District of Columbia ruled that the U.S. Army Corps of Engineers violated federal environmental law when it permitted Energy Transfer LP to construct the portion of the pipeline that travels beneath Lake Oahe, and determined that the Dakota Access Pipeline should be shut down by August 5th, 2020. See: Jaceyy Fortin and Lisa Friedman, "Dakota Access Pipeline to Shut Down Pending Review, Federal Judge Rules," *New York Times* (July 6, 2020), https://www.nytimes.com/2020/07/06/us/dakota-access-pipeline.html. In a subsequent ruling the U.S. Court of Appeals ruled that the pipeline does not have to be shut down while legal proceedings continue. See: "Dakota Access pipeline can keep running amid legal fight: U.S. Court," *Reuters Business News* (July 14, 2020), https://www.reuters.com/article/us-usa-pipeline-energy-transfer-idUSKCN24F309. In September 2020 the Army Corps of Engineers began an environmental review of the disputed section of the Dakota Access Pipeline. See: Blake Nicholson, "Corps of Engineers formally launches Dakota Access Pipeline study," *Bismarck Tribune* (September 10, 2020), https://bismarcktribune.com/news/state-and-regional/corps-of-engineers-formally-launches-dakota-access-pipeline-study/article_f73c6a9b-397b-54da-92f1-4e6ef03598a3.html.

[Figure 3] *No DAPL*, 2016, Archival Inkjet Print, 16"x20"
The protests against the routing of the Dakota Access Pipeline near the water intake for the Standing Rock Sioux reservation drew supporters from across the country to North Dakota in the Fall of 2016; this image shows a view of one group of campsites just north of the Cannonball River (image credit: Meghan Kirkwood)

[Figure 4] *Housing outside Williston*, 2019, Archival Inkjet Print, 20"x24"
This image was taken of a new development just north of Williston, North Dakota; considered something of the "epicenter" of the oil boom, Williston has grown rapidly in response to industry activity, necessitating the need for new housing (image credit: Meghan Kirkwood)

[Figure 5] *Dust, Truck*, 2017, Archival Inkjet Print, 16"x20"
The impacts from dust stirred up from increased truck traffic are of great concern for farmers and residents in the Bakken region of North Dakota; this image seeks to represent something of this tension (image credit: Meghan Kirkwood)

[Figure 6] *Pipeline Scar*, 2017, Archival Inkjet Print, 16"x20"
Taken in September of 2016 this photograph shows a view of the Dakota Access Pipeline just outside of Tioga, North Dakota (image credit: Meghan Kirkwood)

[Figure 7] *Lines in the Sand*, 2016, Archival Inkjet Print, 16"x20"
During the construction of the Dakota Access Pipeline in North Dakota, orange lines of fence visible at a great distance signaled the outline of the route; the bright chroma pulsed on the rural landscapes and though spectacular to look at, often felt at odds with the hues of the state's agricultural fields (image credit: Meghan Kirkwood)

[Figure 8] *Ruptured Rangelands*, South Dakota, 2019, Archival Inkjet Print, 20"x24"
This photograph visualizes the continued impacts of the pipeline on its surroundings even years post-construction; the visible outline of the pipeline route shows how pasture areas such as this changed in relation to adjacent areas (image credit: Meghan Kirkwood)

[Figure 9] *Pumpjack, Church*, 2018, Archival Inkjet Print, 16"x20"
One of the striking aspects of the oil boom in northwestern North Dakota was the way in which the interface between settlements and oil infrastructure grew thinner and more porous; here, a pumpjack sits alongside the entrance to a church and housing development (image credit: Meghan Kirkwood)

[Figure 10] *Construction in the Grain Field*, 2016, Archival Inkjet Print, 16"x20"
The faint outline of the orange fence shows the narrow barrier between a farmer's field and the pipeline construction (image credit: Meghan Kirkwood)

[Figure 11] *Stop Eminent Domain Abuse*, 2020, Archival Inkjet Print, 16"x20"
This painted trailer is visible from highway 30 in central Iowa, an area in which there was substantial litigation from landowners involving the pipeline route (image credit: Meghan Kirkwood)

[Figure 12] *Pipeline Scar, Iowa*, 2020, Archival Inkjet Print, 20"x24"
(image credit: Meghan Kirkwood)

Territory 02: Upper Mississippi, Ohio, and Tennessee River Basins

Territory 02 Plan

The Upper Mississippi River and its two major eastern tributaries, the Ohio and Tennessee Rivers, are distinct river systems that each provide a critical ecological and infrastructural function to the watershed. The main stem of the Upper Mississippi River has a total length of 1,300 miles and includes the run from its source in upper Minnesota to the three-point border between Missouri, Illinois, and Kentucky.[1] Its watershed drains an area of 189,000 square miles, and nearly 60 percent of the land is used for agriculture.[2] A 2003 study estimated that the total population living in the Upper Mississippi River Basin was 30 million, with 80 percent living in urbanized areas.[3] The Mississippi River joins the Illinois and Missouri Rivers near St. Louis and the Ohio and Tennessee Rivers near the end of its run. Before its confluence with the Ohio River, the Upper Mississippi has an average discharge of 204,800 cubic feet per second (cfs). This number more than doubles after the confluence with the Ohio River, which contributes 281,000 cfs—nearly half of all the water in the Mississippi River Basin.[4] Many of the Mississippi's physical attributes allow it to be an ideal corridor for commercial navigation. Since the 19th century, the U.S. Army Corps of Engineers (USACE) has engineered the Mississippi

Melvin Price Locks & Dam, Alton, Illinois, 2017 (image credit: Derek Hoeferlin)

River and its tributaries to create and maintain a navigable channel through the American Midwest.[5] Currently, a total of 29 locks and dams are operational in the main branch of the Mississippi River with an additional 6 on the Illinois River that links to Chicago and the Great Lakes.[6] The Ohio River has similarly been outfitted with 21 locks and dams that allow navigation upstream to Pittsburgh.[7] Many of the Ohio River locks and dams are equipped with hydroelectric plants that provide power to the region, but the most significant act of watershed management took place in its tributary, the Tennessee River. In 1933, the New Deal founded the Tennessee Valley Authority (TVA), and charged it with improving the quality of life for all residents in the Tennessee Valley.[8] Endowed with the power of government and imbued with the nimbleness of private practice, the TVA both developed the river's hydrologic potential and reorganized land-use patterns around its water resources to transform the Tennessee Valley into a cohesive network.[9] Since its founding, the TVA has constructed 48 dams along the main stem of the Tennessee river and its tributaries for flood control and irrigation, 31 of which also produce hydroelectric power.[10] The Upper Mississippi, Ohio, and Tennessee River Basins are invaluable river systems that have helped to shape the country's history with their important contributions as an agricultural, industrial, and economically productive region.

Territory 02 Section G-G

In the effort to facilitate navigation on the Upper Mississippi River, it has been transformed into a precisely controlled system. Starting from the Lake Itasca headwaters, the river descends more than 1,100 feet to a surface elevation of approximately 300 feet as it crosses from the Upper to Lower Mississippi River Basins at the confluence with the Ohio River. The river runs within bluffs that provide a natural barrier, but levees are frequently constructed within the floodplains between the bluffs for additional flood protection, particularly for farmlands that tend to occupy former wetland and backwater landscapes. In its current state, the Upper Mississippi River has been channelized through a complex network of levees, floodwalls, and a series of 29 locks and dams that control the water and facilitate navigation between St. Paul and St. Louis.[11] The locks and dams have transformed the Upper Mississippi River from a free-flowing river into a series of slack-water pools with a staircase-like profile that spans from Minneapolis to St. Louis. While it has become a key piece of transportation infrastructure in the country, the natural state of the Upper Mississippi River was unreliable for navigation due to its shallow depth and craggy riverbed. In 1930, near the beginning of the Great Depression, the USACE submitted a proposal to create a navigable path in the Upper Mississippi River, called the "9-foot Channel Project." The project was approved and received funding for initial procedures through the "Rivers and Harbors Act."[12] Three years later, the 9-foot Channel received full funding from the New Deal as it promised to be both a significant source of employment and an invaluable project for the country.[13] The original plan, consisting of 26 locks and dams between St. Paul, Minnesota, and Alton, Illinois (north of St. Louis), was completed in 1940, and three additional locks and dams were built in the 1950s and 1960s to extend the channel to Minneapolis and St. Louis.[14] In its current state, interbasin navigation is possible between the Upper Mississippi, Ohio, and Lower Missouri River, and it is also linked to the Saint Lawrence River through its connection to the Great Lakes. The lock and dam system is designed to facilitate smooth passage of modern 15-barge tows which can hold the equivalent capacity of 1,050 semitrucks.[15] A 1999 study discovered that 125 million tons of goods were shipped in the Upper Mississippi River system, generating $1 billion in revenue.[16] However, the amount of engineering and interconnectivity has consequences for the natural environment. In one particularly disastrous example, multiple invasive species of carp were accidentally brought into the Upper Mississippi River from Asia, and research indicates that their proliferation will come at the expense of native fish and plant populations—leading to a decline in the health of the river.[17] Nearly a century after completion of the 9-foot Channel Project, the Upper Mississippi River remains essential to the country's economy, but has incurred unintended and significant consequences as a result.

Upper St. Anthony's Falls

Lower St. Anthony's Falls

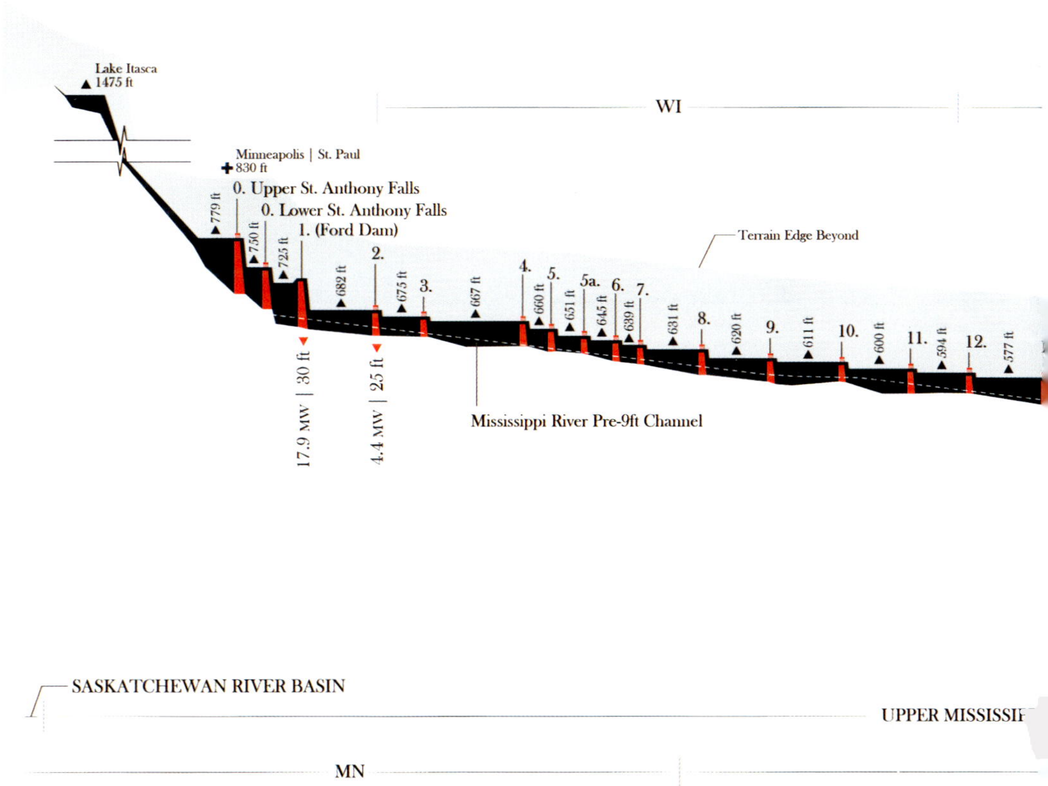
Lake Itasca
1475 ft
WI
Minneapolis | St. Paul
830 ft
0. Upper St. Anthony Falls
0. Lower St. Anthony Falls
1. (Ford Dam)
Terrain Edge Beyond
779 ft
750 ft
725 ft
682 ft
2.
675 ft
3.
667 ft
4.
660 ft
5.
651 ft
5a.
645 ft
6.
639 ft
7.
631 ft
8.
620 ft
9.
611 ft
10.
600 ft
11.
594 ft
12.
577 ft
17.9 MW | 30 ft
4.4 MW | 25 ft
Mississippi River Pre-9ft Channel
SASKATCHEWAN RIVER BASIN
UPPER MISSISSIP
MN

TERRITORY 02

UPPER MISSISSIPPI, OHIO AND TENNESSEE RIVER BASINS

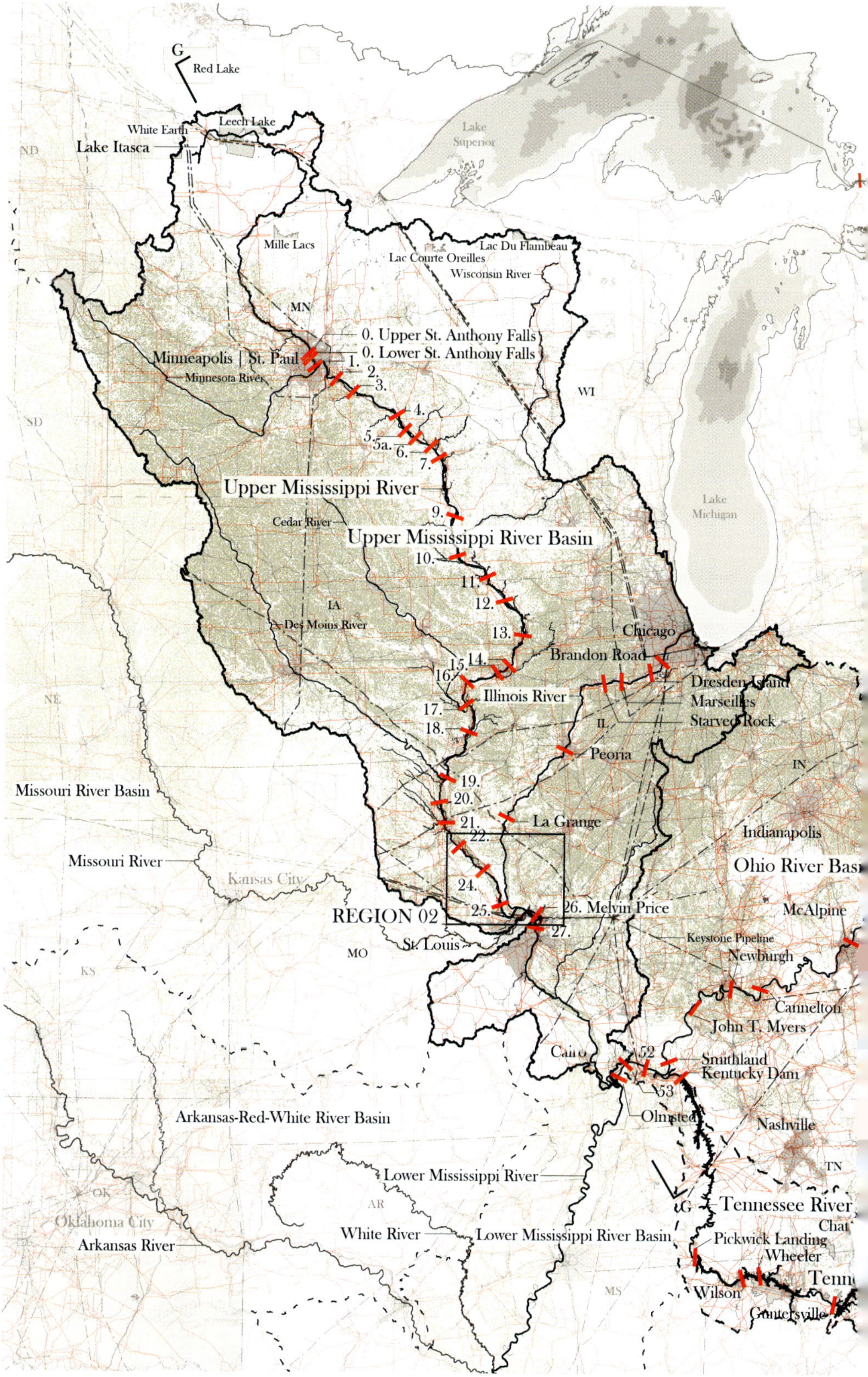

G
Red Lake
Leech Lake
White Earth
Lake Itasca
ND
Lake Superior
Mille Lacs
Lac Du Flambeau
Lac Courte Oreilles
Wisconsin River
MN
0. Upper St. Anthony Falls
0. Lower St. Anthony Falls
Minneapolis | St. Paul
Minnesota River
1.
2.
3.
4.
5.
5a.
6.
7.
SD
WI
Upper Mississippi River
9.
Cedar River
Upper Mississippi River Basin
Lake Michigan
10.
11.
12.
IA
Des Moins River
13.
Chicago
14.
Brandon Road
15.
16.
Dresden Island
Illinois River
Marseilles
17.
Starved Rock
18.
IL
NE
Peoria
IN
19.
Missouri River Basin
20.
21.
La Grange
Indianapolis
22.
Missouri River
Kansas City
Ohio River Basi
24.
McAlpine
25.
26. Melvin Price
REGION 02
27.
Keystone Pipeline
St. Louis
MO
Newburgh
KS
Cannelton
John T. Myers
Cairo
52
Smithland
Kentucky Dam
53
Olmsted
Arkansas-Red-White River Basin
Nashville
TN
Lower Mississippi River
G
Tennessee River
OK
AR
Chat
Oklahoma City
White River
Lower Mississippi River Basin
Pickwick Landing
Arkansas River
Wheeler
MS
Tenn
Wilson
Guntersville

Lock & Dam 19

Pool 22

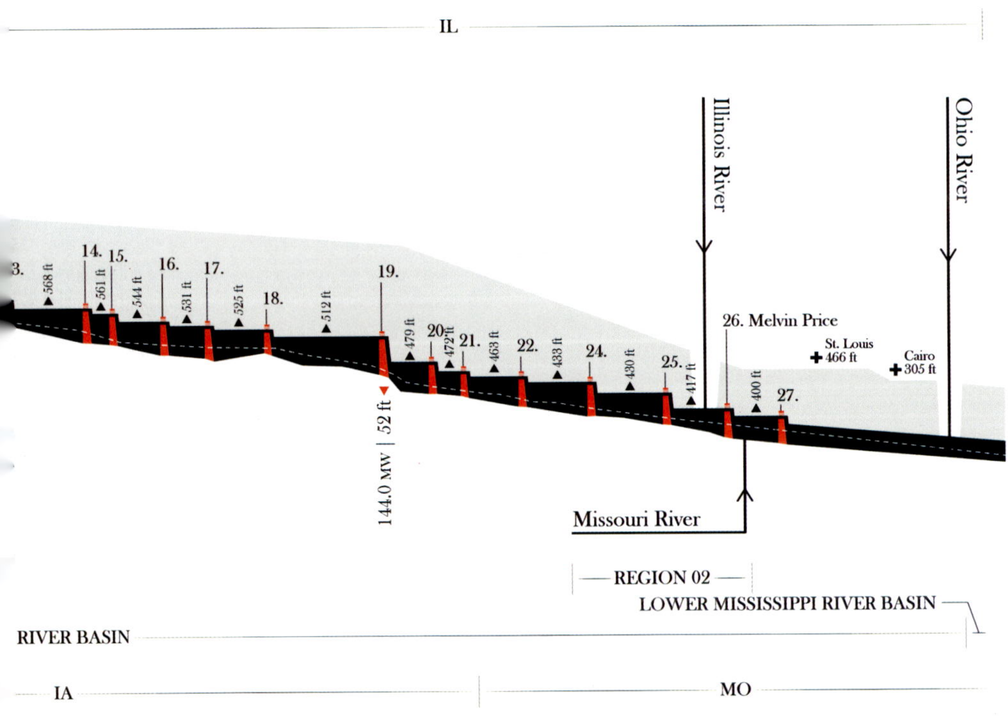

SECTION G-G

FOLLOWING THE PATH OF THE UPPER MISSISSIPPI RIVER

Region 02: Confluences of the Illinois, Mississippi, & Missouri Rivers

Region 02 Plan

The process of creating the 9-foot Channel Project included the construction of 29 locks and dams as well as countless dikes and other river control structures that have together irreversibly altered the character of the Upper Mississippi River. By far the most significant physical change was the inundation of the river into 29 sections that the USACE has named "pools."[18] The pool is defined as the area between the dams and the natural bluffs adjacent to the river, and each one is associated with the downstream dam that has impounded it. Each pool features the riverine landscape—islands, wetlands, sandbars—as well as a significant amount of land that was reclaimed from the riparian zone into agricultural and urbanized land. The "9-foot Channel" refers specifically to a designated path on the main-stem Upper Mississippi River. At the head of the pool, the river is thin and splits into multiple channels as it courses around islands in a seemingly natural state, but near the downstream dam, the effects of the inundation become evident as the surface of the river increases and overtakes natural riverine archipelagos and wetlands. Importantly, the dams manage the amount of water flowing through the river to maintain a stable water level for year-round navigation regardless of natural water flows.[19] However, the physical changes to the river as well as the land-use practices in the 20th century would have negative consequences for future flood safety. Natural floodplains were removed to facilitate the 9-foot Channel, or reclaimed into agricultural or urbanized areas.[20] Without natural buffers, flood protection structures like levees have been constructed along the edge of the river to protect the residential and agrarian areas that were reclaimed from the floodplain. Even with flood protection, many areas were still unprepared for extreme events like the Great Flood of 1993.[21] That year, the Missouri and Mississippi Rivers reached record water

Pool 25, Mississippi River, Missouri/Illinois, 2017 (image credit: Derek Hoeferlin)

levels that affected tens of thousands of people and incurred damages that cost between $15 and $20 billion.[22] An overwhelming majority of the inundated land was agricultural, but most urban areas remained safe behind more robust flood prevention networks.[23] St. Louis, located at a high-risk zone near the confluence of the Mississippi, Illinois, and Missouri Rivers, was luckily safeguarded by its floodwalls and artificial reservoirs.[24] The transformation of the Upper Mississippi River and its riparian landscape into its current state has led to precious and disruptive land-use practices both socially and ecologically.

Region 02 Section H-H

While the UMRB has been primarily adapted for navigation and agriculture, the main-stem river has recently become an important site for conservation. The Upper Mississippi River is one of North America's most important natural waterways. For example, nearly 40 percent of all North American migratory birds pass through the river annually, and a quarter of all the continent's fish species are native to the river basin. It is estimated that 15 million people rely on the Upper Mississippi and its tributaries for water.[25]As the Upper Mississippi River approaches St. Louis, the 9-foot Channel is diverted to the Chain of Rocks Canal, an adjacent channel of water, to bypass an unnavigable stretch of the river near the city. A majority of the commodities shipped through the Upper Mississippi River are agricultural. Nitrogen-based fertilizers are brought upstream to support corn and soybean production which is in turn transported downstream to ports in Louisiana for global export.[26] However, the proliferation of industries along the Mississippi River has caused a decline in the health of the river because of the pollution discharged from these activities, especially fertilizer runoff.[27] The declining water quality is detrimental to the ecosystem and the wellbeing of residents along the river. Through the Water Resources Development Act of 1986, Congress recognized the Upper Mississippi River as both a "nationally significant ecosystem and a nationally significant commercial navigation system," and created the Environmental Management Program (EMP) to address the declining health of the river along with other concerns raised by environmentalists.[28] A key initiative of the EMP is the restoration and the preservation of riverine habitats like islands, wetlands, marshes, and ancillary channels.[29] The U.S. Army Corps of Engineers primarily developed these projects, and many of the seemingly natural islands and wetlands have actually been artificially reconstructed. The preservation of the Upper Mississippi River's natural environment arguably has become as important as the economic and industrial activities that have dominated the river.

Pool 26

Chain of Rocks Low Water Dam

Melvin Price Lock & Dam

Locks 27 (southernmost lock)

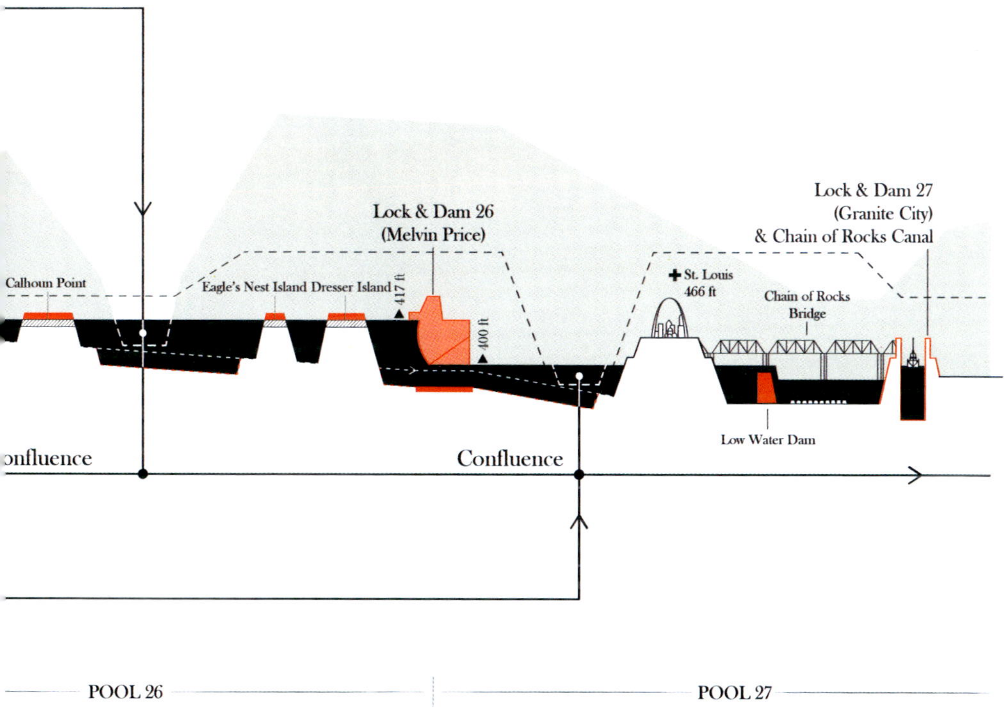

SECTION H-H

SECTION THROUGH POOL 25, UPPER MISSISSIPPI RIVER BASIN

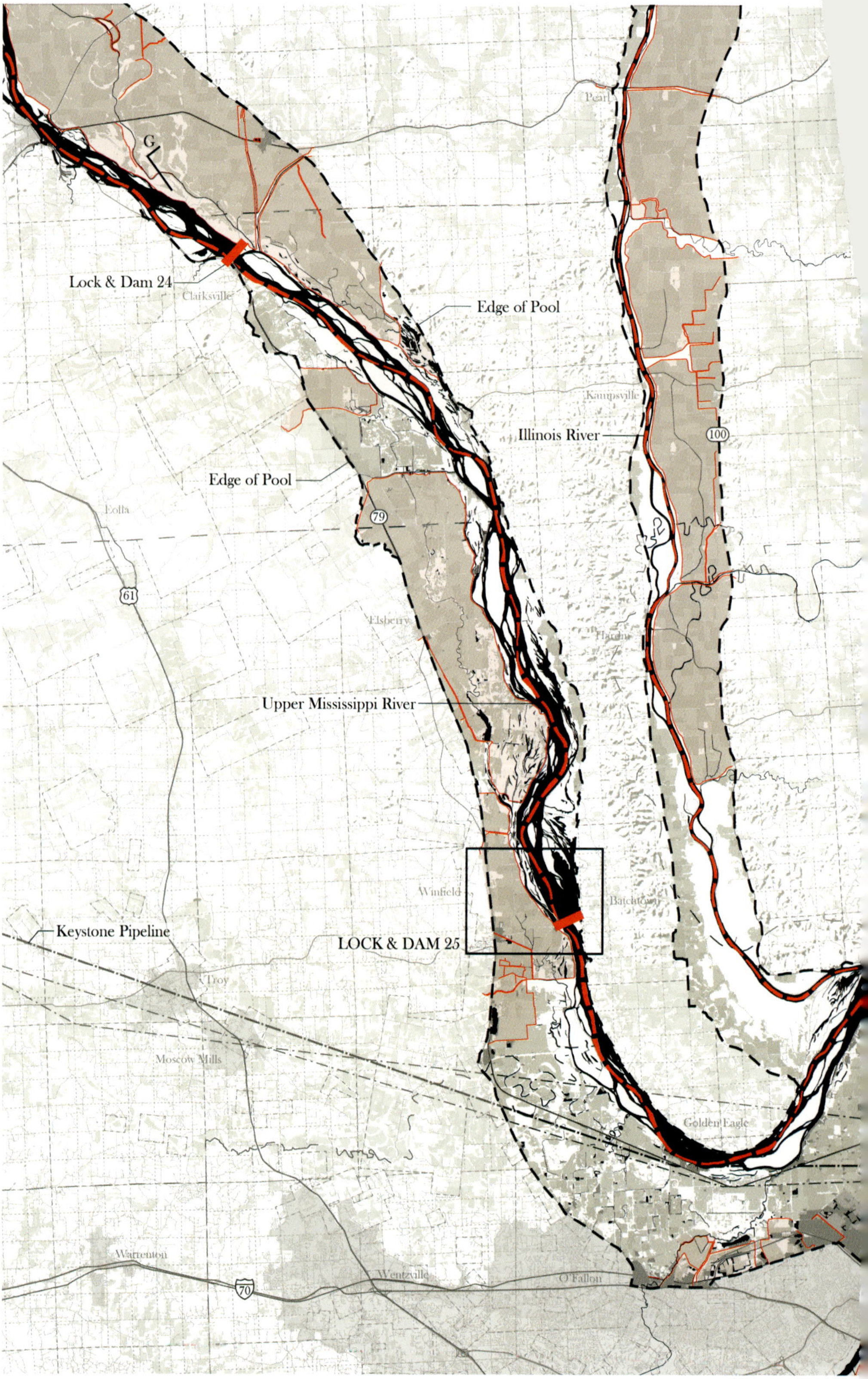

Pearl
G
Lock & Dam 24
Clarksville
Edge of Pool
Kampsville
Illinois River
100
Edge of Pool
79
Eolia
61
Elsberry
Hardin
Upper Mississippi River
Winfield
Batchtown
Keystone Pipeline
LOCK & DAM 25
Troy
Moscow Mills
Golden Eagle
Warrenton
70
Wentzville
O'Fallon

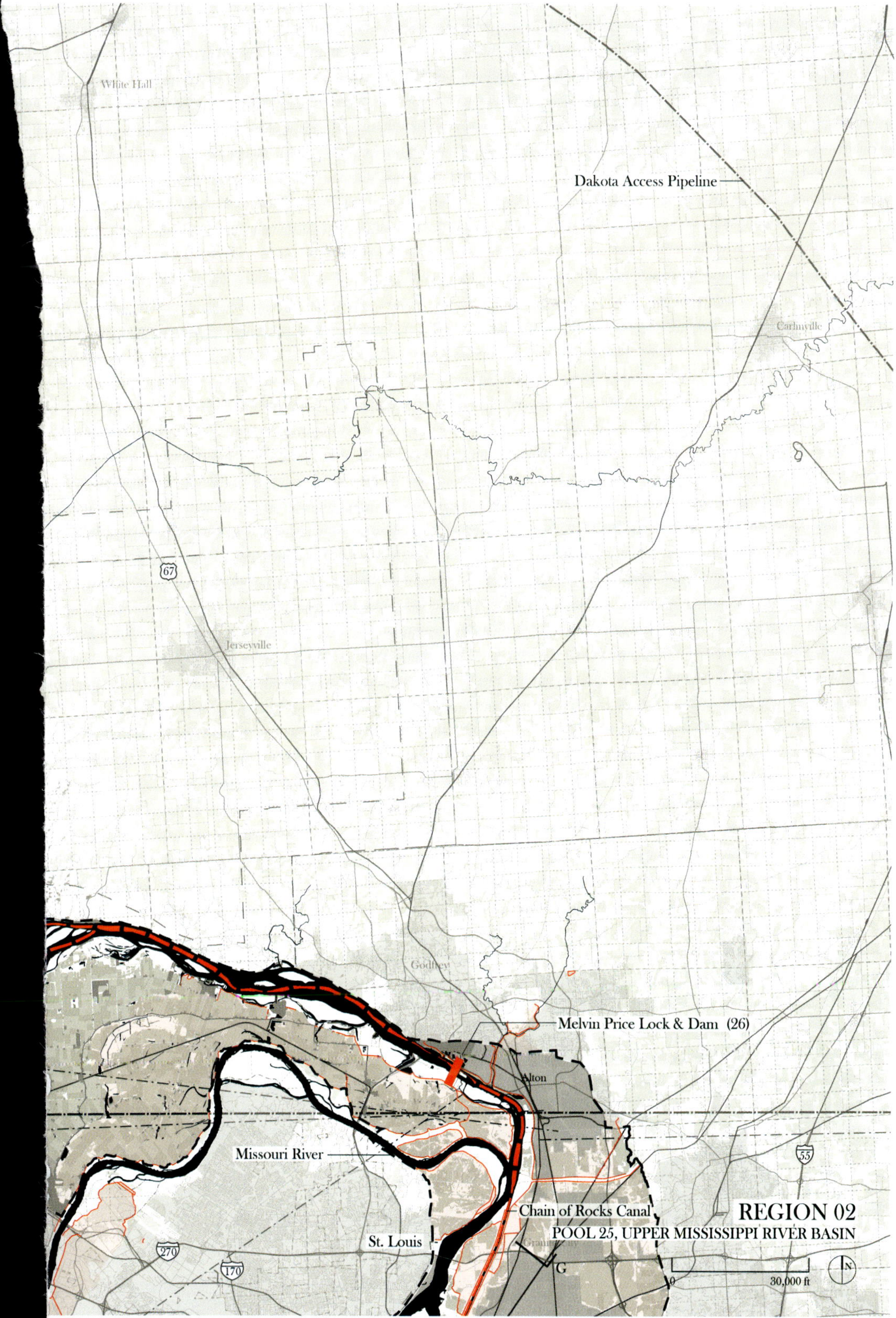

REGION 02
POOL 25, UPPER MISSISSIPPI RIVER BASIN

Pool 24

Pool 25

Lock & Dam 24

Lock & Dam 25

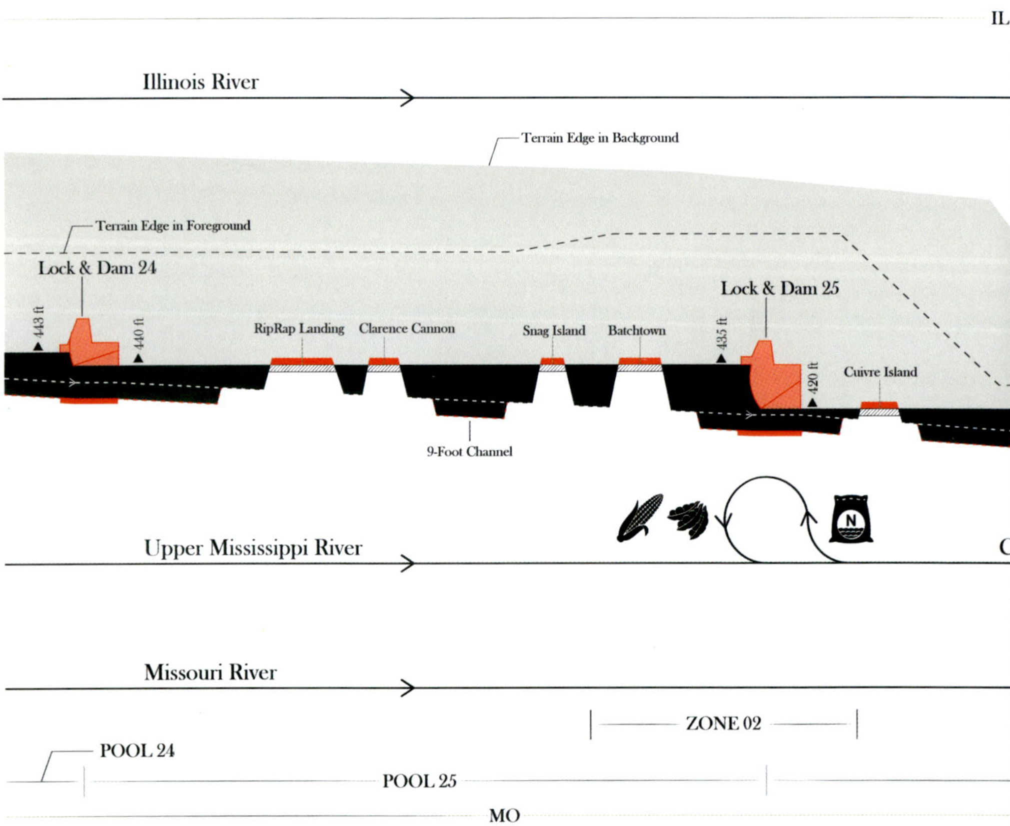
IL
Illinois River
Terrain Edge in Background
Terrain Edge in Foreground
Lock & Dam 24
443 ft
440 ft
RipRap Landing
Clarence Cannon
Snag Island
Batchtown
435 ft
Lock & Dam 25
420 ft
Cuivre Island
9-Foot Channel
N
Upper Mississippi River
Missouri River
ZONE 02
POOL 24
POOL 25
MO

Zone 02:

Lock and Dam 25

Zone 02 Plan

The landscape in the pools is a patchwork of different environments, delineated through artificial barriers. The line of the two bluffs and Lock and Dams 24 and 25 define Pool 25. As the river approaches Lock and Dam 25, the eastern flank of the river runs up against the bluffs, while the western riverbank meets an agricultural levee that protects fields and a small residential area in the floodplain. The Sandy Slough dike was erected to channelize water towards the 9-foot Channel, but it has disconnected the Sandy Slough from the Mississippi River.[30] The layout and design of Lock and Dam 25 is a typical example of all locks and dams in the Upper Mississippi River. The project consists of a lock, a 1,300-foot spillway, and a 2,600-foot overflow dike that connects to the eastern riverbank. The 9-foot Channel follows the bathymetry of the river and directs vessels between each of the 29 locks in the Upper Mississippi River. The chevron dikes adjacent to the 9-foot Channel are a recent infrastructural addition that channelize the river without being obstructive.[31] To be more ecologically attuned, the chevrons have sectional profiles that allow them to be submersible, which has the added benefit of providing habitats for fish and wildlife.[32] While the USACE's responsibility is maintaining the navigation channel and infrastructure, it has recently been engaged with conservation and managing land-use practices in the riparian landscape. Leading up to the 1993 flood, half of the floodplains had been cut off from the river by agricultural levees. The channelization of the water to maintain the 9-foot Channel disconnected the main channel from adjacent streams of water.[33] Due to the modifications to the river by the construction of new infrastructure, the Upper Mississippi River has been constricted—leading to amplified floodwater peaks.[34] In response to the 1993 flood, the USACE has prioritized floodplain management in the Upper Mississippi River and has adapted land-use practices to reduce potential damages in future inundation events, like the reconversion of risk farmlands back into wetlands.[35] The USACE also engages in conservation projects like the one at the Batchtown Fish and Waterfowl Management Area. Due in part to poor environmental management, the 3,490-acre site nearly disappeared.[36] The project included a full rehabilitation of the formation's wetland forests and sand islands as well as the installation of water pumps and outflow gates to protect the area from future decline.[37] In addition to their benefits to the natural environment, the conservation and river restoration projects are important initiatives for the long-term sustainability and viability of both recreational and commercial activities.

Lock and Dam 25, Mississippi River, Missouri/Illinois, 2017 (image credit: Derek Hoeferlin)

Zone 02 Section I-I, J-J

Lock and Dam 25 has been constantly utilized daily since its completion in 1939. The lock consists of a chamber between two gates that can be isolated from the surrounding body of water in order to adjust the surface elevation. A series of underground valves direct the flow of water either into the lock for upstream travel or out of the chamber to allow boats to continue downstream. Lock and Dam 25 has a 15-foot elevation change from the end of Pool 25 to the beginning of Pool 26. On average, the lock operates at least a dozen times every day, with annual lockages ranging from 4,000 to 6,000 times a year in the last decade.[38] Both the structure and the navigation channel have deteriorated due to age, natural factors, and usage. The USACE's maintenance efforts include repairs to the lock and dams as well as dredging in the navigation channel to remove trapped sediment.[39] The structure's spillway consists of 14 tainter gates and 3 roller gates designed to regulate excess flow. To facilitate the 9-foot Channel, water levels in the Upper Mississippi River are raised by 5 to 20 feet and kept at a constant surface elevation.[40] In 1994, after the adoption of the Environmental Pool Management program, Pool 25 was the first test of a drawdown where the water level would be lowered 2 feet for a month in the summer and gradually return to its typical level.[41] This test mimicked the seasonal water cycle, and restored many fish and waterfowl habitats in the pool that had been in decline.[42] With no expense to navigation, the drawdowns have become an annual event in Pools 24, 25, and 26 for habitat rehabilitation, and it has been tested in more pools throughout the Upper Mississippi River.[43] The extensive conservation projects are also important for attracting people to visit the river. It is estimated that tourism and outdoor activities on the Upper Mississippi River generate $6.6 billion annually.[44] Lock and Dam 25 has become a popular staging area for recreation due to its proximity to St. Louis and its ease of access to conservation areas like Sandy Island and Batchtown.[45] With the restoration of natural habitats, it has become an ideal and accessible location for birdwatching, hunting, fishing, and canoeing.[46] The locks and dams have become central to all activities that take place on the Upper Mississippi River.

1. "River and Basin Facts," River Facts, Upper Mississippi River Basin Association (January 2003), accessed January 23, 2021, https://www.umrba.org/facts.htm.

2. Ibid.

3. Ibid.

4. Ibid.; "Flows of Largest U.S. River: Length, Discharge, and Drainage Area" (Suitland: U.S. Census Bureau, 2011), accessed January 23, 2021, https://www2.census.gov/library/publications/2010/compendia/statab/130ed/tables/11s0361.pdf.

5. O'Brien et al., *Gateways to Commerce*, 19.

6. Ibid., 13–14.

7. "Navigation on the Ohio River," U.S. Army Corps of Engineers Great Lakes and Ohio River Division, accessed December 7, 2020, https://www.lrd.usace.army.mil/Missions/Navigation/Ohio-River/.

8. U.S. Congress, *Tennessee Valley Authority Act of 1933*, 48 Stat. 58–59, 16 U.S.C. sec. 831.

9. Morgan, *The Making of the TVA*, 3.

10. "Hydroelectric," Our Power System, Tennessee Valley Authority, accessed December 7, 2020, https://www.tva.com/energy/our-power-system/hydroelectric.

11. "Upper Mississippi River: Locks & Dams" (Vicksburg: U.S. Army Corps of Engineers Mississippi Valley Division: 2018), accessed December 8, 2020, https://usace.contentdm.oclc.org/utils/getfile/collection/p16021coll11/id/3033, 2.

12. John O. Anfinson, *The River We Have Wrought: A History of the Upper Mississippi* (Minneapolis: University of Minnesota Press, 2003), 269.

13. Ibid., 269–272.

14. Ibid., 274.

15. "Upper Mississippi River: Locks & Dams," 1.

16. Robert Black et al., *Economic Profile of the Upper Mississippi River Region* (Cambridge: Industrial Economics Incorporated, March 1999), accessed January 23, 2021, https://training.fws.gov/Pubs3/economicprofile_miss99.pdf, ii.

17. Todd M. Koel, Kevin S. Irons, and Eric Ratcliff, "Asian Carp Invasion of the Upper Mississippi River System" (La Crosse: Upper Midwest Environmental Sciences Center, November 2000), accessed January 23, 2021, https://www.researchgate.net/publication/330325584_Asian_Carp_Invasion_of_the_Upper_Mississippi_River_System, 1–2.

18. "A River That Works and a Working River" (Carbondale: Upper Mississippi River Conservation

Committee, 2000), accessed December 8, 2020, https://www.umrcc.org/publications, 5.

19. Ibid., 21.

20. Ibid., 7.

21. "Floodplain Management Assessment of the Upper Mississippi River and Lower Missouri Rivers and Tributaries," (Washington, DC: U.S. Army Corps of Engineers, June 1995), accessed December 8, 2020, https://apps.dtic.mil/dtic/tr/fulltext/u2/a297674.pdf, 4.

22. Ibid., ATT 1_11.

23. Ibid., 3.

24. Ibid., 1_7.

25. "A River That Works," 4.

26. Anfinson, *The River We Have Wrought*, 277.

27. Ibid., 280.

28. Ibid., 288.

29. Ibid., 289.

30. "Project Fact Sheet: Lock and Dam 25 Dam Safety" (St. Louis: U.S. Army Corps of Engineers, St. Louis District, February 19, 2015), accessed December 8, 2020, https://www.mvs.usace.army.mil/Portals/54/docs/pm/2016%20Project%20Fact%20Sheets/CG/ProjectFactSheet-LD25DamSafety.pdf.

31. "Inland Navigation: Channel Training Works" (Reston: American Society of Civil Engineers Manuals of Practice, 2012), accessed December 8, 2020, https://ascelibrary.org/doi/book/10.1061/9780784412534, 87.

32. Ibid.

33. "A River That Works," 5.

34. Ibid., 21.

35. "Floodplain Management Assessment," 12_5.

36. "2016 Report to Congress: Upper Mississippi River Restoration Program" (Rock Island, U.S. Army Corps of Engineers, 2016), accessed December 8, 2020, https://www.umesc.usgs.gov/ltrmp/documents/2016_umrr_rtc_%20final.pdf, vi.

37. Ibid., 13.

38. "Upper Mississippi River: Locks & Dams," 58.

39. "Project Fact Sheet: Lock and Dam 25 Safety"; "Lock and Dam 25 Overflow Dike Scour: Interim Risk Reduction Measure," (St. Louis: U.S. Army Corps of Engineers, St. Louis District, November 2014), accessed December 8, 2020, https://www.mvs.usace.army.mil/Portals/54/docs/pm/Reports/EA/LD%20 25%20Spillway%20Scour%20Repair%20Draft%20EA%20and%20Unsigned%20FONSI%202014%20 Combined%20Documents.pdf, EA-8.

40. K.P. Kenow et al., "Process, Policy, and Implementation of Pool-Wide Drawdowns on the Upper Mississippi River: A Promising Approach for Ecological Restoration of Large Impounded Rivers," *River Research and Applications* 31, iss. 3, (2016): 295–308, accessed December 8, 2020, https://www.fws.gov/uploadedFiles/Kenow_et_al-2016-River_Research_and_Applications.pdf, 296.

41. Ibid., 298.

42. Ibid., 298.

43. Ibid., 298; "Environmental Pool Management," Water Control Management, U.S. Army Corps of Engineers, St. Louis District, accessed December 8, 2020, https://www.mvs-wc.usace.army.mil/epm/epmindex.html.

44. "A River That Works," 4.

45. "Lock and Dam 25 Overflow Dike Scour," EA_12.

46. Ibid., EA_12.

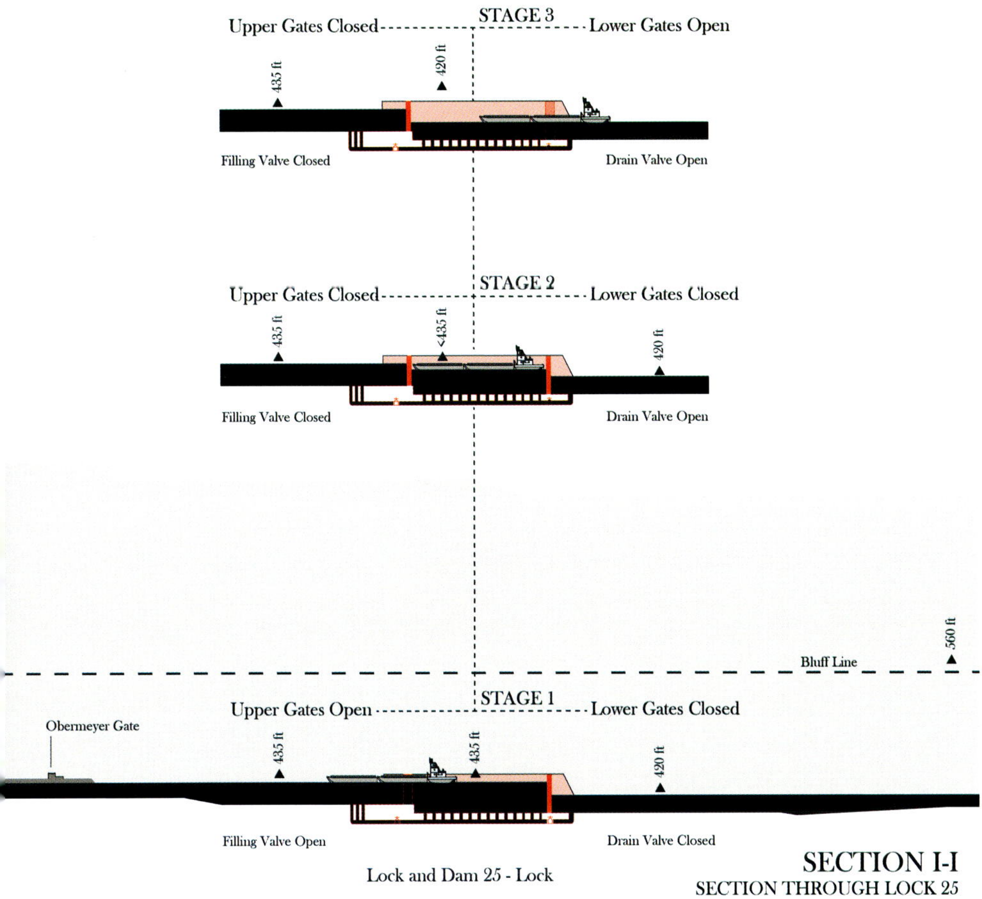

SECTION I-I

SECTION THROUGH LOCK 25

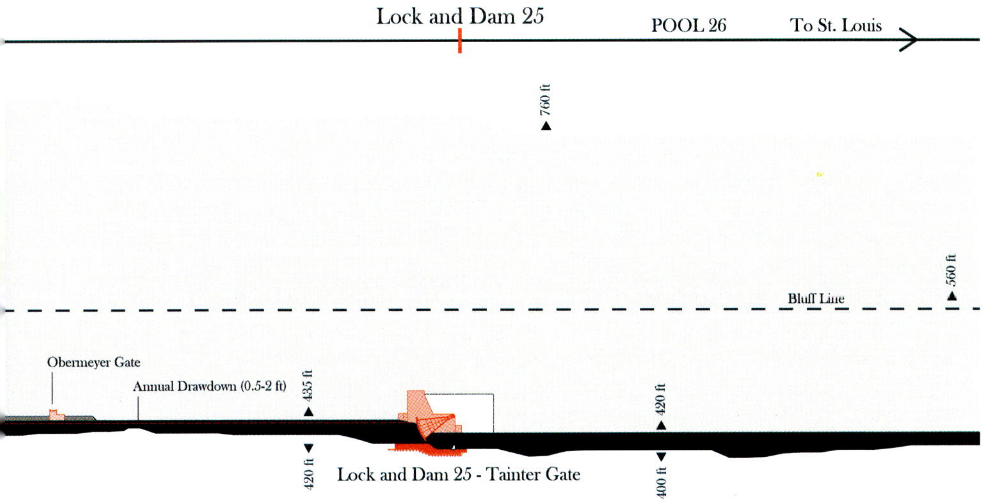

SECTION J-J

SECTION THROUGH THE DAM 25 SPILLWAY

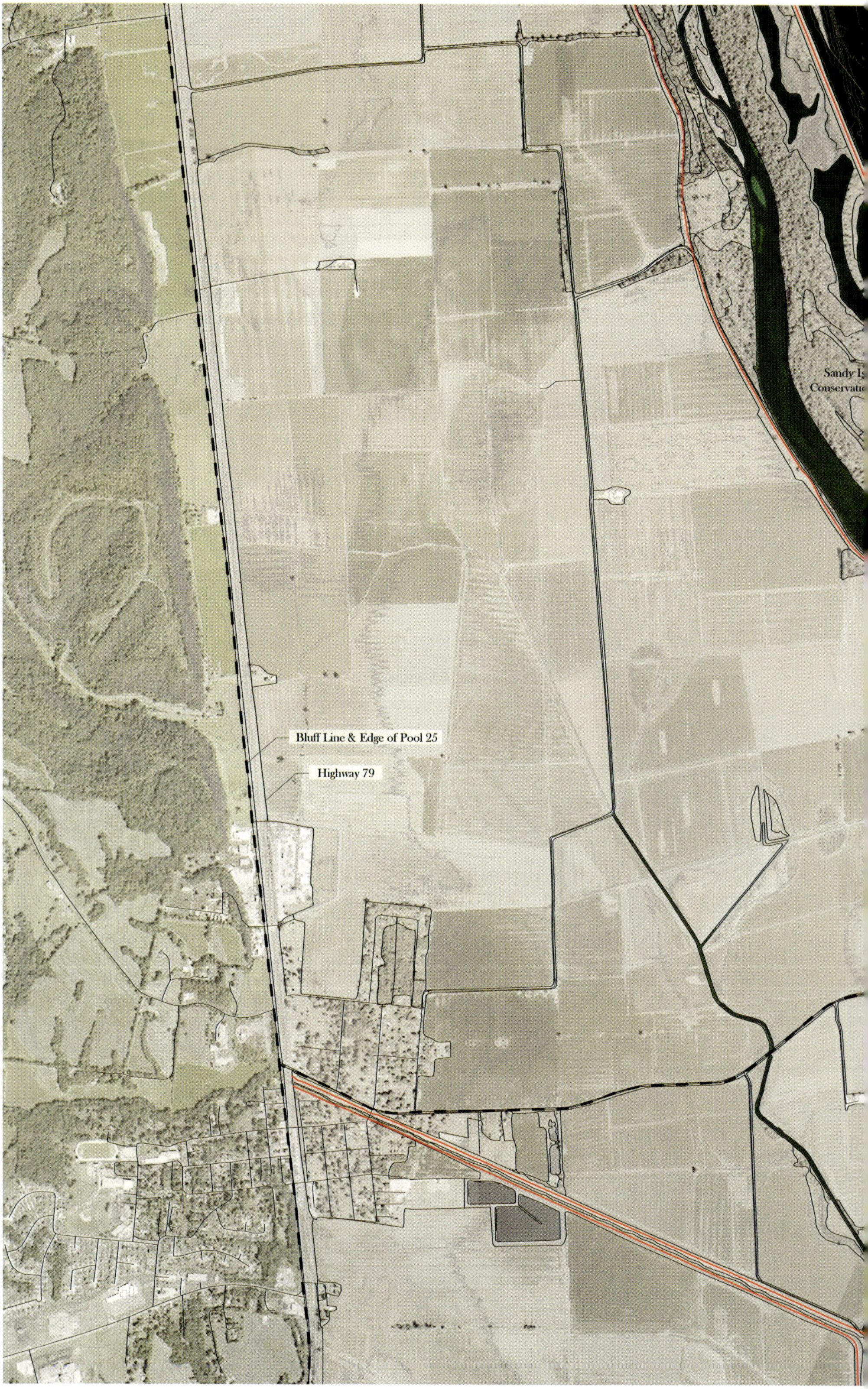

Bluff Line & Edge of Pool 25
Highway 79

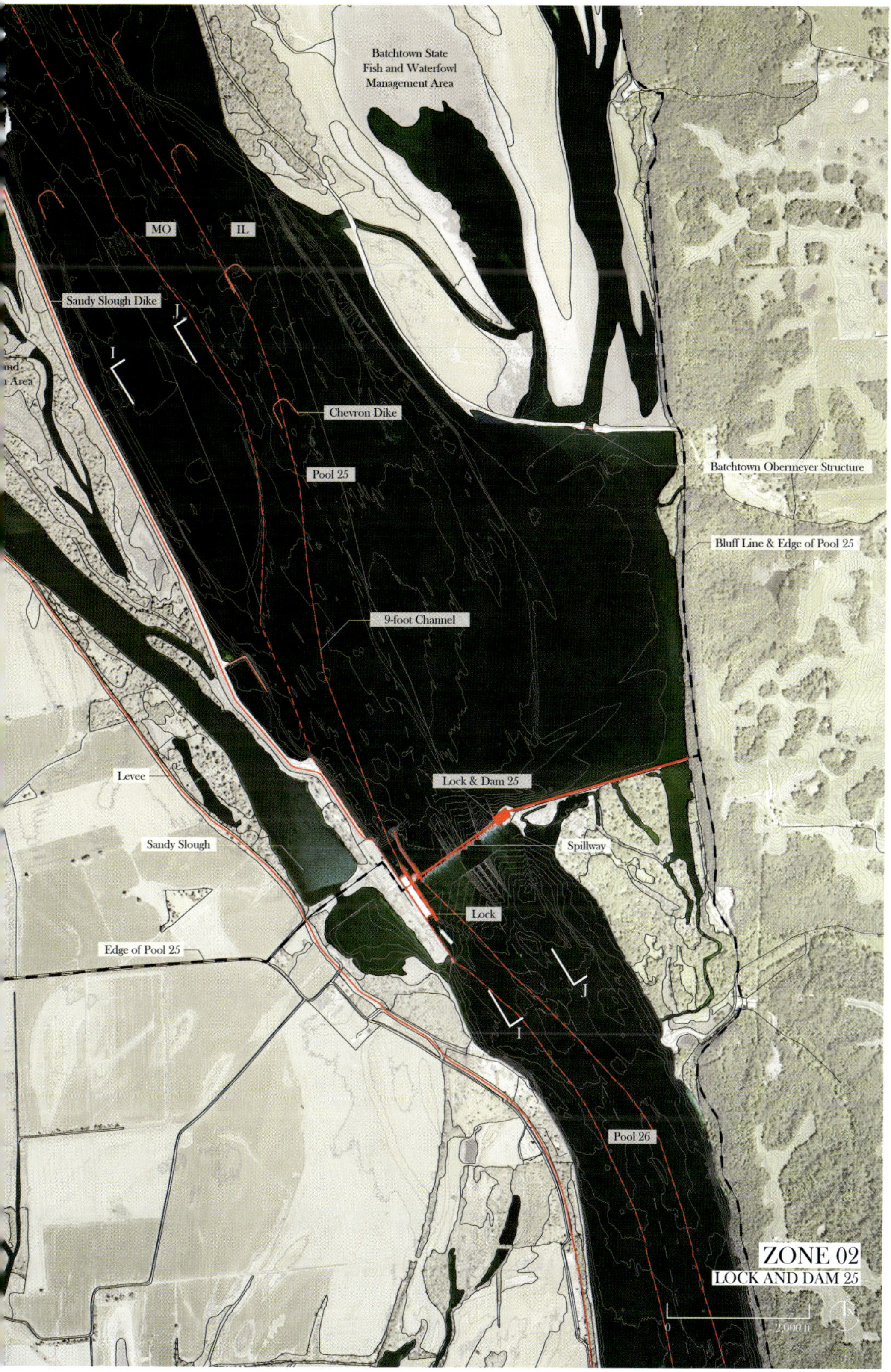

ZONE 02
LOCK AND DAM 25

Lower Gates Opening

Lower Gates Closed

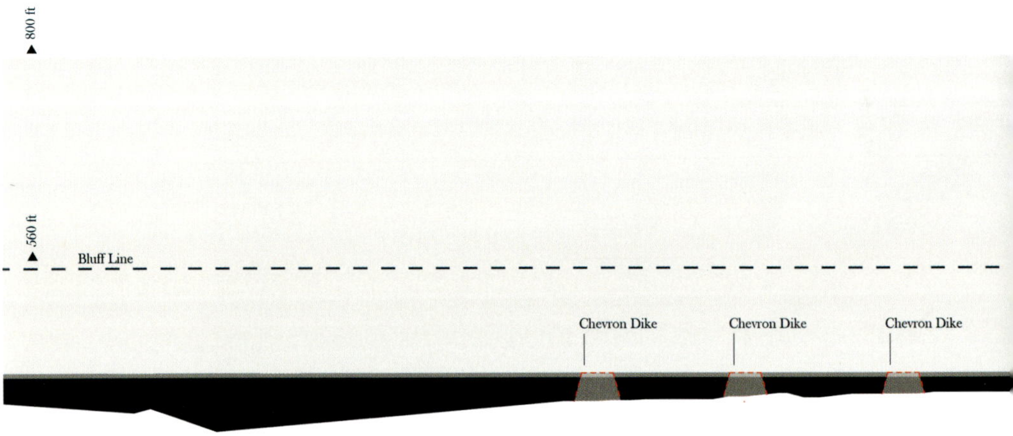

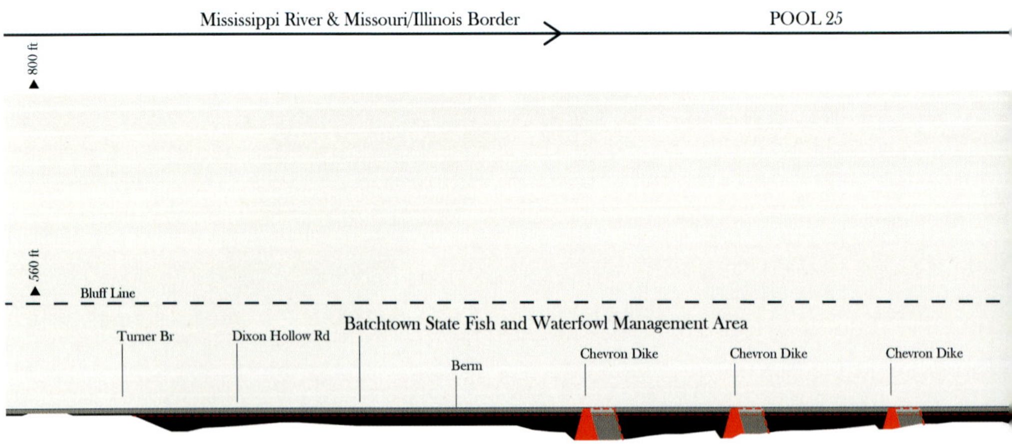

(UPPER RIGHT) Floodwall, St. Louis, Missouri, 2013
(BACKGROUND) Gateway Arch, Eads Bridge, Floodwall, East St. Louis, Missouri, 2010 (image credit: Derek Hoeferlin)

(UPPER RIGHT) Chain of Rocks Canal, high water level, Illinois, 2019
(BACKGROUND) Chain of Rocks Canal, low water level, Illinois, 2019 (image credit: Derek Hoeferlin)

Cultivate Foods

(UPPER RIGHT) Agricultural equipment, St. Charles County, Missouri, 2013
(BACKGROUND) Agriculture levee and farmland between the Mississippi and Missouri Rivers, St. Charles County, Missouri, 2013 (image credit: Derek Hoeferlin)

Transport Cargos

(UPPER RIGHT) Barges at Bellerive Park, St. Louis, Missouri, 2012
(BACKGROUND) Barge tow transporting petrochemicals upriver on the Mississippi River, St. Louis, Missouri, 2019 (image credit: Derek Hoeferlin)

Reconnection

Adaptive Management for Levee and Drainage Districts

Chuck Theiling

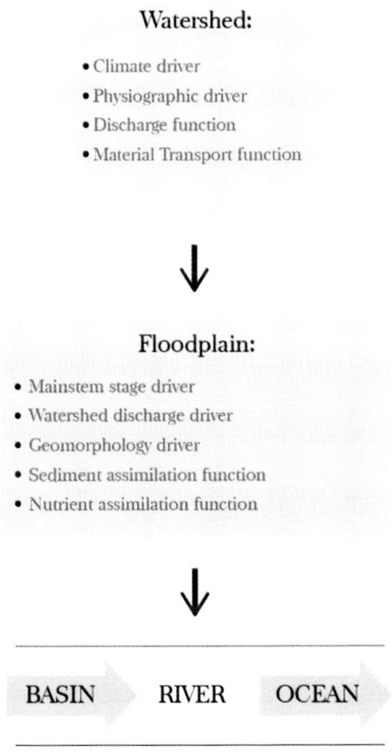

[Figure 1] Hydrologic Cycle (image credit: Chuck Theiling, re-drawn by Chenyu Zhang)

[Figure 2] Chuck Theiling explaining to Derek Hoeferlin's Washington University in St. Louis students how the most recent glacial stage shaped the Upper Mississippi River Basin, 2017 (image credit: Derek Hoeferlin)

[Figure 3] Chuck Theiling guiding Derek Hoeferlin's Washington University in St. Louis through the backwaters of the Mississippi River, 2017 (image credit: Derek Hoeferlin)

The classical hydrologic cycle image has water moving from clouds to rain, land, streams, rivers, and the ocean, and over again. Rivers progressively widen and may have island and delta formations and a green, lined, or gray border representing nature, farms, or cities, respectively. The cycle illustrates a climate driver (precipitation and runoff) and landscape drivers (watersheds and river valleys), which create river flow and watershed material transport functions. **[Figure 1]**

The general models, and many water management strategies, however, do not emphasize the role of floodplains as the final node in watershed material transport and assimilation. They therefore compartmentalize and underestimate the value of flood storage, sediment and nutrient assimilation, fish and wildlife habit, and other ecosystem goods and services that floodplains provide when they prioritize development and river regulation over natural function. Floodplains are often overlooked by watershed planners who focus on uplands and stop their planning at the river bluffs, as well as river planners who typically work only in river channels. The floodplains between the bluffs and rivers are often overlooked, and this typical oversight undervalues them as such. Flood risk planning mostly focuses on human protection and economic development, not on ecological connectivity and integrative design. My collaborative efforts and research focus on these overlooked floodplains and their correlating ecologically beneficial landscapes. **[Figure 2]**

Floodplain Challenges

Policies and practices dating to the Swampland Act of 1850 established federal intent to drain and develop floodplains.[1] Significant public-private investment had built and now maintains the existing systems as a mix of federal, municipal, private-public, and private levee systems. Regional flooding conditions that were used to design Upper Mississippi and Illinois River levee and drainage districts 100 years ago have changed. This means we cannot use historic hydrology to predict future hydrology, that is, at least, with certainty. Floods are larger. Floods are more frequent. Floods occur at different times of the year. Floods last longer than in the recent past. And the pattern is expected to continue.[2] "Levee wars" have ensued when landowners heighten levees during extreme floods and never remove them, referred to as "flood fighting." This results in illegal levee raises that threaten neighbors who abide by the rules and remove the material.[3]

Floodplain Isolation

Local landowners established the footprint of Upper Mississippi and Illinois Rivers levee and drainage districts by 1920, despite some concern for the environmental impact of constricting the ancient glacial floodway or from draining wetlands and clearing floodplain ecological buffers that assimilated water, sediment, and nutrients.[4] **[Figure 3]** Upland drainage to get rainwater off cropland quickly expanded with a similar rush toward the agricultural development of the Midwest landscape. Wetlands were drained with ditches and subsurface drains, i.e., drain tiles, which increased watershed runoff and added to the downstream cumulative impact with more water moving faster, delivering more material through watersheds to their respective sinks. Levee developers channelized tributary channels with tieback levees from river to bluff, constricting tributary channels into narrow flumes for all the material in a watershed to be flushed directly to the main-stem river. This floodplain isolation eliminates the absorptive capacity of floodplains, which become sediment- and nutrient-starved, while rivers get nutrient and sediment enrichment. The result is floodway filling, local eutrophication, and Gulf of Mexico hypoxia, which is oxygen depletion resulting from the microbial decay of algal blooms in the gulf caused by nitrogen from Midwestern farms.[5] **[Figure 4]**

Existing seasonal floodplain connectivity ranges from floodwater access to the entire floodplain to complete isolation behind levees, depending on location in the river system. The uppermost reach of the Upper Mississippi River has very few levees; the midsection and lower Illinois River are 50 percent leveed; and the reach below St. Louis is greater than 80 percent leveed. **[Figure 5]** The midreach Upper Mississippi and Illinois River levee districts offer unique management opportunities because the dams were built after the levee districts, and the impoundment effects of navigation dams hold river levels higher than ground elevations in low parts of some levee and drainage districts. That means low areas would flood if landowners did not pump groundwater against the head of the dam year-round. **[Figure 6]**

Managed Connectivity

Managed floodplain connectivity using existing infrastructure offers alternatives to increase local ecosystem goods-and-service benefits and reduce impacts to main-stem rivers and oceans. Managed hydraulic connectivity for wetland habitat is a long-practiced wildlife management tool.[6] It is a popular agricultural Best Management Practice.[7] And it is a common stormwater management treatment.[8] Treatment wetland microbes and algae are used in many municipal and emerging waste management applications.[9,10] Several former Illinois River levee districts and other private lands have been converted to managed wetlands, which demonstrates their multifunction potential.[11,12]

The view of floodplain management began to broaden after the Great Flood of 1993.[13] After more flooding in 2008, 2010, and 2011, new environmental stakeholders became involved in river planning. Informal planning efforts developed relationships with floodplain landowners, farmers, and engineers through the Upper Mississippi, Illinois, and Missouri Rivers Association. This area represents floodplain levee and drainage districts in planning and policy initiatives. Meeting with landowners, learning their land and water management opportunities, and identifying "early adopters," including Eileen Shader from American Rivers, became crucial to building these new relationships.[14] Additional on-the-ground input was received from local Midwest landowners and farmers, such as Brent Hoerr of Palmyra, Missouri. **[Figure 7]** This led to exploring alternative management plans to integrate more floodplain function into agricultural levee districts while still maintaining crops on the landscape. Some concepts are passive; some are highly engineered; some displace crops; some adopt seasonal function; some increase habitat; and some use alternative crops to harvest nutrients and produce feedstock materials. Each of the floodplain management alternatives discussed here is based on common environmental management tools applied to a unique floodplain system with high-potential hydraulic connectivity and significant water management capacity. With a small amount of funding from the initial allocations of

[Figure 4] Soybean farm, South River, Missouri, 2017 (image credit: Derek Hoeferlin)

the USACE Navigation and Ecosystem Sustainability Program (NESP) in 2011, I conceptualized alternative management plans for levee and drainage districts at the Fabius River confluence at the Mississippi River, across from Quincy, Illinois.[15] **[Figure 8]**.

Research and Development funding in 2016 provided resources to quantify the nutrient reduction potential of the alternatives. The predevelopment condition was floodplain forest and prairie toward the bluff (a). The existing condition is crops behind perimeter levees with ditches, a forebay lake, and electric or diesel pump drainage systems (b). One simple alternative water-management approach is to reduce pumping and let wetlands develop in the inundated low spots near ditches and pump stations (c). Nitrates seeping into low-elevation depressions with groundwater would be reduced by sediment bacteria in the expanded basin area. If wetlands are allowed to develop, nutrient reduction potential would increase even more. Controlled tributary diversions during the noncrop season could provide large flood detention basins that can assimilate the "first flush" of watershed nutrients and sediment from the winter landscape (d). And most of these adaptations are additive, in that they can be used in the same levee district together or seasonally; for example, the wetland and detention basin alternatives are compatible. Nutrient farming can be achieved by connecting main-stem surface water to interior drainage systems(e).[16] This in turn flows nutrient laden water through assimilative ditch systems.[17] Simply running water through ditches provides nutrient assimilation by naturally occurring sediment and water bacteria. Assimilation capacity can be enhanced with hydroponic systems like floating treatment wetlands or algal turf scrubbers (f).[18] Algal turf scrubbers grow wild-stock mat algae in shallow raceways which could be constructed adjacent to levee district ditches (g).A ten-foot-wide raceway, one mile long, is approximately one acre of surface area that can sequester nutrients at a rate twelve times greater than corn. The carbon, nitrogen, and phosphorus could be valuable commodities on nutrient credit markets, and new algal products ranging from soil to biofuel have been conceived for algae. Nutrient credit markets (see below) were established to place caps on total nutrient discharge from a region where polluters can buy, sell, or trade pollution credits to achieve overall nutrient reduction goals for the region. New algal products include biofuels, biofertilizers, bioplastics, and animal feed supplements, among others. Floating treatment wetlands in pump house forebay impoundments or ditches can grow food or biomass crops. Removing the entire plant for food/feed, fuel fermentation, or composting removes the most nutrients. Integrating several compatible approaches can increase ecosystem goods-and-service potential with nutrient sequestration and habitat provision (h). Detention basins would not be compatible with algal turf scrubber investments because detention basin flooding would inundate algal systems, rendering them inoperable for that period and allowing silt to settle onto the algal growth surface. If carbon and nutrient credit payment systems were successful, investments in nutrient sequestration might replace row crops. **[Figure 9]**

Innovative concepts move to process simulation modeling, i.e., water-quality models, before implementation. Planners and engineers have many tools for documenting the purposes, costs, benefits, and impacts of water projects. Model complexity varies with the size of a project, its planning stage, the risk of new techniques or uncertain consequences, the location of projects, and many other factors. The screening level analyses presented here used the best available information for desktop integration and evaluations, which is demonstrated in GIS imagery of the Fabius and Marion County Levee and Drainage Districts, to the north of Palmyra, Missouri. Three images illustrate: a) the existing condition, b) a detention basin simulation using the 50-percent-probability flood (i.e., two-year flood) stage to simulate the impacts of a seasonal detention basin; and, c) a dam-controlled river stage used to simulate the "pumps-off" condition, whereby low areas in the L&DDs would be inundated by groundwater levels maintained by Upper Mississippi River System Lock and Dam 21. **[Figure 10]**

A rapid desktop evaluation comparing literature-derived nutrient reduction rates with potential ditch and surface water area revealed that the area of influence has a great effect on potential benefits delivered. In this case, for example, the predevelopment and detention basin scenarios have low efficiency, but they operate over very large areas to add significant nutrient sequestration potential. Floating treatment wetlands and algal turf scrubbers have the highest nutrient sequestration performance among alternatives. Combining them for dual stream phytoremediation benefits, i.e., floating treatment wetlands and algal turf scrubbers, yields the highest nitrate removal rate. Incorporating a pumps-off managed wetland reduces algal turf scrubber denitrification efficiency but increases the total area for denitrification substantially. The managed wetland gains habitat benefits that are not achieved by other alternatives but displaces agriculture that other alternatives do not. Preplanting season detention alternatives had moderate denitrification and sediment retention benefits, but sediment deposition on roads, ditches, and other structures in mixed-use areas could be challenging.

Ecosystem Services and Nutrient Trading Markets

"Benefit stacking" multiple ecosystem services may provide adequate economic offset to support land use change where traditional environmental cost-benefit evaluation has not.[19] Ecosystem services are the many and varied benefits to humans provided by healthy ecosystems. Ecosystems provide such things as natural pollination of crops, clean water, extreme weather mitigation, and human mental and physical well-being. Implementing multifunctional levee district management can also generate many ecosystem services beyond denitrification potential. A comprehensive ecosystem service analysis is warranted. Deriving beneficial products, balancing flood risk, creating wetlands, and supporting urban nutrient reduction objectives could offer great economic incentives for integrated floodplain management.

Nutrient trading markets are necessary to support large-scale nutrient remediation. They were established to place caps on total nutrient discharge from a region where polluters can buy, sell, or trade pollution credits to achieve the overall nutrient reduction goals for the region.[20] The social and ecological motivation for increased sediment and nutrient management is strong, but the costs are high and the responsibility is diffuse. The Environmental Protection Agency nutrient credit trading policy established in 2003 stated that "the most effective and economical way to reduce pollution is to provide incentives to encourage action by those who can achieve reductions easily and cost-effectively."[21] Large river levee districts are ideally located at tributary deltas to provide this function for large watershed regions. These floodplain management alternatives offer nutrient sequestration options that are compatible with contemporary agriculture and natural resource management objectives. The alternatives presented here, and the floodplain landmass available for such actions, could greatly enhance the capacity of a nutrient market by expanding the physical space for nutrient remediation actions, but also by incorporating efficient tools that can produce economic value.

Conclusion

Noted Upper Mississippi River historian John Anfinson discusses the future of a "Fourth River" shaped by integrated management.[22] Donald Hey coined the term "nutrient farming," and his essay "Thinking Like a River" envisions a riverine national park with enhanced river-floodplain connectivity at major tributary confluences to support critical EGS functions.[23] The potential income from land set-asides or algal feedstock production could significantly change the approach to Upper Mississippi River Basin water management. Raw material in the form of nutrient-laden river water can be managed by innovative bottomland "nutrient farmers" looking for new economic opportunities, who also have a desire to improve water quality. Societal benefits would accrue through nutrient and sediment management, leading to improved water quality and sustainability, increased habitat potential, and new economic markets. If aggregated as an integrated system and potentially a new ecological industry, these adaptations would have impactful benefits, and at multiple scales, reinstating a healthier Mississippi River Basin.

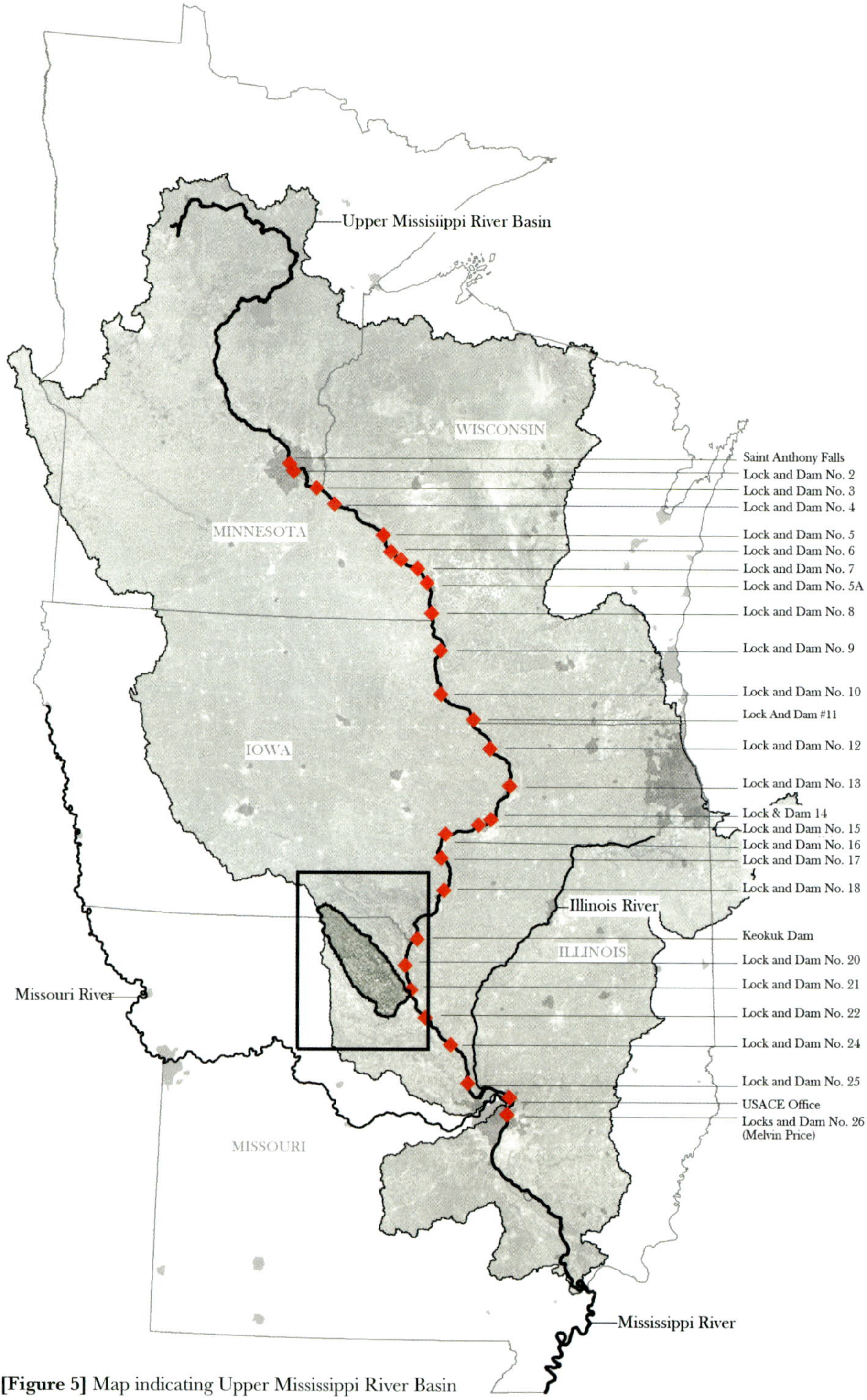

[Figure 5] Map indicating Upper Mississippi River Basin with Locks and Dams; and, North Fabius Watershed, South Fabius River Watershed, and North River Watershed indicated in box (image credit: Chuck Theiling, re-drawn by Wendy Stradley and Chenyu Zhang)

[Figure 6] Pumphouse, Bay De Charles, north of Hannibal, Missouri, 2017 (image credit: Derek Hoeferlin)

[Figure 7] Brent Hoerr explaining the management of water levels between agricultural and ecological zones near the Mississippi River, 2017 (image credit: Derek Hoeferlin)

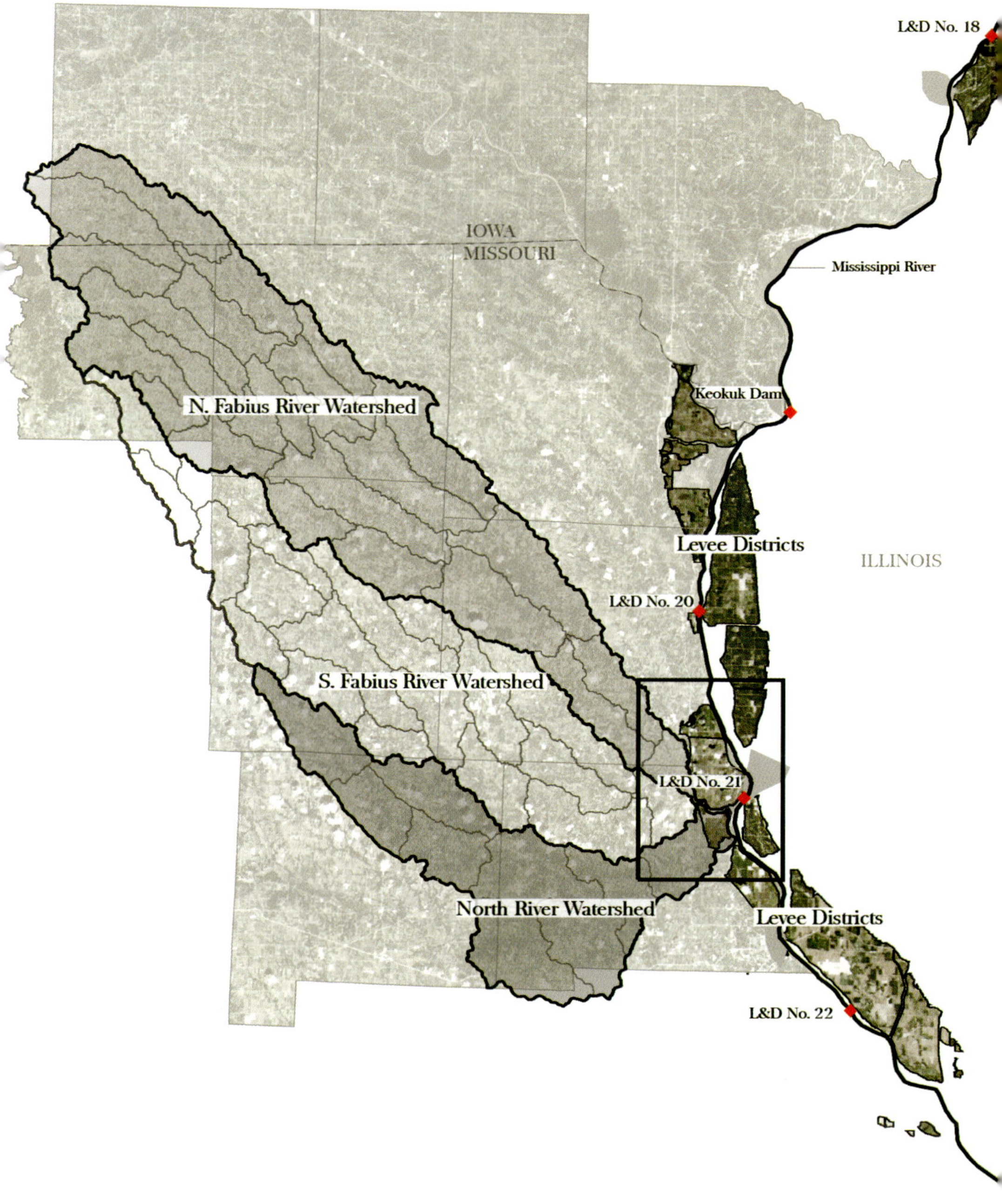

[Figure 8] Levee and drainage districts at the Fabius and Mississippi Rivers confluence across from Quincy, Illinois (image credit: Chuck Theiling, re-drawn by Wendy Stradley and Chenyu Zhang)

Indian Grave
Drainage District South
(Lower)
Mississippi
River
ILLINOIS
MISSOURI
LEWIS COUNTY
MARION COUNTY
Fabius River
Drainage District
N. Fabius River
Lock and Dam No. 21
S. Fabius River
Marion County
Drainage District
South Quincy
North River
South River
Drainage
District

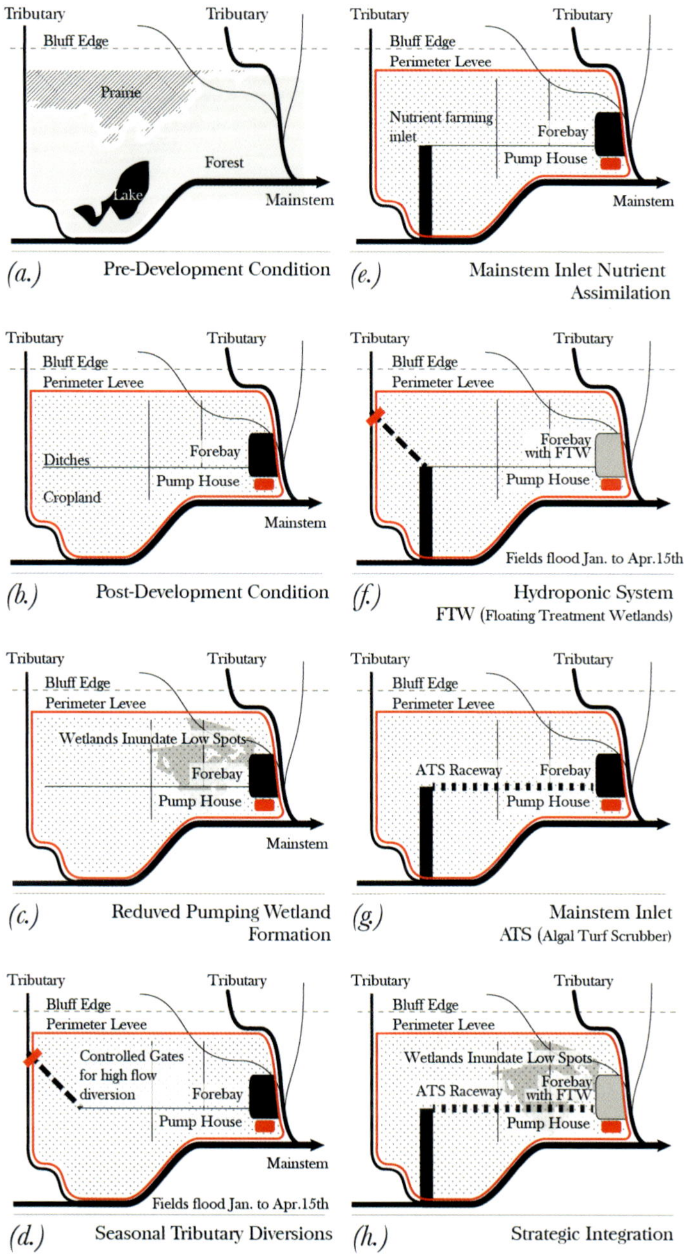

[Figure 9] Chuck Theiling's alternative management plans proposal for levee and drainage districts, in sequence from pre-development condition to strategic integration (A-H).
(image credit: Chuck Theiling, re-drawn by Wendy Stradley and Chenyu Zhang)

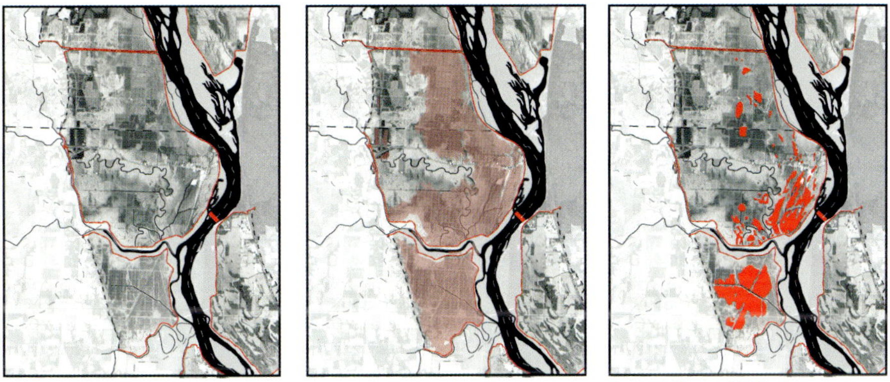

Levee Districts at L & D No.21

(a.)

Potential Detention Areas

(b.)

Potential Managed Wetlands

(c.)

[Figure 10] Existing Fabius and Marion County Levee and Drainage Districts with potential detention areas and potential managed wetlands (image credit: Chuck Theiling, re-drawn by Wendy Stradley and Chenyu Zhang)

1. "43 USC Ch. 23: Grants of Swamp and Overflowed Lands," Swampland Act of 1850, accessed November 13, 2020, https://uscode.house.gov/view.xhtml?hl=false&edition=prelim&path=%2Fprelim%40title43%2Fchapter23&req=granuleid%3AUSC-prelim-title43-chapter23&num=0&saved=L3ByZWxpbUB0aXRsZTQzL2NoYXB0ZXIyMw%3D%3D%7CZ3JhbnVsZWlkOlVTQy1wcmVsaW0tdGl0bGU0My1jaGFwdGVyMjM%3D%7C%7C%7C0%7Cfalse%7Cprelim.

2. "Midwest," National Climate Change Assessment, accessed November 13, 2020, https://nca2014.globalchange.gov/highlights/regions/midwest.

3. Jacob Barker, "Levee wars: Missouri residents complain Illinois levee was built higher without approval," St. Louis Post-Dispatch, accessed November 13, 2020, https://www.stltoday.com/business/local/levee-wars-missouri-residents-complain-illinois-levee-was-built-higher/article_8c59fbba-ce1b-5cb1-a828-222a5509f78c.html.

4. John Thompson, *Case studies in drainage and levee district formation on the floodplain of the lower Illinois River, 1890s to 1930s, Special Report 016* (Champaign, Illinois: University of Illinois Water Resources Center), 152.

5. "Hypoxia 101: What is hypoxia and what causes it?" United States Environmental Protection Agency, accessed November 13, 2020, https://www.epa.gov/ms-htf/hypoxia-101.

6. Leigh Fredrickson, "13.4.6. Strategies for Water Level Manipulations in Moist Soil Systems," *Waterfowl Management Handbook* (Washington DC: U.S. Fish and Wildlife Service, 1991), 9.

7. Tom Miller et al., *The Agricultural BMP Handbook for Minnesota* (Saint Paul: Minnesota Department of Agriculture, 2012).

8. "Storm Water Technology Fact Sheet Wet Detention Ponds," U.S. Environmental Protection Agency (Washington DC: EPA 832-F-99-048, Office of Water, 1999).

9. U.S. Environmental Protection Agency, "Primer for Municipal Wastewater Treatment Systems" (Washington DC: EPA 832-R-04-001, Office of Water, Office of Wastewater Management, 2004).

10. Walter Adey, Patrick Kangas, and Walter Mulbry, "Algal Turf Scrubbing: Cleaning Surface Waters with Solar Energy While Producing a Biofuel" *BioScience* 61 (June 1, 2011): 434–441.

11. "The Nature Conservancy," accessed November 13, 2020, https://www.nature.org/en-us/get-involved/how-to-help/places-we-protect/emiquon/; and "The Wetlands Initiative," accessed November 13, 2020, http://www.wetlands-initiative.org/dixon-waterfowl-refuge-hh.

12. "Major Illinois River Valley Program Launched: Ducks Unlimited to lead 13,000-acre effort," accessed November 14, 2020, https://www.ducks.org/press-room/news-releases/major-illinois-river-valley-program-launched.

13. "The Great Flood of 1993," U.S. Geological Survey, accessed November 14, 2020, (multiple reports) https://www.usgs.gov/centers/cm-water/science/great-flood-1993?qt-science_center_objects=3#qt-science_center_objects.

14. "Eileen Shader, Director, River Restoration, American Rivers," accessed November 14, 2020, https://www.americanrivers.org/about/staff/eileen-shader/.

15. "U.S. Army Corps of Engineers Navigation and Ecosystem Sustainability Program," accessed November 14, 2020, https://www.mvr.usace.army.mil/Missions/Navigation/NESP/.

16. Donald Hey, Jill Kostel, and Laura Urban, "Nutrient Farming: The business of environmental management," *Ecological Engineering* 24 (2005): 279–287.

17. Giuseppe Castadelli et al., "Vegetated canals mitigate nitrogen surplus in agricultural watersheds," *Agriculture, Ecosystems and Environment* 212 (2015): 253–262.

18. T.R. Headly and C.C. Tanner, "Constructed Wetlands with Floating Emergent Macrophytes: An Innovative Stormwater Treatment Technology," *Critical Reviews in Environmental Science and Technology* 42 (2012): 2261–2310.

19. Morgan Robertson et al., "Stacking ecosystem services," *Frontiers in Ecology and the Environment* 12 (2014):186–193.

20. "National Pollutant Discharge Elimination System (NPDES): Water Quality Trading," U.S. Environmental Protection Agency, accessed November 14, 2020, https://www.epa.gov/npdes/water-quality-trading.

21. U.S. Environmental Protection Agency, "Working in Partnership with States to Address Phosphorus and Nitrogen Pollution through Use of a Framework for State Nutrient Reductions (Washington DC, Office of Water, 2011).

22. John Anfinson, *The River We Have Wrought: A History of the Upper Mississippi* (University of Minnesota Press, 2005), 388.

23. Donald Hey and Paul Heltne, "Thinking Like a River: A Riverine National Park for the Upper Mississippi River," *Ecological Engineering* 6 (2014): 8–13.

(RIGHT)
Geology of the American Bottom, showing surficial geology and test-well locations
(image credit: Bergstrom, Robert E. and Theodore R. Walker, *Groundwater Geology of the East St. Louis Area, Illinois*, Urbana: University of Illinois Press, 1956)

Depth

Floodplain Media in the American Bottom

Jesse Vogler

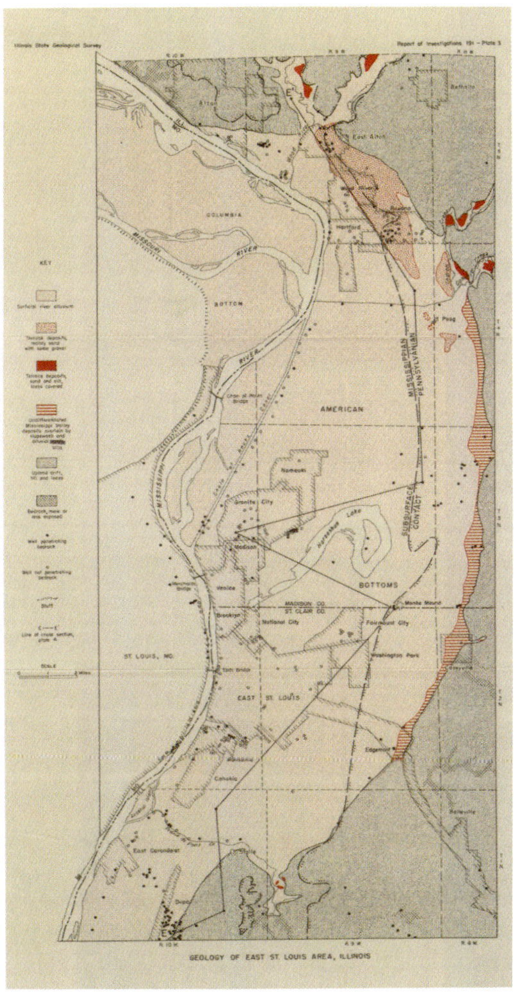

Rivers get all the attention. They are the thing of poets' reveries, they shape narratives of national identity, occupy engineers' dreams of control, and hold a unique space in global geographic imaginaries. Yet it is the floodplain that is the river's own memory: a deposition of watershed chemistry; an archive of geological time interwoven with unmistakable sedimentation of human and nonhuman activities; a surface of inscription, a depth of recording, and a medium of transmission. Floodplain as media: signal, noise, all the rest. Our attempts to live within its dynamics, to inscribe into the saturated land our ditches and canals, to wall off the river's freshets with giant levees and floodwalls, and to dwell in the liminal space created by these temporary fluvial reconciliations, are all part of a long history of cultural technologies for translating and remaking the floodplain.[1]

There is something fundamentally disruptive in a floodplain: challenging the engineered clarity of a modern sensibility of space, disturbing the controlled wildness of the picturesque imaginary, and undermining even the certainties of soil itself. This disruption holds sway not only upon the aesthetic register of landscape—for a floodplain is a manifestly vital and untamed land when compared to the cultivated wildness of even the most eccentric pastoral landscapes—but, more significantly, upon the political register of property. Embodiment and ownership, and the narratives of discreteness, uniqueness, and separation that undergirds each, are destabilized in the dynamic processes of floodplain ecology.

As a landscape, the floodplain is quite simply a difficult landscape to *see.* "Forbidding both to the eye and hand," writes the author of an 1881 floodplain account.[2] And with this forbidding, also understood as a withholding, aesthetic and narrative closure is deferred. Which is to say, the floodplain is an irreducible landscape. Irreducible to any of the easy theoretical and aesthetic categories that inhabit our ways of thinking through landscapes—natural/manmade, human/nonhuman, productive/waste. It is a landscape that, through the visible presence of traces and active processes of re-inscription, resists easy closure.

In the floodplains of the Upper Mississippi and its tributaries, the history of cultural technologies of inhabitation are indeed long. The dynamic constructions of pre-European Native American mound-building cultures dates back thousands of years—with names archeologists have advanced like Hopewell, Adena, and Mississippian standing in for an heterogenous and perhaps unknowable cycle of habitation, cultural landscape construction, and meaning reproduction in the river valleys and adjacent uplands throughout the middle of North America.[3] The cultural technology of the mound is of course only the most visible trace of this long history of floodplain inhabitation. Innumerable midden heaps, borrow pits, lodge poles, house trenches, levelled platforms, and fecal piles are recorded in the geologic cross section; and as they are unearthed by the archeologist's trowel, the blade of earthmoving equipment, or the domestic well, new reading and inevitable (mis)interpretations emerge. All these histories continue to collide, mingle, write, and overwrite that-and-those who came before. It is an often-violent collision of meaning and values, as the hubris, neglect, bias, hatred, and forgetfulness of a settler colonial ideology of improvement ignores and effaces the many meanings that were there before. Even their own.

This essay asks us to read the Mississippi River through one of its most significant floodplains—the American Bottom. To think and see the river through its topographic flatness as well as its geologic and historical depth. To interpret and scrutinize the many discourses and practices that have allowed us to recover the floodplain history—geologic, human, and more than human—as one chain in a broader fluvial technology. This essay moves through the region sectionally, like Henri Hus's "Ecological Cross Section of the Mississippi River in the Region of St. Louis,"[4] Isaiah Bowman's study for the Illinois State Geological Survey,[5] or Robert Bergstrom and Theodore Walker's "Groundwater Geology of the East St. Louis Area."[6] **[Figures 1-3]** In doing so it attempts to render material the imperatives of "thick description" by attending to the unseen geologies and metabolic flows that humans, current and past, have attached themselves to.[7] All the while, staying attentive to the ways in which this industrial geology is itself an agent in landscape effacement, erasure, and extraction—establishing the conditions for one of the largest concentrations of industrial production in the country and the many uneven legacies of pollution, contamination, and disruption that attend such patterns.[8]

The American Bottom

Few regions in the United States exhibit a social and spatial fragmentation as extreme as that of the vast Mississippi River flood plain of the East St Louis region. As a coherent geographic interval stretching from the confluence of the Missouri and Mississippi rivers down to the confluence with the Kaskaskia River, this floodplain—known to geographers and anthropologists as the American Bottom—is site to the social and spatial aspirations of pre-contact Native Americans, 19th-century industrial expansion, 20th-century infrastructural consolidation, and 21st-century ecological precarity. Yet this is a region currently defined less by its inherent ecological and geological continuities and more by the industrial patterns that have effectively fractured this region into closed parcels of extraction, production, and displacement. It is a territory where UNESCO heritage sites abut Superfund sites, and where the first African-American incorporated town in the U.S. abuts the site of one of the country's most violent race riots. Through this rather compact region, then, an entire history of North American settlement, aspiration, and anxiety can be told.[9] **[Figure 4]**

As a singular, coherent, geographic interval, the American Bottom is one of the more clearly defined geographic units in the Midwest. It is a floodplain defined on its edge by sharp limestone bluffs that rise 40 to 200 feet from the bottomlands, and is defined in its basin by a consistent geological section of alluvium, groundwater, and now, habitation. Along the Mississippi River, more people now live behind the levees of the American Bottom than anywhere outside of the greater New Orleans area.

Early European explorers describe a patchwork landscape of dense floodplain forests, rich meadows, and wide expanses of bottomland lakes, swamps, and wetlands **[Figure 5]**, with associated plant and animal communities that sustained waves of inhabitation and

[Figure 1] Ideal Cross Section of the Mississippi River based on the St. Louis Directrix (image credit: Hus, Henry, "An Ecological Cross Section of the Mississippi River in the Region of St. Louis, Missouri" Missouri Botanical Garden Annual Report (1908): 127–258)

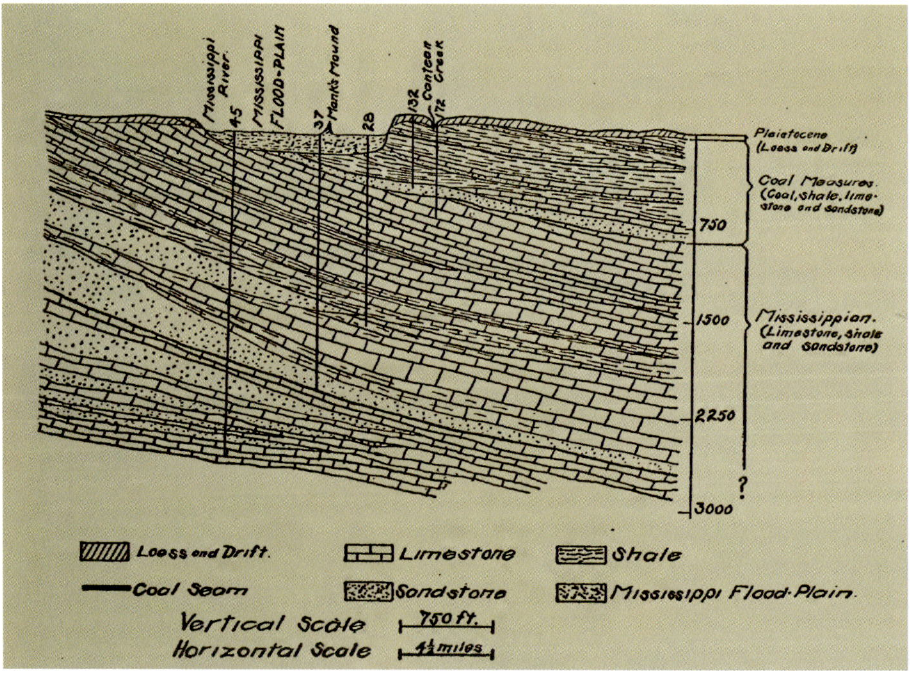

[Figure 2] Geological cross section from east to west across the central part of the East St. Louis district (image credit: Bowman, Isaiah, *Water Resources of the East St. Louis District*, Urbana: University of Illinois Press, 1907)

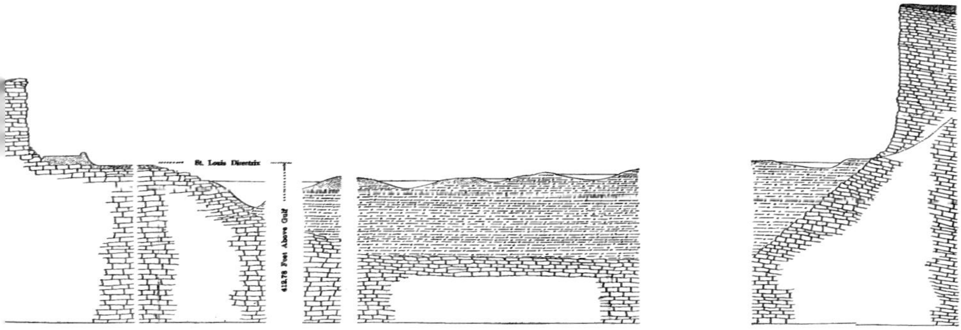

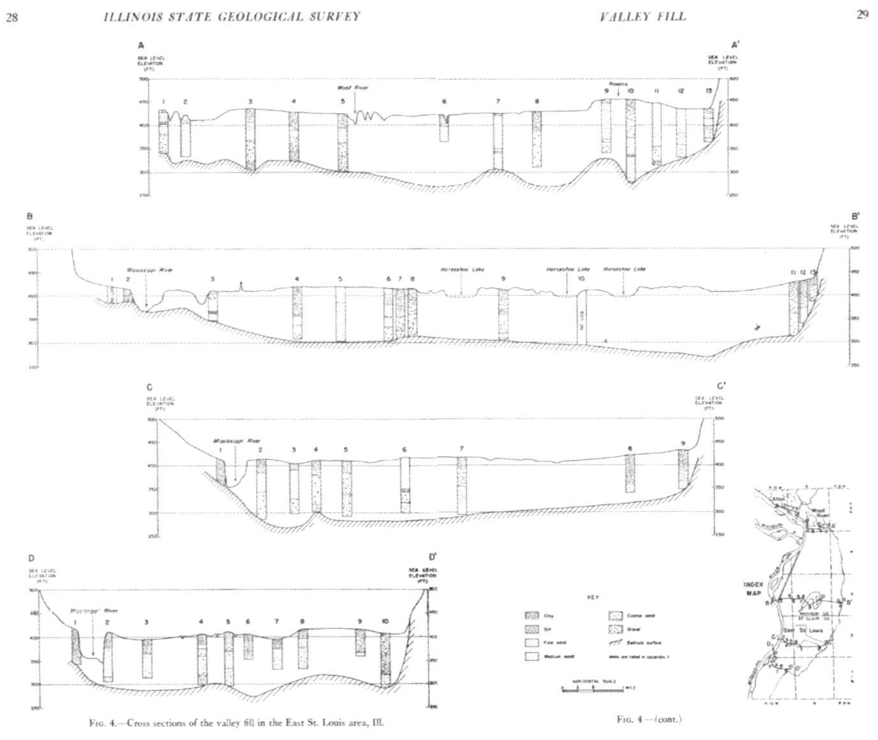

[Figure 3] Cross Section of the valley fill in the East St. Louis area (image credit: Bergstrom, Robert E. and Theodore R. Walker, *Groundwater Geology of the East St. Louis Area*, Illinois, Urbana: University of Illinois Press, 1956)

[Figure 4] Drainage districts of the American Bottom (image credit: Southwestern Illinois Metropolitan Area Planning Commission, "Drainage in Southwestern Illinois," Courtesy Missouri History Museum)

colonization across precontact and historical periods. "Bottoms low & level & very full of heavy wood," the GLO surveyors reported in 1817,[10] while French colonists, the first European group to both record and leave traces of their imperial design on the region, regularly constructed their vertical wooden-post cabins with deaf, windowless walls facing in the direction of large bodies of water—to help block the deafening calls of the geese and other fowl that were described as covering every last inch of open water. It was, according to one early account, the "Elysium of America."

Across the 70-mile length of the bottomlands, the Mississippi River falls about six inches per mile. Flat. Bisecting the river at this stretch is an anticlinal bedrock formation that makes navigation above this point unpredictable in low-water conditions. For barge captains and river engineers, this anticline—known as the Great Chain of Rocks—marks a significant hinge in the river's management, a place where the river can be divided in two: above the American Bottom, the river can be likened to a chain of pools—with levels managed and controlled through a series of dams and other flood control apparatuses; below, the river is undammed—with the low-sinuosity of the upper Mississippi giving way to the high-sinuosity of the River's gulf plain near Cairo, Illinois, 100 miles to the south.

Depth

Despite the topographical flatness of the American Bottom, the true nature of this floodplain is *depth*. Attempts have been made to manage away the groundwater through ditches, canals, levees, and railroad grades. The ridge and swale geology of sand, silt, and clay—deposited in its arcing strips across the floodplain—has been evened out by the plow of the farmer. Yet dig deep enough—sometimes not at all—and it is still there: the river. Graham Taylor, in his seminal work on the industrial satellite city, aptly describes the many settlements of the American Bottom as "amphibious" in their mingling of soggy ecologies and unkempt urbanism.[11] This is a landscape of saturation. It was across this thick, saturated alluvium that Charles Dickens traveled, in the late April rains of 1861, "through one unbroken slough of black mud and water," a landscape which he characterized as having "no variety but in depth."[12]

> *A dismal swamp, on which half-built houses rot away: cleared here and there for the space of a few yards; teeming then, with rank unwholesome vegetation … the hateful Mississippi circling and eddying before it … a hotbed of disease, and ugly sepulcher, a grave by any gleam of promise: a place without one single quality, in earth, air, or water, to commend it.*

Dickens hated it. "Everywhere," he wrote, "was stagnant, slimy, rotten, filthy water." But of course he would. What could be more of an affront to his Victorian sensibilities than the flat fecundity of the floodplain? Confronted with some of the most Dickensian qualities imaginable, the actual Dickens was repulsed.

Yet it is a depth that has, by now, been partially robbed of its water, of its saturation. Levees, drainage canals, and fill dirt have all been mobilized to convert this once complex ecosystem of backwaters and sloughs into real estate and infrastructure. Surface hydrology was cut off from the Mississippi in the systematic levee building starting in the

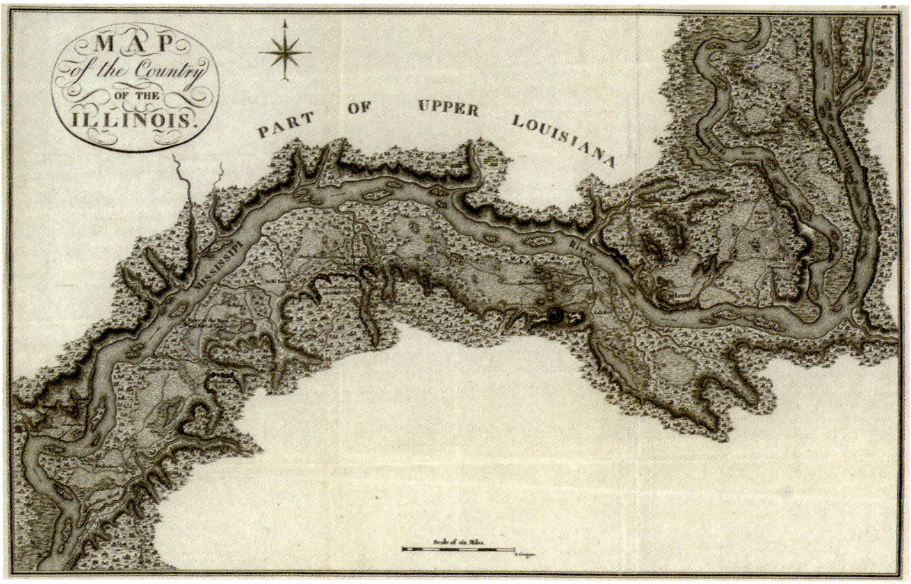

[Figure 5] Map of the Country of the Illinois (image credit: Collot, Victor, "Map of the Country of the Illinois," In Journey in North America, Paris, Arthus Bertrand: 1796)

first decade of the 20th century, severing fundamental floodplain dynamics that linked bottomland lakes with the regular freshets that overtopped the banks to invigorate soil- and seed-banks, and to recharge groundwater reserves. **[Figure 6]**

Prior to these large-scale levee and drainage works, the groundwater level was a few centimeters below the soil surface.[13] In the first half of the 20th century, the natural lake area of the American Bottom decreased by more than 40 percent as miles of drainage ditches were dug and the groundwater level dropped between two and twelve feet across the bottomlands.[14] In this draining we can map the transformation of ecologies to economies, through the engineer's alchemical designs that transmute riparian qualities to real-estate quantities. Below this amphibious alluvium, below Dickens's "dismal swamp," lie the traces of geological processes that give shape to the deep-time of the continent. In sinking the piers for the St. Louis (later Eads) Bridge in 1873—the first railroad bridge to cross the Mississippi River, whose engineering and construction so captured the popular imagination of the country at the time—Eads improved upon the pneumatic caisson technology he witnessed while convalescing earlier in France. The technology, coupled with Eads's new sand vacuum, allowed the workers—more than twelve of whom lost their lives in the first careless months of construction—to reach bedrock below the river. After suctioning out 76 feet of alluvium below the river bottom, they finally reached the valley floor of St. Louis limestone, some 110 feet below the river's surface. After vacuuming the surface clean, the workers stood upon the dark bedrock, never before seen by human eyes, scoured by the great flood events during the last glacial advance and retreat, 15 to 50 thousand years ago.[15]

The bedrock was polished smooth.

Upon this smooth lens lies first a layer of glacial outwash—the valley-train that causes well drillers to hit massive underground boulders at a depth of 80 to 90 feet throughout the American Bottom. Atop this, the unconsolidated alluvium of silt, sand, and gravel—the relatively recent deposition from across the eroded watershed. Here, the geologist's description is most succinct:

> *The valley fill has an average thickness of 120 feet and ranges in thickness from a feather edge, near the bluff boundaries of the area and along the Chain of Rocks Reach of the Mississippi River, to more than 170 feet near the city of Wood River. The thickness of the valley fill exceeds 120 feet in places near the center of a buried bedrock valley that bisects the area.*[16]

A buried bedrock valley, filled with roughly a trillion cubic feet of alluvial sediment. Montana is here. Minnesota is here. The soil itself carries the minerals and memories of its upstream course. The soil of the floodplain has a liminal quality to it—on its way somewhere, but stuck. And in the geological time that renders our levees and river-training structures comically insignificant, the floodplain is just a pause on its way to the gulf. **[Figures 7-8]**

But this alluvial cross section is far from static. Coursing through the stratum are millions of gallons of groundwater—some tied to the rise and fall of the river, others caught within relatively impermeable pockets forming second- or even third-tier aquifers. Large supplies of groundwater, primarily for industrial use, are withdrawn from the permeable sand and gravel in the unconsolidated valley fill of the East St. Louis area. At one time in the industrial height of the region, Wood River, Granite City, National City, and the village of Monsanto extracted over 110 million gallons of water per day from this saturated, water-storage sponge. Localized pumping creates groundwater depressions that draw the level down in a steep curve around deep municipal wells—with groundwater "craters" of 40 or more feet in National City and Monsanto, Illinois. [17] And while the general gradient of groundwater slants gently from the valley edge downward to the river, once this level drops below the river level a kind of reversal occurs—induced infiltration pulls the river water itself through its permeable banks, through the porous ground, and down into the well trough. **[Figure 9]**

Along with this unseen groundwater contour is the dynamic piezometric surface—an imaginary topology of pressures uncontained. Geological texts ask us to visualize this surface as the level to which the constrained aquifers would rise if it were punctured by an infinite number of wells. A subterranean groundwater voodoo that releases the geologic pressures of the aquifer. Itself highly variable in both time and space, the piezometric surface rises and falls depending on time of year, recent discharge stages of the river and local streams, the nature of the aquifer and its alluvial top-strata, and the extent of localized pumping.[18] It is, along with the groundwater gradient, a dynamic but unseen continuity across and within this landscape of depth.

[Figure 6] Flood of June 1903, looking east across The American Bottom (image credit: Howe, Albert, 1903, Courtesy Missouri History Museum)

Floodplain Politics

Reading across this bottomland archive, then, there might be something we call a *politics of the floodplain*—one where landscape takes a more overt position in the struggle for meaning and value. While all landscapes may be read as symptoms of wider political imperatives, rarely are they as concretely the central focus of such efforts. Unlike the tracts of farmland at the edge of many American cities, where land-use transformations depend primarily on individual speculative interest, the floodplain requires concerted political action to affect the transition from land to real estate. Levees, drainage ditches, pumps, and floodwalls are all the things of combined political action. Their value and need are rightly challenged by conservationists and ecologists, but their ultimate political nature, and responsibility, is unambiguous.

The combined result of floodplain politics, as it is currently practiced, is precisely a denial of the depth and floodplain memory this essay seeks to highlight. Floodplain politics, and its infrastructural support, attempts to force the bottomlands into surficial categories of square feet and planar parcel geometry. Flood insurance maps are one index of this transformation. For those living behind a FEMA accredited levee, flood insurance is simply not required. While the territory may be some of the lowest-lying and most risk-prone land, the presence of a levee obviates this natural condition and renders it a mere technicality. The levees and related infrastructure promote a kind of forgetfulness—where the combined imaginaries pairing qualities and risk are cancelled.

But like all landscapes, the floodplain challenges even these certainties of geometry, of the cadastre, of ground, and maybe even of society itself. It is a thoroughly constructed landscape—synthetic through and through–but one that is rarely acknowledged as such. And it is here, in this precarity and paradox, where the floodplain gains its real

currency—its language, meaning, and memory. From the dramatic overtopping of levees during increasingly common flood events to the regular seepage and localized flooding that the communities in the bottomlands routinely experience, even the technologies of flood management are not failsafe and routinely give way to the dynamic nature of the landscape. And it is perhaps here, in the future resurgent floodplains, in its newly resaturated media, where we may one day be reading the assumptions, values, and concerns of our present.

1. On media theory and cultural techniques as they relate to the built environment, see: Friedrich Kittler, "The City Is a Medium," *New Literary History* (1996): 717–729; and Bernhard Siegert, "Doors: On the Materiality of the Symbolic," *Grey Room* (2012): 6–23.

2. *History of St. Claire County, Illinois* (Philadelphia, Brink, McDonough: 1881.

3. For an introduction to both archeological findings as well as interpretive frameworks, alongside extensive bibliographies, see Kelly, John and James Brown. "Cahokia: The Process and Principles of the Creation of an Early Mississippian City." In *Making Ancient Cities: Space and Place in Early Urban Societies*, edited by Andrew Creekmore III and Kevin Fisher, 292-336. Cambridge, Cambridge University Press: 2014; and Pauketat, Timothy. "Refiguring the Archeology of Greater Cahokia." *Journal of Archeological Research* (1998): 45-89.

4. Hus, Henri. "An Ecological Cross Section of the Mississippi River in the Region of St. Louis, Missouri." *Missouri Botanical Garden Annual Report* (1908): 127-258.

5. Bowman, Isaiah. *Water Resources of the East St. Louis District. Illinois State Geological Survey Bulletin No. 5.* Urbana, University of Illinois 1907.

6. Bergstrom, Robert and Theodore Walker. *Groundwater Geology of the East St. Louis Area, Illinois. State Geological Survey Report of Investigations 191.* Urbana, Illinois. 1956.

7. Gertz, Clifford. *Interpretation of Cultures*. New York, Basic Books: 1973

8. Yusof, Kathryn. *A Billion Black Anthropocenes or None.* Minneapolis, University of Minnesota Press: 2019. See

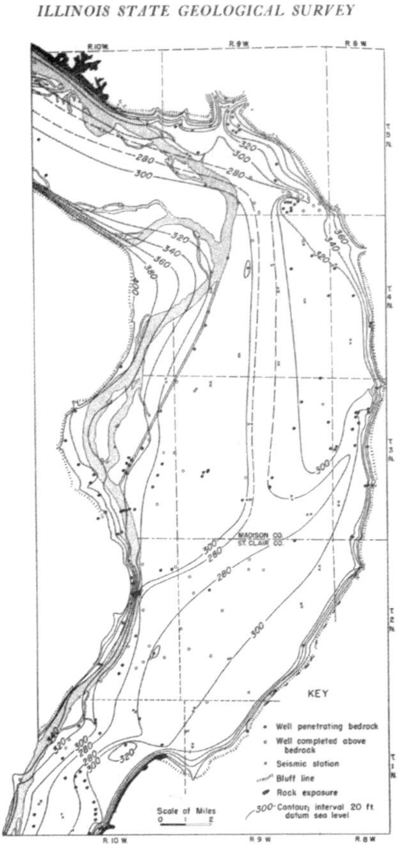

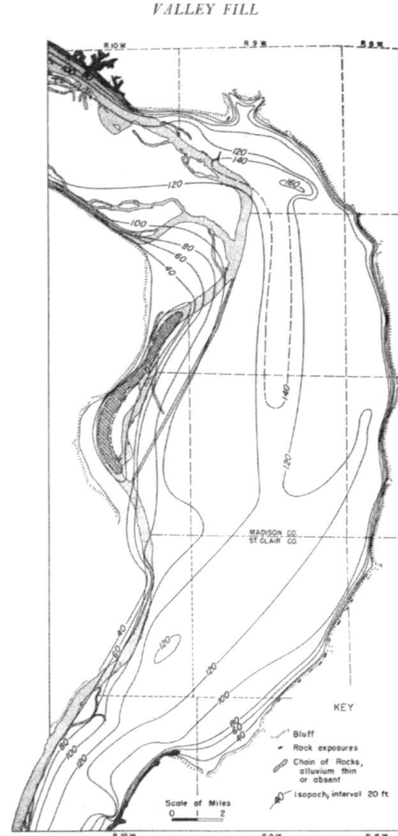

[Figure 7] Bedrock surface map (image credit: Bergstrom, Robert E. and Theodore R. Walker, Groundwater Geology of the East St. Louis Area, Illinois, Urbana: University of Illinois Press, 1956)

(RIGHT)

[Figure 8] Thickness of the valley fill (image credit: Bergstrom, Robert E. and Theodore R. Walker, Groundwater Geology of the East St. Louis Area, Illinois, Urbana: University of Illinois Press, 1956)

(NEXT PAGE)

[Figure 9] Slope of ground water (image credit: Bowman, Isaiah, Water Resources of the East St. Louis District, Urbana: University of Illinois Press, 1907) also Colten, Craig. "Environmental Development in the East St. Louis Region, 1890-1970." *Environmental History Review*. (Spring-Summer, 1990): 92-114

9. For additional framing and interpretation of the American Bottom, and an extensive regional bibliography, see Vogler, Jesse and Matthew Fluharty. "Charting the American Bottom," The American Bottom Project, 2017. http://theamericanbottom.org.

10. Bureau of Land Management. "Field Notes Search," digital image, *General Land Office Records*. 1817.

11. Taylor, Graham. *Satellite Cities: A Study of Industrial Suburbs.* New York: D. Appleton and Company, 1915.

12. Dickens, Charles. *American Notes.* London, Chapman & Hall: 1842.

13. Giedeman, Charles. "Restoration Potential of Farmed Bottomland in the American Bottom of the Mississippi River near St. Louis, Missouri." PhD diss., SIUE, 1999.

14. Schicht, R. J. *Ground Water Development in East St. Louis Area, Illinois. Illinois State Water Survey, Report of Investigation 51.* Urbana, Illinois: 1965. See also: Coulter, Samuel Monds. "An Ecological Comparison of some Typical Swamp Areas." *Missouri Botanical Garden Annual Report.* (1904): 39-71.

15. Woodward, C. M. *A History of the St. Louis Bridge.* St. Louis: G.I. Jones and Company, 1881.

16. Schicht. *Ground Water Development*, 8.

17. Ibid, 1.

18. Ibid, 20.

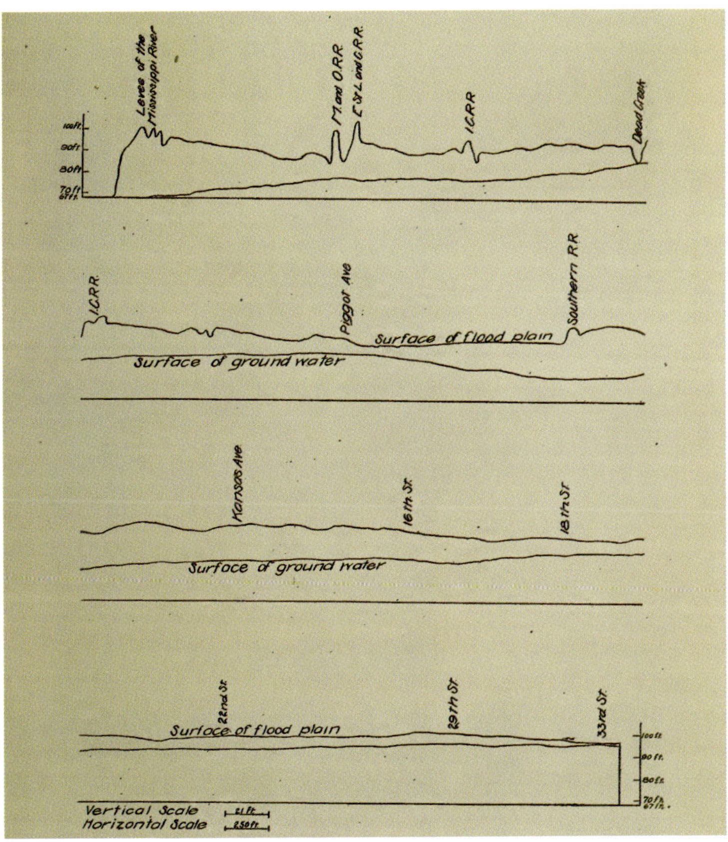

Between

The Levee and the River

Jennifer Colten

The space between the levee and the river is a forgotten zone—transitions marked mostly by regular cycles of flooding and changes of season. At first encounter, this place seems inhospitable—made more so because of its proximity to and entanglement with industrial and toxic histories. This is a landscape of erasures and deeply hidden histories.

These are damaged woods where the remnants of 20th-century infrastructure are being swallowed by the earth, mounds of residue from coal production and stone pilings that stand like sentinels, recalling the area's complex and distant past. Here too can be found the demarcations of vegetation where emergence and decay find an uncertain balance.

This segment along the Mississippi River was once a significant hub of commerce, industrial growth, and transport activity. The levee protects the surrounding community of strip clubs and chemical plants, and runs parallel to one of the remaining railroad lines that skirt across the region. It is this space *in-between*, deep in the fragile woods where no one looks, that I wander.

Photography is the ideal medium to explore this landscape in which the marks of human intervention are hidden in plain sight. A photograph can be shrewd in its deception; it can appear to operate as a neutral document with an unbiased perspective while simultaneously expressing individual and acute observations. This paradoxical condition calls attention to expectations and opens questions about what we think we believe. I use this duality embedded in the medium to address the environmental precarities of our time.

Mound.8714 (image credit: Jennifer Colten)

AB.8221 (image credit: Jennifer Colten)

AB.8027 (image credit: Jennifer Colten)

AB.8447 (image credit: Jennifer Colten)

Above

The 2019 Flood

Jess Vanecek and Derek Hoeferlin

In June of 2019, the Mississippi River in the St. Louis region experienced its second-highest river levels in recorded history, second only to the Great Flood of 1993. Using a drone, we documented the peak crests with the intent of revealing the fragility of flood protection, currently engineered as a straightened series of "single-line" defense mechanisms via floodwalls and levees. The aerial images expose vulnerabilities, yet provide opportunistic perspectives or resiliencies that emerge from flood conditions.

Water on both sides of an untopped levee questions infrastructural performance, while creating ambiguities regarding what should or should not be flooded. One side still maintains the navigation channel. The other side is allowed to flood, replenishing the wetland ecologies adjacent to the Mississippi main stem nearby. **[Figure 1]**

A concrete mixing plant submerges on the "unprotected" side of a floodwall as raw sewage seeps up on the "protected" side due to high-water-induced pump failure. Its instable condition opens up opportunities for future re-inhabitation since it is close to nearby downtown St. Louis. **[Figure 2]**

High velocity currents threaten vegetation and habitation as the river swells towards the floodwall, yet power, rail, and other infrastructures continue operations as usual. **[Figure 3]**

Water encroaches upon a gas station and places pressure on underground gasoline tanks, while pop-up programming emerges in the form of a fish market, produce stand, and impromptu tourism. **[Figure 4]**

[Figure 1] Levee separating Chain of Rocks Canal (left) and Chouteau Island (right), Illinois, 2019 (image credit: Jess Vanecek and Derek Hoeferlin)

[Figure 2] Floodwall separating Mississippi River (left) and Chouteau's Landing (right), St. Louis, Missouri, 2019 (image credit: Jess Vanecek and Derek Hoeferlin)

[Figure 3] Floodwall separating Mississippi River (left) and East St. Louis (right), Illinois, 2019
(image credit: Jess Vanecek and Derek Hoeferlin)

[Figure 4] Gas Station at Alton Slough, West Alton, Missouri, 2019
(image credit: Jess Vanecek and Derek Hoeferlin)

Territory 03: Lower Mississippi & Arkansas-White-Red River Basins

Territory 03 Plan

The shift from the Upper to the Lower Mississippi River Basin (LMRB) marks a dramatic change to the physical terrain and hydrology, but retains many core agricultural and navigational functions. Beginning after the confluence of the Mississippi and Ohio Rivers, the lower Mississippi River includes the remainder of the river's path. Continuing south towards the delta region, where it empties into the Gulf of Mexico, it is nicknamed the "Birds Foot." The lower Mississippi River has a length of 950 miles, and the watershed has a catchment area of 71,000 square miles.[1] A 2004 study estimated that 6.5 million people live in the lower Mississippi Basin.[2] While there are small cities along the entire path of the river, the two largest cities, Baton Rouge and New Orleans, are near the mouth of the river. On average, the Mississippi River discharges 593,000 cubic feet of water per second, with nearly the full cumulative flow present for the entirety of the lower Mississippi River's run. Due in part to the higher water volume, the Lower Mississippi River Basin is navigable without locks and dams and remains mostly free-flowing. However, the basin is particularly susceptible to flooding at high water stages due to the wider floodplain in the low terrain and the accumulation of upstream water. After the devastating flood of 1927, Congress passed the Flood Control Act of 1928, which authorized the U.S. Army Corps of Engineers to develop the Mississippi River and Tributaries (MR&T) Project in an effort to mitigate flood risk.[3] The MR&T Project resulted in localized and basin-wide protection measures like levees and floodwalls as well as four significant spillways and river control structures to manage flooding and to maintain navigation. These four are the Birds Point–New Madrid Floodway, the Old River Control Structure, the

Morganza and Atchafalaya Floodways, and the Bonnet Carré Spillway. A continuous levee system was constructed and reinforced between 1928 and 1973 in order to protect a significant amount of agricultural lands and cities like Baton Rouge and New Orleans.[4] The Arkansas-White-Red River Basin is a collection of rivers to the west of the LMRB, and navigation between the two sub-basins was achieved through lock and dam systems deployed in both the Red River Waterway Project and the McClellan-Kerr Arkansas River Navigation System (MKARNS) on the Arkansas-White River. Before the Mississippi River arcs east and arrives in the delta, part of the river diverges from the main path into the Atchafalaya River. The Atchafalaya is a distributary of the Mississippi River and continues directly south instead of passing through New Orleans. The accumulation of water in the lower Mississippi River has led it to be a unique and hydrologically intense landscape that has been developed primarily to mitigate the risk of flood for existing land uses and urbanization patterns.

Territory 03 Section K-K

Along with its natural hydraulic functions, the LMRB is a heavily industrialized territory dependent on the management of the river. The lower Mississippi River begins with a surface elevation of 350 feet and gradually descends to sea level as it arrives in its delta. It is an economically active corridor. A 2004 study estimated that economic activities directly related to the lower Mississippi River have generated $128 billion in revenue, $87 billion of which comes from the manufacturing and processing of chemicals, petroleum, and food.[5] That year, 470 million tons were shipped through the lower Mississippi River, earning $6 billion from Commercial Navigation.[6] Three of the country's most prolific ports are located in Louisiana near the end of the Mississippi River: the ports of Baton Rouge, New Orleans, and South Louisiana.[7] The floodplain in the lower Mississippi River Basin is both wider and less steep, and does not feature a reliable natural buffer against floodwater like the bluffs in the Upper Mississippi River. Instead, a near continuous network of levees lines the riverbank and peaks at 25 to 55 feet higher than the normal flood stage, prepared to address a one-hundred-year flood event.[8] In addition to the levees, the four relief and control structures are at key locations in the river, regulating water flow to further reduce the flood risk. The first structure is the Birds Point–New Madrid floodway positioned just downstream of the confluence with the Ohio River. It diverts and stores floodwaters from the Upper Mississippi and the Ohio River into a temporary holding area, before gradually releasing it back into the river once it is safe to do so. Much further south is the Old River Control Complex (ORCC), located at the junction between the Mississippi, Red, and Atchafalaya Rivers. The ORCC is a unique series of structures built to manage a diversion rate of water between the Mississippi River and its distributary, the Atchafalaya River. It maintains a strict discharge rate of 30 percent from the Mississippi towards the Atchafalaya Basin and allows the remaining 70 percent of the water from the Mississippi to continue downstream towards the delta. Without this water management procedure, the Atchafalaya River would overtake the flow of water and eventually redirect the Mississippi River to the Atchafalaya Basin, and the current path of the river would cease to receive water. The remaining two projects are the Morganza Spillway and Floodway and the Bonnet Carré Spillway, which both divert

Oxbow Lake, New Madrid Floodway, Missouri, 2020 (image credit: Derek Hoeferlin)

water from the Mississippi River to alternative destinations. Completed in 1953, the Morganza Spillway and Floodway redirects surge waters down a guided path through the Atchafalaya Basin. It has only been opened in 1973 and 2011.[9] The Bonnet Carré Spillway, located in the delta, relieves overflow from the Mississippi River and moves it towards the estuary, Lake Pontchartrain. Responsible for protecting New Orleans, the structure has been utilized 18 times since its construction, and at a rapidly accelerating rate. The structure was opened 12 times between 1937 and 2008 with six more openings since then, and was even opened twice during the 2019 floods.[10] Both a site of immense economic production and hydraulic accumulation, the lower Mississippi River remains an intricately managed and controlled water system.

Cairo, Illinois

New Madrid Floodway, Missouri

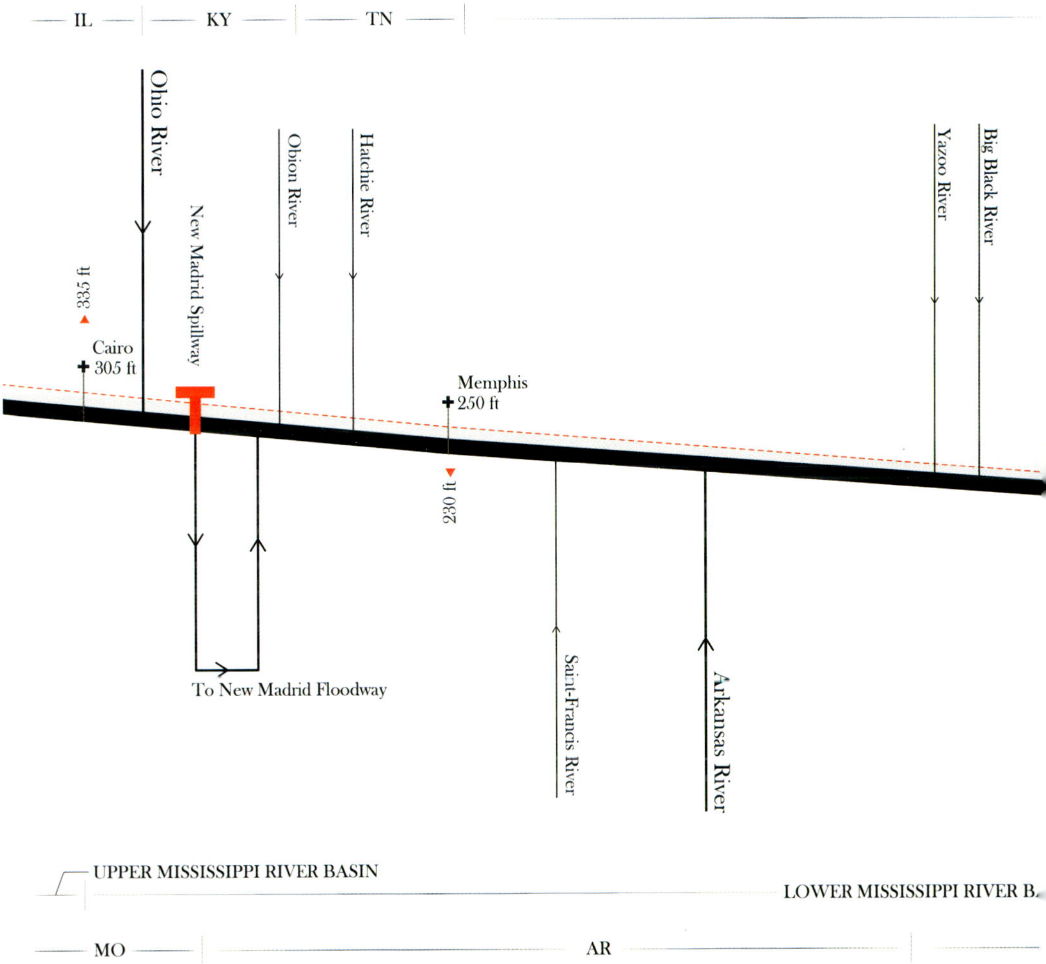

TERRITORY 03

LOWER MISSISSIPPI & ARKANSAS–WHITE–RED RIVER BASINS

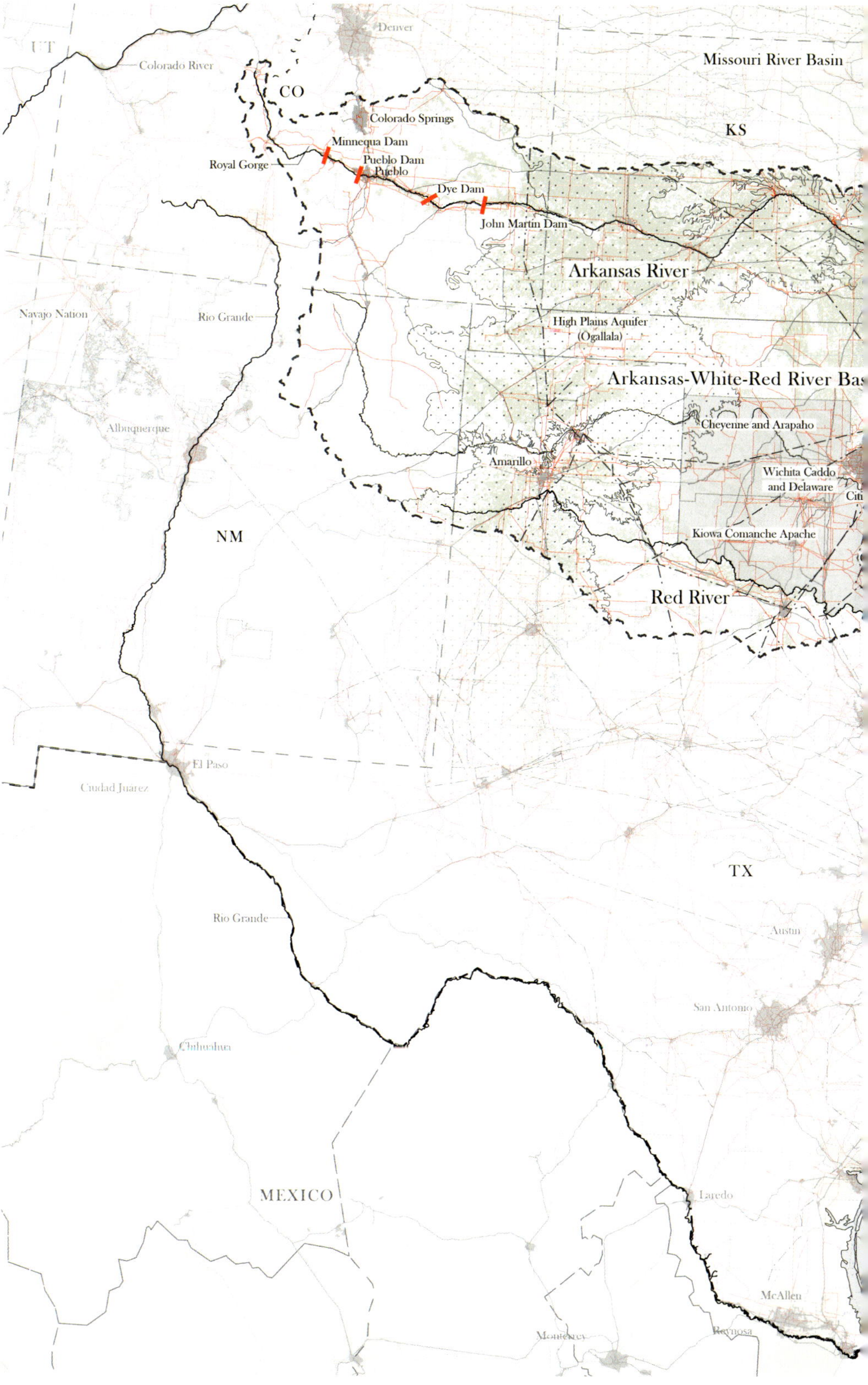

UT
Colorado River
Denver
CO
Colorado Springs
Missouri River Basin
KS
Minnequa Dam
Royal Gorge
Pueblo Dam
Pueblo
Dye Dam
John Martin Dam
Arkansas River
Navajo Nation
Rio Grande
High Plains Aquifer
(Ogallala)
Arkansas-White-Red River Bas
Albuquerque
Cheyenne and Arapaho
Amarillo
Wichita Caddo
and Delaware
Kiowa Comanche Apache
NM
Red River
El Paso
Ciudad Juarez
TX
Rio Grande
Austin
San Antonio
Chihuahua
MEXICO
Laredo
McAllen
Monterrey
Reynosa

Mississippi River Basin Model, Mississippi

Bonnet Carre Spillway, Louisiana

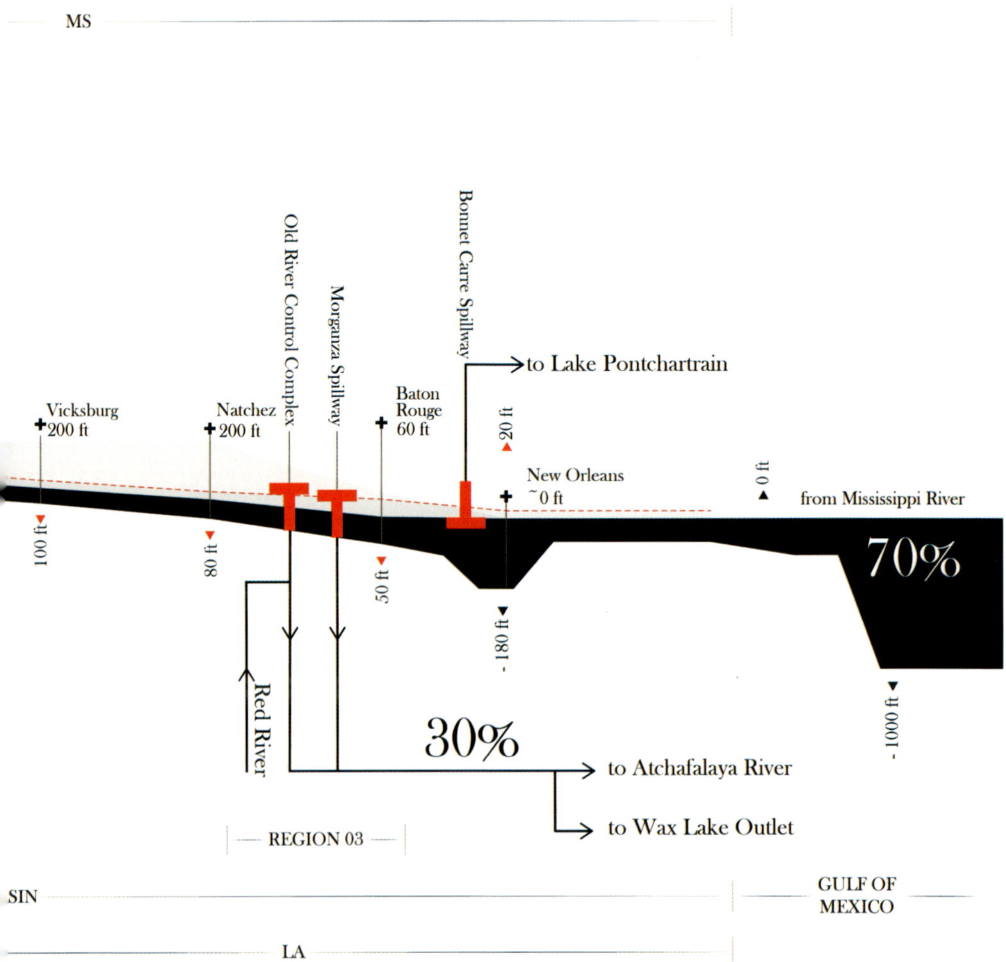

SECTION K-K

FOLLOWING THE PATH OF THE LOWER MISSISSIPPI RIVER

Region 03: Mississippi, Red, and Atchafalaya Rivers

Region 03 Plan

Historically, the lower Mississippi River meandered through the landscape both figuratively and literally, and it has become the setting of a complex hydrologic network between the Mississippi, Red, and Atchafalaya Rivers. The path of the river constantly changed as bends in the river were frequently created and abandoned for new ones, and many of the oxbow lakes have been identified as a prior path that has since been disconnected from the river. The geomorphology of the Mississippi has been rigorously studied and catalogued, for example, in the iconic Fisk maps. Until the 15th century, the Red and Mississippi Rivers were separate, parallel streams. The two joined when the Mississippi River's path arced west before returning south, creating the Turnbell Bend. It transformed the Red River into a tributary of the Mississippi River, and the remainder of the Red River's old path became the Atchafalaya River. The 19th century was a period of significant human intervention in the lower Mississippi to facilitate navigation. In 1831, a shortcut, which remains the modern path of the Mississippi River, bypassed the narrow Turnbell Bend. The bend was renamed the Upper and Lower Old Rivers and ceased to direct water in a loop, causing the Red River to stop feeding into the Mississippi. Eight years later, the state began efforts to remove a natural logjam in the Atchafalaya that had fully obstructed the distributary.[11] These two decisions inadvertently altered the complex hydrology of the site. Cleared of obstructions, the Atchafalaya River began to capture water from the Mississippi River at an accelerating rate. Eventually, all of the water from the Mississippi could have flowed down the Atchafalaya River, effectively changing its course and abandoning its existing path southeast towards New Orleans. In order to preserve its current path, the USACE built the Old River Control Complex (ORCC) at the Old River in the 1960s to maintain the annual latitude flow towards the Atchafalaya Basin at 30 percent and a main-stem flow for the Mississippi River at 70 percent.[12] The USACE constructed three control structures and a hydropower plant in the north end of the complex in order to regulate the flow to the Atchafalaya River in the Outflow Channel. To the south,

Old River Control Complex, Louisiana, 2019 (image credit: Derek Hoeferlin)

a lock and dam structure connects the Lower Old River to the navigation channels of the Mississippi, Atchafalaya, and Red Rivers. The Red River Waterway District consists of five public ports on the Red and Atchafalaya Rivers, and is a driving force in the regional economy.[13] As an emergency relief, the Morganza Spillway, to the south of the Old River Control Complex, is an artificial floodway that can redirect water surges to the southwest towards the West Atchafalaya Floodway. Both the Old River Control Complex and Morganza Spillway possess floodways that hold floodwaters for a predictable amount of time before reaching New Orleans, thus ensuring a safe evacuation of high-risk areas. The water security guaranteed by the ORCC also supports more than 2,500 acres of public land, including the Richard K. Yancey Wildlife Management Area, which offers seasonal outdoor activities like fishing and hunting.[14] In the last few centuries, the changes to the Mississippi River have been a result of artificial control that preserve the status quo.

Region 03 Section L-L

The challenging hydrologic interactions between the Mississippi, Red, and Atchafalaya Rivers were a result of shortsighted river modifications, and they remain checked by more significant pieces of infrastructure. The modifications to the LMRB in the 19th century inadvertently caused the Atchafalaya River to begin overtaking the flow of water from the Mississippi River, threatening to change the course of the Mississippi. Recognizing an impending social and environmental disaster, the U.S. Army Corps of Engineers built the Old River Control Complex to manage the flow distribution between the two rivers. In its current state, the Mississippi River connects to the Red and Atchafalaya Rivers through two active streams that are both managed by the Old River Control Complex (ORCC). The primary control devices are located in the upper stream, called the outflow channel, where a series of four structures—the Sydney Murray Hydropower Plant, the Over Bank Structure, the Low Sill Structure, and the Auxiliary Structure—precisely redirect water from the Mississippi River towards the Atchafalaya River. Each structure is independently connected to the outflow channel, allowing for a high level of precision in water control. The southern half of the complex uses the path of the Lower Old River and features a lock and dam structure, facilitating and maintaining navigation between the Mississippi and the Atchafalaya–Red Rivers. More prolific than the 9-Foot Channel in its Upper Mississippi counterpart, the Lower Old River Lock is used an average of 15 times per day, and most shipped goods consist of petrochemical, agricultural, and aggregate products.[15] The diversion between the Mississippi and Atchafalaya Rivers is also the site for the Morganza Spillway and Floodway. Built before the ORCC, the project was an emergency flood prevention system that released surge water from the Mississippi down a guided path along the Atchafalaya Basin. A continuous levee system surrounds both the ORCC and Morganza control structures to protect areas beyond riverbanks and to guide the floodwater along the floodway. The Morganza Spillway has only been opened twice, in 1973 and 2011.[16] Despite its use in the 1973 floods, the Low Sill Structure and Overbank Structure both sustained damage in the process. The Auxiliary Structure was built in 1986 to provide relief for the existing structure and add to the ORCC's management capabilities.[17] In 1990, the Sidney Murray Hydropower Plant was constructed to support the energy needs in the region, especially the nearby city of Vidalia.[18] Beginning as a site for flood control, the infrastructure between the Mississippi and Atchafalaya–Red Rivers has adapted over time to address the region's complex hydrology and economic needs.

1. Robert Black, Stephanie Hutchinson, and Chris Warshaw, *Economic Profile of the Lower Mississippi River Region*, (Cambridge: Industrial Economics Incorporated, January 2004), accessed January 23, 2021, http://www.lmrcc.org/wp-content/uploads/2013/06/economic-profile.pdf, 1_1.
2. Ibid., 1_1-2.
3. "Mississippi River and Tributaries Project," Mississippi River Commission, U.S. Army Corps of Engineers Mississippi Valley Division, accessed October 27, 2020, https://www.mvd.usace.army.mil/About/Mississippi-River-Commission-MRC/Mississippi-River-Tributaries-Project-MR-T/.
4. "History of the Lower Mississippi Levee System," (Vicksburg, U.S. Army Corps of Engineers Mississippi Valley Division), accessed December 8, 2020, https://www.mvd.usace.army.mil/Portals/52/docs/MRC/MRT_Levees.pdf?ver=2017-07-27-141912-910.
5. Black et al., *Economic Profile of the Lower Mississippi River Region*, ES_3.
6. Ibid.
7. Ibid., 9_4.
8. "The Mississippi River & Tributary Project: Controlling the Project Flood" (Vicksburg, Mississippi River Commission, 2007), accessed December 8, 2020, https://www.mvd.usace.army.mil/Portals/52/docs/Controlling%20the%20Project%20Flood%20info%20paper.pdf, 5.
9. "Morganza Floodway Overview," U.S. Army Corps of Engineers New Orleans District, accessed October 27, 2020. https://www.mvn.usace.army.mil/Missions/Mississippi-River-Flood-Control/Morganza-Floodway-Overview/#:~:text=Intended%20to%20operate%20during%20emergency,River%20into%20the%20Atchafalaya%20Basin.
10. "Historic Operation of Bonnet Carré," U.S. Army Corps of Engineers New Orleans District, accessed October 27, 2020. https://www.mvn.usace.army.mil/Missions/Mississippi-River-Flood-Control/Bonnet-Carre-Spillway-Overview/Historic-Operation-of-Bonnet-Carre/.
11. "Old River Control," (New Orleans: U.S. Army Corps of Engineers New Orleans District, January 2009), accessed December 12, 2020, https://www.mvn.usace.army.mil/Portals/56/docs/PAO/Brochures/OldRiverControlBrochure.pdf, 4.
12. "Louisiana Old River Control Complex and Mississippi River Flood Protection,"America's Wetland Foundation Resource Center, July 1, 2012, http://www.americaswetlandresources.com/background_facts/detailedstory/LouisianaRiverControl.html.
13. "Economic Development Handout: Red River Waterway District," (Natchitoches, Red River Waterway Commission), accessed December 8, 2020, https://www.redriverwaterway.com/sites/default/files/pdf/EconomicDevelopmenthandout.pdf, 1-2.
14. "Old River Control," 13.
15. Ibid., 9.
16. "Morganza Floodway Overview."
17. "Old River Control," 10–12.
18. Ibid, 15.
19. Ibid., 8.
20. Ibid,. 12.
21. Ibid.
22. Ibid., 9.
23. Ibid., 10–12.
24. "Review of Soils Design, Construction and Performance Observations: Overbank Structure, Old River Control," (Vicksburg: U.S. Army Corps of Engineers Waterways Experiment Station, February 1964), accessed December 12, 2020, https://usace.contentdm.oclc.org/digital/collection/p266001coll1/id/3128/, 14.

Hydropower Plant

Overbank Structure

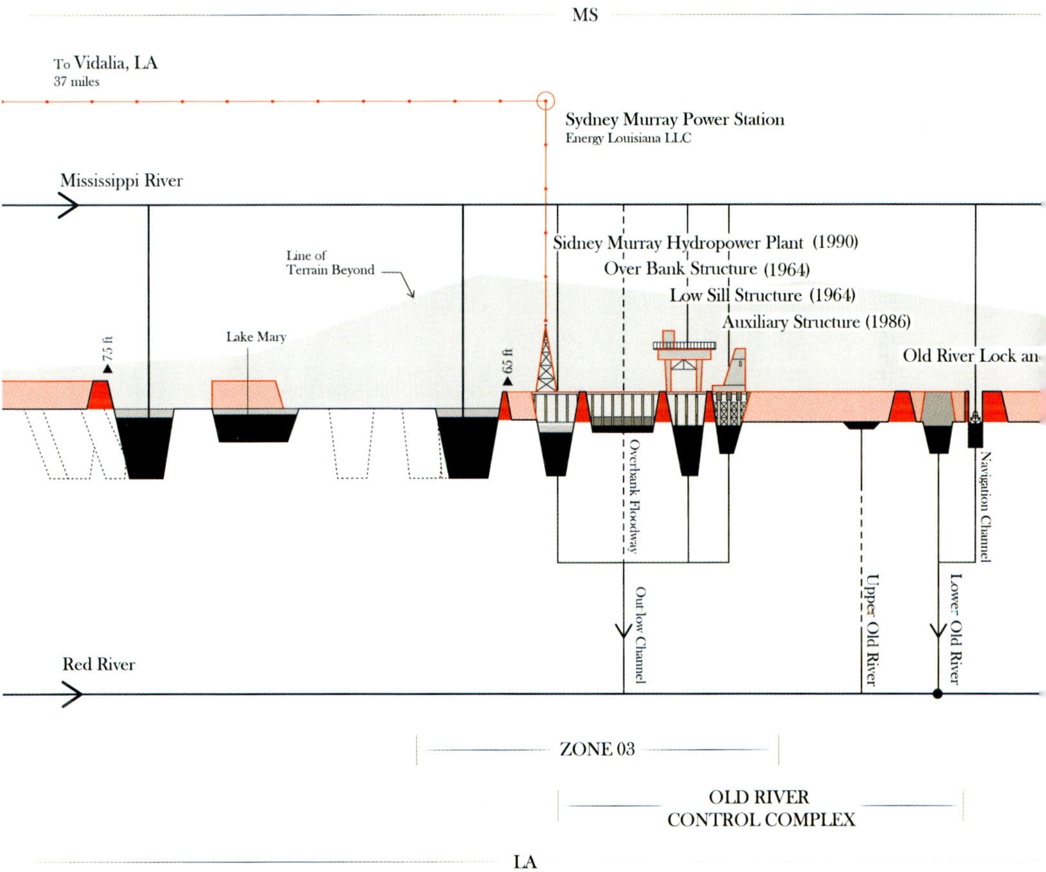

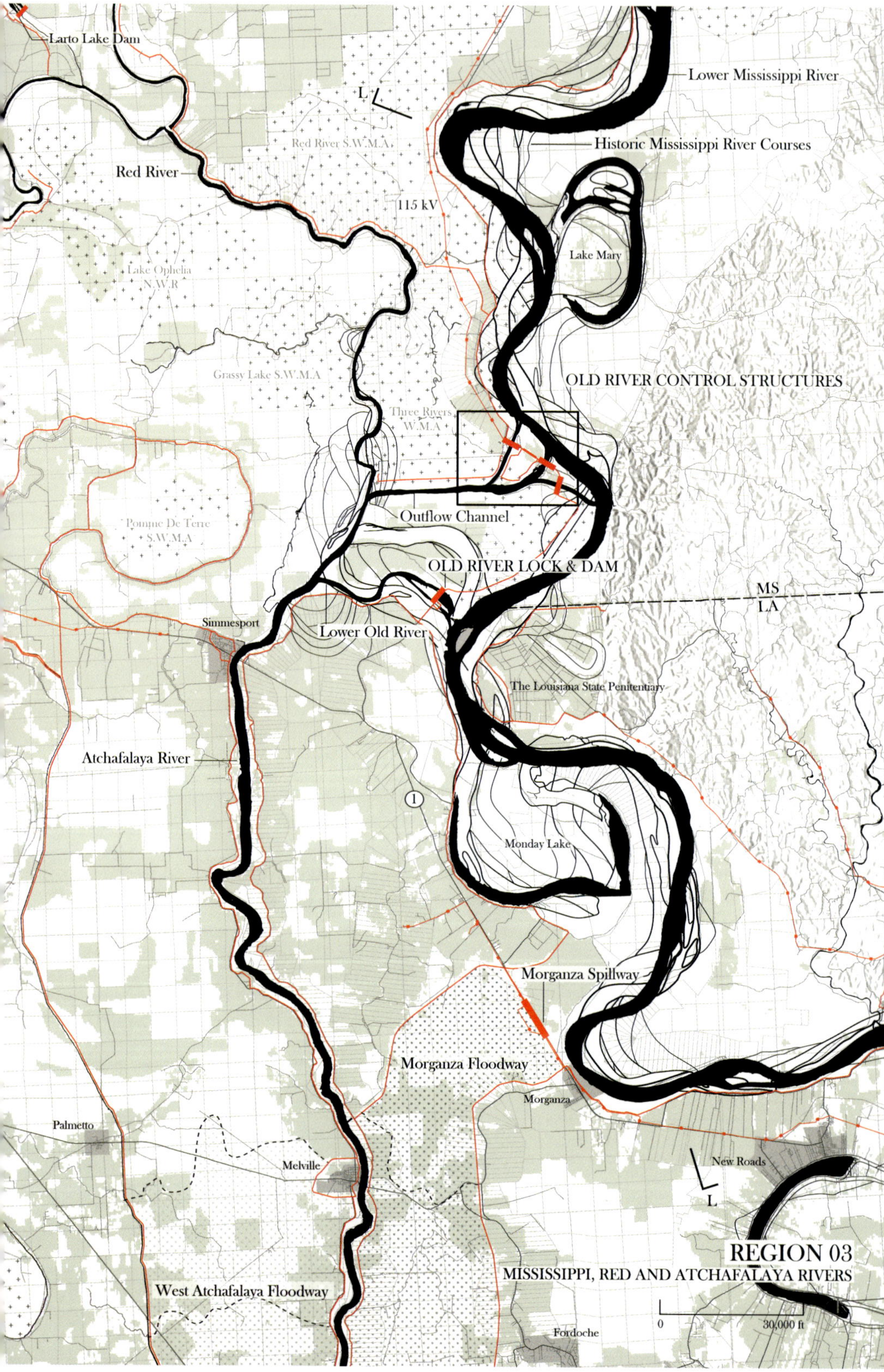
Larto Lake Dam
Lower Mississippi River
Historic Mississippi River Courses
Red River S.W.M.A.
Red River
115 kV
Lake Mary
Lake Ophelia
N.W.R
Grassy Lake S.W.M.A
OLD RIVER CONTROL STRUCTURES
Three Rivers
W.M.A
Outflow Channel
Pomme De Terre
S.W.M.A
OLD RIVER LOCK & DAM
MS
LA
Simmesport
Lower Old River
The Louisiana State Penitentiary
Atchafalaya River
1
Monday Lake
Morganza Spillway
Morganza Floodway
Morganza
Palmetto
Melville
New Roads
REGION 03
MISSISSIPPI, RED AND ATCHAFALAYA RIVERS
West Atchafalaya Floodway
0
30,000 ft
Fordoche

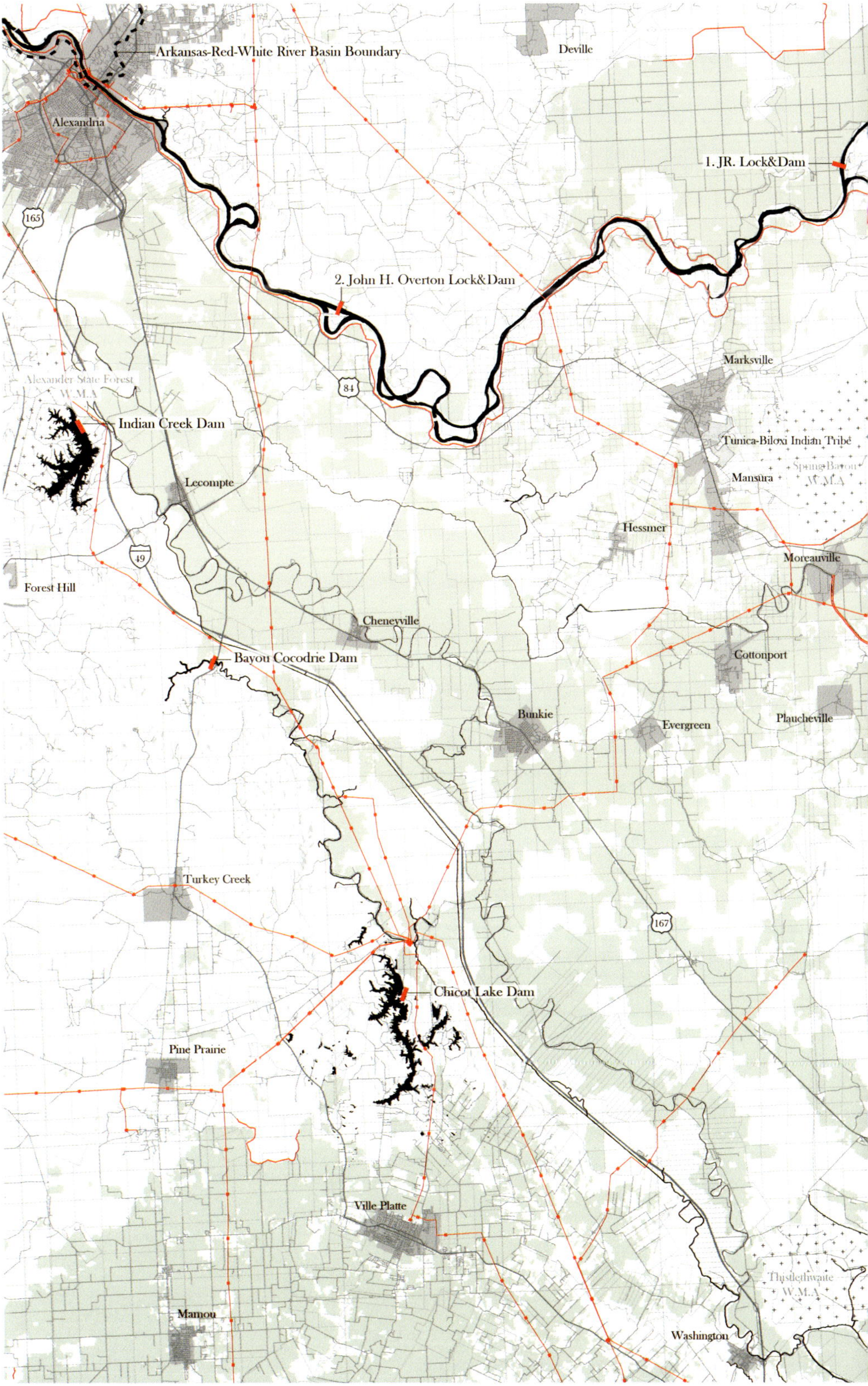
Arkansas-Red-White River Basin Boundary
Deville
Alexandria
165
1. JR. Lock&Dam
2. John H. Overton Lock&Dam
84
Marksville
Alexander State Forest
W.M.A
Indian Creek Dam
Tunica-Biloxi Indian Tribe
Spring Bayou
W.M.A
Mansura
Lecompte
Hessmer
49
Moreauville
Forest Hill
Cheneyville
Bayou Cocodrie Dam
Cottonport
Bunkie
Evergreen
Plaucheville
Turkey Creek
167
Chicot Lake Dam
Pine Prairie
Ville Platte
Thistlethwaite
W.M.A
Mamou
Washington

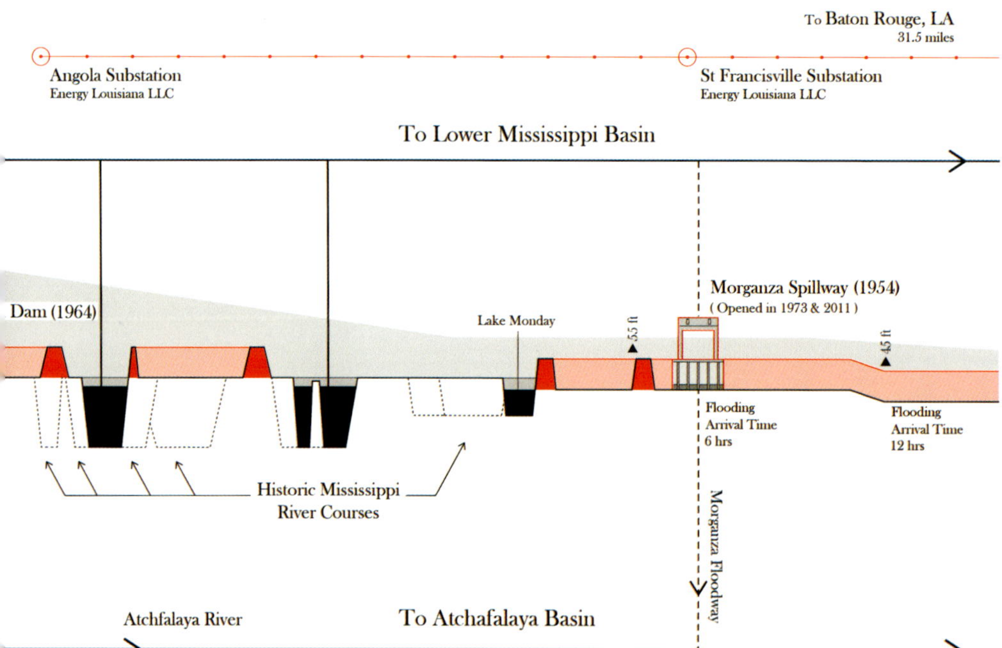

MORGANZA
SPILLWAY & FLOODWAY

SECTION L-L

SECTION THROUGH THE MISSISSIPPI, RED AND ATCHAFALAYA RIVERS & OLD RIVER CONTROL COMPLEX

25. "Old River Control," 15.

26. Ibid.

27. "Old River Low Sill Structure: Downpull Forces on Vertical-lift Gates," (Vicksburg: U.S. Army Corps of Engineers Waterways Experiment Station, December 1956), accessed December 9, 2020, https://usace.contentdm.oclc.org/digital/collection/p266001coll1/id/1698/, 6.

28. B.P. Fletcher and J.L. Grace Jr., "Hydrodynamic Forces on Tainter Gates and Stilling Basin Old River Control Auxiliary Structure" (Vicksburg: U.S. Army Corps of Engineers Waterways Experiment Station, February 1988), accessed December 9, 2020, https://apps.dtic.mil/dtic/tr/fulltext/u2/a192262.pdf, 8.

29. "Old River Control," 10–12.

30. Ibid., 12.

31. Ibid., 15.

32. Ibid.

33. U.S. Corps of Engineers, "Access Machine Case History: Louisiana Hydropower," Internet Archive Wayback Machine, accessed on October 27, 2020, https://web.archive.org/web/20090105211049/http://accessware.org/Case/LH/LH.htm.

34. "Review of Soils Design, Construction and Performance Observations," 14.

35. "Old River Control," 12.

Zone 03: Old River Control Complex

Zone 03 Plan

The Old River Control Complex features a series of four structures that critically manage the flow of water from the lower Mississippi River to its distributary, the Atchafalaya. It specifically diverts 30 percent of the flow towards the Atchafalaya Basin while the remaining 70 percent continues downstream.[19] From north to south, the complex consists of the Sidney Murray Hydropower Plant, Overbank Structure, Low Sill Structure, and Auxiliary Structure, all of which linearly connect to the 500-year levee system. Built in 1964, the 3,356-foot-long Overbank Structure is the longest structure in the complex.[20] It is a controlled spillway with 73 bays running across drylands, where its floodway is bounded by levees that guide water to the outflow channel.[21] Completed at the same time, the Low Sill Structure was once the only full-year-run control structure. Both structures began construction in 1955 by the USACE and became operational in 1962, after the channels between the Mississippi and Red Rivers were stabilized.[22] Due to damages sustained during the Mississippi flood of 1973, the Auxiliary Structure was built in 1986 to reduce the stress on the Low Sill Structure.[23] Currently, the Low Sill Structure and Auxiliary Structures are the primary control structures operating year-round, while the Overbank Structure only operates during major flood events.[24] The Sidney Murray Hydropower Plant was completed in 1990, finishing the series of four structures in the Old River Control Complex.[25] The power plant was fabricated off-site in New Orleans, and fittingly shipped upstream by barge, to be installed at the ORCC. At the time of its completion, it was both the single largest item ever shipped on the Mississippi River and the world's largest prefabricated power plant.[26] The ORCC both maintains balance between the Mississippi and Atchafalaya Rivers and serves additional infrastructural functions to provide flood safety and hydroelectricity.

Zone 03 Sections M-M, N-N, O-O, P-P

The Old River Control Complex is an invaluable piece of infrastructure. The USACE manually opens and closes the control structures' gates to regulate the water flow. The Low Sill Structure is a regulating dam with 11 vertical-lift gates, having three weir crests at -5 feet and eight weir crests at 10 feet.[27] Another regulating dam, the Auxiliary Structure, has six tainter gates with all weir crests at -5 feet to ensure discharge to the Atchafalaya Basin.[28] The 1973 flooding scoured a 50-feet-deep cavity under the Low Sill Structure where the alluvial foundation is prone to erosion.[29] In addition to the repairs to the foundation, the USACE constructed the Auxiliary Structure and a new inflow channel to supplement the existing structure's capacities and to prevent similar damages to be potentially sustained.[30] The Sidney Murray Hydropower Plant is a run-of-the-river power plant, relying on the large volume of water flow as well as an 8-to-20-foot elevation drop from the Mississippi River to the Atchafalaya River.[31] Eight bulb turbines equip the plant with a total capacity of 192,000 kWh.[32] It is also integrated with the flow distribution system and must maintain a minimum flow of 40 percent, even when it is not producing electricity.[33] The Overbank Structure is a spillway consisting of 73 hinged-timber gates, having all weir crests at 52 feet for discharge during flood flow.[34] Unlike the other three structures, the Overbank Structure is only opened during high-water stages to relieve the pressure off the two main control structures in order to protect the structures like in the 1973 floods. Together, the four structures have a maximum discharge capacity of 700,000 cubic feet per second. They critically maintain the 70 to 30 percent water distribution between the Mississippi and the Atchafalaya Deltas without jeopardizing navigation, flood safety, or ecology.[35] The ORCC remains an iterative, and arguably controversial, process in river engineering that addresses the increasing complexity of the site that is in constant pursuit of preserving both the lower Mississippi River's path, as well as its invaluable socioeconomic and environmental positions.

Low Sill Structure, Old River Control Complex, Louisiana, 2019 (image credit: Derek Hoeferlin)

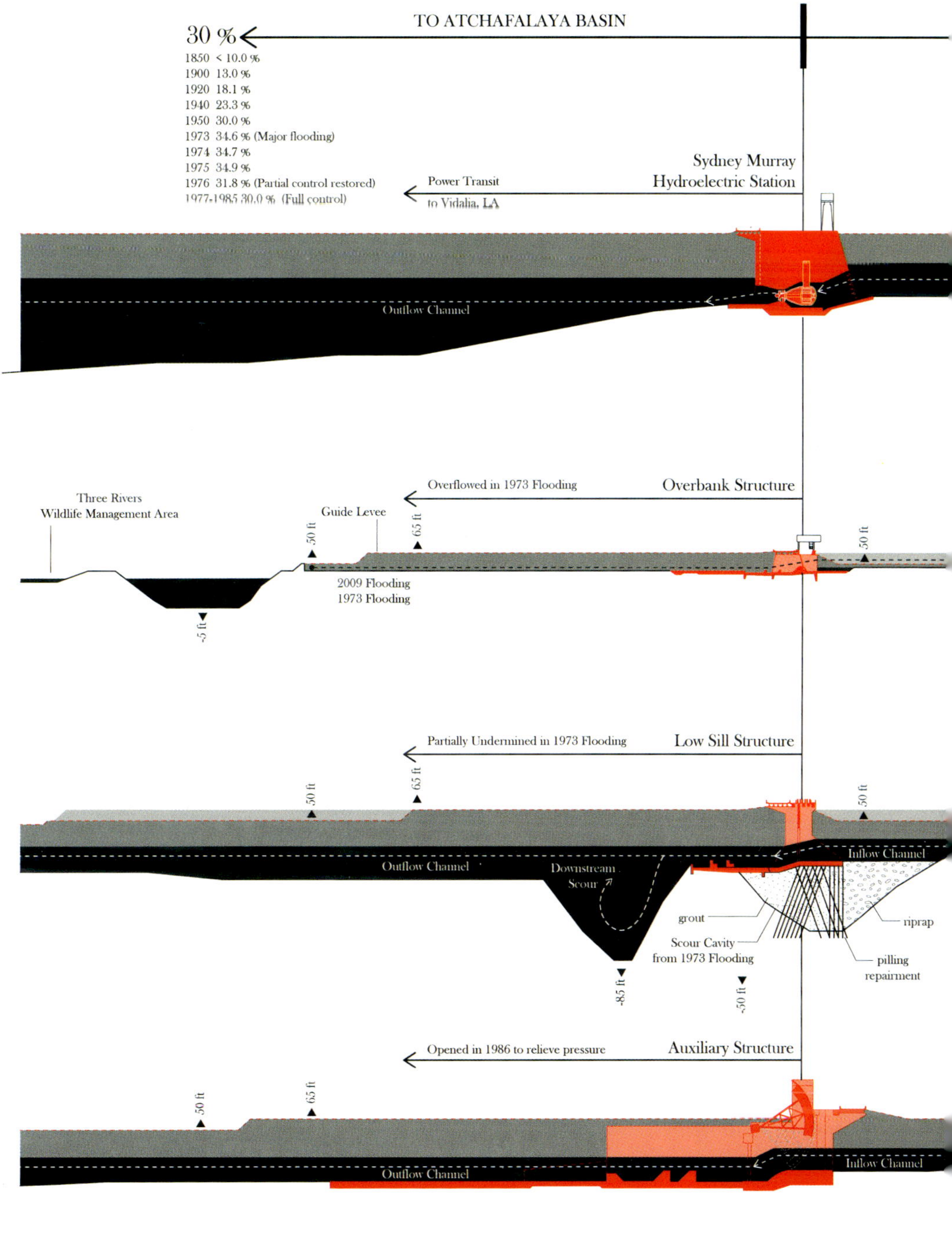

OLD RIVER CONTROL COMPLEX

ZONE 03
OLD RIVER CONTROL COMPLEX

115kV Transmission Lines
500 Year Levee
Sidney Murray Hydroelectric Station
Outflow Channel

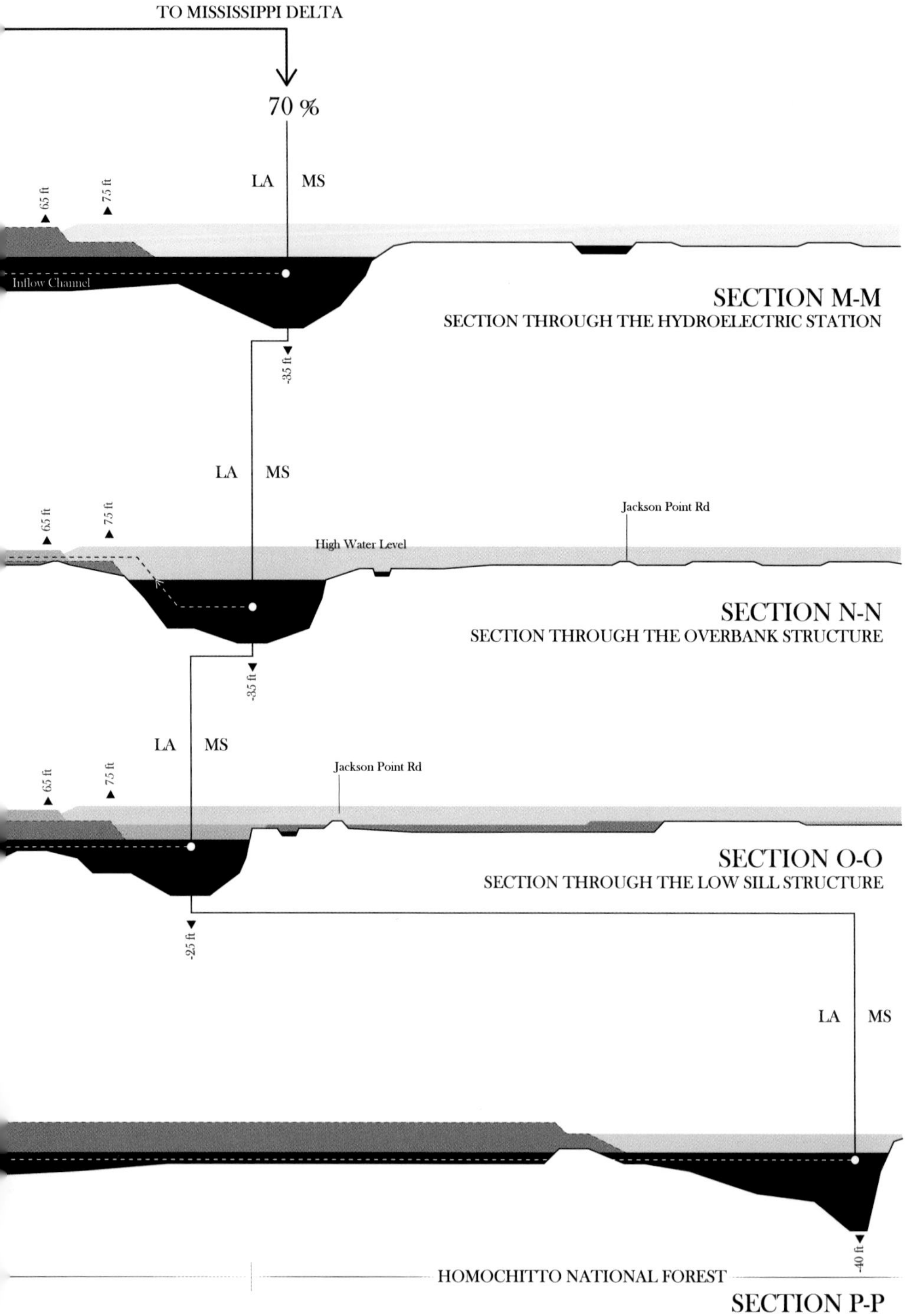

SECTION M-M
SECTION THROUGH THE HYDROELECTRIC STATION

SECTION N-N
SECTION THROUGH THE OVERBANK STRUCTURE

SECTION O-O
SECTION THROUGH THE LOW SILL STRUCTURE

SECTION P-P
SECTION THROUGH THE AUXILIARY STRUCTURE

Divert Flows

(UPPER RIGHT) Auxiliary Structure, Old River Control Complex, Louisiana, 2020
(BACKGROUND) Bonnet Carré Spillway, Norco, Louisiana, 2019 (image credit: Derek Hoeferlin)

Refine Resources

(UPPER RIGHT) Valero Refinery, Good Hope, Louisiana, 2020
(BACKGROUND) View across Mississippi River to Dow Chemical Plant from Montz Park, Louisiana, 2020 (image credit: Derek Hoeferlin)

Erase Lands

(UPPER RIGHT) Manchac Wildlife Management Area, Louisiana, 2012. (BACKGROUND) Example of coastal wetland loss somewhere above the Mississippi River Delta, Louisiana, 2011.

Ship Goods

(UPPER RIGHT) View of Mississippi River from Crescent Park, New Orleans, Louisiana, 2020
(BACKGROUND) View of Mississippi River from Bonnet Carré Spillway, Norco, Louisiana, 2020
(image credit: Derek Hoeferlin)

Splitting

Aquaculture & Migratory Birds in the Yazoo-Mississippi Floodplain (the Delta)

Forbes Lipschitz and Justine Holzman

[Figure 1] Saturated agricultural land in the Mississippi Alluvial Valley, 2020 (image credit: Derek Hoeferlin)

Introduction

More than 300 bird species migrate annually along the Mississippi Flyway, the longest overland flyway in North America. Every year, waterfowl and other waterbirds depart their breeding grounds in the Arctic Circle, where the short summers provide ample food for new nestlings, and fly southward to the Gulf of Mexico. Historically, a rich complex of wetlands, lakes, and rivers provided suitable habitat to support their journey along the flyway. The draining of lands for agricultural expansion and intensification is the leading cause of wetland loss across the continent, where migratory birds must now compete for increasingly scarce resources. A critical confluence of birds traveling the Mississippi Flyway emerges at the terminus of the Mississippi River watershed within a region defined by its damp and watery landscapes, the Mississippi Alluvial Valley (MAV). The MAV in particular has lost 80 percent of its wetlands to agriculture and settlement, including forested wetlands, swamps, cypress-tupelo brakes, scrub-shrub wetlands and emergent wetlands.[1] **[Figure 1]** Far more narratives and imagery of this erasure center on the Gulf Coast, where the causes, effects, and risks of the land-loss crisis readily appear. However, the lost and degraded wetlands that comprise the Gulf Coast are part of a much larger, irrevocably altered landscape—the Lower Mississippi River Basin (LMRB)—wherein the adverse hydrologic effects of drowning and draining lands have been compounded and amplified throughout the basin. This process of wetland erasure is particularly intense in the Yazoo-Mississippi floodplain, an area within the AV also known as the Delta.

The Delta spreads across the boundaries of Arkansas, Mississippi, and Louisiana, where the confluence of the Mississippi and Ohio Rivers constitutes the beginning of the Lower Mississippi River Basin. Once a densely forested and frequently flooded swampland, the Delta was among one of the most biologically diverse forests of 19th-century America. The combined and contingent efforts of agricultural expansion and hydrologic alteration drained 7.2 million hectares of bottomland hardwood forest, resulting in a range of profound ecological consequences, including habitat loss and fragmentation, water quality degradation due to non-point source runoff and intensified downstream flooding.[2] This immense project of land reclamation was accomplished through the dispossession of indigenous peoples from their land, an abundant supply of slave labor in a plantation economy, and post-emancipation racist agricultural exploitation through convict leasing and a sharecropping system that kept tenant farmers in debt.[3] The Delta landscape is known for some of the most brutal and violent histories of racism and oppression of Black life alongside the celebrated emergence of Delta blues music. The financialization and extraction of nature, bodies, and labor are woven into the plantation landscape. Expansive row crop agriculture emerged out of a long history of anti-Black racism and racist policies. In the contemporary iteration of the plantation landscape, distribution of farmland remains inequitable.[4] Most farmland is owned by large corporations and often unavailable to small farmers due to discriminatory loan policies.

This extractive agricultural model, based on the exploitation of people and ecosystems, has resulted in a monoculture landscape. Interrupting the vast fields of commodity crops are the isolated ponds of catfish farming. Though still a legacy of the region's complex history, these ponds represent some of the only remaining "wet" lands in the Delta. During winter in the MAV, waterbirds, specifically waterfowl, spend a large portion of their energy foraging for seeds, tubers, hard mast, and invertebrates. While the annual vegetation of seasonally emergent wetlands and bottomland hardwood wetlands once provided food resources for these migratory species, the monocultural nature of row crop agriculture fails to provide the biomass or variety of food sources necessary for bird survival.[5] **[Figures 2 & 3]**

Catfish Farming in the Delta

In an area that has undergone major declines in natural permanent and seasonal wetlands, catfish ponds have created a novel regional ecology, providing a substantial area of artificial wetland for waterfowl.[6] Catfish farming in the Delta emerged during the 1960s as a way to make areas of Sharkey clay soils productive. Known colloquially as "gumbo" soils, the high clay content and sticky red-brown consistency prevent infiltration, an ideal trait for holding water, but unsuitable for most production crops, especially cotton. Idled catfish ponds provide critical wintering waterfowl and autumn shorebird habitat—the shallowly flooded cracked clay soil approximating an inland shoreline in what is otherwise a sea of drained cropland. In recent years, the catfish aquaculture industry has undergone considerable consolidation, resulting in a decline in acreage and changes to aquaculture practices. Escalating production costs combined with volatile annual prices and weakened demand caused many producers in Arkansas, Louisiana, and Mississippi Delta regions to take their ponds out of production. There were only 36,000 acres of catfish ponds in Mississippi in 2019, down from a peak of 113,000 in 2001. This consolidation reconfigured landscape patterns and in turn impacted waterbird habitat availability.[7] In an effort to remain competitive, some catfish farmers have started using intensive, outdoor production systems called *split-ponds*.[8] **[Figure 4]**

As its name suggests, split-pond systems are divided into two sections, a *fish cell* and a *waste treatment cell*. The fish cell, having deeper waters and comprising 20 percent of the pond's area, is used to contain the fish as they are fed, aerated, and harvested. A barrier prevents fish from entering the other section, a larger and shallower area of the pond used to aerate and filter the water. In a typical ten-acre split pond, two acres are dedicated to fish production and harvesting, while eight acres are reserved for waste treatment only. This separation of active (productive) and passive (performative) use provides a unique opportunity for split-pond adopting catfish farms to provide ecological benefits. With many of the prior constraints of catfish farming shifted to a smaller portion of the typical pond, the design of the waste treatment cell can be modified to become multibenefit. Can strategic regrading and plant selection provide additional habitat for birds and pollinators without negatively influencing the productive capacity of the connected fish cell? How might a new multibenefit pond network create compound ecological benefits at the farm and regional scale? The following design concepts explore such opportunities for multibenefit and multispecies design at the pond, farm and Delta scales. **[Figure 5]**

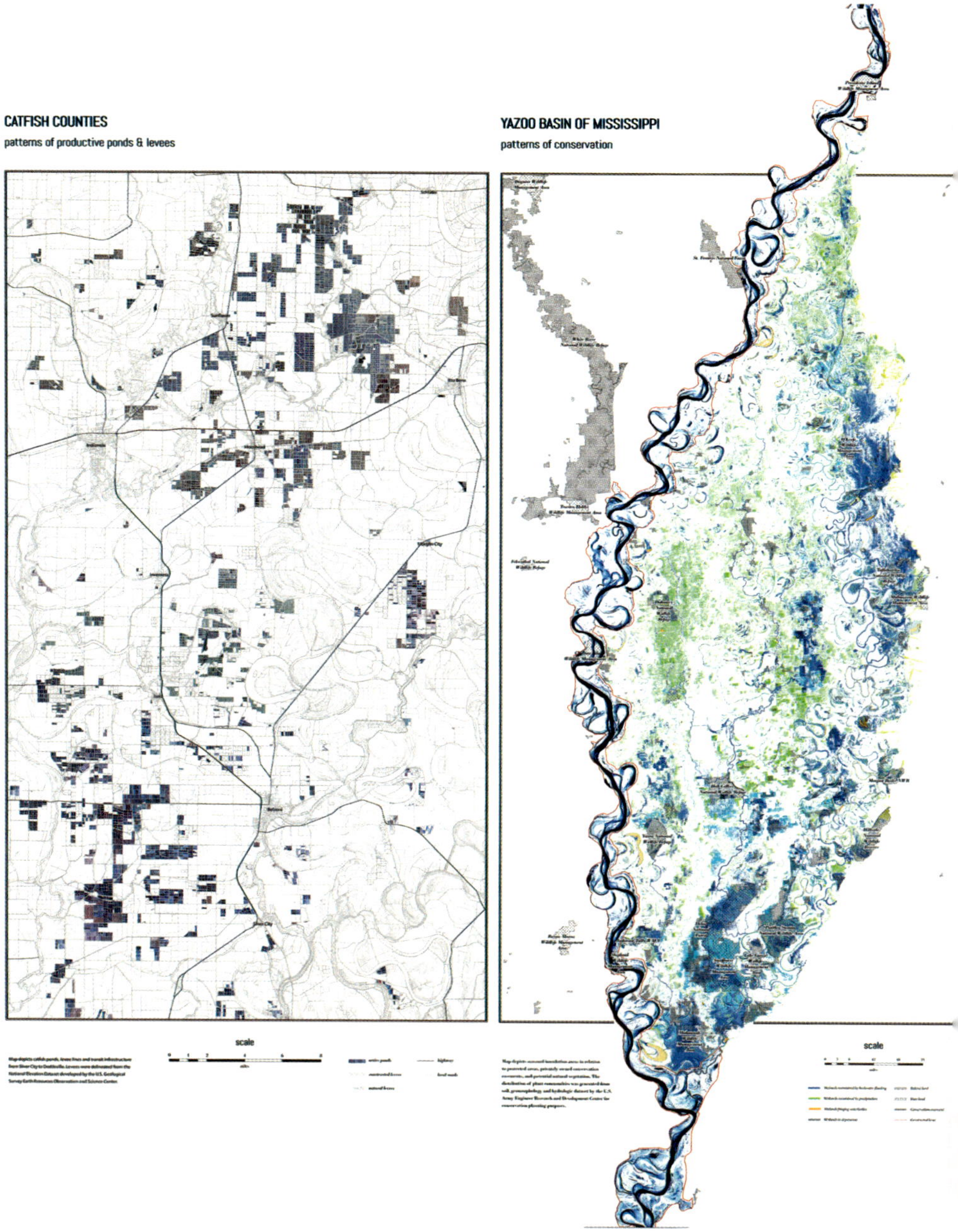

[Figure 2] Moving left to right: Catfish Country; The Yazoo-Mississippi Basin with conservation areas; Historic Inundation of the Mississippi Alluvial Valley; and the Mississippi Flyway (image credits: Forbes Lipschitz and Justine Holzman, 2016)

PPI ALLUVIAL VALLEY

inundation

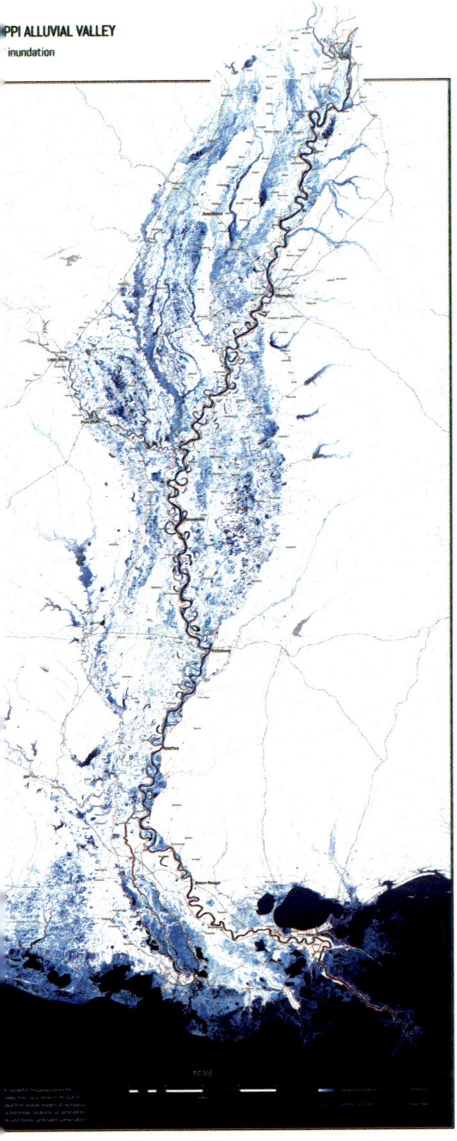

MISSISSIPPI FLYWAY

patterns of migration

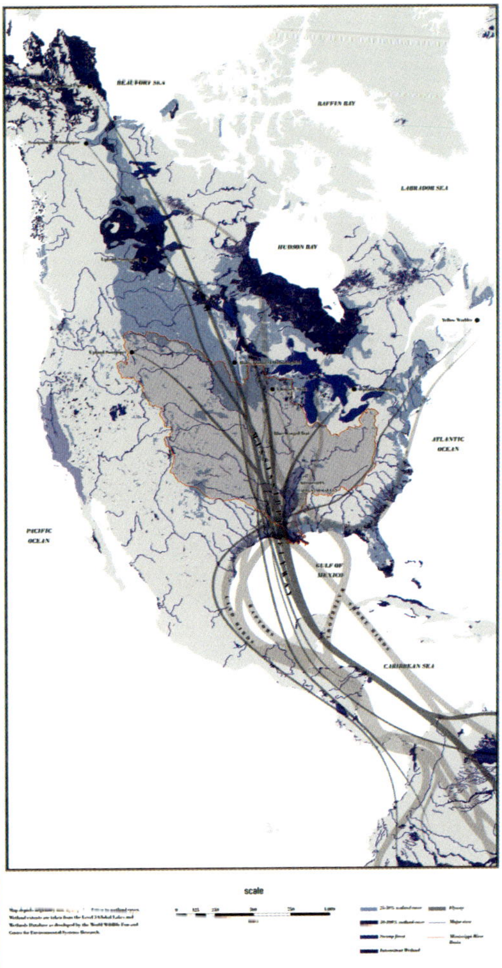

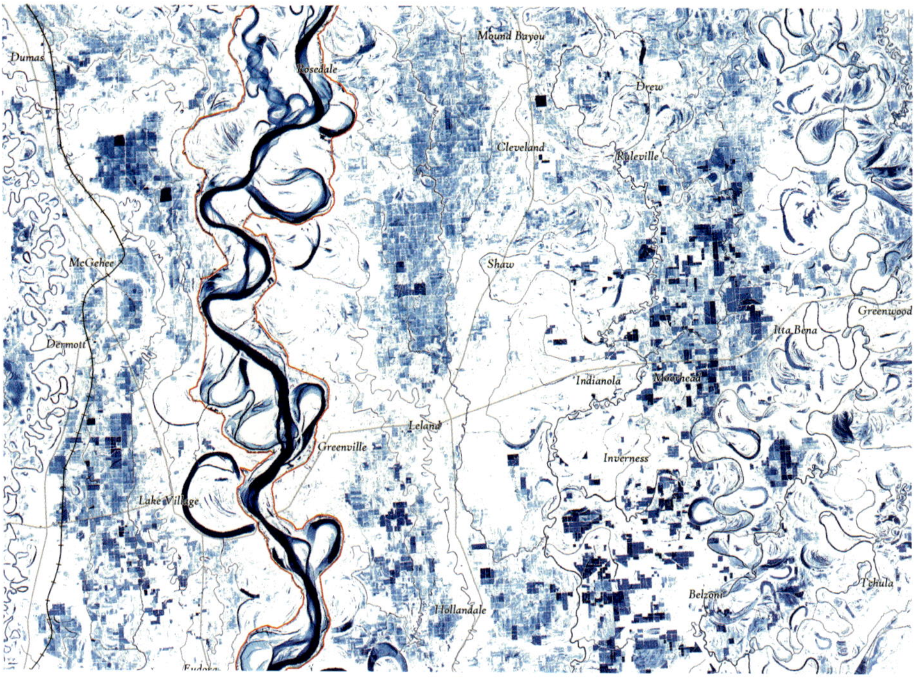

[Figure 3] Detail of the Mississippi Alluvial Valley (MAV) Patterns of Inundation (image credits: Forbes Lipschitz and Justine Holzman)

The Pond

At the pond scale, material changes to pond design can work to create desirable conditions for waterbirds, providing seasonally specific mixtures of open water at varying depths, wetlands, mudflats, vegetated edges, and vegetated islands. The relatively large area of the waste treatment cell presents fewer constraints compared to the fish cell. This space can accommodate various topographic and vegetative changes that would otherwise be restricted in catfish cultivation because of pests and harvesting methods. Four speculative approaches to vegetative and/or topographic change of the waste treatment cell involve altering the standard split-pond design through modifications of the interior, the edge, and the baffle. **[Figure 6]**

A "floating wetlands" design could increase area for vegetation throughout the pond without altering its topography, using floating geotextile mats that can be seeded and relocated. However, relative to other designs, floating wetlands do not capture potential benefits offered by the shallow water state. An "augmented edge" design increases edge length and vegetated area by reducing the slope and crenellating the outer edge of the pond. The gentler sloping edges could mimic the shoreline and mudflat habitats that exist in shallow waters. A "branching baffle" design involves topographic manipulation of the baffle that runs through the midline of a split pond. As conventional ponds are converted to split ponds, augmenting the design of the baffle might streamline construction efforts while further separating the constructed habitat elements from the maintenance road. Moreover, this could allow for varied vegetation growth of shrubs and scrub on top of the baffle. An "isolated islands" design utilizes a cut-and-fill strategy to provide topographic variation within the pond. This design leaves major elements of the split pond intact, excavating material from the bottom of the pond to create islands with enough elevation to support shrubs and trees. When drained, this design could produce small ponds in excavated areas surrounded by mudflat or fallow land.

The multibenefit split pond designs present multiple possibilities for habitat depending on water level. Pond maintenance and operations would occur alongside the needs of migrating birds, aiming to time productive and idled cycles with the stopover needs of different species. In general, high water levels during production would create habitat for waterfowl and low water levels of idle ponds would create habitat for shorebirds. The primary species found in active (in-production) catfish ponds are those that typically frequent open-water habitats that are around one meter deep, a similar depth to most catfish ponds. These include lesser scaup, double crested cormorant, and ruddy duck, as well as generalist species like northern shoveler, American coot, great blue heron, and great egret.[9] Idled (out-of-production) ponds have greater vegetation and water level diversity than production ponds, and have been shown to attract more than thirty species of waterbirds from fall to early spring. Idled ponds are frequented by species associated with shallow emergent wetlands, such as northern pintail, gadwall, and American green-winged teal.[10] Preliminary designs would need to be tested at full scale on working farms to assess ecological and habitat value alongside the effective production of catfish. **[Figure 7]**

The Farm

With these potential design standards, farmers could create a variety of multibenefit split ponds by converting conventional ponds or modifying existing split ponds. A combination of multibenefit split ponds could create a midscale landscape capable of supporting a range of waterbird species throughout the year. The proposed split pond designs are flexible. A farm-scale masterplan could accommodate specific amounts of edge length, open water, and vegetation to meet the habitat requirements of targeted species. Maintenance of the novel plant communities in the passive ponds must be compatible with the daily operations of the active ponds. A key challenge to establishing more diverse plant and insect communities in ponds has been maintaining the health of the catfish, considering their susceptibility to bacterial infection. Though predatory birds are unlikely disease vectors, their tendency to feed on sickly fish can result in the transfer of infected fish from one pond to another.[11] **[Figure 7]**

The Delta

Although this design work focuses on the scale of the pond, it has territorial ambition. Given that catfish farming occupies a relatively large area of the Delta, the opportunity to improve migratory bird habitat across this region is significant. Conservation and restoration initiatives have incentivized farmers both large and small to take their land

[Figure 4] America's Catch, a large catfish farm in the Delta
(image credits: Forbes Lipschitz and Justine Holzman)

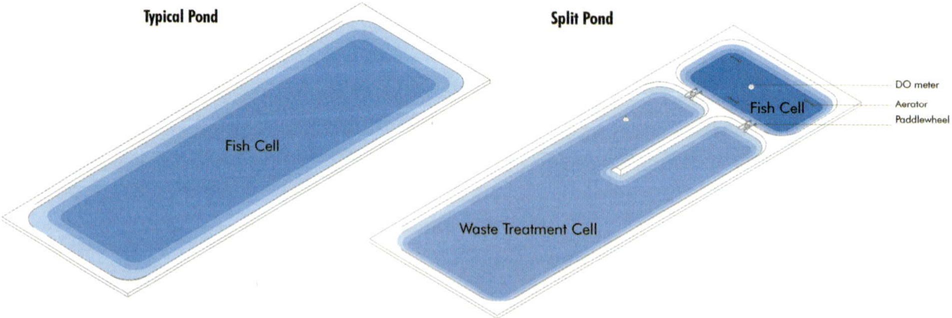

[Figure 5] Diagram of a conventional catfish pond design compared to a conventional split-pond design
(image credits: Forbes Lipschitz and Justine Holzman)
(RIGHT)
[Figure 6] Diagrams of multi-benefit split-pond design concepts.
(image credits: Forbes Lipschitz and Justine Holzman)

Floating Wetlands
Open water area: 12 686 m2
Vegetated area: 7 457 m2
Edge Length 1 480 m

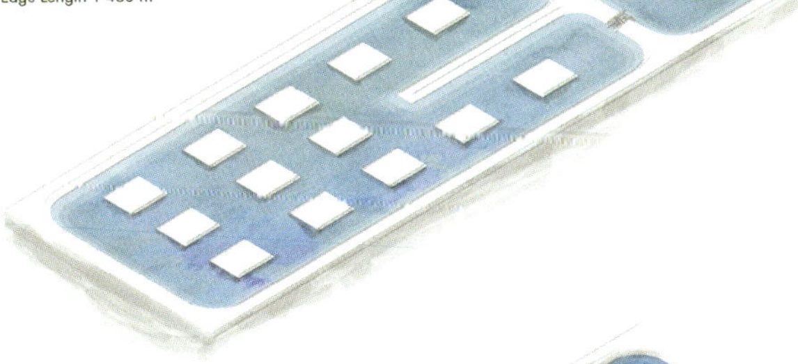

Augmented Edge
open water 28 487m2
vegetated area: 8 400m2
edge length 1 570m

Branching Baffle
Open water area: 33 764 m2
Vegetated area: 2 337m2
Edge Length 1 260m

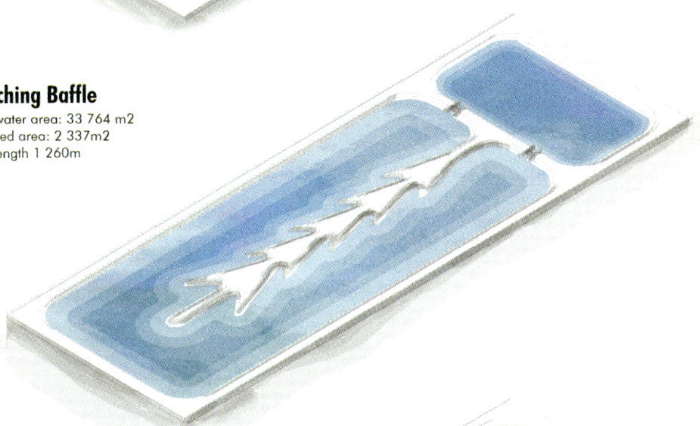

Isolated Islands
Open water area: 28 526m2
Vegetated area: 7 697m2
Edge Length 4 080m

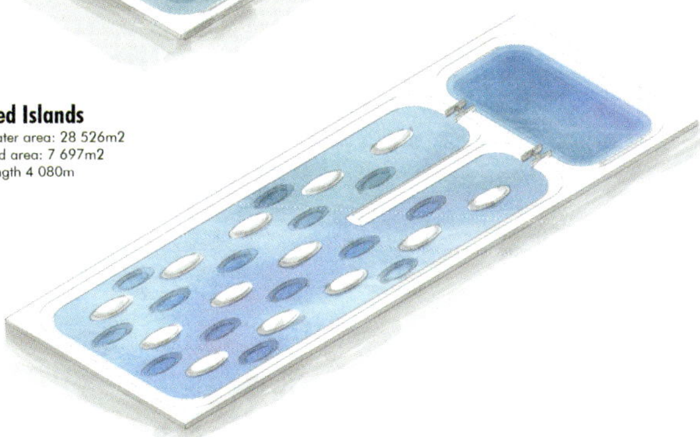

out of production in order to achieve local and federal conservation goals with private land. The Conservation Reserve Program administered by the U.S. Department of Agriculture's Farm Service Agency has successfully converted former catfish ponds back into wetland and bottomland hardwood forest. Providing similar support for farmers who improve ecological and habitat conditions on in-production farmlands would increase the possibility of addressing larger, more interconnected ecological issues.

From the MAV to the MRB

Expanding beyond the aquaculture landscapes of the Delta back out to the MAV, and further, to the full extent of the Mississippi River Basin (MRB)—this strategy of intervening in the standards of production can be applied to a variety of different agricultural contexts and address major ecological issues in this vast watershed. The standardization of agricultural landscapes affords the opportunity for transformative ecological change. Whether improving migratory bird habitat on a catfish farm in Mississippi or reducing nonpoint source runoff on a cornfield in Iowa, finding space for water in the agricultural landscape is essential.[12] Soil degradation and erosion, seasonal flooding, nonpoint source pollution and the dead zone in the Gulf could all be addressed by changes to water management in agricultural landscapes.

Conclusion

Agriculture is a leading cause of habitat loss, degradation, and fragmentation.[13] If we value natural ecosystems and wildlife we must integrate cost-effective and sustainable conservation practices into mainstream agricultural production systems worldwide. Scholarship in landscape architecture has examined the necessity of multibenefit green infrastructure in agricultural and aquacultural landscapes, but has yet to influence mainstream agricultural practices.[14] Working in the agricultural landscape at a broad scale and without a specific client is notoriously difficult and falls outside of typical landscape architectural practice.[15] In an effort to find new ways to cultivate and care for these formerly wet lands, strategies for integrating habitat and multibenefit landscape infrastructure without sacrificing economies of scale or productive capacity must make their way to farmers and into the working landscape. Advancing green/blue infrastructure design means working with policymakers, engaging government bodies at multiple scales and collaborating with the people who live and work in these landscapes. Future work should examine opportunities for federal policies to improve social equity as well as environmental outcomes. The Delta figures prominently in the U.S. history of slavery, anti-Black racism, economic growth and decline, agriculture, and hydrologic transformation. Because of these issues and the ecological importance of the Mississippi Flyway, the region demands more attention.

Acknowledgments

This research was made possible by the Graham Foundation for Advanced Studies in the Fine Arts. We are grateful to America's Catch Catfish Farm for permission to conduct fieldwork and for generously answering questions related to production, pond design, and pond management. And, we thank Emiley Switzer-Martell for research assistance as part of the University of Toronto work-study program.

[Figure 7] Speculative birds eye view of a catfish farm that has adopted split pond design concepts for waterbird habitat (image credits: Forbes Lipschitz and Justine Holzman)

1. "Mississippi Alluvial Valley," Ducks Unlimited, accessed May 15, 2020, http://www.ducks.org/Conservation/Where-Ducks-Unlimited-Works/Mississippi-Alluvial-Valley/poe/SO14.

2. S.L. King, D.J. Twedt, and R.R. Wilson, "The Role of the Wetland Reserve Program in Conservation Efforts in the Mississippi Alluvial Valley," *Wildlife Society Bulletin* 34 (2016): 914–920; Robert E. Turner and Nancy N. Rabalais, "Changes in Mississippi River Water Quality this Century: Implications for Coastal Food Webs," *BioScience* 53 (1991): 563–572.

3. Clyde Woods, *Development Arrested: Race, Power, and the Blues in the Mississippi Delta* (New York: Verso, 1998); W.E.B. Du Bois, *The Souls of Black Folk: Essays and Sketches*, introduction by Shawn Leigh Alexander (University of Massachusetts Press, 2018); Ira Berlin, *Many Thousands Gone: The First Two Centuries of Slavery in North America* (Cambridge, MA: Belknap Press of Harvard University Press, 1988).

4. Vann R. Newkirk II, "This Land Was Our Land: How Nearly One Million Black Farmers Were Robbed of Their Livelihood," *The Atlantic* (September 2019): 74–85.

5. H.M. Hagy and R.M. Kaminski, "Winter Waterbird and Food Dynamics in Autumn-Managed Moist-Soil Wetlands in the Mississippi Alluvial Valley," *Wildlife Society Bulletin* 36 (2012): 512–523.

6. Mark W. Christopher, Edward P. Hill, and David E. Steffen, "Use of Catfish Ponds by Water-Fowl Wintering in Mississippi," *Waterfowl in Winter*, ed. Milton Webster Weller (Minneapolis: University of Minnesota Press, 1988): 413–418.

7. Brian S. Dorr et al., "Double-Crested Cormorant Distribution on Catfish Aquaculture in the Yazoo River Basin of Mississippi," *Wildlife Society Bulletin* 36, no. 1 (2012): 70–77.

8. Craig. S. Tucker, David E. Brune, and Eugene L. Torrans, "Partitioned Pond Aquaculture Systems," *Journal of the World Aquaculture Society* 6 (2014): 9–17.

9. James A. Dubovsky and Richard M. Kaminski, "Waterfowl and American Coots Habitat Associations with

Mississippi Catfish Ponds," *Proceedings of Southeastern Association of Fish and Wildlife Agencies* 46 (1992): 10–17.

10. Sarah E. Lehnen and David G. Krementz, "Use of Aquaculture Ponds and Other Habitats by Autumn Migrating Shorebirds Along the Lower Mississippi River," *Environmental Management* 52, no. 2 (2013): 417–426.

11. Bruce A. Wagner, "The Epidemiology of Bacterial Diseases in Food-Size Channel Catfish," *Journal of Aquatic Animal Health* 14 (2002): 263–272.

12. Justine Holzman and Sandra Cook, "Wet Lands: Agroecological Experimentation in Essex County," in *Fresh Water*, eds. Mary Pat McGuire and Jessica M. Henson (San Francisco: Applied Research + Design Publishing, 2019), 162–171; Forbes Lipschitz, "From Drain to Delta: Green Infrastructure for Working Landscapes," in *Fresh Water*, eds. Mary Pat McGuire and Jessica M. Henson (San Francisco: Applied Research + Design Publishing, 2019), 71–81.

13. R.L. Stanton, C.A. Morrissey, and R.G. Clark, "Analysis of Trends and Agricultural Drivers of Farmland Bird Declines in North America: A Review," *Agriculture, Ecosystems & Environment* 254 (2018): 244–254; T. Tscharntke et al., "Landscape Perspectives on Agricultural Intensification and Biodiversity Ecosystem Service Management," *Ecology Letters* 8, no. 8 (2005): 857–874; Tim G. Benton et al., "Linking Agricultural Practice to Insect and Bird Populations: A Historical Study over Three Decades," *Journal of Applied Ecology* 39, no. 4 (2002): 673–687.

14. Joan Iverson Nassauer, Mary V. Santelmann, and Donald Scavia, eds., *From the Corn Belt to the Gulf: Societal and Environmental Implications of Alternative Agricultural Futures* (Washington, DC: Resources for the Future, 2007); Michael Ezban, *Aquaculture Landscapes: Fish Farms and the Public Realm* (New York: Routledge, 2020).

15. Billy Fleming speaks to this specifically, using the Army Corps as the governmental organization and "singular force" determining the form and future of water infrastructure in the U.S. despite the work of early and contemporary landscape architects who have advised otherwise. Billy Fleming, "Boxed In, Boxed Out: Water, Policy, and Design in Landscape Architecture" in *Fresh Water*, 20–25. Rob Holmes attributes this to a fixation on solutionism, while offering a number of hopeful pathways for landscape architecture to engage in landscape infrastructure: Rob Holmes, "The Problem with Solutions," *Places* (July 2020), accessed September 14, 2020, https://doi.org/10.22269/200714.

Shifting

Adjustments & Weak Spots in the Mississippi River Delta

Alexander S. Kolker

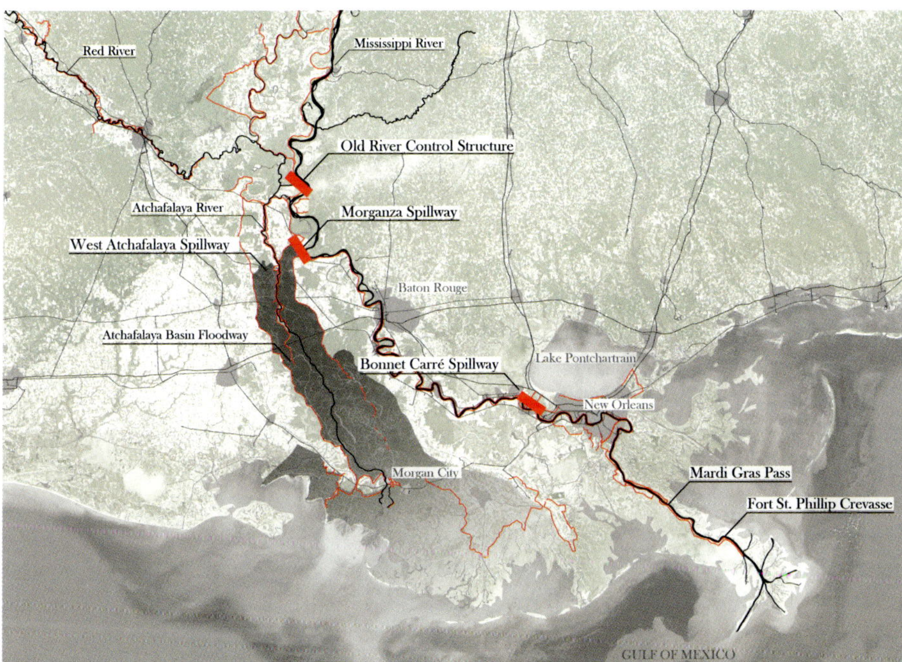

[Figure 1] Map of southeast Louisiana, featuring the Atchafalaya Basin Floodway in gray; delineating major river control structures such as Old River Control, Morganza, West Atchafalaya and Bonnet Carré Spillways and the overall levee systems, which includes "Morganza to the Gulf," in red; and, locating Mardi Gras Pass and Fort St. Philip crevasse downriver from New Orleans (image credit: Alex Kolker, Derek Hoeferlin, Chenyu Zhang)

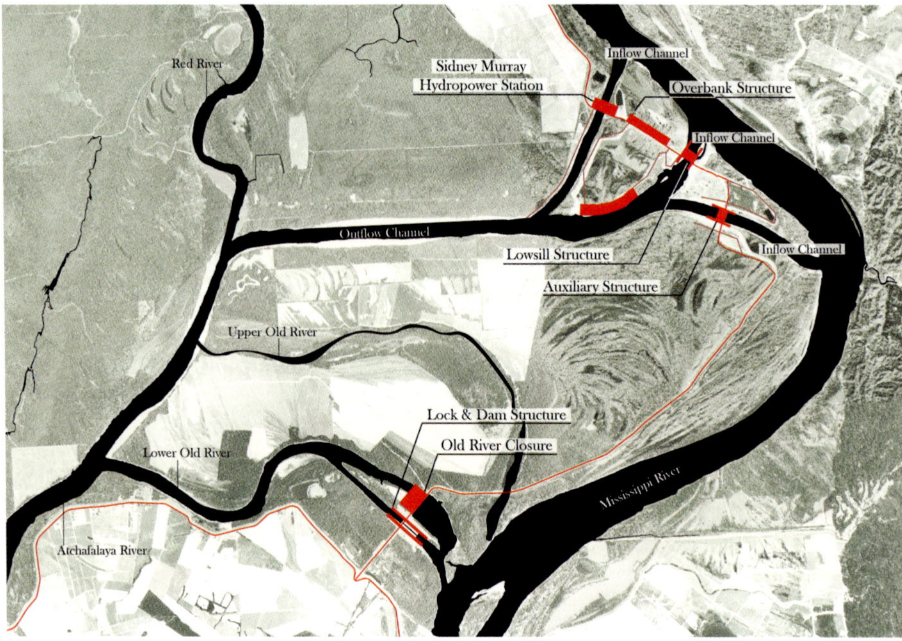

[Figure 2] Plan of Old River Control Complex, comprised of multiple structures, Louisiana (image credit: Alex Kolker, Derek Hoeferlin, Chenyu Zhang)

People who study the Mississippi River will often say that the river is likely to jump down the Atchafalaya River, switching course near the Old River Control Structure in northeastern Louisiana. If this happened, that change to the region would be dramatic. The main stem of the Mississippi River would transform into a tidal, saltwater channel, which would likely silt up, impacting shipping conditions along this heavily industrialized corridor, mostly between the urbanized areas of Baton Rouge and New Orleans. As saltwater moved up the Mississippi River, the drinking water supply for New Orleans would be impacted, likely requiring intensive desalinization efforts. The increased salinities would change the ecology of the region, transforming many freshwater and brackish systems into high salinity ones. And the lack of sediment carried by the river would make restoration in many parts of Louisiana more difficult. At the same time, such a shift would raise water levels—and river flood threats—in Morgan City in the Atchafalaya Basin. It would also increase the amount of sediment moving through the Atchafalaya Basin, resulting in large quantities of new land developing in southwest Louisiana. **[Figure 1]**

The idea that the Mississippi River will change course down the Atchafalaya is backed by important historical studies. Starting in the mid-19th century, the Atchafalaya started receiving an increasing amount of water from the Mississippi River. By the early 1950s, between 20 and 30 percent of the flow of the Mississippi River flowed through the Atchafalaya.[1] Seeing that a channel switch was likely, the U.S. Army Corps of Engineers (USACE)—at the direction of the U.S. Congress—constructed a water control structure at Old River.

The Old River Control Structure maintains the flow distribution of the two rivers at its mid-20th century condition. Seventy percent of the combined flow of the Mississippi and Red Rivers run down the main stem of the Mississippi River, and thirty percent runs down the Atchafalaya. But the Atchafalaya is a shorter distance to the Gulf than the river's main stem, making it a hydrodynamically more favorable, shorter, and steeper route. Furthermore, the Mississippi River's channel has been filling in downstream of the Old River Control Structure (likely a result of slower currents that occur after the water loss), raising the potential for a shift.[2]

This evidence suggests that a channel switch is likely. One almost occurred during the 1973 flood, as beautifully documented in John McPhee's *The Control of Nature*. McPhee writes:

> *When Dugie himself went to look at the guide wall, he looked at it for the last time. "It was slipping into the river, into the inflow channel." Slowly it dipped, sank, broke. Its foundations were gone. There was nothing below it but water. Professor Kazmann likes to say that this was when the Corps became "scared green." Whatever the engineers may have felt, as soon as the water began to recede they set about learning the dimensions of the damage. The structure was obviously undermined, but how much so, and where? What was solid, what was not? What was directly below the gates and the roadway? With a diamond drill, in a central position, they bored the first of many holes into the structure. When they had penetrated to basal levels, they lowered a television camera into the hole. They saw fish.*[3]

There are also good reasons to think that a change of course here is not imminent. First, the Old River Control Structure is a massive and well-monitored complex. **[Figure 2]** The Old River Control Structure is actually a combination of multiple separate structures: Low Sill Structure, Auxiliary Structure, Overbank Structure, and Sidney Murray Hydropower Station, totaling over 4,300 feet in length, with the capability of moving nearly 700,000 cubic feet of water per second. **[Figures 3-6]** The Auxiliary Structure was added and made operational in 1986 to relieve pressure on the system, thereby reducing the repeat likelihood of the kind of event that occurred during the 1973 flood. The furthest upstream of these three structures also functions as the hydroelectric plant. Since the Old River Control Structure is a gated system, the flow can be managed when the river gets high. The presence of the Morganza Spillway, which can carry almost as much water as can flow through the Old River Control Structure, offers another way to reduce water pressures just to the south. **[Figure 7]** Further west, the West Atchafalaya Spillway adds another relief valve. Sedimentation along the main stem of the Mississippi River could probably be removed with a large dredging project. A channel switch near Old River would probably require both a large flood and a large level of neglect. While the literature does not have an exact figure on the level of neglect or the size of the flood required to cause a channel switch, moderate to large floods have occurred every one to two years over the past decade, with little overall threat to the stability of the Old River Control Structure.

(TOP)

[Figure 3] Low Sill Structure **[Figure 4]** Auxiliary Structure

(BOTTOM)

[Figure 5] Overbank Structure **[Figure 6]** Sidney Murray Hydropower Station

(image credit: Derek Hoeferlin)

So where else might the river switch course?
Are there other weak spots in the system?

The notion that there might be multiple points of instability is hardly farfetched. Before the modern era of levee building, there were nearly 70 outflow channels along the Mississippi River.[4] **[Figure 8]** These channels sent water, sediment, and energy away from the main channel, often reducing the likelihood of a major jump downstream. Today, depending on exactly how one counts channels, there are fewer than two dozen—mostly near the river's mouth. Aside from the rarely used used Morganza and Bonnet Carré Spillways and two small river diversions (the Caernarvon and Davis Pond Freshwater Diversions), there are no outflow channels in the nearly 250-mile reach between the Old River Control Structure and the Bohemia Spillway, which is about 70 miles downstream of New Orleans.

So where are these points of instability?

One of the largest points of instability is the crevasse complex at Fort St. Philip, located about 75 miles downstream of New Orleans. This opened around the time of the 1973 flood. Over the intervening decades, it has evolved from a small cut to a large

(TOP)

[Figure 7] Morganza Spillway (image credit: Derek Hoeferlin) **[Figure 8]** Historic channels in the lower Mississippi River Delta (image credit: Welder, F.A., 1955, *Deltaic Processes in Cubits Gap Area, Plaquemines Parish, Louisiana*, Louisiana State University, Baton Rouge, pp119)

(BOTTOM)

[Figure 9] Fort St. Philip crevase complex (image credit: Alex Kolker, in association with Southwings)

[Figure 10] Mardi Gras Pass (image credit: Alex Kolker, in association with Southwings)

system with nearly a dozen channels, many of which carry 10,000 to 25,000 cubic feet per second of water. **[Figure 9]** At high flow the total flow of the channels reaches 150,000 cubic feet per second, and possibly more, making that flow approximately one of the ten largest rivers in the United States.[5] A few miles north of Fort St. Philip is a smaller but publicized system called the Mardi Gras Pass, which has some similar hydrological features. **[Figure 10]**

While the Fort St. Philip crevasse complex is highly understudied, we have some insights into its potential for an avulsion (the technical term for a channel switch). On one hand, the system has grown substantially over the last four decades. This growth follows some of the typical patterns of avulsion development. As channels grow, they draw more water from the main river, which erodes the surrounding river bank and bed, causing the system to grow, which causes more erosion. This leads to a feedback loop that only stops once the channel has switched completely, and land begins to build on the downstream side.[6] Given the rapid growth of the complex, one must assume

[Figure 11] High Mississippi River stage, Crescent Park, Bywater, New Orleans, Louisiana, 2019 (image credit: Derek Hoeferlin)

[Figure 12] High Mississippi River stage, French Quarter, New Orleans, Louisiana, 2019 (image credit: Derek Hoeferlin)

that this process is at least partially underway.[7] That said, many of the channels by Fort St. Philip and the surrounding banks of the Mississippi River are armored with a combination of rocks and concrete, a low-tech solution that has prevented a major switch. Given the multiple high-river events that have occurred along the Mississippi River in the past decade, it's possible that this armoring has done the trick. A final possibility is that a switch might only occur when there are multiple high-water events occurring at the same time, like a hurricane striking while the river is high. This would not only stress the crevasses at Fort St. Philip, but it would also put pressures on the levees across the Lower Mississippi River.

The Mississippi River and Tributaries System—the bureaucratic name for the system of levees and outlets along the Lower Mississippi River—is well-designed to handle a large river flood. Indeed, across the region the system can handle about 10 percent more water than the 1927 flood, which is the largest flood on record. Near New Orleans, this means that water levels are kept below a river stage of 17 feet, and the levees are rated to protect the city to floods of 20 feet high. **[Figures 11 & 12]**

But there is a weak spot. The system is not designed to manage a large river volume and a tropical storm striking at the same time. Hurricanes can send a storm surge up the Mississippi River. Hurricane Katrina pushed a roughly 14-foot surge up the river, and Hurricane Isaac pushed an 8-foot surge up the river.[8] These storms did not stress the Mississippi River levees, as they occurred when the Mississippi River was low. (During Katrina, of course, other poorly constructed levees across the region failed.) Should a hurricane cause an 8 or 10-foot surge along the Mississippi River, coupled with a 15-foot river stage (a level common during floods), the result could be highly problematic, stressing crevasses like Fort St. Philip and river levees across south Louisiana.

There are important climatic controls on floods, and the chance of a hurricane and a river flood occurring simultaneously is somewhat unlikely. River floods typically occur in spring when the tropics are quiet, and hurricanes tend to occur in late summer when the river is low. However, as climate warms and the global hydrological cycle intensifies, the chances of this double threat increase. Furthermore, rising sea levels, sinking lands, and channel infilling along the Mississippi River can all raise water heights in the channel relative to the same volume of flow, further pressuring river levees.[9]

While levees along the Mississippi River reduce the day-to-day risk of flooding, they can also increase stress on the system. By preventing water from leaving the river's channel, levees along the Mississippi River raise the height of the water in the river's channel.[10] This creates additional pressure on the levees themselves. The Mississippi River and Tributaries System is engineered to account for these additional stresses on a day-to-day basis, and in most floods.[11] This effect becomes more concerning in conditions like the co-occurrence of a river flood and hurricane, the development of a natural crevasse like Mardi Gras Pass, or the Fort St. Philip crevasse complex, or, as mentioned below, seepage underneath the levee.

While water flowing over levees is a concern, water flowing under levees can sometimes be a bigger one. Water that flows under levees can undermine them, leading to a blowout. This water flow is by nature hard to detect, and yet it can occur across the river. Groundwater flow along the Mississippi River appears to be a function of both the modern human-made levees and the historic geology of the Mississippi River. The Mississippi River's levees keep river water elevated—often higher than the surrounding land. Near New Orleans, the difference between the river's height at flood stage and the surrounding wetlands and urban areas is about 15 feet, and sometimes more. Near St. Francisville, that difference can approach 40 feet. This height differential creates a lot of water pressure. Under this pressure, water will try to find a weak spot through which it can flow. These weak spots are often sand bodies left behind by old river courses, or pockets of debris. When water and sand flow through to the dry side of the levee, the system is referred to as a sand boil. Sand boils, if left unattended, can grow, and lead to a collapse of the levee. **[Figure 13]**

Will such a break happen, and can anything be done to prevent them? On one hand, the federal standards for fill material to build levees call for very high clay contents, which reduces the possibility of structural problems. These standards were increased after Hurricane Katrina, as water flowing underneath the levees was one of the likely causes of levee collapse. On the other hand, the Mississippi River levees represent over 150 years of construction, and weak spots from earlier times may exist.[12]

The potential for a sand boil can be reduced through river operations. For example, certain activities along the Mississippi River, like driving piles for construction, are forbidden near the river when it is high. The USACE also regularly monitors for sand boils when the river is high. If sand boils do occur, there are things that can be done to prevent them, such as drilling relief wells, or using construction techniques to equilibrate the pressure. The near-term chance of a catastrophic sand boil is probably low. However, large volumes of water, possibly as much as 10 percent of the river at high water, flow underneath the river levees and into the surrounding bays and wetlands. Since much of the area around the river is wetland and water, finding sand boils here may be difficult. The Mississippi River levee system incurred nearly $2 billion in damages during the large 2011 flood, and part of that damage was from sand boils.

Conclusion

There is a saying that water will eventually find a way around an obstacle. In the modern Mississippi River, it may be more accurate to say that water is always searching for a way. The river carries a massive amount of water. Several times this century the combined flow of the Mississippi and Atchafalaya Rivers has exceeded two million cubic feet per second. When this quantity of water is kept elevated behind levees, it leads to massive water pressure, and river water searches for the lower ground, and the lower pressure.

There are many places where water's search for lower pressure is taking place: at the Old River Control Structure, at Fort St. Philip, at Mardi Gras Pass, and in sandy or organic-filled channels underneath the river levee. Whether it will find a way depends on both the physics of the water, and the actions—or inactions—of humankind. These actions are substantial and involve everything from large-scale construction projects to complex hydrodynamic computer models. We do not always know if water will find a troubling pathway to lower ground, but we know it is searching for a way.

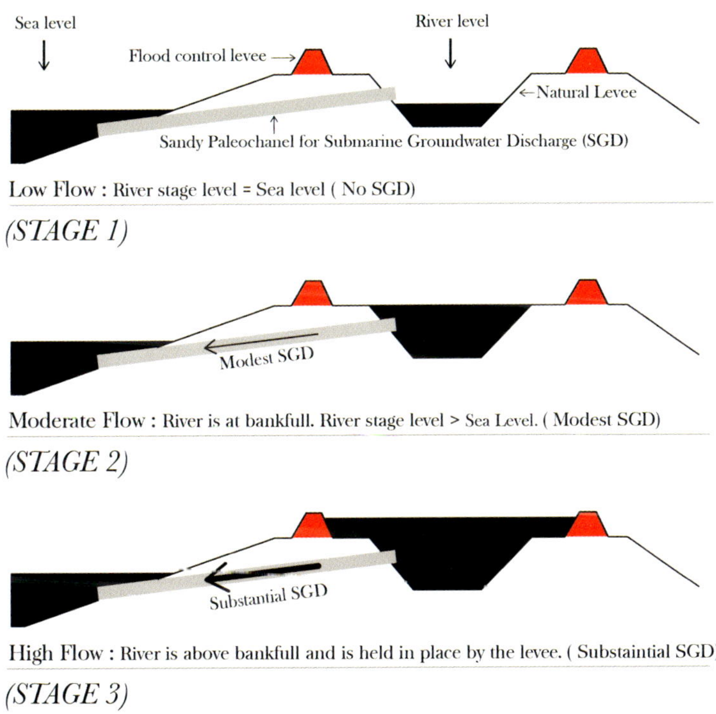

[Figure 13] Schematic of how water from the Mississippi River flows underneath levees, potentially create areas of seepage and structure weakness (image credit: Alex Kolker, et al., 2013, re-drawn by Chenyu Zhang)

1. Robert H. Meade and John A. Moody, "Causes for the decline of suspended-sediment discharge in the Mississippi River system, 1940–2007," *Hydrological Processes* 24 (2010): 35–49; and Waterways Experiment Station, United States Army Corps of Engineers, and U.S.E.D., *Geological Investigation of the Atchafalaya Basin and the Problem of Mississippi River Diversion* (Vicksburg, Mississippi: 1952).

2. Bo Wang, Y. Jun Xu, Wei Xu, Heqin Cheng, Zhongyuan Chen, Weiguo Zhang, "Riverbed Changes of the Uppermost Atchafalaya River, USA—A Case Study of Channel Dynamics in Large Man-Controlled Alluvial River Confluences," *Water* 12, no. 8, 2139 (July 2020).

3. John McPhee, *The Control of Nature* (New York: Farrar, Straus, and Giroux, 1989).

4. Jaia Syvitski and Yoshiki Saito, "Morphodynamics of Deltas under the Influence of Humans," *Global and Planetary Change* 57, no 3-4 (2007): 261–282.

5. H. Dallon Weathers, III, Mead A. Allison, C.G. Ramachandiran, and Brendan Yuill, "Water and Sediment Dynamics in the Fort St. Philip Crevasse During the 2016 Highwater Event," *State of the Coast Conference* (2016).

6. Harry H. Roberts, "Dynamic Changes of the Holocene Mississippi River Delta Plain: The Delta Cycle," *Journal of Coastal Research* 13 (1997): 605–627.

7. Glenn M. Suir, William R. Jones, Adrienne L. Garber, John A. Barras, 2014, "Pictorial account and landscape evolution of the Crevasses near Fort St. Philip, Louisiana," *Mississippi River Geomorphology & Potomology Program* Report #2 (2014).

8. Data were accessed from rivergauges.com for the Mississippi River at New Orleans (Carrolton), and from waterdata.usgs.gov/la/nwis/ for the Mississippi River at Belle Chasse.

9. Alexander S. Kolker, Jaye E. Cable, Karen H. Johannesson, Mead A. Allison, Lorna V. Inniss, "Pathways and processes associated with the transport of groundwater in deltaic systems," *Journal of Hydrology* 498 (2013): 319–334; and, Charles D. Little, Jr., David Biedenharn, "Mississippi River Hydrodynamic and Delta Management Study (MRHDM) Geomorphic Assessment," U.S. Army Corps of Engineers, Engineer Research and Development Center (2014): 309.

10. Jonathan A. Ashley, James W. Lewis, "Executive summary Mississippi River and Tributaries flowline assessment," *Mississippi River Geomorphology & Potomology Program,* Tech Note no. 7 (2018).

11. An Li, Frank T.-C. Tsai, Brendan Yuill, Chenliang Wu, "A three-dimensional stratigraphic model of the Mississippi River Delta, USA: implications for river deltaic hydrogeology," *Hydrogeology Journal* 28 (2020): 2341–2358.

12. Jason S. Alexander, Richard C. Wilson, W. Reed Green, "A brief history and summary of the effects of river engineering and dams on the Mississippi River System and Delta," *Circular 1375, U.S. Geological Survey* (2012).

(NEXT PAGE)

Waters of the Mississippi River (image credit: Derek Hoeferlin)

Mekong River Basin & the World

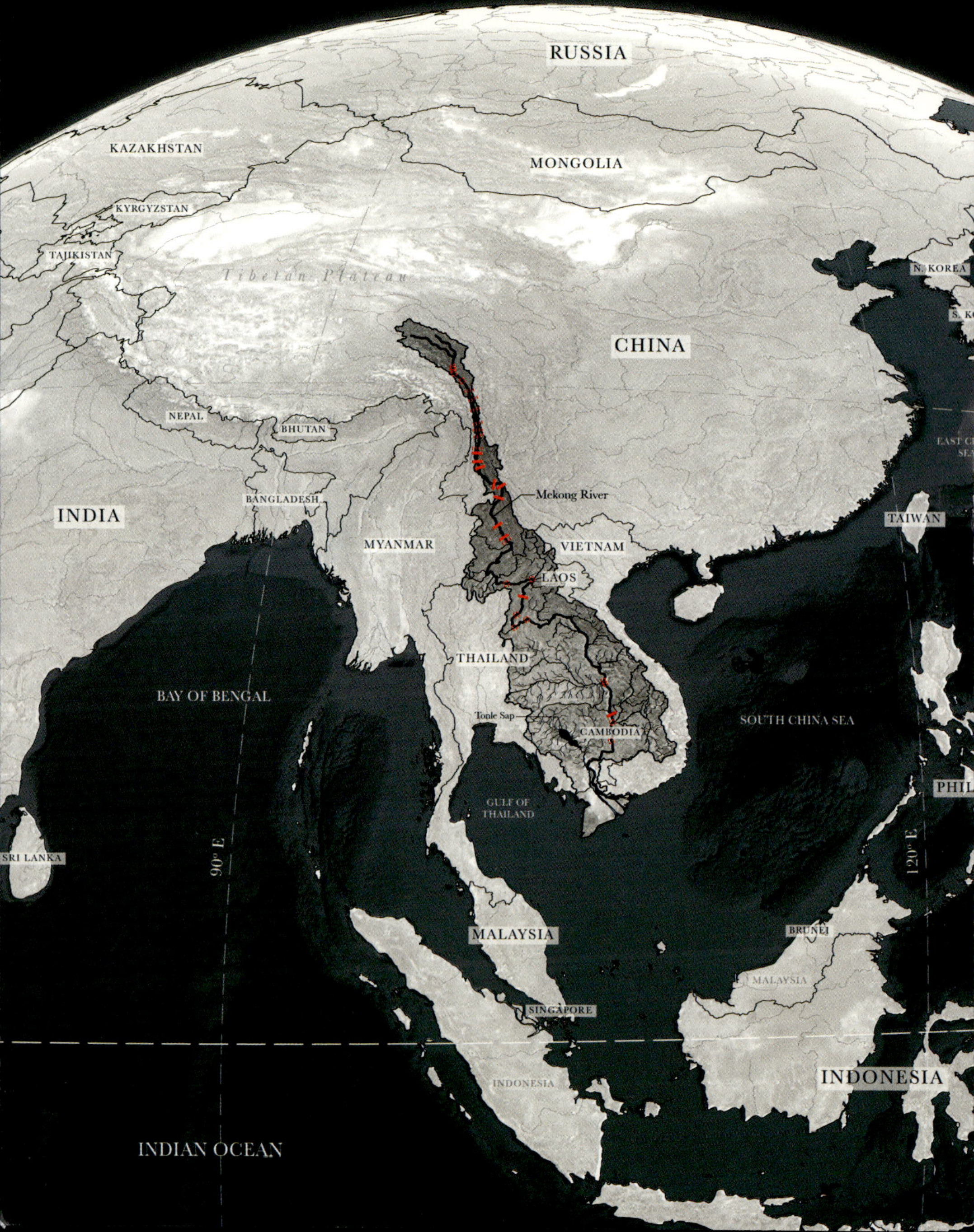

Quoting the Mekong River Commission:

Among the world's river basins, only the Amazon possesses a greater diversity of plants and animals [than the Mekong, which has the world's largest inland fishery]. On average, an astounding 15,000 cubic meters of water flow into the Mekong mainstream from the surrounding basin area every second—enough to meet the daily needs of 100,000 people. The water irrigates large tracts of forest and wetlands that produce building materials, medicines, and food and serve as habitats for thousands of species.

Continent 02: Mekong River Basin & Asia

Continent 02 Plan

The Mekong River Basin (MRB) is a crucial river system for Southeast Asia. From source to mouth, the Mekong River has a total length of 3,000 miles, and its watershed has a total catchment area of 307,000 square miles.[1] The Mekong River travels in a north-south direction through Southeast Asia and discharges into the Pacific Ocean. Divided into a lower and upper section, it travels through six countries: China, Myanmar, Laos, Thailand, Cambodia, and Vietnam. The Mekong shares its source in the Tibetan Plateau, nicknamed the "Third Pole," with many other significant river systems originating in Asia. On average, the Mekong River discharges 570,000 cubic feet of water every second, but this number fluctuates as the volume of precipitation changes seasonally.[2] In comparison to the Mississippi River, the Mekong River is almost identical in length and water volume but the watershed is at a quarter the size, making the Mekong similarly abundant in water resources at a higher concentration and intensity due to its smaller basin. The MRB is one of the most biodiverse rivers in the world and as well as one of the most productive in terms of fisheries.[3] A 2005 study estimated that the population living in the MRB was over 72 million and projected to grow in the 21st century.[4] Energy demand is also increasing, as economies adjust alongside human populations.[5] Currently, the main stem of the Mekong River is undergoing a dramatic change in character. The first main-stem hydroelectric dam was completed in the mid-1990s.[6] By 2020, 10 main-stem hydroelectric dams were constructed with an additional 21 either under construction or planned for the near future. Of the completed projects, eight are in China on the upper Mekong River and the two most recent dams were completed on the lower Mekong River in Laos. While the development of the Mekong's hydroelectric potential has undoubtedly benefited the continent's growing energy needs, it also is criticized for not fully addressing the impact on the environment, ecology, and hydrology of the river, and the resulting consequences on social and political dynamics in the basin.[7] The damming of the Mekong River will have immeasurable effects on the environment and politics of Southeast Asia for the foreseeable future.

Continent 02 Section A-A

With the ongoing construction of main-stem dams, the Mekong River is in a transformative state, and the management of its water resources has become a vital issue. Depending on various interest groups' agendas, whether it attempts to develop projects responsibly is uncertain. The Mekong River begins its journey in the Tibetan Plateau, surrounded by many of Asia's most significant rivers, including the Brahmaputra, Irrawaddy, Ganges, Yangtze, and Yellow. By the time it discharges into the Pacific Ocean, the Mekong passes through six countries. Both a challenge and an opportunity, the Mekong is the longest river in Southeast Asia and the most transboundary. In the beginning, all main-stem projects were solely led by China. But the Mekong River Commission (MRC) has recently emerged as the leading intergovernmental body responsible for managing the Mekong River Basin.[8] The core countries that comprise the MRC are Laos, Thailand, Cambodia, and Vietnam, while China and Myanmar are involved as dialogue partners.[9] In addition to generating hydropower, the dams offer additional benefits and security for irrigation, navigation, flood control, and recreation.[10] In an effort to reduce ecological risk while maximizing the economic benefits of developing the Mekong, the MRC created a comprehensive basin plan, which is primarily designed for its core members, and is consistently updated. The main priority of the MRC is to establish a framework for cooperation and coordination of main-stem dam development in order to ensure it is done responsibly, equitably, and sustainably.[11] However, the assumption that dam construction will be profitable has been disputed by critics who argue that the opposite could happen. The potential disruption to the water cycle could very well lead to a decline in the Mekong's natural resources, with a significant impact on fisheries. Ultimately, this will create a net negative economic outlook.[12] In 2020, the Mekong experienced its second consecutive year of record low water flows in the dry season and a delayed start to the wet season, a particularly devastating event for farmers in the delta region.[13] Early studies into the 2020 drought blame the construction of dams for withholding water during this period, exacerbating the effects of the drought.[14] Historically "water rich," the Mekong now suffers from the effects of water scarcities as well. While the damming of the Mekong River undeniably offers burgeoning economies many of the obvious benefits of "modernization," the recent droughts begin to underscore the importance of cooperation between all six countries in the responsible development and sustainable utilization of Southeast Asia's shared water resources.

Song Dao canal, Chau Doc near Bassac River, An Giang Province, Mekong Delta, Vietnam, 2011
(image credit: Derek Hoeferlin)

Yangtze River, Yunnan Province, China (2007)

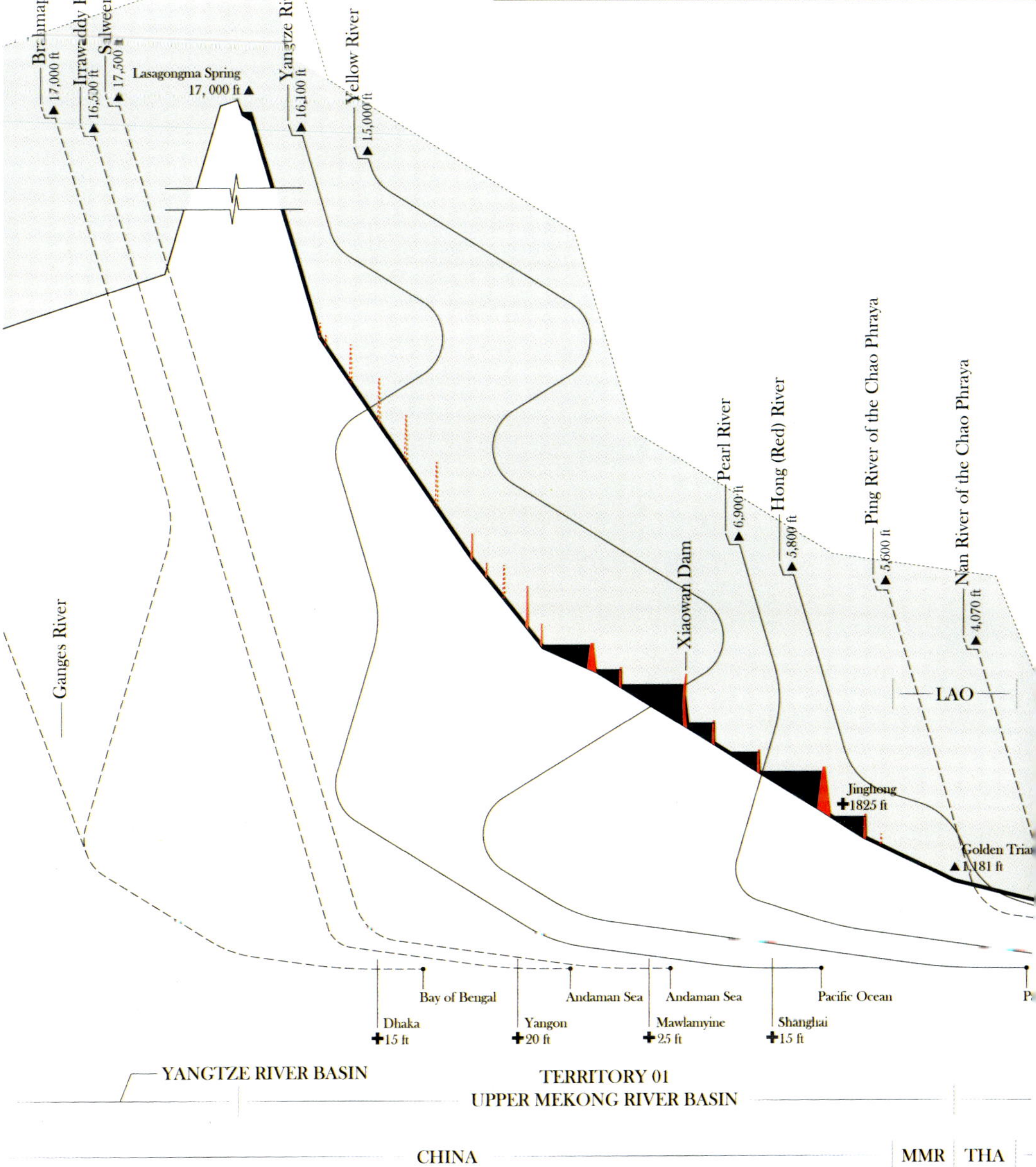

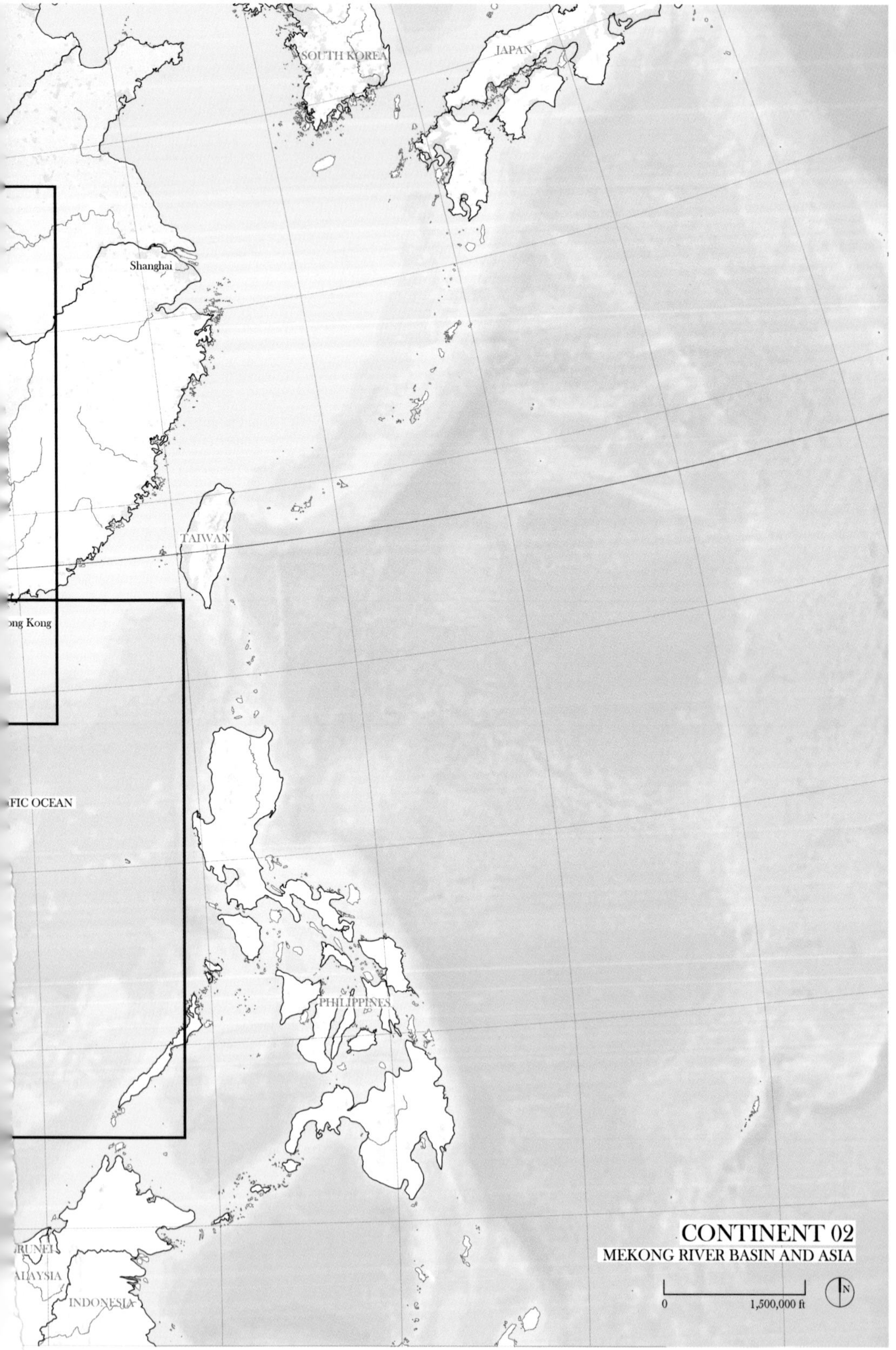

CONTINENT 02

MEKONG RIVER BASIN AND ASIA

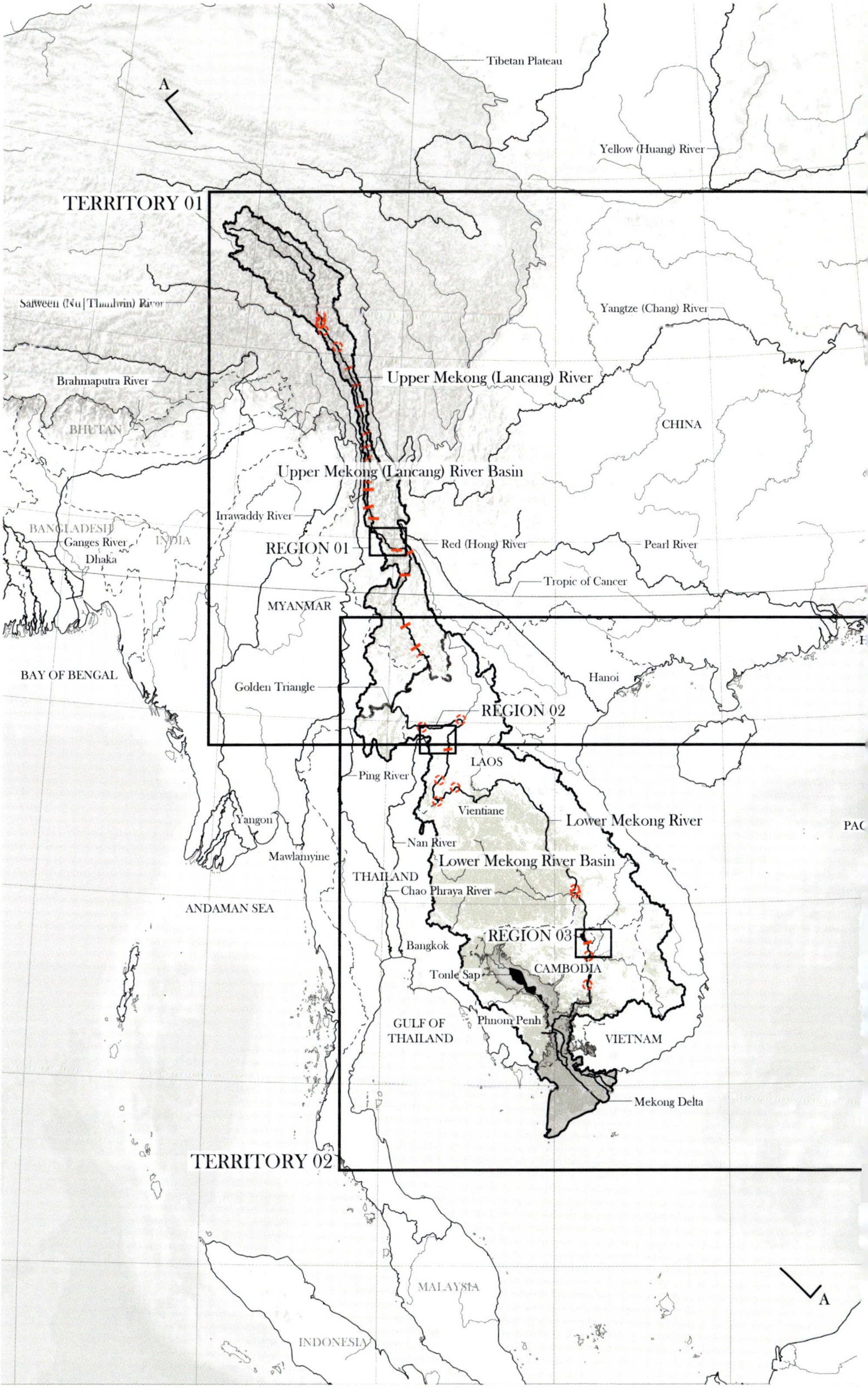

Tibetan Plateau
A
Yellow (Huang) River
TERRITORY 01
Salween (Nu|Thanlwin) River
Yangtze (Chang) River
Upper Mekong (Lancang) River
Brahmaputra River
BHUTAN
CHINA
Upper Mekong (Lancang) River Basin
Irrawaddy River
BANGLADESH
Ganges River
INDIA
Dhaka
REGION 01
Red (Hong) River
Pearl River
Tropic of Cancer
MYANMAR
BAY OF BENGAL
Golden Triangle
Hanoi
REGION 02
LAOS
Ping River
Vientiane
Lower Mekong River
Yangon
Nan River
Mawlamyine
Lower Mekong River Basin
THAILAND
Chao Phraya River
ANDAMAN SEA
REGION 03
Bangkok
CAMBODIA
Tonle Sap
GULF OF THAILAND
Phnom Penh
VIETNAM
Mekong Delta
TERRITORY 02
MALAYSIA
A
INDONESIA

Mekong River, Laos (2019)

Sluice Gate, Mekong Delta, Vietnam (2011)

SECTION A-A

FOLLOWING THE PATH OF THE MEKONG RIVER

1. *Planning Atlas of the Lower Mekong River Basin* (Vientiane: Mekong River Commission, 2011), accessed January 25, 2021, https://www.mrcmekong.org/assets/Publications/basin-reports/BDP-Atlas-Final-2011.pdf, 3.
2. "The Flow of the Mekong" (Vientiane: Mekong River Commission, November 2009), accessed November 9, 2020, http://www.mrcmekong.org/assets/Publications/report-management-develop/MRC-IM-No2-the-flow-of-the-mekong.pdf, 4.
3. Kirk Winemiller et al., "Balancing Hydropower and Biodiversity in the Amazon, Congo, and Mekong," *Science* 351, no. 6269, (January 8, 2016): 128–29; Robin Welcomme et al., "Fisheries of the Rivers of Southeast Asia," in *Freshwater Fisheries Ecology*, 1st ed., 363–76 (Hoboken, NJ: Wiley, 2016), 373.
4. Sokhem Pech and Kengo Sunada, "Population Growth and Natural Resources Pressures in the Mekong River Basin," *Ambio* 37, no. 3 (May 2008): 219–24.
5. "Integrated Water Resources Management-Based Basin Development Strategy: For the Lower Mekong Basin" (Vientiane: Mekong River Commission, April 20, 2012), accessed November 9, 2020, http://www.mrcmekong.org/assets/Publications/strategies-workprog/BDP-Basin-Dev-Strategy-2013-Eng.pdf, 14.
6. "1995 Mekong Agreement and Procedural Rules" (Vientiane: Mekong River Commission, May 21, 2018), accessed November 9, 2020, https://www.mrcmekong.org/assets/Publications/MRC-1995-Agreement-n-procedures.pdf, iv.
7. Robert Constanza et al., "Planning Approaches for Water Resources Development in the Lower Mekong Basin" (Portland: Portland State University Institute for Sustainable Solutions, July 1, 2011), accessed November 9, 2020, https://pdxscholar.library.pdx.edu/cgi/viewcontent.cgi?article=1006&context=iss_pub, 40.
8. "1995 Mekong Agreement and Procedural Rules," 3.
9. Ibid., i.
10. Ibid., 6.
11. Ibid., 4.
12. Richard Frankel, Apisom Intralawan, and David Wood, "Economic Evaluations of Hydropower Projects in the Lower Mekong Basin" (Vientiane: Mekong River Commission, 2017), accessed November 9, 2020, https://www.mrcmekong.org/assets/Uploads/Final-report-Mekong-Study-March-2017-8.pdf, 13–14.
13. "Situation Report: Hydrological Conditions in the Lower Mekong River Basin in January-July 2020" (Vientiane: Mekong River Commission, August 2020), accessed November 9, 2020, https://www.mrcmekong.org/assets/Publications/Situation-report-Jan-Jul-2020.pdf, 1.
14. Hannah Beech, "China Limited the Mekong's Flow. Other Countries Suffered a Drought," *New York Times* (September 25, 2020), accessed November 9, 2020, https://www.nytimes.com/2020/04/13/world/asia/china-mekong-drought.html.

Development

Geopolitics and Regionalism in Southeast Asia

Dorothy Tang

[Figure 1] Example of new infrastructure on the Mekong River, Laos, 2019 (image credit: Derek Hoeferlin)

"Have you seen the water levels of the Mekong?" my guide asked me. "It has never been so low before!" Throughout my fieldwork in Phnom Penh in early 2020, observations of the historic and perilously low water levels of the Mekong River were a constant conversation starter whether with friends, interlocutors, or local scholars. There was no clear consensus of the cause. Some thought it was an unusually dry year, while others blamed dam building on the upper reaches of the river in China. Suspicion of China's role in the severe drought in the Mekong Region seemed to be confirmed in April when American climatologists released a report suggesting that the Chinese government had indeed withheld water resources on the upper reaches of the Lancang River in 2019, resulting in a record low of water flow in the Lower Mekong Basin.[1] What ensued was a battle of scientific data between U.S.-backed scientists and Chinese researchers, each calling for transparency and claiming legitimacy,[2] all the while rekindling the embers of geopolitical conflict along the Mekong from the Cold War.[3]

Southeast Asia, particularly the Mekong Region, has long been a theater for competing global powers. Thailand's modern borders were demarcated as a result of confrontations with British Burma and French Indochina in the 19th century when Siam adopted Western surveying and mapping technologies to delineate once porous border regions with other Southeast Asian kingdoms.[4] Japanese imperialist ambitions in the region during the Second World War renewed its geopolitical significance.[5] This resulted in proxy wars during the Cold War, especially evident in the Vietnam War (1955–1975), where China-backed Communist troops were in direct conflict with the U.S. It was during this time that the Committee for the Coordination of the Investigations of the Lower Mekong Basin (known as the Mekong Committee)—an alliance of the riparian nations of Vietnam, Laos, Cambodia, and Thailand—was formed to manage the abundant and untapped water resources of the Mekong River.

The Mekong Committee, now known as the Mekong River Commission, is the precursor to infrastructure-led international cooperation within mainland Southeast Asia. New regional development projects have since formed, acknowledging the full extent of the Mekong's watershed region, such as the Asian Development Bank's (ADB) Greater Mekong Subregion Economic Corridors in 1992, and the Chinese-led Lancang Mekong Cooperation Project from 2016. Both have promoted economic development and international cooperation through infrastructural investment. China's sweeping Belt and Road Initiative (BRI) of 2013 aims to reconnect historic maritime and overland silk roads connecting to Western Europe and Eastern Africa. Southeast Asia is a key site for the BRI not only due to the territorial disputes along the South China Sea, but more importantly because of the terrestrial connection between China's relatively underdeveloped southwest provinces to the Mekong Region.[6] The BRI, despite its lack of coordination and ineffective impact, has been largely criticized by the West as blatantly imperialist and a vehicle for debt-trap diplomacy—a scenario in which borrowing countries cede strategic assets or political leverage due to predatory sovereign loans.[7] In the Mekong Region, Laos and Cambodia tacitly acknowledge China's hold over upstream water resources and have readily complied with Beijing's development push.[8] Thailand and Vietnam are able to maintain a fragile independence due to their locations in the watershed. **[Figure 1]**

How did transnational infrastructure come to feature so prominently in international cooperation and diplomacy? With increased conflict over scarce freshwater resources due to climate change, equitable water management and infrastructure development are important levers for negotiation and regional cooperation. How will water futures shape the geopolitics of the region? This essay explores the histories of how infrastructure defined the spatiality of the Mekong Region, the promise of modernist regional planning in addressing resource conflicts, and how globalization and discourses of free trade replaced the primacy of the watershed as a unit for economic planning.

The Functional Region and Modernist Regional Planning

> *Now, the human region existed as a fact, long before the political state know it came into existence.... In each of these natural regions, certain modes of life have arisen in adaptation to the fundamental conditions.... Regional planning ... begins with the region as a whole and it seeks to bring every capacity of the region up to its fullest state of cultivation or use.*
> *—Lewis Mumford* [9]

Regions are a critical unit for modernist urban thinkers in North America and Europe. Inspired by the biological sciences and methods of sampling along a transect, Patrick Geddes's iconic *Valley Section* of 1909 positions different human settlement patterns within its landscape context along the valley of a river from its source to the sea. **[Figure 2]** By correlating different types of settlement from primitive to civilized within specific geographies, the *Valley Section* depicts human settlement as an evolutionary process and also serves as a critique of the early 20th-century city that ignored its relationship to the natural environment.[10] This conception of cities as the evolutionary product of its landscape setting informed Lewis Mumford's work on regionalism and regional planning leading up to the New Deal. For Mumford, the region becomes a legible unit when settlements are configured based on the specificities of physical geographies and economic functions.[11] These functional regions—typically defined by natural systems such as topographical ranges or biomes—were considered the ideal scale for planning in order to manage its natural and economic resources most effectively.[12]

New Deal–era infrastructure projects such as the Hoover Dam and Tennessee Valley Authority (TVA) revolutionized the scale of engineering rivers, and also introduced a new understanding of entire river basins as productive resources and symbols for nation-building.[13] More than an infrastructure project, the TVA was framed as a regional planning effort. The TVA developed watershed management regimes that enlisted local farmers and novel forms of regional governance. Mumford and his colleagues at the Regional Planning Association of America played an influential role in these processes. All of these successful innovations made the TVA an exemplar of engineering (led by the U.S. Bureau of Reclamation), governance, economic development, poverty alleviation, and regional planning.

Despite these triumphs, postwar America emerged with a radically changed political and economic landscape. In a society that was confronting rapid urbanization, increased environmental awareness, and diminished federal capital, regional projects at

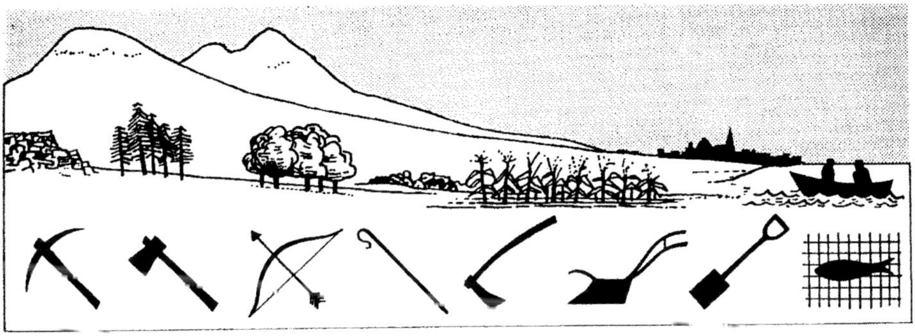

[Figure 2] "The Valley Section," (image credit: Patrick Geddes, 1909, public domain)

the scale of TVA were no longer feasible. Instead, capital and expertise were redirected to postwar reconstruction efforts abroad in the form of monetary and technical aid, and the U.S. State Department directed engineers from the Bureau of Reclamation to develop mega-infrastructure projects internationally to further U.S. diplomacy.[14] The "untapped" potential of the Mekong River Basin and U.S. interests in Southeast Asia became the perfect laboratory for TVA alumni to test the limits of comprehensive water basin management and regional planning across a fractured transnational region.

Integrated Water Basin Planning and Peace Building

> *[R]egionalism ... is above all a technique for applying science and technology systematically to a multinational region. Development of a country is inherently a process of technological application toward an economic result. Regionalism—or more precisely, regional development—introduces the idea of a system within which technology is applied more coherently to a geographic unit than to a political unit.*
> *—Franklin P. Huddle, U.S. Congressional Research Services* [15]

Established in 1957 with the express support of the United Nations and the U.S., member nations of the Mekong Committee recognized the "interdependency" of infrastructure projects along the Mekong River Basin that required unified coordination in order to effectively harness its economic potential for hydropower, irrigation, and navigation.[16] As such, the main mission of the Mekong Committee, active from 1957 to 1975, with the institutional support provided by the United Nations, was to conduct the hydrological surveys, mapping, and data collection necessary for the engineering and planning of top priority proposals—Pa Mong Dam on the border of Laos and Thailand, and the Sambor and Tonlé Sap Dams in Cambodia. With tacit acknowledgement of the ongoing Vietnam War, the UN promoted the project as "more than a symbol of international cooperation in a troubled world," with the promise of improved livelihoods and economic development for inhabitants of the Lower Mekong River Basin.[17] It implied that this massive infrastructure project of managing the Mekong River Basin transcended the geopolitical tensions that at the time were playing out in the Mekong Region, thinly disguising the ideological project of limiting the spread of Communism.

However, this ideological rhetoric to regionalism was shrouded in the apolitical language of rational planning and a scientific approach. Leading up to the UN's "decade of development" of the 1960s, the United Nations Economic Commission for Asia and the Far East (ECAFE) identified the scale of entire river basins as sites with great development potential. ECAFE published a series of technical manuals outlining the procedures of carrying out a "multiple-purpose river basin development plan" and inventories of major "international rivers" that fit well under the UN's mandate for international cooperation and development.[18] Multiple-purpose river basin development plans—following the TVA model—were distinct from prior single-purpose water resource development projects due to the technological advances of large-scale and complex engineered systems and novel forms of financing from Bretton Woods institutions such as the World Bank. This would produce power while improving river navigation; account for the ecological health of a watershed region while still providing for irrigation and water supply; and most importantly, provide an economic infrastructure for developing nations to industrialize.

These ambitious watershed-scale plans for development were made possible by the establishment of new multilateral financial institutions and the emergence of international development aid in the wake of World War II. The World Bank was established to finance postwar reconstruction and development through administering sovereign loans. This promoted the development pathways of the U.S. and Europe as a blueprint, and provided an unprecedented scale of financing available for economic infrastructure in developing nations. This momentum for building large-scale projects was furthered by bilateral and multilateral development aid—through financing and technical assistance—and motivated by postwar reparations and Cold War geopolitical competition. The U.S. played an outsized role in shaping the infrastructure development agenda in the Mekong Region through funding and technical aid, but also through its influence over the UN and the World Bank. However, Japan also gained a foothold in the Mekong Region during this time due to war reparations and as an American ally, paving the way for sustained involvement in the development and geopolitics of the region. With the convergence of technical expertise, financing, and political interests, the Mekong Committee and the ECAFE were well positioned to execute a real-time experiment in transnational river basin planning.

Given the geographical scope and scale of large river basins, the ECAFE and its collaborators were optimistic that a scientific and technologically driven approach to transboundary river basin development would form the basis for international cooperation. For the technocrats of this era, a development plan with a strong scientific basis would provide neutral ground for resource negotiations that would ultimately overcome political conflict.[19] After all, they assumed any rational process would prioritize objective interests for all parties rather than fall victim to petty politics. It is under these auspices that the Mekong Project became a flagship project for the UN and U.S. development aid.

This technological optimism found its way into two key aspects in the early work of the Mekong Committee. First, the Mekong Committee established a decision-making process that required unanimous agreement amongst all four riparian states—Thailand, Laos, Cambodia, and Vietnam—for any development project along the Mekong. This unanimous rule was intended to ensure that the extraction of water resources was equitable throughout the basin and to preserve sovereignty and self-determination amongst the four riparian nations. Furthermore, this created a nonhierarchical relationship between the four members regardless of economic or political status and a highly negotiated process that ensured progress.[20] Notably, even with the geopolitical conflict in the region and hostility between the four riparian states, the Mekong Committee did meet regularly until 1975, when Cambodia withdrew its membership under the Khmer Rouge regime. Second, the Mekong Committee received significant technical aid in the form of mappings, surveys, and monitoring, specifically from developed nations, to provide a sound scientific basis for the river basin development plan. By the late 1960s, the U.S. had committed to providing a hydrographic survey and longitudinal hydrological monitoring data. Canada carried out aerial surveys over the region, Japan surveyed the major tributaries to identify development potential, Australia created detailed geologic mapping at proposed dam sites, and France conducted soil and mineral surveys of the region.[21]

Despite the international technical aid, the accomplishments of the Mekong Committee were quite limited because of the lengthy negotiations required by unanimous rule. Only one mega-infrastructure project, the Nam Ngum Hydroelectric Scheme in Laos **[Figure 3]**, resulted from the intergovernmental efforts of the Mekong Committee, and there were some small-scale irrigation projects carried out during this time.[22] Despite this, the four riparian nations were able to complete a joint declaration regarding the utilization of water resources in the Lower Mekong Basin in 1975, guiding the development of water resources in the following decades. However, the geopolitical turbulence and realignment in Southeast Asia during the second half of the Cold War completely disrupted the coordination between the original riparian states. Although there was an Interim Mekong Committee (1978–1995) established to continue coordination of water resources, no meaningful progress was made due to the conflicting priorities of the member states, compounded by the lack of Cambodian participation.[23]

The U.S. began a long process of normalizing relations with the People's Republic of China in the late 1970s, but the ending of the Cold War in 1991 was the most significant turning point in the geopolitics of the region. With peace talks in Cambodia and friendlier relations between Vietnam and its neighbors, Thailand became a prominent economic force in the region, and China emerged as a major political and economic regional player as well. The 1990s were also a time when neoliberal fiscal policies and the global networks of post-Fordist production were coming of age. The World Bank and the IMF had begun implementing Structural Adjustment Programs (SAP) that promoted privatization, trade liberalization, and foreign investment. The focus for international financing shifted from physical infrastructure projects to other development projects, such as poverty alleviation and public health. These changes in

[Figure 3] Nam Ngum Dam, Laos (image credit: Chaoborus, CC BY-SA 3.0)

development policies, in addition to the rise of the "sustainability" discourse as a result of the environmental movement, had a longlasting influence on the new regime of river basin management in the Mekong.

The Interim Mekong Committee negotiated a new set of terms and priorities and established the Mekong River Commission (MRC) in 1995 to promote the "sustainable development" of water resources in the region. Palakorn Chanbanyong and Simon Krohn's essay in this volume detail a thorough explanation of the Mekong River Commission's activities in regard to hydropower development during this period. But it is important to note a subtle but significant conceptual shift about the role of the Mekong River. Early discussion about resources in the Mekong River Basin conceived of it as a vital natural resource ready for extraction through infrastructure development. Under the new premise of "sustainable" development, the river is no longer an economic engine, but a shared resource to be conserved and managed over time. Economic development policies now privileged infrastructure that facilitated global trade and foreign investment—and its spatial expression from the inwardly oriented river systems to externally connected forms of transportation infrastructure and urban spaces to accommodate trade and investment. With MRC's redefined role focused on the monitoring and environmental stewardship of river resources, there is no longer a political mandate for cooperation amongst the four riparian nations. Consequently, each of the riparian nations must individually manage their relationships with the U.S., China, and other global powers. Without a united front or political mandate, the MRC has little leverage in negotiating with China regarding upstream development.

Regionalism and Cooperation through Economic Corridors

Despite the decline of the Mekong River as the spatial focus of development in the mainland Southeast Asia, the geographic identity of the watershed region looms large in recent efforts for economic cooperation in the region. In 1992, the Japanese-led Asian Development Bank (ADB) initiated the "Greater Mekong Subregion (GMS)" program, expanding the scope of regional cooperation in the Mekong Basin to include

Yunnan Province (in southwest China) and Myanmar in addition to the four original riparian nations. The program proposed three sets of economic corridors crisscrossing the region to strengthen interconnectivity through transportation infrastructure projects accompanied by improved cross-border trade policies. The networked region promised to improve transnational economic exchanges and encourage foreign direct investment. The plans for each of these corridors are anchored by ports and connected to new industrial zones and existing urban centers through major transnational highways, cross-border logistical facilities, and improved communications technologies.

However, the grand vision of a hyper-connected Greater Mekong Subregion remains elusive. Its realization is uneven and fragmented due to economic disparities between nations, decentralized financing mechanisms, and the lack of a binding regional governance structure to coordinate its implementation. Although the ADB has provided technical assistance to develop a master plan for the GMS program and some financing, individual member states are still responsible for securing their own financing and implementation—the Greater Mekong Subregion Economic Corridors exists as a vision plan organized by an international policy bank and held together by a loose coalition of member states that happen to be in the watershed of the Mekong Region.

Over time, Japan has become one of the most important allies in realizing the GMS program. Japan's obligations for postwar reparations combined with strong commercial interests in the region have motivated many bilateral development assistance agreements and built a formidable pipeline for Japanese expertise, goods, and services in formerly occupied territories.[24] This engagement increased in the 1980s as Japan sought new locations for offshore manufacturing. By the end of the Cold War, Japanese institutions like the Japanese Bank for International Cooperation and the Japanese International Cooperation Agency (JICA) were major contributors to infrastructure development in the Mekong Region. More importantly, as the technical arm of development assistance, JICA has continued to promote infrastructure-led development even after its Western counterparts primarily shifted to "social" infrastructures.[25] However, the promise of physical infrastructure as an effective instrument for development and economic stimulus has endured, especially in Southeast Asia.[26] Infrastructure financing from institutions like the World Bank now have stricter financial, environmental, and social standards, making it more difficult to acquire funding for large infrastructure projects. The ADB estimates that there is an infrastructure funding gap of $27 trillion USD in Asia.[27] Japan's emphasis on economic infrastructure and robust technical assistance have partially bridged this gap. In addition, China's Belt and Road Initiative is now a major contributor to infrastructure financing, and the rhetoric of political "noninterference" and the lack of codified regulations is particularly appealing to many developing nations.[28]

The BRI's "belt" includes six economic corridors radiating from China's border regions and a maritime "road" connecting to Africa. In Southeast Asia, the China-Indochina Peninsula Economic Corridor (CICPEC) connects the southwest provinces of Yunnan, Guangxi, and Guangdong through the Mekong Region, eventually extending south to the Malaysian peninsula and Singapore. Through the BRI, China has financed major transnational projects such as the China-Laos Railway that connects Yunnan to Vientiane **[Figure 4]**, significant national projects such as the Phnom Penh–Sihanoukville expressway in Cambodia, and special economic zones for manufacturing scattered throughout Southeast Asia. However, it is worth noting that the BRI has not yet produced a master plan that publicly communicates their priorities for infrastructural investment. Upon further examination, many Chinese-financed projects in the Mekong Region are consistent with ADB's plans for the GMS economic corridors established more than a decade prior—supporting one view that the BRI is merely a vehicle to export China's excess capital and construction capacity rather than a cohesive geopolitical strategy for global influence.[29]

The BRI has challenged Japan's historical dominance in Southeast Asia, and this geopolitical rivalry is evident in the predominantly north-south corridors with Chinese financing and east-west corridors funded by the Japanese.[30] **[Figure 5]** With the rise in Sino-American tensions since 2018, the infrastructure-based BRI is a popular target for Western criticism of Chinese "economic aggression."[31] Alarmed by the increase in global infrastructure financing through the BRI, the U.S. State Department has launched its own infrastructure program in Southeast Asia[32] and has used strong language to condemn Chinese-funded projects as a threat to freedom and democracy.[33] However, U.S. influence in the Mekong Region waned during the Trump administration's "America First" agenda. The U.S. committed a paltry $113 million USD[34] to infrastructure investments in Southeast Asia in 2018, compared to China's $255 billion USD and Japan's $367 billion USD in 2019.[35] Although Japan has been a close U.S. ally since World War II, the world's third-largest economy has its own geopolitical and economic interests in the Mekong Region. Japan's tensions with China over the Senkaku/Diaoyu Islands in the East China Sea were compounded by the supply-chain disruptions of COVID-19, and prompted a national strategy to relocate industries from China to Southeast Asia, particularly Vietnam and Thailand.[36]

Conclusion: Geopolitics and Infrastructure in the Mekong

The GMS economic corridors and the BRI are both examples of how the global financial capital and offshoring have reconfigured economic regions. Rather than a shared interest in resource extraction—exemplified by the early works of the Mekong Committee—commonality is found in trade liberalization and in exploiting minute differences in labor costs. Cross-border Special Economic Zones, Industrial Estates, and other spaces of exception[37] now dominate strategies for cooperation and development. The promise of unimpeded transnational corridors as instruments of economic growth and progress[38] has structured an alternative spatial logic of urban development, land speculation, and industrialization. Moreover, the public investments in infrastructure have generated unplanned spatial products such as the opulent Golden Triangle Digital Special Economic Zone developed by an alleged Chinese drug lord in Laos **[Figures 6 & 7]**, or a construction boom in the crime-ridden Chinese gambling haven of Sihanoukville in Cambodia. The modernist functional region exists as a geographical imaginary but no longer as a development rationale; the rhetoric of regional cooperation is no longer centered on sharing resources, but rather in infrastructure that enables individual nation-states to compete for foreign investment—in all shapes and forms.

However, even with a departure from river resources as economic development, hydropolitics remain central in the Mekong Region. In 2019, the Mekong-U.S. Partnership, funded by the U.S. State Department and supported by over 60 international organizations, launched the Mekong Water Data Initiative[39] that supports the MRC through the collection and analysis of water resource data to effectively manage the Mekong River Basin. Specifically, the Mekong Dam Monitor[40] launched in December 2020, utilizes satellite imagery to monitor near-real time environmental impacts and identify anomalies in the upstream dams in China. China eventually succumbed to geopolitical pressure and has promised to provide the dam and flow data from the Upper Lancang River Dams to the MRC to facilitate international cooperation and appease lower riparian states[41], however, the provision of data does not necessarily mean a commitment to equitable management of water resources.

With the increased hostility that resulted between the U.S. and China during the Trump administration, the two nations are once again using the Mekong Region as a site for proxy wars—albeit one of data transparency. With a U.S. shift in power to the Biden administration's commitment to a return to international diplomacy, the question still remains if the U.S. and China will even attempt to normalize relations in regard to the Mekong Region. Regardless, at the heart of the problem lies a question of agency. Who is monitoring? Who funds these monitoring protocols? What technologies are deployed? And what are the political gains from these competing monitoring regimes? Given the funding sources and technologies used, the power of information and data remains in the hands of global powers such as the U.S., China, and to some degree, Japan. Other than the short period of self-determination exercised by the Mekong Committee during the Cold War, the four riparian states of the Mekong Region are now further subjected to the geopolitical and economic interests of others. Over the past two decades, each nation has chosen different alliances. Laos and Cambodia have the weakest economies and depend on China's financing for development and infrastructure. They are also the two riparian nations that are most reliant on infrastructure development along the Mekong. Vietnam has territorial disputes with China in the South China Sea, and thus leverages a productive relationship with Japan to stand their ground. Thailand, on the other hand, has one of the strongest economies in the GMS, and despite its turbulent internal politics has remained a strong U.S. ally.

The fractured geopolitics is reflected in how infrastructure is financed and the management of water resources in the Mekong River Basin. The region of the Mekong was originally made legible through the extensive monitoring, surveying, and mapping of its potential water resources throughout the 20th century, enduring bitter colonial rivalries between the British and the French, Japanese imperialism, and American efforts to contain Communism. Ironically, the same instruments are still in use to monitor the Mekong River Basin as a geographical expression of current Sino-American tensions, potentially splintering the fragile alliances and individual sovereignty of the Mekong Riparian States once again.

[Figure 4] China-Laos Railway bridge under construction, Mekong River, near Luang Prabang, Laos, 2019 (image credit: Derek Hoeferlin)

1. Alan Basist and Claude Williams, "Monitoring the Quantity of Water Flowing Through the Mekong Basin Through Natural (Unimpeded) Conditions" (Bangkok: Sustainable Infrastructure Partnership, April 10, 2020), https://558353b6-da87-4596-a181-b1f20782dd18.filesusr.com/ugd/81dff2_68504848510349d6a827c6a433122275.pdf?index=true.
2. Brian Eyler, Regan Kwan, and Courtney Weatherby, "New Evidence: How China Turned Off the Tap on the Mekong River," Stimson Center (April 13, 2020), https://www.stimson.org/2020/new-evidence-how-china-turned-off-the-mekong-tap/.
3. Kay Johnson, "Water Wars: Mekong River Another Front in U.S.-China Rivalry," Reuters (July 24, 2020), https://www.reuters.com/article/us-mekong-river-diplomacy-insight-idUSKCN24P0K7.
4. Thongchai Winichakul, "Maps and the Formation of the Geo-Body of Siam," in Asian Forms of the Nation, eds. Hans Antlov and Stein Tonnesson, Studies on Asian Topics (Richmond, Surrey: Curzon, 1996), 67–91.
5. Hiromi Mizuno, "A Kula Ring for the Flying Geese: Japan's Technology Aid and Postwar Asia," Engineering Asia: Technology, Colonial Development and the Cold War Order, ed. Hiromi Mizuno, Aaron Stephen Moore, and John Paul DiMoia (London: Bloomsbury Academic, 2018): 1–40.
6. Tim Summers, "China's 'New Silk Roads': Sub-National Regions and Networks of Global Political Economy," Third World Quarterly 37, no. 9 (September 1, 2016): 1628–43, https://doi.org/10.1080/01436597.2016.1153415.
7. Jonathan E. Hillman, The Emperor's New Road: China and the Project of the Century, Emperor's New Road (New Haven: Yale University Press, 2020); Deborah Bräutigam, "Is China the World's Loan Shark?" New York Times (April 29, 2019), sec. Opinion, https://www.nytimes.com/2019/04/26/opinion/china-

belt-road-initiative.html.

8. Richard P Cronin, "China and the Geopolitics of the Mekong River Basin: Part I," World Politics Review (March 22, 2012), https://www.worldpoliticsreview.com/articles/11761/china-and-the-geopolitics-of-the-mekong-river-basin-part-i; Richard P Cronin, "China and the Geopolitics of the Mekong River Basin: Part II," World Politics Review (March 23, 2012), https://www.worldpoliticsreview.com/articles/11766/china-and-the-geopolitics-of-the-mekong-river-basin-part-ii.

9. Lewis Mumford, "Regional Planning," Architectural Regionalism: Collected Writings on Place, Identity, Modernity, and Tradition, ed. Vincent B. Canizaro (1931; repr., New York: Princeton Architectural Press, 2006), 238, 240.

10. Volker Welter, Biopolis: Patrick Geddes and the City of Life (Cambridge, MA: MIT Press, 2002).

11. Lewis Mumford, "Regionalism and Irregionalism," Sociological Review 19, no. 4 (1927): 277–88.

12. Lewis Mumford, "The Theory and Practice of Regionalism," Sociological Review 20, no. 2 (1928): 131–41.

13. Christopher Sneddon, Concrete Revolution: Large Dams, Cold War Geopolitics, and the U.S. Bureau of Reclamation (Chicago: University of Chicago Press, 2015).

14. Ibid.

15. Franklin P. Huddle, The Mekong Project: Opportunities and Problems of Regionalism, Science, Technology, and American Diplomacy v, 70 p. (Washington: U.S. Govt. Print. Off., 1972), 1, //catalog.hathitrust.org/Record/003209381.

16. UN ECAFE, "Development of Water Resources in the Lower Mekong Basin," Flood Control Series (Bangkok: United Nations Economic Commission for Asia and the Far East, 1957), A X(5-012): 627.51 Uni No.12, United Nations ECAFE Library.

17. UN ECAFE, "Committee for the Coordination of Investigations of the Lower Mekong Basin: Cambodia, Laos, Thailand, Republic of Viet-Nam" (Pamphlet), 1966.

18. UN ECAFE, "Multiple-Purpose River Basin Development: Part 1: Manual of River Basin Planning" (New York: United Nations Economic Commission for Asia and the Far East, 1955); UN ECAFE, "A Compendium of Major International Rivers in the ECAFE Region," Water Resources Series (Bangkok: United Nations Economic Commission for Asia and the Far East, 1966).

19. W.R. Derrick Sewell, "The Mekong Scheme: Guideline for a Solution to Strife in Southeast Asia," Asian Survey 8, no. 6 (1968): 448–55.

20. Abigail Makim, "Resources for Security and Stability? The Politics of Regional Cooperation on the Mekong, 1957–2001," Journal of Environment & Development 11, no. 1 (2002): 5–52, http://www.jstor.org/stable/44318030.

21. United States Engineer Agency for Resources Inventories, Atlas of Physical, Economic, and Social Resources of the Lower Mekong Basin (New York: United Nations, 1968).

22. Jeffrey W. Jacobs, "Mekong Committee History and Lessons for River Basin Development," Geographical Journal 161, no. 2 (July 1995): 135, https://doi.org/10.2307/3059971.

23. Makim, "Resources for Security and Stability?"

24. Mizuno, "A Kula Ring for the Flying Geese."

25. Compared to Western nations, Japanese ODA favors "economic infrastructure"—physical infrastructure and economic policy—over other forms of "social infrastructure" such as education, poverty alleviation, and public health. For further data, see OECD, "Official Development Assistance (ODA)," OECD, 2020, http://data.oecd.org/oda/net-oda.htm.

26. Jago Dodson, "The Global Infrastructure Turn and Urban Practice," Urban Policy and Research 35, no. 1 (January 2, 2017): 87–92, https://doi.org/10.1080/08111146.2017.1284036.

27. Asian Development Bank, "Meeting Asia's Infrastructure Needs," 0 ed. (Manila, Philippines: Asian

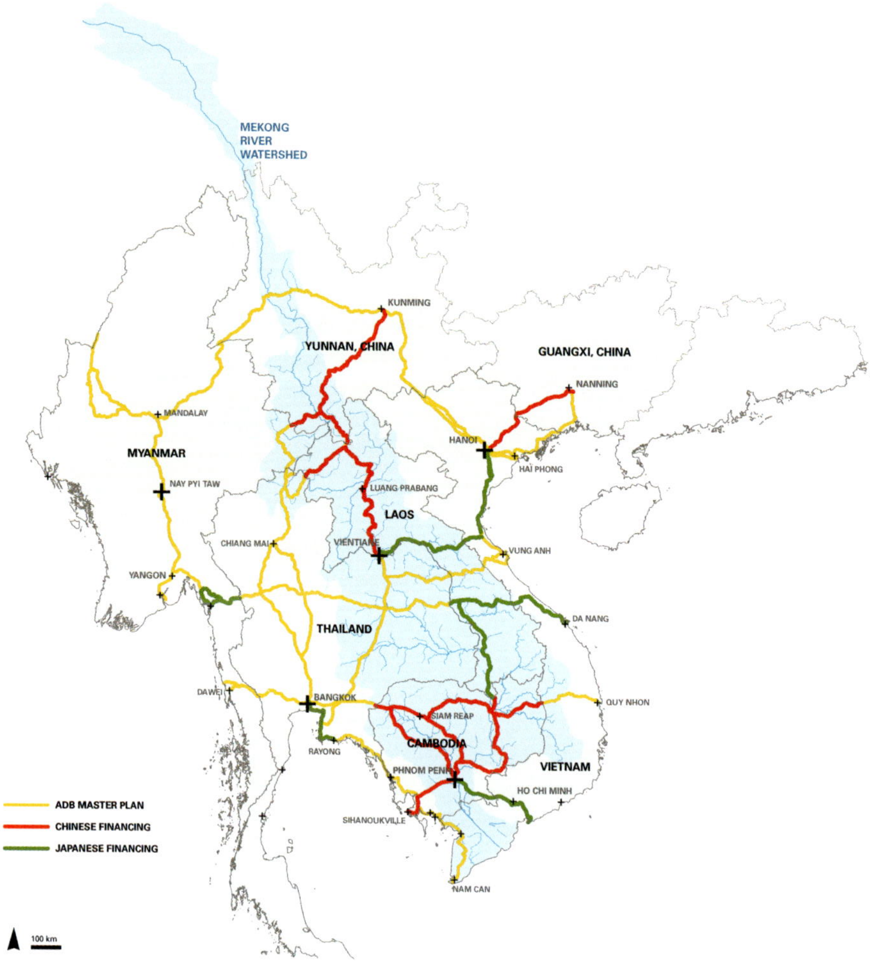

[Figure 5] Great Mekong Sub-Region Economic Corridors (image credits: sources: Stimson Center Mekong Infrastructure Tracker and Asian Development Bank; drawing by Dorothy Tang)

Development Bank, February 1, 2017), https://doi.org/10.22617/FLS168388-2.

28. Ministry of Foreign Affairs, "Vision and Actions on Jointly Building Silk Road Economic Belt and 21st-Century Maritime Silk Road," Ministry of Foreign Affairs of the People's Republic of China, 2015, http://www.fmprc.gov.cn/mfa_eng/zxxx_662805/t1249618.shtml.

29. Scholars have argued that many Chinese-funded projects are initiated by local governments and stakeholders, although often Chinese financing requires the use of a Chinese contractor and goods. Additionally, Western journalists have observed that BRI projects are poorly implemented and uncoordinated. For example, see Jonathan E. Hillman, "The Imperial Overreach of China's Belt and Road Initiative," Wall Street Journal (October 1, 2020), sec. Life, https://www.wsj.com/articles/the-imperial-overreach-of-chinas-belt-and-road-initiative-11601558851; Zhengli Huang and Xiangming Chen, "Is China Building Africa?" European Financial Review (July 2016): 7–13, http://www.europeanfinancialreview.com/?p=6110.

[Figure 6] Golden Triangle Digital Special Economic Zone, 2019 (image credit: Derek Hoeferlin)

30. Corey Wallace, "Leaving (North-East) Asia? Japan's Southern Strategy," International Affairs 94, no. 4 (July 1, 2018): 883–904, https://doi.org/10.1093/ia/iiy027.

31. The OECD's analysis of the BRI highlights U.S. concerns of Chinese "economic aggression" in various forms of infrastructure development, and calls for other nations to step in to bridge the global infrastructure gap. See OECD, "The Belt and Road Initiative in Global Trade, Investment and Finance Landscape," OECD Business and Finance Outlook 2018 (Paris: OECD, 20138), https://doi.org/10.1787/bus_fin_out-2018-6-en; White House, "How China's Economic Aggression Threatens the Technologies and Intellectual Property of the United States and the World" (Washington DC: White House Office of Trade and Manufacturing Policy, June 2018), https://www.whitehouse.gov/briefings-statements/office-trade-manufacturing-policy-report-chinas-economic-aggression-threatens-technologies-intellectual-property-united-states-world/.

32. David Brunnstrom and Lesley Wroughton, "Wary of China's Rise, Pompeo Announces U.S. Initiatives in Emerging Asia," Reuters (July 30, 2018), https://fr.reuters.com/article/us-usa-trade-idUSKBN1KK0V5.

33. Numerous exchanges between the U.S. State Department and China's Foreign Ministry illustrate the symbolic and rhetorical role of infrastructure as Sino-American tensions escalate. Michael R. Pompeo, "Secretary Michael R. Pompeo at the Three Seas Virtual Summit and Web Forum," United States Department of State, accessed January 5, 2021, https://www.state.gov/secretary-michael-r-pompeo-at-the-three-seas-virtual-summit-and-web-forum/; "Pompeo's Comments on Chinese Infrastructure in Laos Lambasted," Global Times (October 21, 2020), https://www.globaltimes.cn/content/1204256.shtml.

34. Brunnstrom and Wroughton, "Wary of China's Rise, Pompeo Announces U.S. Initiatives in Emerging Asia."

35. Bloomberg, "Japan Still Leads in Southeast Asia Infrastructure Race, Even as China Ramps up Belt and Road Investments: Report," South China Morning Post (June 23, 2019), https://www.scmp.com/news/asia/southeast-asia/article/3015732/japan-still-leads-southeast-asia-infrastructure-race-even.

[Figure 7] Golden Triangle Digital Special Economic Zone, aka "Laos Vegas," with Kings Roman Casino under construction, Laos, 2019 (image credit: Derek Hoeferlin)

36. {Citation}
37. Keller Easterling, "Zone," in Extrastatecraft: The Power of Infrastructure Space (New York: Verso, 2014), 25–70.
38. Penny Harvey and Hannah Knox, "The Enchantments of Infrastructure," Mobilities 7, no. 4 (November 2012): 521–36.we trace the disruptive and destabilising processes through which roads come to hold the promise of transformation. We approach roads with curiosity as to their capacity to enchant with respect to three specific promises: speed, political integration and economic connectivity. We suggest that whilst the abstractions of engineering and politics are provisional attempts to demarcate the capacity of roads to bring about the enhancement of international trade, promote the growth of national economies and provide economic opportunity for those prepared to engage with the road's potential, that these practices alone are not sufficient to explain the passionate promise that roads hold in Peruvian society. We suggest, rather, that the promise of stability is invigorated by mundane engagements with unruly forces that threaten to subvert the best laid plans of politicians and engineers. We argue that such forces are integral to the ways in which roads come to endure as enchanted sites of contemporary state-craft despite their capacity to disappoint and/or the likelihood of generating negative consequences. The political and material process of creating roads, calls forth competing, unauthorised and openly unstable dimensions of being – shifting soils and water courses, side-roads and short-cuts which both challenge and reinvigorate the promises of speed, integration and connectivity. [ABSTRACT FROM AUTHOR]","archive":"a9h","container-title":"Mobilities","ISSN":"17450101","issue":"4","journalAbbreviation":"Mobilities","page":"521-536","source":"EBSCOhost","title":"The Enchantments of Infrastructure.","volume":"7","author":[{"family":"Harvey","given":"Penny"},{"family":"Knox","given":"Hannah"}],"issued":{"date-parts":[["2012",1-

1]]}}}],"schema":"https://github.com/citation-style-language/schema/raw/master/csl-citation.json"}
39."Mekong Water Data Initiative," MWDI, accessed December 15, 2020, https://www.mekongwater.org.
40. Stimson Center and Eyes on Earth, "Mekong Mainstream Dam Monitor," accessed December 15, 2020, https://monitor.mekongwater.org/virtual-gauges/.
41. Kay Johnson and Matthew Tostevin, "Chinese Dams under U.S. Scrutiny in Mekong Rivalry," Reuters (December 14, 2020), https://www.reuters.com/article/mekong-river-idUSKBN28N0N4.

Territory 01: Upper Mekong River Basin

Territory 01 Plan
The Upper Mekong River Basin (UMRB) is a long and narrow territory, geologically shaped by the region's steep terrain, and altered by recent main-stem developments. The path of the upper portion of the Mekong River begins in China's Qinhai Province in the Tibetan Plateau and concludes at the tri-border point of Myanmar, Thailand, and Laos, known as the "Golden Triangle." The upper stretch is approximately 1,400 miles and drains an area of 73,000 square miles.[1] It accounts for more than half of the total length of the entire river, but only a quarter of the drainage basin. Both the upper Mekong River and its watershed are almost entirely located in China, which has a regional name for the river, the "Lancang." The river's headwaters, the Lasagongma Springs, originate in the Sanjiangyuan (or "Source of the Three Rivers"), where the Yellow and Yangtze Rivers also begin. While the Yellow and Yangtze travel to the east and remain exclusively in China, the Mekong travels in a southeast direction, where it is flanked by the Irrawaddy and Hong (Red) Rivers. Due to the mountainous terrain in this UMRB, only a few small cities have been established in the watershed, but countless villages are dotted along its riverbanks. In total, the UMRB contributes 16 percent of the annual water flow in the river, which peaks at 40 percent during the dry season, and it also supplies up to half of all the sediment in the Mekong River.[2] As a result, the UMRB has been disproportionately developed in terms of main-stem hydropower. Since the late 20th century, China has been constructing hydroelectric dams in the Lancang to address both regional and national growth.[3] By 2020, seven main-stem hydroelectric dams were completed, with five currently under construction, and seven more planned. All nineteen main-stem upper Mekong River dams are located in China. In the early 2000s, the Chinese government created the state-owned corporation Hydrolancang, which has been rebranded to Huaneng Lancang River Hydropower Inc., tasked to be the sole legal entity responsible for the coordination and development of hydroelectric projects in the Mekong River.[4] While China has undeniably benefited from the hydroelectricity generated from the UMRB, a 2008

study estimated that the rate of construction would displace 300,000 people by 2020.[5] The majority of people who live along the riverbank of the Mekong who have been displaced by the dams are ethnic minorities.[6] A developing story strikingly similar to the Mississippi River Basin's history, the past, present, and future damming of the UMRB will irreversibly change the character of the Mekong River Basin, privileging development, urbanization, and modernization above all else.

Territory 01 Section B-B

Steep and confined in a narrow gorge, the Upper Mekong River Basin is a formidable and impressive landscape. The upper Mekong River begins at an estimated elevation of 17,000 feet, descends 15,800 feet through the mountainous terrain in the Tibetan Plateau and Yunnan Province, then travels as the border between Laos and Myanmar, ending at the "Golden Triangle" intersection of Laos, Myanmar, and Thailand. While the Upper Mekong River Basin only contributes 16 percent of the water to the entire basin, the steep slope grants the main-stem river a significant amount of hydroelectric potential. In Yunnan Province, it is estimated that the main stem of the river has the potential to generate up to 25,000 MW of hydroelectricity.[7] By 2020, the seven completed hydroelectric projects were all located in Yunnan Province, and each one is different in size and typology. The hydroelectric projects in the Lancang form a staircase-like cascade of integrated reservoirs, designed to take full advantage of its water storage and maximize hydroelectric generation regardless of the seasonal water flow into the river.[8] Together, the seven projects have a combined capacity of 17,000 MW. These projects are part of China's goal to develop infrastructural projects in its western territories, and have a key role in the West-East Electricity Transfer (WEET) project, concurrently being developed.[9] The WEET project consists of new transmission lines that will export power generated from China's western territories to its urban centers in the east. The power generated in the UMRB will be exported to the southeastern provinces of Guangxi and Guangdong.[10] For regional growth, the dams and reservoirs manage downstream flows to also facilitate improved irrigation, navigation, and flood regulation.[11] Throughout the process of creating the dams, the projects were criticized for potentially disrupting or harming fish populations and water flows, especially downstream in the Lower Mekong River Basin.[12] A recent study of sedimentation in the Mekong River between 1965 and 2003 concluded that main-stem Lancang dam construction decreased the sediment load being discharged into the Pacific Ocean by nearly 25 percent, and expects such phenomena to be worse in the future.[13] As a result, the Chinese government has been intensely scrutinized by transboundary activists for its perceived irresponsible decisions.[14] In a rare critique from a government leader, the Vietnamese president, Truong Tan Sang, implied of China's Lancang developments, "Dam construction and stream adjustments by some countries in upstream rivers constitute a growing concern for many countries and implicitly impinge on relations between relevant countries."[15] While China has undoubtedly benefited from the damming of the UMRB, these infrastructural projects strain both the natural environment and political dynamics in Southeast Asia.

Golden Triangle, Mekong River, Laos/Myanmar/Thailand, 2019 (image credit: Derek Hoeferlin)

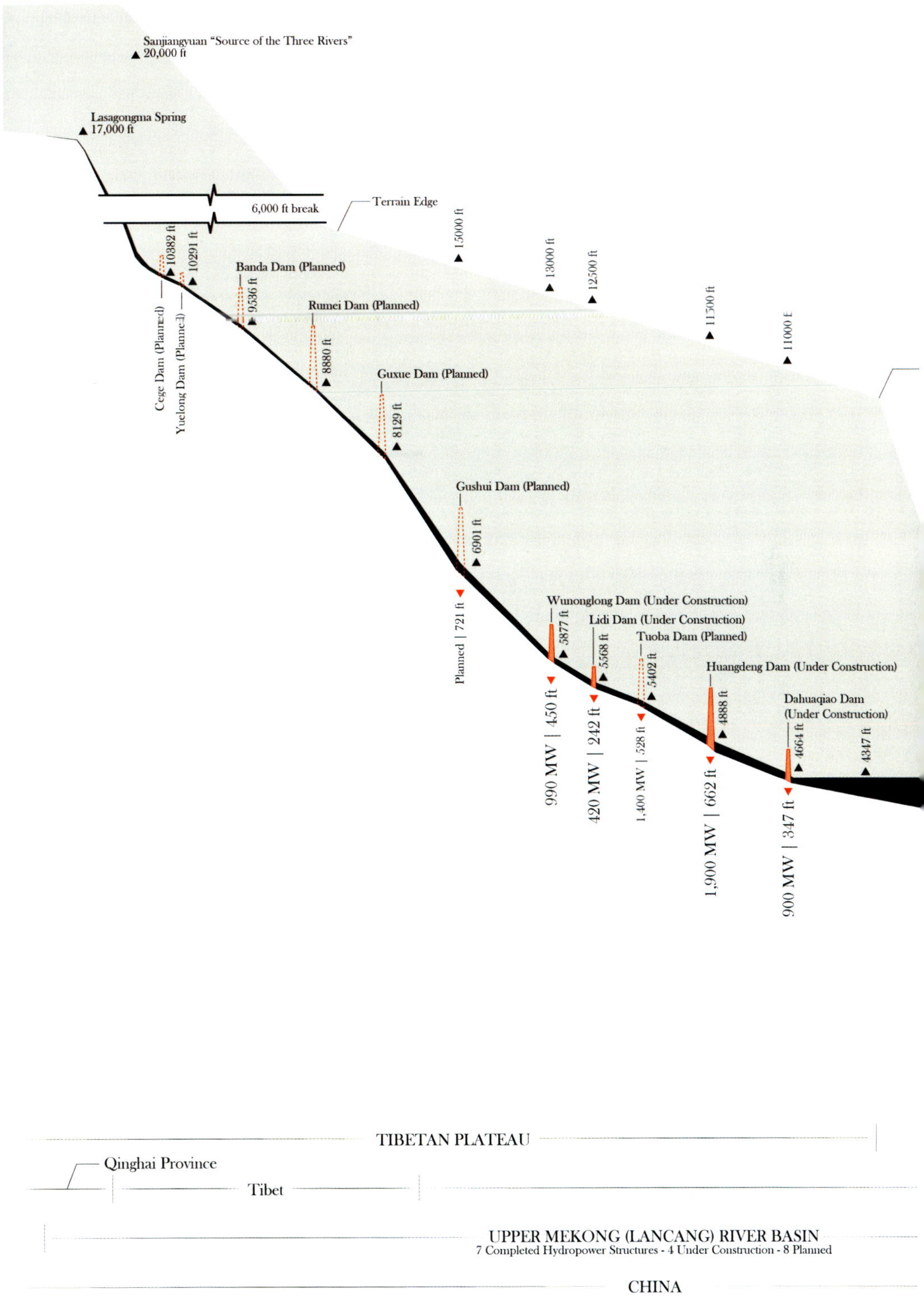

Sanjiangyuan "Source of the Three Rivers"
20,000 ft
Lasagongma Spring
17,000 ft
6,000 ft break
Terrain Edge
10382 ft
10291 ft
Cege Dam (Planned)
Yuelong Dam (Planned)
Banda Dam (Planned)
9536 ft
Rumei Dam (Planned)
8880 ft
Guxue Dam (Planned)
8129 ft
Gushui Dam (Planned)
6901 ft
Planned | 721 ft
15000 ft
13000 ft
12500 ft
11500 ft
11000 ft
Wunonglong Dam (Under Construction)
5877 ft
990 MW | 450 ft
Lidi Dam (Under Construction)
5568 ft
420 MW | 242 ft
Tuoba Dam (Planned)
5402 ft
1,400 MW | 528 ft
Huangdeng Dam (Under Construction)
4888 ft
1,900 MW | 662 ft
Dahuaqiao Dam
(Under Construction)
4664 ft
900 MW | 347 ft
4347 ft
TIBETAN PLATEAU
Qinghai Province
Tibet
UPPER MEKONG (LANCANG) RIVER BASIN
7 Completed Hydropower Structures - 4 Under Construction - 8 Planned
CHINA

TERRITORY 01

UPPER MEKONG RIVER BASIN

The Golden Triangle, confluence of the Ruak and Mekong rivers, Laos/Myanmar/Thailand, 2019

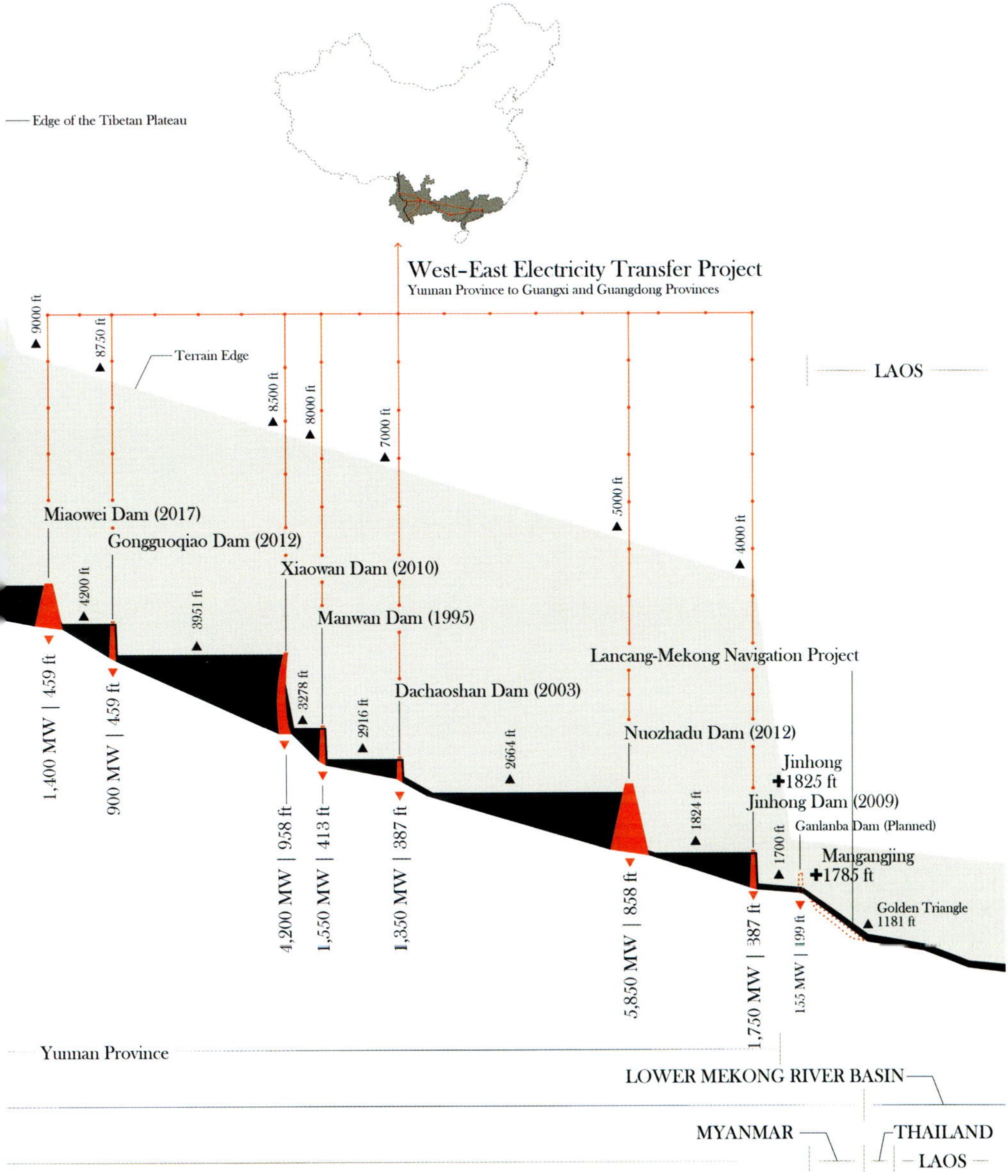

REGION 01

SECTION B-B

FOLLOWING THE PATH OF THE UPPER MEKONG RIVER

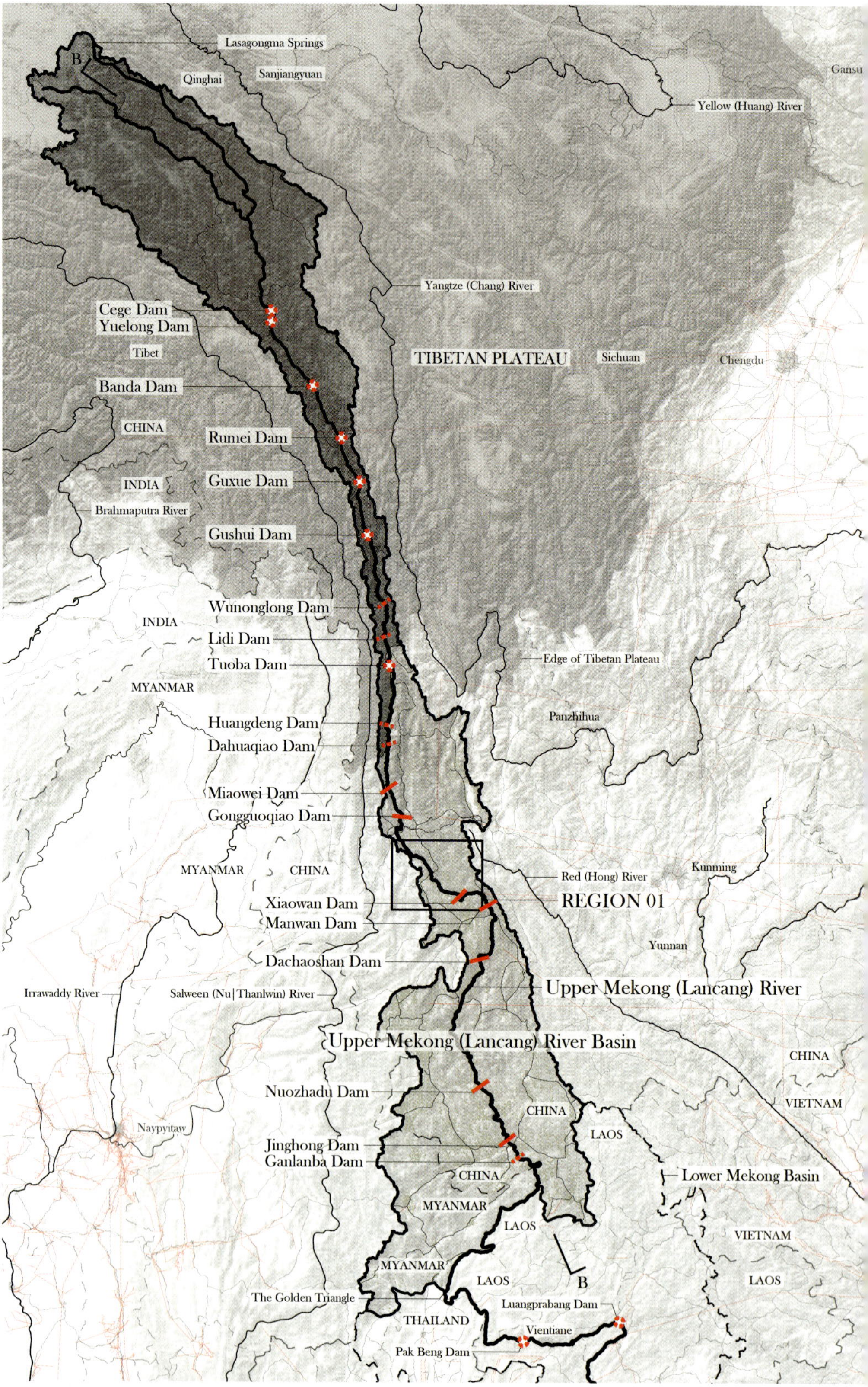
Lasagongma Springs
B
Qinghai
Sanjiangyuan
Gansu
Yellow (Huang) River
Yangtze (Chang) River
Cege Dam
Yuelong Dam
Tibet
TIBETAN PLATEAU
Sichuan
Chengdu
Banda Dam
CHINA
Rumei Dam
INDIA
Guxue Dam
Brahmaputra River
Gushui Dam
Wunonglong Dam
INDIA
Lidi Dam
Tuoba Dam
Edge of Tibetan Plateau
MYANMAR
Huangdeng Dam
Panzhihua
Dahuaqiao Dam
Miaowei Dam
Gongguoqiao Dam
MYANMAR
CHINA
Red (Hong) River
Kunming
Xiaowan Dam
REGION 01
Manwan Dam
Yunnan
Dachaoshan Dam
Irrawaddy River
Salween (Nu|Thanlwin) River
Upper Mekong (Lancang) River
Upper Mekong (Lancang) River Basin
CHINA
Nuozhadu Dam
VIETNAM
CHINA
Naypyitaw
LAOS
Jinghong Dam
Ganlanba Dam
CHINA
Lower Mekong Basin
MYANMAR
LAOS
VIETNAM
MYANMAR
LAOS
B
LAOS
The Golden Triangle
Luangprabang Dam
THAILAND
Vientiane
Pak Beng Dam

Region 01: Mekong & Yangbi Rivers, Yunnan Province, China

Region 01 Plan

Still an imposing landscape, the terrain becomes more accessible in the middle portion of the Upper Mekong River Basin. The basin maintains a slim but gradually widening profile. Flanked by the Salween and the Red (Hong) Rivers, the western edge overlaps with the China-Thailand border. Due to the steep terrain in the Hengduan Mountain Ranges, the agricultural areas are small and scattered around the rivers, while cities are only able to exist in the flatter areas near the edge of the river basin. In its current state, all seven of the completed main-stem hydroelectric dams are located in the middle to lower reaches of the upper Mekong River in Yunnan Province. The seven dams are integrated in China's West–East Electricity Transmission (WEET) project and operate in two cascade systems. The Xiaowan Dam is third in the line of dams, and belongs to the second level of the Middle-Low Lancang River cascade system. Located one mile downstream from the confluence of the Mekong and Yangbi Rivers, the process of creating the reservoir inundated both rivers, submerging 75 square miles of land in the process.[16] At maximum capacity, the reservoir will extend nearly 100 miles upstream to Erhai Lake, near the historic town of Dali.[17] Since the economic reformation strategy implemented in 1978, the rapidly developed urban areas along the country's east coast demanded increased needs for electricity. This is especially the case in Guangdong Province far to the east, projected in 2010 to face supply shortage if it did not import power.[18] Completed in 2010, the Xiaowan Dam is a key hydropower station for the national WEET project and an important regional initiative for stimulating localized industry and tourism opportunities. Near the Xiaowan Dam, two highways have also been commissioned in this region, the Changbao and Yunfeng Highways that are

The "Three Pagodas" at Dali, with Erhai Lake in background, Yunnan Province, China, 2007 (image credit: Derek Hoeferlin)

planned to be completed by 2020.[19] Upon completion, the two connected highways, with a total length of 55 miles, will bring Fengqing and Changning counties near the Xiaowan Dam into the national highway system.[20] To create the dam and reservoir, 40,000 people were displaced and relocated to areas away from the river. They were compensated monetarily and allegedly with improved socio-economic conditions offered by the dams, like better farming conditions.[21] However, many argue that the reparations are inadequate and that the damming has deteriorated the health of the environment by introducing industrial activities, causing pollution and erosion along the river, which in turn worsens the social stability of the region.[22] The government justifies the development in part by claiming that projects stimulate economic growth in a sustainable manner by claiming that hydropower is "clean energy."[23] Regardless of the controversy, the main-stem Lancang River dams have become impactful initiatives in China's regional and national growth.

Region 01 Section C-C

Running through Hengduan Mountain Ranges, the steep gorges impressively tower thousands of feet over the surface of the river. A series of bridges were built across the river to connect settlements from the two sides of the ranges. However, the region is difficult to access because of the mountainous terrain and partly the reason why western China has lagged in development, but its abundant water resources and hydroelectric potential have made the Lancang a key area for regional and national developments. This includes China's WEET project, which was initiated in 1996.[24] Hydroelectric dams along the Chinese portion of the Mekong are tapped into the national power grid under the electricity transfer agreement made between Yunnan and Guangdong provinces in 2000, supporting the nationwide WEET project.[25] The installation of Xiaowan Dam added a staggering 3,000 MW of generating capacity to the existing 4,800 MW supplied by the Manwan and Dachaoshan Dams downstream.[26] The hydroelectricity is pooled in Yunnan Province where it is distributed regionally and sent east to Guangdong Province. In order to reach a minimum operating level for the Xiaowan Dam power plant, the water level was raised 703 feet.[27] The Xiaowan Dam reservoir has a maximum capacity of 12,267,730 acre-feet, significantly more than the 745,857-acre-feet reservoir for Manwan Dam.[28] The Xiaowan Dam maintains a minimum operating capacity of 8,022,000 acre-feet by storing water over the course of the wet season that is released during the dry months.[29] When water is released from the Xiaowan Dam's immense reservoir, it feeds directly into all subsequent projects and aids in maximizing the power generation in the main-stem Lancang cascade. The combined annual production ratio of the three downstream dams, including Manwan Dam, nearly doubled from 46.4 percent to 85.6 percent after the completion of the Xiaowan Dam.[30] However, by storing water over the wet season and releasing it over the course of the year, it both causes a decrease in wet season water discharge and a reciprocal increase in the dry, which counterintuitively disrupts the natural water cycle.[31] The Mekong River Commission believes that the emergency release of Lancang reservoir water ameliorated conditions in the lower Mekong River Basin during the 2016 drought.[32] Four years later, however, critics believe that the 2019 and 2020 lower Mekong droughts were exacerbated by the retention of water by the Lancang cascades, directly contradicting the MRC.[33]

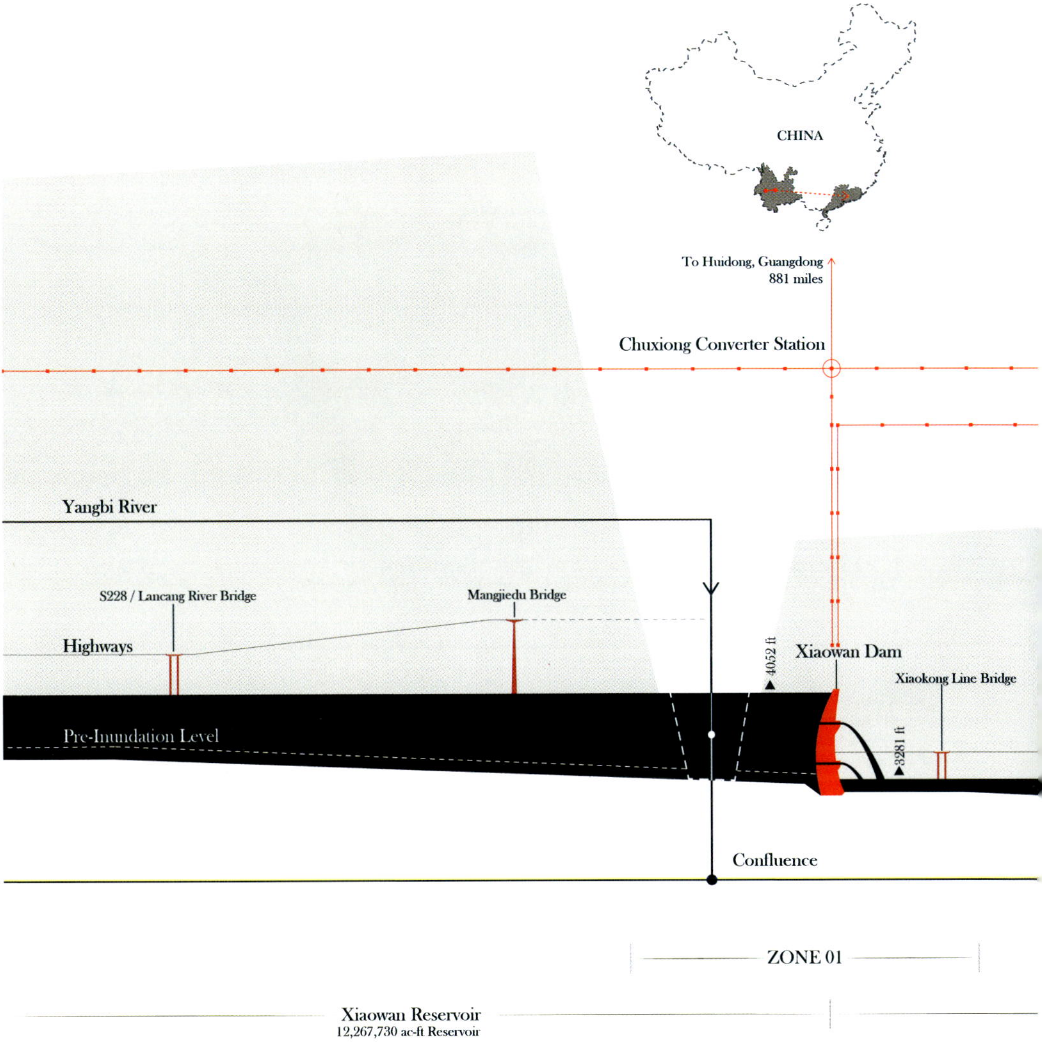
CHINA
To Huidong, Guangdong
881 miles
Chuxiong Converter Station
Yangbi River
S228 / Lancang River Bridge
Mangjiedu Bridge
Highways
4052 ft
Xiaowan Dam
Xiaokong Line Bridge
Pre-Inundation Level
3281 ft
Confluence
ZONE 01
Xiaowan Reservoir
12,267,730 ac-ft Reservoir

REGION 01
MEKONG & YANGBI RIVERS, YUNNAN PROVINCE, CHINA

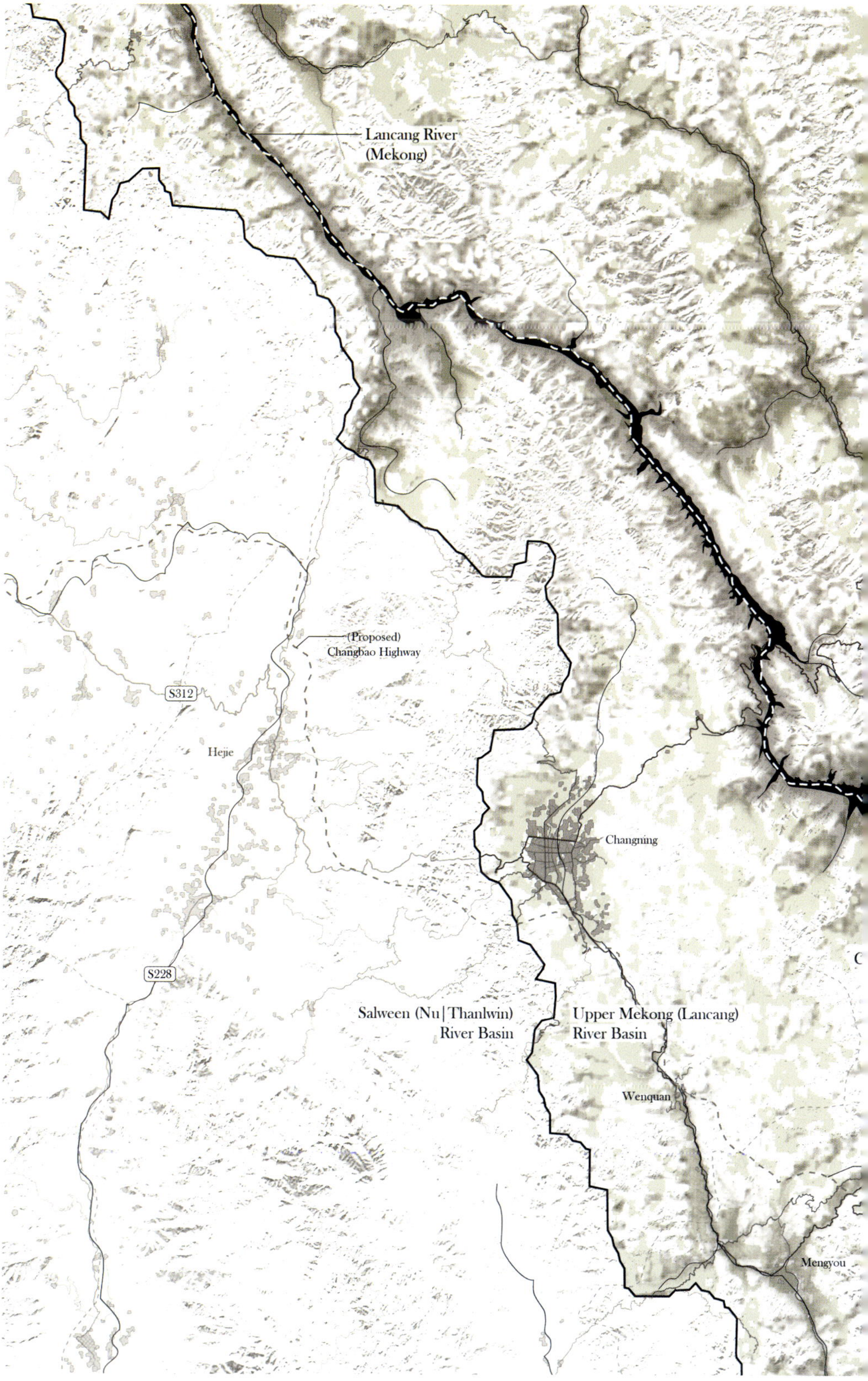
Lancang River
(Mekong)
(Proposed)
Changbao Highway
S312
Hejie
Changning
S228
Salween (Nu|Thanlwin)
River Basin
Upper Mekong (Lancang)
River Basin
Wenquan
Mengyou

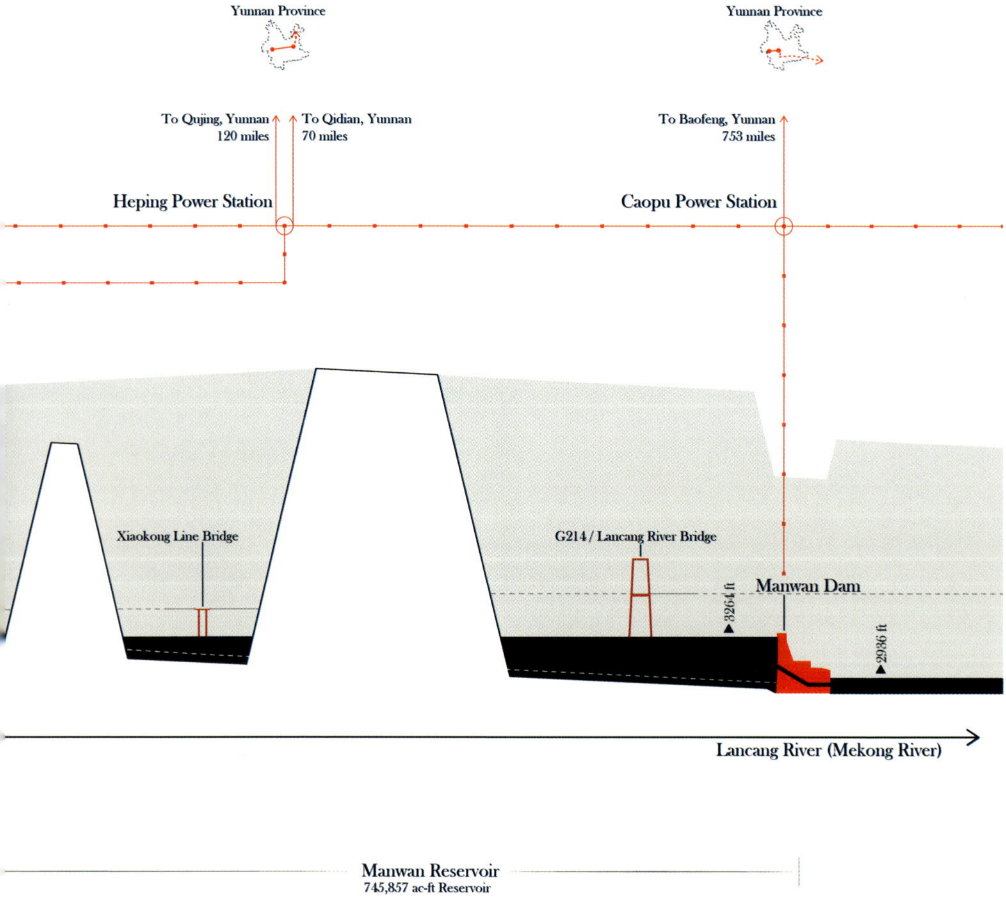

SECTION C-C

SECTION THROUGH THE MEKONG & YANGBI RIVERS, YUNNAN PROVINCE, CHINA

Zone 01:

Xiaowan Dam

Zone 01 Plan

The Xiaowan Dam is the largest structure in the Mekong River Basin (MRB). Completed in 2011, the Xiaowan Dam introduced a scale of engineering unprecedented in the MRB, both for an individual project and a basinwide management system.[34] The Xiaowan Dam is a concrete, double-curvature arch design, buttressed into the valley in the Hengduan mountain range. Located one mile downstream from the confluence of the Yangbi and Lancang Rivers near the middle of the upper Mekong River, in steep, mountainous terrain, it is only accessible via local roads that navigate the difficult terrain. Villages are small and scattered throughout the region. The project consists of the dam, an underground powerhouse, and five discharge tunnels.[35] Located in a seismically active region, the dam is designed to maximize stability.[36] It has a double curvature shape that is arched towards the reservoir. The force of water presses against the convex shape of the dam and embeds the structure into the mountains. After the completion of the dam, the upstream river valley was inundated to create the 8,022,000-acre-feet reservoir.[37] The river increased from a width of 328 feet to 2,624 feet at its normal storage level.[38] Following the natural water cycle in the Mekong River, the volume of water in the reservoir reaches its maximum levels during the wet months. Stored during that time, the water is gradually released over the course of the year. The Xiaowan Dam's powerhouse engages underneath the western valley and has a total installed capacity of 4,200 MW.[39] It is the second-largest power plant in the MRB, contributing nearly 25 percent of all the power generated on the main-stem Mekong River.[40] As a part of China's WEET project, the electricity generated by the dam transmits to the east of China. While the dam is designed primarily for hydropower, it also has flood control capabilities. A set of flood control and diversion tunnels were built into the eastern mountainside, managing the reservoir's water level during flood events. It can reduce flood peaks by 12 percent to safeguard the Xiaowan project, as well as the cascade of dams downstream.[41] The Xiaowan Dam is an impressive feat of engineering both in its individual qualities and in its ability to enable the cascade of dams downstream.

Zone 01 Sections D-D, E-E

The Xiaowan Dam is one of the most consequential projects in the MRB. It was constructed by the Chinese national energy company, Huaneng Power International, which is also responsible for its operation. Spanning the two valleys surrounding the Lancang River, the Xiaowan Dam is 2,926 feet in length and reaches a maximum height of 958 feet.[42] It is by far the tallest dam in the MRB, and the third-tallest dam in the world.[43] After the completion of the arched structure, the reservoir took a year to fill with water.[44] Raising the river 942 feet at the end of the reservoir, it maintains a minimum operating surface elevation of 4,068 feet that increases by 8 feet during the wet season.[45] There are three sets of outlets that discharge water from the reservoir. Two sets of tunnels are embedded into the mountainside. To the west, a set of tunnels directs a constant flow of water into the powerhouse, while a flood discharge tunnel and two diversion tunnels in the eastern slope manage floodwaters.[46] The dam is also designed with multiple orifices, engaged in the main structure. These open individually based on need between five surface spillways, six middle orifices, and two bottom outlets.[47] During the height of the flood season, the dam has a maximum discharge capacity of 731,331 cubic feet per second.[48] The water is stored for use for the rest of the year and will drop a maximum of 8 feet before the wet season replenishes it again. With an average slope of 40 degrees, the mountains rise more than 3,000 feet starting from the riverbed, which has an approximate elevation of 3,200 feet, to the nearby peaks that are as high as 6,500 feet above.[49] While roads are forced to meander through the contours of the mountainside, the transmission lines are able to freely travel through the steep terrain, transferring the power to urban areas in Yunnan Province or outside the basin to China's southeast coast. While the Chinese government has been heavily criticized for causing immense environmental and social harm in constructing the Lancang Dams, the Mekong River Commission (MRC) has publicly defended China's water management strategy.[50] In 2010, a delegation of government officials from the lower Mekong countries and the Mekong River Commission secretariat made a symbolic visit to the Xiaowan Dam to bring about cooperation between China and the lower Mekong countries.[51] In many ways, the Xiaowan Dam has become a monument to the efforts to develop the Mekong River.

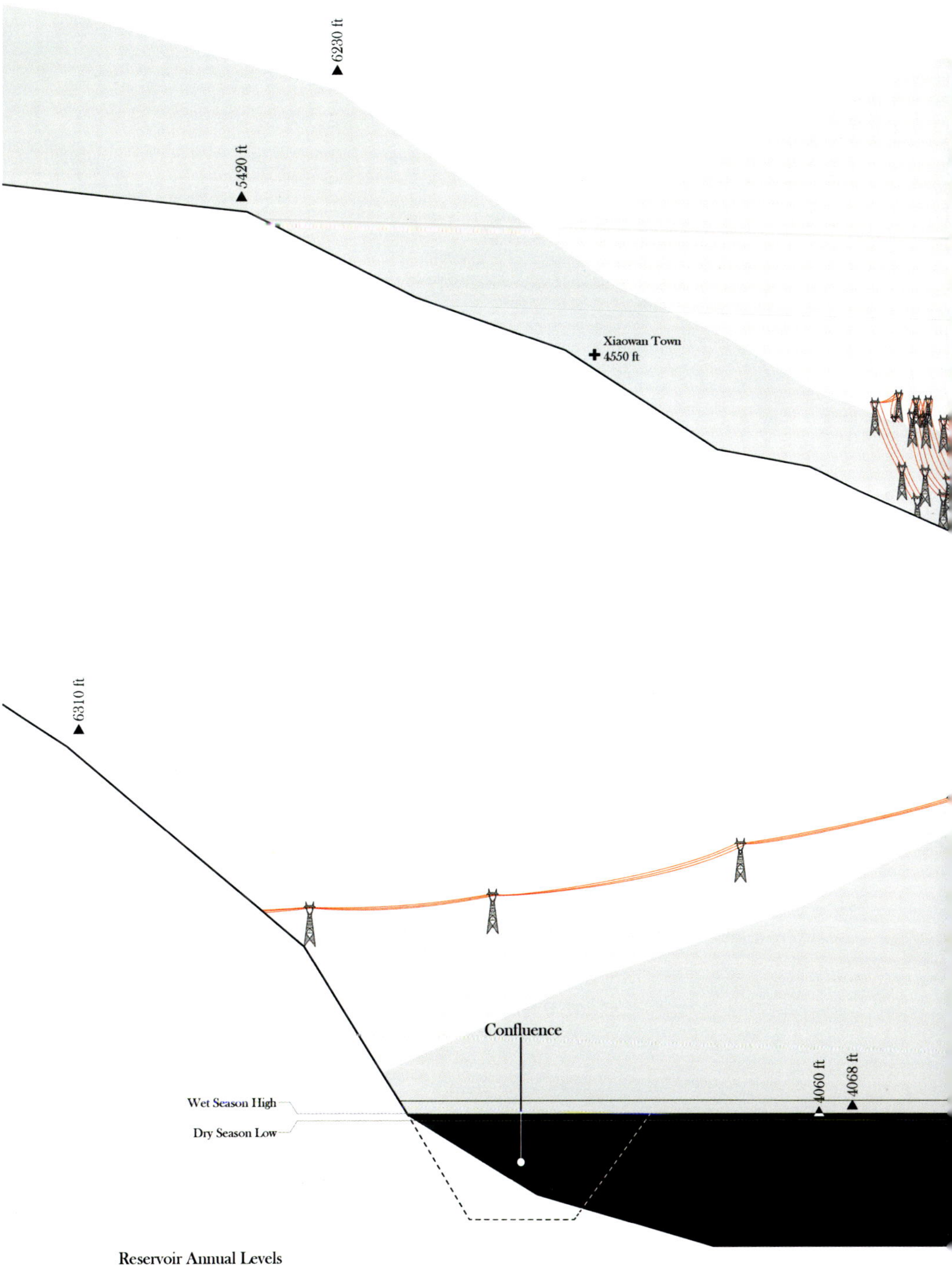

Reservoir Annual Levels

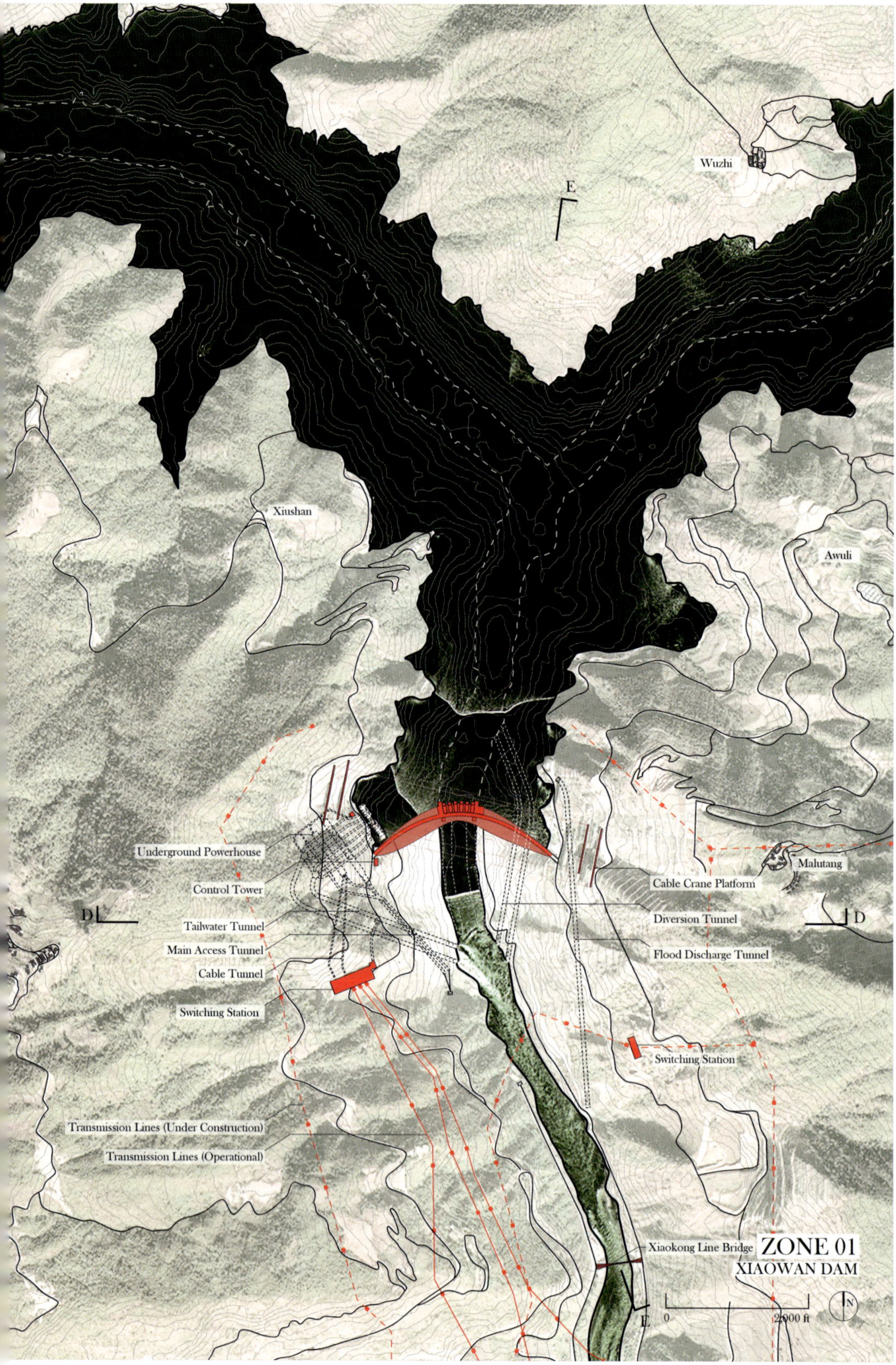
Wuzhi
E
Xiushan
Awuli
Underground Powerhouse
Control Tower
Tailwater Tunnel
Main Access Tunnel
Cable Tunnel
Switching Station
D
Malutang
Cable Crane Platform
Diversion Tunnel
Flood Discharge Tunnel
D
Switching Station
Transmission Lines (Under Construction)
Transmission Lines (Operational)
Xiaokong Line Bridge
ZONE 01
XIAOWAN DAM
0
2000 ft
N
E

Lancang River (Mekong)
Pre-Inundation Width
Akeming
Maduozi
Xiushan Cun
Amoshan
Juecai Cun
Shizhulin

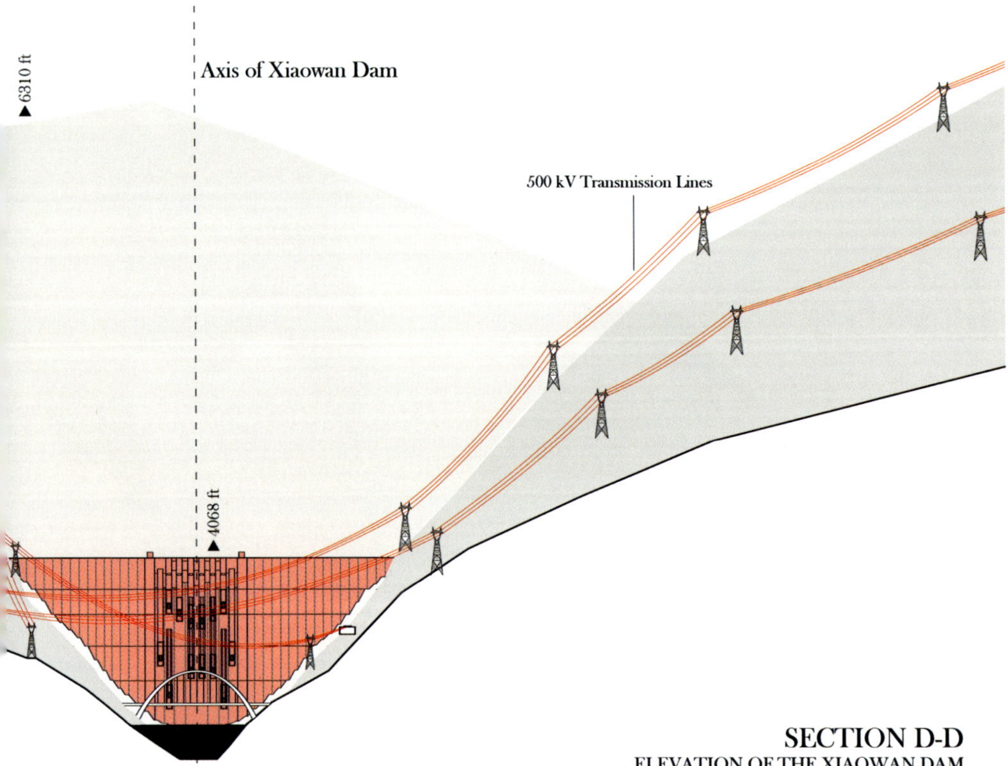

SECTION D-D
ELEVATION OF THE XIAOWAN DAM

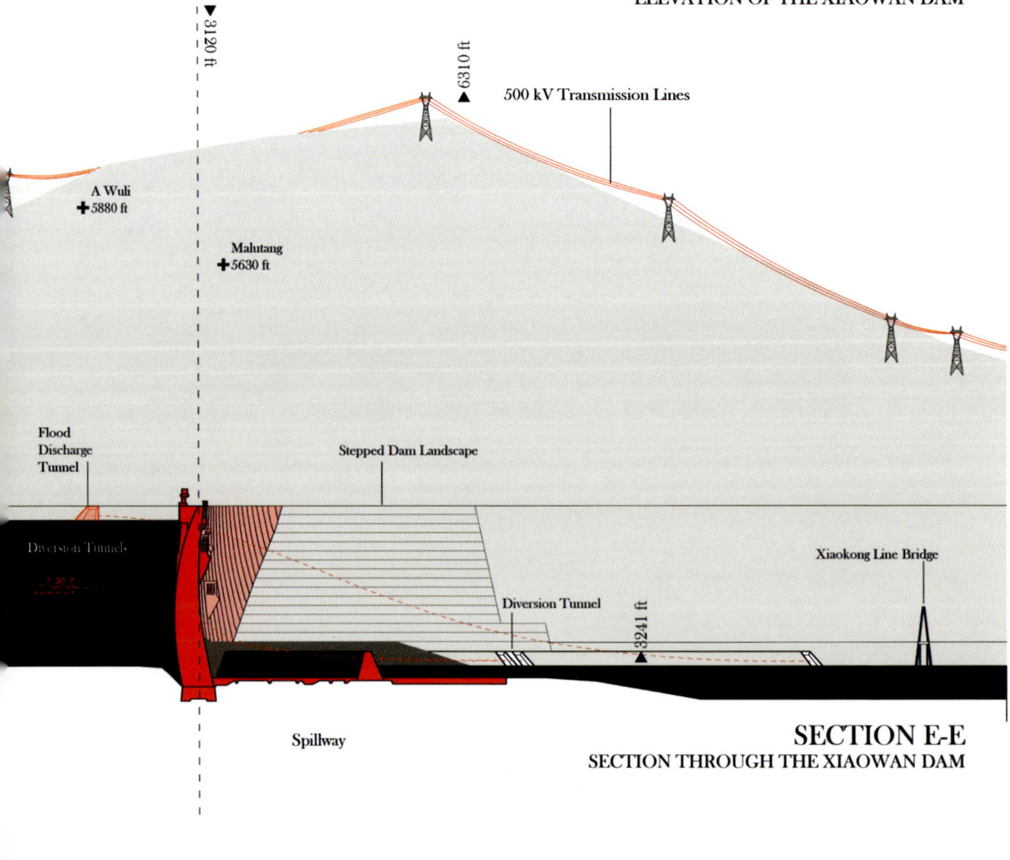

SECTION E-E
SECTION THROUGH THE XIAOWAN DAM

Territory 02: Lower Mekong River Basin

Territory 02 Plan

The Lower Mekong River Basin (LMRB) is a water-abundant and fertile landscape that is beginning to be developed to take advantage of its immense hydroelectric potential. The lower Mekong River begins at the Golden Triangle, the tri-border area of Laos, Myanmar, and Thailand, and concludes at the delta region where it empties into the Pacific Ocean. Flowing 1,500 miles in length, it drains a total area of 233,000 square miles.[52] The shape of the LMRB begins narrow in area, but quickly expands to cover nearly all of Southeast Asia before shrinking in size as it enters the distributive context of the delta. Depending on the season, the upper Mekong River will contribute 15 to 20 percent of water in river; it will have accumulated an average flow of 570,000 cubic feet per second as it discharges through the delta.[53] The lower Mekong River passes through five countries—Myanmar, Thailand, Laos, Cambodia, and Vietnam—and in 2010, it was estimated that 60 million people were living in the LMRB.[54] The LMRB's vast fish, irrigation, and natural resources depend on the seasonal dry-wet water flow cycle.[55] As much as 90 percent of the year's water flows through the river from June to November.[56] This flooding is the key event that replenishes the basin with water, and it also physically changes the character of the river. Nutrient-rich sediment scatters throughout the basin's floodplains. Fish migrate to spawning habitats upstream, triggered by the swelling of the river.[57] In 2010, it was estimated that a total of 3.6 million tonnes of fish were captured in the LMRB, and 1 million tonnes were exported.[58] Driven by modernization, Laos's vice minister of energy and mines stated in a 2014 interview that Laos will realize the hydroelectric potential in the Mekong and become the "battery of Southeast Asia."[59] Through a global effort, the first two dams in the Lower Mekong were recently completed in Laos in 2019 and 2020. Eight more main-stem dams are planned throughout the basin. Even before the first completed project in the lower Mekong, it was already demonstrated that the upstream main-stem Lancang dams have altered seasonal water flows. The addition of more main-stem projects in the LMRB will have more disruptive effects on cycles, including impeding migration paths and trapping even more sediment.[60] In a 2010 study prepared for the Mekong River Commission, it was

Salt Flat Farm, Mekong Delta Vietnam, 2011 (image credit: Derek Hoeferlin)

discovered that nearly half of the population in the LMRB is located within 10 miles of the Mekong River, and more than two million people are living on sites that will be directly affected by the main-stem dams and their reservoirs.[61] Furthermore, it's estimated that more than 70 percent of the region's population is considered rural and depends almost entirely on the Mekong River for their resource and food security.[62] The lower Mekong River is an invaluable natural system and a source of social security. Main-stem damming is a risk for the environment and an existential threat for millions of people.

Territory 02 Sections F-F, G-G

The lower Mekong River and its tributaries provide invaluable resources to Southeast Asia. As the lower Mekong River charts through the subcontinent, the landscape undergoes significant, and at times unique, changes that allow it to be more easily inhabitable and environmentally productive than the UMRB. From the Golden Triangle to the Mekong Delta region, the river descends 1,181 feet to sea level. Many countries share both the main stem of the river and its drainage basin. The main path of the river will occasionally form the border between two countries; for instance, between Laos and Thailand. The terrain at the beginning of the basin is steep, but the western riverbank suddenly drops and remains flat across the Khorat Plateau. The eastern mountain ranges level out near the Laos-Cambodia border, which coincides with a series of archipelagos, punctuated by waterfalls. Near the end of its course in Cambodia is an idiosyncratic hydrological phenomenon that takes place on its tributary, the Tonlé Sap River. During the monsoon season, water from the Mekong will flow into the Tonlé Sap River and its nearby lake until the dry season, when the course of the water flow is switched and the tributary drains back into the main stem of the Mekong River.[63] More than a natural system, the lower Mekong River has shaped urbanization on the continent. Countless villages are located along the riverbanks, along with many of the largest cities on the continent, such as Vientiane and Phnom Penh, the capital cities of Laos and Cambodia, respectively, and where the Mekong River Commission (MRC) is jointly headquartered. A 2010 report prepared for the MRC stated that the four countries that share the lower Mekong River will experience above-average population growth which will lead to an estimated increase in electricity use by 6 to 7 percent annually.[64] To meet this growing demand, it is expected that the development of the lower Mekong River's immense hydroelectric potential, estimated at 30,000 MW, will be one of the most pressing issues in the territory.[65] In its current state, there will be eleven main-stem hydroelectric dams that will have a combined capacity of 13,000 MW—over five times the amount installed by the Pick-Sloan Program in the Missouri River Basin.[66] As of 2020, there are two hydroelectric dams completed on the main stem of the lower Mekong River, with eight more planned—seven in Laos and two in Cambodia. A 2010 study conducted by Thai academics, however, disputes the MRC's claim that dams will have a net positive economic impact, stating that the loss of fisheries and agricultural productivity along with social displacement would far exceed any benefits of dams.[67] Confronted by the threat of climate change in the 2019 and 2020 droughts, Cambodia has decided to put a moratorium on constructing its two dams until 2030.[68] The damming of the LMRB is one of the pivotal developments that will dictate the future of Southeast Asia, and this recent moratorium allows crucial time for fundamental and sustainable planning both in the short and long term.

Palm oil farming, Thailand(2019)

Rice farming, Luang Prabang, Laos (2019)

Near site of proposed Sambor Dam, Cambodia (2011)

Coastal armoring at development site, Vietnam (2011)

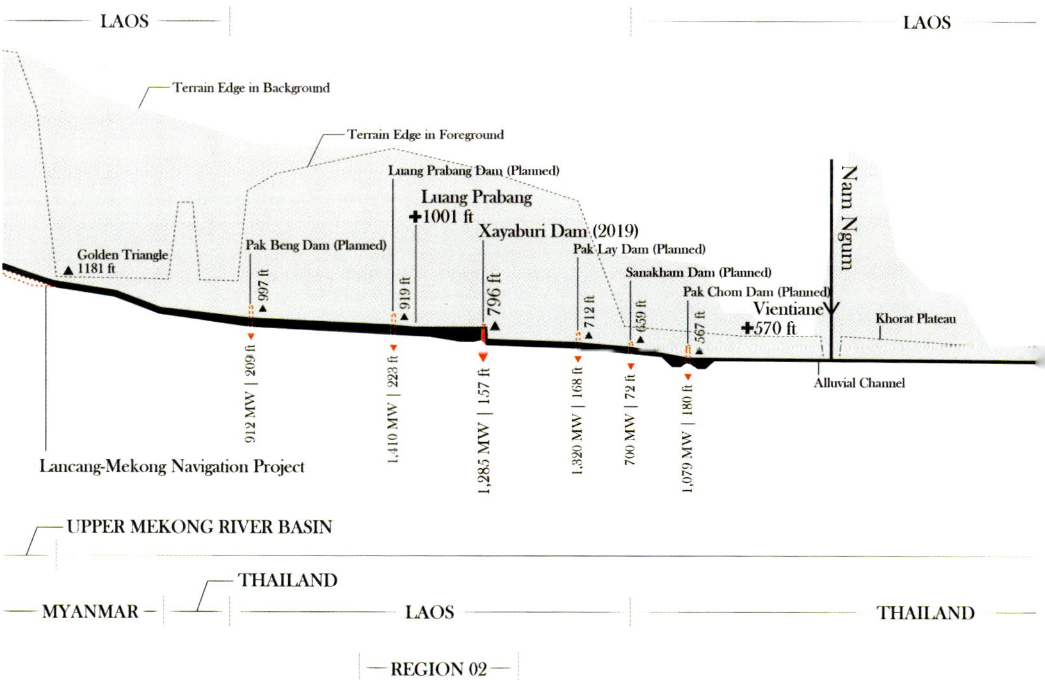

Hong Kong
Hainan
PACIFIC OCEAN
Operational Dam
Dam Under Construction
Planned Dam
TERRITORY 02
LOWER MEKONG RIVER BASIN
0
600,000 ft
N

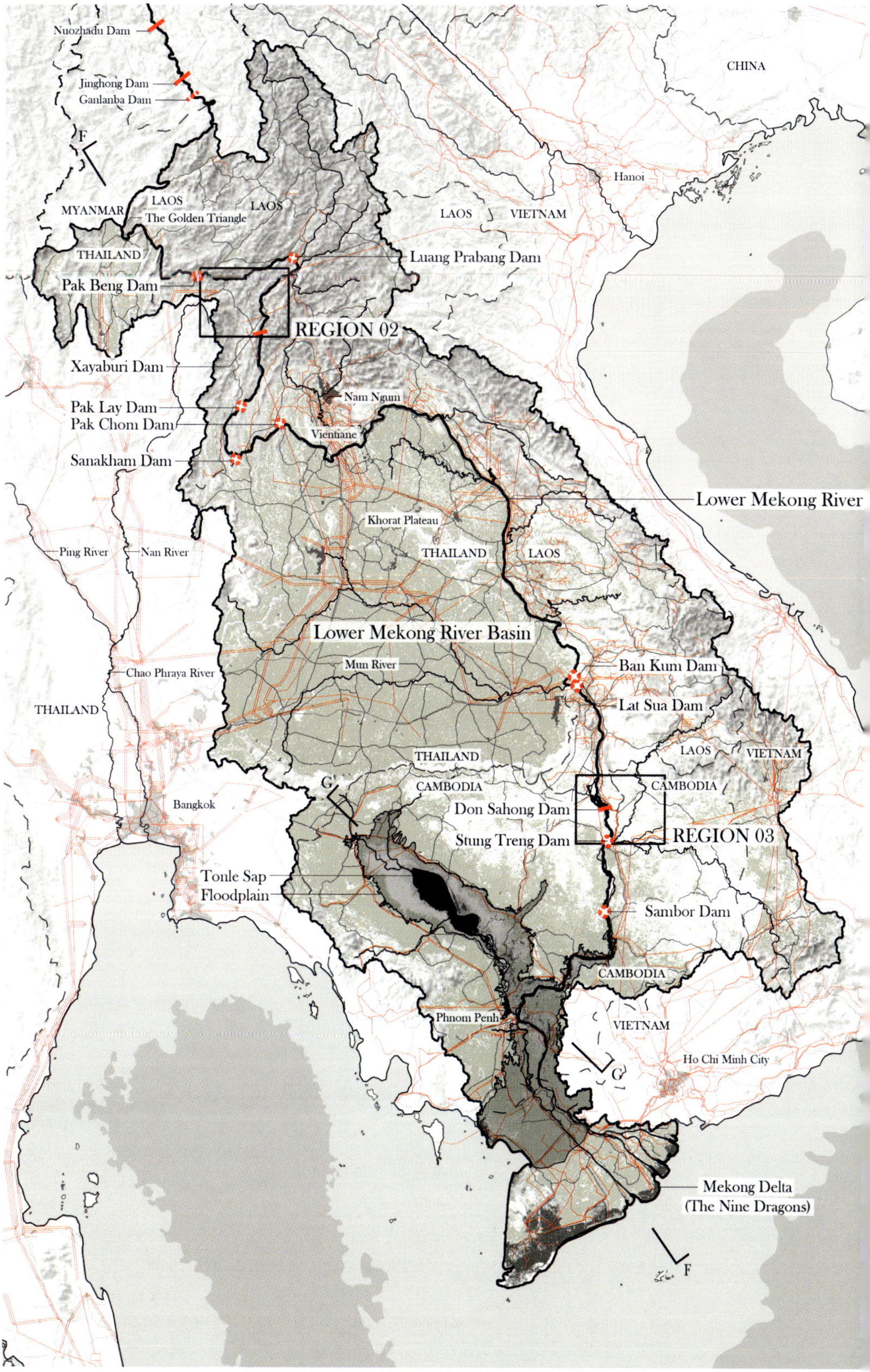

Nuozhadu Dam
Jinghong Dam
Ganlanba Dam
CHINA
F
Hanoi
LAOS
LAOS
MYANMAR
The Golden Triangle
LAOS
VIETNAM
THAILAND
Luang Prabang Dam
Pak Beng Dam
REGION 02
Xayaburi Dam
Nam Ngum
Pak Lay Dam
Pak Chom Dam
Vientiane
Sanakham Dam
Lower Mekong River
Khorat Plateau
Ping River
Nan River
THAILAND
LAOS
Lower Mekong River Basin
Mun River
Ban Kum Dam
Chao Phraya River
Lat Sua Dam
THAILAND
THAILAND
LAOS
VIETNAM
G
CAMBODIA
CAMBODIA
Bangkok
Don Sahong Dam
Stung Treng Dam
REGION 03
Tonle Sap
Floodplain
Sambor Dam
CAMBODIA
Phnom Penh
VIETNAM
Ho Chi Minh City
G
Mekong Delta
(The Nine Dragons)
F

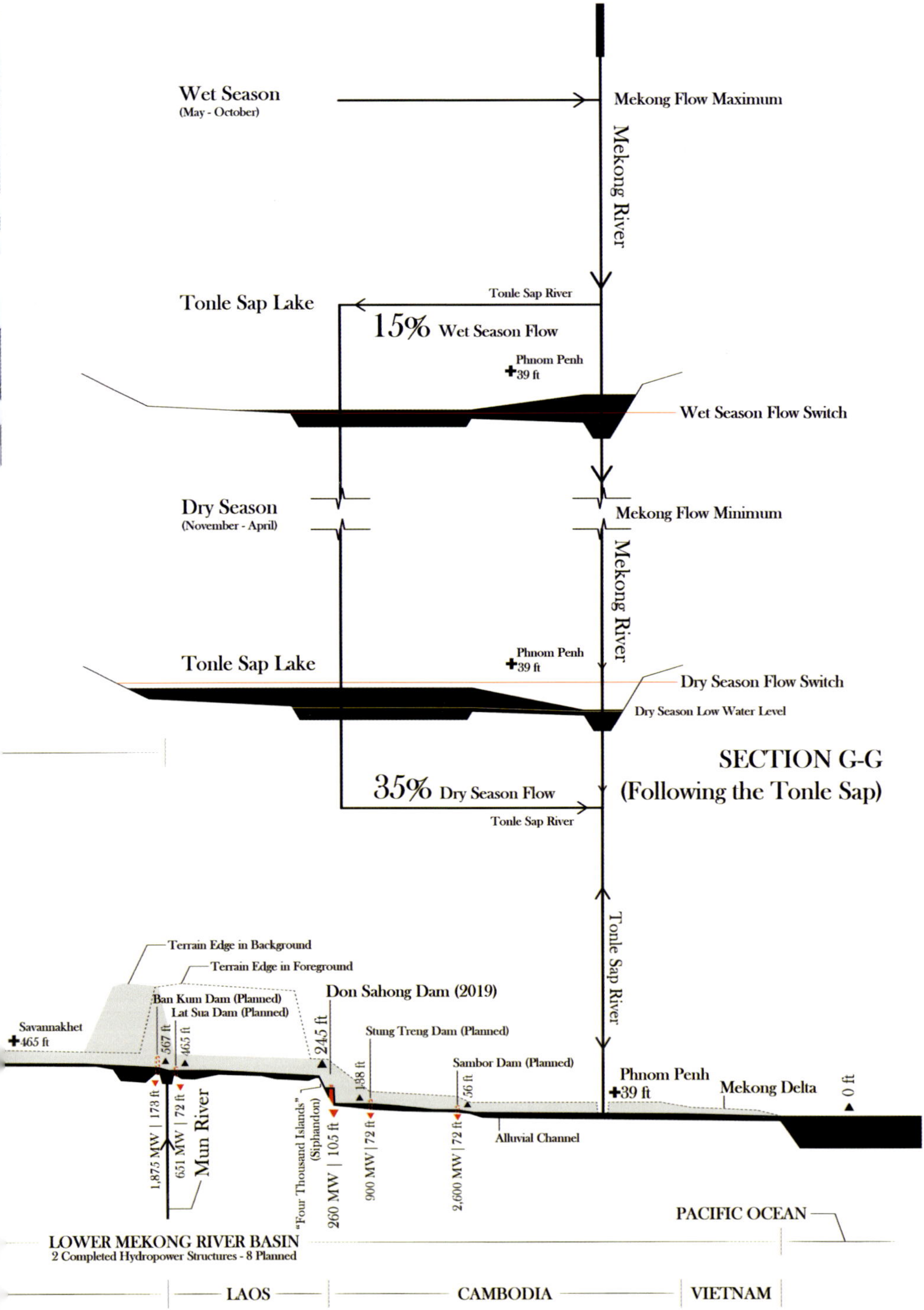

REGION 03

SECTION F-F

FOLLOWING THE PATH OF THE LOWER MEKONG RIVER

Region 02: Xayaboury & Luang Prabang Provinces

Region 02 Plan

Upper Laos is a mountainous, forested landscape that has largely remained in its natural state. In this region, the Mekong River runs solely in Laos, guided by the Luang Prabang mountain range, traveling northeast before looping back south. A mountain ridge marks the edge of the watershed and overlaps with the Laos-Thailand border. Most of the population in the region lives in small towns or villages near the river, including the provincial capitals, Xayaboury and Luang Prabang. Both cities have become important cultural and environmental designations. UNESCO granted Luang Prabang the status of World Heritage Site for its rich cultural sites. Additionally, the Nam Phouy National Biodiversity Conservation Area is managed out of Xayaboury, which crucially features a 775-square-mile elephant conservation center.[69] A notable exception to this trend is Hongsa, an industrial town featuring a coal power plant with the capacity to generate 1,878 MW of electricity that primarily exports energy to Thailand.[70] The few large agricultural fields or plantations in this area are located near these cities. Upper Laos is the site for the Xayaburi Dam, the first completed main-stem hydroelectric dam in the LMRB. Xayaburi Dam is the third dam in the line of a proposed cascade of six main-stem hydroelectric projects that start with the Pak Beng Dam and conclude with the Pak Chom Dam, which will be sited near Vientiane, the national capital of Laos. While the natural environment remains largely untouched, recent reporting has uncovered a significant decrease in tree cover throughout the country due to poor forest management and the proliferation of illegal logging operations.[71] The report specifically attributes the ongoing deforestation to the construction of infrastructure, including hydroelectric dams, roads, and mines.[72] However, these activities have not been pursued solely under Laotian discretion. The Xayaburi Dam was funded primarily by Thailand which, like the Hongsa coal power plant, will be the recipient of most of the energy generated by the project.[73] In a symbolic threat, UNESCO has warned that Luang Prabang will lose its World Heritage designation if main-stem dam construction continues and causes the city to "[become] a 'lakeside' town and no longer a riverside town," something that experts believe will undermine the authenticity of the site.[74] More than just the river, the entire

China-Laos Railway Bridge under construction across Mekong River, north of Luang Prabang, Laos, 2019 (image credit: Derek Hoeferlin)

Mekong River Basin is undergoing a period of rapid modernization that is taxing the environment and existing cultural practices.

Region 02 Section H-H

The mountainous landscape in Upper Laos creates conditions that dictate settlement patterns and the direction of main-stem river developments in a similar manner to the UMRB. While the terrain in the Luang Prabang range is both less steep and shorter than Yunnan Province, it is nonetheless imposing for inhabitation and industrial development. Luang Prabang is an exception, located on a relatively large valley clearing adjacent to the river. Most of the population distributes throughout the riparian landscape. More than 50 villages are located on the riverbanks between Luang Prabang and Xayaboury. The sediment carried in the river has many benefits for the LMRB. It builds and maintains many natural features in the river, like islands, floodplains, and wetlands. Combined, these provide habitats and stabilize the morphology in the river, which prevents the loss of land or erosion.[75] Sediment is an invaluable supply of nutrition for the ecosystem and sustains the watershed's large plant and fish populations.[76] Completed in 2019, the Xayaburi Dam has the capacity to generate 1,285 MW of energy. In the contract, 95 percent of the energy produced by the project will be exported to Thailand, which is expected to supply power to three million people. While only 5 percent will remain in Laos, the lower usage should allow one million people to benefit from the project.[77] In the process, the project has impounded the river to create a 1,054,000-acre-feet reservoir over an area of 105,000 square miles that will extend upstream to the planned dam near the city of Luang Prabang.[78] The plan to construct six main-stem hydroelectric dams in this region aims to implement an integrated water management strategy that will utilize a hydroelectric cascade similar to the ones in the upper Mekong and the Missouri Rivers.[79] The Laotian government commissioned the Compagnie Nationale du Rhône, a private French hydroelectric utility company, to perform a study on the feasibility and impact of a six-dam cascade.[80] Before construction began on the Xayaburi Dam, the Mekong River Commission made a series of projections for the impact of main-stem hydroelectric dams on the LMRB. In their "definite future" scenario, which accounts for the construction of the six Upper Laos cascade dams, the MRC predicts that 55 to 65 percent of all the sediment in the basin will be trapped by dams and will be unable to escape the main-stem Lancang reservoirs. They project that there will be a 20 to 45 percent reduction in the nutrition carried in the river which will lead to reduced ecological and agricultural productivity in the lower Mekong River.[81] The disruption to fish migrations is twofold. Not only will the dams impede movement upstream, the reduced water volume and velocity in the river will trap larvae and prevent them from journeying downstream.[82] The potential risks for the natural environment and their implications for the social security of the watershed's population has been explored by the MRC and made clear to all parties interested in developing main-stem hydroelectric dams in the Mekong River.

Near site of proposed Pak Beng Dam, Laos (2019)

Mekong reservoir due to Xayaburi Dam, Laos (2019)

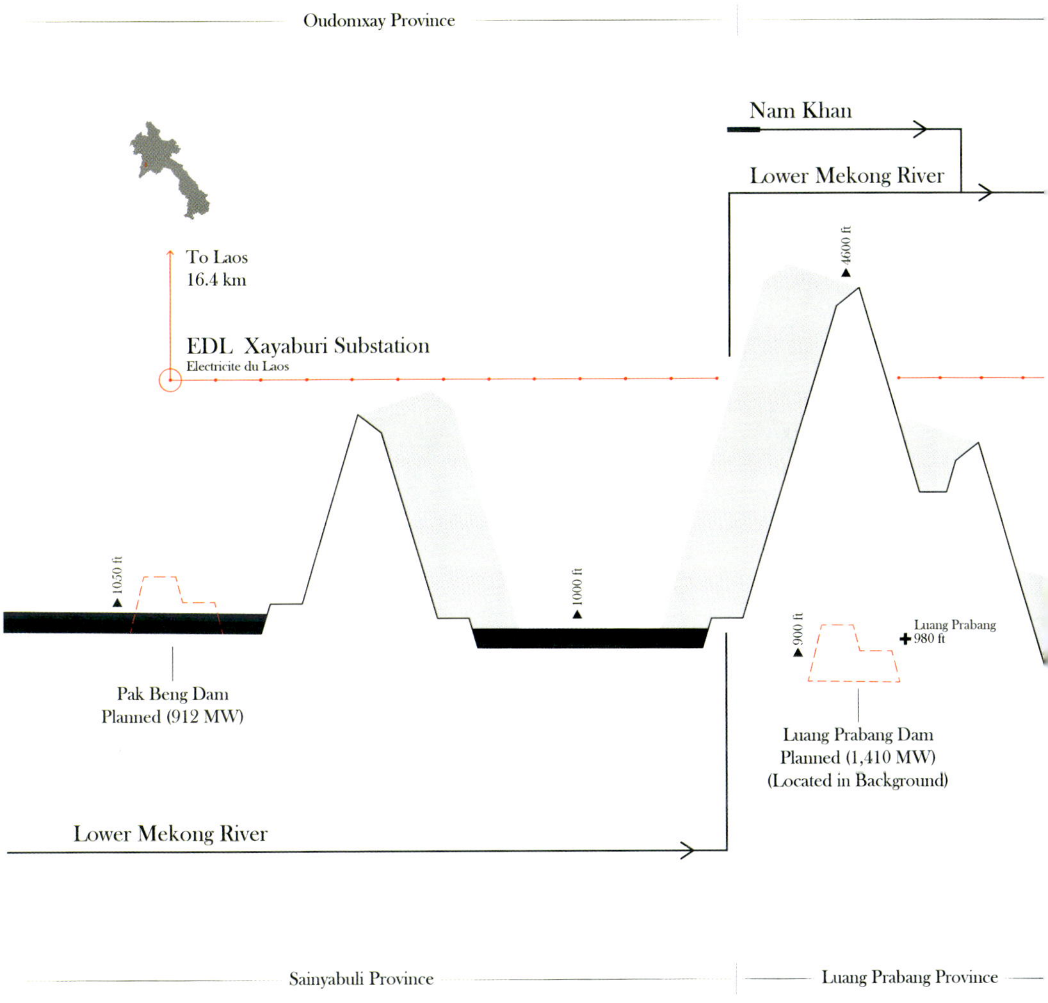

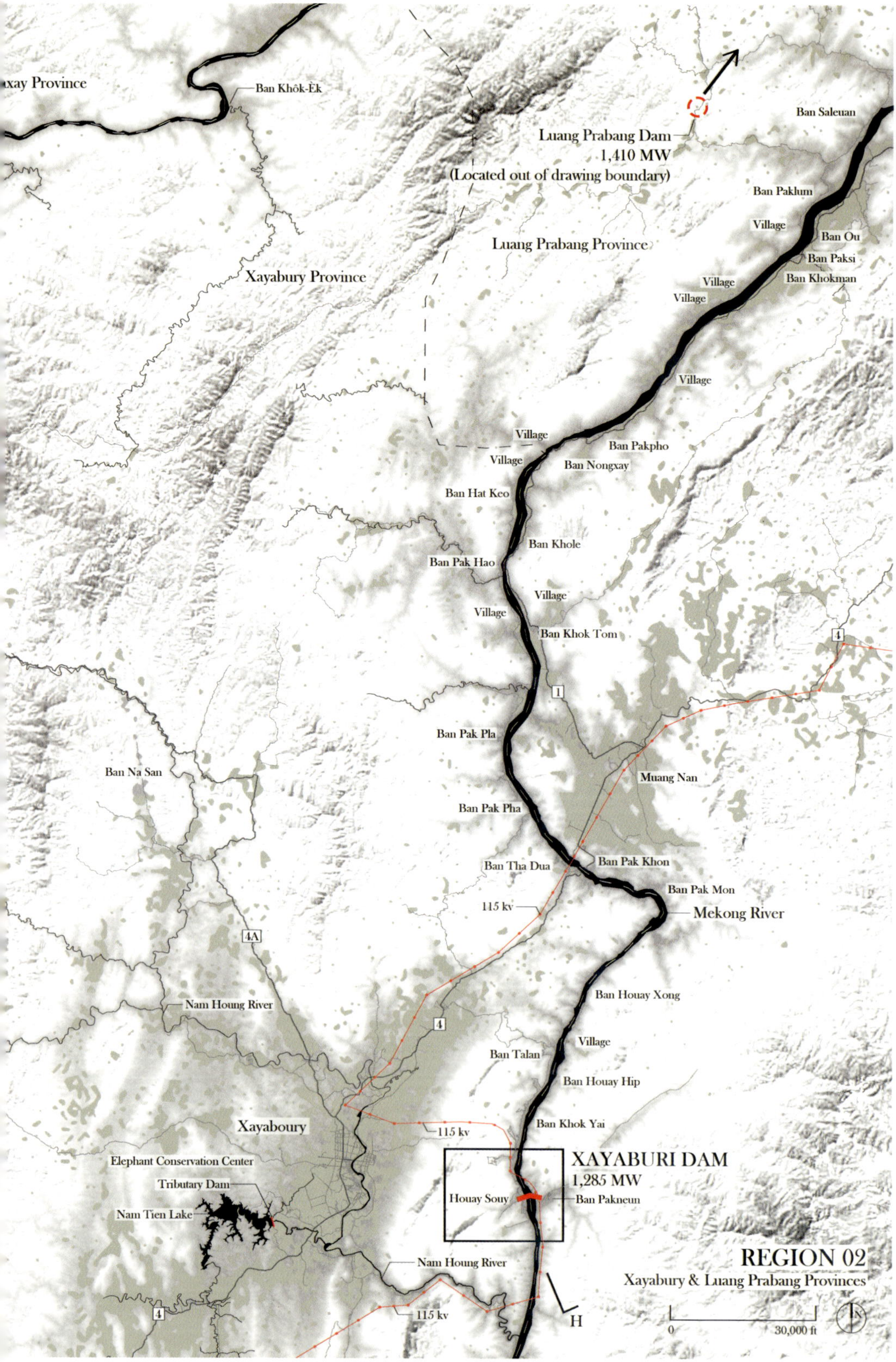

xay Province
Ban Khôk-Èk
Luang Prabang Dam
1,410 MW
(Located out of drawing boundary)
Ban Saleuan
Ban Paklum
Village
Ban Ou
Ban Paksi
Ban Khokman
Luang Prabang Province
Xayabury Province
Village
Village
Village
Village
Village
Ban Pakpho
Ban Nongxay
Ban Hat Keo
Ban Khole
Ban Pak Hao
Village
Village
Ban Khok Tom
4
1
Ban Pak Pla
Muang Nan
Ban Na San
Ban Pak Pha
Ban Tha Dua
Ban Pak Khon
Ban Pak Mon
115 kv
Mekong River
4A
Nam Houng River
Ban Houay Xong
4
Village
Ban Talan
Ban Houay Hip
Ban Khok Yai
Xayaboury
115 kv
Elephant Conservation Center
XAYABURI DAM
1,285 MW
Tributary Dam
Houay Souy
Ban Pakneun
Nam Tien Lake
Nam Houng River
REGION 02
Xayabury & Luang Prabang Provinces
4
115 kv
H
0
30,000 ft

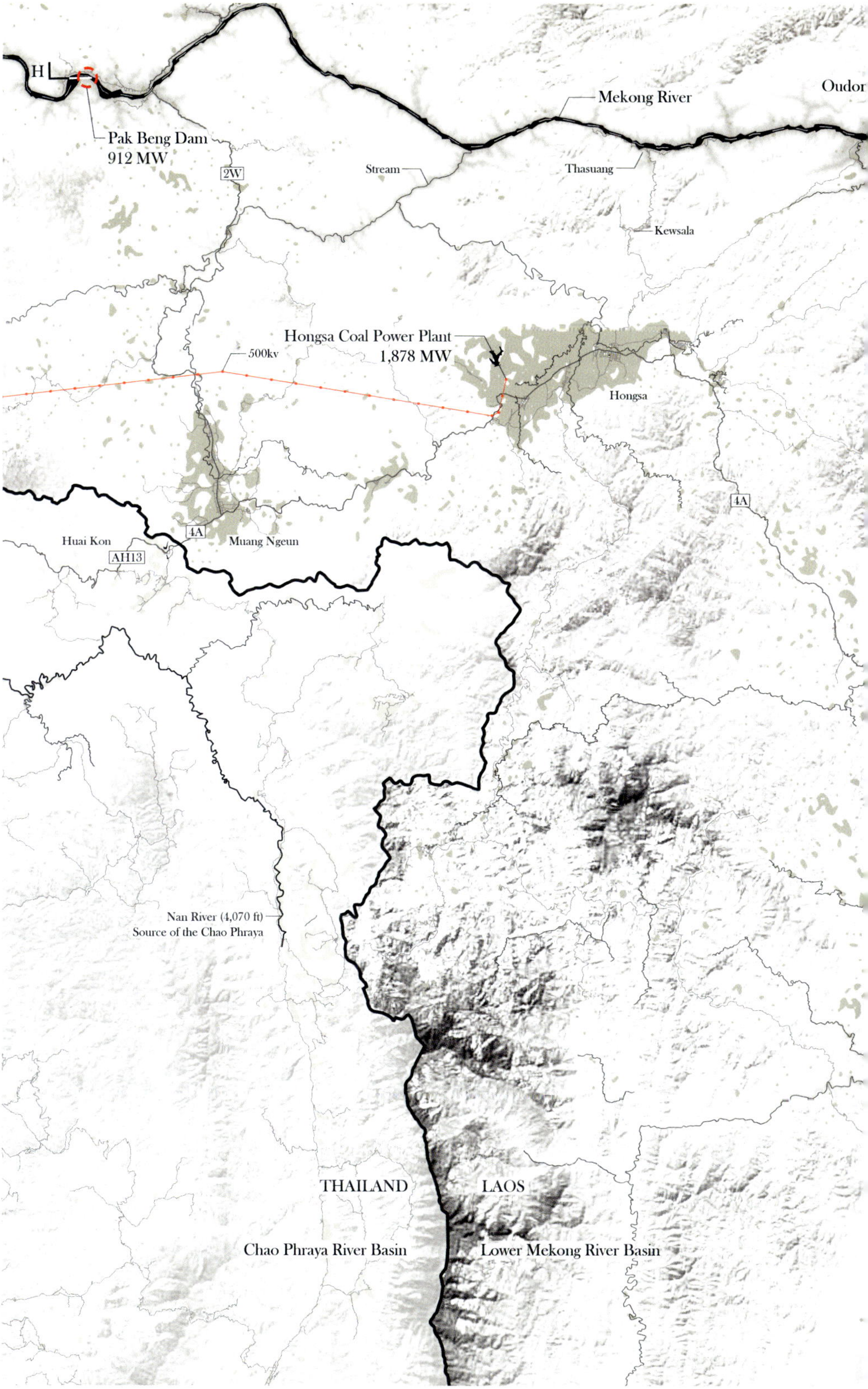

H
Pak Beng Dam
912 MW
Mekong River
Oudor
2W
Stream
Thasuang
Kewsala
Hongsa Coal Power Plant
1,878 MW
500kv
Hongsa
4A
Huai Kon
AH13
4A
Muang Ngeun
Nan River (4,070 ft)
Source of the Chao Phraya
THAILAND
LAOS
Chao Phraya River Basin
Lower Mekong River Basin

Mekong Bridge, Laos (2019)

Relocated village due to reservoir, Laos (2019)

Luang Prabang Province

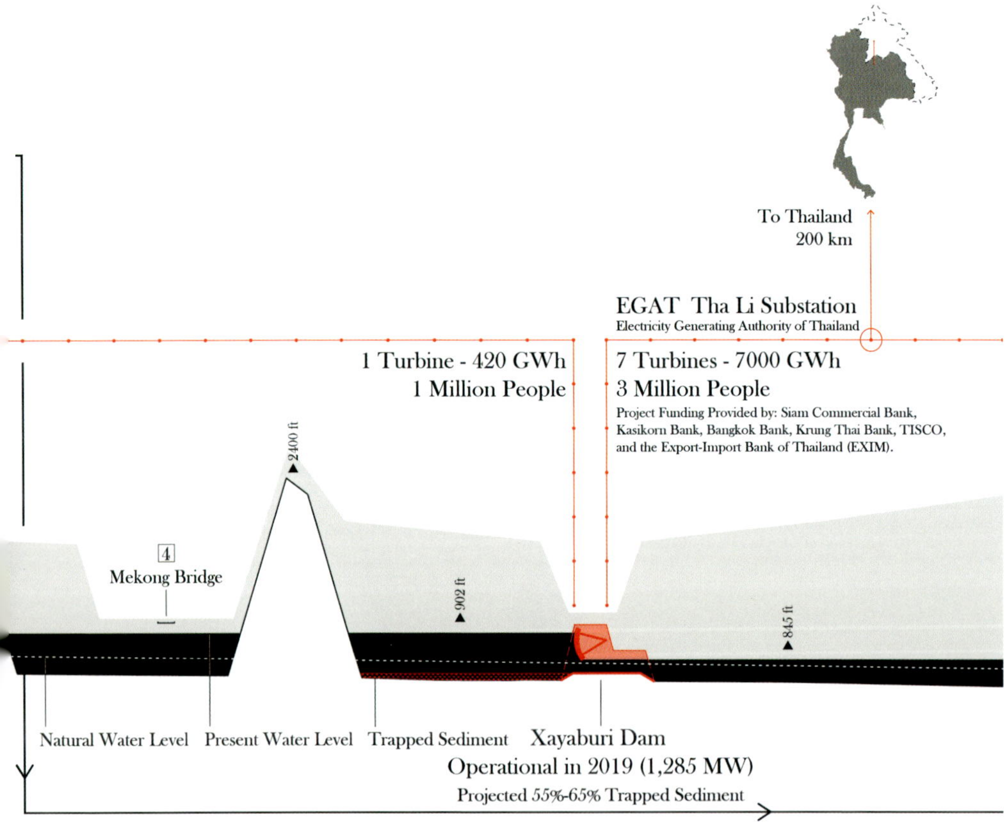

ZONE 02

Sainyabuli Province

SECTION H-H

SECTION THROUGH UPPER LAOS

main-stem dams in the Mekong River.[88] The Xayaburi Dam has not only reshaped the natural environment, it has undermined the institutions that sought to enforce responsible and equitable development in the Mekong River Basin.

Zone 02 Sections I-I, J-J, K-K, L-L

As the first completed dam in the lower Mekong River, the Xayaburi Dam was an important test in the Mekong River Commission's capacity to facilitate transboundary cooperation for sustainable development. Compared to the main-stem Lancang project, the Xayaburi Dam is much smaller in size and different in typology. The water level only drops 57 feet from the headpond to the discharge elevation, and the dam has a reported height of 157 feet. Despite its size, it has the capacity to generate 1,285 MW of energy, which is on par with many of the dams in the Lancang cascades. The Xayaburi Dam was a global effort. It was designed by Poyry, a Finnish engineering firm, which received input and reviews from the Compagnie Nationale du Rhône that helped create a toll fee strategy for the Xayaburi Dam based off lockage precedents on the Rhine and Rhone Rivers. Finally, Thai banks funded the project and the national Thai contracting company, CH Karnchang PCL, built the project. In the built design, a few adaptations were implemented to address concerns over blocked sedimentation and migration. A sediment flush was integrated into the power plant, and a low-level spillway typology was introduced to allow better sediment release. Originally lacking any migration passages, a fish ladder was ultimately built and integrated with the design of the power plant. In their final review of the design however, the Mekong River Commission stated that there was not enough information provided about the operation of the sediment passages or the fish ladder to come to a conclusion as to whether these changes will be effective.[89] Given the diversity in fish sizes and the vast populations, the MRC still believes that fish migrations, even with the ladder, will continue to be disrupted.[90] The MRC admits that their official procedures in 2011 did not lead to "any agreed measures to avoid, minimize, or mitigate the potential impacts, or establish any record of the proposed use once commenced."[91] The Xayaburi Dam has privileged energy and economic growth at the expense of ecological and social sustainability in the basin. It is a watershed project that will have lasting impacts throughout Southeast Asia.

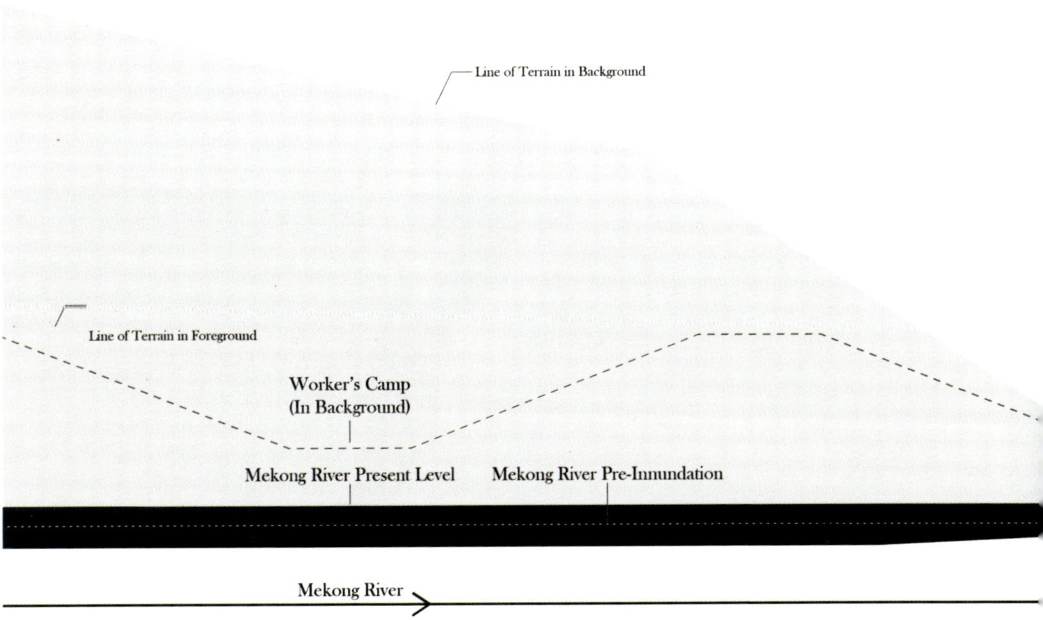

Line of Terrain in Background
Line of Terrain in Foreground
Worker's Camp
(In Background)
Mekong River Present Level
Mekong River Pre-Innundation
Mekong River

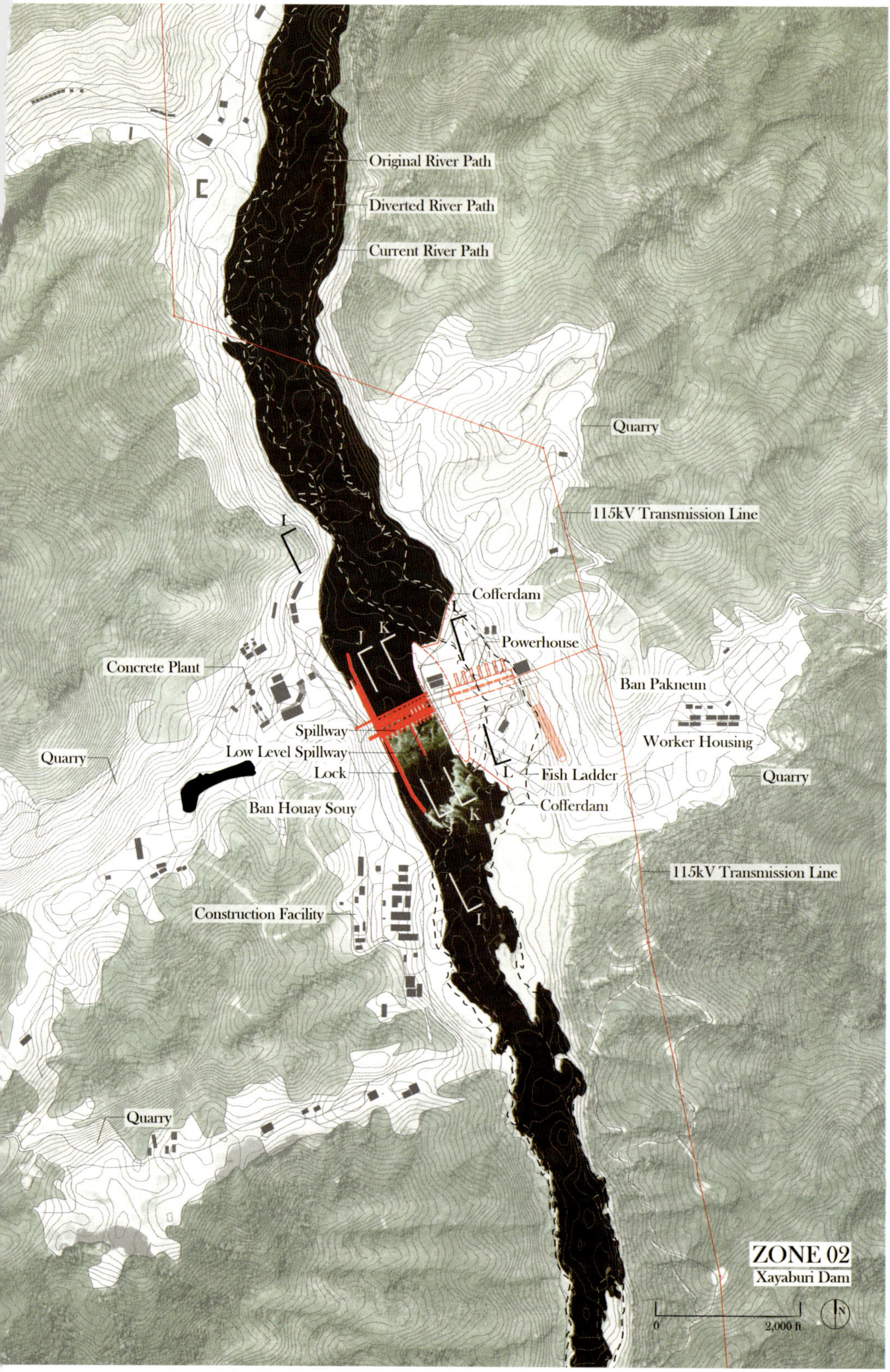

Original River Path
Diverted River Path
Current River Path
Quarry
115kV Transmission Line
Cofferdam
Powerhouse
Concrete Plant
Ban Pakneun
Spillway
Worker Housing
Quarry
Low Level Spillway
Lock
Fish Ladder
Quarry
Cofferdam
Ban Houay Souy
115kV Transmission Line
Construction Facility
Quarry
ZONE 02
Xayaburi Dam
0
2,000 ft
N

Worker Housing
Lock, dam and reservoir (2019)
Concrete Plant (2019)
Spillway, powerhouse, fishladder & transmission line
Construction facility (2019)

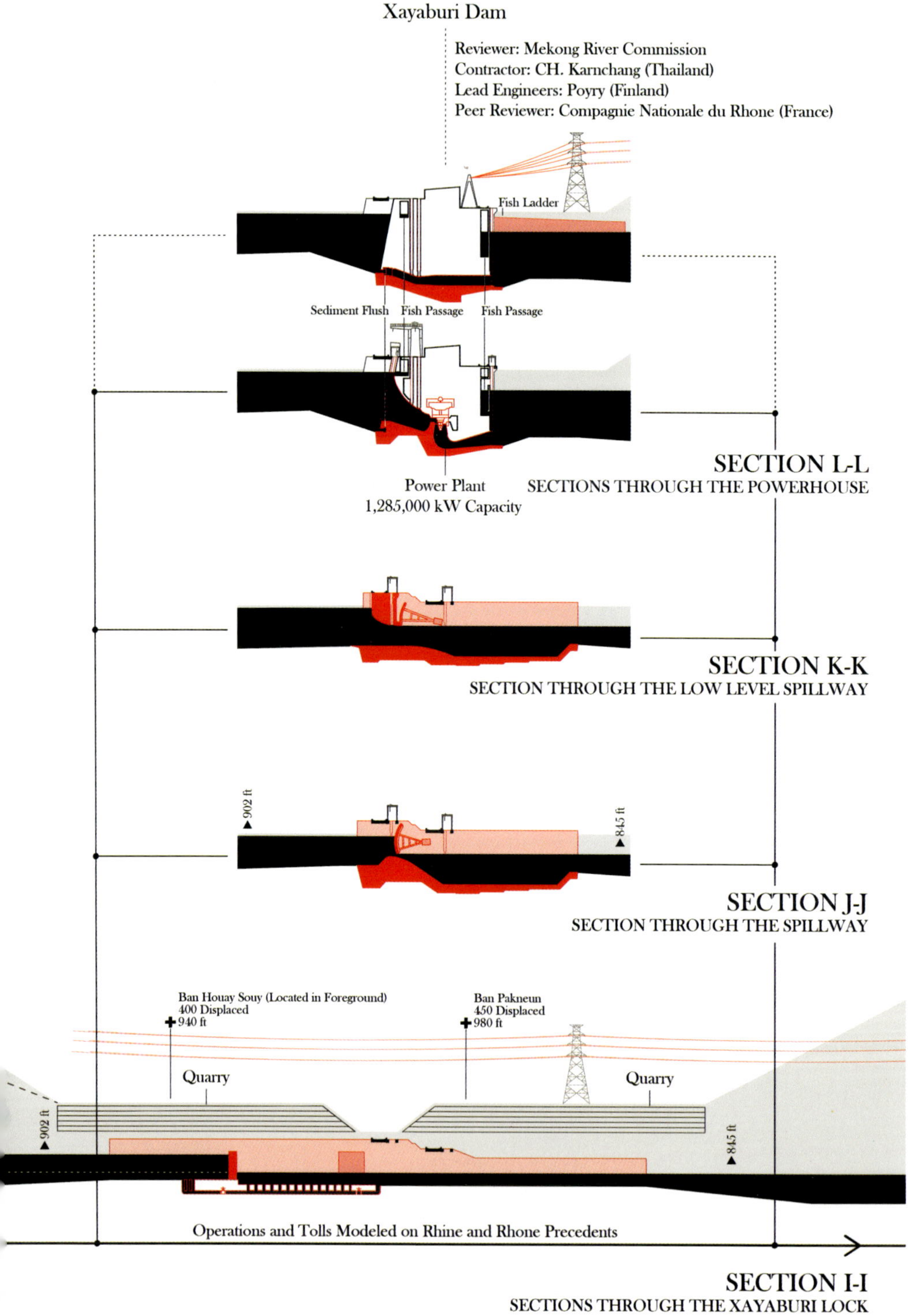
Xayaburi Dam
Reviewer: Mekong River Commission
Contractor: CH. Karnchang (Thailand)
Lead Engineers: Poyry (Finland)
Peer Reviewer: Compagnie Nationale du Rhone (France)
Fish Ladder
Sediment Flush
Fish Passage
Fish Passage
Power Plant
1,285,000 kW Capacity
SECTION L-L
SECTIONS THROUGH THE POWERHOUSE
SECTION K-K
SECTION THROUGH THE LOW LEVEL SPILLWAY
902 ft
845 ft
SECTION J-J
SECTION THROUGH THE SPILLWAY
Ban Houay Souy (Located in Foreground)
400 Displaced
940 ft
Ban Pakneun
450 Displaced
980 ft
Quarry
Quarry
902 ft
845 ft
Operations and Tolls Modeled on Rhine and Rhone Precedents
SECTION I-I
SECTIONS THROUGH THE XAYABURI LOCK

Region 03: Laos & Cambodia Border

Region 03 Plan
At the edge of the Laos and Cambodia border, the Mekong River dramatically transforms into a riverine archipelago called the Si Phan Don, or the "Four Thousand Islands." It is a hydrologically complex region with extreme variation throughout the year, and it has become the site for the second main-stem hydroelectric project, the Don Sahong Dam. During the dry season, most of the streams are either dried up or shallow, with few options for traversing the area, but becoming navigable for large fish migrations upstream when the water level rises in the wet season.[92] This area concludes with a series of rapids and waterfalls before the strands re-form into a single stream as it crosses the border into Cambodia. Completed in 2020, the Don Sahong Dam occupies one of the branches in the lower archipelago, between two of the larger islands. Twenty-five miles south of the national border is the proposed site for the first main-stem Mekong River project in Cambodia, the Stung Treng Dam. These two main-stem projects are potential nodes for the proposed Greater Mekong Subregion Power Trade Project, which will create a cross-border transmission line to link the two projects and their respective country's power grids.[93] Near the site of the Stung Treng Dam is the Lower Sesan 2 Dam, a notable tributary dam that was completed in 2019. Both the Don Sahong Dam and Lower Sesan 2 Dam have been controversial for the displacement of villages to facilitate their construction.[94] Studies have repeatedly shown that any disruption to the watershed's ecology or hydrology will risk threatening the food and social security of millions of people who live nearby and depend on the river.[95] Due to the 2019 and 2020 Mekong River droughts, which are believed to have been exacerbated by the water storage strategies upstream in the upper Mekong River, the Cambodian government placed a 10-year moratorium on all main-stem dam construction while it explores other options to meet its energy needs.[96] The recent droughts and mass displacement that have been attributed to damming have challenged the notion that development engenders progress, at a localized, and potentially larger, scale.

Home of endangered Irrawaddy Dolphins, just south of Don Sahong Dam site Preah Rumkel, Cambodia/Laos border, 2011 (image credit: Derek Hoeferlin)

Zone 02: Xayaburi Dam

Zone 02 Plan

While many of the risks and impacts of the Xayaburi Dam will take time to manifest, its construction has left an immediate mark on both the landscape and the politics in the watershed. No longer densely forested, the land surrounding the project has been transformed into an industrial site. Two villages were removed to clear the project area, displacing a total of 2,100 people.[83] New roads have been paved along the river to access the project, and a series of new transmission lines has been erected to connect to the Thai and Laotian power grids. Many of the natural materials were mined directly from the hillside. Most of the fabrication facilities are located on the western bank of the river, and a small permanent worker community was established in a valley on the eastern riverbank. The project took seven years to complete, starting in 2012 and becoming operational in 2019. From west to east, the Xayaburi Dam consists of a lock, an 800-foot spillway, a 900-foot power plant, and a fish ladder. The structure was constructed in two phases to allow the river to flow freely during this time.[84] First, a series of cofferdams were temporarily installed on the western half of the site to redirect water from the construction zone in order to build the lock and spillways. Upon their completion, the cofferdams were removed, and the river was redirected to flow unimpeded through the dam. The first step was repeated on the opposite side of the river to assemble the power plant and the fish ladder. By the time the Xayaburi Dam broke ground in 2012, the project had been closely scrutinized for two years. The 1995 Mekong Agreement established the "Procedure for Notification, Prior Consultation, and Agreement" (PNPCA), an intergovernmental negotiation process for the development of main-stem projects in the lower Mekong. This process officially began in 2010 after the original design was submitted, and for six months, the four countries and the MRC were engaged in a consultation period where concerns were raised and recommendations made.[85] The PNPCA ended in 2011 without an agreement to begin work on the project. Instead, Vietnam and Cambodia issued a moratorium to allow more time for environmental studies and more substantial redesigns.[86] However, Laos unilaterally made the decision to continue with the project and broke ground in 2012, a decision that the Vietnamese and Cambodian governments roundly criticized.[87] A 2020 academic study of the Xayaburi PNPCA observed that the nationalistic development goals were left unchecked by the MRC's procedures, leading the authors to conclude that the PNPCA failed to meet the MRC's goals of facilitating cooperation in building

Xayaburi Dam under construction, nearing full operation status, 2019 (image credit: Derek Hoeferlin)

Region 03 Sections M-M, N-N

Other than the Tonlé Sap Lake region, more than any other site in the river, the Si Phan Don most clearly demonstrates the physical effect of the hydrologic cycle on the Mekong River Basin. As the Mekong River passes through the archipelago, the riverbed transforms into a large blanket of basalt outcroppings, with which the river coexists. Over the course of the year, the amount of water flowing in the Mekong River dramatically varies. In August, over 990,800 cubic feet per second of water will pass through the region, almost double the average annual discharge. During the height of the dry season, the water volume shrinks nearly tenfold to 100,600 cubic feet per second.[97] The fluctuation in water volume and the unique landscape leads to a dynamic terrain and flow pattern. During the dry season, the western reach reduces to small trickles of water, and at many points fully exposes the riverbed. The majority of the water will travel through the deeper eastern channel, Hou Phapheng.[98] As the volume of water increases over the course of the wet season, the western branch re-forms into a single large stream, and with a higher capacity, the western branch overtakes the flow of water in the archipelago.[99] Generally shallow and narrow, the Si Phan Don is a natural obstruction in the river for fish migrations. Only the Hou Sahong channel has the depth, width, and water volume to facilitate year-round migrations en masse, making it an invaluable passage for the watershed's fish population.[100] However, the Hou Sahong is now obstructed by the Don Sahong Dam, and its impact on the Mekong River Basin's fisheries is potentially devastating.[101] The Si Phan Don is also a natural habitat for a declining population of critically endangered Mekong Irrawaddy dolphins that travel between the Tonlé Sap and the archipelago.[102] Considered sacred in Laotian and Cambodian lore because they are believed to have descended from humans, they are at risk of extinction because of main-stem damming.[103] Additionally, the development of main-stem projects in this region, including the Laos-Cambodia transmission line, reveals a different type of transboundary influence. Like the Xayaburi project, the Don Sahong Dam and Lower Sesan 2 Dam are projects involving multiple countries in addition to their hosts, Cambodia and Laos. The Don Sahong Power Company owns the Don Sahong Dam, which is a subsidiary of the Mega First Corporation Berhad, a Malaysian power corporation. Sinohydro China, a Chinese contractor, built the dam, and the energy will be primarily sold to Thailand.[104] The Lower Sesan 2 Dam was a joint venture between China, Vietnam, and Cambodia, with a majority of the funding and construction provided by the Chinese state-owned corporation, Hydrolancang (or Huaneng Lancang River Hydropower Inc.).[105] Engendered by international policies, the main-stem damming of the Mekong River has disrupted both the watershed's hydrologic cycle and its natural processes.

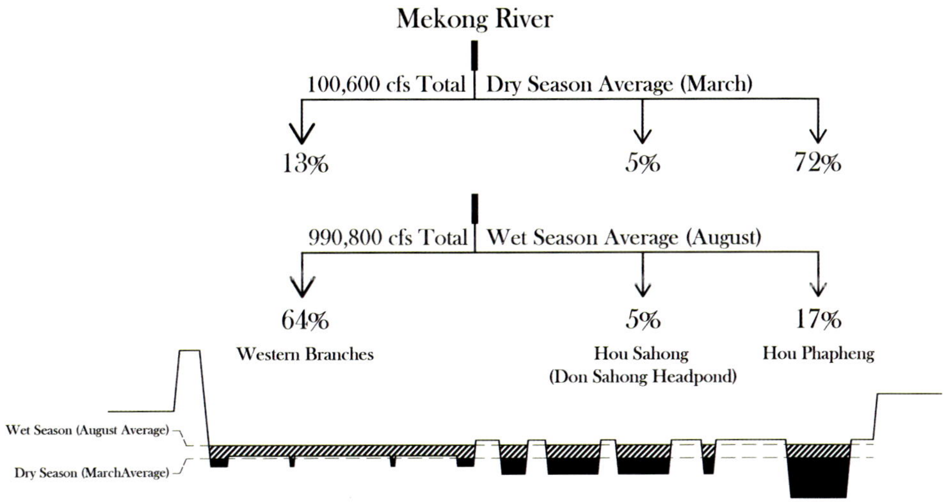

SECTION M-M

TRANSECT THROUGH THE LOWER ARCHIPELAGO PRE-DAMMING

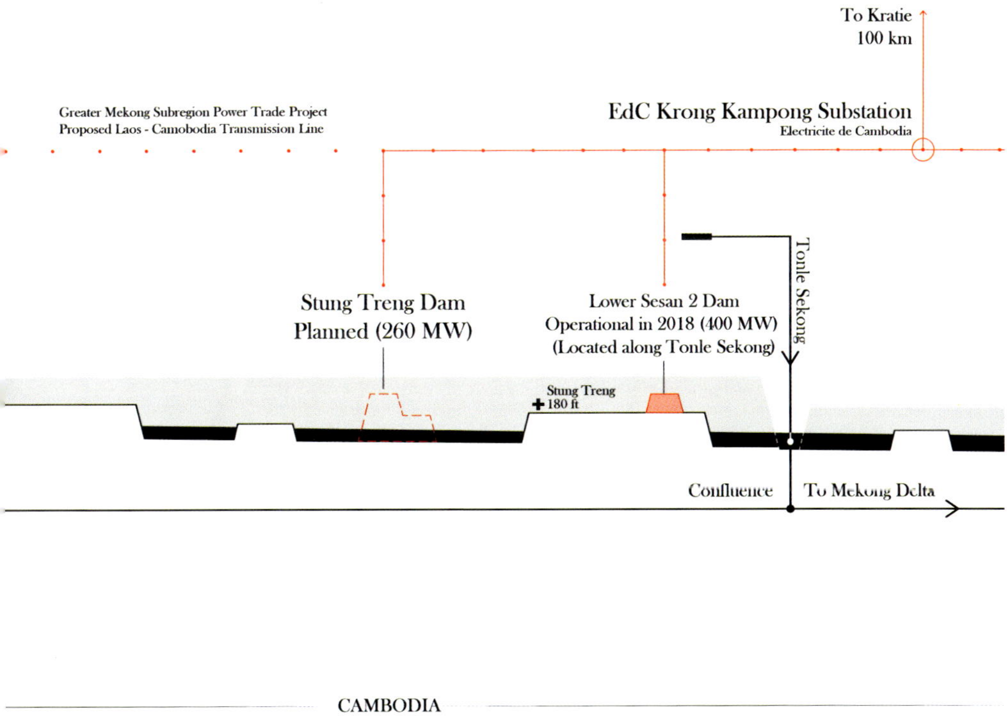

SECTION N-N

SECTION THROUGH THE LAOS & CAMBODIA BORDER

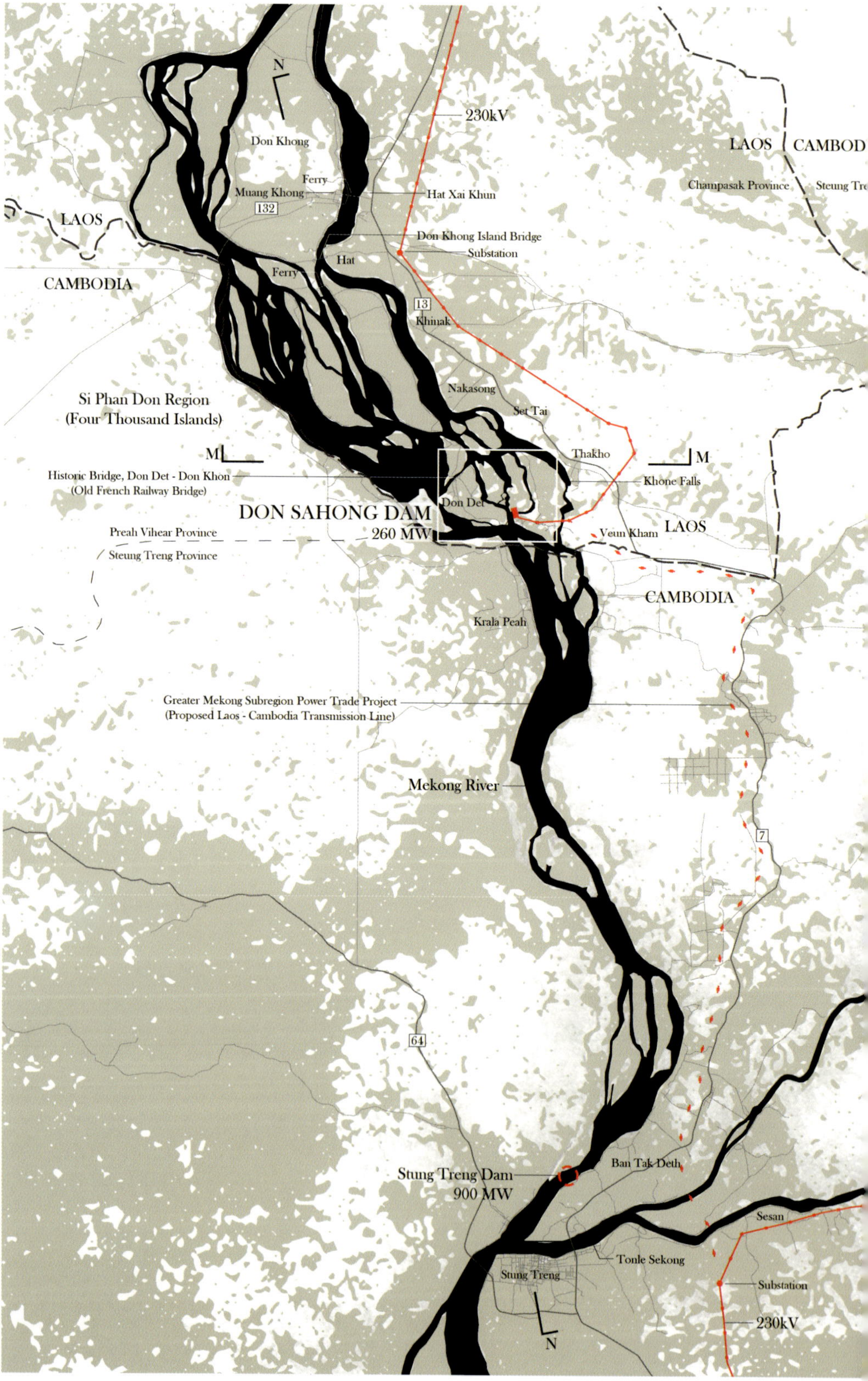

N
230kV
Don Khong
LAOS
CAMBOD
Ferry
Muang Khong
132
Hat Xai Khun
Champasak Province
Steung Tre
LAOS
Don Khong Island Bridge
Substation
Hat
Ferry
CAMBODIA
13
Khinak
Nakasong
Si Phan Don Region
(Four Thousand Islands)
Set Tai
M
Thakho
M
Historic Bridge, Don Det - Don Khon
(Old French Railway Bridge)
Khone Falls
Don Det
DON SAHONG DAM
260 MW
Veun Kham
LAOS
Preah Vihear Province
Steung Treng Province
CAMBODIA
Krala Peah
Greater Mekong Subregion Power Trade Project
(Proposed Laos - Cambodia Transmission Line)
Mekong River
7
64
Ban Tak Deth
Stung Treng Dam
900 MW
Sesan
Tonle Sekong
Stung Treng
Substation
230kV
N

Si Phon Don Region
Dry season
Siem Pang
Si Phon Don Region
Wet season
Tonle Kong River
Nhoun
Khsach Thmei
Tonle San River
Phumi Khsach Thmei
Steung Treng Province
Ratanakiri Province
Lower Sesan 2 Dam
400 MW
Tonle Srepok River
REGION 03
LAOS & CAMBODIA BORDER
0
30,000 ft
N

River level gauge, Cambodia (2011)

Low river stage, Cambodia (2011)

Near site of proposed Stung Treng Dam, Cambodia (2011)

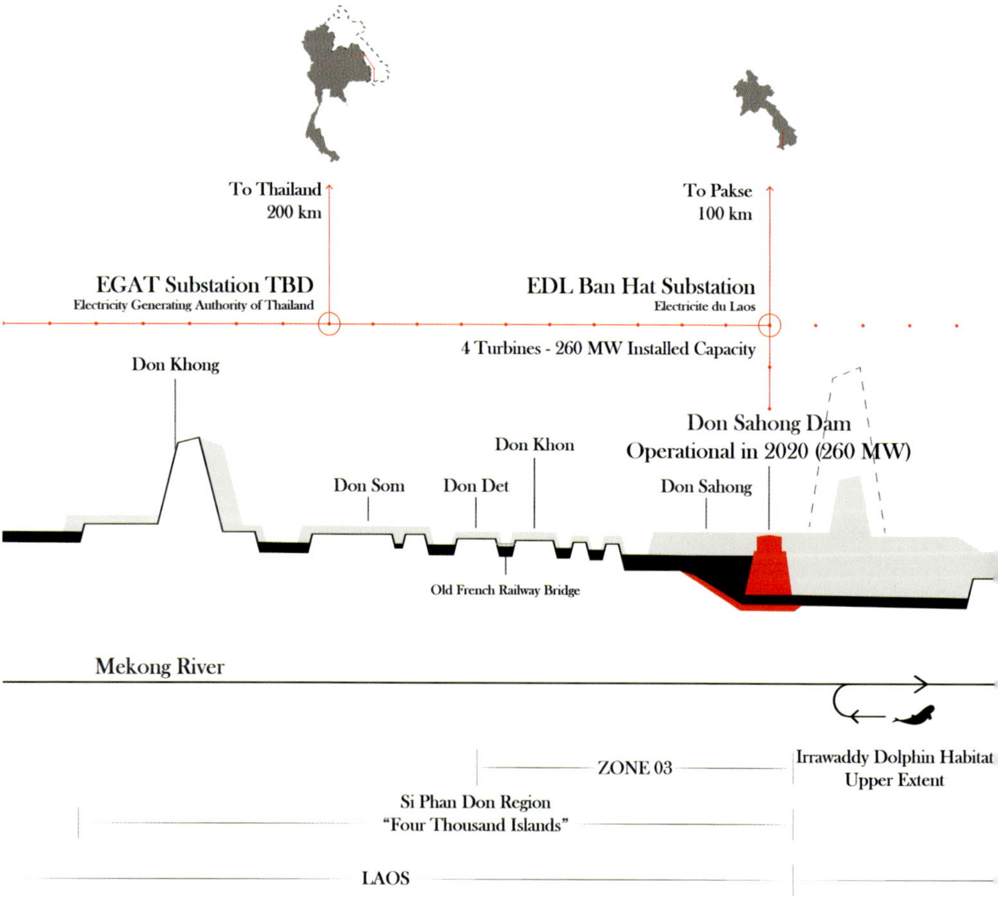

Zone 03: Si Phan Don & Don Sahong Dam

Zone 03 Plan

The lower Si Phan Don is a sublime and formidable landscape that has been developed nonetheless. In this region, the Mekong River splits into seven main channels of water. A line of cascades and waterfalls cuts through the middle of the site, and the river begins to re-form into a single strand after descending these features. Completed in 2020, the Don Sahong Dam is the second main-stem hydroelectric project in Laos and the lower Mekong River. Unlike typical main-stem dams that impound the entire river, the Don Sahong Dam only partially obstructs the river by occupying a single channel in the branching site, the Hou Sahong, located between the islands of Don Sahong and Don Sadam. According to the developer, the project is typologically a "diversion" dam, and is expected to utilize only 15 percent of the river's water flow.[106] The only feature in the dam is a power plant that has the capacity to generate 260 MW of energy, and the reservoir for the project extends to the channel's inlet.[107] The construction site locates mostly on the lower half of Don Sahong with the switchyard being situated on the southern tip of Don Sadam. A worker community was also established on Don Sadam on a small plateau. Regardless of its diminutive size and scope in comparison to the main-stem dams on the Mekong River, the Don Sahong Project has left a significant and irreversible impact on the landscape. In the process of creating the reservoir, the natural riverbed was excavated, and a line of embankments was erected to achieve a minimum operating water level.[108] Two villages, one on each island, were displaced and relocated to an uninhabited site on Don Sahong.[109] While the anticipated disruption to the water flow is small, the channel that the project has impounded, the Hou Sahong, was an invaluable passage for fish migrations. The fluctuation in water volume prevents all of the channels, except for the Hou Sahong, from facilitating year-round fish migration.[110] Its loss is potentially devastating to fish population and a sociocultural disaster for populations dependent on the river's fisheries.[111] In an effort to ameliorate the situation, the developer has dredged the two adjacent streams, Hou Xang Peuk and Hou Sadam, to create artificial passages that they claim will facilitate future year-round

Li Phi Falls/Tat Somphamit Waterfall, Cambodia/Laos border, "dry season," 2011
(image credit: Derek Hoeferlin)

migrations.[112] However, the Mekong River Commission's review of the project noted that this alternative was unsubstantiated and highly unlikely to fully compensate for the lost passage.[113] Developed as a less disruptive project, the Don Sahong Dam's impact on the delicate and crucial site has comparable, if not greater, consequences as a main-stem Mekong dam.

Zone 03 Sections O-O, P-P, Q-Q

The lower archipelago is a branching site that has been dramatically altered by the Don Sahong Dam project despite its diminutive presence. In spite of the area's imposing natural features, it is a relatively populated region. There are villages on both sides of the riverbank and along the edges of the islands. A few locations have been cultivated, but the land largely remains in its natural state. Transportation in the archipelago mostly consists of ferry routes, but a bridge was recently constructed between the Don Sahong Dam project site and the eastern riverbank. Until now, only a single bridge had been erected in this area, the Old French Railway Bridge between Don Det and Don Khon. This locomotive bridge is a ruin from the French Indochina empire and its failed attempt to traverse the waterfalls in a larger effort to navigate the full extent of the Mekong River from the delta to China.[114] There is a minor risk of unexploded ordinance from the CIA's "Secret War."[115] Approaching the lower archipelago, the Mekong River splits into two branches, the western channel and a "primary" branch that feeds into the remaining six streams. The site for the structure is at the end of the Hou Sahong stream between the Don Sahong and Sadam islands, and it houses a relatively small 240 MW power plant. Its diminutive reservoir was transformed from the natural channel which required significant modifications to the physical terrain and the flow patterns. First, the capacity in the reservoir was increased by digging out the bottom of the approach and by constructing embankments along both sides of the pond. A deflector was installed on the riverbed to redirect coarse sediment and prevent the loss of storage capacity over time to sediment accumulation. First, the inlet was widened to improve water diversion into the reservoir. In the wet season, the flow into the reservoir will increase by 19 percent, which is siphoned from the main channel, leading to a 27 percent decrease in the eastern channel, the Hou Phapheng.[116] By decreasing its allocation, the Hou Phapheng has the ability to absorb excess water during flood events and effectively become the Don Sahong Dam's spillway.[117] The modified pattern is more extreme in the dry months. At the height of the dry season in March, 61 percent of the water from the Hou Phapheng will be diverted to the Don Sahong Dam's reservoir, increasing its water intake by 815 percent. The project will be utilizing more than half of the water in the Mekong during this period. While it may be true that the reservoir will only utilize 15 percent of the water over the course of the year, this notion subverts the natural hydrologic cycle. Ostensibly not a main-stem dam, the Don Sahong Dam has nevertheless had the potential to have a devastating impact on the Mekong River Basin.

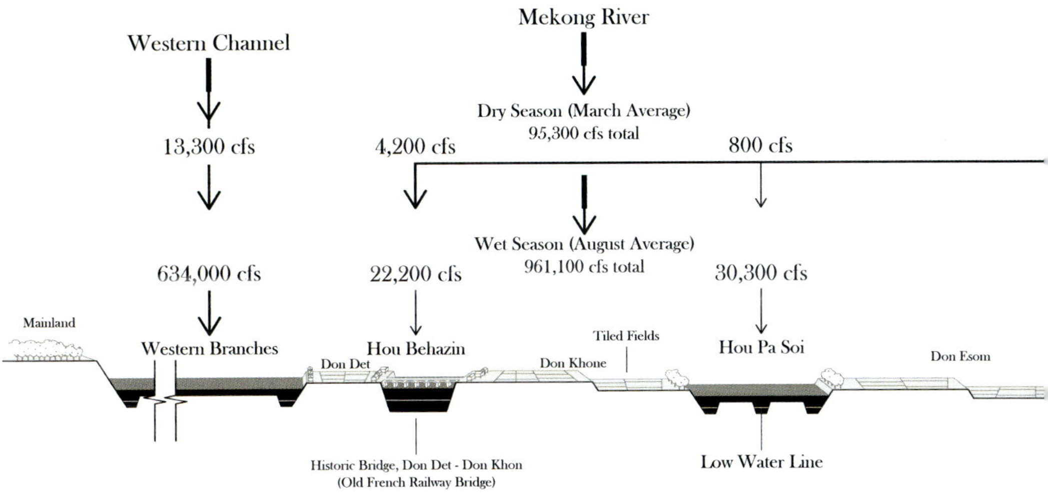
Mekong River
Western Channel
Dry Season (March Average)
95,300 cfs total
13,300 cfs
4,200 cfs
800 cfs
Wet Season (August Average)
961,100 cfs total
634,000 cfs
22,200 cfs
30,300 cfs
Mainland
Western Branches
Hou Behazin
Tiled Fields
Hou Pa Soi
Don Det
Don Khone
Don Esom
Historic Bridge, Don Det - Don Khon
(Old French Railway Bridge)
Low Water Line

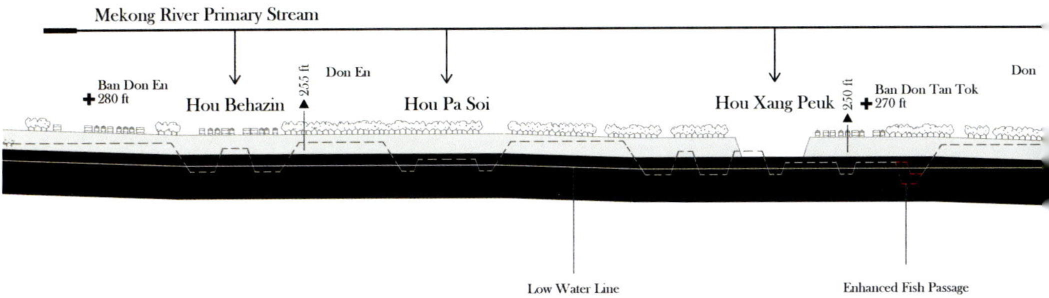
Mekong River Primary Stream
Ban Don En
280 ft
Hou Behazin
255 ft
Don En
Hou Pa Soi
Hou Xang Peuk
250 ft
Ban Don Tan Tok
270 ft
Don
Low Water Line
Enhanced Fish Passage

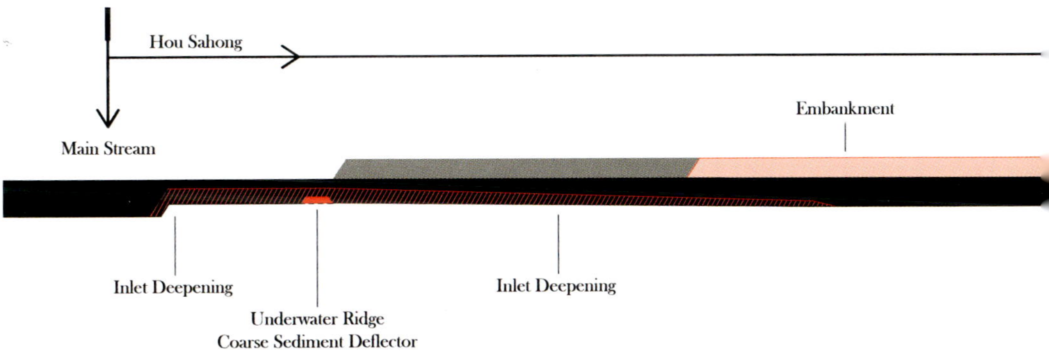
Hou Sahong
Main Stream
Embankment
Inlet Deepening
Underwater Ridge
Coarse Sediment Deflector
Inlet Deepening

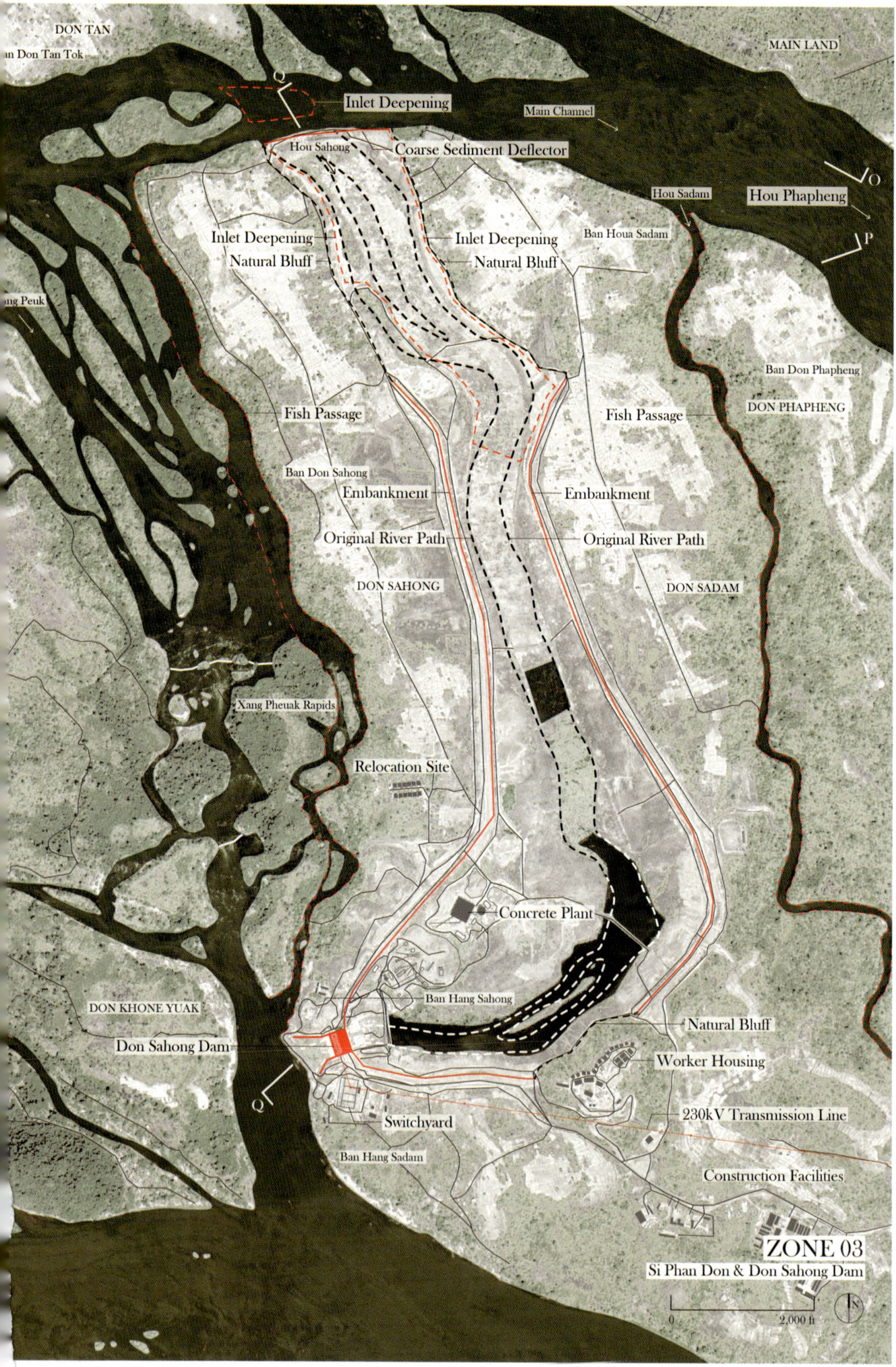

DON TAN
an Don Tan Tok
MAIN LAND
Inlet Deepening
Main Channel
Hou Sahong
Coarse Sediment Deflector
Hou Sadam
Hou Phapheng
O
P
Q
Inlet Deepening
Natural Bluff
Inlet Deepening
Natural Bluff
Ban Houa Sadam
ng Peuk
Ban Don Phapheng
DON PHAPHENG
Fish Passage
Fish Passage
Ban Don Sahong
Embankment
Embankment
Original River Path
Original River Path
DON SAHONG
DON SADAM
Xang Pheuak Rapids
Relocation Site
Concrete Plant
Ban Hang Sahong
DON KHONE YUAK
Natural Bluff
Don Sahong Dam
Worker Housing
Q
Switchyard
230kV Transmission Line
Ban Hang Sadam
Construction Facilities
ZONE 03
Si Phan Don & Don Sahong Dam
0
2,000 ft
N

Old French Port, Don Det
Ban Don En
DON EN
O
Ban Don Det Tok
Main Channel
Hou X
Western Branches
DON DET
Hou Behazin
Hou Pa Soi
Ban Don Det Oke
Ban Khone Neua
Ban Don I-Som
Historic Bridge, Don Det - Don Khon
(Old French Railway Bridge)
DON ESOM
P
Ban Khone Tai
Khone Pa Soi Rapids
DON KHONE
Somphamit Waterfall
Ban Hang Khone

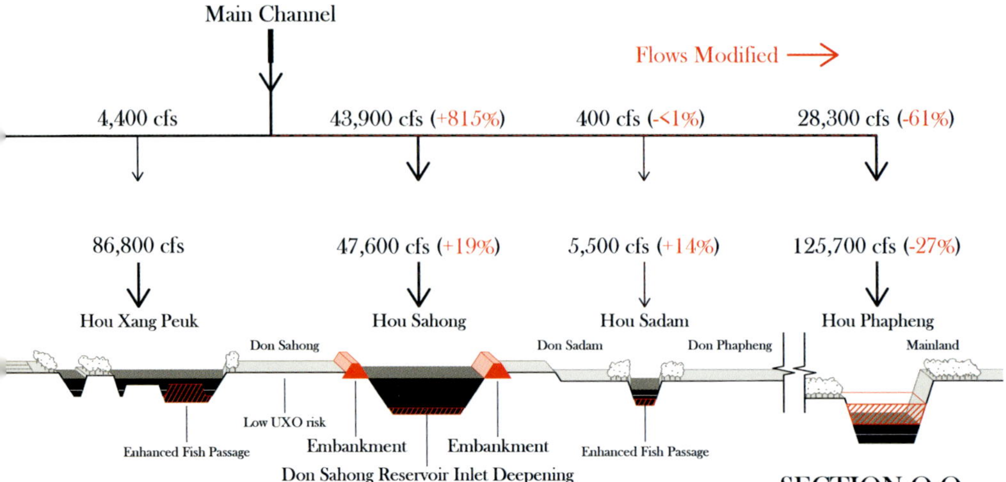

SECTION O-O
TRANSECT THROUGH THE SI PHAN DON POST DAMMING

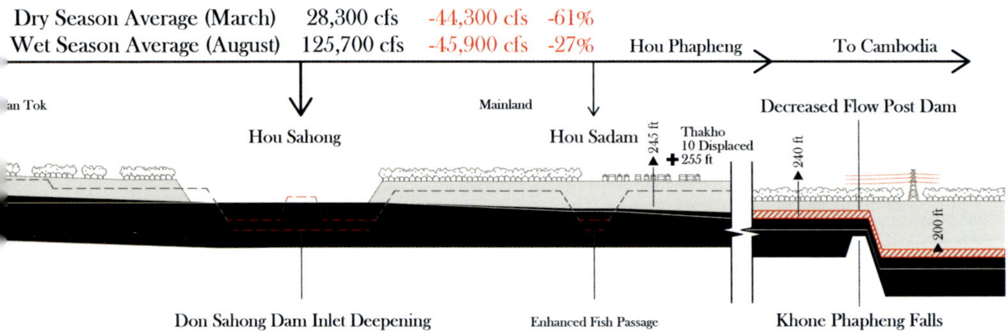

SECTION P-P
SECTION THROUGH THE MAIN CHANNEL

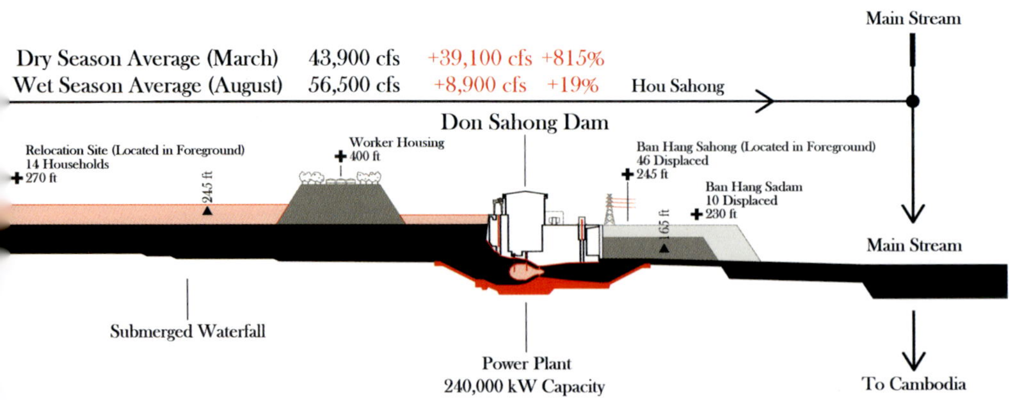

SECTION Q-Q
SECTION THROUGH HOU SAHONG AND DON SAHONG DAM

1. Cheng Liu, Yun He, Des E. Walling, and Jianjun Wang, "Changes in the sediment load of the Lancang-Mekong River over the period 1965–2003," *Science China Technological Sciences* 56, no. 4 (April 2013): 843–852.
2. "The Flow of the Mekong," 4; "Overview of the Hydrology of the Mekong Basin" (Vientiane: Mekong River Commission, November 2005), accessed November 9, 2020, http://www.mekonginfo.org/assets/midocs/0001968-inland-waters-overview-of-the-hydrology-of-the-mekong-basin.pdf, 1.
3. Yongnan Zhu et al., "Water Transfer and Losses Embodied in the West-East Electricity Transmission Project in China," *Applied Energy* 275 (October 1, 2020): 1–2.
4. Darrin L. Magee, "Powershed Politics: Yunnan Hydropower Under Great Western Development," *China Quarterly* 185 (March 2006): 23–41.
5. Lihui Chen, "Contradictions in Dam Building in Yunnan, China: Cultural Impacts versus Economic Growth," *China Report* 44, no. 2 (May 2008): 97–110.
6. Bryan Tilt and Drew Gerkey, "Dams and Population Displacement on China's Upper Mekong River: Implications for Social Capital and Social-Ecological Resilience," *Global Environmental Change* 36 (January 2016): 153–62.
7. Magee, "Powershed Politics," 29.
8. Ibid., 38.
9. Yongnan Zhu et al., "Water Transfer and Losses," 5.
10. Ibid., 5, 7.
11. Magee, "Powershed Politics," 30.
12. Yuichiro Yoshida et al., "Impacts of Mainstream Hydropower Dams on Fisheries and Agriculture in Lower Mekong Basin," *Sustainability* 12, no. 6 (March 2020): 3.
13. Cheng Liu et. al., "Changes in the sediment load," 851–852.
14. Pichamon Yeophantong, "China's Lancang Dam Cascade and Transnational Activism in the Mekong Region: Who's Got the Power," *Asian Survey* 54, no. 4 (2014): 700–724.
15. Ibid., 714; Parameswaran Ponnudurai, "Water Wars Feared Over Mekong," *Radio Free Asia*, September 30, 2012, accessed November 9, 2020, https://www.rfa.org/english/commentaries/east-asia-beat/mekong-09302012160353.html.
16. Yang Yafeng and Shao Xiaolu, "Introduction to the Resettlement Planning of the Lancang River Xiaowan Project (in Chinese) *Yunnan Water Power* 18, no. 1 (2002): 19; Yang Haiqing, Zhu Zhaocai, and Wu Jinliang, "Practice of the 'Land-Resources-Based' Agricultural Resettlement Method at Xiaowan Hydropower Station," (in Chinese) *Yunnan Water Power* 35, no. 5 (2019): 7.
17. Brian Eyler, Regan Kwan, Courtney Weatherby, "Mekong Reservoirs in Yunnan Province, China," *Stimson Center*, July 7, 2020, accessed February 2, 2021, https://www.stimson.org/2020/mekong-reservoirs-in-yunnan-province-china/.
18. Li Qing, "The Important Role of Xiaowan Hydropower Station in the Power Transmission from West to East and the Development of Economy in Yunnan Province," (in Chinese) *Water Power* 30, no. 10 (October 2004): 17.
19. Zhang Guojun, "Changbao Highway Expected to be Completed and Opened to Traffic by the End of 2020," (in Chinese) *Baoshan Daily*, August 28, 2019, accessed November 9, 2020, http://www.baoshandaily.com/html/20190828/content_156698238166499.html; Fengqing County Transportation Bureau, "Fengqing County Transportation Bureau 2020 Annual Budget Disclosure," (in Chinese) People's Government of Fengqing County, June 14, 2020, accessed November 9, 2020, http://www.ynfq.gov.cn/fqxrmzf/xxgk72/czyjsbg/523761/index.html.
20. Guojun, "Changbao Highway"; Fengqing County Transportation Bureau.
21. Yafeng and Xiaolu, "Introduction to the Resettlement Planning of the Lancang River," 7, 11.
22. Yeophantong, "China's Lancang Dam Cascade," 721.

23. Ibid., 722.

24. Tan Weimin, "Actively Promote the Implementation of the National Hydropower Strategy of 'West–East Electricity Transmission' and Facilitate Western Development with Hydropower Development," (in Chinese) *Chinese Hydraulic Engineering Society 2000 Annual Conference*, 2000, 366.

25. "To Speed up the Implementation of 'Yunnan-Guangdong Electricity Transmission' Yunnan and Guangdong Provinces Reached Agreements on Economic Cooperation Framework," (in Chinese) *Yunnan Electric Power News*, August 3, 2001.

26. Li Qing, "Important Role of Xiaowan Hydropower Station in the Power Transmission from West to East and the Development of Economy in Yunnan Province," (in Chinese) *Water Power* 30, no. 10 (October 2004), 18.

27. Li Honggang, "Analysis on the Initial Impoundment of Xiaowan Hydropower Station," (in Chinese) *Yunnan Water Power* 26, no. 6 (2010): 5–7.

28. Ibid., 5.; "Manwan Hydropower Station," (in Chinese) *Yunnan Water Power* 31, no. 2 (1993): 30.

29. Chen Xuezhen and Fu Shuhong, "Layout of the Hydro-junction of Xiaowan Hydropower Station," (in Chinese) *Yunnan Water Power*, no. 1 (March 1996): 43.

30. Li Qing, "Important Role of Xiaowan Hydropower Station," 18.

31. "The Effects of Chinese dams on water flows in the Lower Mekong Basin," News and Events, Mekong River Commission, June 6, 2017, accessed January 26, 2021, https://www.mrcmekong.org/news-and-events/news/the-effects-of-chinese-dams-on-water-flows-in-the-lower-mekong-basin/.

32. Ibid.

33. Beech, "China Limited the Mekong's Flow."

34. Yang Haiqing, Zhu Zhaocai, Wu Jinliang, "Practice of the 'Land-Resources-Based' Agricultural Resettlement Method at Xiaowan Hydropower Station," (in Chinese) *Yunnan Water Power* 35, no. 5 (2019), 7.

35. "Dam Information: Xiaowan Hydropower Project" (Beijing: China National Committee on Large Dams, May 21, 2008), accessed November 9, 2020, http://www.chincold.org.cn/dams/rootfiles/2010/07/20/1279253974169481-1279253974171370.pdf, 1.

36. Xuezhen and Shuhong, "Layout of the Hydro-junction of Xiaowan Hydropower Station," 44.

37. Ibid.

38. Ibid.

39. Ibid.

40. Board of Directors of Huaneng Lancang River Hydropower Incorporate, "Huaneng Lancang River Hydropower Inc. Announcement of Annual Power Production Performance in 2017" (in Chinese), *China Securities Journal*, January 14, 2018, accessed November 9, 2020, http://epaper.zqrb.cn/html/2018-01/24/content_77609.htm; Board of Directors of Huaneng Lancang River Hydropower Incorporate, "Huaneng Lancang River Hydropower Inc. Announcement of Annual Power Production Performance in 2019," (in Chinese) *China Securities Journal*, January 4, 2020, accessed November 9, 2020, http://epaper.zqrb.cn/html/2020-01/04/content_552000.htm.

41. "Classic Hydropower Project 16: Xiaowan Hydropower Station" (in Chinese), (Guangzhou: Guangdong Society for Hydropower Engineering, September 10, 2014) accessed November 9, 2020, http://www.gdshe.org/Item/2949.aspx.

42. Yang Haiqing et al., "Practice of the 'Land-Resources-Based' Agricultural Resettlement Method at Xiaowan Hydropower Station," 7.

43. Joyce Chepkemoi, "World's Tallest Dams," World Atlas, April 25, 2017, accessed November 9, 2020, https://www.worldatlas.com/articles/the-world-s-tallest-dams.html.

44. Honggang, "Analysis on the Initial Impoundment of Xiaowan Hydropower Station," 5–7.

45. Ibid., 5.

46. “Dam Information: Xiaowan Hydropower Project,” 1.

47. Ibid., 2.

48. Ibid., 1.

49. Xuezhen and Shuhong, “Layout of the Hydro-junction of Xiaowan Hydropower Station,” 43.

50. “The Effects of Chinese Dams on Water Flows in the Lower Mekong Basin.”

51. “Mekong Commission visits China dams and will discuss future cooperation,” News and Events, Mekong River Commission, June 7, 2010, accessed January 25, 2021, https://www.mrcmekong.org/news-and-events/news/mekong-commission-visits-china-dams-and-will-discuss-future-cooperation/.

52. Planning Atlas of the Lower Mekong River Basin, 3.

53. Ibid., 3.

54. Ibid., 13.

55. “The Flow of the Mekong,” 2.

56. “Hydrology,” Mekong River Commission.

57. Ibid.

58. “Fisheries Programme 2011–2015” (Vientiane: Mekong River Commission, 31 December 2010), accessed November 9, 2020, https://www.mrcmekong.org/assets/FP-2011-2015-Document-FINAL.pdf, 8.

59. Florence Tan, Interview with Viraphonh Viravong, Interview—Laos's Hydropower Generation Capacity to Jump Almost Four-Fold by 2020, Reuters, 28 October 2014, accessed November 9, 2020, https://www.reuters.com/article/laos-energy-minister/interview-laos-hydropower-generation-capacity-to-jump-almost-four-fold-by-2020-idUKL4N0SL0EG20141028.

60. Yoshida et al., 3–4, 17.

61. ICEM Australia, *Strategic Environmental Assessment of Hydropower on the Mekong Mainstream: Summary of the Final Report* (Vientiane: Mekong River Commission 14 October 2010), accessed November 9, 2020, http://www.mrcmekong.org/assets/Publications/Consultations/SEA-Hydropower/SEA-FR-summary-13oct.pdf, 16.

62. Ibid., 14.

63. Matti Kummu and Juha Sarkkula, “Impact of the Mekong River Flow Alteration on the Tonlé Sap Flood Pulse,” *AMBIO: A Journal of the Human Environment* 37, no. 3 (May 2008): 185–92.

64. ICEM Australia, “Strategic Environmental Assessment of Hydropower on the Mekong Mainstream,” 9.

65. Ibid., 4, 9.

66. Frankel, Intralawan, and Wood, “Economic Evaluations of Hydropower Projects in the Lower Mekong Basin,” 4.

67. Ibid., 1.

68. Leonie Kijewski, “Cambodia Halts Hydropower Construction on Mekong River Until 2030” (VOA News, April 1, 2020) accessed November 9, 2020, https://www.voanews.com/east-asia-pacific/cambodia-halts-hydropower-construction-mekong-river-until-2030.

69. “Town of Luang Prabang,” World Heritage List, United Nations Educational, Scientific and Cultural Organization, https://whc.unesco.org/en/list/479/; “Protecting Wild Elephants and Their Habitat in Laos,” Nam Pouy National Protected Area Management, Elephant Conservation Center, accessed January 27, 2021, https://www.elephantconservationcenter.com/ranger-patrols/.

70. “Hongsa Power Plant and Mining Project,” EarthRights International, August 15, 2017, accessed November 9, 2020, https://earthrights.org/what-we-do/extractive-industries/hongsa-power-plant-and-mining-project/.

71. Ethan Harfenist, “Leaked report reveals massive illegal logging in Laos,” *Mongabay* (November 6, 2015), https://news.mongabay.com/2015/11/leaked-report-reveals-massive-illegal-logging-in-laos/.

72. Ibid.

73. Ame Trandem, "Xayaburi Dam: Laos" (Nijmegen: BankTrack, October 12, 2016), accessed November 9, 2020, https://www.banktrack.org/project/xayaburi_dam/pdf, 4-5.

74. Tom Fawthorp, "Hydropower vs Heritage: Will Laos Lose Luang Prabang?" *Diplomat* (December 23, 2020), https://thediplomat.com/2020/12/hydropower-vs-heritage-will-laos-lose-luang-prabang/.

75. *Proposed Xayaburi Dam Project—Mekong River: Prior Consultation Project Review Report* (Vientiane: Mekong River Commission Secretariat, March 24, 2011), accessed November 9, 2020, http://www.mrcmekong.org/assets/Publications/Reports/PC-Proj-Review-Report-Xaiyaburi-24-3-11.pdf, 44-45.

76. Ibid., 43.

77. Poyry, "Xayaburi Run-of-River HPP Presentation to Government of Lao PDR and Other Interested Stakeholders" (Presentation, Xayaburi Dam Procedure for Notification, Prior Consultation and Agreement, July 16, 2012, Luang Prabang), https://www.slideshare.net/sarodp/xiyaburi-dam-project-poyry-july2012v03, 28.

78. Knut Sierotzki, "Experiences with the Preliminary Design Guidelines in the Design of Xayaburi Hydroelectric Power Project," (Vientiane: MRC Forum on Sustainable Hydropower, August 11, 2017), accessed November 9, 2020, http://www.mrcmekong.org/assets/Uploads/7.-Poyry-Experience-with-PDG.pdf, 5.

79. "Proposed Xayaburi Dam Project," 5.

80. Ibid., 5.

81. Ibid., 6.

82. Ibid., 92–93.

83. Kirk Herbertson, *The Xayaburi Dam: Threatening Food Security in the Mekong* (Oakland: International Rivers, September 2012), accessed January 27, 2021, https://archive.internationalrivers.org/resources/the-xayaburi-dam-threatening-food-security-in-the-mekong-7675, 4.

84. Poyry, "Xayaburi Run-of-River HPP Presentation" (Luang Prabang: July 16, 2012), accessed November 9, 2020, https://www.slideshare.net/sarodp/xiyaburi-dam-project-poyry-july2012v03, 29.

85. "Review of the Design Changes Made for Xayaburi Hydropower Project: Technical Reference Paper No. 65" (Vientiane: Mekong River Commission, January 2019), accessed January 27, 2021, https://www.mrcmekong.org/assets/Publications/Review-of-the-design-change-made-for-Xayaburi-hydropower-project_technical-ref-paper_2019.pdf, 1.

86. Richard Grunwald, Wenling Wang, and Yan Feng, "Modified Transboundary Water Interaction Nexus (TWINS): Xayaburi Dam Case Study," *Water* 12, iss. 3 (2020), accessed December 16, 2020, https://www.mdpi.com/2073-4441/12/3/710, 10.

87. Ibid., 11.

88. Ibid., 13.

89. "Review of the Design Changes Made for Xayaburi Hydropower Project: Technical Reference Paper No. 65," 2.

90. Ibid., 12.

91. Ibid., 5.

92. Vu Vi An, et al., *Prior Consultation for the Proposed Don Sahong Hydropower Project Technical Assessment Report: Fish Passage and Fisheries Ecology* (Vientiane: Mekong River Commission, December 2014), accessed November 9, 2020, https://www.mrcmekong.org/assets/Publications/Consultations/Don-Sahong/Annex-C-Fisheries-Report.pdf, C_5.

93. Korea Electric Power Corporation, "Initial Environmental Examination and Environmental Management Plan for Greater Mekong Sub-Region Power Trade Project: Ban Hat in Champasak Province (Laos) to Stung Treng (Cambodia)" (Phnom Penh: Kingdom of Cambodia Ministry of Industry, Mines and Energy, December 2011), accessed November 9, 2020, http://documents1.worldbank.org/curated/en/844841468044952343/pdf/E15970V30EAP1E10Box358333B01PUBLIC1.pdf, 6. 90.

94. Stephanie Jensen-Cormier, "Watered Down: How Do Big Hydropower Companies Adhere to Social

and Environmental Policies and Best Practices" (Oakland: International Rivers, November 2019), accessed November 9, 2020, https://3waryu2g9363hdvii1ci666p-wpengine.netdna-ssl.com/wp-content/uploads/sites/86/2020/10/watered-down-full-report-english-compressed.pdf, 115.

95. ICEM Australia, "Strategic Environmental Assessment of Hydropower on the Mekong Mainstream," 14.

96. Leonie Kijewski, "Cambodia Halts Hydropower Construction on Mekong River Until 2030," *VOA News* (April 1, 2020), accessed November 9, 2020, https://www.voanews.com/east-asia-pacific/cambodia-halts-hydropower-construction-mekong-river-until-2030.

97. SMEC New Zealand Limited, "Hydrology of the Khone Falls: Don Sahong Hydropower Project" (Vientiane: Don Sahong Power Company Ltd, 19 September 2016), accessed November 9, 2020, http://dshpp.com/wp-content/uploads/2016/09/2016-09-16-DSHP-Hydrology-of-the-Khone-Falls.pdf, 38.

98. Ibid., 2.

99. Ibid., 38.

100. *Technical Review Report: Prior Consultation for the Proposed Don Sahong Hydropower Project* (Vientiane: Mekong River Commission, February 6, 2015), accessed November 9, 2020, http://www.mrcmekong.org/assets/Publications/Consultations/Don-Sahong/Technical-Review-Report-DSHPP-040315.pdf, 17.

101. An et al., "Prior Consultation for the Proposed Don Sahong Hydropower Project Technical Assessment Report: Fish Passage and Fisheries Ecology," C_5.

102. Isabel Beasley, "Review of the Mekong Dolphin Population Status and Potential Impacts of the Proposed Don Sahong Hydropower Project: In Support of the Prior Consultation Process" (Vientiane: Mekong River Commission, December 7, 2014), accessed November 9, 2020, http://www.mrcmekong.org/assets/Publications/Consultations/Don-Sahong/Annex-D-Dolphin-Report.pdf, D-3.

103. Ibid., 20.

104. National Consulting Company Vientiane, Lao PDR, "Don Sahong Hydropower Project, Lao PDR: Environmental Impact Assessment" (Petaling Jaya: MEGA First Corporation Berhad, January 2013), accessed November 9, 2020, https://www.mrcmekong.org/assets/Other-Documents/Don-Sahong/DSHPP-EIA-FINAL.pdf, 2_7; Johan Frijns, "Don Sahong Hydropower Project: Laos" (Nijmegen: BankTrack, November 1, 2016), accessed November 9, 2020, https://www.banktrack.org/project/don_sahong_dam/pdf, 3.

105. Jensen-Cormier, "Watered Down," 116.

106. *Don Sahong Hydropower Project: Engineering Status Report Vol. 1,* (Auckland: AECOM New Zealand Limited, 27 September 2011), accessed January 23, 2021, https://www.mrcmekong.org/news-and-events/consultations/pnpca-prior-consultations/don-sahong-hydropower-project/, xiii.

107. Ibid., x; *Technical Review Report: Prior Consultation for the Proposed Don Sahong Hydropower Project*, 8.

108. *Technical Review Report: Prior Consultation for the Proposed Don Sahong Hydropower Project*, 8.

109. National Consulting Company Vientiane, Lao PDR, "Don Sahong Hydropower Project, Lao PDR: Environmental Impact Assessment," 6_1.

110. An et al., *Prior Consultation for the Proposed Don Sahong Hydropower Project Technical Assessment Report: Fish Passage and Fisheries Ecology*, C_5.

111. Ibid., C_5.

112. *Technical Review Report: Prior Consultation for the Proposed Don Sahong Hydropower Project*, 9.

113. Ibid., 18, 23.

114. John Keay, "The Mekong Exploration Commission, 1866–68: Anglo-French Rivalry in South East Asia" (*Asian Affairs* XXXVI, no. III, November 2005): 289–312.

115. "Don Sahong Hydropower Project," xiii.

116. SMEC New Zealand Limited, "Hydrology of the Khone Falls," 51.

117. Ibid., 51, 57.

(LOWER LEFT) Mekong River water levels during "dry season," near Cambodia/Laos border, 2011
(BACKGROUND) Example of Mekong Delta houses designed to adjust heights based on water levels, Vietnam, 2011(image credit: Derek Hoeferlin)

(LOWER LEFT) Fishing village, Mekong Delta, Vietnam, 2011
(BACKGROUND) Fishing net, Mekong Delta, Vietnam, 2011(image credit: Derek Hoeferlin)

Farm Fresh-Saline

(LOWER LEFT) Drying rice, Mekong Delta, Vietnam, 2011
(BACKGROUND) Harvested salt, Mekong Delta, Vietnam, 2011
(image credit: Derek Hoeferlin)

Mine Sand

(LOWER LEFT) Sand mining site on Mekong River, Cambodia, 2011
(BACKGROUND) Mekong River bank erosion, Cambodia, 2011 (image credit: Derek Hoeferlin)

Balance

Sustainable Hydropower Development and Management in the Lower Mekong Basin

Palakorn Chanbanyong & Simon Krohn

Disclaimer:

"The views expressed are those of the authors and not necessarily the views of the MRC member countries, secretariat, or partners."

[Figure 1] Example of riverbank community and farming threatened by hydropower development, Stung Treng, Cambodia, 2011 (image credit: Derek Hoeferlin)

Introduction

Over the last decade, the Mekong River has come under increasing threat from climate change and water resources development projects such as hydropower dams, irrigation projects, and sand mining. **[Figure 1]** These challenges, along with demographic changes, are set out in the MRC's State of the Basin Report 2018 (SOBR)[1] and Council Study.[2] The 1995 Mekong Agreement[3] provides the legal mandate of the Mekong River Commission (MRC). It defines the scope of the work and the cooperation required for joint planning to achieve balanced and socially just development in the Mekong River Basin while protecting the environment and maintaining the region's ecological balance.

About the Mekong River Commission

The MRC is the only intergovernmental organization that works directly with the governments of Cambodia, Lao PDR, Thailand, and Vietnam to jointly manage the shared water resources and sustainable development of the Mekong River. China and Myanmar, the upstream countries of the Mekong River Basin, are Dialogue Partners of the MRC. The commission also engages a wide range of stakeholders in its strategies, plans, and work. The MRC is a platform for water diplomacy and regional cooperation in which member states share the benefits of common water resources despite different national interests. It also acts as a regional knowledge hub on water resources management that helps to inform the decision-making process based on scientific evidence. The MRC works across all sectors, including fisheries sustainability, identification of opportunities for agriculture, freedom of navigation, sustainable hydropower, flood management, and the preservation and conservation of important ecosystems. It also helps its member states face the future effects of more extreme floods, and prolonged drought and sea level rise associated with climate change. In providing its advice, the MRC aims to facilitate dialogue among governments, the private sector, and civil society. It is one of the few international organizations that is governed by a specific set of rules developed to coordinate technical cooperation among its members. Since its establishment in 1995 by the signing of the Mekong Agreement, the MRC has adopted a series of procedures, namely the Procedures for Water Quality; Procedures for Data and Information Exchange and Sharing; Procedures for Water Use Monitoring; Procedures for Notification, Prior Consultation and Agreement; and Procedures for Maintenance of Flows on the Mainstream, to provide a systematic and uniform process for the implementation of this accord.

Needs for Sustainable Hydropower in the Lower Mekong Basin (LMB)

An increase in power demand, volatile prices in international energy markets and concerns over carbon emissions have intensified interest in hydropower development—the Mekong's indigenous renewable energy resource. Hydropower development in the Lower Mekong Basin (LMB) has an important role to play in achieving development goals across the spectrum, from the global level (notably, the Sustainable Development Goals, SDGs), through the regional goals of the MRC, to the national goals of the Member Countries (MCs). Hydropower development in the Lower Mekong Basin is, however, a sensitive topic attracting a range of stakeholder views. Certain stakeholders propose a moratorium on all projects on the Mekong mainstream, while others support this development to boost national economic growth. Many hydropower projects in the Lower Mekong export their electricity to neighboring countries. Governments see these potential earnings from hydropower development as a means of reducing poverty, lowering national debts, and achieving regional economic prosperity and energy security. Over the past decade, the Mekong has arrived at a crossroads—whereas hydropower presents great economic and energy gains, at the same time, concerns have intensified over the potential cumulative impacts proposed schemes have on the environment, fisheries, and people's livelihoods in the Lower Mekong Basin.

Hydropower Development Trends in the LMB Countries

The pace of hydropower development in the Lower Mekong Basin has accelerated in recent years with growing demand for low-cost electricity to support economic development. In 2001, there were approximately 17 hydropower projects in operation in the LMB with a cumulative capacity of less than 1,400 MW[4]. From 2002 to 2015, an additional 40 hydropower projects with a capacity of 6,442 MW were commissioned. A further 14 dams with a total capacity of 3,000 MW are scheduled to commission by 2020, and another 30 dams with a total capacity of around 6,653 MW are in the development process, with most having completed feasibility studies. Upstream of the LMB, China has completed 9 major hydropower dams on the Upper Mekong (Lancang), with a capacity of 15,700 MW. A further 11 projects are under construction with a capacity of 11,800 MW. Another 10 projects are planned in the upper basin with a capacity of 3,800 MW. The scale of storage in these Upper Mekong Basin dams, when combined with the smaller storage in the Lower Mekong dams, has resulted in changes to the seasonal flow patterns in the Mekong. Wet season flows have been reduced and dry season flows increased. In addition, sediments have been trapped in these dams, significantly reducing the supply into the lower reaches of the river. **[Figure 2]** Provides the location of commissioned, under-construction, and planned projects based on the MRC hydropower database as updated in 2017 for the MRC Council Study. In **[Figure 3]**, commissioned projects are those already in operation (2019), while the committed projects are either under construction or have existing concession agreements and power purchase agreements in the LMB. Note that the "candidate" potential represented is indicative of the potential development opportunity only. It is not currently representative of the power demand that is required to be met by hydropower over the next 20 years across the region.

Balancing Benefits and Risks of Hydropower Development

Energy Security and Economic Benefits

Energy security and economic growth are strategic priorities for all MRC member countries. Multiple recent studies find that hydropower development in LMB may deliver net economic benefits across the region. The savings in electricity supply costs relative to alternatives, such as new coal- and gas-fired generation, are significant. In addition, lower-cost alternative renewable sources (solar and wind) may be combined with hydropower to provide low-cost energy security for member countries. These economic benefits are further supplemented by royalties, taxes, and profits accruing to governments, and the benefits from employment, flood mitigation and management, irrigation, and local economic development. To enhance the net benefits (i.e., benefits minus costs) arising from the range of energy development options available to member countries, detailed regional dialogue on water and energy plan alternatives is needed.

Environmental Risks

The economic benefits must, of course, be considered in light of the substantive risk of negative impacts. These include the loss of livelihoods (notably through falling capture fisheries), declines in sediment flows, and the loss of environmentally important wetlands and forests. The MRC studies have confirmed the projected risks to the ecosystems and the reductions in capture fisheries and sediment transport resulting from existing and planned hydropower. These changes are already being measured in the basin—for example, the reduction in sediment transport. There are also major, but unquantifiable, risks related to the disruption to ecosystems and the loss of the region's valuable and unique biodiversity. The impacts of hydropower development on the biodiversity of the Mekong River Basin has emerged as one of the critical elements of sustainability in the hydropower sector. However, putting an economic value on the biodiversity loss (or gain) is difficult. Basin scale monitoring is underway by MRC to understand the changes that are occurring within the basin due to existing and under-construction hydropower and other developments. Adaptive management of the hydropower mitigation operations should then be undertaken to reduce measured impacts. This monitoring will also allow impact mitigation solutions to be adapted to the Mekong context.

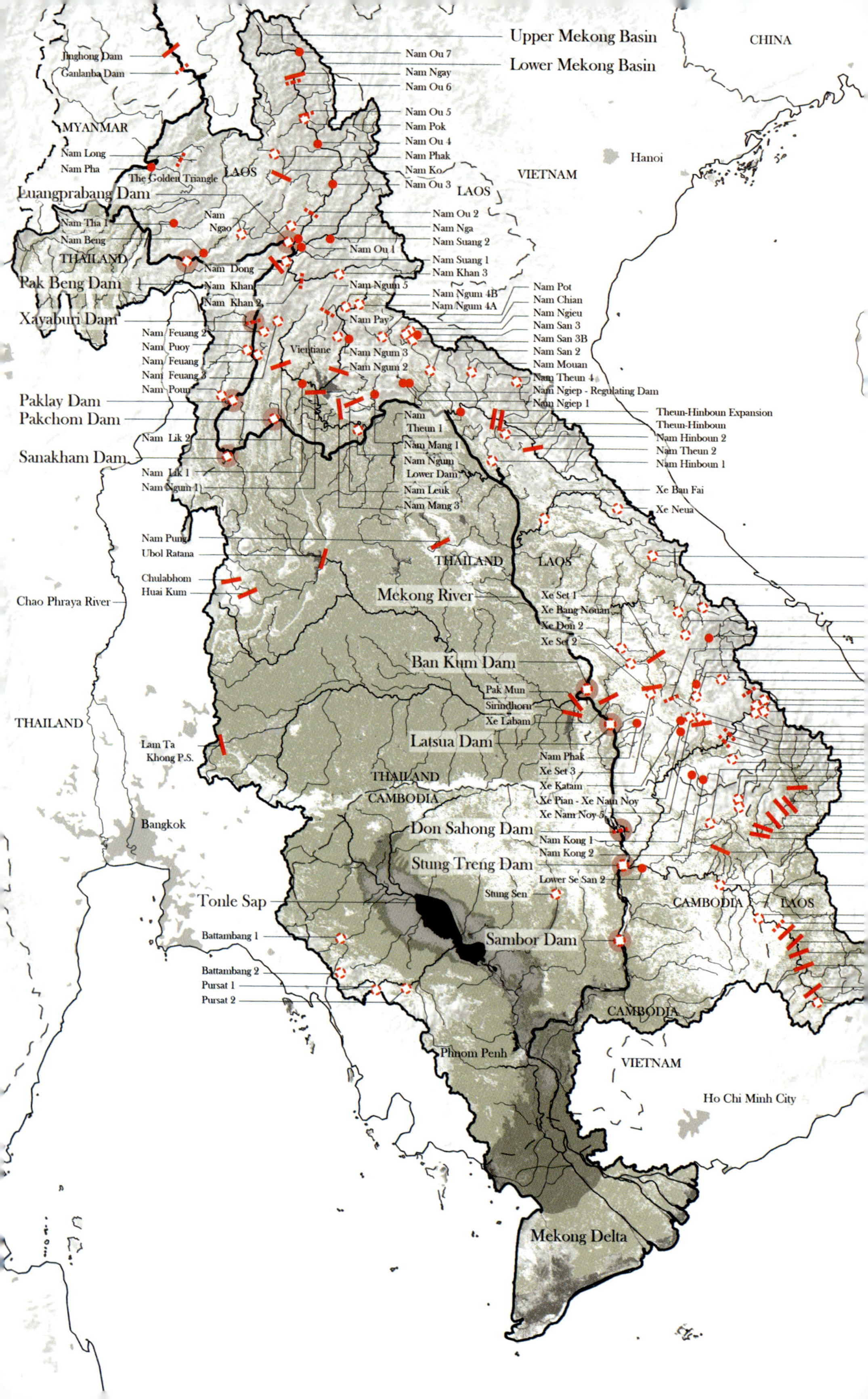

Upper Mekong Basin
Lower Mekong Basin
CHINA
Jinghong Dam
Ganlanba Dam
Nam Ou 7
Nam Ngay
Nam Ou 6
Nam Ou 5
Nam Pok
Nam Ou 4
Nam Phak
Nam Ko
Nam Ou 3
MYANMAR
Nam Long
Nam Pha
The Golden Triangle
LAOS
Hanoi
VIETNAM
LAOS
Luangprabang Dam
Nam Tha 1
Nam Beng
Nam Ngao
THAILAND
Nam Ou 2
Nam Nga
Nam Suang 2
Nam Ou 1
Nam Suang 1
Nam Khan 3
Pak Beng Dam
Nam Dong
Nam Khan
Nam Khan 2
Nam Ngum 5
Nam Ngum 4B
Nam Ngum 4A
Nam Pot
Nam Chian
Nam Ngieu
Nam San 3
Nam San 3B
Nam San 2
Nam Mouan
Nam Theun 4
Nam Ngiep - Regulating Dam
Nam Ngiep 1
Xayaburi Dam
Nam Pay
Nam Feuang 2
Nam Puoy
Nam Feuang 1
Nam Feuang 3
Nam Poun
Vientiane
Nam Ngum 3
Nam Ngum 2
Paklay Dam
Pakchom Dam
Nam Theun 1
Theun-Hinboun Expansion
Theun-Hinboun
Nam Hinboun 2
Nam Theun 2
Nam Hinboun 1
Nam Lik 2
Nam Mang 1
Sanakham Dam
Nam Ngum Lower Dam
Nam Lik 1
Nam Ngum 1
Nam Leuk
Nam Mang 3
Xe Ban Fai
Xe Neua
Nam Pung
Ubol Ratana
THAILAND
LAOS
Chulabhom
Huai Kum
Mekong River
Chao Phraya River
Xe Set 1
Xe Bang Nouan
Xe Don 2
Xe Set 2
Ban Kum Dam
Pak Mun
Sirindhorn
Xe Labam
THAILAND
Latsua Dam
Lam Ta Khong P.S.
Nam Phak
Xe Set 3
Xe Katam
THAILAND
CAMBODIA
Xe Pian - Xe Nam Noy
Xe Nam Noy 5
Bangkok
Don Sahong Dam
Nam Kong 1
Nam Kong 2
Stung Treng Dam
Lower Se San 2
Stung Sen
Tonle Sap
CAMBODIA
LAOS
Battambang 1
Sambor Dam
Battambang 2
Pursat 1
Pursat 2
CAMBODIA
Phnom Penh
VIETNAM
Ho Chi Minh City
Mekong Delta

[Figure 2] Map of commissioned, committed, and proposed hydropower (image credit: Mekong River Commission, re-drawn by Wendy Stradley and Chenyu Zhang)

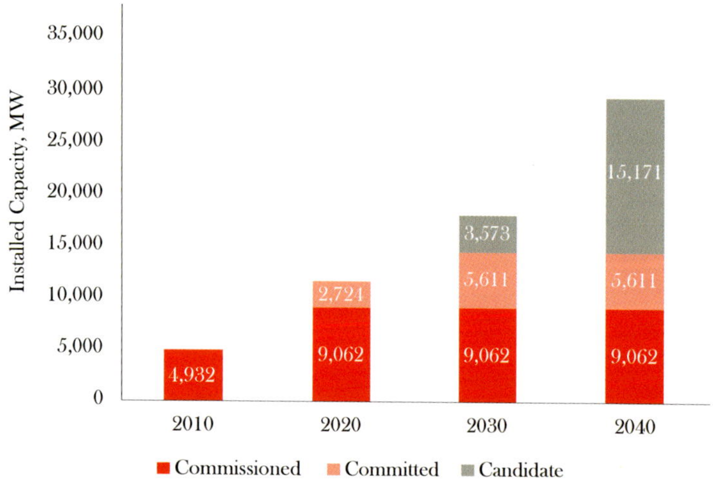

[Figure 3] Commissioned, committed, and candidate Lower Mekong Basin hydropower capacity (image credit: Sustainable Hydropower Development Study, ECA, 2019, re-drawn by Chenyu Zhang)

Social Risks

If all currently planned projects were to be developed, more than 100,000 people would be displaced between 2020 and 2040, and 3 million people downstream would be affected,[5] including from the resulting flood risk from dam failures. Well-designed resettlement, compensation, and income restoration programs may mitigate the adverse impacts and may even raise the economic status of affected communities to a higher level than the pre-project situation. Care in the design of these programs to minimize the social risk is critical. Ongoing and adequately supported resettlement programs and programs to compensate impacted communities, should be designed to ensure these communities are substantially better for the life of the project operation. Even with effective resettlement and compensation programs, such displacement is inevitably disruptive to existing cultural and social arrangements, and households will take time to adjust. These impacts fall disproportionately on women, children, and ethnic minorities. In the Mekong River Basin, women generally tend to be responsible for managing households, and as a result, their livelihoods may be most vulnerable to changes in river use, such as lost access to sources of firewood and the flooding of riverbank gardens. The transboundary effects of these major infrastructure developments require that MRC member countries cooperate on suitable impact assessment, mitigation, and adaptive management approaches. Dialogue on the implementation of the recommended approach set out in the MRC's Preliminary Design Guidance (PDG) and the Rapid Hydropower Sustainability Assessment Tool (RSAT), are aimed at seeking practical solutions to mitigate these risks.

Climate Change Opportunities and Risks

Hydropower, along with other renewable energy sources, is seen by many, including the Intergovernmental Panel on Climate Change (IPCC), as a key component of

Reservoir created by Xayaburi Dam, Mekong River, Laos, 2019 (image credit: Derek Hoeferlin)

climate change mitigation. In the Mekong this opportunity to reduce greenhouse gases is substantial if these renewable energy resources are prioritized in the power development plans (PDPs) of the member countries. The MRC studies have shown that, if these GHG reductions are able to be monetized in the future, for example through carbon pricing, they may provide a considerable additional economic benefit for the region. Multipurpose hydropower reservoirs may be utilized for a range of purposes including irrigation and flood and drought mitigation and management. They therefore have the opportunity to play a role in climate change adaptation if these aspects are built into the design and operations of the reservoir. However, uncertainties as to the impact of climate change on hydropower production variability, as well as extremes of drought and flood, must be considered. MRC studies[6] have shown that there are risks associated with potential greater variability in wet and dry seasons, with resulting uncertain risks to downstream communities. At a basin scale, these climate change opportunities and risks need to be built into dialogue on hydropower development within the context of basin planning.

Benefits of Basin Scale Planning on Hydropower Development and Management

The MRC's studies highlight the need for member countries to strike an appropriate balance between regional and national equity and risk reduction. The economic benefits at the national and regional levels must be carefully considered. Downstream countries may already be exposed to negative transboundary impacts from existing developments. On the other hand, they have not yet been able to realize the potential benefits of their own hydropower due to the later starting dates of their development. The studies have found that, at a national and regional level, the benefits may be enhanced and the risks of further negative impacts may be reduced by cooperation and information-sharing on plans for energy and water development. The MRC strategies and guidelines seek to improve the balance between benefits and risks by facilitating careful project selection, siting, and design during the feasibility study stage. Careful selection or improved design of projects to be developed may enhance national and regional outcomes as a whole.

Design, Construction, and Operation for Sustainable Hydropower Enhancement

Recent studies by the MRC on hydropower risk mitigation[7] have emphasized the importance of implementing regionally relevant approaches to the avoidance, minimization, and mitigation of hydropower risks. This work has emphasized the need for both individual project mitigation and also the critical role of cascade operations to ensure the transmission of sediments and the safe passage of extreme floods. The intensity of hydropower development in the Mekong basin mainstream and tributaries has meant that joint operation of cascades of projects, with potentially different owners, is now critical. Clearly this is important to optimize production, but it is also essential for the coordination of flood management, sediment transmission during flushing operations, navigation, and riparian community safety.

Working Together Towards a More Sustainable Hydropower Future

At present, only 10 percent of the estimated hydroelectric potential in the Lower Mekong Basin is developed. How Mekong countries decide to pursue future hydropower development is perhaps one of the most challenging strategic decisions they have faced since the signing of the 1995 Mekong Agreement. It is important that member countries work together to balance sustainability with development opportunities. In response to this dynamic situation, the MRC focuses on advancing regional cooperation for the sustainable management of the growing number of hydropower projects from a river basin management perspective. This includes drawing effectively on international experiences, developing regional technical knowledge, and sharing best practices relevant to all stages of planning. To avoid transboundary impacts, the MRC is exploring sustainable options to hydropower development. Sustainable hydropower development moves away from narrowly approaching infrastructure as a way to meet the growing needs of energy services and focuses on thinking about the overall effectiveness of projects within a basinwide perspective. In the 1995 Mekong Agreement, the MRC member countries agreed to "*cooperate in all fields of sustainable development, utilisation, management and conservation of the water and related resources of the Mekong River Basin including… hydropower…in a manner to optimise the multiple-use and mutual benefits of all riparians and to minimise the harmful effects.*" While each country plans and implements hydropower projects nationally, the MRC has a mandate to assess and guide the development of projects from a basinwide perspective, in order to optimize transboundary benefits and minimize adverse transboundary impacts.

It should be emphasized that **decision-making with respect to hydropower development and operations rests with the member countries**, although MRC has a role to play in working with member countries on hydropower development strategies and policies, coordinated and integrated impact assessments, and consistent and fair mitigation measures, especially those related to transboundary issues. MRC seeks to complement national and other international institutions involved in hydropower development in the Mekong River Basin and, more generally, in power development in the region. Co-operation with institutions involved in hydropower and water resources management in the region is emphasized, in order to create a more coherent and effective coordination mechanism that ensures joint efforts to tackle the opportunities and challenges while drawing on the experience of other River Basin Organizations.

Key ongoing MRC's project - Pilot program to monitor impacts from Xayaburi and Don Sahong (Joint Environmental Monitoring)
The Xayaburi and Don Sahong are the first two dams already built on the mainstream of the lower Mekong River in Lao PDR. During their six-month prior consultation process[8] under the MRC procedures and throughout their construction stage, Cambodia, Thailand and Viet Nam and other concerned stakeholders called for a program to properly and systematically assess impacts from the dams once they go online. Currently, MRC is working on the pilot program Joint Environment Monitoring of Mekong Mainstream Hydropower Projects (JEM) which is a response to the call to provide the standard operating procedures for joint environment monitoring of Mekong mainstream hydropower projects. The monitoring process, which runs from 2020 – 2021, will allow testing teams to trial and refine proposed monitoring approaches and methodologies that can later be applied at a basin-wide scale and incorporated into the MRC's core monitoring work in order to monitor the Mekong River condition and support on decision making on river planning and management.

Conclusion
The 1995 Mekong Agreement, MRC procedures and related guidelines encourage member countries and their developers to make significant efforts and investments towards addressing the concerns raised by other MRC members and relevant stakeholders. The cumulative impacts of infrastructure development in the Mekong, analyzed by the MRC's Council Study, indicate major adverse effects on Mekong River System, and riparian communities if all proposed developments in the basin proceeds. This reinforces the need for joint monitoring, analysis and dialogue on regional strategies in the water, food and energy sectors to meet all the Member Countries development needs.

1. http://interactive.mrcmekong.org/sobr-2018-findings/sobr-2018-findings/

2. http://interactive.mrcmekong.org/council-study-findings/council-study-findings/

3. http://www.mrcmekong.org/assets/Publications/MRC-1995-Agreement-n-procedures.pdf

4. a unit of power equal to one million watts, especially as a measure of the output of a power station. As a comparison, the peak demand for a city like Bangkok is 30,000MW.

5. Affected persons are defined as all those living downstream within 5km of the river up to the point where the increase in flows resulting from a dam falls below 130% of pre-dam levels).

6. Basin-Wide Assessment of Climate Change Impacts on Hydropower Production, MRC 2018.

7. Development of Guidelines for Hydropower Environmental Impact Mitigation and Risk Management in the Lower Mekong Mainstream and Tributaries (Case Study), MRC 2018.

8. http://www.mrcmekong.org/topics/pnpca-prior-consultation/

Adapt

Flood Pulse Urbanization: Phnom Penh and the Tonlé Sap

Shelby Elizabeth Doyle

Water does not constitute one object of analysis but rather an intersecting set of processes, practices, and meanings that cuts across existing disciplinary boundaries.

—Matthew Gandy, The Fabric of Space: Water, Modernity, and the Urban Imagination[1]

[Figure 1] Chaktomuk or the "Four Faces," indicating the four branches of the three rivers or as the French termed the area the Quatre Bras or "the four arms." (image credit: Shelby Elizabeth Doyle)

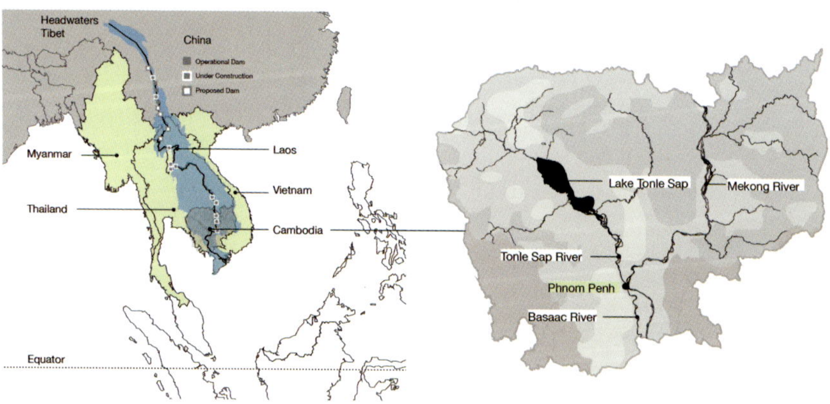

[Figure 2]

(LEFT)

Mekong River Basin in blue, adjacent countries in green; Dams (operational, under construction, proposed) indicated by key

(RIGHT)

Map of Cambodia's major rivers and identifying Phnom Penh at the confluence of the Mekong, Tonlé Sap and Bassac Rivers, known as Chaktomuk, the Four Faces

(image credits: source, Mekong River Commission, illustration by Shelby Elizabeth Doyle)

The fan-shaped Chaktomuk Conference Hall marks the confluence of the Bassac, Tonlé Sap, and Mekong Rivers.[2] Designed by Cambodian modernist Vann Molyvann, the arced façade offers a 270-degree view of the moment where the Mekong River meets the Tonlé Sap and Bassac Rivers. In Khmer, this intersection is called Chaktomuk, or the "Four Faces," indicating the four branches of the three rivers, or as the French later termed the area, the Quatre Bras or "the four arms." During the dry season, the Tonlé Sap and Mekong Rivers flow into the confluence from the northwest and north respectively, then the Mekong and Bassac Rivers flow out of the confluence to the southeast and south respectively During the wet season the Mekong River flows into the confluence with such force and volume that the Tonlé Sap River reverses flow—returning to the northwest—bringing water, fish, and sediment into the country's midlands. **[Figure 1]**

Annually, since the 12th century, the Tonlé Sap's reversal is celebrated during Bon Om Touk (Water & Moon Festival) during the week of the full moon in late October or early November.[3] The cultural and hydrological importance of Chaktomuk cannot be overstated: the wet-season reversal of the Tonlé Sap at Chaktomuk is essential to the environmental health of Cambodia.

Phnom Penh, the capital of Cambodia, is located at Chaktomuk, and home to nearly two million people, many of whom live and work along the banks of the Mekong River. [4] [5] Millions more people are sustained by the basin's flood cycles and deltaic system. The result is a topography defined by an intense interdependence between the inhabitants of the region and its rivers. Stretching from the glaciers of the Tibetan Qinghai Plateau to the South China Sea, the Mekong descends 2,700 miles through six countries—China, Myanmar (Burma), Laos, Thailand, Cambodia, and Vietnam.[6] The river is an overlapping series of infrastructures that provides water, food, irrigation, hydropower, transportation, and commerce to hundreds of millions of people.[7] **[Figure 2]** Much of the terrain in the Lower Mekong Basin varies no more than three feet in height, creating a flat, dense, illegible landscape. Each rainy season (May-October), monsoon rains and snowmelt cause the Mekong River to flow into the Tonlé Sap with such force that the latter reverses its flow. During the dry season, the Tonlé Sap is approximately three feet deep; with an area of around 1,000 square miles; during the wet season, the Tonlé Sap swells to nearly five times its dry-season size volume, changing in depth from as low as three feet to as high as forty feet.[8] **[Figure 3]** Consequently, Phnom Penh and the surrounding region experience a dramatic swing in flood levels from dry to wet season. Although the floods are destructive, they also support one of the most delicate and diverse ecosystems in the world. This seasonal flood pulse sustains the region: fisheries are replenished, floodwater is stored for use in the dry season, flood-deposited sediments improve soil fertility across the region, and groundwater aquifers are recharged.[9] Conversely, severe flooding results in the loss of life, damage to agriculture, property, and infrastructure, and can cause the disruption of social and economic activities throughout the Lower Mekong Basin. Flood events in Phnom Penh are twofold—there are almost daily rainy season flood events and episodic larger-scale river flood events. During the rainy season, monsoon rains inundate low-lying streets, some with nearly three feet of

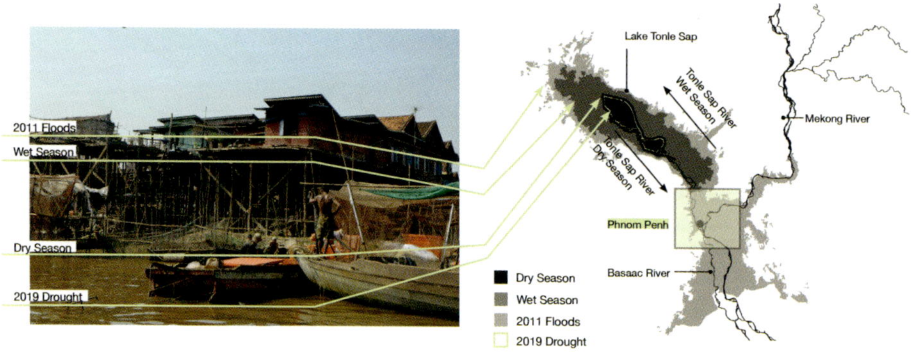

[Figure 3]

(LEFT) Kampong Khleang a floating and stilted village on the Tonlé Sap Lake; dry season, wet season, and 2011 flood levels indicated; villages, such as this one, are dependent upon the Tonlé Sap flood surge for fishing and agriculture

(RIGHT) Map of a typical wet/dry season Tonlé Sap Flood Surge and the extent of the 2011 floods, redrawn by author from a United Nations Map (image credits: source, United Nations Institute for Training and Research, photograph and illustration by Shelby Elizabeth Doyle)

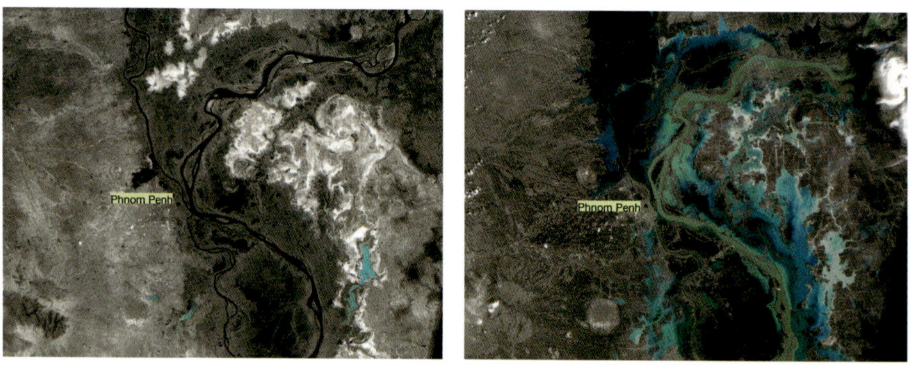

[Figure 4]: Present day Phnom Penh boundaries indicated in white (LEFT) Dry season, February (RIGHT) Wet season, October (image credit: USGS Earthshots)

water.[10] According to the Mekong River Commission, the economic benefits of this flood pulse far outweigh its consequences. Average annual flooding costs range from $60 to $70 million, while the benefits of the flood annually range from $8 to $10 billion.[11] Therefore, the city must mediate a delicate balance to preserve the benefits of the flooding while reducing the costs and impacts to life and property. **[Figure 4]**

This convergence demonstrates the friction between ecology, landscape, infrastructure, economic development, and political power. The city of Phnom Penh provides evidence of centuries of water-control strategies. The Cambodian urban record began with the 12th-century Khmer capital of Angkor and accelerates in the mid-19th century when Cambodia became a French protectorate, followed by a brief period of independence, and, in rapid succession, the Second Indochine War to the east, a civil war within, the depredations of the Khmer Rouge regime, followed by Vietnamese occupation, and the present-day autocracy of the Cambodian's People Party.[12] The legacy of Cambodia's numerous political regimes reveals an evolving relationship with water and the politics of water control through urban design and planning policies. Each of these political evolutions demanded a simplified model of water management that created an abstracted, administrative ordering of nature and society, and each of these models failed to represent the environment and the complications of human occupation of that environment.[13]

In the context of this book, Phnom Penh provides an example of how architecture, as a detail scale of urbanization, is intrinsically connected to its watershed, the Mekong River Basin, providing evidence of the need for Derek Hoeferlin's theory and practice of "Watershed Architecture."

Today, the very existence of the flood pulse is threatened by an expanding number of upstream hydrologic dams, which are delineated and discussed in Hoeferlin's "Mekong River Basin Atlas." As thoroughly explained in Dorothy Tang's essay in this book, Mekong damming stems from a proliferation of water management expertise commenced in the 1950s by the U.S. Bureau of Reclamation, an agency of the United States Department of Interior, and continued today by Chinese corporations. The Bureau's aim was to transfer technical knowledge of water resources to "developing" regions such as Southeast Asia. In the context of the Bureau's efforts in Southeast Asia during the 1960s, the particular characteristics of the Mekong River basin (the "natural resources" waiting to be "developed") were calculated and simplified under the impetus of the Bureau's particular expertise in water resources and river basin development as well as a means for combatting the spread of Communism in the region. Damming has now become an instrument of Chinese economic expansion.[14] Efforts to turn upstream Laos into the "Battery of Southeast Asia" have created the worst drought conditions in one hundred years on the Tonlé Sap, threatening the food source and livelihood of millions.[15] In 2019 and 2020, the reversal of the river came a month later than average, causing economic hardship and food scarcity in the region.[16]

In the context of Asia's rapidly urbanizing port megacities, such as Jakarta and Ho Chi Minh City, Phnom Penh is a small and often overlooked topic of study. However, the city presents a unique and relevant record of living and building with water, and more importantly, this history reveals methods for making legible the deep entanglement of politics and water. From the crisis in Flint,[17] to the hurricanes of New Orleans[18] and New York City,[19] to the disappearing Colorado River,[20] the scale and complexities of water infrastructure have never so urgently demanded examination. Reflecting upon Phnom Penh is a method for contemplating architecture's contemporary role in water polemics. Cambodia is often referred to in the parlance of humanitarian development as "Third World," "a developing nation," or more recently as part of the "Global South." This measurement of its development or "modernization" is often expressed in relation to its transformation and mastery of water. As Gandy writes, "infrastructure is presented as modernity itself."[21]

[Figure 5] Street 51 during an afternoon monsoon, 2012 (image credit: Shelby Elizabeth Doyle)

Modernity as it is used here is a concept derived from European experience, codified by the French colonial project, and relying heavily upon an Enlightenment compulsion to impose universal technocratic models upon the environment without regard for the cultural, political, and environmental complexities of non-European urban contexts. Thus, the episodic hydrological cycle of Cambodia provided a hostile context for the imposition of French and later Modernist urban planning models antagonistic to the environmental rhythm of Cambodia. The ecological health of Cambodia relies upon the significant swing of the monsoon season from the dry northeast monsoon to the wet southwest monsoon and their corresponding changes in precipitation. This condition does not align well with notions of the environment as a consistent and legible condition interlocking with its architectural counterpart: that which is "not architecture" is environment. The environment of Cambodia is not a background condition to urbanism; rather it expresses the slow, viscous matter of the Southeast Asian climate as a resistance to technocratic ambitions.

Despite efforts to "control" water, flood events in Phnom Penh remain twofold—almost daily rainy season flood events and episodic larger-scale flood plain events. During the rainy season (May-October), monsoon rains fill low-lying streets, some to nearly four feet deep. The near-daily floods during the rainy season reframe the experience of inhabiting the city, altering its landscape and blurring the distinction between water and

[Figure 6] Representative section of the edge between the wetlands and the ring road levee in southern Phnom Penh. (image credits: Shelby Elizabeth Doyle)

land. Roads become waterways and sidewalks disappear beneath the muddy waters. Curbs and tree roots are hidden from view, hindering walking and driving. Businesses unfurl overhangs, open umbrellas, and hang tarps, expanding available dry space. Traffic slows to a near stop as cars, motos (small motorcycles), and bicycles navigate the water and intermittently stall out or dip into deep, unseen potholes. **[Figure 5]**

The population anticipates the rains, adapting to the accompanying flooding and its perceived cleansing effects. Floods necessitate a pause and they disrupt the flow of daily business and activity. Additionally, flooded streets carry potential disease as the stormwater mixes with human waste, and street drains are blocked by municipal trash, slowing drainage and posing a possible public health threat. As for larger-scale flood events, Phnom Penh was founded in the alluvial plain of the Mekong River, which varies upwards of 12 meters (nearly 36 feet) in depth between the dry and wet seasons. The most devastating flood risk comes from the Mekong River cresting over its natural berm into the city. The volume of water produced by a Mekong flood could take weeks or even months to recede, evaporate, or penetrate into the ground. The factors contributing to the potential for increased flooding in Phnom Penh are deforestation, the unknown impacts of climate change, overbuilding in catchment areas, the damming and diversion of natural waterways, and the infill of canals and lakes, combined with no formally accepted or followed master plan.[22]

Historically Phnom Penh was surrounded by wetlands which provided catchment areas for floodwater and now are becoming infilled to create developable land. **[Figure 6]** is a representative section of the edge between the wetlands of Boeung Cheung Ek and the ring road levee in southern Phnom Penh. There is no formal wastewater treatment in the city. Instead, sewage and other wastewater from households, businesses, and industries dump into a series of covered and open canals that flow through the city and combine with seasonal rainwater and floods. Wastewater is indicated in pink and potable water in green. This system of sewage and wastewater removal is shown in the figure, first enclosed in subsurface piping then emptying into the lake beneath the occupied edge. Boeung Cheung Ek (BCE) Lake is the largest of the water bodies that receives human waste and industrial effluents.[23] The lake covers 3,400 hectares of land in an area five kilometers south of the city center. Eighty percent of the wastewater from the city including untreated effluent from three thousand small- and large-scale industrial enterprises ends up in this body of water. Boeung Cheung Ek Lake is an effective, low-cost means of biological treatment for the city's wastewater through its aquatic vegetable production.[24]

Housing and small businesses occupy the edge of the levee connecting the city to a network of wetlands, streams, and ponds into which more than one million cubic meters of the city's household wastewater and stormwater are discharged daily. These structures perch on the non-protected side of the levee creating a three-dimensional grid of inhabited space. This grid negotiates the section between the economic space of the street and the agricultural space of the wetlands. At the left edge of the illustration, dry and wet season wetlands water levels are marked. To the right is the heavily trafficked ring road levee where cars, motorbikes, and bicycles compete for space. The road is lined with small shops selling everyday items such as cell phone cards, drinks, and toiletries.

Habitation of the structure adapts to the water levels in the adjacent wetlands. Lower grid quadrants are abandoned during floods for higher spaces. The structures are built of loose pieces of wood, tarps, corrugated metal, and construction debris. There is limited access to electricity; spaces are unconditioned; rainwater is collected for washing; drinking water is boiled or purchased; and wastewater empties directly into the wetlands. When soaked by rain the structures air-dry, and when destroyed by flooding, they are rebuilt with available debris, creating a patchwork architectural sieve at the edge of the city connecting it to the episodic cycles of the monsoon and the flood pulse of the Mekong and Tonlé Sap Rivers.

Hoeferlin writes in *The Watershed Architecture of the Mekong River Basin,* "the need for transboundary cooperation and design solutions is critical in the future of adaptive, water-based design, especially when it comes to a better understanding of coupling the challenges of climate change and dam infrastructure across entire river basins."[25] Phnom Penh's "Flood Pulse Urbanization" offers both unique and universal contributions to water-based design discourse. Undoubtedly, the Tonlé Sap flood reversal is exceptional, unique to the specific hydrological conditions of Chaktomuk. Simultaneously, the architecture of Phnom Penh, a small portion of which is described here, provides evidence of centuries of design adaptations for living within the time and space of the flood pulse. In this context, the flood is not a force to be controlled through technocratic ambitions, but rather an environmental rhythm to be inhabited and even celebrated. This Cambodian watershed architecture offers vital lessons for flood urbanization far beyond Chaktomuk.

Acknowledgments

This research was supported by Khmer Architecture Tours and funded through the 2011–2012 United States Fulbright Scholars Program in Phnom Penh, Cambodia. The resulting project, *City of Water: Architecture, Infrastructure, and the Floods of Phnom Penh*, and additional documentation can be found at: www.cityofwater.wordpress.com. Earlier versions of this chapter can be found in *Phnom Penh: Rescue Archeology: Contemporary Art and Urban Change in Cambodia,* edited by Erin Gleeson, and *Nakhara Journal of Environmental Design Planning* volume 8 (2012), edited by Niall Kirkwood and Pat Seeumpornroj. A longer analysis of the environmental politics of Phnom Penh's urbanization is available in *Genealogy of Bassac* (2021), edited by Sereypagna Penh and Brian McGrath.

1. Matthew Gandy, *The Fabric of Space: Water, Modernity, and the Urban Imagination* (Cambridge: MIT Press, 2014).
2. Sereypagna Pen, "Chaktomuk Conference Hall," *Vann Molyvann Project*, accessed February 29, 2020, http://www.vannmolyvannproject.org/archive#/new-page-1/.
3. Fred Pearce, *When the Rivers Run Dry: Water—The Defining Crisis of the Twenty-First Century* (Boston: Beacon Press, 2018).
4. For additional information on the architectural and urban history of Phnom Penh see: Vann Molyvann, *Modern Khmer Cities* (Chicago: Art Media Resources Ltd, 2003); Helen Grant Ross and Darryl Leon Collins, *Building Cambodia: "New Khmer Architecture" 1953-1970* (Bangkok: The Key Publishing Company Limited, 2006); and, Penny Edwards, *Cambodge: The Cultivation of a Nation 1860-1945*, (Honolulu: University of Hawaii Press, 2008).
5. United States Central Intelligence Agency (CIA). "The World Factbook Cambodia," *CIA The World Factbook*, accessed February 23, 2020, https://www.cia.gov/the-world-factbook/countries/cambodia/.
6. Mekong River Commission, "About the Mekong River Basin," *Mekong River Commission for Sustainable Development*, accessed February 23, 2020, https://www.mrcmekong.org/about/mrc/.
7. Karen Frenken, ed., "Mekong Aquastat Water Report 37 2012," *Food and Agriculture Organization of The United Nations*, accessed February 29, 2020, http://www.fao.org/docrep/016/i2809e/i2809e.pdf.
8. Chris Berkik, "Of Fish, Monsoons and the Future: A Push to Save Cambodia's Tonle Sap Lake," *New York Times* (June 9, 2014), http://www.nytimes.com/2014/06/10/science/of-fish-monsoons-and-the-future.html.
9. Mekong River Commission, "Mekong River Commission Lower Mekong River Basin Flood and Drought Data," *Mekong River Commission for Sustainable Development*, accessed February 29, 2020, http://www.mrcmekong.org/topics/flood-and-drought/.
10. Jennyl Estil, "Interactive Flood Map of Phnom Penh," *Jennyl Estil Flood Demo*, accessed February 29, 2020, http://flooddemo.estil-jennyl.com/.
11. Mekong Aquastat Water Report, 2012.
12. David Chandler, *A History of Cambodia* (New York: Routledge, 2018).
13. James C. Scott, *Seeing Like a State: How Certain Schemes to Improve the Human Condition Have Failed* (New Haven: Yale University Press, 1998).

14. Chris Sneddon, "The 'sinew of development': Cold War geopolitics, technical expertise, and water resource development in Southeast Asia, 1954–1975," *Social Studies of Science* 42, no. 4 (2012): 564–590.
15. Stefan Lovgren, "Mekong River at its lowest in 100 years, threatening food supply," *National Geographic* (July 31, 2019), accessed February 29, 2020, https://www.nationalgeographic.com/environment/2019/07/mekong-river-lowest-levels-100-years-food-shortages/.
16. Prak Chan Thul, "Fishermen without fish as Cambodia's river reversal runs late, *Reuters* (July 21, 2020), accessed July 27, 2020, https://www.reuters.com/article/us-mekong-river-cambodia/fishermen-without-fish-as-cambodias-river-reversal-runs-late-idUSKCN24M1T3.
17. Merit Kennedy, "Lead-Laced Water in Flint: A Step-By-Step Look at the Makings of a Crisis," *National Public Radio* (April 20, 2016), http://www.npr.org/sections/thetwo-way/2016/04/20/465545378/lead-laced-water-in-flint-a-step-by-step-look-at-the-makings-of-a-crisis.
18. Douglas Brinkley, *The Great Deluge: Hurricane Katrina, New Orleans, and the Mississippi Gulf Coast* (New York: Harper Perrenial 2006).
19. Kathryn Miles, *Superstorm: Nine Days Inside Hurricane Sandy* (New York: Penguin, 2014).
20. David Owen, "Where the River Runs Dry: The Colorado and America's water crisis," *The New Yorker* (May 25, 2015), http://www.newyorker.com/magazine/2015/05/25/the-disappearing-river.
21. Matthew Gandy, *The Fabric of Space: Water, Modernity, and the Urban Imagination* (Cambridge: MIT Press, 2014).
22. Karen Frenken, ed., "Mekong Aquastat Water Report 37 2012," *Food and Agriculture Organization of The United Nations*, accessed February 29, 2020, http://www.fao.org/docrep/016/i2809e/i2809e.pdf.
23. Kuong Khov et al., "Periurban Aquatic Food Production Systems in Phnom Penh,"*Urban Agriculture Magazine*, no. 14 (2005): 13–16.
24. Wim Van Der Hoek et al., "Skin Diseases Among People Using Urban Wastewater in Phnom Penh," *Urban Agriculture Magazine*, no. 14, (2005), 30–31.
25. Derek Hoeferlin, "The Watershed Architecture of the Mekong River Basin," *Journal of Architectural Education*, 74, no.1, (2020): 70-82.

Phnom Penh, Cambodia, 2011 (image credit: Derek Hoeferlin)

Tonle Sap Lake during "dry season," 2010 (image credit: Derek Hoeferlin)

Monitor

Community Engagement Project to Reduce Salinity Impacts in the Mekong Delta

Dr. Duong Van Ni

[Figure 1] Typical example of a healthy and productive rice farm in the Mekong Delta, Can Tho, Vietnam, 2011 (image credit: Derek Hoeferlin)

As of 2011, the Mekong Delta contained 17.33 million inhabitants, and it has been growing slowly since then.[1] These communities live within approximately four million hectares of extremely low-lying land, mainly at elevations of less than two meters above mean sea level.[2] The Mekong Delta is one of several mega-deltas worldwide that have been identified as highly vulnerable to the impacts of climate change and sea-level rise.[3] With changes in precipitation as well as increasing rates of sea-level rise that are predicted to occur in climate change models, salinity levels in the Mekong Delta are likely to increase and move further inland. Further exacerbated by alterations to the built environment, these will continue to negatively impact local communities and their livelihoods. **[Figure 1]**

The goal of this project was to reduce salinity impacts by developing a community-based environmental monitoring program through a variety of activities. To select an appropriate representation of participants, we worked with stakeholder organizations in local communities that included local governments, women's unions, farmers' associations, youth organizations, schools, and others. The project was a true collaboration that merged our team's "scientific expertise" with important aspects of public participation, known as "citizen science." We trained participants to measure salinity; to exchange information and experiences on adaptation strategies; and finally, to consolidate their findings about various challenges and send them back to our team in real time, via the chosen modality of text messaging. We implemented the work in six provinces in the Mekong Delta where environmental problems such as climate change and sea-level rise, canal and sea dike construction, mangrove forest degradation, land use alteration, and sluice operation all combine to affect rice production, aquaculture, cash crops, fruit gardens, animal husbandry production, and water supplies within communities. Salinity increase has affected 85 percent of the villagers, and salinity levels are expected to increase according to climate change scenarios. During the period of 2012–2013, 333 participants joined the project. Salinity measurements were used to inform second-level water resource management decisions in the local communities. Salinity information collected during this study was shared throughout the community through personal communications, local institutions, local authorities, and schools. As a result, salinity adaptation strategies were adopted to protect rice crops, aquaculture, cash crops, fruit gardens, livestock, and drinking water supplies. Dozens of text messages were sent daily, which were incorporated into a salinity database. Frequently updated or near real-time salinity data is of great interest to the rice farming and aquaculture communities in the Mekong Delta of Vietnam. Salinity data is also important for managing drinking water supplies, and has implications for the productivity of freshwater fisheries within the delta's river and canal systems. Salinity levels are closely related to seasonal rainfall and flooding patterns as well as sea-level rise and tidal variations in the East Sea and the Gulf of Thailand.

During the annual dry season, decreased river flow results in less fresh water to dilute the influx of saline water from the sea.[4] Seawater enters a network of rivers and canal systems and moves upstream, increasing salinity levels. Because the water from the rivers and canals is the main water resource for irrigation, increased salinity can result in saltwater contamination of rice fields and fish ponds and reduced agricultural productivity. **[Figure 2]** Salinity control projects implemented in the 1980s and 1990s, such as levees and sluice gates, are used to help prevent salt intrusion during the dry season to improve agricultural production. **[Figure 3]**

However, these canals and sluice systems have made salinity in the coastal areas of the Mekong Delta more complicated and difficult to predict. Mekong Delta communities lack access to environmental information, especially about saline water intrusion, and therefore crop production has historically relied only on their available experiences. Unfortunately, their knowledge of saline water intrusion was based on knowledge of local landscape conditions prior to the construction of disturbances such as canals, sea dikes, and sluices in the area. In the meantime, salinity information is collected by governmental agencies, but the release of information to the public is limited and delayed.

Therefore, providing local communities with access to salinity monitoring data at the provincial level is important from both a climate change and food security perspective. Salinity monitoring data can be used by local farming communities to identify where to plant rice varieties that have greater salt tolerance, change rice cropping calendars, and apply other farming techniques to adapt to changes in salinity levels, such as extensive polyculture practices. In addition, dikes and sluice gates are used in the Mekong Delta to manage salinity levels, and salinity monitoring data could be used by communities and farmers to operate these systems more effectively. In the Vietnamese portion of the Mekong Delta, 78 percent of the land use in 2000 was dedicated to rice production.[5] Vietnam is the third-largest exporter of rice worldwide, after India (1) and Thailand (2).[6] Safeguarding agricultural productivity, especially rice production, is critical to the food security of the region and the economy of Vietnam.

The three objectives of this project were to: 1) develop a community-based salinity monitoring system; 2) build a local network to exchange information and adapt to salinity changes; and 3) facilitate teacher capacity to integrate salinity data to their curriculum in secondary schools and high schools to strengthen scientific capacity and understanding of environmental changes. The coastal zone study area included Ben Tre, Tra Vinh, Soc Trang, Bac Lieu, Ca Mau, and Kien Giang provinces of the Mekong Delta. **[Figure 4]** These provinces are located along the coast of the delta where saline water typically intrudes inland during the dry season from December to May, and fresh water is prevalent during the wet season from June to November. In general, the topography of the study area is zero to two meters above sea level. The coastal areas often consist of tidally influenced mangrove forests; further inland the elevation becomes gradually higher, with the highest found along sandy beach ridges. **[Figure 5]**

Land use in this area is dependent on topography and water quality. At higher elevations, perennial crops such as longan (dragon eyes) and coconut are grown and are dependent on rainfed water supplies. At lower elevations, cash crops and paddy rice fields are found; and in the lowest areas aquaculture is common, mainly shrimp farms. Drinking water

[Figure 2] Paddy rice field affected by fish kills (LEFT) and saline water (RIGHT) (images credit: Southern Water Resource Planning Institute)

supply for animals and humans is dependent on rainwater, canals, and groundwater. About 60 percent of the delta population is dependent on canals for drinking water, which is the only water source during the dry season in the rural areas. **[Figure 6]**

Beginning in 1992, a pilot salinity monitoring project was initiated by the Hoa An Biodiversity Research Station of Can Tho University (Can Tho, Vietnam) to assist farmers and provincial government officials with understanding and managing salinity intrusion. As the director of the Hoa An Biodiversity Research Station, I implemented salinity monitoring by using a network of women and young students throughout the study area to measure salinity samples using gravity meters that are simple, inexpensive pieces of equipment manufactured locally in Vietnam. **[Figure 7]** The salinity levels were measured on a regular basis at specific sampling sites, and the data were reported to me via phone calls. Data were recorded one phone call at a time, and the information was used to develop salinity contour maps of the Mekong Delta—by hand. Although the individuals in the rural network collected the salinity data in a reliable manner, the project was too labor intensive to continue over the long term. The fact that the salinity readings had to be recorded manually—one at a time—into a central database made the data aggregation extremely time consuming. In addition, mapping the salinity contours by hand was laborious and produced less rigorous data than statistical mapping techniques such as interpolation, which are available in most GIS software packages. Finally, because of the bottleneck caused by the manual data aggregation, the salinity contour maps could not be produced quickly enough to be used to inform day-to-day water management decisions, such as opening or closing a sluice gate in response to changing salinity levels or planting a different rice variety in certain fields.

Advancements in technology in recent years, such as the proliferation of cell networks and text messaging in Vietnam, as well as the availability of web-based mapping software, have made it possible to automate the data aggregation and mapping tasks

[Figure 3] Sluice gate, Mekong Delta, Vietnam, 2011 (image credit: Derek Hoeferlin)

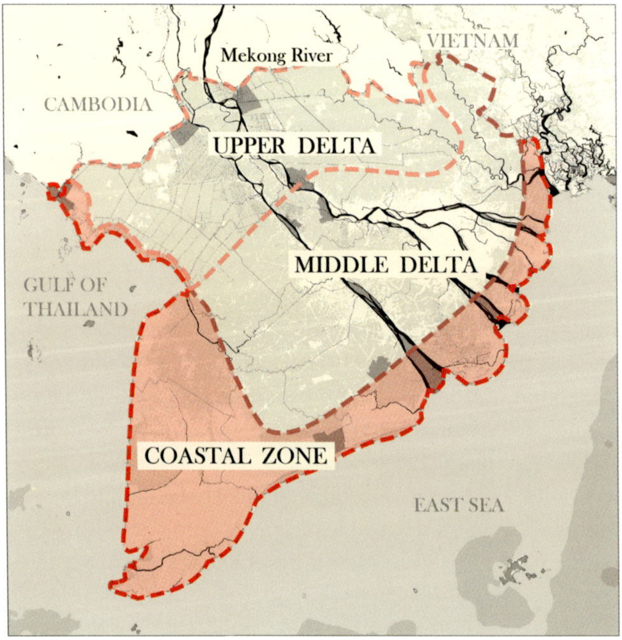

[Figure 4] Mekong Delta map indicating project study area in Coastal Zone (image credits: Mekong Delta Project-ver.0.1; re-drawn by Chenyu Zhang)

[Figure 5] Coastal mangrove, Mekong Delta, Vietnam, 2011 (image credit: Derek Hoeferlin)

[Figure 6] House over canal, Mekong Delta, Vietnam, 2011 (image credit: Derek Hoeferlin)

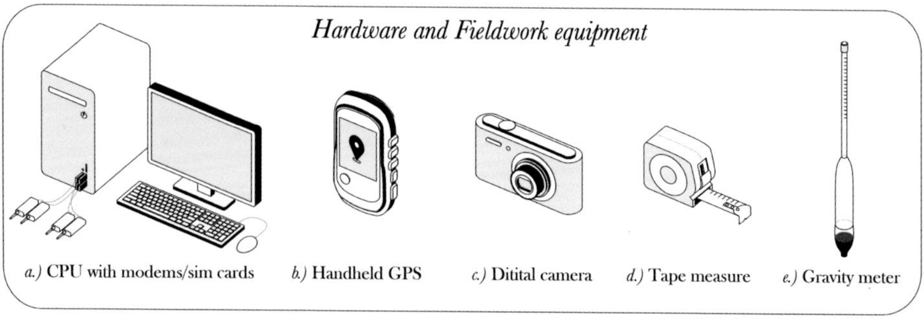

[Figure 7] Hardware unit with CPU and modems/sim cards (left), field work equipment to identify sampling locations (middle), and salinity measure equipment (RIGHT) (image credit: Duong Van Ni, et. al.; re-drawn by Chenyu Zhang)

described above to a much more inexpensive and efficient manner. For this project, the salinity data were collected by individuals in rural communities (as in the previous pilot project) on a daily basis. However, the measurement values were sent by text message and incorporated into a database through an automated process. These advancements helped to expand the monitoring network to up to one thousand individuals collecting salinity observations on a daily basis. A commercial application programming interface was used to develop an application to receive and relay text messages into a database, with each sampling location associated with a unique ID and geographic coordinates. The sampling locations and associated salinity data were displayed on an interactive, user-friendly web mapping application developed using ArcGIS Server software and Google Maps, with new data continually added on a daily or weekly basis. The up-to-date raw salinity data, time series charts, and salinity contour maps were made available to farmers, provincial leaders, the scientific community, and anyone else with internet access. As the database accumulated, the dynamics of salinity intrusion into a specific area could be predicted using computer models and early informing text messages could be sent back to the participants.

Our project worked with the local government and villagers to target areas that exhibited salinity problems yearly. We then mapped the area and collected the baseline information to select locations for salinity measurement and to determine their positions with GPS. Our team selected participants to measure salinity, noting their names, addresses, and cellphone numbers. Each participant was asked to be responsible for one sampling location, and in return we provided equipment and trained participants on taking salinity measurements and sending text messages for the database and website. We sent hard copies of the results back to participants or extension workers at sites without internet access. We trained participants, teachers, and local villagers to view results on the website at sites with internet access. Using phone calls, direct visits, workshops, and suggestions from participants to identify difficulties in collecting and sending salinity data, we provided further training for

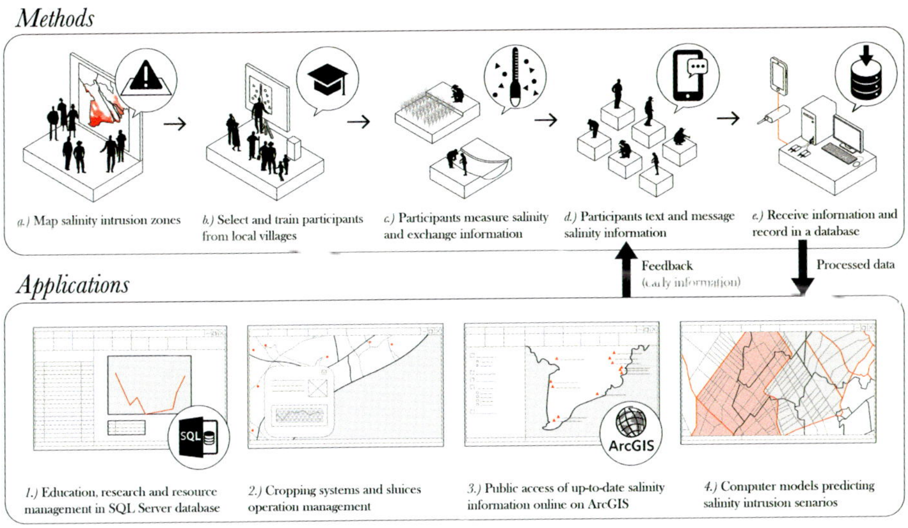

[Figure 8] A summary of methods and applications developed in the community-based salinity monitoring project (image credit: Duong Van Ni, et. al.; re-drawn by Chenyu Zhang)

using field equipment. By exchanging information about local salinity adaptation, we improved the procedures and techniques to satisfy the participants' needs and plans for project expansion. **[Figure 8]**

The ultimate goal of the project was to help develop applications and alternatives for the local communities to adapt to the effects of salinity variations on their crops, animals, trees, fish, and drinking water. Another priority outcome was the sharing of salinity values among relatives, neighbors, friends, local authorities, and institutions such as women's unions or farmers' organizations to identify cropping system alternatives, how to operate sluices to reduce salinity, and how to manage drinking water supplies. To accomplish this, a team on salinity was established at Can Tho University. It consisted of experts on agriculture, especially rice and cash crops; natural fish populations and shrimp aquaculture; animal husbandry of chickens, ducks, and pigs; tree crops, especially coconut, mango, and longan; and wetland ecosystems. These experts played a role in consulting with the local communities on agricultural and salinity management issues. As directed by Vietnamese policy, each institution, such as schools, universities, and various administrative levels including provinces, districts, communes, and hamlets, must have youth, women, and farmer organization participation. These organizations meet regularly to implement policies and exchange experiences. Additional stakeholders focus on different local interests such as sugarcane, shrimp, pig, and duck production. Our project approached as many of these groups as possible to encourage their participation in measuring salinity, exchanging information on adaptation experiences, and identifying alternative income resources.

An additional important aspect of the project became education. This included the university level, particularly Can Tho University, which until 2000 was the only university in the entire Mekong Delta. Engaging the large Can Tho University alumni network, which ranges from the highest levels of the Communist Party to the grassroots levels of farmers' associations and women's unions, is a crucial bridge to local communities, netting the important building of social capital resources and community buy-in. Also, the project advocated for resources for teachers to integrate salinity data into their curriculum in secondary schools and high schools, in turn strengthening scientific capacity and a better understanding of environmental changes and challenges. In fact, we encouraged teachers to teach different subjects to form new, innovative teaching groups. Each group was led by a group leader, conducting joint, interdisciplinary seminars on the salinity project objectives, salinity measurement protocols, and developing applications for salinity information under the leadership of the team of salinity experts from Can Tho University. New curriculums were developed in relation to salinity information. Local indigenous knowledge emerged from the salinity project. For example, during physics classes on specific gravity, the teachers demonstrated how to measure the specific gravity of fresh and saline water using gravity meters in the classroom. After salinity measurements were introduced, teachers asked students about how high and low salinity values affected their livelihoods. Students were asked to interview their parents about salinity adaptation strategies and to present these applications in class. Encouraged to form active learning groups, students brought knowledge from the classroom to the community as living laboratories. Both the teachers and farmers became their instructors in theory and in practice. Students living near intake waterways, canal crossings, or sluices were selected to participate in the salinity monitoring program. These students then received training on measuring salinity and sending text messages, received a gravity meter, and determined the position of sampling sites with the assistance of their teachers.

The United States Geological Survey (USGS) National Wetlands Research Center Advanced Applications group developed web mapping applications and data management technology that could be used to automate the salinity data processing and mapping. To build the human resources for further research development of Vietnam, the Vietnamese staff developed the database and web mapping technology to automate the data aggregation and salinity mapping. USGS worked closely with the Vietnamese staff to write a final report and communicate the results to both the local rural community and to the scientific community. This group developed a computer program to receive text messages and integrate the messages into a database. The computer program was developed to receive salinity data and other environmental information such as water levels, acidity, air temperatures, rainfall levels, and disease incidences. The system also identified errors in the text messages and provided a simple statistical summary of incoming messages. The modeling group used the salinity monitoring data to run different models to predict salinity intrusion and favorable conditions for the development of certain diseases. The modeling results formed the basis for an early warning text messaging system that could send information to the project participants automatically.

The basic strategy of the project was to promote the participant's understanding of the environmental changes through collecting salinity measurements in order to develop adaptation strategies and reduce the impact on crops. Some of these strategies can be carried out by individual participants, some by participants working together through local organizations, and others by schools. It is notable that school students and their teachers in the local communities were enthusiastic to participate. For the farmers, accessing salinity information was helpful for crop management, but taking measurements daily was a challenge. In many cases, children in the family were taking the water samples, measuring salinity levels, and text messaging under the supervision of their parents. Teachers and students, for example, used the project to demonstrate the positive impact that a citizen-science effort can have on students, farmers, and the local community as a way to "open the eyes" of parents and community organizations as to what is possible and the benefits that can accrue to them. Schools that initiated salinity measurement and collected experiences on adaptation, for example, were followed up by seminars and workshops conducted by the salinity experts at Can Tho University, who used the opportunity to approach parents and farmers to stimulate household involvement.

Salinity experts also worked directly with farmers through workshops on salinity that covered topics such as salt-tolerant crop varieties, crop management and alternatives, water management projects, and aquaculture projects. They also worked indirectly with many farmers in targeted provinces by providing support through phone calls to local supervisors to relay information about salinity levels. A key condition for participation was that these farmers exchanged information about salinity measurements and adaptation strategies through visits to other farmers or through local media releases. Teachers were involved in both approaches as a way to improve school capacity by linking community experiences to the curriculum and promoting a hands-on approach to student learning. For example, teachers participated in workshops that directly trained farmers in specific adaptations including mechanisms of salinity tolerant varieties, adjusting cropping systems, and water management strategies. They then connected themes to lessons in the classroom on topics such as osmotic pressure in biology or biodiversity and ecosystem management. As a result, this salinity measurement project was conducted on different ecosystems and land uses in various communities and served as an assignment for student study trips to integrate curricular knowledge with real-life experiences. The result was a true collaboration of theory and research meeting reality and practice.

Acknowledgments
I would like to gratefully acknowledge my other partners on this project who also assisted in the production of this essay: Ngo Thao Nguyen (The College of Environment and Natural Resources [CENRes], Can Tho University [CTU], Vietnam), Truong Quoc Dinh, Lam Chi Nguyen (The College of Information & Communication Technology [CICT], Can Tho University), Cindy Thatcher, Scott Wilson (The U.S. Geological Survey [USGS]). I would also like to especially thank the volunteers who collected salinity measurements in the Mekong Delta. A special thanks to Bryan "Rick" Switzer of the U.S. Department of State for his support and assistance. This study was funded by USAID through USGS and Can Tho University.

1. General Statistics Office, *Statistical Yearbook of Vietnam 2011* (Statistical Publishing House, Hanoi, Vietnam, 2012).

2. Reiner Wassmann et al., "Sea Level Rise Affecting the Vietnamese Mekong Delta: Water Elevation in the Flood Season and Implications for Rice Production," *Climate Change* 66 (2004): 89–107.

3. Intergovernmental Panel on Climate Change, *Climate Change 2007: Impacts, Adaptation and Vulnerability, Contribution of Working Group II to the Fourth Assessment Report of the Intergovernmental Panel on Climate Change* (Geneva, Switzerland: 2007).

4. Toshihiro Sakamoto et al., "Spatio-Temporal Distribution of Rice Phenology and Cropping Systems in the Mekong Delta with Special Reference to the Seasonal Water Flow of the Mekong and Bassac Rivers," *Remote Sensing of Environment* 100 (2005): 1–16.

5. Wassmann et al., "Sea Level Rise," 89–107.

6. United States Department of Agriculture, Foreign Agricultural Service, "Grain: World Markets and Trade," accessed December 23, 2020, http://www.fas.usda.gov/psdonline/circulars/grain.pdf

Example of small-scale agriculture, aquaculture and water management in the Mekong Delta, Vietnam, 2011 (images credit: Derek Hoeferlin)

(NEXT PAGE)
Waters of the Mekong River (image credit: Derek Hoeferlin)

Rhine River Basin & The World

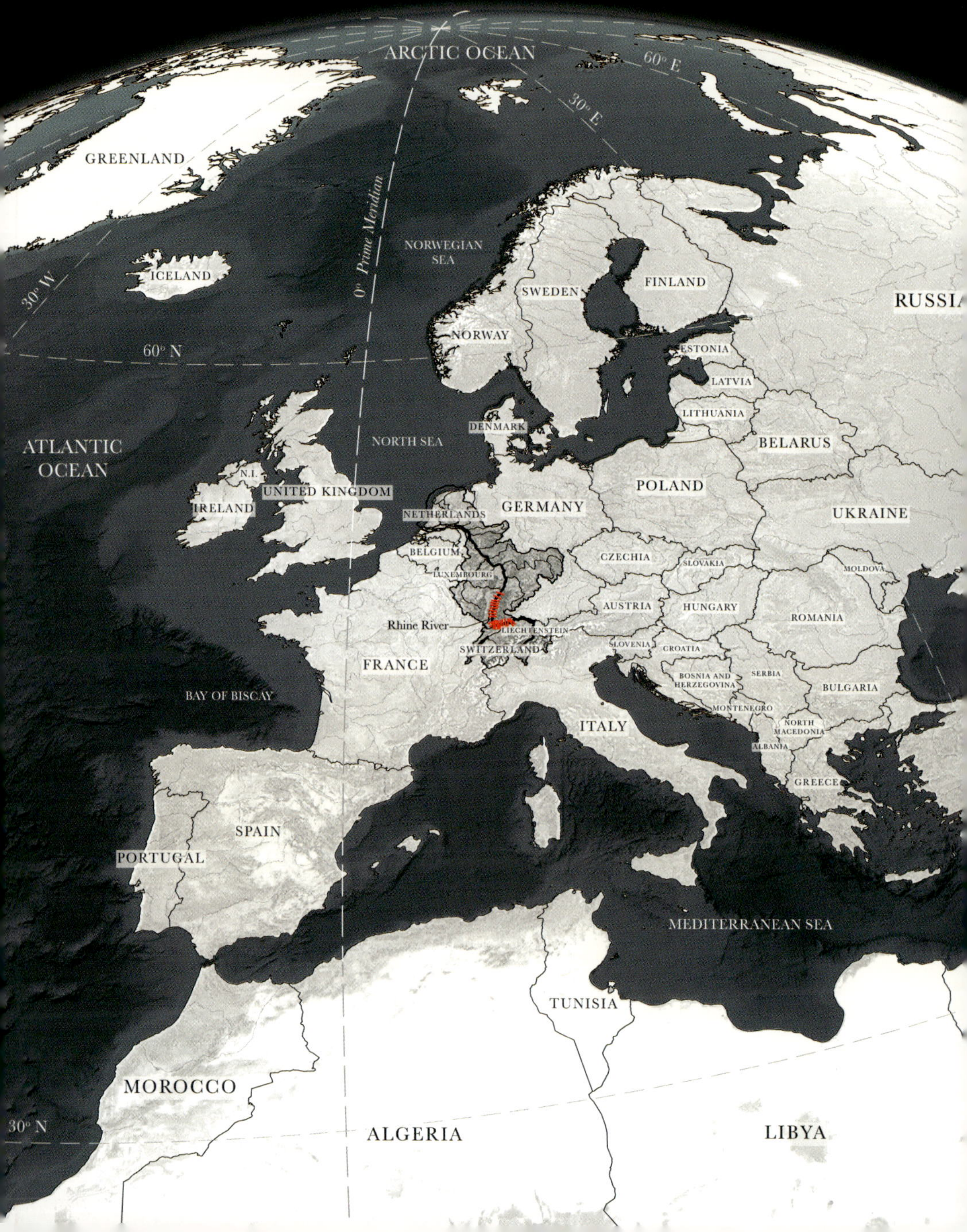

Quoting the International Commission for the Protection of the Rhine:

The Rhine connects the Alps to the North Sea and represents the most important cultural and economic axis in Middle Europe. Its use is more intensive and varied than that of all other European rivers. In its watershed, [approximately] 60 million people are living in nine different [countries]. With its tributaries, uncounted brooks, lakes, wetlands, and groundwater the Rhine forms a widely ramified network of water bodies, in which water flows in all directions, always following the slope towards the North Sea.

Continent 03: Rhine River Basin & Europe/Middle East/North Africa

Continent 03 Plan

The Rhine River Basin (RRB) historically is one of western Europe's most important river basins, established as a vital part of the modern European community. A 2009 study estimated that 58 million people live in the RRB, and a majority of the watershed's largest urban centers are along the riverbanks.[1] The Rhine River has a total length of 765 miles and a catchment area of 85,000 square miles.[2] For comparative context, it is a quarter of the length of the Mekong, and the entirety of the RRB can fit in the Upper Mississippi River Basin, but it is still one of the largest river basins in western Europe. Nine countries are in the Rhine River Basin's drainage area: Austria, Belgium, France, Germany, Italy, Lichtenstein, Luxembourg, Switzerland, and the Netherlands. The average mainstream discharge of the Rhine River is 81,200 cubic feet per second, a fraction of the Mississippi and the Mekong.[3] Despite its compact size and smaller water resources, the RRB is one of the most important river basins in terms of global trade. In 2013, 332 million tonnes of freight were transported through the Rhine, which accounts for nearly two-thirds of all inland waterway transportation in Europe.[4] The port of Rotterdam moves the highest volume of freight in all of Europe.[5] The main stem of the Rhine River has been engineered for navigation to an even greater extent than the Mississippi River. In addition to interbasin navigation, a robust network of waterways both within and surrounding the continent facilitates cross-border and global exchange.[6] To the southeast, the Suez Canal creates a shortcut to the ports in the east by connecting the Red Sea to the Mediterranean Sea. The Rhine River's access to the North Sea and the Mediterranean cements its presence in the European and global economies. Within its boundary, the Rhine has also been engineered to prevent destructive floods and to withstand the effects of global climate change. In particular, the efforts by the Dutch to integrate its cities with the Rhine River and its tributaries and distributaries through integrated river basin management, has demonstrated a model of interdisciplinary design that has pushed the discourse on watershed management.[7] It is also important to point out that the RRB spatially and economically ties into the Meuse and Scheldt Rivers as part of a more robust, urbanized system. Within the last 25 years, this has been part of a new field of study defined as "Delta Urbanism," developed by Han Meyer and others at TU Delft.[8] Despite its smaller size, the Rhine River Basin maintains a global presence through its economic activities, and has become one of Europe's most valuable river basins.

Continent 03 Section A-A

The Rhine River is one of the longest rivers in Europe, helping to shape a European identity by facilitating exchange. While the length and area of the Rhine River Basin are a fraction of the Mississippi and Mekong, the Rhine exerts a tremendous presence on the ecologies, economics, and politics of Europe. The source of the Rhine is near the center of the European continent in the Swiss Alps. Beginning at an elevation of 7,694 feet, the Rhine is the only major alpine river that discharges into the North Sea.[9] The main stem of the Rhine River flows through five countries: Austria, Switzerland, Germany, France, and the Netherlands. The Rhine is primarily managed by the Central Commission for the Navigation of the Rhine (CCNR). Established by the Treaty of Vienna in 1815, it remains the oldest international organization and consists of five member states: Belgium, France, Germany, Switzerland, and the Netherlands.[10] Its mission is to ensure and preserve open navigation on the Rhine River by developing projects and negotiating the use of the Rhine between its members.[11] In 2006, the CCNR committed to cooperation with the European Union and its riverine navigation initiatives.[12] The chemical industry, particularly petrochemicals and energy, dominate international shipping on the Rhine.[13] A line of ten locks and barrages facilitate barge navigation from the North Sea to Basel, where the industry is centered.[14] Various canals connect the main stem of the Rhine River to neighboring rivers including the Seine, Rhone, Ems, Elbe, Scheldt, and most importantly, the Danube River, through its tributary, the Main River.[15] The Danube River discharges into the Black Sea and is navigable from its mouth to the beginning of the canal near the German city of Passau.[16] Completed in 1992, the Rhine-Main-Danube canal connected the two rivers along with 15 riparian countries. Importantly, it created an inland waterway between the North Sea and the Mediterranean through the Black Sea.[17] In 2014, 4.74 million tonnes (a little more than 1 percent of the total tonnage in the Rhine River) were shipped through the canal, consisting mostly of agricultural products and metals.[18] As a site of exchange through the European continent, the Rhine River has helped to foster cooperation, first between riparian countries, and gradually throughout the European continent and around the world.

1. Urs Uehlinger, Karl M. Wantzen, Hartmut Arndt, and Rob S.E.W. Leuven, "The Rhine River Basin," in Rivers of Europe 1st ed. (London: Academic Press, 2009): 199–245, accessed November 19, 2020, https://www.researchgate.net/publication/30019497_The_Rhine_River_Basin.

2. Alice F.A. Mutton, "Rhine River," Encyclopædia Britannica, accessed October 27, 2020, https://www.britannica.com/place/Rhine-River.

3. Uehlinger et al., "Rhine River Basin," 199.

4. "Inland Navigation in Europe: Market Observation 2014" (Strasbourg: Central Commission for the Navigation of the Rhine, September 8, 2014), 13, accessed November 13, 2020, https://www.ccr-zkr.org/files/documents/om/om14_en.pdf.

5. Jeroen Rijke, Sebastiaan van Herk, Chris Zevenbergen, and Richard Ashley, "Room for the River: Delivering Integrated River Basin Management in the Netherlands," International Journal of River Basin Management, no. 4 (October 2012): 1, 8; accessed November 19, 2020, https://www.researchgate.net/publication/234111926_Room_for_the_River_Delivering_integrated_river_basin_management_in_the_Netherlands.

6. Uehlinger et al., "Rhine River Basin," 205.

7. Rijke et al., "Room for the River," 1, 8.

8. Taneha Kuzniecow Bacchin, Fransje Hooimeijer, Baukje Kothuis, "Delta Urbanism Premises," Journal of Delta Urbanism 1, (2020): 4–5, accessed February 5, 2021, https://journals.open.tudelft.nl/jdu/issue/view/759/Premises.

9. Uehlinger et al., "Rhine River Basin," 205.

10. Dale S. Collinson, "The Rhine Regime in Transition: Relations between the European Communities and the Central Commission for Rhine Navigation," Columbia Law Review 72, no. 3 (March 1972): 485–516.

11. Ibid., 491.

12. Declaration of the Ministers of the Member States of the Central Commission for Navigation of the Rhine (CCNR) Germany, Belgium, France, Netherlands, and Switzerland: ("Basel Declaration"), 1, opened for signature May 16, 2006, CCNR Declarations and Reports, accessed November 18, 2020, https://www.ccr-zkr.org/files/documents/dbale/dbale_en.pdf.

13. "Inland Navigation in Europe," 54.

14. Uehlinger et. al., "Rhine River Basin," 234.

15. Ibid., 205.

16. "Manual on Danube Navigation" (Vienna: via donau – Österreichische Wasserstraßen-Gesellschaft mbH, January 2013), 103, accessed November 13, 2020, http://ines-danube.info/goto.php?target=file_1545_download&client_id=viailias4.

17. Ibid., 3.

18. "Verkehrsbericht 2014/2015" (Berlin: Wasserstraßen und Schifffahrt des Bundes, November 2016), (in German), 92, accessed November 16, 2020, https://www.gdws.wsv.bund.de/SharedDocs/Downloads/DE/Verkehrsberichte/Verkehrsbericht_2014_2015.pdf?__blob=publicationFile&v=3.

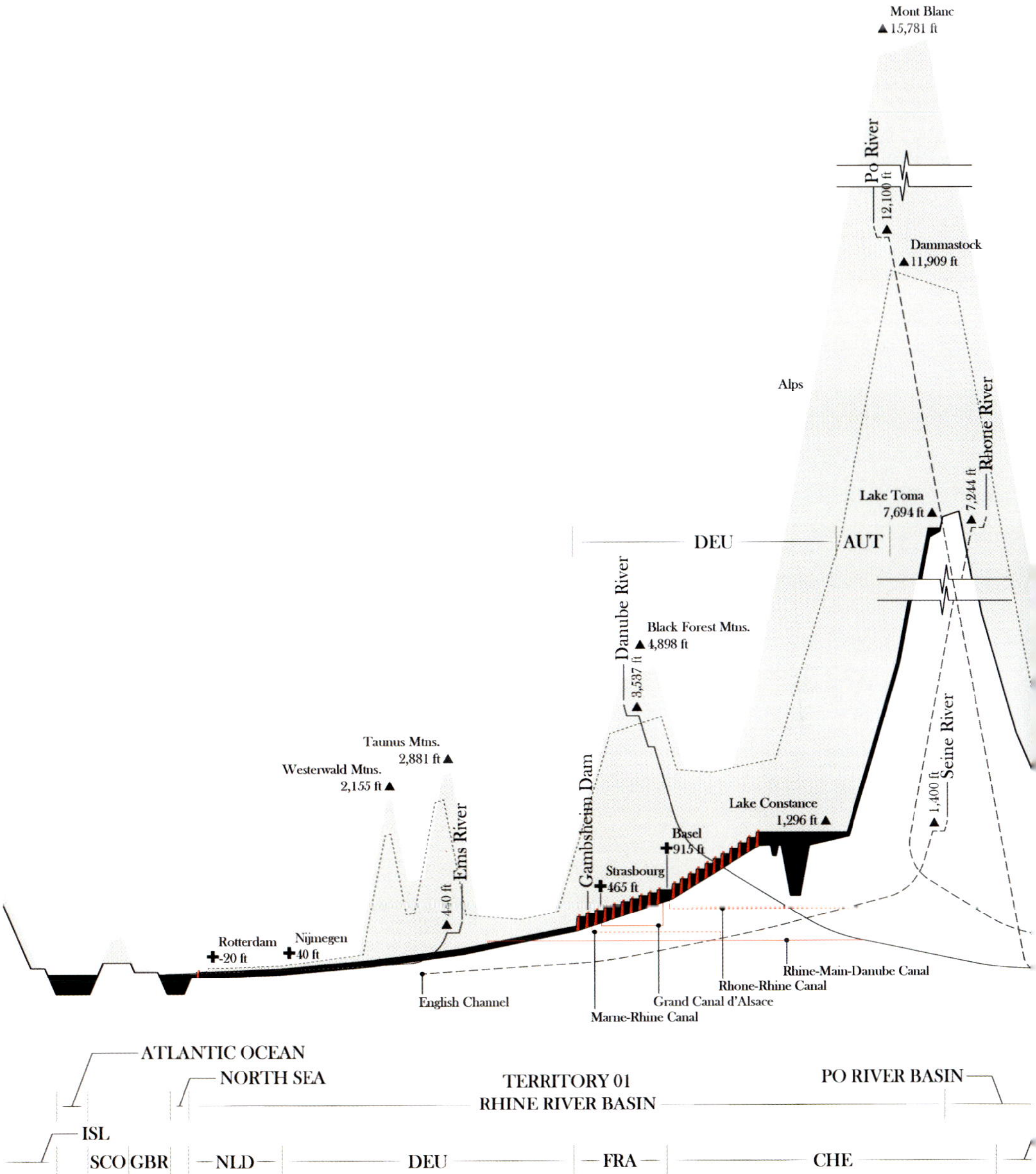

Mont Blanc
15,781 ft
Po River
12,100 ft
Dammastock
11,909 ft
Alps
Rhone River
Lake Toma
7,694 ft
7,244 ft
DEU
AUT
Danube River
Black Forest Mtns.
4,898 ft
3,537 ft
Seine River
1,400 ft
Taunus Mtns.
2,881 ft
Westerwald Mtns.
2,155 ft
Ems River
Gambsheim Dam
Lake Constance
1,296 ft
Basel
915 ft
Strasbourg
465 ft
Rotterdam
-20 ft
Nijmegen
40 ft
English Channel
Marne-Rhine Canal
Grand Canal d'Alsace
Rhone-Rhine Canal
Rhine-Main-Danube Canal
ATLANTIC OCEAN
NORTH SEA
TERRITORY 01
RHINE RIVER BASIN
PO RIVER BASIN
ISL
SCO
GBR
NLD
DEU
FRA
CHE

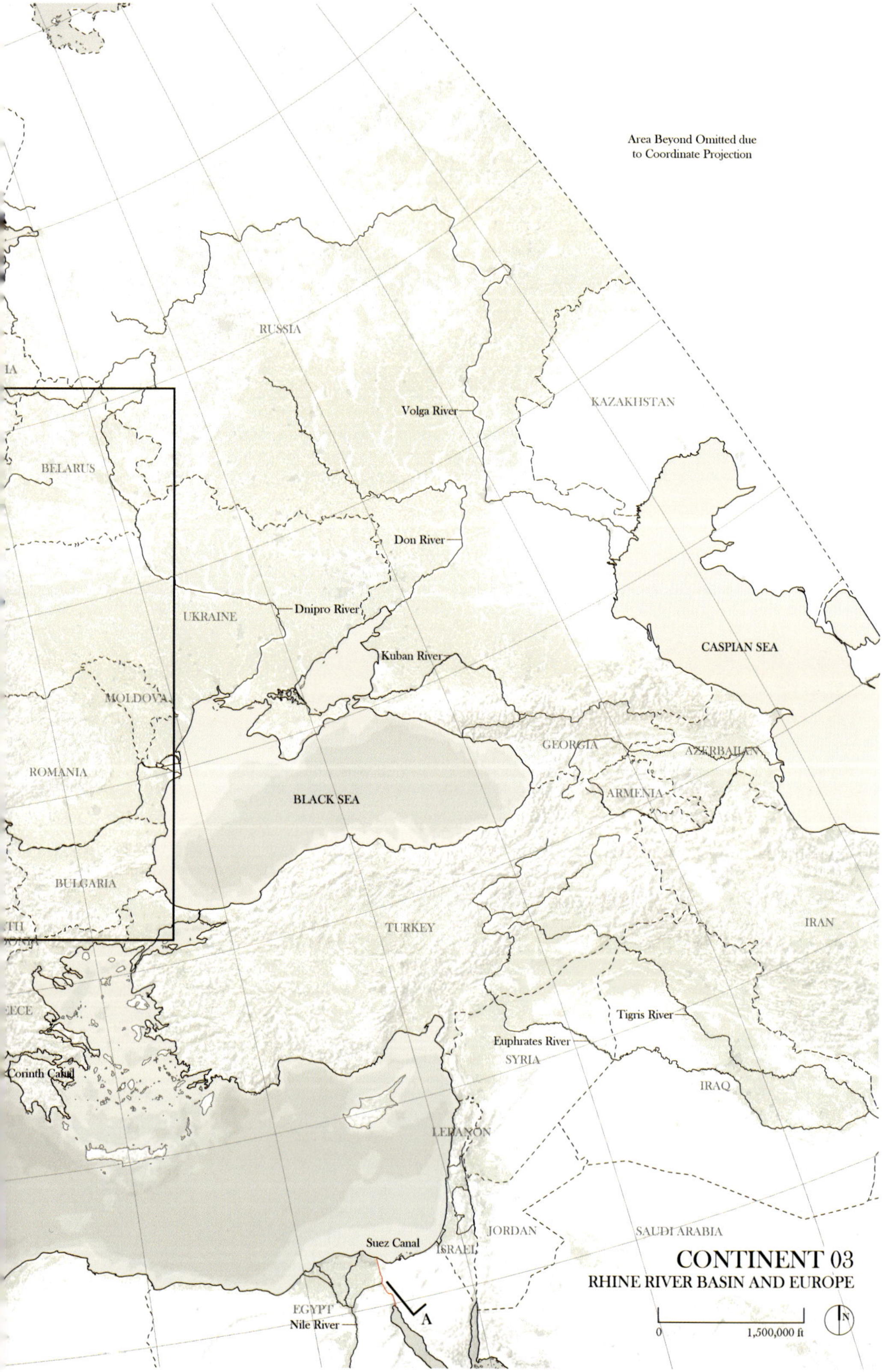

CONTINENT 03
RHINE RIVER BASIN AND EUROPE

ICELAND
A
ATLANTIC OCEAN
NORWAY
SWEDEN
FINLAND
ESTONIA
SCOTLAND
NORTHERN IRELAND
IRELAND
UNITED KINGDOM
DENMARK
LITHUANIA
NORTH SEA
NETHERLANDS
Ems River
Elbe River
POLAND
REGION 02
GERMANY
Rhine-Herne Canal
BELGIUM
English Channel
Rhine River
LUXEMBOURG
Rhine River Basin
CZECHIA
Rhine-Marne Canal
Rhine-Main-Danube Canal
SLOVAKIA
Seine River
REGION 01
Danube River
Rhine-Rhone Canal
AUSTRIA
HUNGARY
FRANCE
SWITZERLAND
SLOVENIA
CROATIA
Rhone River
Po River
BOSNIA AND HERZEGOVINA
SERBIA
MONACO
MONTENEGRO
ANDORRA
ITALY
ADRIATIC SEA
TERRITORY 01
ALBANIA
SPAIN
PORTUGAL
Strait of Gibraltar
MEDITERRANEAN SEA
MOROCCO
ALGERIA
TUNISIA
LIBYA

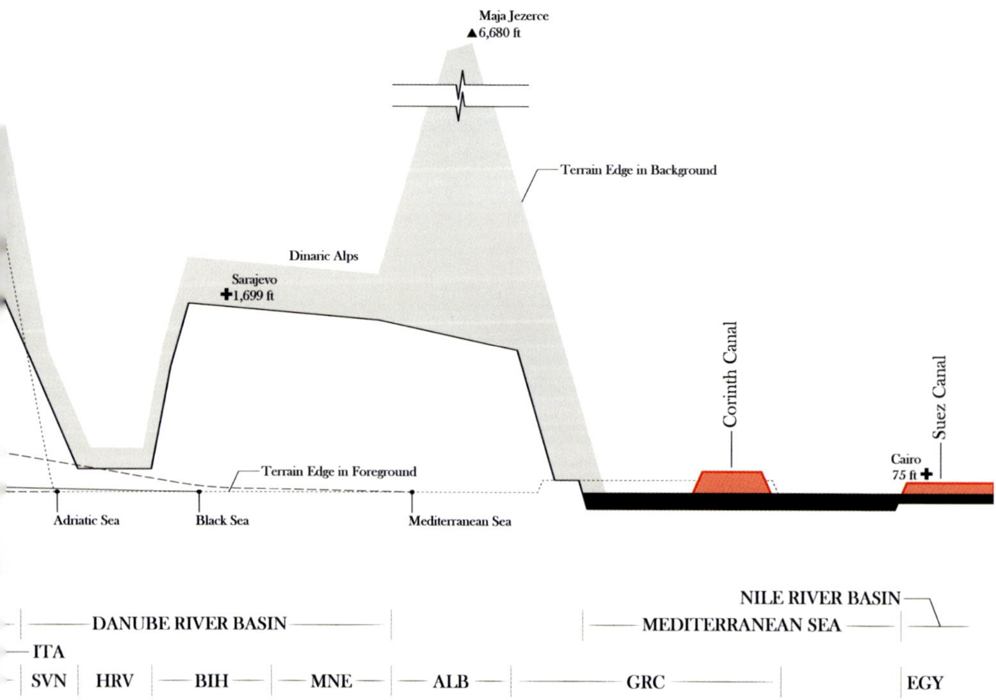

SECTION A-A
FOLLOWING THE PATH OF THE RHINE RIVER

View towards Caldic Chemical Plant, Europoort Rotterdam, Calandkanaal, Rotterdam, Netherlands, 2010 (image credit: Derek Hoeferlin)

Transform

The Rhine: A European River

Han Meyer

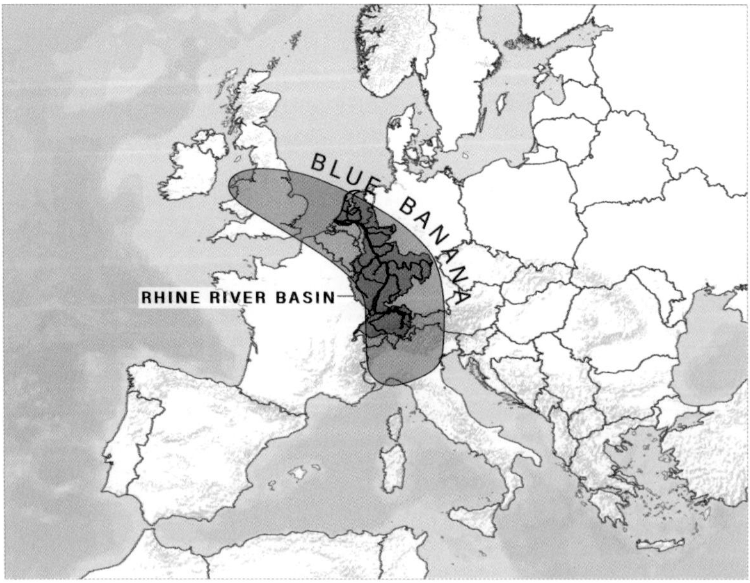

[Figure 1] "The Blue Banana," as imagined by Roger Brunet, indicating the central industrial and urban corridor, stretching from Italy to Great Britain, following the course of the Rhine River (image credit: Roger Brunet, re-drawn by Paul Wu)

Understanding and writing about the Rhine River and its delta are impossible without paying attention to the important role of this river and its catchment area—the Rhine River Basin—in the economic and urban development of Europe, past, present, and future. The term "Blue Banana," coined by the French geographer Roger Brunet in 1989,[1] refers to this central industrial and urban corridor of Europe and the banana-like form of its course. **[Figure 1]** The close relationship between the river basin and Europe's main economic and urban structure was not always self-evident. On the contrary, in different historical periods, the Rhine River has been characterized by different economic and technological conditions, including several important interventions in the water system that were necessary to create and improve conditions for economic development in the river basin area. In turn, these interventions in the water system also created new conditions and possibilities for urban development. At the same time, the transnational character of the Rhine, with its basin covering territories in six different European countries, often led to monetary, political, and military conflicts, which deeply frustrated the prospects for transnational water management.

Nevertheless, the net result of several transitions and interventions is that the Rhine River became the foremost inland waterway of the world with the most populous agglomerations of Europe from the end of the 19th century to the present.

The transformation of the Rhine into a transport corridor was an important condition for the growth of economic productivity and welfare in Europe, but it took also its toll. The subjection of the natural processes of the river to economic purposes led to a dramatic increase in problems, including pollution, ecological damage, the disappearance of highly valued cultural landscapes and urban waterfronts, floods, and salt intrusion.

Before the Rhine took on its role as transport corridor, the river was hardly usable as a navigation channel for large-scale vessels, up until the mid-19th century. In the transformation of the Rhine from a natural river to an industrial transport corridor, three events played a significant part: 1) the "rectification" of the Upper Rhine during the first half of the nineteenth century, 2) the effects of this rectification on the Lower Rhine and the delta; and, 3) the rise of a huge industrial center in the German Ruhr area. The interaction of these three events is still important today.

From the mid-19th century until the present, a series of interventions in the river system has been applied, aiming to get the river—and especially its delta—under control. This essay will describe four important transition phases in this process. Each phase or period has been characterized by the strong mutual influences of economic development and energy supply, port development, hydraulic works, and urban development. The fourth period is the current (and future) one: we are again facing a fundamental transition regarding economic systems and energy supply, and we are confronted with the necessity of adapting to climate change and an increase in extreme weather conditions, with serious impacts on the state of the river. The central question is: after two centuries of subjecting the river system to economic goals, how can we turn this one-sided focus on the economy into a new balance of economy, river landscape, ecology, and climate?

Rhine River as Transport Corridor: Opening the Delta as a Crucial Transition

Until the mid-19th century, the Rhine was hardly usable as transport infrastructure. When Germany began to address the need for an efficient transport infrastructure for its fast-developing industrial economy, several regions struggled with problems, including the shallowness of large parts of the river and the vulnerability of cities and agricultural fields to flooding alongside the river. The course of the Rhine through and alongside four different countries (seven if we include all its tributaries) created additional problems in terms of monetary (toll rates), political, and military tensions. Also, the different countries did not show any central coordination in water management at a national level. The Netherlands, for instance, counted more than 2,000 regional and local water boards, without any coordination at the national level.

It was during and directly after the Napoleonic period that this situation changed. In 1798, during the French occupation of the Netherlands, a National Water Agency (later renamed "Rijkswaterstaat") was established.[2] In 1815, during the Congress of Vienna, the victorious nations drew a new, post-Napoleonic map of Europe. Also, the international Central Committee for Navigation on the Rhine (CCNR) was founded, aiming to create favorable conditions for free and unobstructed navigation on the river.

"Unobstructed navigation" on the Rhine was especially relevant for two parts of the river: in the Upper Rhine, between the cities of Basel and Karlsruhe, and in the delta, from the Dutch-German border to the sea. In both sections, the water was not flowing through one main channel, but through marshlands. These could be several miles wide and very shallow, with meandering and interweaving creeks that changed their courses after every flood. These landscapes were ideal grounds for fish species such as salmon, sturgeon, and trout, leading to a flourishing fishing industry. But both regions struggled with floods in periods of high discharge, making navigation for large river vessels impossible.

The German engineer Johann Gottfried Tulla was the man who "tamed the wild Rhine."[3] His "Rhine rectification" was the largest civil engineering project ever undertaken in Germany. The project commenced in 1817 and led to the shortening of the meandering river between Basel and Worms, from 220 to 170 miles. The final result did indeed improve the flow of the river, but it resulted in a number of unintended consequences. The transformation of wide marshlands with meandering branches into one central river channel resulted in a dramatic drop in groundwater levels in the Upper Rhine region. This caused the death of vegetation and the disappearance of breeding grounds for fish. Tulla's interventions did not do much for navigation. The speed of the river flow was so high that navigation was almost impossible. To solve this problem, a lateral canal—the Grand Canal d'Alsace—was built. This canal runs through (regained) French territory, but had a large economic impact on Germany and

Switzerland. Because of the complex negotiations over this transnational question, the Canal d'Alsace was not completed until 1959, well over a century later.[4]

But there was one more problem Tulla did not pay attention to, even though he had already been warned. Local authorities and farmers in the Upper Rhine region had already started to reclaim the floodplains after the rectification, leading to a loss of more than 85 percent of the floodplain of the Upper Rhine.[5] The result was that the floodplain no longer absorbed and retained rainwater, but rather discharged directly through the river channel. The accelerated and increased river discharge led to many problems in the downstream river sections. German cities like Bonn and Cologne, and especially cities and polders in the Dutch delta, were confronted with an increase in high-water events from the beginning of Tulla's Upper Rhine rectification. During this period, a series of serious floods ravaged the central river landscape of the Netherlands, resulting in many deaths and catastrophic economic damage.

Solving the imbalance between increased discharge volumes and shallow riverbeds was important for another reason. The discovery and mining of large amounts of coal in the region of the Rhine-tributary Ruhr River had led to the rise of the Ruhr area as Europe's main industrial center. The development of an industrial economy in this region, and especially the rise of a steel industry, was only possible with the existence of an efficient infrastructure for the export of excess coal and the import of iron. Railroads seemed to deliver the best conditions, considering the absence of navigable waterways. The result was an increasing monopoly position of railroad companies for the transport of iron ore to, and coal from, the Ruhr area. Antwerp, Hamburg, and Bremen became the most important seaports because they were well-sited to connect to railroad networks.[6] As such, Antwerp was expected to become Europe's leading seaport. The need for cheaper transport conditions led to increased pressure by the CCNR, then dominated by Germany, to "normalize" the Rhine as a navigation channel. This was especially Germany's desire, since the distributaries in the Dutch delta possessed such shallow riverbeds, creating blockages for navigation routes. Ongoing sedimentation in the distributaries of the delta has led to repeated changes of the main discharge channels, with a general tendency to slowly move the main discharge channel southward. After the silting up of the mouth of the Rhine near Katwijk (currently the "Old Rhine," 40 kilometers north of Rotterdam) during the 10th century, the "Nieuwe Maas" (New Meuse River) became the main discharge channel of the delta in the 11th century, enabling conditions for the rise of Rotterdam as a new seaport. However, after the 17th century, the New Meuse also started to silt up, and Rotterdam became increasingly inaccessible for large sea vessels. The Haringvliet estuary then became the main discharge channel.

The combination of increased flood risk in the river area and the pressure for navigation by the CCNR created the basis for an extensive program of river normalization projects in the Rhine-Meuse delta. This program included the massive construction of groynes in the streambeds of rivers in order to increase the currents' speed and prevent the rivers from silting up, as well as the digging of new channels

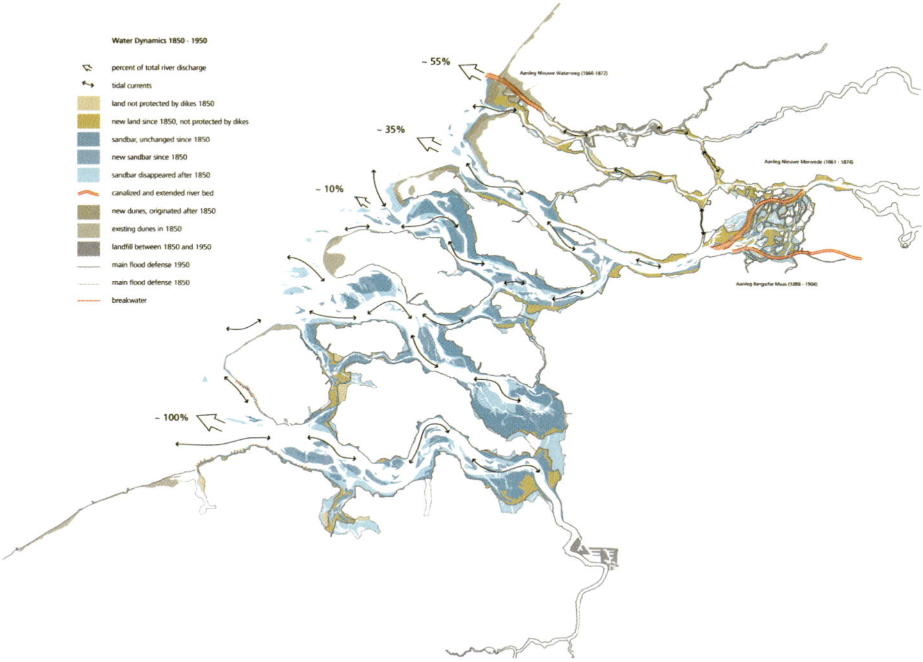

[Figure 2] River discharge in the Rhine delta after construction of Nieuwe Waterweg, Bergsche Maas and Nieuwe Merwede (image credit: © MUST Stedebouw, IPDD/NOW)

in the delta to improve the discharge of river water. These included the Nieuwe Merwede, the Bergsche Maas, and the Nieuwe Waterweg (New Waterway). The New Waterway was a particularly major intervention as an attempt to counter the increasing shallowness of the New Meuse river mouth, which was the main access from the sea to the port of Rotterdam. By digging a new opening to the sea, the New Waterway was an intervention to force the river to reuse the New Meuse, with its harbor basins of the port of Rotterdam becoming once again the main discharge channel. **[Figure 2]**

After digging the New Waterway, the transport of bulk cargo by river barges from Rotterdam to the Ruhr area and vice versa increased, and freight rates plunged by 80 percent. The port—and consequently also the city of Rotterdam—extended explosively and became Germany's most important seaport. River transport surpassed rail transport and, consequently, Rotterdam surpassed Antwerp as Europe's largest seaport. Rotterdam specialized in the transshipment of bulk cargo. This particularly included iron imported from overseas countries to be used in the Ruhr area's steel factories, and coal, originating from the Ruhr area, to be exported to overseas countries.

The French economic geographer Lucien Febvre explains how the main corridor of the new industrial economy of Europe was based on a simple spatial system: a strongly normalized and rationalized Rhine River between the North Sea mouth and Mainz,

Germany, with Rotterdam as the most important transit port, and with Duisburg as the center of the Ruhr area with the largest inland port in the world.[7] **[Figure 3]**

The importance of Rotterdam for the German economy in this period becomes clearer if we consider the number of German firms that settled in the Rotterdam port area, including Thyssen, Müller, Deka Hanno, and others. At the local level, the growth of Rotterdam as a transit port transformed the relationship between city and river fundamentally. The 17th-century riverfront of the city, considered one of the most stylish and beautiful in Europe, changed into a sidewalk-as-transport highway, flanked by transshipment terminals for coal, ore, oil, and cereals. Moreover, because of the construction of the New Waterway and the increased influence of the sea's high tides, urban areas outside the dikes became more vulnerable to flooding.

At the mouth of one of the other distributaries of the delta, the IJssel, the sea-inlet Zuiderzee was dammed and transformed into the freshwater lake IJsselmeer. A part of the IJsselmeer was reclaimed, which heralded a period of rationalization of the agricultural economy in the Netherlands. Summing up the period from the 19th to the early 20th century, we can say that the Tulla project of Upper Rhine rectification, accompanied by the rise of the coal and steel industries in the Ruhr region, contributed to an acceleration of the "normalization" of the river branches in the delta. This was of decisive importance for the development of the Rhine into an efficient and cheap transport corridor and for industrial and urban development in the whole basin area. The Ruhr area became the main industrial center, and Rotterdam became the main connection between continental and intercontinental transport.

Industrialization of the Rhine River Basin and Regulation of River Discharge in the Delta

After World War II, the relationship between Rotterdam and Germany changed. The Dutch and Rotterdam governments wanted to be less dependent on coal-oriented industries in Germany, not only due to Germany's role as a former enemy that had ruined the inner city of Rotterdam, but especially because the transit of bulk goods did not produce much added value for the local economy. The Netherlands wanted to modernize and industrialize the national economy, especially the Rotterdam port area. The rise of oil as a new energy supply offered new perspectives. Rotterdam was considered to be a serious candidate not only for the transshipment and distribution of oil and oil products in all of Europe, but also for processing.

In 1953, southwest Netherlands was hit by a heavy storm surge, resulting in a serious flood. The construction of the Delta Works afterwards was not only an answer to reduce flood risk in this region, but also accelerated the development of the Rotterdam port area as a petrochemical center. American oil companies were looking for a strategic settlement in a northwest European seaport. The Delta Works created large freshwater stocks near the port area, which was—and still is—crucial for the cooling water installations of petrochemical industries. **[Figure 4]**

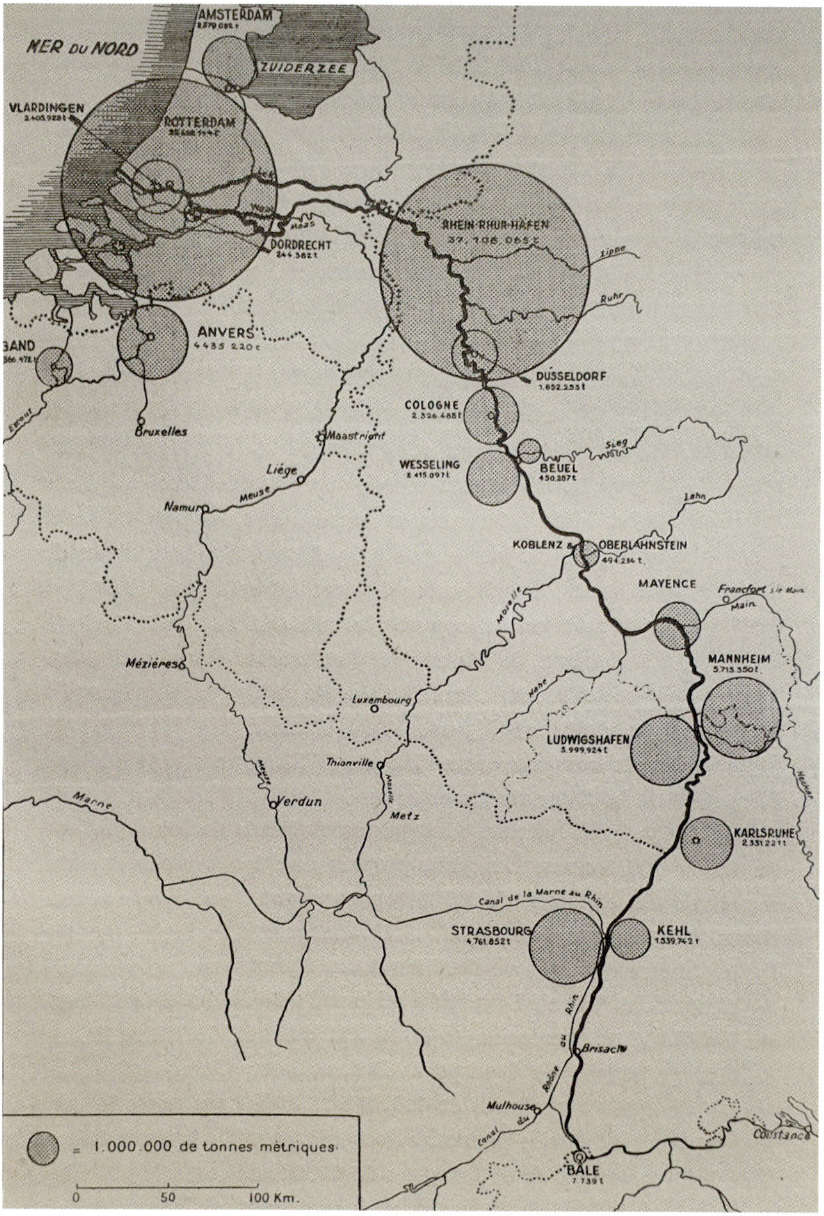

[Figure 3] As explained by Lucien Febvre, the economic system of a rationalized Rhine River corridor, with two largest circles indicating Rotterdam as most important transit port and Duisburg as the center of the Ruhr area with largest inland port of the world (image credit: Demangeon and Febvre, 1935)

The Delta Works also provided a fast and tidal-free navigation route between Rotterdam and Antwerp via the Scheldt-Rhine canal. This canal makes it possible to combine Rotterdam's connections with the hinterland by water and Antwerp's connections with the hinterland by train. Currently, the Scheldt-Rhine canal is the busiest inland canal in the world. Moreover, the Delta Works, together with a number of weirs and moveable dams, resulted in a sophisticated regulation system for discharging river water in the whole delta territory and, consequently, for maintaining deep water channels in the main distributaries. Also, the amount of water discharge through the New Waterway can be regulated in a rather precise way, which is important for the permanent accessibility of the port of Rotterdam as well as for stopping saltwater intrusion. **[Figure 5]**

During the postwar decades, the emphasis for Dutch (and many other European) politics focused on combining economic growth and increasing prosperity through social and physical safety—building the welfare state. The combination of industrialization with an emphasis on flood risk reduction was an important characteristic of building the welfare state in the Netherlands, with a huge impact on land use and the spatial organization of cities and regions. One example was the changing relationship between city and river in Rotterdam: a new dike with a motorway at the riverbanks created a spectacular entry to the city for motorists, but blocked the city's view to the river completely. **[Figure 6]**

With its new emphasis on oil, the Rotterdam port had increased its global reach. The Ruhr area was still the main customer of oil products, but it was no longer the only one. The Rhine was still the main transport corridor, but it was supplemented with roads, railroads, and especially pipe networks; and new industrial centers developed across the river basin. Moreover, the Rhine played an important role in building a European-wide electricity network. The first-generation hydropower plants were built in the High Rhine region, on the border of Switzerland and Germany, during the early 1900s. More were built in the Canal d'Alsace and became the central key in this electricity network.[8]

As a result, the "simple system" of Rotterdam–Rhine–Duisburg transformed into a much more diffuse and complex system of industrial plants, infrastructure networks, and urbanization patterns. The large-scale hydraulic works of Delta Works and additional weirs in the distributaries played a main role in the transition of the whole Rhine River Basin into an oil-based industrial and densely urbanized region. The river itself was considered and treated like an industrial transport corridor, resulting in the disappearance of the spatial orientation of the river in cities like Rotterdam, and in the narrowing of the riverbed in many places. This condition sped up the river currents and deepened the navigation channel.

Globalization and the Rise of Widespread Concerns for the Environment

The third transition was not based on a new energy supply, but on two revolutionary developments. The first took place in transport logistics, caused by the introduction and massive application of the shipping container, leading to a massive automatization of ports and navigation. This resulted in a dramatic reduction in freight costs for general cargo.[9]

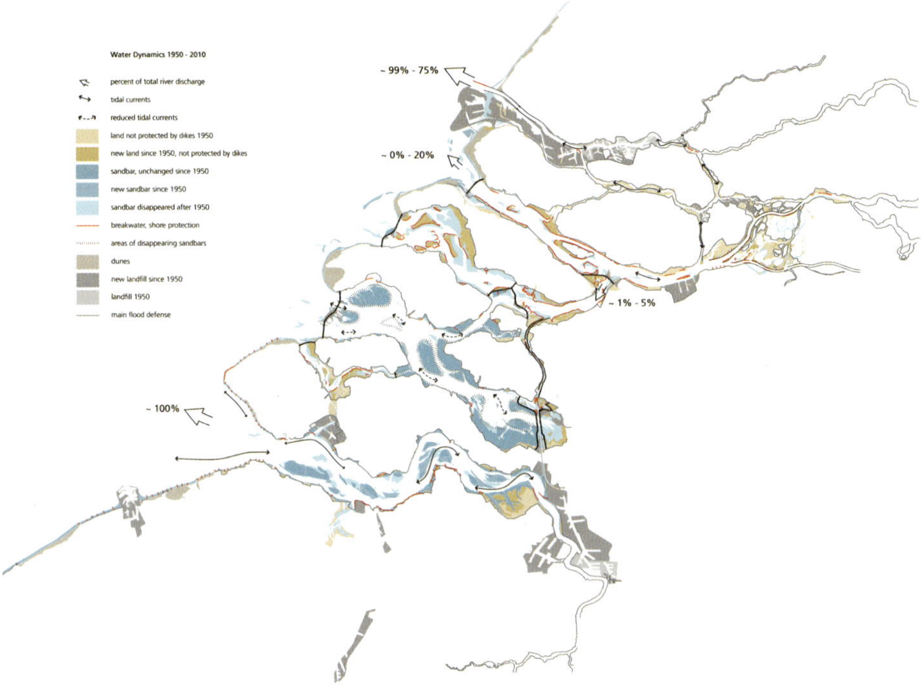

[Figure 4] River discharge in the Rhine delta after construction of the Delta Works
(image credit: © MUST Stedebouw, IPDD/NOW)

After the transshipment of the first container in 1966, Rotterdam became the first large container port in Europe, which led to the growth of its role as a distribution port. The port developed as a hub in the worldwide distribution network of raw materials, semifinished products, and final products. Together with digitalization, the new transport conditions were the driving force for globalization, defined as a diffusion of economic activity without regard for national borders, and revolutionizing trade patterns and industrial locations.[10]

Because of the container, new logistics led to the increased interweaving of transport by river, motorway, railroad, and pipeline. The Rhine basin maintained its role as the main transport corridor of Europe; however, it was no longer just the river itself, but the whole river basin as a corridor with a complex and diffuse system of different transport modalities. This system was accompanied by an additional complex and diffuse pattern of urban and industrial developments and inland container ports.

As part of this globalization trend, industries in western Europe, and especially in the Ruhr area, moved production facilities to low-income countries in Asia and Eastern Europe. The relics of heavy industry in the Ruhr area itself were transformed into

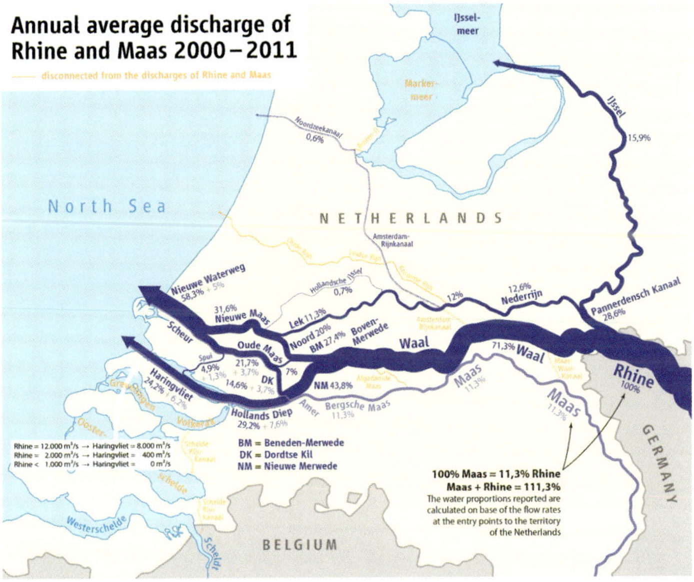

[Figure 5] Regulation of discharge through the different distributaries of the Rhine-Meuse delta, 2016 (image credit: Dörrbecker (Chumwa)

[Figure 6] Construction of new dike in Rotterdam, alongside the river New Meuse, 1960 (image credit: J.E.H. Roovers)

cultural and leisure destinations. The Emscher Landscape Park near Duisburg, built between 1991 and 2002, is one of the most notable examples of transforming industrial areas—coal mines, steel factories, and railway yards—into cultural areas, in this case, museums, theaters, and recreational spaces.

Parallel to this process of the rise of the container and globalization (from the 1960s to the 1990s), another revolutionary change took place: the rise of an awareness by academics, politicians, and the public at large of the disastrous effects of industrialization and large-scale infrastructures on the natural environment. An important part of the exposure of the international debate on this issue was the publication of the report *The Limits to Growth* (1972).[11]

In the Netherlands, the increasing concern for the environment resulted in the cancellation of several initiatives for new industrial plants in the Rotterdam port area, as well as the cancellation of the last reclamation project in the IJsselmeer (the Markerwaard). In the southwest delta, a dam to close off the East Scheldt estuary was changed into a storm surge barrier. Planned enhancements of the flood defense system in the river area were also cancelled due to widespread protests against the destruction of cultural and ecological values of the river landscape.

An important aspect of this increased concern for the environment was the initiative of the Dutch government and the Rotterdam Port Authority for new international negotiations that aimed to stop the serious pollution of the Rhine by industrial wastewater. This resulted in a new International Treaty on the Rhine (1976) to make the river cleaner and more accessible for migratory fish, by stopping industrial wastewater deposits in the river and reopening the closed estuaries in the Dutch delta. (Cynical detail: the treaty was a result of Dutch initiative, but the Dutch were the last ones to implement the appointed agreements.)

The economic changes in industry and transport in the 1970s were the first signs of the rise of an economic system based on automatization and digitalization, logistics, extended supporting services (logistics, finance, assurance), and a new "creative industry."[12] In order to create better conditions for this rising economy, cities at the Rhine embankments, like Rotterdam, wanted to eliminate the one-sided economic dependency of ports and industries, and try to present themselves as global cities. They rediscovered the river as an important trump card in this process, which led to a revaluation of the river as an urban feature, with a focus on the design and development of new urban waterfronts. **[Figure 7]**

Related to the increasing attention to nature and the environment and pushed forward by protests against new canalization projects and dike enhancements in the central river area of the Netherlands, new experiments concerning the river area were developed. These pleaded for the end of the domination of economic arguments in river management and advocated for more attention to the environmental and cultural value of rivers. An important moment in this process was the Eo Wijers design

[Figure 7] New urban waterfronts in Rotterdam, 1995
(image credit: drawing by Arjan Knoester, City planning department Rotterdam)

[Figure 8] The "Blue Room" project near Wageningen, 2000 (image credit: Beeldbank Rijkswaterstaat)

[Figure 9] Rhone-Rhine Canal lock, structure designed by architect Le Corbusier, Niffer, France (image credit: Derek Hoeferlin)

competition[13] in 1986, dedicated to the future of the river area. The winning entry in this competition was "Plan Stork," which was a plea for a 180-degree turn in river management methodology. Instead of making rivers narrower and heightening dikes for flood protection, the riverbeds should be widened as a basic condition for the repair and restoration of the typical ecosystems of the river area. The disappearance of the stork was one of the most alarming signs of the degradation of river ecosystems, and its return was considered an indication of the restoration of the river ecosystem as a whole. As an experiment and pilot project, the essence of the idea of Plan Stork was implemented in a small part of the Lower Rhine, west of the town of Wageningen, which resulted in a new landscape park called Blauwe Kamer (Blue Room). **[Figure 8]** Indeed, creating a wider riverbed by making several cuts in the main river dike, and building a new dike at a greater distance from the river, resulted in the recovery of a disappeared river landscape. This principle would be widely applied in the next decades. During the 19th and 20th centuries, several attempts were made to extend the water network of the Rhine by connecting it with the Danube and the Rhone. The connection of the Rhine and the Danube is an old dream—Charles the Great tried to realize it as far back as the 8th century, without success. In the 20th century, the Rhine-Donau canal was built, opening in 1992. The expectations concerning freight transport were very high, but the results were disappointing. Passing through the many locks in the canal proved to be too time-consuming and costly. That is all the more true for the 236-kilometer Rhone-Rhine canal, realized in 1833 and numbering 133 locks. Both canals are mainly used today by pleasure craft and cruise ships. **[Figure 9]**

[Figure 10] Overview of projects of the "Room for the River Program," 2005–2015 (image credit: Rijkswaterstaat)

We can say that the Rhine corridor shows a complex transition in this period. On the one hand, the Rhine became a more diffuse pattern of urban and economic development, including new infrastructural networks. But on the other hand, a "rediscovery" of the cultural and ecologic values of the river resulted in new urban waterfront projects and riverbed restorations.

Climate Change, Rising Waters, Energy Transition: New Challenges, New Opportunities

The last episode in this story has most recently been increasingly dominated by climate change impacts, and particularly the adverse effects of global rising temperatures on sea-level rise and river discharges. These lead to the need for a fundamental energy transition in the future.

While the warnings of *The Limits to Growth* have led to more attention being paid to the restoration and maintenance of natural landscape features and the reduction of environmental pollution, the warnings on climate change by the IPCC (founded in 1988), will have a deep impact on economies and land-use patterns worldwide, and throughout the Rhine River Basin, and its delta especially.

In the Dutch delta, the awareness of the seriousness of climate change started with two critical high-water events in the rivers in the 1990s. These made clear that prevailing assumptions about possible discharge volumes needed a serious revision, based on new insights into the consequences of accelerated climate change for river discharges.

[Figure 11] "Demountable Flood Defence in Cologne," a system of mobile parts consisting of posts and dam beams, easily and rapidly erected during flood events (TOP) Anchoring supports along Cologne's waterfront (MIDDLE) Dr. Marlene Willkomm of Stadtentwässerungsbetriebe Köln, AöR explaining the concept to Dutch landscape architect Stijn Koole and architect Derek Hoeferlin (BOTTOM) The system stored as pallets under the Deutz Suspension Bridge (images credit: Derek Hoeferlin)

The awareness of the serious nature of global warming has led to two strategies: 1) adaptation that aims to anticipate the effects of climate change; and, 2) mitigation that aims to reduce climate change's effects of warming temperatures through the reduction of greenhouse gas emissions.

Concerning adaptation, two important programs were developed in the Dutch delta: "Room for the River" and the Dutch "Delta program." The Room for the River program was developed after the high-water events of the 1990s, and aimed to combine the adaptation of the riverbed to higher discharge volumes with the intention of paying more attention to ecological and cultural values, as proposed by Plan Stork in 1986 and tested by the Blue Room project near Wageningen. The Room for the River program was implemented between 2005 and 2015, and resulted in 39 projects where the riverbed was widened or provided with bypasses. **[Figure 10]** In all these projects, a special quality-assessment committee played an important role in advising and controlling the spatial and ecological quality of the outcomes.[14] In most projects, radical rearrangements of land use and urban patterns proved necessary. Because of extensive public debates at the local level, and the relative freedom and flexibility of local authorities to develop tailor-made solutions, the whole program could be implemented. During an extreme high-water event in February 2020, most of the recently widened riverbeds and bypasses were flooded, without any physical damage or victims.

Although the implementation of these integrated projects proved the concept of the Room for the River program, the question remains as to whether the approach of giving more room to the water system by reorganizing land use could be continued in other (upstream) parts of the Rhine River Basin, as well as in the densely urbanized and industrialized areas of the mouth of the river.

Concerning the upstream regions, the structure of river management in different countries and jurisdictions is quite fragmented. Complicating matters in Germany, every state has its own policy on flood risk reduction.[15] Flood control standards are much lower in Germany than in the Netherlands, and the catastrophic flooding during the summer of 2021 emphasizes the need for stronger standards and coordination structures. Adaptation measures in the German Lower Rhine are limited to a number of incidental improvements of urban waterfronts, like Duisburg, Dusseldorf, and Cologne.[16] In Cologne, for instance, due to the compactness and density of the urban waterfront, "demountable flood defense barriers" are erected during high river stages. While these temporary fortifications work quite well for the local condition, in reality, the walls may force more water faster downstream (to the delta). **[Figure 11]** During extreme high-water events, it is indeed possible that the Dutch river dikes are prepared to withstand the high-water levels, but the German dikes, just east of the Dutch-German border, can be submerged. The final result will be that the eastern parts of the Netherlands will be flooded. Dutch-German negotiations have been started to resolve this problem, but have yet to result in final agreements.[17]

For the Dutch delta as a whole, and especially for the river mouth, the approach of

Room for the River became globally relevant in 2005 when Hurricane Katrina destroyed a large portion of the New Orleans region. This catastrophic event of infrastructural failure was a wake-up call in the Netherlands, raising awareness for the need to update the Dutch delta's flood control system. A new Delta Committee was installed by the Dutch government in the same year and published its final report in 2008, titled *Working Together with Water*. A core tenet of this report pleads for more attention to be paid to the natural "behavior" of water and water systems.[18] The advice of the Delta Committee resulted in the start of the Dutch Delta program in 2009. These first steps toward a new comprehensive delta program looked promising, building on the same ideas as Room for the River, along with elaborating its philosophy and approach.

One of the most important conclusions of the Delta Committee was the recognition of the extreme vulnerability of the Rotterdam region, and the urgency of finding sufficient long-term solutions. The increased vulnerability for flood risk is caused by the construction and pursuant frequent deepening of the New Waterway. This process has made the urbanized areas of the region gradually more vulnerable to high water events from the sea. Moreover, also increasing peak discharges of the rivers can become a problem for the region. The worst-case scenario is a simultaneous storm surge from the sea and a peak river discharge.

Additionally, the Delta Program not only focuses on rising sea levels and increasing flood risk, but also other aspects of climate change, including extremely low water levels in the riverbeds during periods of drought. These low water levels lead to increasing saltwater intrusion in the surface- and groundwater of the delta, creating problems for navigation on the rivers. Saltwater intrusion creates problems for the availability of fresh water for drinking, agriculture, and process industries, and has been worsened in the Rotterdam region by the construction and frequent deepening of the artificial river mouth New Waterway.

Next to a series of proposed and partially implemented interventions alongside the coast and in the river system, the Delta Committee defined the Rotterdam region as the most complex and critical region. Sea-level rise and the increasing peak discharges of the rivers led to higher flood risk, coupled with increased saltwater intrusion. The obvious answer is to design a long-term robust and sustainable solution that combines the urgency of adaptation with a policy of mitigation via energy transition, resulting in a high impact on the land-use pattern near the port of Rotterdam. Sixty percent of the 12,000-hectare port territory in the Rotterdam region is occupied by fossil fuel installations for storage, transshipment, and processing. Combined, these fossil fuel land uses constitute 17 percent of the greenhouse gas emissions of the Netherlands. The path towards energy transition will have a huge impact on the land use and spatial structure of the port territory. In relation to energy transition, we can also expect a transformation of transport modalities. Containerization had led to a modal split in favor of road transport, accounting for almost 60 percent of all freight cargo in the Rotterdam-Duisburg corridor (2014),[19] and responsible for 83 percent of greenhouse gas emissions of all transport modalities (road, railroad, water, pipelines). A change towards more transport by other modalities is necessary but difficult because of the limited capacity of railroads and increasing problems with shallow waterways during droughts.

A central dilemma in this respect will be the future of the mouth of the river. On the one hand, a "status quo" scenario of the intensification of transport by water would mean ongoing dredging and the deepening of navigation channels, including the New Waterway. This would create the need to raise the existing dikes in the urbanized areas of the delta region, or the construction of a lock system in the river mouth, in order to protect the safety of more than two million people in this region.

On the other hand, a scenario of building on the new adage "working together with water" would mean that the river mouth should recover its quality as an estuary. Several international research projects have shown that natural estuaries, featuring broad, shallow, and funnel-shaped river mouths, function as solid and sustainable barriers against floods and sea-level rise, as well as against saltwater intrusion.[20] For the Rhine this would mean that the Haringvliet should be recovered as its main estuary. In this option, the New Waterway would lose its role as the main discharge channel and could silt up and "degrade" to a small side estuary. Dredging activities could be decreased substantially. With a shallower riverbed, high waters from the sea would have less influence on the upriver areas. Saltwater intrusion would be reduced as well. This scenario builds on several recent interventions in the river mouth system. The first step in the recovery of the Haringvliet as an estuary is the "ajar decision" for the Haringvliet locks. Since 2019, these locks have been left ajar, allowing fish to migrate from the sea to the river and vice versa, which re-establishes a more brackish, estuary-like environment in the Haringvliet. Simultaneously, the recovery of the New Meuse–New Waterway as a tidal river has already been started by the "River as a Tidal Park" program, initiated by environmental organizations like the World Wildlife Fund, ARK Nature Development, and the City of Rotterdam.

Building on these initiatives, a new future vision for the Rotterdam region was presented recently. This vision shows the transformation of the New Meuse–New Waterway from a monofunctional navigation channel to a multifunctional estuary, creating conditions for a natural river mouth ecosystem, for a nature-friendly port and adapted shipping activities, for new types of river-oriented urban patterns, and for a natural barrier against high tides and saltwater intrusion. **[Figure 12]**

Conclusion

The story of the Rhine of the last two centuries is a story of subjecting the natural system of the entire Rhine River Basin to the goals of building a modern, industrialized society. This story is coming to a close for two reasons: 1) the subjection of the natural system has reached its absolute limits, and 2) the character of industrialized society is already changing and needs to change more radically, both in concept and in implementation strategies. The driving forces in this transformation must include alternate futures of energy transition, climate adaptation, the rise of a circular economy, and different intermodalities such as digitalization and robotization. New types of navigation such as different vessel sizes should be designed. Returned cultural connections to river systems and landscapes should be encouraged. Sustainable transboundary agreements should be negotiated. And finally, a reimagining of the Rhine River Basin as an economic and historic center of Europe should be championed. All of these possibilities will be further explored in the Rhine River Basin speculation later in this book.

1. Roger Brunet, *Les Villes 'Européennes': Rapport pour la DATAR,* Délégation à *l'Aménagement du Territoire et à l'Action Regionale* (Paris: Documentations Française, 1989).

2. A. Bosch, W. Van der Ham, *Twee eeuwen Rijkswaterstaat 1798–1998* (Baarn: Europese Bibliotheek, 1998).

3. David Blackbourn, *The Conquest of Nature: Water, Landscape, and the Making of Modern Germany* (New York/ London: Routledge, 2006), 77.

4. Vincent Lagendijk, "Europe's Rhine power: connections, borders, and flows," *Journal of Water History* 8 (2016): 23–39.

5. Pham Thi Minh Thu, *A Hydrodynamic-Numerical Model of the River Rhine* (Karlsruhe: Institut für Wasserwirtschaft und Kulturtechnik Universität Karlsruhe, 2002) .

6. Marten Boon, Hein A.M. Klemann, Ben Wubs, *Transnational Regions in Historical Perspective* (London/New York: Routledge, 2020).

7. A. Demangeon, L. Febvre, Le Rhin, *Problèmes d'Histoire et d'Économie* (Paris: Librairie Armand Colin, 1935).

8. Lagendijk, "Europe's Rhine power."

9. Marten Boon, Hein A.M. Klemann, Ben Wubs, *Transnational Regions in Historical Perspective* (London/New York: Routledge, 2020).

10. Hein A.M. Klemann, Ben Wubs, *River Dependence: Creating a Transnational Rhine Economy 1850–2000* (Rotterdam: Erasmus University, 2013).

11. Donella H. Meadows, Dennis L. Meadows, Jørgen Randers, William W. Behrens III, *The Limits to Growth: A Report for the Club of Rome's Project on the Predicament of Mankind* (New York: Universe Books, 1972).

12. Charles Landry, *The Creative City: A Toolkit for Urban Innovators* (London: Earthscan, 2000); and Richard Florida, *The Rise of the Creative Class: And How It's Transforming Work, Leisure, Community and Everyday Life* (New York: Perseus Books/Basic Books, 2002).

13. Eo Wijers was a director of the Dutch National Planning Agency in the 1960s and Professor of Regional Design in Delft in the 1970s. After his death, his pupils started the Eo Wijers Foundation, which organizes a competition every two years, aiming to create more attention for the importance of design at the regional scale. See https://eowijers.nl/.

14. F. Klijn et al., "Design Quality of Room-for-the-River Measures in the Netherlands: Role and Assessment of the Quality Team (Q-team)," *International Journal of River Basin Management* 11, no. 3 (2013): 287–299; and Dirk Sijmons et al., *Room for the River: Safe and Attractive Landscapes* (Wageningen: Blauwdruk, 2017).

15. Judith Janssen, *Mein Rhein, dein Rhein, onze Rijn? Nederlands-Duitse samenwerking rond hoogwaterbescherming in het stroomgebied van de Rijn* (Enschede: Universiteit Twente, 2004); and Cornelia Redeker, *Rhine Cities—Urban Flood Integration (UFI)* (Delft: TU Delft, 2013).

16. Redeker, *Rhine Cities.*

17. Janssen, *Mein Rhein.*

18. Delta Committee, *Working Together with Water: A Living Land Builds for Its Future* (The Hague: 2008).

19. Luc De Vries, *Top Corridors: An Integral, Multimodal and Collaborative Approach for Logistics Corridors* (The Hague: Ministry of Infrastructure and Water Management, 2019).

20. R. Costanza et al., "The Value of the World's Ecosystem Services and Natural Capital," *Nature* no. 387 (May 1997): 253–260; and Jasper R.F.W. Leuven et al., "Sea-Level-Rise-Induced Threats Depend on the Size of Tide-Influenced Estuaries Worldwide, *Nature Climate Change* 9 (2019): 986–992.

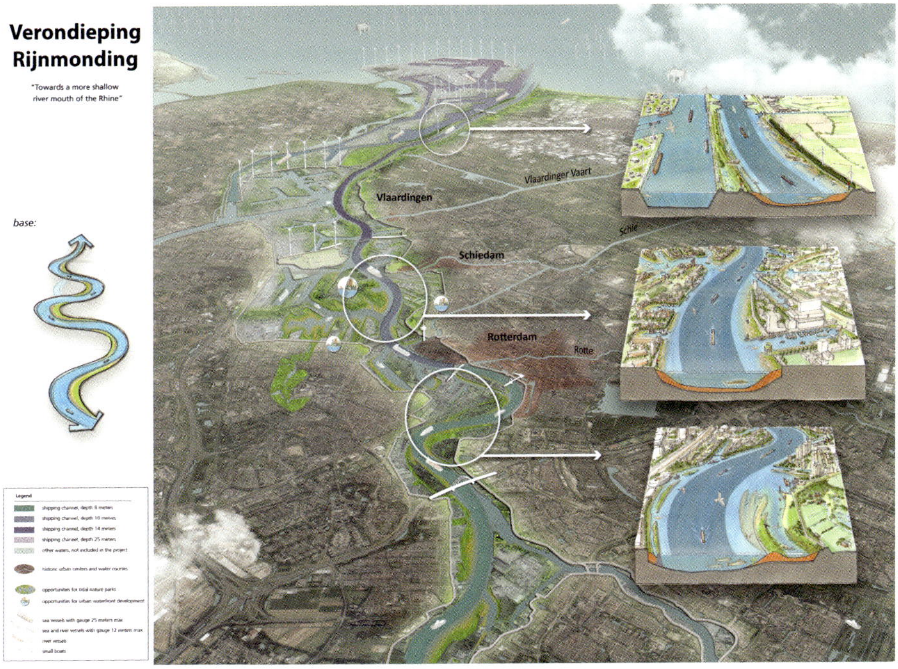

[Figure 12] Birds eye view of the Rotterdam region, with New Meuse and New Waterway, seen from the east, exploring the possibilities of making the riverbed more shallow and broader (image credit: concept by ARK Nature development, Bureau Stroming and Han Meyer, drawing by Dirk Oomen en Peter Veldt (Bureau Stroming)

Maeslantkering storm surge barrier, Nieuwe Waterweg, Netherlands, 2010 (image credit: Derek Hoeferlin, with Stijn Koole)

Rhine Falls, Schaffhausen, Switzerland, 2018 (image credit: Derek Hoeferlin)

Territory 01: Rhine River Basin

Territory 01 Plan

The Rhine River Basin has adapted to Europe's changing paradigms. It is the source of drinking water for 25 million people, but it must balance its function as a transportation corridor, as well as a site for energy production. Currently, the Rhine is canalized from the end of Lake Constance through the line of 21 mainstream hydroelectric dams, after which the river remains free-flowing for the remainder of its path.[1] The first mainstream hydroelectric dam was completed in 1866 at the Swiss town of Schaffhausen. It was replaced in the 1960s after a century of use.[2] Together, the 21 hydroelectric dams have a total capacity of 2,186 MW, almost matching the six mega dams in the Missouri River. The first European interconnected energy grid was created after WWI in the High Rhine Valley. The river's hydroelectric potential and central location in Europe made the region an important site for both the production and transfer of energy.[3] Energy exchange and power grid interconnectedness were a tool for building and solidifying alliances during the Cold War, and have continued to be a pressing matter for the European Union.[4] In addition to the 21 mainstream dams, 2,000 hydroelectric dams have been constructed throughout the watershed, as well as 10 nuclear powerplants that have a total capacity of 19,000 MW, cooled directly by water drawn from the Rhine River and its tributaries.[5] Historically, people have been concerned about water quality and damage to the river's ecology as early as the 15th century, but chemical production and navigation in the 20th century polluted the Rhine to the point where it was considered the "sewer of Europe."[6] In 1950, Switzerland, France, Germany, Luxembourg, and the Netherlands cofounded the International Commission for the Protection of the Rhine (ICPR) to address the worsening condition of the Rhine, and the European Commission joined the ICPR in 1976. However, no meaningful measures were taken by the ICPR until the Sandoz Chemical Spill in 1986.[7] On the night of the first of November, a fire broke out in a warehouse upstream of Basel. The firefighting efforts caused 30 tonnes of pesticides and 200 kilos of mercury to be dumped into the Rhine, turning the river red and decimating riverine wildlife as far as 400 kilometers downstream.[8] As a result of this disaster, the ICPR enacted plans that put in place strict environmental protection policies and enacted conservation programs throughout the Rhine.[9] The Rhine River has been central to the formation of modern European society, but it has been historically neglected and poorly managed. Through improved leadership and environmental consciousness, the current state of the Rhine has greatly improved and continues to be an invaluable cultural and economic corridor in Europe.

NETHERLANDS

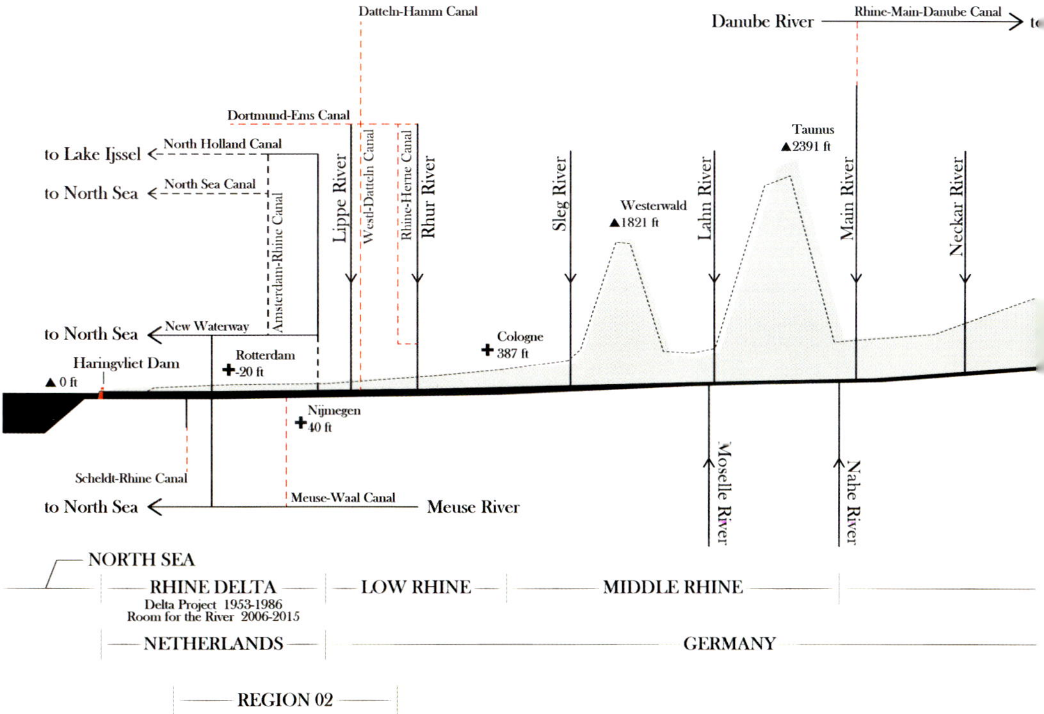

TERRITORY 01
RHINE RIVER BASIN

SWEDEN
DENMARK
Copenhagen
NORTH SEA
UNITED KINGDOM
Hamburg
Ems River
GERMANY
Berlin
North Holland Canal
North Sea Canal
B
NETHERLANDS
REGION 02
Amsterdam-Rhine Canal
Rotterdam
Dortmund-Ems Canal
Harvingvliet Dam
Westl-Datteln Canal
Lippe River
Scheldt-Rhine Canal
Datteln-Hamm Canal
Rhine-Herne Canal
Meuse-Waal Canal
Antwerp
Leipzig
Rhur River
Cologne
LUXEMBOURG
BELGIUM
Scheldt River
Prague
Main River
Meuse River
Moselle River
CZECHIA
Seine River
Paris
Marne River
REGION 01
Rhine-Main-Danube Canal
Rhine-Marne Canal Ouest
Iffezheim Barrage
Rhine-Marne Canal
Strasbourg
Gambsheim Barrage
Strasbourg Barrage
Gerstheim Barrage
Rhinau Barrage
Munich
Marckolsheim Barrage
Grand Canal d'Alsace
Fessenheim Dam
Vogelgrun Dam
Augst Dam
Ottmarsheim Dam
Ryburg Dam
Kembs Dam
Birsfelden Dam
Basel
Schaffhausen Dam
AUSTRIA
Rheinfelden Dam
Rhemau Dam
Rhone-Rhine Canal
Eglisau Dam
Sackingen Dam
Laufenburg Dam
Laufenburg Dam
Alps
Albbruck-Dogern Dam
SWITZERLAND
FRANCE
Saone River
SLOVENIA
B
Lyon
Milan
Rhone River
ITALY
MONACO
Marseille
ADRIATI
SEA
LIGURIAN
SEA

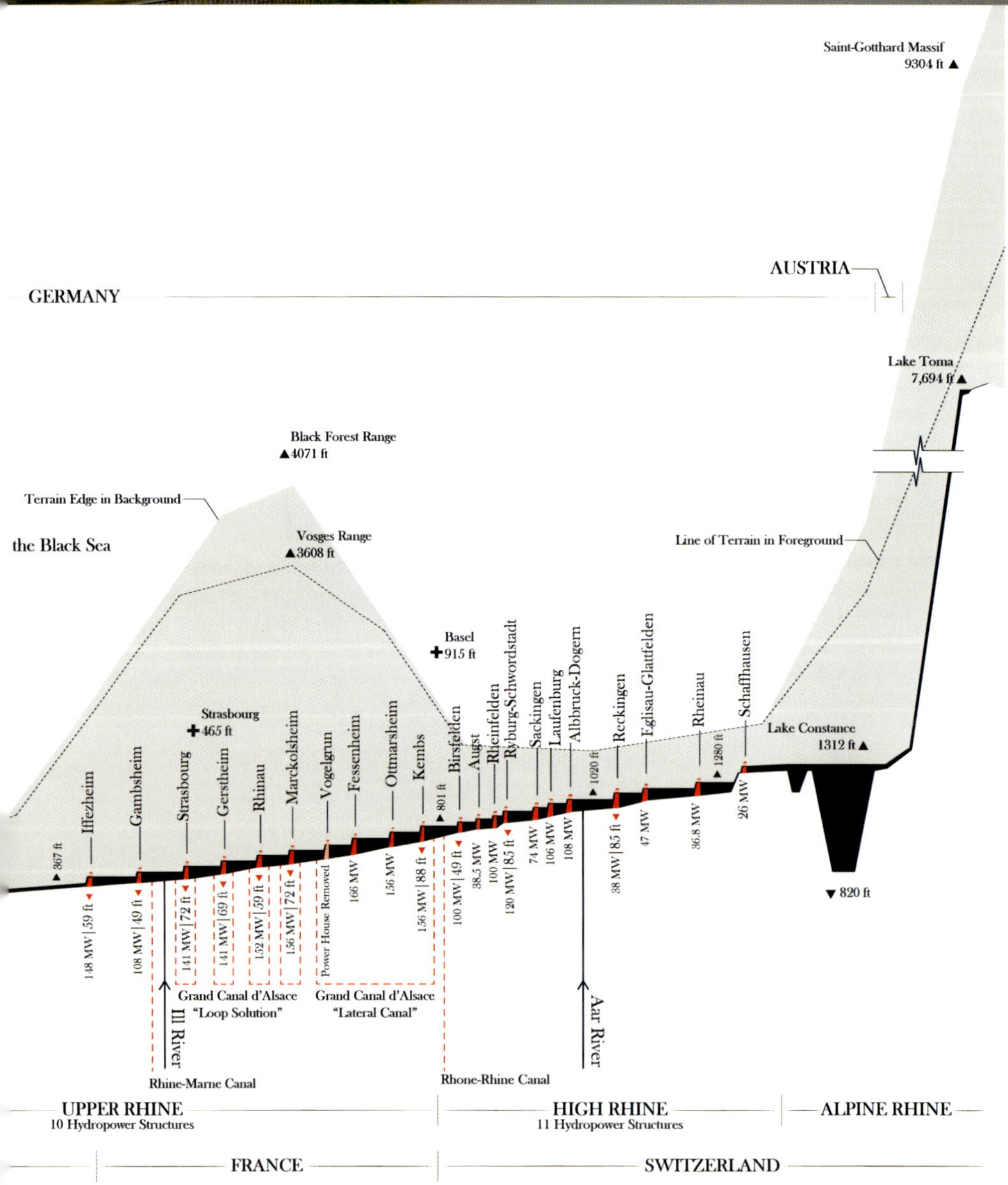

REGION 01

SECTION B-B
FOLLOWING THE PATH OF THE RHINE RIVER

Territory 01 Section B-B

Sectionally, the Rhine River resembles the Mississippi in infrastructure buildup while having a trans-boundary character like the Mekong. The main stem of the Rhine consists of six distinct sections, developed independently of each other. Starting from the glaciers in the Saint-Gotthard Massif and discharging into the North Sea, the Rhine River divides into the following reaches, from source to mouth: Alpine, High, Upper, Middle, Low, and Delta.[10] The Alpine Rhine stretches from the river's source in the Alps to where it pools in Lake Constance. Following Lake Constance, Switzerland, Germany, and France share the High and Upper Rhine stretches. In these two sections, the river descends 945 feet, making it suitable for producing hydroelectricity. Currently, there are 21 hydroelectric dams, 11 in the High Rhine and 10 in the Upper Rhine, with the last one completed in 1977.[11] The 10 projects in the Upper Rhine additionally feature locks and barrages to facilitate barge navigation to Basel.[12] In addition to the mainstem dams, the path of the Upper Rhine has been extensively modified to consolidate and control the path of the river.[13] The Middle and Low Rhine are significantly less developed in terms of infrastructure, and run entirely in Germany. In these sections, the river joins its largest tributaries including the Ruhr, Sleg, Lahn, and Moselle Rivers. Many of Germany's largest cities are located along its riverbanks, including Düsseldorf, Cologne, and Duisburg. This portion of the Rhine was pivotal to Germany's industrialization in the 20th century. The coal and steel industries transformed the Middle and Low Rhine, in particular the Ruhr valley, into the most industrialized valley in western Europe.[14] The transition to the Rhine Delta is marked by the German-Dutch border and a change in character as the Rhine River branches into different distributaries that empty towards the North Sea. It is an area that has been at constant risk of flooding from both inland and tidal surges, which in recent years have been exacerbated by climate change and sea-level rise.[15] Initiated in 1953 after the North Sea Flood, the Dutch Delta Works Project placed barriers along the delta to limit the size of the coast and control the flow of water to protect against tidal surges.[16] A series of dams were built at the end of many outlets, most notably the Haringvlietdam which features a series of 17 sluices that span five kilometers at the end of Lek distributary.[17] Following the Delta Works, the Dutch government implemented the "Room for the River Programme" in 2006 to ameliorate inland water levels through channel expansion and dike reinforcement.[18] The current state of the Rhine River reflects centuries of modification that has reflected regional developments.

Region 01: Strasbourg Region & France-Germany Border

Region 01 Plan
The Upper Rhine has been subject to centuries of engineering efforts that have had ecological and political consequences throughout the basin. Navigation is the Upper Rhine's primary function, and the key piece of infrastructure that manages the river is the Grand Canal d'Alsace.[19] Spanning almost the entire run of the upper Rhine River from Village-Neuf to Strasbourg, the Grand Canal diverts a channel of water that runs parallel to the main path of the Rhine River and directs water to 8 of the 10 hydroelectric locks and hydroelectric dams in the Upper Rhine. These projects are typologically different from the dams in the Mississippi and Mekong. Instead of creating reservoirs or pooled areas, they rely on the canal to provide the volume and velocity of water to operate.[20] A set of barrages and weirs accompanies each project. Located on the mainstem of the Rhine River, they assist in directing water to the canal, while slowing the speed of water to prevent flooding during the higher-volume water seasons.[21] Politically, the current state of the Upper Rhine reflects the conditions outlined in the Treaty of Versailles. With its ratification in 1920, the mainstem of the Rhine River permanently became the border between France and Germany. France received control of all territories on the west bank of the Rhine, and importantly, it also gave France the exclusive right to develop projects in the river.[22] The Grand Canal d'Alsace is not only an act of engineering, but also a political tool that gives France control of the Rhine River by drawing water away from the border into its territories. This gives France sole possession of the hydroelectric dams and locks in the process.[23] Nine of the locks and hydroelectric dams in the Upper Rhine operate exclusively to the French, and only one project was conceded to Germany in the 1970s.[24] The Grand

Hydroelectric Station at Gambsheim Dam, France/Germany border, 2018
(image credit: Derek Hoeferlin)

Canal d'Alsace is not only the most prominent act of river engineering in the region, it is also a political tool that seized control of the Upper Rhine for France.

Region 01 Section C-C

The immense amount of engineering in the Upper Rhine has caused unintended consequences throughout the region. In its natural state, the Upper Rhine River broke into countless strands and enveloped the area with marshlands.[25] The river was unpredictable, especially during the flood seasons, and the wetlands were breeding grounds for diseases such as malaria, two attributes that threatened settlements along its path. Beginning in the 19th century, the Rhine was consolidated into a single thin, fast-flowing stream of uniform width for navigation, and the surrounding wetlands were eliminated and reclaimed to support agriculture and urban expansion.[26] While this established the Upper Rhine as the industrial core of Europe, it created new threats for the region. The increased speed of the river eroded the riverbed which lowered the water table, and caused more damaging floods downstream in the Middle Rhine.[27] The Grand Canal d'Alsace draws water from the Rhine into a parallel path. Because the path of the Rhine River is the national border between France and Germany, the diversion of water away from the mainstem river gives control of the water and the infrastructure to the French government.[28] Designed in two phases, the first stretch from Village-Neuf to Vogelrun features a typical parallel canal, while the second phase implemented between Marckolsheim and Strasbourg accounts for the threats in the "loop solution."[29] In the "loop solution," the canal weaves in and out of the river to maximize the amount of water in the main stem and to slow the river.[30] However, this was not enough to fully remedy the issue, and two additional dams were completed downstream of the canal to halt the degradation of the riverbed in the Upper Rhine.[31] In turn, these two dams magnified the threats of trapping sedimentation in the Upper Rhine, which requires annual dredging to remove the buildup.[32] The political influence in the engineering of the Upper Rhine has caused a cascade of unintentional harm to the river that undermines the Rhine's capacity to facilitate trade and the overall health of the environment.

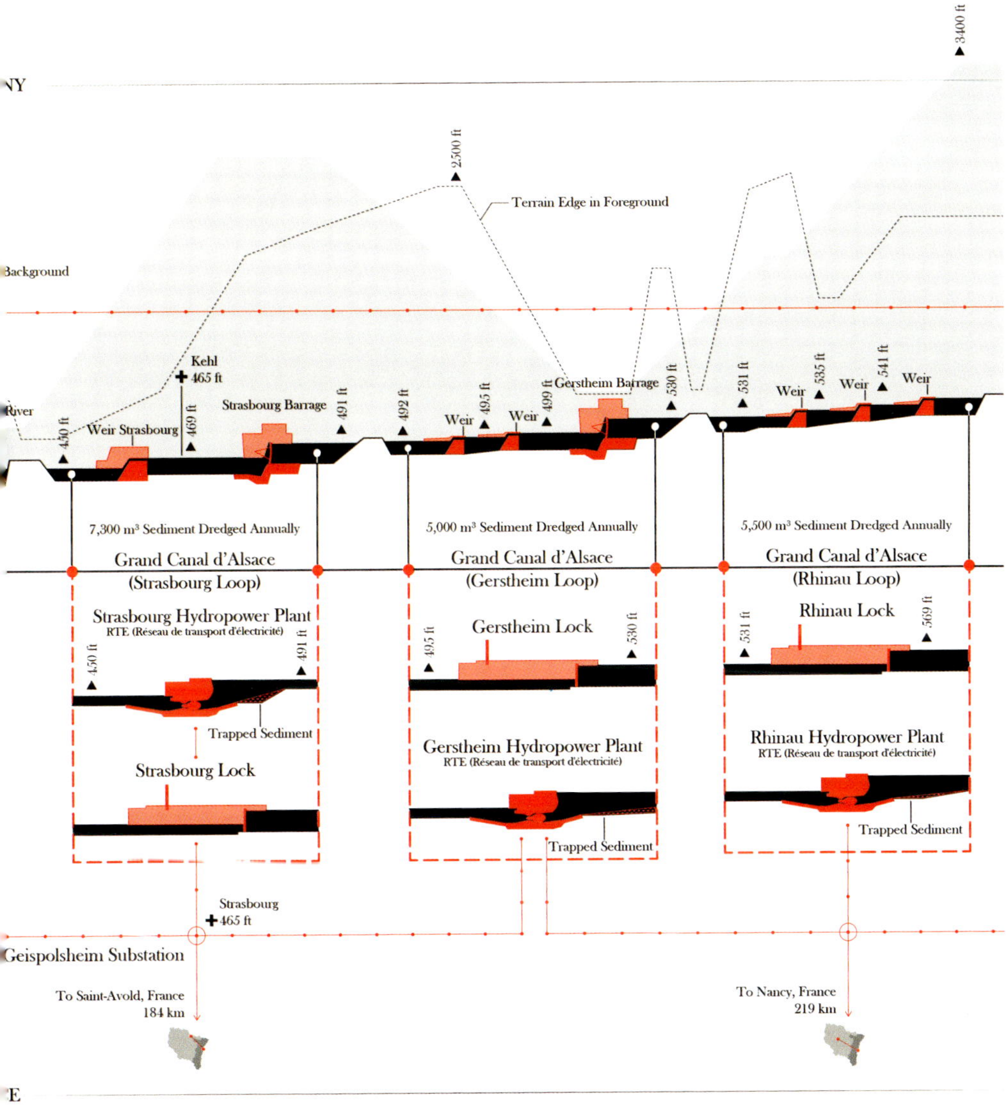

SECTION C-C

SECTIONS THROUGH THE STRASBOURG REGION

D661
A4
N4
Marne-Rhine Canal
19
20
21
22
23
24
25
26
27
28
29
30
31
32
33
34
35
36
37
38
39
40
GRTgaz Pipeline Oltingue-Blaregnies
Molsheim
D1420
A35
D420
N59

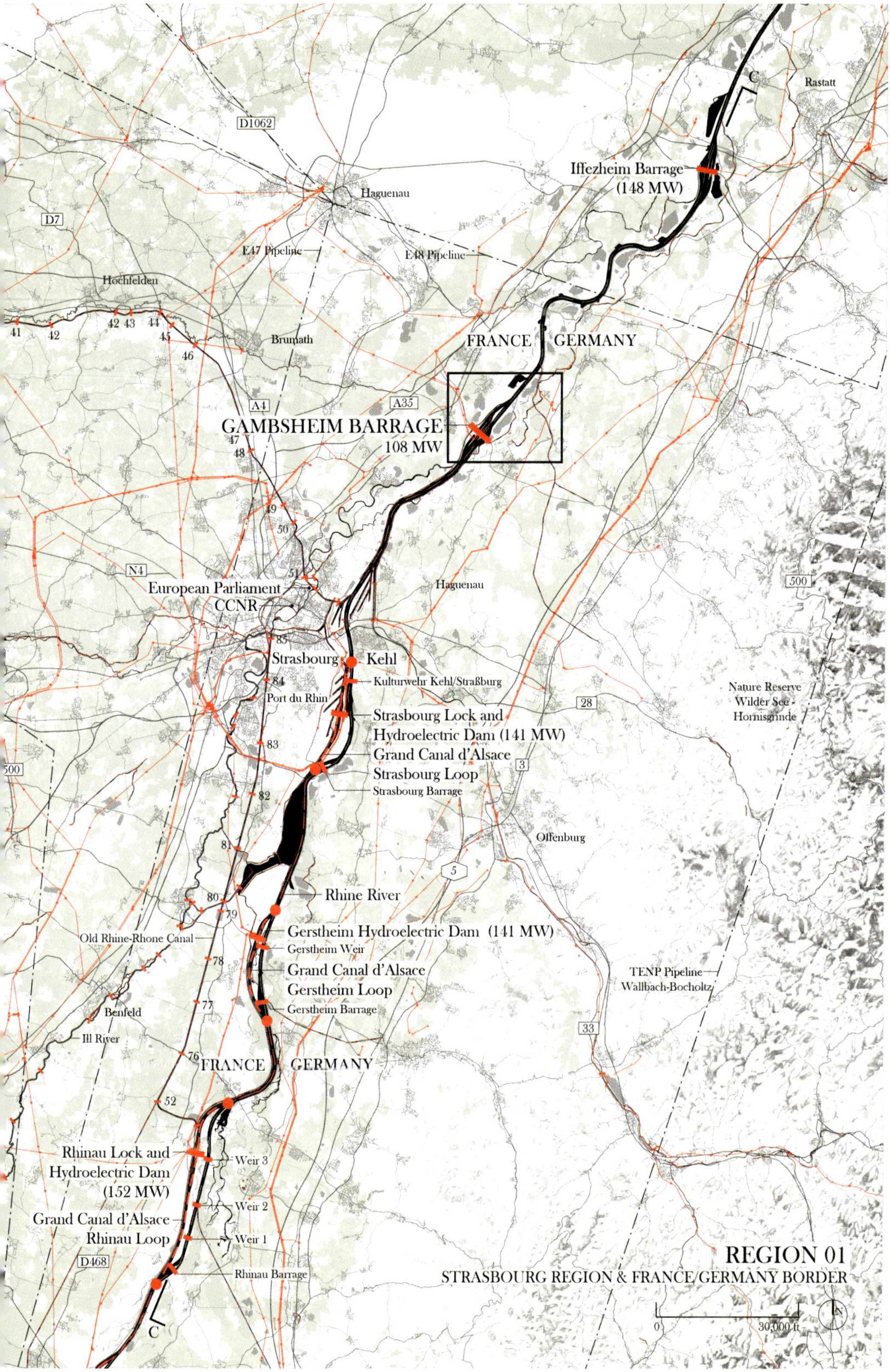

D1062
Rastatt
Iffezheim Barrage
(148 MW)
Haguenau
D7
E47 Pipeline
E48 Pipeline
Hochfelden
41
42
42 43
44
45
46
Brumath
FRANCE
GERMANY
A4
A35
GAMBSHEIM BARRAGE
108 MW
47
48
49
50
N4
51
European Parliament
CCNR
Haguenau
500
85
Strasbourg
Kehl
84
Kulturwehr Kehl/Straßburg
Port du Rhin
Strasbourg Lock and
Hydroelectric Dam (141 MW)
28
Nature Reserve
Wilder See -
Hornisgrinde
83
Grand Canal d'Alsace
Strasbourg Loop
3
500
Strasbourg Barrage
82
Offenburg
81
5
80
Rhine River
79
Old Rhine-Rhone Canal
Gerstheim Hydroelectric Dam (141 MW)
Gerstheim Weir
78
Grand Canal d'Alsace
Gerstheim Loop
TENP Pipeline
Wallbach-Bocholtz
77
Benfeld
Gerstheim Barrage
33
Ill River
76
FRANCE
GERMANY
52
Rhinau Lock and
Hydroelectric Dam
(152 MW)
Weir 3
Weir 2
Grand Canal d'Alsace
Rhinau Loop
Weir 1
D468
Rhinau Barrage
C
C
REGION 01
STRASBOURG REGION & FRANCE/GERMANY BORDER
0
30,000 ft
N

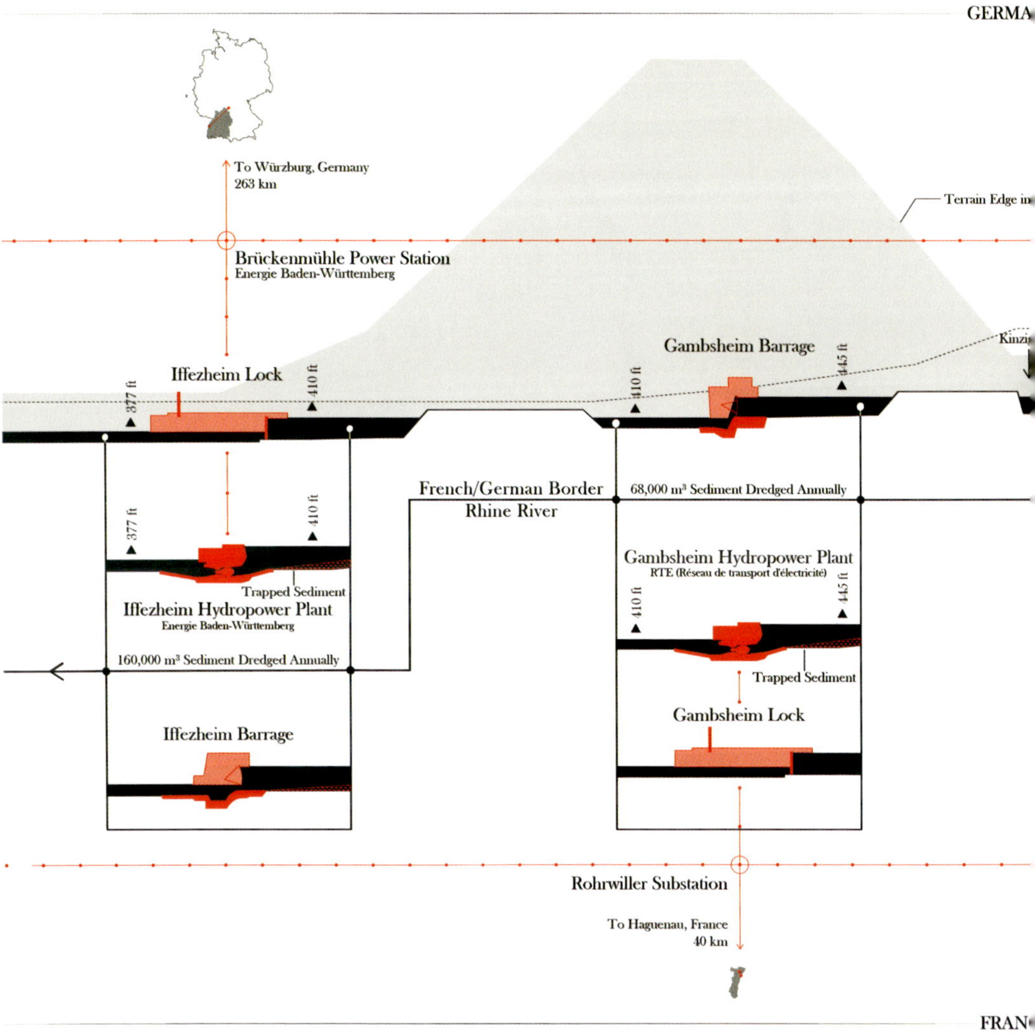
GERMA
FRAN
To Würzburg, Germany
263 km
Terrain Edge in
Brückenmühle Power Station
Energie Baden-Württemberg
Kinzi
Gambsheim Barrage
Iffezheim Lock
377 ft
410 ft
445 ft
French/German Border
Rhine River
68,000 m³ Sediment Dredged Annually
Gambsheim Hydropower Plant
RTE (Réseau de transport d'électricité)
Trapped Sediment
Iffezheim Hydropower Plant
Energie Baden-Württemberg
160,000 m³ Sediment Dredged Annually
Gambsheim Lock
Iffezheim Barrage
Rohrwiller Substation
To Haguenau, France
40 km

ZONE 01

Zone 01: Gambsheim Barrage

Zone 01 Plan

The project at Gambsheim was one of a pair of projects commissioned after the completion of the Grand Canal d'Alsace. Along with the project at Iffezheim, the Gambsheim Barrage consists of a lock, hydroelectric dam, and moveable weir.[33] Conceived in 1969, the two projects at Gambsheim and Iffezheim were realized through a joint effort between Germany and France to address the environmental and hydrological concerns that were magnified by the construction of the Grand Canal d'Alsace.[34] The primary purpose of both projects is to slow the speed of water in the Upper Rhine before it transitions into the Middle Rhine.[35] Gambsheim was completed in 1974, followed by Iffezheim three years later, and fish ladders were later installed to both projects in 2006.[36] Located downstream from the Grand Canal, the project crosses the Rhine River where the strands of the river combine back into a single path. The linear arrangement of both projects is a more typical design, unlike the distributed typology in the Grand Canal. Named after the nearby town of Gambsheim, the regional road for vehicular traffic also crosses on top of the project. The line of the French and German border passes through the midpoint of the project and divides ownership of the different pieces of infrastructure. France has possession of the lock and hydroelectric dam while Germany is responsible for the moveable weir, and in a concession to Germany, this layout mirrors downstream at the Iffezheim project where the control of the project flips.[37] Germany's sole hydroelectric power plant and lock in the Upper Rhine are at the Iffezheim project. While Iffezheim and Gambsheim Barrages are smaller in scale and scope compared to the engineering in the Grand Canal d'Alsace, their additions are a productive development in facilitating the cooperative management on the Rhine River.

Zone 01 Sections D-D, E-E, F-F, G-G, H-H

Despite being commissioned to address the hydrological harm caused by the damming and canalization of the Upper Rhine, the two projects at Gambsheim and Iffezheim have exacerbated other threats to the river. Downstream of the Grand Canal, their primary purpose of decreasing the velocity of the water in the channel was an effort to halt the degradation of the riverbed, but the creation of two new obstructions in the river has particularly exacerbated the sediment buildup in the Upper Rhine. Since their completion, Iffezheim and Gambsheim Barrages have caused a 25 percent drop

Gambsheim Lock, France/Germany border, 2018 (Image credit: Derek Hoeferlin)

in the sediment concentration and suspended load in the Upper Rhine River.[38] The two barrages have caused a significant increase in sediment accumulation along the riverbed, and have accounted for over 85 percent of the sediment dredged from all ten projects in the Upper Rhine.[39] As a result, the Middle Rhine is losing sediment. However, the sediment removed from the Upper Rhine cannot be transferred downstream to replenish the Middle Rhine due to the presence of HCB and other toxins in the sediment from the 1989 Sandoz chemical spill.[40] After the disaster, the International Commission for the Protection of the Rhine (ICPR) enacted a basin-wide environmental plan, the Rhine Action Programme (RAP), that aimed to restore and preserve the health of the river.[41] It addressed ecosystem conservation along with strict environmental regulations, and one program in particular has become a symbol of their progress—the reintroduction of salmon to the Rhine.[42] While the native Rhine salmon population had been declining for centuries due to overfishing and habitat destruction from river engineering, the chemical spill was the event that lead to its extinction.[43] The "Salmon 2000" project, which was half funded by the European Commission, was a holistic conservation project that sought to restore the ecology to the point where salmon could inhabit the Rhine River again.[44] It was seemingly a success, and every fall, visitors to the fish ladder have the opportunity to watch salmon migrate upstream to reach spawning grounds.[45] Ironically, what now swims through the Rhine are Atlantic salmon, an international breed brought to the river from its neighbors as far away as Scotland.[46] While the Rhine River has partially recovered, much of the Rhine's natural state has been irreversibly lost.

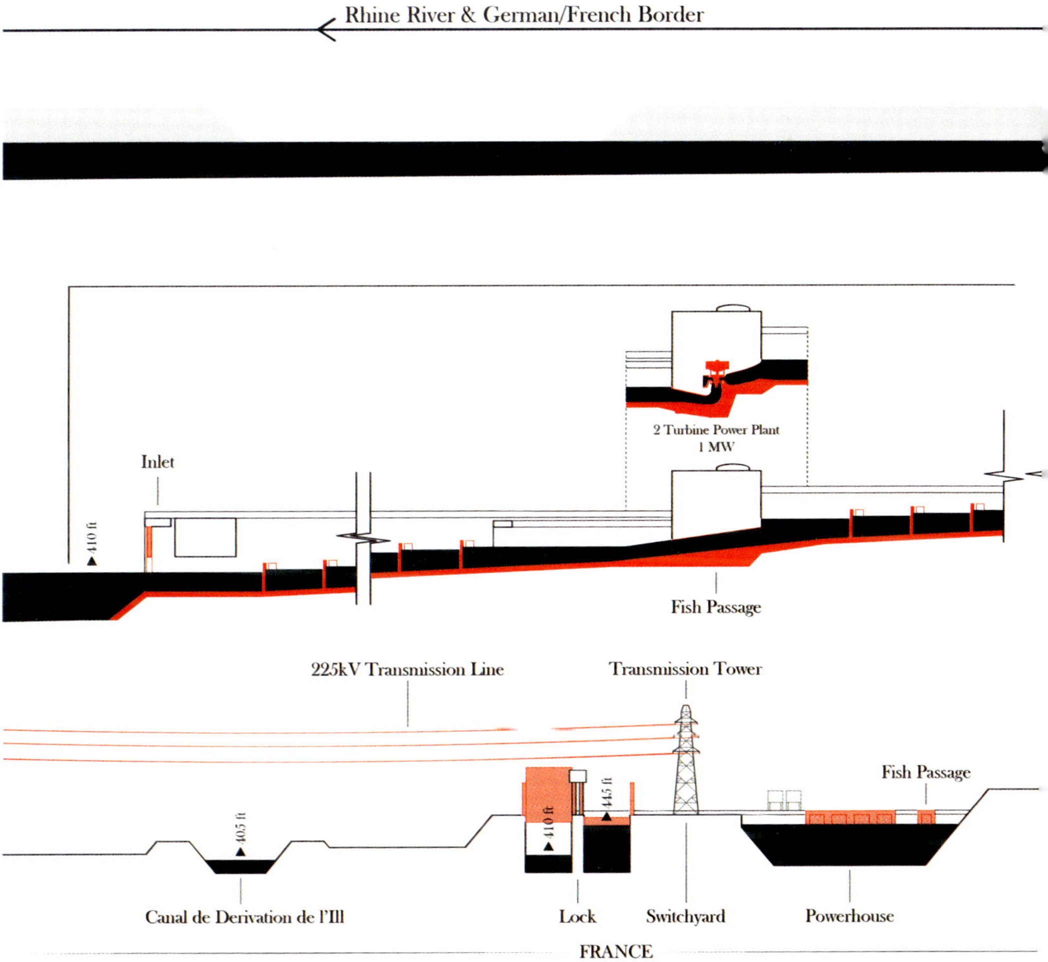
Rhine River & German/French Border
Inlet
410 ft
2 Turbine Power Plant
1 MW
Fish Passage
225kV Transmission Line
Transmission Tower
40.5 ft
410 ft
44.5 ft
Fish Passage
Canal de Derivation de l'Ill
Lock
Switchyard
Powerhouse
FRANCE

FRANCE
GERMANY
Baggersee Helmligen
HELMLINGEN
Renchdamm
110kV
GERMANY
FREISTETT
ZONE 01
GAMBSHEIM BARRAGE
0
2,000 ft
N

D468
OFFENDORF
GAMBSHEIM
D29
225kV
225kV
D2
F
E
D
H
G
Lock
Powerhouse
Fish Ladder
Switchyard
Canal de Dérivation de l'Ill
Movable Weir
G
F
E
D
H
Rheinseitenkanal
L87
FRANCE
Rhine River
GERMANY

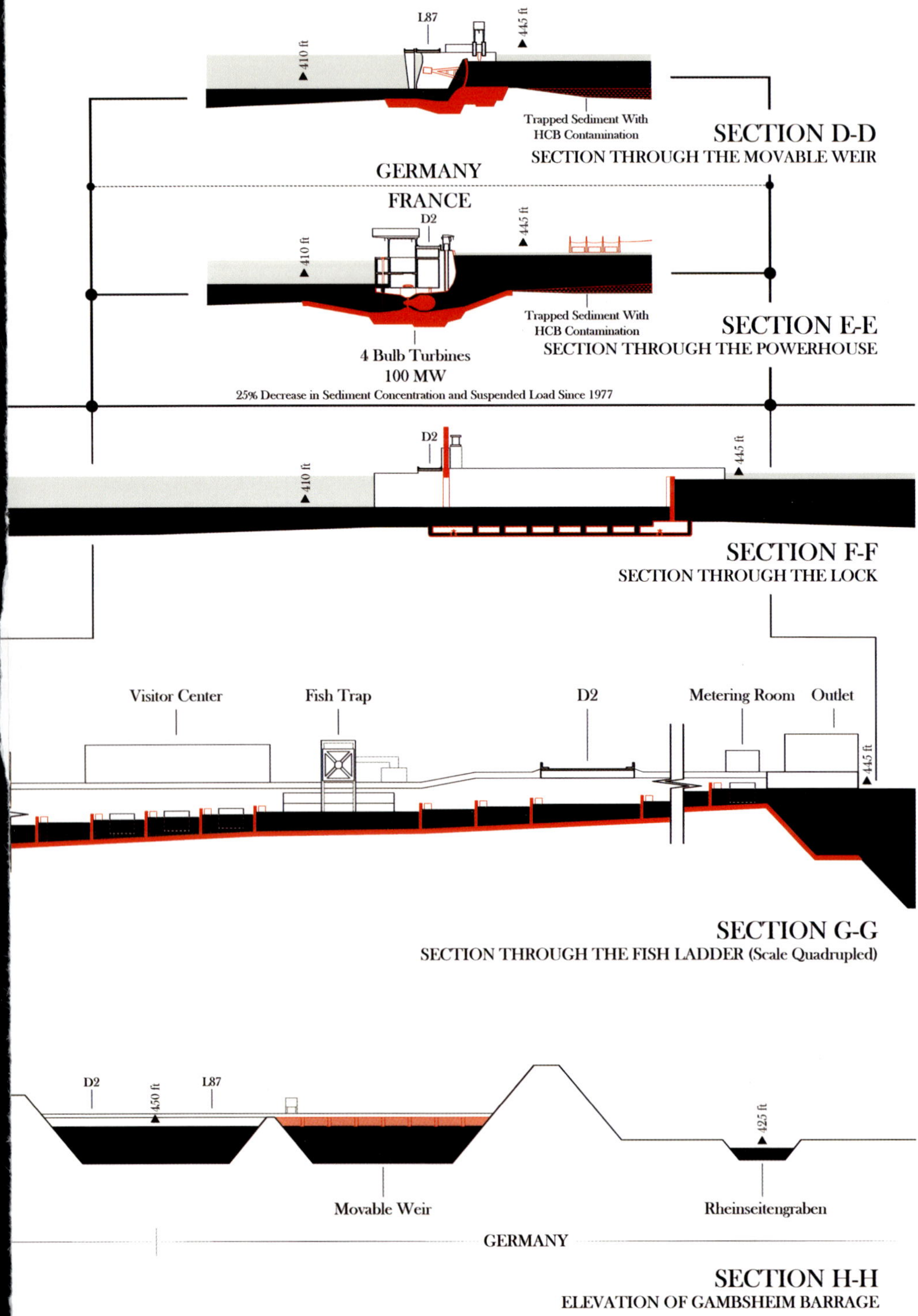

L87
445 ft
410 ft
Trapped Sediment With
HCB Contamination
SECTION D-D
SECTION THROUGH THE MOVABLE WEIR
GERMANY
FRANCE
D2
445 ft
410 ft
Trapped Sediment With
HCB Contamination
SECTION E-E
SECTION THROUGH THE POWERHOUSE
4 Bulb Turbines
100 MW
25% Decrease in Sediment Concentration and Suspended Load Since 1977
D2
445 ft
410 ft
SECTION F-F
SECTION THROUGH THE LOCK
Visitor Center
Fish Trap
D2
Metering Room
Outlet
445 ft
SECTION G-G
SECTION THROUGH THE FISH LADDER (Scale Quadrupled)
D2
450 ft
L87
425 ft
Movable Weir
Rheinseitengraben
GERMANY
SECTION H-H
ELEVATION OF GAMBSHEIM BARRAGE

Region 02: Rhine River Split: Waal, Nederrijn/ Lek, & IJssel Rivers

Region 02 Plan

The Rhine Delta begins as the river crosses the German-Dutch border into the Netherlands. It is a hydrologically complex region that has undergone centuries of river modification to support urbanization in the Rhine Delta. Immediately downstream of the border, the Rhine River meets the Pannerdensche Kop bifurcation point. Created in 1707, the Pannerdensch Canal was the first significant act of river control, and it redirected water from the Rhine and the Waal, its natural distributary, into the artificial path.[47] At the end of the Pannerdensch Canal, a second bifurcation point further splits the river into Nederrijn/Lek and IJssel distributaries, which started receiving water from the Waal in order to supplement its water level to remain viable waterways and natural defenses.[48] Starting in the 19th century, the Dutch began canalizing the Rhine to improve its navigability in order to stimulate economic growth.[49] An extensive network of inland transportation has been established both within and outside the Rhine River Basin. This network connects the river's multiple distributaries and links it to nearby rivers like the Meuse and the Scheldt. However, the engineering of the Rhine Delta primarily addresses the flooding that can be devastating throughout the delta. According to the PBL Netherlands Environmental Assessment Agency, about 59 percent of the Dutch land surface is susceptible to flooding.[50] While various flood control measures have been developed by the Dutch, the Room for the River Programme marks a turning point in national strategy to address the increasing flood risk under the pressure of climate change.[51] Rather than continuing the traditional method of increasing dike levels, through radical efforts of "de-poldering," this new strategy seeks to expand the river to uptake more discharge

Pannerden Canal (left) and Waal River (right) splitting off from Rhine River
Fort Pannerden, The Netherlands, 2018 (image credit: Derek Hoeferlin)

without worsening the future flood impact. These projects were also expected to improve urban landscapes and environmental conditions, exemplified by the successful transformation at Nijmegen.[52] Over 30 projects were implemented along the Rhine River's main distributaries and Meuse River, with measures differentiated according to the characteristics of the river section, yet coordinated as an integrated spatial planning strategy.[53] The Rhine (and Meuse-Scheldt) Delta has developed to address social needs of the region, including both navigational purposes and resiliency.

Region 02 Section I-I

The Rhine Delta is an intricate web of interconnected water systems. Two splits of the Rhine River characterize the inland portion of the Rhine Delta, creating three major distributaries: the Waal, Nederrijn/Lek, and IJssel. These distributaries also connect to numerous canals with navigational locks which improve both the Rhine River's navigability to the North Sea and the inland transportation network to nearby rivers and cities. For example, Sint Andries Canal and Meuse-Rhine Canal both provide navigational shortcuts to the Meuse River. Two of Europe's largest ports are in this region, Rotterdam and Antwerp. The volume of water flowing into each of the Rhine's distributaries is precisely managed: 63 percent of the Rhine's flow is carried by the Waal River at the first bifurcation point which flows west towards the North Sea; 12 percent to Nederrijn/Lek, which also discharges in the North Sea; and, 15 percent to the IJssel which empties into the inland bay known as Lake IJssel.[54] It is crucial to maintain these ratios because dike levels downstream are designed according to the safety discharge along each channel.[55] Three weirs along the Nederrijn/Lek help to regulate the distribution ratio, and their operation depends on the water level measured at the Dutch village Lobith on the Dutch-German border.[56] The Room for the River Programme increases the river's capacity for water by expanding the river laterally. New ancillary channels were created along bends in the river at key locations like Nijmegen and Millingerwaard. This increases the river's capacity for water at key points, which ameliorates the threat of inundation.[57] With the completion of the Room for the River Programme projects, the amount of water discharged in the Rhine Delta is designed to increase from 530 cubic feet per second to 565 cubic feet per second.[58] Existing dikes were relocated to facilitate the new ancillary channels, and the Room for the River Programme has helped to influence the end of the unsustainable dike improvement cycle. In other words, the dikes are no longer required to be regularly raised even as the threat of climate change intensifies.[59] The Rhine Delta has been meticulously engineered into a cogent regional water system.

LANDS

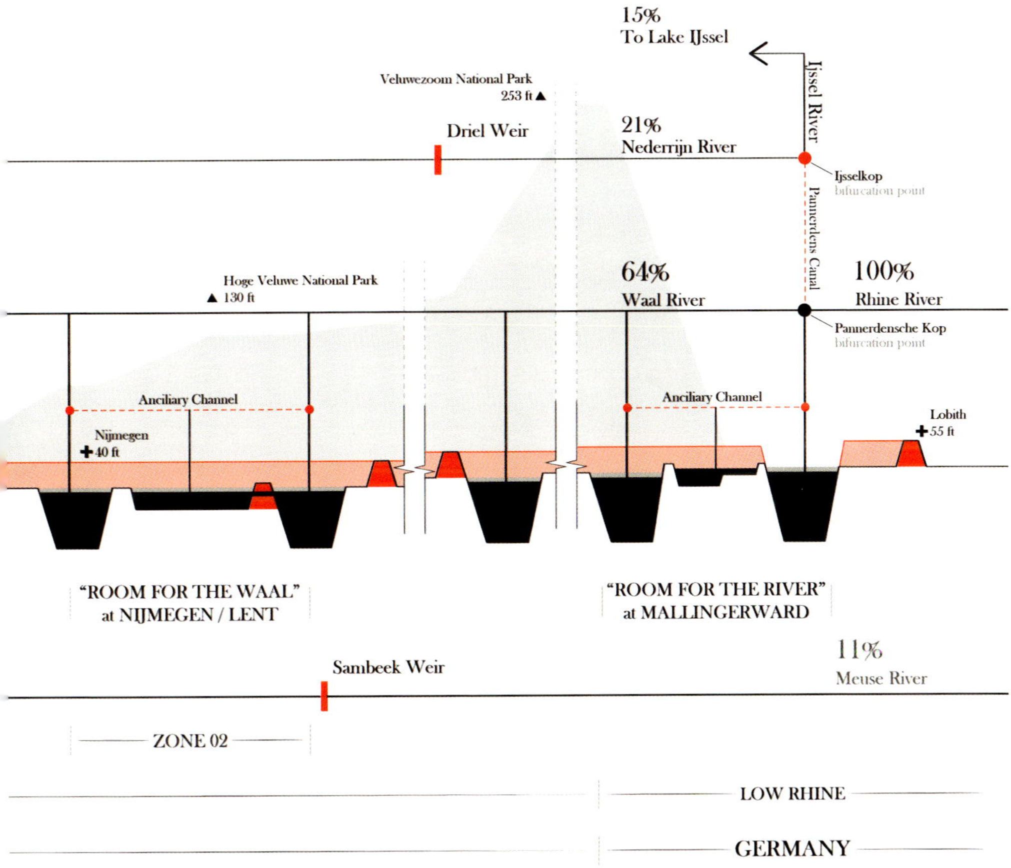

SECTION I-I

SECTION THROUGH THE NETHERLANDS/GERMANY BORDER

Amersfoort
Utrecht
Utrecht-Heuvelrug National Park
A27
A30
Nieuwegein
RFTR: BOSSENWAARD / PONTWAARD
Amsterdam-Rhine Canal
Ede
Veenendaal
RFTR: ALBLASSERWAARD
RFTR: MACHINISTENSCHOOL ELST
Hagestein Weir
Lock Pr. Irenesluis
Amerongen Weir
RFTR: DE TOLLEWAARD
RFTR: MIDDELWAARD
Lock Marijkesluis
RFTR: LEK / BETUWE / TIELER-EN CULEMBORGERWAARD
Merwede Canal
RFTR: NEDERRIJN / BETUWE / TIELER-EN CULEMBORGERWAARD
Lock Prins Bernhardsluizen
RFTR: AVELINGEN
A15
RFTR: MIDDEN-WAAL
RFTR: MUNNIKENLAND
RFTR: BENDEN-WAAL
RFTR: WAAL FORT ST. ANDRIES
Afgedamde Maas
St. Andries Lock
Prinses Maxima Weir
St. Andries Canal
RFTR: MEINERSWIJK
Oss
Sluis Empel Weir
A50
Meuse River
Zuid-Willemsvaart Canal
s-Hertogenbosch
Drainage Canal
s-Hertogenbosch-Drongelen
Loonse-Drunense-Duinen National Park
Lock Schijndel
Tilburg
Wilhelmina Canal

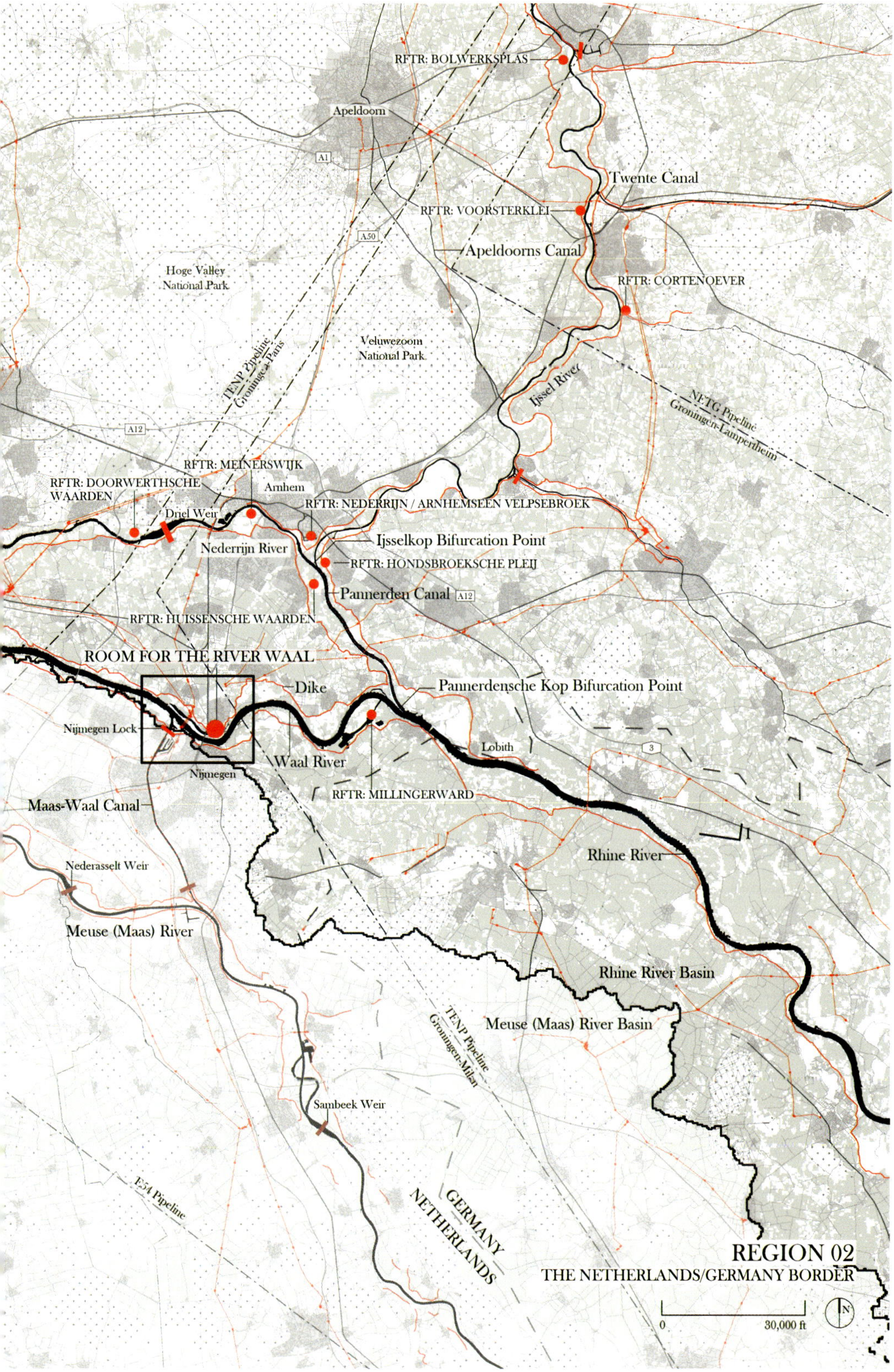
RFTR: BOLWERKSPLAS
Apeldoorn
A1
Twente Canal
RFTR: VOORSTERKLEI
A50
Apeldoorns Canal
Hoge Valley National Park
RFTR: CORTENOEVER
Veluwezoom National Park
TENP Pipeline Groningen-Paris
Ijssel River
NETG Pipeline Groningen-Lampertheim
A12
RFTR: MEINERSWIJK
RFTR: DOORWERTHSCHE WAARDEN
Arnhem
RFTR: NEDERRIJN / ARNHEMSEEN VELPSEBROEK
Driel Weir
Ijsselkop Bifurcation Point
Nederrijn River
RFTR: HONDSBROEKSCHE PLEIJ
Pannerden Canal
A12
RFTR: HUISSENSCHE WAARDEN
ROOM FOR THE RIVER WAAL
Dike
Pannerdensche Kop Bifurcation Point
Nijmegen Lock
Lobith
3
Waal River
Nijmegen
RFTR: MILLINGERWARD
Maas-Waal Canal
Rhine River
Nederasselt Weir
Meuse (Maas) River
Rhine River Basin
Meuse (Maas) River Basin
TENP Pipeline Groningen-Milan
Sambeek Weir
E54 Pipeline
GERMANY
NETHERLANDS
REGION 02
THE NETHERLANDS/GERMANY BORDER
0
30,000 ft
N

NETHER

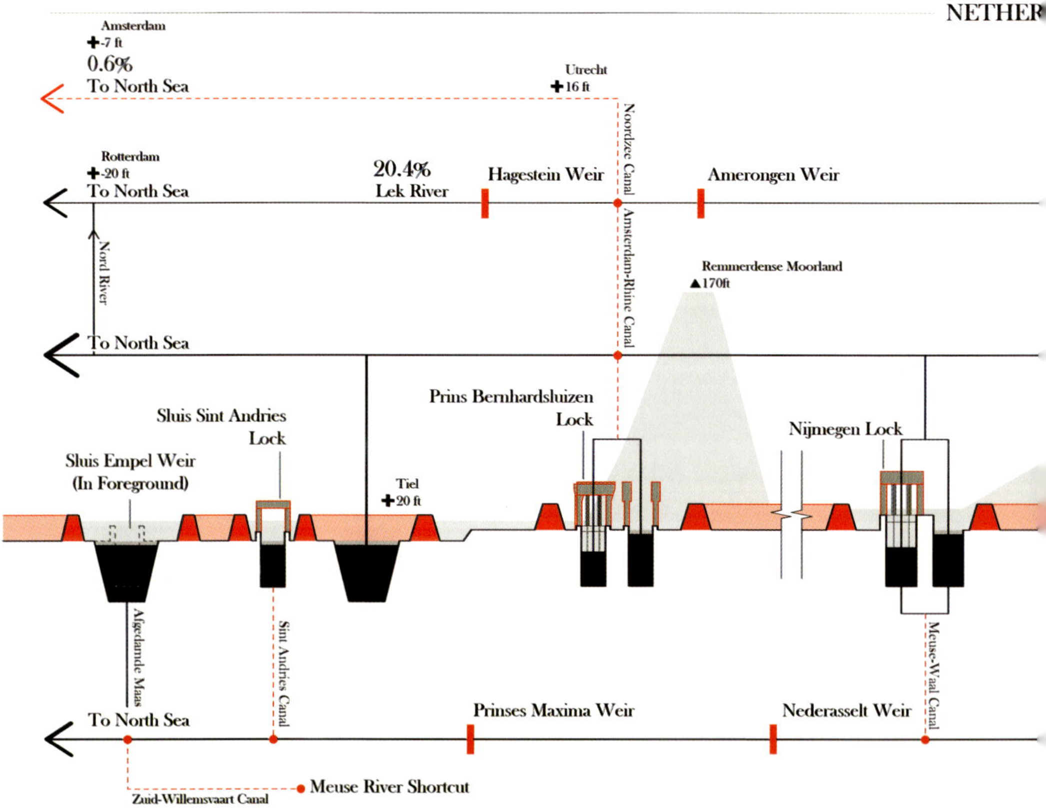

RHINE DELTA

NETHERLANDS

Zone 02: "Room for the Waal" Project at Nijmegen & Lent

Zone 02 Plan

The Room for the Waal project at Nijmegen and Lent was a comprehensive project that utilized the hydraulic engineering of the Rhine to improve the urbanization and landscape of the city. In 1993 and 1995, the Rhine River was inundated from high precipitation and flooded a significant amount of land in the Netherlands. These catastrophes, as well as global ones such as Hurricane Katrina ten years later in 2005, prompted the Dutch government to undertake the Room for the River Programme to enact a new flood mitigation strategy that could prepare for the threats posed by climate change.[60] Nijmegen and Lent are two moderately sized cities located along the largest distributary of the Rhine, the river Waal, at a sharp bend in the river where the water flow is constricted, leading to a higher risk of inundation.[61] The old dike line previously ran adjacent along the entire run of the river. In this particularly unique project, the northern dikes were relocated to the edge of the city Lent, and a new ancillary channel was dredged between the bend in the river.[62] The land previously occupied by the old dike line was transformed into an island, called the Veur-Lent, which separates the two channels of water. An inlet structure at the head of the channel regulates the amount of water allowed in the ancillary channel, and a series of new bridges and extensions connect the cities of Nijmegen and Lent. During the planning phase for the project, it was discovered that the initial Room for the River Waal plan conflicted with municipal urban design projects, specifically Lent's new housing program, which used the same site.[63] Undeterred, local stakeholders and designers engaged with the national infrastructure plan, and integrated the Room for the River Programme with the two cities' vision for urban design and planning.[64] The

Rivierpark Nijmegen Waal, The Netherlands, 2018 (image credit: Derek Hoeferlin)

conflict in land use was resolved, and the cities used the scale of the project to enrich its waterfronts and create a park on the Veur-Lent island.[65] The realized design of the Room for the River Waal in Nijmegen and Lent is important for both managing national and local interests and for utilizing flood safety infrastructure to holistically improve the quality of life in the city.

Zone 02 Sections J-J, K-K, L-L, M-M, N-N, O-O, P-P

This complex project was a collaborative effort across scales and disciplines, coordinated by H+N+S Landscape Architects. Initially conceived by a team of engineers and hydrologists, the site-specific application of the project's framework in Nijmegen and Lent would enlist urban planners, urban designers, landscape architects, and architects. A key feature of the project was the relocation of the dike line inward towards the city to accommodate the ancillary channel that has a maximum shift of 1,148 feet.[66] This changed the relationship between the city and the river. To link the existing and unchanged portions of the dikes, a new quay was created along the southern edge of Lent that is intended to be the city's riverfront urban park.[67] The Veur-Lent island consists of a small residential corridor and a new park that establishes a connection between the two cities of Nijmegen and Lent.[68] During low water stages, the inlet structure only diverts 1.5 percent of the Waal River into the channel, but this increases to 30 percent during surges.[69] Not only is the Veur-Lent park a new recreational space for the cities, it is also designed to be submersible, thereby mimicking the natural wetlands.[70] In a collaboration between engineers and architects, three new bridges were constructed (the Oversteek, Citadel, and Lentloper) and the two existing bridges (the Nijmegen Railway and Waalbrug) were modified to cross the ancillary channel.[71] The Nijmegen Railway bridge was reinforced at the new channel crossing and the Waalbrug was extended. Located at the far end of the submersible park, the Oversteek Bridge is a new construction that connects the historic city of Nijmegen with the upcoming housing development in Lent. This supports both cities' growth and relieves traffic. The Citadel and Lentloper are two new bridges that only span the ancillary channel between the island and Lent. Adjacent to the Oversteek Bridge, the Citadel Bridge is submersible and only accessible to pedestrians. The Lentloper connects the quay to the residential part of the island for pedestrians and vehicles. A 2015 study on the process of creating the RFTR project at Nijmegen concluded that designers, in addition to their contributions to the built form, were valuable intermediaries between different groups of people both within the project team and the local community, and they were considered vital to the project's process.[72] The Room for the Waal at Nijmegen and Lent is considered a success in many terms. It is an important development for riverine infrastructure and resilience that was completed on time and within budget. Most importantly, it negotiated national and municipal interests through an interdisciplinary team that gave agency to designers and local actors. The Room for the River Programme was an infrastructural initiative that integrated cities with the river to improve the quality of life for its residents.

1. Roy M. Frings et al., "From source to mouth: Basin-scale morphodynamics of the Rhine River," *Earth-Science Reviews* 196, (September 2019), accessed November 19, 2020, https://www.sciencedirect.com/science/article/pii/S0012825216304585?via%3Dihub, 5.

2. Urs Uehlinger et al., "The Rhine River Basin," *Rivers of Europe*, (London: Academic Press, 2009), 210.

3. Susanne Nies, *Gouvernance Européenne et Géopolitique de l'énergie: At the Speed of Light? Electricity Interconnections for Europe*, Tome 5, (Paris: Institut Français des Relations Internationales, 2009), accessed November 16, 2020, https://www.ifri.org/sites/default/files/atoms/files/intersnfinal1_1.pdf, 58-59.

4. Ibid., 65 & 76.

5. Uehlinger et al., "The Rhine River Basin," 234.

6. Koos Wieriks and Anne Schulte-Wülwer-Leidig, "Integrated Water Management for the Rhine River Basin: From Pollution Prevention to Ecosystem Improvement," *Natural Resources Forum* 21, no.2 (October 9, 1997): 147–156, accessed November 16, 2020, https://www.academia.edu/30863297/Integrated_water_management_for_the_Rhine_river_basin_from_pollution_prevention_to_ecosystem_improvement, 147-149.

7. Ibid., 150–151.

8. "The Rhine: 30 Years After Sandoz" (Koblenz: International Commission for the Protection of the Rhine, 17 October 2016), accessed November 16, 2020, https://www.iksr.org/fileadmin/user_upload/Dokumente_en/Press_Releases/30_Jahre_nach_SANDOZ_Hintergrund.docx_de-DE_en-GB.pdf, 1.

9. Wieriks and Schulte-Wülwer-Leidig, "Integrated Water Management for the Rhine River Basin," 151–153.

10. Uehlinger et al., "The Rhine River Basin," 200.

11. Frings et al., "From Source to Mouth," 4.

12. "Erosion, Transport and Deposition of Sediment: Case Study Rhine" (Utrecht: International Commission for the Hydrology of the Rhine Basin, October 13, 2009), accessed November 19, 2020, https://www.oieau.org/eaudoc/system/files/documents/44/224441/224441_doc.pdf, 195.

13. Ibid., 195.

14. Uehlinger, "The Rhine River Basin," 240.

15. Anna Wesselink, Wiebe E. Bijker, Huib de Vriend, and Maarten S. Krol, "Dutch Dealings with the Delta," *Nature and Culture* 2, issue 2 (September 2007): 4, 12, 188–209.

16. Ibid., 3.

17. Ibid., 3; "Haringvliet Dam," Deltawerken, accessed November 19, 2020, http://www.deltawerken.com/Haringvliet-Dam/327.html.

18. Rijke et al., "Room for the River," 2.

19. Stefan Vollmer and Emil Goelz, "Sediment Monitoring and Sediment Management in the Rhine River" in *Sediment Dynamics and the Hydromorphology of Fluvial Systems* (Kolenz: Federal Institute of Hydrology [BfG], 2006): 231–40.

20. Ibid., 232.

21. Ibid., 234.

22. Vincent Lagendijk, "Europe's Rhine Power: Connections, Borders, and Flows" (Berlin: Springerlink, September 5, 2015): 29.

23. Ibid., 29–30.

24. "Convention Between the French Republic and the Federal Republic of Germany Concerning Development of the Rhine Between Strasbourg/Kehl and Lauterbourg/Neuburweir," opened for signature 4 July 1969, *International Water Law Project* https://www.internationalwaterlaw.org/documents/regionaldocs/rhine_river1969.html.

25. "Erosion, Transport and Deposition of Sediment: Case Study Rhine," 14.

26. Ibid., 15.

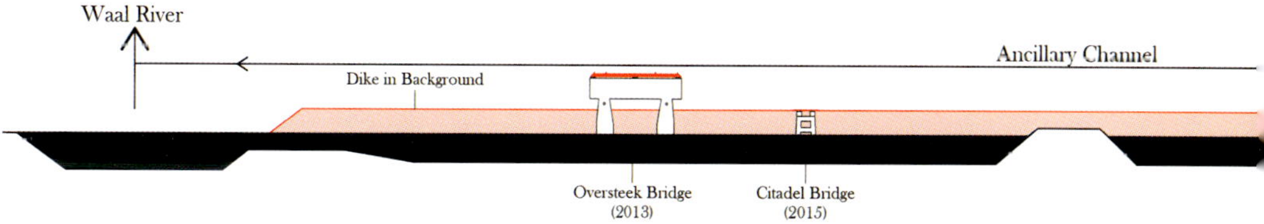

Waal River
Ancillary Channel
Dike in Background
Oversteek Bridge (2013)
Citadel Bridge (2015)

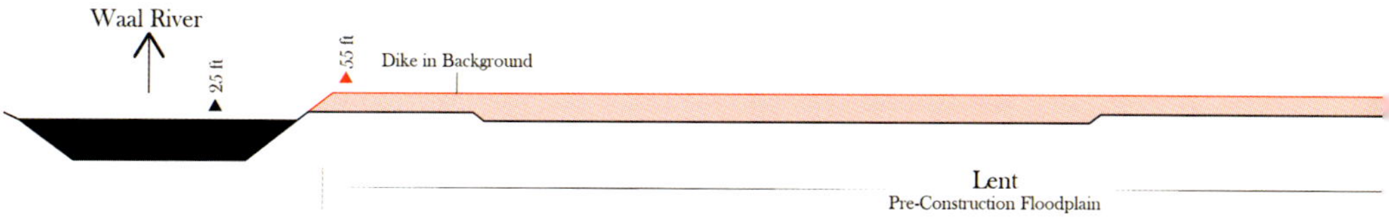

Waal River
25 ft
55 ft
Dike in Background
Lent
Pre-Construction Floodplain

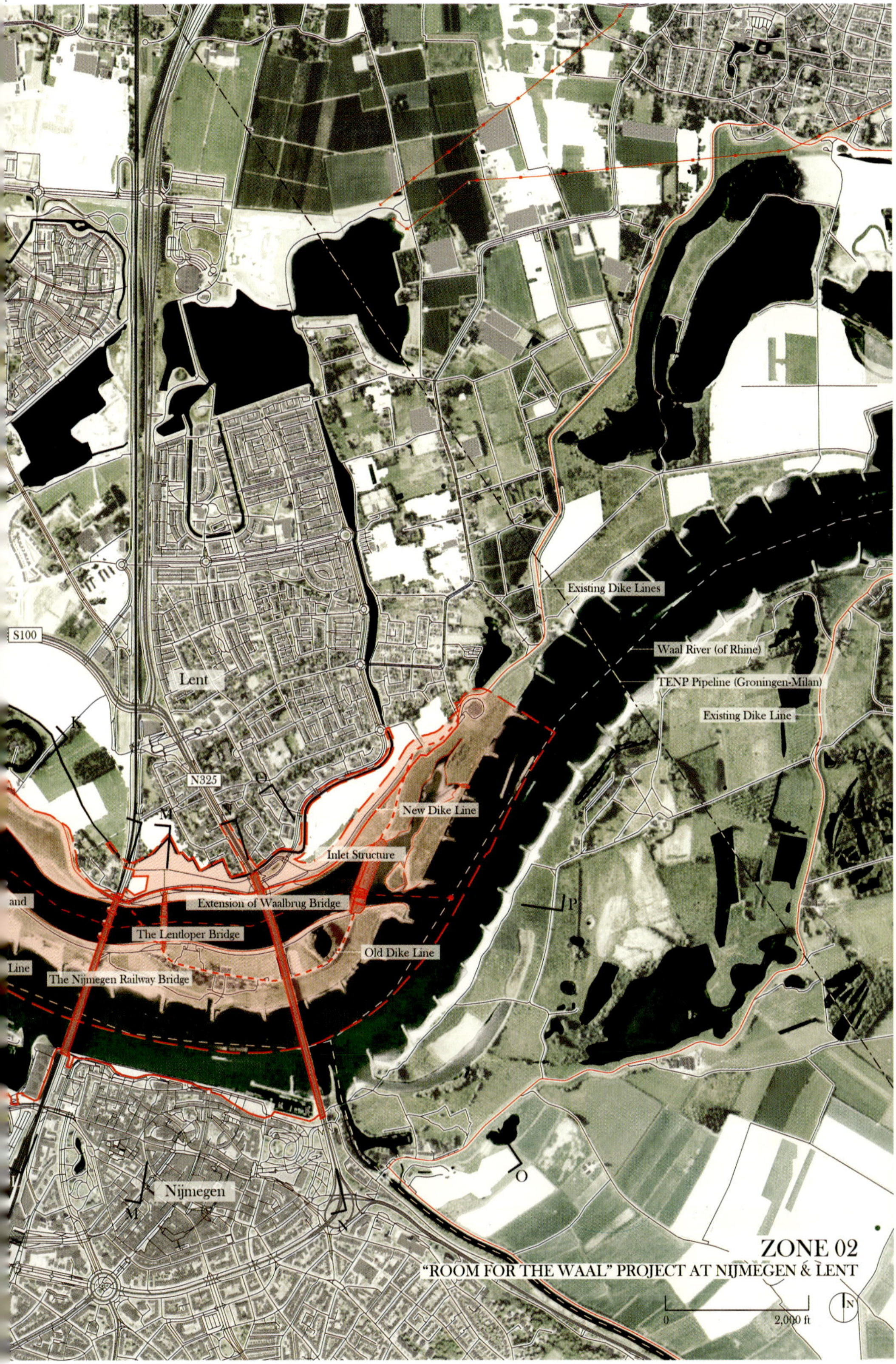

Existing Dike Lines
Waal River (of Rhine)
TENP Pipeline (Groningen-Milan)
Existing Dike Line
S100
Lent
N325
New Dike Line
Inlet Structure
Extension of Waalbrug Bridge
and
The Lentloper Bridge
Old Dike Line
Line
The Nijmegen Railway Bridge
Nijmegen
ZONE 02
"ROOM FOR THE WAAL" PROJECT AT NIJMEGEN & LENT
0
2,000 ft
N

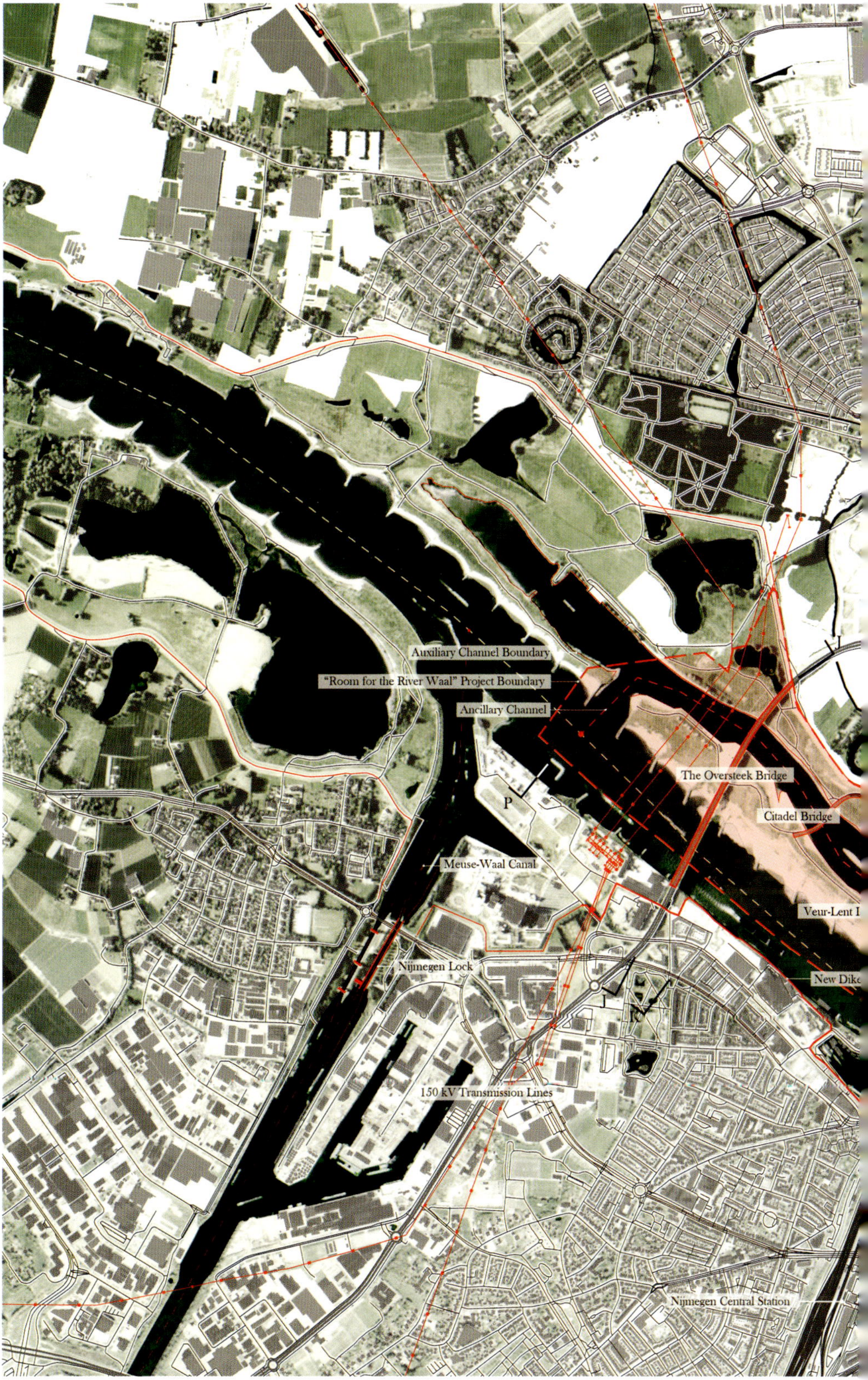

Auxiliary Channel Boundary
"Room for the River Waal" Project Boundary
Ancillary Channel
P
The Oversteek Bridge
Citadel Bridge
Meuse-Waal Canal
Veur-Lent I
Nijmegen Lock
New Dike
J
K
150 kV Transmission Lines
Nijmegen Central Station

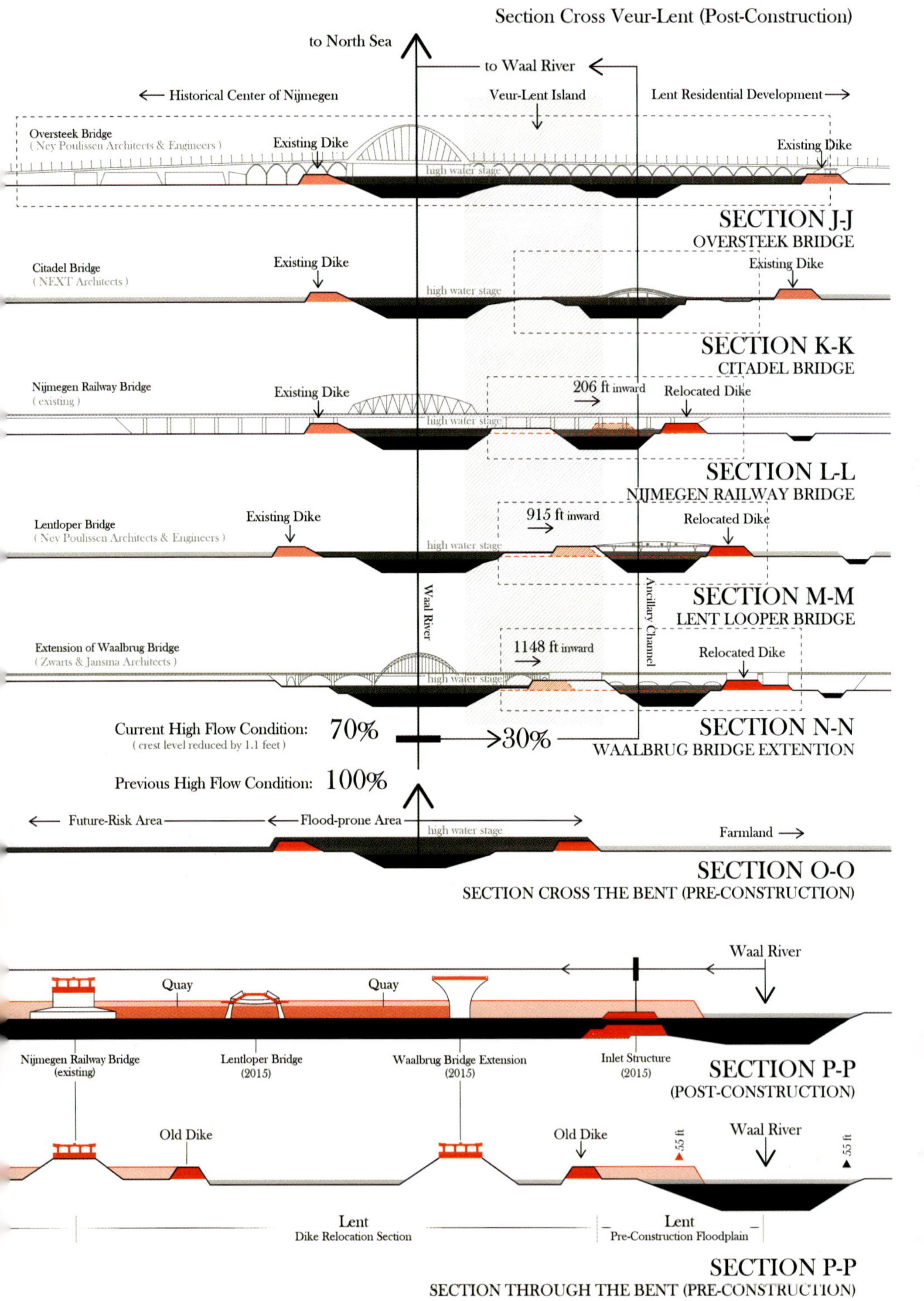

Section Cross Veur-Lent (Post-Construction)
to North Sea
to Waal River
Historical Center of Nijmegen
Veur-Lent Island
Lent Residential Development
Oversteek Bridge
(Ney Poulissen Architects & Engineers)
Existing Dike
Existing Dike
high water stage
SECTION J-J
OVERSTEEK BRIDGE
Citadel Bridge
(NEXT Architects)
Existing Dike
Existing Dike
high water stage
SECTION K-K
CITADEL BRIDGE
Nijmegen Railway Bridge
(existing)
Existing Dike
206 ft inward
Relocated Dike
high water stage
SECTION L-L
NIJMEGEN RAILWAY BRIDGE
Lentloper Bridge
(Ney Poulissen Architects & Engineers)
Existing Dike
915 ft inward
Relocated Dike
high water stage
SECTION M-M
LENT LOOPER BRIDGE
Waal River
Ancillary Channel
Extension of Waalbrug Bridge
(Zwarts & Jansma Architects)
1148 ft inward
Relocated Dike
high water stage
SECTION N-N
WAALBRUG BRIDGE EXTENTION
Current High Flow Condition:
(crest level reduced by 1.1 feet)
70%
30%
Previous High Flow Condition:
100%
Future-Risk Area
Flood-prone Area
high water stage
Farmland
SECTION O-O
SECTION CROSS THE BENT (PRE-CONSTRUCTION)
Waal River
Quay
Quay
Nijmegen Railway Bridge
(existing)
Lentloper Bridge
(2015)
Waalbrug Bridge Extension
(2015)
Inlet Structure
(2015)
SECTION P-P
(POST-CONSTRUCTION)
Old Dike
Old Dike
.55 ft
Waal River
.55 ft
Lent
Dike Relocation Section
Lent
Pre-Construction Floodplain
SECTION P-P
SECTION THROUGH THE BENT (PRE-CONSTRUCTION)

27. Ibid., 16.
28. Lagendijk, "Europe's Rhine Power," 29–30.
29. "Erosion, Transport and Deposition of Sediment: Case Study Rhine," 15.
30. Ibid., 15 & 195.
31. Ibid., 195.
32. Ibid., 196.
33. "Convention Between the French Republic and the Federal Republic of Germany."
34. Ibid.
35. Ibid.
36. Barbara Froehlich-Schmitt, "Rhine Salmon 2020," (Koblenz: International Commission for the Protection of the Rhine, 29 November 2004): 4; "Les Aménagements Hydroélectriques du Rhin: Franco-Allemand" (Paris: Électricité de France, 17 January 2013): 9.
37. "Convention Between the French Republic and the Federal Republic of Germany."
38. "Erosion, Transport and Deposition of Sediment: Case Study Rhine" (Utrecht: International Commission for the Hydrology of the Rhine Basin, 13 October 2009): 197.
39. Vollmer and Goelz, "Sediment Monitoring and Sediment Management in the Rhine River," 235.
40. Ibid., 235.
41. Wieriks and Schulte-Wülwer-Leidig, "Integrated Water Management for the Rhine River Basin," 151.
42. Ibid., 151–152.
43. Uehlinger et al., "The Rhine River Basin," 231; "The Rhine: 30 Years After Sandoz," 2.
44. "Salmon 2000: Return to the Rhine of Long Distance Migratory Fish" (Brussels: European Commission), accessed November 19, 2020, https://ec.europa.eu/environment/life/project/Projects/index.cfm?fuseaction=search.dspPage&n_proj_id=1105&docType=pdf, 1.
45. "Passage 309: Site Rhénan / Rheinareal Gambsheim Rheinau" (Gambsheim: Passage 309, May 13, 2013), accessed November 19, 2020, http://www.passage309.eu/downloads/aktuelles/passage_flyer_fischtreppe_v0410web_e_1572.pdf, 2.
46. Richard Bernstein, "Rhine Has Fish Again, but It's Not as It Was," *New York Times* (April 20, 2006), accessed November 19, 2020, https://www.nytimes.com/2006/04/20/world/europe/rhine-has-fish-again-but-its-not-as-it-was.html.
47. Piet H. Nienhuis, *Environmental History of the Rhine-Meuse Delta: An ecological story on evolving human environmental relations coping with climate change and sea-level rise* (Berlin: Springer Science & Business Media, 2008), accessed November 20, 2020, https://www.researchgate.net/publication/242024465_Environmental_History_of_the_Rhine-Meuse_Delta_An_Ecological_Story_on_Evolving_Human-Environmental_Relations_Coping_with_Climate_Change_and_Sea-level_Rise, 96 & 110.
48. Ibid., 113.
49. Ibid., 117–118.
50. PBL Netherlands Environmental Assessment Agency, Deltares, HKV Consultants and Blueland, "Low probabilities: Large Consequences," PBL Netherlands Environmental Assessment Agency, accessed November 3, 2020, https://themasites.pbl.nl/o/flood-risks/.
51. "Room for the River," (in Dutch) Rijkswaterstaat: Ministry of Infrastructure and Water Management, accessed November 3, 2020, https://www.rijkswaterstaat.nl/water/waterbeheer/bescherming-tegen-het-water/maatregelen-om-overstromingen-te-voorkomen/ruimte-voor-de-rivieren/index.aspx.
52. Ibid.
53. Rijke et al., "Room for the River," 3–4.
54. "Dynamic Control of the Discharge Distributions of the Rhine River in the Netherlands," *Proceedings of*

River Flow 2008: Fourth International Conference on Fluvial Hydraulics (Ankara: Kubaba Congress Department and Travel Services, September 2008): 395–404.

55. Ibid.

56. "Renovatie stuwensemble Nederrijn en Lek" (project brochure, Rijkswaterstaat, March 2014): 2–3; Bart Reeze et al., "Watersysteemrapportage Rijntakken 1990–2015" (Bart Reeze Water & Ecologies, April 2017): 11–12.

57. "Dutch Water Program Room for the River" (project factsheet, Room for the River, July 2012), accessed November 23, 2020, https://dredging.org/media/ceda/org/documents/events/ceda/room%20for%20the%20river.pdf, 1.

58. Ibid., 1.

59. Rijke et al., "Room for the River," 12.

60. Municipality of Nijmegen, "Room for the River Waal Nijmegen" (Nijmegen: Municipality of Nijmegen Room for the River Waal, May 2014), accessed November 25, 2020, http://www.ruimtevoordewaal.nl/nl/actueel, 1.

61. Ibid., 1.

62. Ibid., 2.

63. Niels Heeres, Terry van Dijk, Jos Art, and Taede Tillema, "Coping with Interrelatedness and Fragmentation at the Infrastructure/Land-use Interface: The Potential Merits of a Design Approach," *The Journal of Transport and Land Use* 10, no. 1 (2017), accessed November 25, 2020, https://conservancy.umn.edu/handle/11299/187855, 422.

64. Ibid., 422.

65. Ibid., 423.

66. Municipality of Nijmegen, "Room for the River Waal Nijmegen," 1.

67. Ibid., 2.

68. Ibid.

69. Ibid.

70. H+N+S Landscape Architects, "Room for the Waal in Nijmegen, The Netherlands," *Landscape Architecture Frontiers* 6, no. 4 (October 2018): 86–97, accessed November 25, 2020, http://journal.hep.com.cn/laf/EN/10.15302/J-LAF-20180409#1, 95.

71. Ibid., 96–97.

72. Heeres et. al., "Coping with Interrelatedness," 423–424.

Integrate Waters

(UPPER RIGHT) Amsterdam, Netherlands, 2011
(BACKGROUND) Ijberg, Netherlands, 2012 (image credit: Derek Hoeferlin)

Bypass Rivers

(UPPER RIGHT) Rhine-Rhone Canal, Niffer, France, 2018
(BACKGROUND) Grand Canal d'Alsace, near Kembs, France, 2018 (image credit: Derek Hoeferlin)

(UPPER RIGHT) Windmills along Eastern Scheldt Storm Surge Barrier (Oosterscheldekering), Netherlands, 2010 (BACKGROUND) Kembs Hydroelectric Powerstation, Grand Canal d'Alsace, France, 2018 (image credit: Derek Hoeferlin)

(UPPER RIGHT) Flood levels marked on "Pegel" water level meter, Rhine River, Koblenz, Germany, 2018 (BACKGROUND) "Pegel" water level meter, Rhine River, Worms, Germany, 2018 (image credit: Derek Hoeferlin)

Revive

Room for the River: Revisited & Relevance to the United States

Robbert de Koning & Dale Morris

[Figure 1] Characteristic image of the Noordwaard before de-poldering, with farmlands and relics of wooded creeks (image credit: Rijkswaterstaat, Joop van Houdt)

At the end of the 20th century, high river water levels and the discussion about climate change prompted the Netherlands government to establish a large-scale flood risk reduction program along the main Dutch rivers. That discussion led to the Room for the River (RfR) Program, which was started in 2002 and completed in 2015 (for a map of RfR projects, see Han Meyer's essay "Transformation," Figure 10). What follows is an assessment of RfR, its dual-goal approach, how a focus on spatial quality can improve the total benefits of flood risk mitigation, and if, how, and how not RfR might be relevant to the United States.

Room for the River: Ambition Yields Results

RfR's strength was a simple dual objective: reduce flood risk and improve the spatial quality of the project area. These objectives broke with previously pursued policies which focused primarily—often solely—on "Flood Risk Mitigation" (FRM), which is also the primary goal of large-scale U.S. riverine FRM projects. RfR's starting point challenged the preexisting orthodoxy that river dikes should be raised. **[Figure 1]** RfR introduced the importance of embracing other interventions on and near river dikes and in river floodplains that would yield flood risk mitigation *and* ecosystem and floodplain restoration *and* landscape "connectivity" *and* achieve other goals that improve spatial quality. This new approach enabled landscape characteristics, environmental benefits, economic, and recreational ambitions to be considered, explored, and designed.

RfR mandated a high level of public engagement from both national (*Rijkswaterstaat*—the peer of the U.S. Army Corps of Engineers), provincial, and local authorities. Stakeholders and citizens were regularly engaged and provided with tools to help them understand river dynamics, flood causation, and risks, which eventually helped to narrow FRM options. RfR was grounded, in part, in citizen science. After an initially suspicious or even angry public response ("what do you mean we're going to give land back to the water?"), especially from to-be-impacted residents, a broader dialogue led to unexpected, surprising, and often beautiful results.

In retrospect, RfR was a tremendous success. Residents in and near the 35 completed RfR projects believe that their flood risks have been reduced and that the river landscape is more beautiful, accessible, and resilient. Moreover, unlike most large, new, and complex government projects which often have significant cost overruns and missed construction deadlines, RfR was completed on time and on budget, notwithstanding its research, design, and public engagement requirements. The Dutch Nature Monitoring programs show that the river area that bisects the Netherlands—where RfR projects are primarily located—is one of the few areas where natural system functioning has improved over the past decade, thanks in part to RfR.

RfR's spatial quality leadership and focus was provided by a Quality Team (Q-Team) embedded in the RfR project office. The Q-Team was comprised of leading specialists in landscape architecture, urban planning, river ecology, and hydraulic design and chaired by the former government advisor on landscape, a senior official in the ministry and special advisor to the minister. The Q-Team regularly visited the projects during their planning and implementation to assess them for spatial quality. Precisely because the concept of spatial quality is sometimes elusive and cannot be mathematically substantiated, project initiators and sponsors were required to think creatively and plan critically on how to realize spatial quality improvements. The Q-Team was instrumental in this planning and helped achieve key project goals.

Given the spatial quality requirement, project initiators (provincial and local government, water authorities, and public works departments) and *Rijkswaterstaat* had to establish project frameworks and processes in which integrated design was self-evident. These frameworks also provided oversight and insight into tasks, opportunities, and bottlenecks. Through effective community engagement and outreach, stakeholders were taken by the hand and enveloped into project designs which they then informed with invaluable regional and local knowledge, needs, and goals. The Dutch colloquialism that "it is not *either/or*, but instead it is *and this and that*" applies here. The community dialogue yielded trust and created shared commitment between the government, local authorities, and impacted residents.

Upon completion in 2015, RfR received several national awards for the achievement of spatial quality including the *Bijhouwerprijs* in 2017 and *Grote Maaskantprijs* in 2018.[1] RfR also became an export product of integrated design and expertise. Thanks to energetic collaborations between the Netherlands and various global cities, including in the United States, much knowledge, experience, and inspiration has been exchanged since RfR's adoption. Thousands of government officials, planners, architects, landscape architects, engineers, and environmental activists have visited *Rijkswaterstaat*'s RfR program office, project initiators, and project sites over the past decade and this, in turn, has made local Dutch authorities, residents and entrepreneurs in the Netherlands enthusiastic about, and even proud of, their RfR projects.

Room for the River for the United States: Governance, Risk, and Culture Argue "Maybe Not"

There are psychological, physical, and governance chasms that would impede a RfR-type program in the United States.

First, flood risk is a notable feature of the Dutch national psyche. Citizens and policymakers understand that FRM is essential because a major flood would be devastating for the Dutch people and for its economy. Dutch FRM is neither an expensive government program benefitting a few, nor is FRM policy stasis a feature of Dutch government. Conversely, floods in the U.S. are regional or local problems, and when the economic impacts are national—as with major Mississippi River floods—they do not threaten to disable the national economy. Thus, a broad RfR-type program in the U.S. would be more difficult to shape, because current river users and nearby landowners would be skeptical of change and because FRM is less nationally salient. Second, many U.S. rivers have more dynamic discharge levels, water flows, and water level fluctuations than the main Dutch rivers. And U.S. river floodplains have more diverse settlement patterns, land uses, and ecosystems, and often are physically larger.

RfR-type interventions would need to be more robust and malleable, complicating already difficult existing political, regulatory, investment, and planning hurdles. Third, the Dutch political system is national, with provincial and municipal governments, as water authorities, in subsidiary roles. This "top-down" nature facilitates implementation. The U.S. federal system, in which (a) states and local governments have considerable autonomy, with (b) authority diffused between numerous federal agencies, and with (c) local prerogatives in planning and concepts of spatial quality jealously guarded, encumbers policy innovation, ambition, design, and implementation. Moreover, notwithstanding public comment periods and environmental impact statement processes in the U.S., it is hard to imagine U.S. authorities—federal, state and local—engaging the public and stakeholders to the degree achieved in RfR. RfR succeeded in part because its engagement was deep and extensive.

Finally, RfR and other recent FRM projects in the Netherlands have benefitted from multiple agencies and stakeholders (national and subnational) designing projects to achieve multiple goals. This multiple-goal approach has required intergovernmental coordination and shared project funding which is more easily arranged. In the U.S., however, the tight *federal* policy, regulatory and targeted appropriation silos impede project designs in which multiple goals can be imagined and achieved. Designing and constructing a project that combined federal funding from the Departments of Transportation, Housing and Urban Development, Agriculture, Interior (National Park Service), and Homeland Security (FEMA), for instance, for multiple goals is hard to imagine. Understaffed, underfunded local agencies who often jealously guard against federal encroachment into local issues further cements policy and project sclerosis. Post Hurricane Sandy there was an acknowledgement of this sclerosis and multiple attempts to create multiple-benefit recovery responses; these attempts, however, were limited in scope, and devolved over time, because of hardened constructs of federalism, institutional inertia, and bureaucratic inflexibility.

A Practical Example, the Depoldering Noordwaard RfR project

The Noordwaard depoldering project was the largest and most complex RfR project.[2] **[Figure 2]** The Noordwaard is a dike ring in the Biesbosch, a striking and sparsely populated river landscape at the confluence of the Maas and Waal rivers. Depoldering is a sensitive subject in the Netherlands. After all, the Dutch first conquered their land and later defended it against the water. To then "give up" the landscape to the water feels at first like a costly retreat. Depoldering lowers the dikes around the polder to enable water to flow across it during high river conditions, thereby reducing both upstream and downstream water levels. Depoldering yields other cost savings as miles of upstream and downstream river dikes do not need to be raised. Depoldering, however, has substantial impacts upon land-use, occupation, and safety conditions within the polder. We note that some river diversion projects in the U.S., along the Mississippi River and its tributaries, and in California's Central Valley, achieve many of the same goals as depoldering, although these diversion channels are used only in periods of severe duress, whereas RfR projects may operate on a more frequent basis. **[Figure 3]**

Depoldering was chosen for Noordwaard for a few reasons. First, Noordwaard's geographical location is favorable, at the confluence of two major rivers. **[Figures 4 & 5]** Because Noordwaard's ground level is relatively low and the Waal has a higher water level than the Maas, during flood conditions water would automatically flow through the polder from the Waal to the Maas if there were no dikes. Second, Noordwaard is a relatively small polder, with relatively few occupants and agriculture as its primary function. Agriculture functions are even more important in nearby polders. Finally, Noordwaard is bordered on three sides by the Biesbosch National Park, a rich national estuarine facility. Reestablishing a more natural wetland landscape in which people can live, that increases water safety for the entire region through a restored natural system, albeit with reduced agriculture, seemed a logical and good alternative.

Depoldering is also special from a policy point of view. Depoldering by definition leads to a large-scale replanning of the landscape. Between 1950 and 1980, spatial planning in the Netherlands attempted to rationalize and optimize the landscape. The Noordwaard was redesigned primarily for agriculture during this period, which saw agricultural plots enlarged partly by closing and filling existing creeks.

Because increasing water safety is a national priority, discussions were held with regional and local authorities in the Noordwaard about where and which river-widening measures should be implemented. Two dominant options took shape. First, either many small areas directly on and near the river dikes would have to be redeveloped on higher ground, which would make the area "safe" for a few decades, after which an additional measure, probably depoldering, would be needed. Or, second, the Noordwaard would be immediately depoldered, creating at least 50 years of safety. With the approval of a struggling regional agricultural sector, the choice was made to depolder the Noordwaard. This decision was of great concern to Noordwaard's residents and farmers, who faced an uncertain future and felt partly abandoned.

It is unique that a 4,000-hectare (10,000-acre) polder like the Noordwaard would undergo a complete transformation. **[Figure 6]** The Dutch landscape is purposefully planned and used, with intense interests and investments. RfR's dual objectives of FRM and spatial quality improvement required Noordwaard's replanning and design process to integrally address both. This deliberate, almost iterative approach made it possible to consider added value for many functions. A tipping point in the early Noordwaard discussions was a direct commitment from the Netherlands government minister in charge, allowing current residents to continue to live in parts of the Noordwaard that were to be depoldered, if they chose to do so. This commitment was remarkable, because the option for ongoing habitation in the project area had not yet been approved by the Noordwaard project team. The impact of this commitment was equal parts substantial and controversial because it further complicated the project and required *Rijkswaterstaat* to actively involve the region, key stakeholders, and design professionals into the project design and engineering processes. This commitment also made it necessary to innovate, integrate, and think creatively about how to balance the FRM and spatial quality tradeoffs. In hindsight, the commitment was a blessing because it seeded

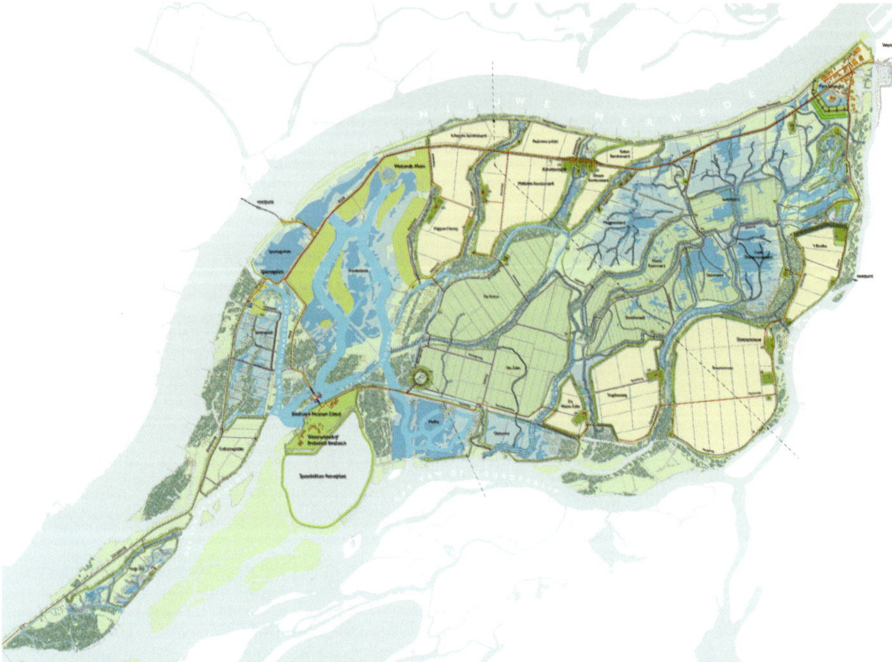

[Figure 2] Site Plan of Noordwaard (image credit: Robbert de Koning, Rijkswaterstaat)

the drive for spatial quality. In other words, simply buying everything and everyone out of the polder was no longer sufficient. *What was needed now was a robust, future-oriented, and multifunctional water landscape for humans and nature, for recreationists and farmers.*

Integrated design issues were discussed with private residents and farmers, often at their homes, in their barns or at their kitchen tables. These close interactions enabled the surfacing of deeply held personal beliefs about the land and about flood safety. It also established a grounding of trust. These were not easy discussions. Business survival was at stake, family ties to the land were in jeopardy, and sometimes, a home or business could not be spared. The input and ideas of Noordwaard's residents were nevertheless indispensable in helping *Rijkswaterstaat,* the project team, and the Q-Team to grasp the polder's unique features and characteristics and incorporate those in the project's design.

From the first strokes of the pen in 2003 to project completion in 2015, Depoldering Noordwaard demanded continued attention, energy, resources and commitment. Today, water dynamics have been reintroduced to the polder. Indeed, the Noordwaard is (again) a landscape in which living with water is central. Agriculture continues in seven small, high-quay polders on the polder's flanks. **[Figure 7]** Different quay heights lead to different "flood protection levels" and different land use possibilities. **[Figure 8]** The flow-through area is naturalized, more beautiful, where livestock can graze in the summer. Parts of Noordwaard now flood annually, although not disruptively and not often in high quayside polders. **[Figure 9]** The system of channels and creeks between the polders is being reestablished. Old creek beds have been dug out and are now flanked by buntings of reed, pilot whale, and willow thickets. **[Figure 10]** The creeks are wooded where possible (in low-flow areas) and open where necessary (in the flow-through area). The landscape aesthetic is strongly colored by the "empty" polders, bordered by green edges of quays and wooded creeks. Farms and barns are iconic landscape elements and accentuate the polder's emptiness. **[Figure 11]** Quays and dikes form the dividing lines *and* the connections between the polders and the creeks. Residents and farmers live on mounds. **[Figure 12]** Many new bridges, designed by West 8, have been built to provide access and connection. **[Figure 13]** New pumping stations, also designed by West 8, have been installed and mounds have been reinforced and erected. **[Figure 14]** All in all, a palette of culture and nature has emerged, of old and new, to benefit a broader set of community goals. **[Figure 15]**

Learning the Lessons of RfR

In hindsight, it is striking that the impact of RfR's success in the current Netherlands' national flood protection program (HWBP) is, at best, moderate, notwithstanding the fact that HWBP's budget is quadruple that of RfR (€9.7 billion versus €2.3 billion). In many ways, the Dutch national government chose a different infrastructure and water management approach after RfR. HWBP decentralized many policy decisions, set fewer regulations, goals, and targets, and enabled or required local authorities to implement many HWBP requirements on their own.

In theory, achieving spatial quality is easier to achieve, or automatically realized, through a decentralized, locally driven approach. Unfortunately, many local water authorities are not well equipped or predisposed to achieve spatial quality goals. Institutional and funding silos, "we don't do that" attitudes, and a reflexive reliance upon traditional FRM practices in which water authorities have skill, competence, and established procedures—like elevating dikes and levees to further constrict the floodplain and accelerate discharge—dominate project approaches. Water management bureaucracies, whether in the Netherlands or in the U.S., are by nature institutionally and professionally reluctant to experiment, whether through fear of liability or fear of change. These bureaucracies tend to prefer proven, familiar, ingrained processes and have leadership focused upon project delivery and not project innovation.

Some Dutch water authorities were, and are, geographically outside the scope of RfR and thus were not subject to its dual-goal mandate and riverine FRM focus. Fortunately, other Dutch water authorities were inspired by and have embraced RfR's integrated approach and have made the achievement of spatial quality a key objective in their project and design approaches.

The benefits of the RfR approach have caught the positive attention from the U.S. Army Corps of Engineers and some state and local water authorities, but, at present, they cannot imagine a similar implementation given federalism (see above), a lack of regional governance structures, federal and state policy, spending silos, the integration of upstream and downstream goals, and a difficulty to approach large rivers as coherent systems instead of as having particular places that flood. This is most obvious in California's San Joaquin and Sacramento River systems and their tributaries. Some U.S. states, however, are developing a partial RfR approach, focusing on river systems mostly or wholly within their jurisdiction, seen best in the Louisiana Watershed Initiative, the Iowa Watershed Approach and the inspiring North Carolina river mapping program. Another quite promising U.S. development is within the Corps's Engineering with Nature (EWN) program. While EWN's focus is not solely riverine FRM, its focus on natural and nature-based features, of multiple benefits and their quantification to support cost-benefit analysis, will clearly have spatial quality and other environmental, economic, and recreation outcomes benefits.

Spatial Quality: What Is It, Exactly?

Two persistent misconceptions exist about spatial quality. The first is that spatial quality always costs more money. That is not always true, and often true only to the extent that current cost-benefit analyses (CBA) do not capture spatial quality benefits. In some ways, this is a matter of math. A design with a high degree of spatial quality offers considerable practical value, amenity value, aesthetic value, social value, ecosystem value, and future value. Spatial quality improvements may be more expensive to implement in a FRM project *over the near term*, but the additional returns in the medium and long terms are most often excluded from typical cost-benefit analyses and calculations. For example, the ecosystem services valuation of nature provisioning, of a natural cyclical wet-dry landscape, or the economic value induced and retained for local hospitality and other businesses as visitors use and enjoy the landscape, and hiking and cycling paths, are not included. In other words, these benefits are not (or not often) quantified as a project outcome and thus the dominant CBA procedures favor typical FRM projects. In the Netherlands and the U.S., these focus on damage to structures and economic activity. When the economic science catches up to the environmental and social sciences, and when CBAs encompass more than structural and economic activity-avoided losses, projects with key spatial quality improvements will likely be less expensive over their project life.

The second misunderstanding is that spatial quality is subjective. Certainly, that is partly true, and maybe that is a good thing. It might not be possible to assign a finite, objective grade of spatial quality. Beauty and benefit are indeed subjective—to whom, for whom, and over what time period. But when innovative architects, designers, planners, and landscape architects find a workable symbiosis between required civil engineering project delivery tasks and FRM goals, and they can deliver a project landscape full of legible character, benefit, and identity that is equitably shared by all—we all win. That requires talent, good education, and experience.

The Culture of Spatial Quality and Thrift

The pursuit of simplicity and logic is in keeping with the Dutch tradition of water and dike and levee construction. The Netherlands' former national landscape and water advisor, Eric Luiten, emphasizes in "Guide to Landscape Integration" that spatial quality is not simply the addition of "bells and whistles." Luiten's guide, which informs

HWBP program management, describes spatial quality as a careful and intentional design of the assignments, whether they are comprehensive and large, or small and detailed. Spatial quality is not "the cherry on the cake," but instead "the yeast in the bread." By striving for simplicity, and using the resources at hand as sensibly as possible, spatial quality often comes into its own, embracing the old Dutch Calvinistic belief that "excess is harmful."

Many believe that RfR's outcomes can and must be better utilized. The Board of Government Advisers (CRA), which advises the minister of Infrastructure and Water Management, recently issued an important directive for the implementation of spatial quality in flood risk management projects. The advice, "from sober and efficient to smart and efficient," references HWBP's dominant credo of "sober and efficient." "Sober" suggests thrift, which is another Dutch Calvinistic tendency, but here it relates to the strict sectoral focus placed on HWBP projects. CRA worries that HWBP's project definitions and processes are approached narrowly, perhaps shortsightedly, instead of integrally, and that the spatial layout is treated as a final task or afterthought. In practice, this approach often yields an unnecessarily long, laborious, linear, check-the-box planning process instead of one in which many goals are pursued. Many RfR projects are deemed successful because they were able to escape this approach.

The CRA makes three recommendations. First, project scopes should be increased in space and time. In many projects, "other goals" are explored only in the project planning phase. It is important in the postplanning phase to retain the ability to explore new or previously unforeseen combinations of flood risk management and other tasks in the project area. Second, CRA argues that water projects must be able to encompass multiple goals. This means breaking down funding and project silos. Some Dutch water boards already try to encompass other goals in addition to water safety, and have defined project effectiveness as one that embraces multiple goal integration. The third recommendation is for regional approaches. Several water boards and provinces have instituted collaborative processes and have integrated regional quality teams. Enabling strategic alliances between parties (for example, between municipalities and the regional water authority), or between upstream-downstream neighbors, can reduce costs and improve project outcome and quality. Municipalities can also play an important role in outreach and engagement with the region's residents, stakeholders, and entrepreneurs.

The minister's response to the CRA advice was that HWBP does not need to be changed, although transforming "sober and efficient" into "sober, smart, and efficient" would be acceptable. The question, however, is what that shift will yield in practice. Local authorities sometimes interpret the term "sober" to mean that they need not pay too much attention to spatial quality, because that is seen as "extra costs," which is by definition neither sober, thrifty, nor efficient. Conversely, other local authorities fear that they will run afoul of HWBP goals. Because localities are reimbursed for 50 percent of the costs of HWBP projects from the national government, they are overly careful, prescriptive, or reticent, which is disastrous for integrated design.

[**Figure 3**] Birds Point-New Madrid Floodway, Missouri, United States, 2020 (image credit: Yiqi Jiang, Derek Hoeferlin, Washington University in St. Louis Master of Landscape Architecture program)

[**Figure 4**] 1850 historic map of Noordwaard's location at the confluence of the Maas and Waal Rivers (image credit: Topografische Dienst, photograph by Derek Hoeferlin, 2012)

[Figure 5] Landscape architect Robbert de Koning explaining design concepts of Noordwaard at the confluence of the Maas and Waal Rivers, 2012 (image credit: Derek Hoeferlin)

[Figure 6] The agricultural polder has been transformed into a tidal freshwater landscape with creeks and small low-quay polders. (Image credit: Rijkswaterstaat, Yourcaptain)

[Figure 7] View over a high quay polder with agriculture, surrounded by creeks (image credit: Robbert de Koning)

[Figure 8] Multiple land-uses of Noordwaard with over a reinforced old mound (front) and a former fortress with a levee combined with wave breaking willow structures (back) (image credit: Robbert de Koning)

[Figure 9] Bridge over a wide creek at the sea side of the Noordwaard
(image credit: Robbert de Koning)

[Figure 10] New bridge over creek flanked by new native plantings that are conducive to wet clay soil
(image credit: Jeroen Bosch)

Following CRA's advice and the lessons learned from RfR, the Lower House of the Dutch Parliament intervened at the end of 2020. Because an update to the Environmental Act will be pursued in 2021, the Lower House approved a motion "requesting the government to explore how attention to spatial quality can be further linked to the water task." This is encouraging and a step in the right direction and could open the door to applying RfR's substantial benefits and improvements to future HBWP projects.

Final Thoughts

Ingrained habits and familiar processes are hard to break even when those habits or processes are not satisfactory and new approaches are promising. "Change is difficult" is a tired, but exact truism. RfR was tremendously successful and must not be seen as an oddity, a one-off success, or a black swan policy coincidence. It is instead a steady, modern integration of FRM and spatial quality, demanded, approved, and applauded by citizens, worthy of affirmation and adoption into the Environmental Act in the Netherlands and into the U.S. FRM vernacular.

We note further that achieving spatial quality is human work. It is also *additive*, demanding collaboration across policy and professional disciplines. Spatial quality, by its very nature, rejects single-purpose approaches and also, again by its very nature, encourages the negotiation of many goals and benefits. It is thus messy, difficult work and will be most successful when the project team openly explores, posits, and confirms shared values and goals, maybe even passions. The design and delivery *process* must be able to embrace and achieve multiple goals; spatial quality specialists must work alongside project planners, engineers, and delivery professions. This change of mindset and approach is hard to imagine and may be even harder to achieve. On the other hand, try pondering a future in which our physical landscapes and the places we occupy are dominated by inefficient, unimaginative, soulless FRM projects devoid of spatial quality. That future might be temporally and physically "safe," but at what cost and at whose expense?

1. The Bijhouwer Prize is awarded once every three years to a person or organization that has made a special and high-quality service in the field of garden and landscape architecture. The prize is set by the NHBos Foundation. The NHBos Foundation aims to support garden and landscape architecture in the Netherlands in a targeted manner (www.nhbos.nl). The Grote Maaskant Prize is named after Hugh Maaskant, a renowned Rotterdam architect (1907–1977). It is a four-yearly *oeuvre* prize for one or more persons who significantly stimulate the debate about architecture, urban development, or landscape design through publications, education, research activities, or commissioning, for example (www.rotterdammaaskant.nl).
2. Noorwaard project credits: Rijkswaterstaat (client), Robbert de Koning Landschapsarchitect (lead designer/supervisor), Dienst Landelijk Gebied (codesigner), Boskalis, Martens Van Oord, Van Hattum en Blankevoort & Gebr. Van Kessel (contractors), IPV Delft and West 8 urban design & landscape architecture (bridges and pumphouses).

[Figure 11] Farms and barns as iconic landscape elements within polders, quays and wooded creeks
(image credit: Jeroen Bosch)

[Figure 12] New mound with a house, as compensation for a demolished house
(image credit: Jeroen Bosch)

[Figure 13] New bridges for various types of connections (image credit: Jeroen Bosch)

[Figure 14] New pumphouse constructed from recycled bricks from demolished barns on-site (image credit: Jeroen Bosch)

[Figure 15] A new cultural and natural landscape benefiting community goals (image credit: Jeroen Bosch)

February 10, 2020: the first time that the threshold (front right) at the riverside
of the Noordwaard overflew, and the flow area functioned as designed (image credit: Robbert de Koning)

Speculate + Synthesize [S+S]

(or the need for transboundary watershed architecture)

In Part Two, Speculate + Synthesize [S+S], and after Ian Caine's introductory essay "Context," I propose transboundary speculative futures for the Mississippi, Mekong, and Rhine River Basins, to stimulate long-term possibilities for sustainable river basin management. These build upon the Appreciate + Analyze [A+A] section, but reciprocally, these speculations have informed content for the [A+A] section as well. They are meant to provoke dialogues and provide graphic road maps of how to later on develop concrete proposals to implement sustainable futures.

[S+S] intends to stimulate both debates and long-term possibilities for multi-scaled river basin issues. Much of the discussion across entire river basins, in its current form, is predominantly rhetorical, rarely propositional, and other than a few noteworthy examples, unfortunately without input from the design disciplines.[1] The [S+S] work ranges from the hyperbolic to the pragmatic. One form of speculation cannot exist without the other. The following "Watershed Architecture" design templates attempt to fill in such a gap.

What emerges from all three of the proposals is a radical reinstating of a notion of localization. Ironic as it sounds, each river basin in effect is proposed to become the localized condition, informing future-forward, 21st-century adaptive measures for each river basin, at multiple scales, and across shared geographies, ecologies, and communities. What if we rethought scales of communities at scales of watersheds? Going a step further, what if the Mississippi, Mekong, and Rhine were collective communities?

Waters of the Rhine River (image credit: Derek Hoeferlin)

The Mississippi proposal, designed with Jonathan Stitelman, Allison Méndez, L. Irene Compadre, and Chad Fisk, is titled "from the Big Six to the Birds Foot." We propose a future ecological industry that transforms what have been considered wastes—excess nutrients and suppressed sediments—into resources as alternative energy sources and wetland restoration practices.

The Mekong proposal, designed with Jess Vanecek and Rob Birch, is titled "from the Third Pole to the Nine Dragons." We propose a reconfiguration of the energy infrastructure that has resulted from current and planned large-scale hydropower dam infrastructure projects throughout the Mekong. These projects are primarily designed with the purpose of exporting power to countries outside of the Mekong. Alternatively, we propose to relocalize the power within the Mekong, and for the Mekong communities in the future.

The Rhine proposal, designed with Jess Vanecek, Paul Wu, and Han Meyer, is titled "from the Rheinquelle to the Leo Hollandicus." Challenged by current uncertainties of climate change and industrialization, we propose a new integration of the energies, economies and environments for a new collective project in the center of Europe.

1. Groups such as America's Watershed Initiative, America's Wetland Foundation, the Nature Conservancy, and Mississippi River Cities and Towns Initiative have been developing venues for transboundary policy discussions across the entire Mississippi River Basin.

Mississippi River Basin rivers and streams, ink on tracing paper, Derek Hoeferlin, 1999 (image credit: Derek Hoeferlin)

Context

Synthetic Utopias for a Post-Katrina Era

Ian Caine

[Figure 1] A map of Thomas More's Utopia (woodcut, November 1518)
(image credits: source: The Folger Shakespeare Library, author: Utopia, Thomas More, 1518)

In Thomas More's 1516 novel *Utopia*, King Utopos initiates the pursuit of architectural utopia with a grand act of separation. He uses water to do it, severing a 15-mile-long isthmus to construct an artificial island called Utopia.[1] By breaking all physical or historical connections to the mainland, the fictional island of Utopia emerges as a powerful metaphor, reminding us that the fundamental impulse of architectural speculation has long been to escape the obligations of physical and political context. If the origins of architectural utopia reside in the power of water to separate, however, in the post-Katrina era water is reemerging as a synthesizing force, prompting urbanists to align their formal speculations with prevailing ecological and sociopolitical realities. Today, the opportunities and constraints associated with water are prompting architects, landscape architects, and urban designers to dramatically recast the parameters of urban speculation, challenging the veracity of the autonomous project in architecture while recovering the best utopian impulses of the Modern project. Within this context, Derek Hoeferlin positions his broad portfolio of work—presented here as Watershed Architecture—as a fully synthetic project, one that aligns urban speculations with the multiple logics of water at the metropolitan, regional, and continental scales. **[Figure 1]**

Defensive Legacies

The word utopia comes from the Greek "ou" and "topos," which refers to a negation of place and translates as "no-where."[2] This etymology underscores More's clear desire to flee the political realities of medieval Europe, an impulse that has characterized most utopian projects since. A specter of fear and concern for military defense permeate More's description of Utopia: the entrance to the island's bay hides submerged rocks which threaten to shipwreck strange or unwelcome ships.[3] A high wall and deep ditch "set thick with thorns" surround the capital city of Amaurot, securing the perimeter against invaders.[4] Such defensive fortifications are common in Renaissance utopias, which typically assume closed, geometric forms. Separation is the fundamental impulse, as utopian thinkers strive to escape the disordered realities of history while concretizing a new "world governed by an immutable, sovereign, definitive order." [5]

Similar instincts fuel Modernist utopian visions: consider Le Corbusier's iconic 1925 Plan Voisin, which dreams of replacing the tangled politics and morphologies of historical Paris with an ideal, geometric, and rational city. The distinct yet inseparable histories of utopia and Modernism reveal a consistent belief that voyages to ideal futures begin with departures from difficult pasts. If a longing to escape political chaos inspired such impulses during the Renaissance and Modern periods, the fear of ecological catastrophe is motivating these desires today. In this regard, Masdar City may be our generation's Palmanova **[Figure 2]**: an attempt to fortify the city against existential threat, to sequester it from the political imperatives of the day.[6]

Such legacies become interesting as we consider the precarious position that New Orleans found itself in as Katrina bore down on the city in August 2005. Remember that New Orleans has long owed its survival to the U.S. Army Corps of Engineers, the agency that leads the federal government's flood control efforts. Incredibly, the origins of the Corps predate the country's founding: George Washington first assigned engineer officers to the Army during the Revolutionary War. Engineers have done combat in every American war since.[7] For much of its history, the Corps has constructed and maintained barricades against armed and environmental threats. Notable examples include the 11-pointed fort that safeguarded New York Harbor during the War of 1812 (now the base of the Statue of Liberty) and much of the flood control infrastructure that protects New Orleans today.[8]

To fulfill such colossal responsibilities, the Corps leverages military-sized budgets and infrastructures—not to mention a Congressional mandate—to protect communities and economies against catastrophic threats from without. Given the agency's military and engineering roots, it should come as no surprise that the Corps has long favored defensive and mechanical fortifications—strategies that sequester vulnerable environments from their ecological and social context. In the case of New Orleans, the Corps's driving motivation has long been a deep-seated and warranted fear of catastrophic flooding. In this scenario, a massive network of levees, floodwalls, pumps, and canals fortifies the city against environmental intrusion, becoming simultaneous instruments of civil defense and urban design. In 2005, Katrina tested the limits of this system, killing almost 2,000 New Orleans residents, inflicting $125 billion of damage, and reconfirming water as the most unforgiving material on earth. **[Figure 3]**

The intellectual foundations for Watershed Architecture lie in the tragic fallout from Katrina. While the aerial images of an underwater New Orleans damaged the reputation of the Corps, they also raised uncomfortable questions about the relevance of architects, landscape architects, and urban designers. When the water receded, the inadequacy of our own professional discourse lay bare, muddied, and exposed. Literally overnight, our disciplinary obsessions with the proportions of streets and blocks became obsolete as decisions about large-scale civil infrastructure—made at multiple levels of local, state, and national government—determined the very life and death of cities. As a speculative project, Watershed Architecture rejects the sufficiency of defensive and mechanical strategies on the one hand, and disciplinary preoccupations with form on the other. Instead, the project commits to forging synthetic relationships between urban and ecological systems, with special attention to the scalar logic of watersheds. If the tragedy of Katrina has taught us anything, it is that water's unforgiving material qualities demand nothing less.

Synthetic Ecologies

The impulse to fortify urban speculations with ecological logic, of course, is not new. In the 19th century, William Morris proposed that a return to nature would remedy the adverse effects of the industrial city. Frederick Law Olmsted offered a different tactic, strategically introducing ecological systems into industrial cities with projects like New York City's Central Park and Boston's Emerald Necklace. In 1915, Patrick Geddes expanded his concept of the Valley Section in *Cities in Evolution*, emphasizing the foundational relationship between topography, vegetation, animal life, and regional planning. In 1969, Ian McHarg extended this logic in *Design with Nature*, leveraging his Potomac River Basin Study to position the physiographic region and river basin

[Figure 2] The late Renaissance town of Palmanova, founded by the Venetian Republic (1593) (image credits: source: wikimedia.org, author: IlirikIlirik)

[Figure 3] New Orleans, Louisiana on August 30, 2005, in the aftermath of Hurricane Katrina (image credit: The U.S. National Archives)

as the organizing framework for ecological planning and design.[9] In 1971, Reyner Banham celebrated the veracity of existing ecologies and infrastructures in *Los Angeles: The Architecture of Four Ecologies*. Since the late 1990s, movements in Landscape and Ecological Urbanism have generated an extensive body of speculative work that leverages a complex interplay between ecological and urban processes. Each of these seminal projects offers a fundamentally synthetic view of the city, one that embraces the primacy of ecological systems and projects urban futures at a regional scale.

Watershed Architecture extends these intellectual trajectories, focusing specifically on the inseparable logics of urban form, hydrology, hydraulics, ecology, and infrastructure at the scale of the watershed. This approach can make it challenging to establish the scale and scope of a given project, as watersheds typically transcend geographic and jurisdictional scales. Consider a single raindrop as it navigates the hydrologic cycle: after falling from the sky, it travels across roofs, downspouts, parking lots, storm sewers, rivers, oceans, and atmospheres before recondensing and beginning the sequence again. During this journey, the raindrop will pass through cities, counties, unincorporated areas, water districts, and multiple regulatory jurisdictions at the local, state, and federal levels.[10] These complexities provoke questions about the critical relationships between ecologies and politics, for example how to best align the boundaries of watersheds and problem-sheds, which are rarely symmetrical.[11]

Today, the ecological imperatives of water are compelling designers to reimagine urban speculations as multiscalar and multidisciplinary endeavors that span watersheds, regions, and even continents. This scenario obliges designers to expand—not to restrict—their understanding of context while confronting issues of scale as they relate to ecologies (what is the boundary of the site?); politics (who are the constituencies?); and strategies (what tactical interventions are appropriate?).

Speculate + Synthesize: The 100-Year Plan

Ian Caine and Derek Hoeferlin (with Michael Heller)

[Figures 4 & 5]

A fundamental reconsideration of the scalar relationship between urban form and watersheds drove an early speculation titled the *100 Year Plan*, my first design collaboration with Derek Hoeferlin. In 2009, in the wake of Katrina, the San Francisco Bay Conservation and Development Commission and AIA San Francisco sponsored *Rising Tides*, an international design competition that explored how cities could adapt to the worst effects of sea-level rise.[12] Derek and I, both nascent practitioners and studio instructors at the time, submitted one of six winning entries to the competition, generating ideas that would guide our respective professional trajectories for the next decade. Our approach to the single competition board (printed on bond, spray-mounted to a piece of foam core, and mailed!) was simple: in lieu of architectural form-making, we submitted a regional plumbing diagram that restored the ecological health and balance of California's watersheds. In our mind, rising tides were merely one symptom of a more daunting regional water crisis.

The *100-Year Plan* was fundamentally a political proposal. We purposefully avoided specific design solutions, instead emphasizing goals and desired outcomes. This approach expanded the architect's role from designer to long-range policy advocate, recognizing that ecological processes do not correspond to project and market cycles. The *100 Year Plan* relied on a public policy toolkit to swap the energy-intensive and environmentally destructive practice of massive water transport—known as "watershed hopping"—for a more localized approach. The project leveraged four organizing principles to manage water in a new way: *re-localizing watersheds*, allowing real issues such as topography, water supply and demand, and the maintenance of local watersheds to dictate policy; *re-plenishing watersheds*, via a controlled re-flooding of the Sacramento–San Joaquin River Delta; *re-powering* water production, using tidal power as a new energy source to run desalination plants; and *re-growing* tidal marshes, regenerating tidal marshes to create storm barriers, restore crucial ecology, and increase local carbon sinks.[13]

Ultimately, the *100 Year Plan* represented an early, schematic attempt to synthesize urban and ecological systems, in effect establishing the early terms of a speculative, synthetic Watershed Architecture. By critically engaging the ever-blurry distinction between the natural and artificial, the *100 Year Plan* contested a Modern narrative that called for the two to remain separate.

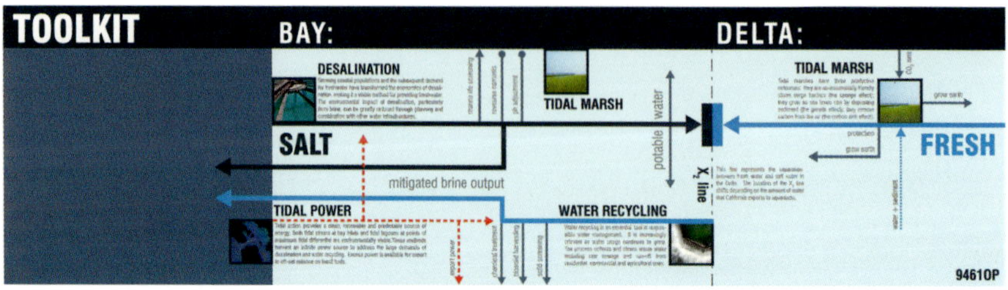

[Figure 4] Toolkit for The 100 Year Plan (image credit: Ian Caine and Derek Hoeferlin with Michael Heller)

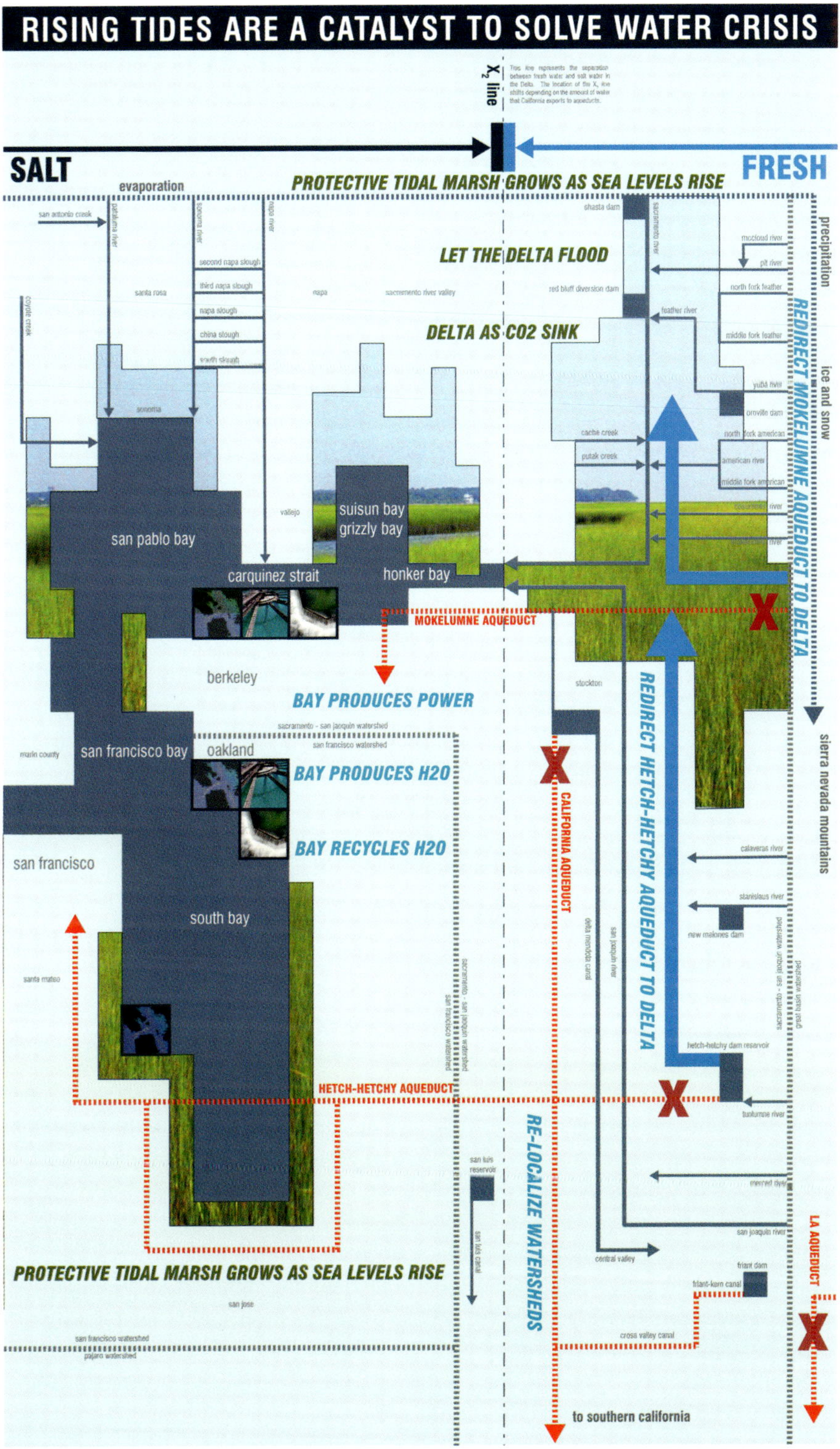

[Figure 5] The 100 Year Plan (image credit: Ian Caine and Derek Hoeferlin with Michael Heller)

Synthetic Politics

Just as the imperatives of water compel ecological synthesis, they oblige designers to pursue political synthesis in the face of often combative struggles over water resources. This means that designers, working across the scale of multiple watersheds, must generate a partisan position in advance of a formal one. This obligation again challenges the intellectual foundations of architectural utopia, which reside in the Renaissance ideal that perfect form can perfect society. This fundamental belief binds an otherwise disparate fabric of historical speculations, from Fillarete's Sforzinda (1465) to Ledoux's Ideal City of Chaux (1773–1806) to Le Corbusier's Plan Voisin (1925) to Lúcio Costa's Brasilia (1957) to Norman Foster's Masdar City (2010 to the present). Form, as it turns out, is never enough. This outcome became especially apparent during the latter stages of the Modern Movement, when the resolute geometries and conceptual rigor of twentieth century utopia gave way to the concrete sense of alienation that these projects, when built, induced in occupants. This also marks the time that the already fraying relationship between architecture and utopia unraveled.[14] This outcome represents an unfortunate departure from the radical political origins of the Modern Movement, which advanced a program of collectivist social transformation across scales, from buildings to cities to regions.[15]

Watershed Architecture seeks to recover the lost relationship between architecture and utopia, while offering that the first obligation of urban speculations must be to establish a political position. In this way, form follows politics. Landscape architect Billy Fleming summarizes the pragmatics of this approach well, advising that politics is downstream from culture and that design is downstream from politics.[16] Watershed Architecture therefore obliges designers to move upstream. Given the critical power dynamics that reside in water politics, designers must begin their work by building allegiances and establishing principles. Who will designers serve and to what end? Landscape architect Pierre Bélanger has a quick answer for such questions, suggesting that his own discipline prioritize marginalized people and territories while reclaiming biophysical processes, repairing damaged watersheds, and reconstructing critical ecosystems. This will require designers to abandon 20th-century urban design practices and refocus on spatial inequalities.[17]

The unpleasant reality here is that while many architects and urban designers pay quick lip service to politics, few engage in real advocacy or take up tangible action. To be fair, our financial dependence on sustained construction gives us every reason to obscure and rationalize our complicity with capital. Still, we have an unfortunate capacity to trivialize even marginal displays of social or environmental activism: the recent fetish with "ruin porn" comes to mind, as does our sudden and conspicuous concern for issues of social justice in the built environment. Billy Fleming rightly dismisses many of today's "activist practices" as a cynical new form of greenwashing.[18] Such critique reminds us that our disciplines would do well to develop a more substantive view of water, one that turns an eye towards the structural roots of the problems we are being paid to solve. With each new "public" seawall, green roof, or floodable park, we obscure systemic vulnerabilities with formal and technical interventions that are designed to distract as much as they are to solve.[19] Watershed Architecture therefore obliges designers to imbue speculations with partisanship, to move upstream and engage the political structures that actually construct cities.

One way that architects and urban designers can better engage political structures is to speculate about urban infrastructures and the institutions that build them. The massive scale of water infrastructure—i.e., dams, reservoirs, levees, pumps, canals, and aqueducts—compels designers to critically engage the bureaucracies that program, finance, and implement these projects. This includes small local utilities, massive federal agencies like the Corps, and every bureaucratic scale in between. In the fallout from Katrina, New Orleans architect David Waggonner developed a compelling model for this, initiating the "Dutch Dialogues" workshops with a diverse array of architects, landscape architects, urban designers, urban planners, architects, environmental engineers, members of the New Orleans Sewage and Water Board, the Corps, and multiple politicians from the city, state, and national levels.[20] These sessions, which ran between the years 2008 and 2010, challenged disciplinary boundaries, fleshed out political positions, and helped establish the principles for the ensuing Greater New Orleans Urban Water Plan, as well as similar efforts throughout the country. In the aftermath of Katrina, such conversations—which were also echoing in the halls of architecture schools throughout the country—became a revelation for a profession that had spurned political and social engagement for decades.

The political imperatives of water are also shifting conversations within the discipline of landscape architecture, which has historically focused more on greening and reprogramming gray infrastructure than on redesigning the social and political institutions that produce it.[21] Recently, landscape architect Kate Orff called out policymakers for managing next-century landscapes with 19th-century policy and "gray" engineering tools. As a counterproposal, Orff suggests a "Teal New Deal" for the country's coastlines, calling on government to remove dams and seawalls, rejoin rivers with their floodplains, and preserve the ecologies of riverbeds and coastal estuaries.[22] Such conversations are kick-starting a new era of urban speculation, one that confronts the real problems of the city with political tools and values that transcend disciplinary boundaries.

Speculate + Synthesize: The Continental Compact
Ian Caine and Derek Hoeferlin
(with Pablo Chavez, Emily Chen, Tiffin Thompson)

[Figures 6-11]

In 2015, Archinect sponsored *Dry Futures*, an international design competition that sought design responses to California's drought. Derek Hoeferlin and I took this opportunity to revisit the regional thinking that we initiated in the *Rising Tides* competition, expanding the scale of the *100 Year Plan* to the continent. *The Continental Compact*, which received an Honorable Mention from the competition jury, challenges decades of public policy that rely on an elaborate network of aqueducts to maintain populations in water-poor locations like Los Angeles, San Diego, San Francisco, Phoenix, and Denver.[23] Given the enormous financial and environmental costs of this status quo, *The Continental Compact* suggests a series of new transnational and transboundary agreements which, taken together, would end the culture of water-trading in western states. The projects adhere to three simple principles: guide population growth towards water; allow water-starved regions to shrink via attrition; and return the river to its hydrologic course. At the time we wrote:

The Continental Compact proposes a new chapter for the American story, one that continues to leverage water resources for public good, but does so in a more ecologically viable way. In this alternative narrative, Americans make a radical retreat from the mythology of westward expansion, opting instead for a massive reinvestment in regions where water resources remain abundant and underutilized... This proposal contends that the next wave of transcontinental migrations will head [back] east, supported by shifting public policies that stop moving water to people and start moving people to water. These transformational policies will forsake a historical desire to exert dominion over natural resources, instead adopting a more pragmatic approach that acknowledges the opportunities and constraints of local watersheds. [24]

The Continental Compact offers a radical policy prescription for the dire ecological contradictions that threaten the viability of cities in the western United States. By discouraging population growth in water-poor regions and encouraging it in water-rich basins near dams, along rivers, and within deltas, the proposal catalyzes novel conurbations at the scale of the river basin. By definition, these urbanisms will not align with local, state, and even national boundaries, thereby suggesting a political restructuring that aligns with the ecology of river basins. While the political costs of this restructuring could be high, the environmental and financial benefits would also be enormous: reducing the demand for energy, cutting carbon emissions, slowing subsidence, slashing infrastructure costs, and regenerating deltas. [25]

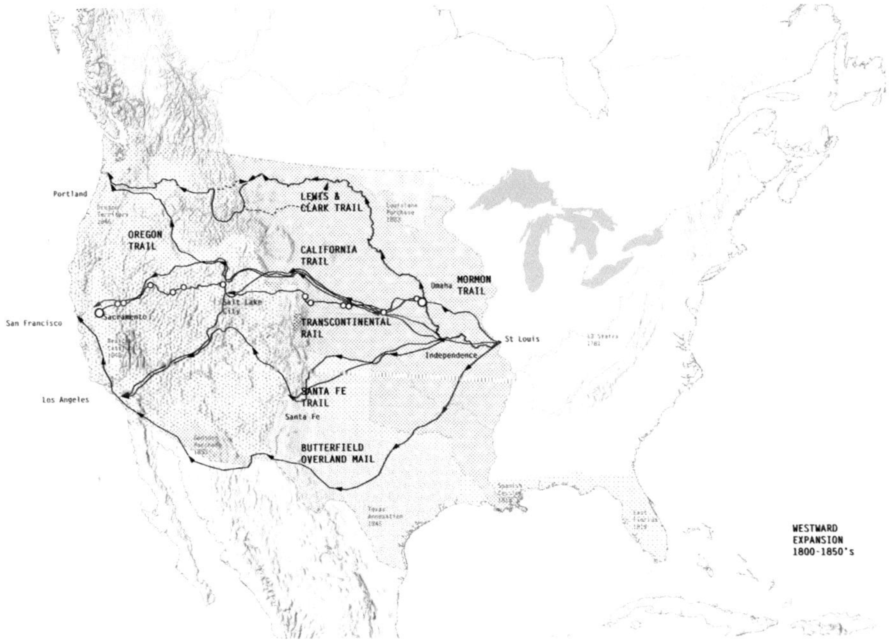

[Figure 6] Westward Expansion 1800–1850s (image credit: Ian Caine and Derek Hoeferlin, with Emily Chen, Tiffin Thompson, Pablo Chavez)

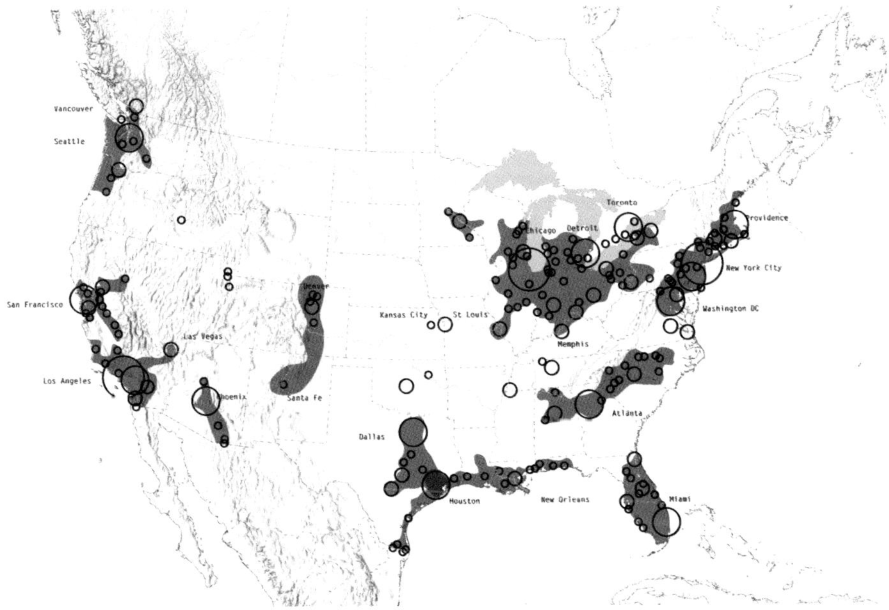

[Figure 7] The Regional Plan Association's projected megaregions for 2050 (image credit: Ian Caine and Derek Hoeferlin, with Emily Chen, Tiffin Thompson, Pablo Chavez)

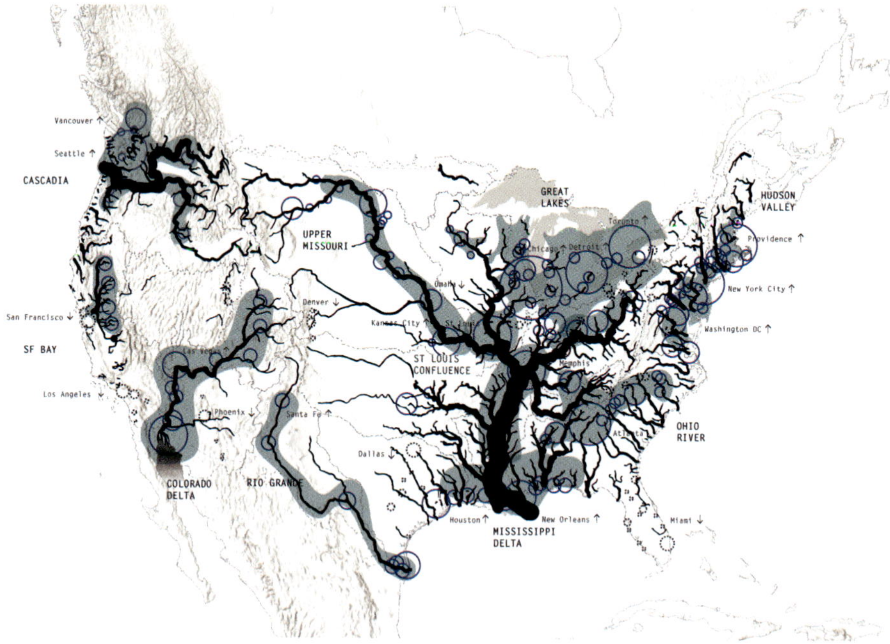

[Figure 8] The Continental Compact's proposed Hydrologic regions for 2050
(image credit: Ian Caine and Derek Hoeferlin, with Emily Chen, Tiffin Thompson, Pablo Chavez)

[Figure 9] The Continental Compact's projected Eastward Migrations
(image credit: Ian Caine and Derek Hoeferlin, with Emily Chen, Tiffin Thompson, Pablo Chavez)

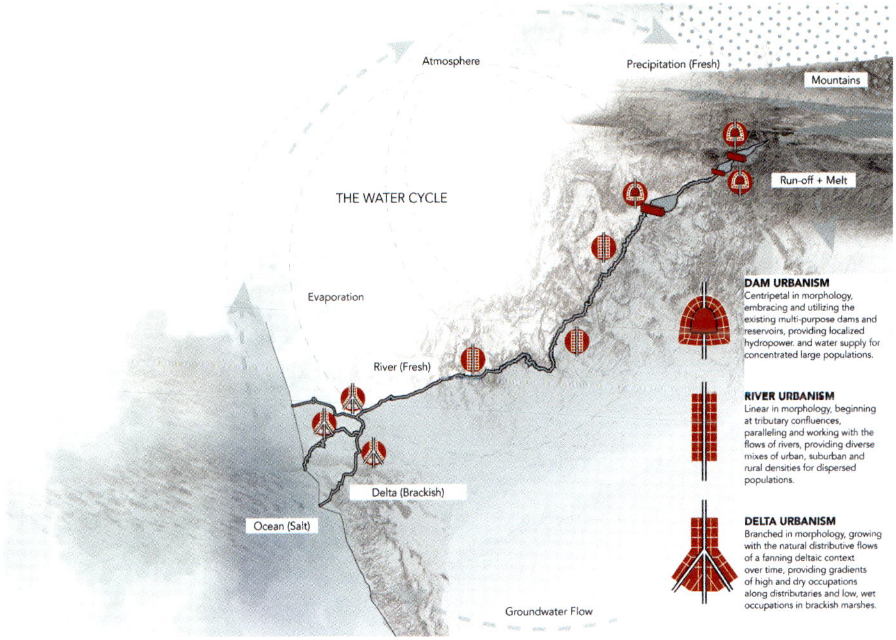

[Figure 10] The Continental Compact's proposed dam, river and delta urbanisms (image credit: Ian Caine and Derek Hoeferlin, with Emily Chen, Tiffin Thompson, Pablo Chavez)

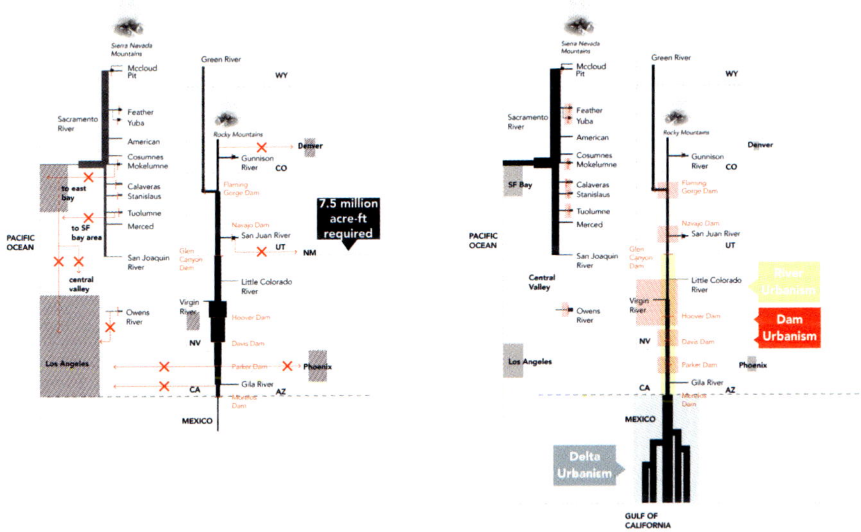

[Figure 11] The Continental Compact's proposed movement from hydraulic urbanism (LEFT) to hydrologic urbanism (RIGHT) (image credit: Ian Caine and Derek Hoeferlin, with Emily Chen, Tiffin Thompson, Pablo Chavez)

Synthetic Utopias

As designers, we crave constraint. Tight budgets and boundaries often inspire our best work. Given the devastation wrought by Hurricane Katrina, and more recently Gustav, Ike, Sandy, Maria, and Harvey, the existential threats associated with water are emerging as the ultimate check on our urban imaginations: while water's most tangible limits are ecological and technical, we are learning—belatedly—that the limits are social and political too. The argument that Derek Hoeferlin presents in *Way Beyond Bigness* is fundamentally a response to the severe ecological and sociopolitical limits of water. The multiscalar, multidisciplinary approach aligns with that of leading practitioners in architecture, landscape architecture, and urban design. Collectively, these practices are leveraging water's inherent ecological and sociopolitical constraints to reengage the utopian trajectories that most abandoned in the latter stages of the Modern project. This period saw Modern architecture surrender its foundational social agenda while diverting attention to issues of postmodern allusion or autonomous formalism. Such detours have pushed architects to the periphery of urban discourse, allowing real estate developers and media to fill the vacuum.[26] This retreat has rendered our discipline incapable of addressing existential environmental threats during the post-Katrina era.

With *Way Beyond Bigness,* Hoeferlin seeks to counter these trends by rehabilitating the Modern project's unfulfilled social agenda. Taken as a whole, the ideas presented in this book contribute to a broader, emerging urban project that begins with the postmodern attention to context, forged by figures like Colin Rowe and Reyner Banham; scales up to meet the regionalist aspirations of Patrick Geddes and Lewis Mumford; leverages the commitment to systems and ecology prescribed by Ian McHarg and James Corner; and embraces the ethical imperatives of environmental justice movements like #NoDAPL, the grassroots campaign to stop the Dakota Access Pipeline. Collectively, this deep and diverse intellectual lineage is supercharging our understanding of context and providing the terms for speculative, transcalar, and transdisciplinary projects like Watershed Architecture.

Architects Joshua Nason and Jeffrey Nesbit recently argued for a "neo-utopian paradox," a concept that defers the utopian impulse to impose prototypes onto a city, replacing it with a commitment to find out what the city is and what it actually needs.[27] This approach seeks to flush the residual tendencies of utopian planning, which rely on external models to inspire urban futures.[28] The authors describe this approach as anti-utopian, though it evokes Henri Lefebvre's call for a critical feedback loop between utopia and reality, a process he terms *Transduction*.[29] As Lefebvre writes: "Transduction assumes an incessant feedback between the conceptual framework used and empirical observations.... It introduces rigour in invention and knowledge in utopia." [30] Watershed Architecture builds on these ideas, embracing the tangible constraints of real ecological systems to help designers generate more informed and synthetic speculations about urban futures. By trading formal prescriptions for the vast opportunities that reside in the multifaceted and inescapable demands of hydrologic systems, Watershed Architecture answers theorist Nathaniel Coleman's challenge to reposition utopia as a "description of responsive capacities rather than a taxonomy of visionary images." [31]

Watershed Architecture finally submits that the future of urban speculation is not about building bigger or better islands; it is not about discovering New Worlds, here on earth or beyond. Instead, it offers that the next utopia will emerge from an expanded definition of context and a more sympathetic alignment between cities, water, and people. That alone is a radical speculation, one sufficient to inspire grand visions of urban futures and a new measure of what it means to think big.

Acknowledgements:
Thank you to Dr. Eric Mumford, Rebecca and John Voyles Professor of Architecture at Washington University, for his invaluable feedback on an early draft of this essay.

1. Franco Borsi, *Architecture and Utopia*, trans. Deke Dusinberre (Paris: Hazan, 1997), 27.
2. Antoine Picon, "Learning From Utopia," *Journal of Architectural Education* 67, no. 1 (2013): 17.
3. Thomas More, *Utopia* (1516). This work is licensed under a Creative Commons Attribution, Noncommercial 3.0 United States License, 51.
4. Ibid., 56.
5. Borsi, *Architecture and Utopia*, 27.
6. In the case of Palmanova, the existential threat was violence; in the case of Masdar City, the existential threat was environmental fallout due to global warming. In the latter case, the gravity of this threat appears to have been exceeded by the financial and political concerns of the project's capital investors and petrostate sponsor.
7. "A Brief History: Introduction," U.S. Army Corps of Engineers, https://www.usace.army.mil/About/History/Brief-History-of-the-Corps/Introduction.
8. "A Brief History: The Beginnings to 1815," U.S. Army Corps of Engineers, https://www.usace.army.mil/About/History/Brief-History-of-the-Corps/Beginnings/.
9. Anne Whiston Spirn, "Ian McHarg, Landscape Architecture, and Environmentalism: Ideas and Methods in Context," in *Environmentalism in Landscape Architecture*, ed. Michael Conan (Washington, DC: Dumbarton Oaks, 2000), 105.
10. For further investigations into the relationship between urban design and water see Jane Wolff, Elise Shelley, Derek Hoeferlin, "Why does the city fight gravity?" Gutter to Gulf: Legible Water Infrastructure for New Orleans, https://guttertogulf.com.
11. Shafiqul Islam and Lawrence Susskind, *Water Diplomacy: A Negotiated Approach to Managing Complex Water Networks* (New York: RFF Press, 2013), 51–52.
12. The multidisciplinary jury for the *Rising Tides* international competition included architect Michael Sorkin, landscape architect Walter Hood, coastal expert Denise Reed, coastal engineer Marcel Stive, and journalist Tracy Metz.
13. Ian Caine and Derek Hoeferlin, "The 100 Year Plan," San Francisco Bay Conservation and Development Commission and AIA San Francisco, *Rising Tides* international competition, 2009.
14. Nathaniel Coleman, "Utopia and Modern Architecture?" *Architectural Research Quarterly* 16, no. 4 (2012): 345.
15. Eric Mumford, *The CIAM Discourse on Urbanism, 1928–1960* (Cambridge: MIT Press, 2000), 12.
16. Billy Fleming, "Boxed In, Boxed Out: Water, Policy, and Design in Landscape Architecture," in *Fresh Water: Design research for inland water territories*, eds. Mary Pat McGuire and Jessica M. Henson (San Francisco: ORO Applied Research + Design, 2019), 21.
17. "The limits of the plan: Pierre Bélanger," Foreground, last revised October 5, 2017, https://www.

foreground.com.au/culture/pierre-belanger/.

18. Fleming, "Boxed In, Boxed Out," 23.

19. Eliyahu Keller and Kelly Leilani Main, "After the Flood: Water, Climate Crisis, and Architectural Imagination," *Journal of Architectural Education* 74, no. 1 (2020): 126.

20. For more information on the "Dutch Dialogues" process see Judith Nemes, "New Orleans architects look to the Netherlands for ideas on living with water," USGBC+, https://plus.usgbc.org/dutch-dialogues/.

21. Fleming, "Boxed In, Boxed Out," 21.

22. Kate Orff, "The Great Mother of Life," *Journal of Architectural Education* 74, no. 1 (2020): 8.

23. The multidisciplinary jury for the *Dry Futures* international competition included Allison Arieff, editorial director of *Spur*; Charles Anderson, founder/principal of Werk; Colleen Tuite and Ian Quate, cofounders of GRNASFCK; Geoff Manaugh, writer, BLDGBLOG; Hadley and Peter Arnold, cofounders/directors of the Arid Lands Institute; Jay Famiglietti, senior water cycle scientist, NASA Jet Propulsion Laboratory Water Initiative; and Peter Zellner, Principal and Design Lead, AECOM Los Angeles.

24. Ian Caine and Derek Hoeferlin, "The Continental Compact: Eastward Migration in a (New) New World," *Scenario Journal* 6: Migration (Summer 2017), https://scenariojournal.com/article/the-continental-compact/.

25. Ibid.

26. Nathaniel Coleman, *Lefebvre for Architects* (New York: Routledge, 2014), 37.

27. Joshua M. Nason and Jeffrey S. Nesbit, "Introduction: Chasing the Neo-Utopian Paradox," in *Chasing the City: Models for Extra-Urban Investigations*, ed. Joshua M. Nason and Jeffrey S. Nesbit (New York: Routledge, 2018), 3.

28. Ibid., 2.

29. Nathaniel Coleman, *Lefebvre for Architects* (New York: Routledge, 2014), 44–45.

30. Henri Lefebvre, *The Right to the City (1968)*, reprinted in *Writings on Cities*, trans. E. Kofman and E. Lebas (Oxford: Wiley-Blackwell, 1996), 151.

31. Nathaniel Coleman, "Utopia and Modern Architecture?" *Architectural Research Quarterly* 16, no. 4 (2012): 347.

from the Big Six to the Birds Foot

transforming the Nutrients, the Sediments, & the Industries in the Mississippi River Basin (1)

with Jonathan Stitelman, Allison Méndez, L. Irene Compadre, & Chad Fisk

From the Big Six to the Birds Foot is a speculative design future informed by complex systems affecting the entire Mississippi River Basin, with direct impact up and down the river network, and more specifically for the degrading Mississippi River Delta and its sinking urbanism of the Greater New Orleans Region.

No longer a natural river system, the Mississippi River Basin has become a controlled conduit system facilitating massive agriculture, commerce, development, and industrialization by prioritizing navigation and the barge industry to deliver it.

Quoting the Mississippi Valley Division:

> *The Mississippi Valley Division's navigation responsibilities include planning and constructing navigation channels, locks, and dams, and dredging to maintain channel depths of the harbors and inland waterways within its 370,000-square-mile boundary. The division operates and maintains 4,200+ miles of navigable channels, 59 locks, 51 shallow-*

draft ports and seven deep-draft ports. In partnership with local port authorities, MVD personnel oversee dredging and construction projects at numerous ports and harbors.[2]

There have been great economic and resource benefits from such river control as agriculture, development, navigation, and flood protection for communities. But adverse ecological byproducts and deindustrialized regions have resulted as well from the 20th-century practices of such things as dam construction by the U.S. Army Corps of Engineers (USACE), along with natural resources challenges and major stresses on flood and drought management.

According to the 2011 *National Water Resources Challenges Facing the U.S. Army Corps of Engineers* report created by the National Research Council (NRC) Committee on U.S. Army Corps of Engineers Water Resources Science, Engineering, and Planning, a new, 21st-century agenda for the Corps entails the following:

In an earlier era of national water development, Corps of Engineers civil works projects focused on construction of dam(s), levees, navigation channels, and other infrastructure. Over time, Congress has greatly broadened the Corps' work program and responsibilities. Future Corps water resources activities will be less dedicated to construction of major new civil works, and more heavily focused on (1) operating, maintaining, rehabilitating, and upgrading existing infrastructure, (2) re-allocating reservoir storage and releases among changing water resources demands and users, and (3) providing some degree of ecosystem restoration and ecological services in heavily altered riparian and aquatic ecosystems. [3]

This proposal argues that any new USACE or basinwide management agenda for the future of the Mississippi River Basin needs to be inextricably linked to future visions for sustainably oriented forms of ecological industries and adaptive land uses along the Mississippi main stem, its tributaries, and its communities. To be fair, the USACE is attempting ecological adaptations in different parts of the basin, such as wetland restoration in the Upper Mississippi's pools. But I argue a much more visionary, coordinated approach is desperately needed, especially in regards to proposing carbon-neutral alternatives to the current status quo reliance on the extractive industries of oil, natural gas, and coal commerce, as well as industrial agriculture and the petrochemical industries.

While the Mississippi River Basin's namesake is the main stem, just as important economically and environmentally are its two predominant tributaries—the Missouri and the Ohio Rivers. The Missouri River supplies the majority of the river basin's sediment. The Ohio River, and by extension the lower portion of the Mississippi River, supply the majority of water volume. **[Figure 1]** In current form, two of the main negative environmental and economic impacts from development of the Mississippi River watershed ultimately manifest in the delta of south Louisiana and the Gulf of Mexico: 1) the "Dead Zone" phenomena caused by algae blooms due to excess nutrients from fertilizer runoff much further upstream; and, 2) wetland loss due to the starvation of sediments and expedited flows of water due to leveeing the river system. Both of these pose interconnected environmental and economic threats not just to the Gulf Coast and the New Orleans region, but also ultimately to the United States at large.

Wastes as Resources: Excess Nutrients, Suppressed Sediments, and Expedited Flows

The Dead Zone is primarily caused by excess levels of nitrogen and phosphorus nutrients discharged into the Mississippi River basin via runoff, creating a hypoxic area. The algae blooms—coupled with the large amounts of fresh water at the surface of the Gulf of Mexico—starve oxygen from reaching important marine life in the lower, heavier, and saltier areas of the gulf. According to the USGS, 70 percent of the nitrogen and phosphorus is the result of large-scale agricultural processes in the Lower Mississippi, Upper Mississippi, and Ohio sub-basins.[4] And 75 percent of all the nitrogen and phosphorus discharged into the river basin originates from only 9 of the 31 states drained by the river basin—Illinois, Iowa, Indiana, Missouri, Arkansas, Kentucky, Tennessee, Ohio, and Mississippi.[5] As these nutrients make their way unmitigated through the river basin, they significantly contribute to the Dead Zone phenomena in the Gulf of Mexico off the coast of Louisiana. The past five-year average size of the Dead Zone has been just under 6,000 square miles, roughly the size of the state of Connecticut.[6] **[Figure 2]**

Wetland loss is caused by a number of factors, such as oil and gas pipeline canals that cut into the natural system, in turn providing a direct conduit for saline intrusion. But more specific to the scale of the river basin, the two significant contributors that contribute to wetland loss are sediment suppression and expedited flows. Due to the damming of the sediment-rich Missouri River far up-river in the basin, a large portion of the sediment never makes its way to south Louisiana to help grow the land with seasonal flooding. **[Figure 3]** Coupling this wetland loss is the extreme leveeing of the majority of the river basin that expedites the flow of the waters and does not allow the river to flood to distribute the sediment (see Mississippi River Basin Atlas maps in the Appreciate + Analyze section of this book). What little sediment resource is left is forced out to the Gulf of Mexico, off the continental shelf, as if going through a hose spigot. **[Figure 4]**

Accepting that the Mississippi River Basin will not return to being a network of natural rivers, the speculation proposes the retrofit of the Mississippi's existing infrastructures and ecologies, at the river basin scale, into a networked "eco-industry" toolkit that holistically reconsiders dynamic relationships, both environmentally and economically, over the next hundred years and beyond. **[Figure 5]**

The intertwined toolkit proposes: filtering nutrients, collecting sediment, farming algae, refining algae fuel, distributing sediment, and distributing fuel. [Figure 6]

To achieve the toolkit, the Mississippi River Basin will be mighty once again by collecting, transforming, and distributing two important resources of the watershed that are currently mismanaged: excess nutrients and suppressed sediments. The speculation proposes physical engagement with existing locks and dams and their proximate underutilized,

de-urbanized spaces and varied land uses within the pools, lakes, and reservoirs along the Upper Mississippi and Missouri Rivers. By extension, it is pragmatic to implement this proposal as a viable option in relation to the backlog of maintenance to the locks and dams, a concern repeatedly expressed by the U.S. Army Corps of Engineers.
From the 2015 article "It's Time to Fix America's Infrastructure. Here's Where to Start,"

> *(Dams are) frightfully expensive to maintain. The US Army Corps of Engineers says it will take more than $25 billion to do all of the maintenance required at the 694 dams it manages, and without an infusion of cash it will take 50 years to complete the repairs. According to the Association of State Dam Safety officials, rehabilitation of all dams categorized as high-hazard would cost some $21 billion.*[7]

Rather than allowing the excess nitrogen and phosphorus to contribute to the algae bloom Dead Zone in the Gulf of Mexico, a series of stations could be placed at each of the locks and dams in the Upper Mississippi River (north of the confluence of the Mississippi and Missouri Rivers). These stations would filter the nutrients into algae biomass that could then be transported to deindustrialized sites along the Mississippi River (such as North St. Louis or East St. Louis, Illinois) to be refined into biofuel for local power use.

The proposed process of transforming nutrient overloads in the Mississippi River to algae fuel includes: (1) extracting nutrients through bacterial filters in underwater barrels to be used as plant food for the algae farm; (2) farming algae into biomass in detachable photobioreactor units strung together on pontoons; (3) transporting biomass via barges to retrofitted industrial sites along the river to refine algae fuel; (4) distributing algae fuel for local alternative energy supplies. **[Figure 7]**

Nutrient-rich Mississippi water flows through a nitrogen extraction filter. The filter consists of an underwater field of barrels containing colonies of bacteria that feed on nitrogen, amplifying the natural nitrogen cycle in the river. The bacterial filter at Mississippi Dam 26 contains 41,000 bacterial colony barrels. Each barrel is capable of removing 17 pounds of nitrogen from the Mississippi River every two weeks. The bacteria, which has concentrated nitrogen, is used as plant food for the algae farm. Algae farms require a great deal of space because algae occur at very low concentrations in water. The algae farm at Mississippi River Dam 26 floats on pontoons over 450 acres of reclaimed water surface on a distributary of the Mississippi River. This reclamation must be balanced with existing recreational, ecological, and migratory species aspects that actively occur in this zone. But if designed and integrated properly, it can be feasible. **[Figure 8]** It is projected that a single acre of algae can yield between 1,000 and 10,000 gallons of biofuel.[8] The algae are grown in photobioreactor units that are strung together into 300-foot bays. The bioreactor units can be easily detached from the bay and brought by boat to a processing facility where the algae are harvested and stored in silos. Algae biomass is transferred from storage silos onto barges docked on the shore of the Mississippi River. Barges bring biomass from the harvest sites along the river to the retrofitted abandoned industrial site in deurbanized, rust-belt cities such as St. Louis. Refined algae biofuel will locally power cities such as St. Louis. **[Figure 9]**

[Figure 1] (UPPER LEFT) Mississippi River Basin, indicating primary sediment from Missouri River (brown) and primary flow from Ohio and Lower Mississippi River (blue) (BACKGROUND) Confluence of the Mississippi River (foreground) and Ohio River (background), 2018 (image credit: Derek Hoeferlin)

[Figure 2] (UPPER LEFT) Mississippi River Basin, indicating areas in purple of excess nitrogen and phosphorous levels, as well as the "Dead Zone" in the Gulf of Mexico (UPPER RIGHT) Prototypical section of run-off from nitrogen and phosphorous sources (background) Typical example of a Midwest soybean farm, St. Charles County, Missouri, 2013 (image credit: Derek Hoeferlin)

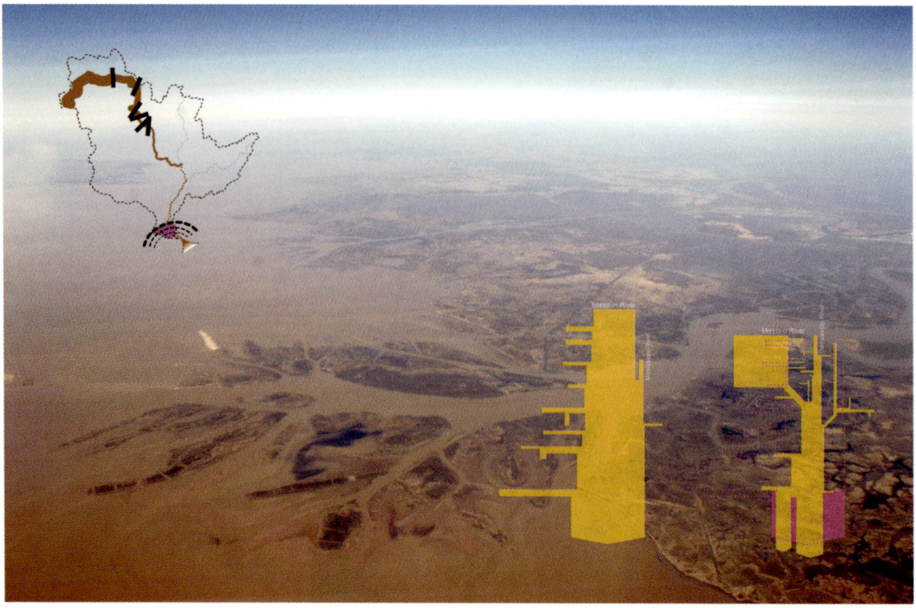

[Figure 3] (UPPER LEFT) Mississippi River Basin, indicating majority source of sediment in brown (LOWER RIGHT) Plumbing diagram schematic of past and present sediment load of Mississippi River Basin (BACKGROUND) Atchafalaya Basin Delta, Louisiana, at the Gulf of Mexico, with sediment discharge, 2010 (image credit: Derek Hoeferlin)

[Figure 4] (UPPER LEFT) Mississippi River Basin, indicating diagrammatic locations of levee system funneling water towards the Gulf of Mexico's Dead Zone (BACKGROUND) View from Eads Bridge of floodwall and Mississippi River during the 2019 flood, East St. Louis, Illinois, 2019 (image credit: Derek Hoeferlin)

The proposal will have different applications in the different sub-basins throughout the Mississippi River Basin. For instance, certain areas will be more conducive to transporting, farming, refining, filtering, and restoring. Each sub-basin over time will go through a transformation of land use as well. **[Figure 10]**

Granted, in the short term, the energy balance resulting from algae fuel may be underwhelming, as with other biofuels, such as soybean biodiesel and corn ethanol. But with more investment in research for alternative energy futures, in the long term algae fuel can be an alternate source of energy for the Mississippi River Basin, if the United States chooses to move towards an alternative energy future. Although there still is a vast amount of oil and gas remaining in both the Gulf of Mexico and the Bakken Shale Formation in the upper reaches of the Missouri River Basin, as well as a continued heavy reliance on coal for power in Midwest states like Missouri, these resources are still finite, polluting, unsustainable methods which have to soon become obsolete, whether it be in time or in policy. **[Figure 11]**

Simultaneously, the speculation proposes to sequester the sediment that is being trapped by the dams along the Missouri River, which carries the largest portion of sediment in the basin and releases it to be utilized as a needed resource for the current and future wetland restoration projects of the Mississippi Delta. There are two potential methods of retrieval and release of the trapped sediment from behind the dams, both coming with their pros and cons, costs, and benefits. One would be to dredge the sediment and ship it downriver to the Gulf Coast via barge, rail, or truck. This would certainly be costly, as well as require enhanced navigation measures, particularly along the Missouri River, and the need for vast quantities of fuel, which in current form is diesel-powered barges. But in the future, new barge fleets should be envisioned that are designed with renewable energies for their power sources. This method would harvest the most sediment at once to be relocated elsewhere for beneficial use. A second technique would be to create a series of "sediment agitators" that would gather the sediment trapped behind the dams across the large reservoirs and deploy it via spillways or valves as adaptive design retrofits to the existing dams. **[Figure 12]** It is important to note that the sediment is not necessarily trapped directly behind the dams. Rather, it usually lies at the opposite end of the reservoir in what is defined as a lacustrine delta. The sediment would have to be removed from these deltas, and transported across the reservoir to be released to the other side of the dams. As hyperbolic as this sounds, there are precedents for sediment management strategies in more recent, large-scale dams around the world, such as in China's Three Gorges Dam, including "storing the clear and releasing the turbid, releasing turbidity contents, sediment flushing, and dredging."[9] The con of this method is loss of sediment in the water column as the sediment makes its way downriver to the Gulf Coast. However, the sediment will be beneficial along the way in restored riparian buffers as a result of this method. In short, the continued coastal wetland loss certainly is an issue of security for the future commerce of the entire Mississippi River Basin, and for the local safety of New Orleans and coastal communities in the face of climate change, sea level rise, and tropical storm surges.

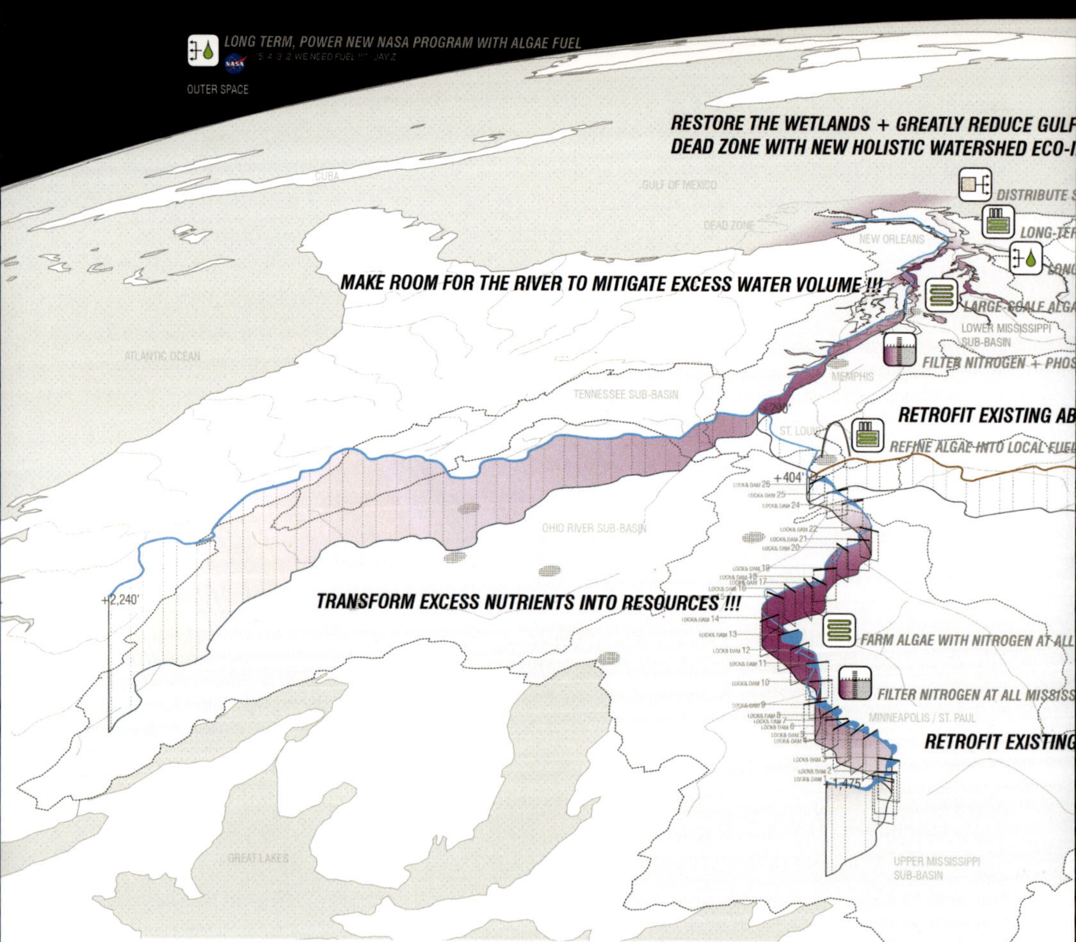

[Figure 5] Globe projection view of "from the Big Six to the Birds Foot" (image credit: Derek Hoeferlin, Jonathan Stitelman, Allison Méndez)

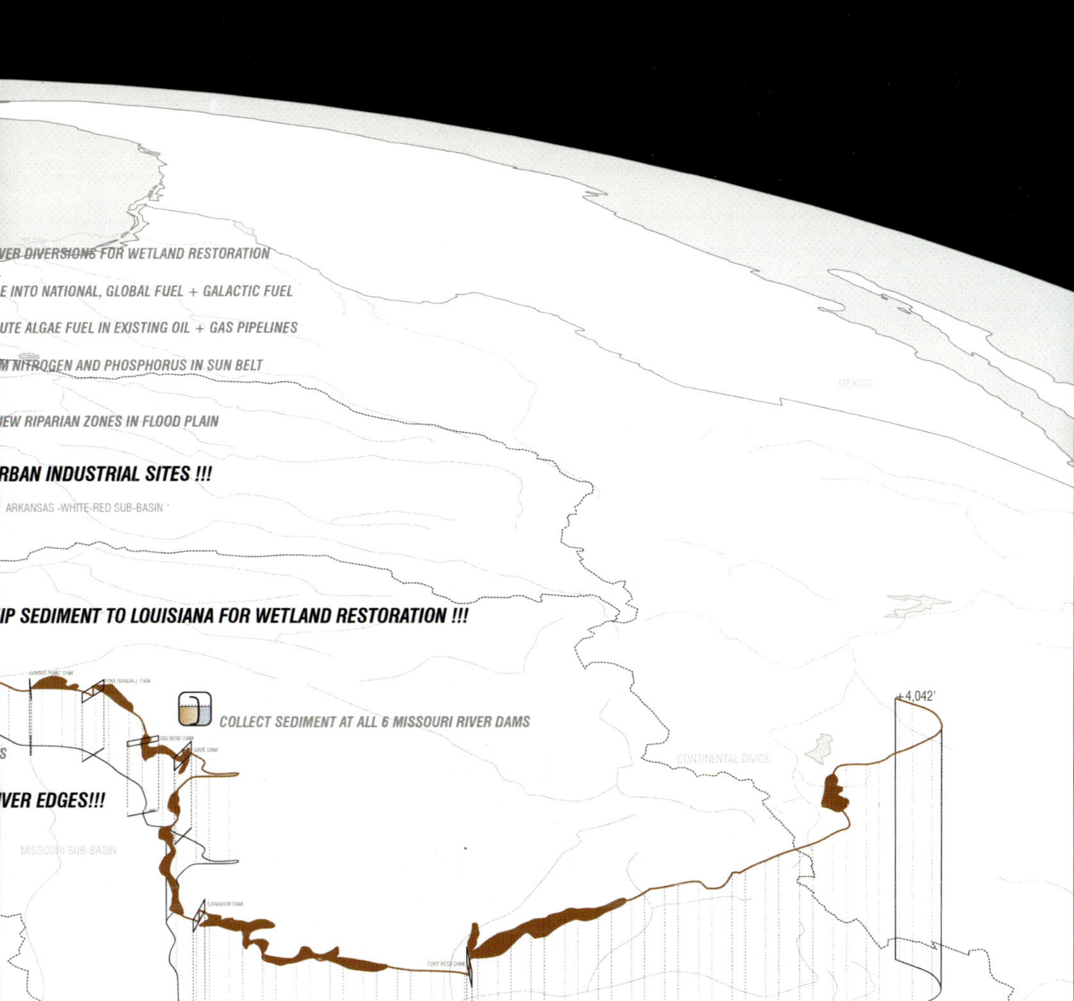

VER DIVERSIONS FOR WETLAND RESTORATION
E INTO NATIONAL, GLOBAL FUEL + GALACTIC FUEL
UTE ALGAE FUEL IN EXISTING OIL + GAS PIPELINES
M NITROGEN AND PHOSPHORUS IN SUN BELT
MEXICO
IEW RIPARIAN ZONES IN FLOOD PLAIN
RBAN INDUSTRIAL SITES !!!
ARKANSAS -WHITE-RED SUB-BASIN
IP SEDIMENT TO LOUISIANA FOR WETLAND RESTORATION !!!
+4,042'
COLLECT SEDIMENT AT ALL 6 MISSOURI RIVER DAMS
CONTINENTAL DIVIDE
VER EDGES!!!
MISSOURI SUB-BASIN

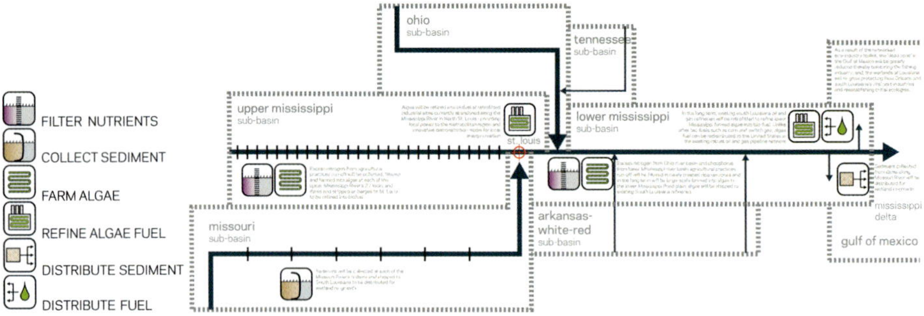

[Figure 6] "Eco-Industry" Toolkit (image credit: Derek Hoeferlin)

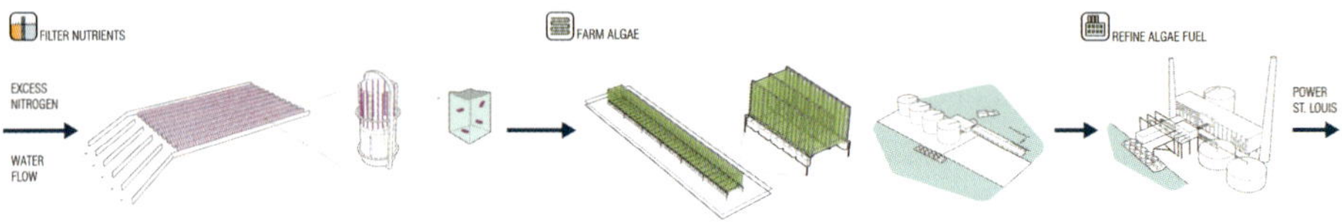

[Figure 7] "Eco-Industry" process of filtering, farming and refining (image credit: Derek Hoeferlin, Jonathan Stitelman)

[Figure 8] Vignette of "Eco-industry Algae Farm" integrating with ecology and recreation in a pooled area of the Mississippi River behind a lock and dam (image credit: Derek Hoeferlin, Allison Méndez)

Combined, this Watershed Architecture speculation could create a massive new eco-industry that adapts to climate extremes such as floods and droughts, and retrofits existing infrastructure networks. In the long term, the algae fuel will be an alternate source of energy for the Mississippi River Basin as the United States moves towards an alternative energy future, since the finite oil and gas resources from the Gulf of Mexico ultimately will become obsolete. Simultaneously, the proposal sequesters the sediment that is being trapped by the dams along the Missouri River and releases it to be utilized as a needed resource for the current and future wetland restoration projects of the Mississippi Delta. The continued coastal wetland loss certainly is an issue of national security for the future commerce of the entire Mississippi River Basin, and for the local safety of New Orleans and coastal communities in the face of climate change, sea level rise, and tropical storm surges. Thus, long-term interventions far "upstream" in the Mississippi River Basin can generate a new hydro-region economy that has local environmental and economic benefits throughout river communities and cities in the river basin, and also will help remediate two of the main threats to the New Orleans deltaic region.

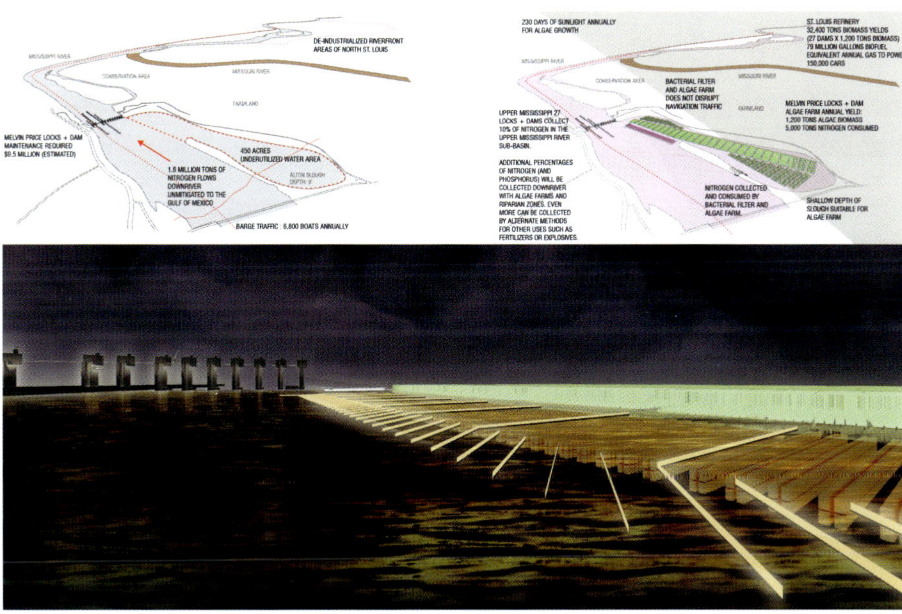

(**[Figure 9]**

ABOVE) Algae farm integrated into St. Louis regional network

(BELOW) Algae farm at Melvin Price Locks & Dam

(image credit: Derek Hoeferlin, Jonathan Stitelman)

[Figure 10] Mississippi River sub-basin retrofit zones (transport, farm, refine, filter, restore) (image credit: Derek Hoeferlin, L. Irene Compadre)

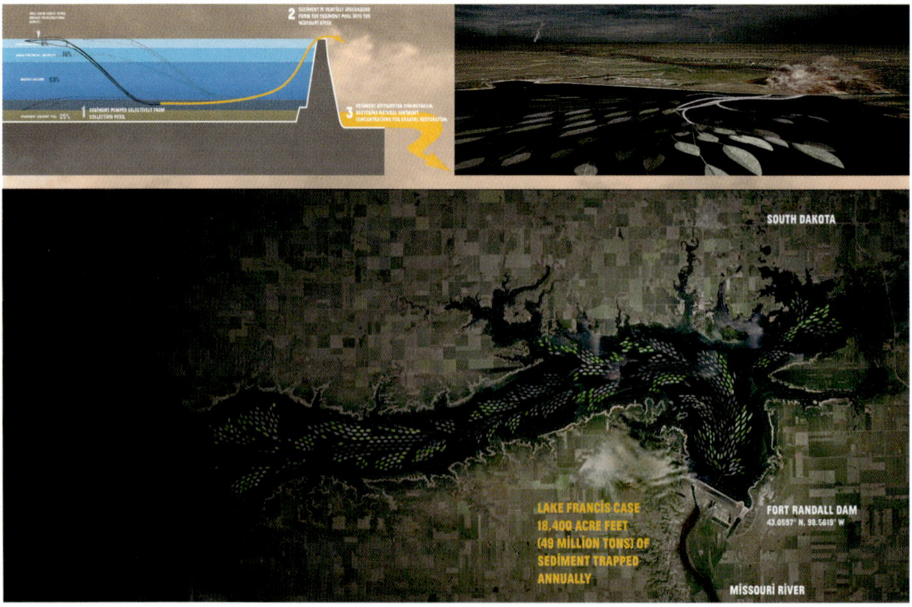

[Figure 11] Proposed "sediment agitators" within Missouri River dam reservoirs (image credit: Derek Hoeferlin, Jonathan Stitelman, Chad Fisk)

[Figure 12] Ameren Energy Company's "Sioux Energy Center" coal-fired power plant along Mississippi River during 2019 flood, West Alton, Missouri, 2019 (image credit: Derek Hoeferlin with Rachel Bartels, Missouri Confluence Waterkeeper)

1. Prior versions of this text and design proposal previously published in: Derek Hoeferlin, "Hey Delta Urbanisms!!! Don't Forget the Watersheds!!! Advocating for Watershed (Not Just Delta) Urbanisms" (Delft, The Netherlands: EAAE/ISUF International Conference Proceedings—New Urban Configurations, 2012); Derek Hoeferlin, L. Irene Compadre, Allison Mendez, Jonathan Stitelman, "from the BLIGHTY MISSISSIPPI to the MIGHTY MISSISSIPPI," in *New Constellations/New Ecologies* (Association of Collegiate Schools of Architecture [ACSA] Conference Proceedings, 2013); Derek Hoeferlin, "Chasing #Antidrone" in *Chasing the City*, eds. Joshua Nason and Jeffrey Nesbit (New York: Routledge, 2018); Derek Hoeferlin, "The Watershed Architecture of the Mississippi River Basin," in *The Anthropocene Review "The Mississippi Issue"* (SAGE Publishing, 2021), 1–12.
2. U.S. Army Corps of Engineers Mississippi Valley Division, accessed February 23, 2021, www.mvd.usace.army.mil/Missions/.
3. For a thorough explanation of the U.S. Army Corps of Engineers' management of the nation's water resources, see "National Water Resources Challenges Facing the U.S. Army Corps of Engineers," accessed February 23, 2021, https://www.nap.edu/read/13136/chapter/3.
4. "Nutrient Delivery to the Gulf of Mexico," U.S. Geological Survey, accessed February 23, 2021, http://water.usgs.gov/nawqa/sparrow/gulf_findings/faq.html.
5. Ibid.
6. https://earthsky.org/earth/dead-zone-gulf-of-mexico-2019, accessed February 23, 2021, and Louisiana State University and LUMCON (Louisiana Universities Marine Consortium) annual summer sampling, funded by NOAA (National Oceanic and Atmospheric Administration).
7. For information regarding U.S. Army Corps of Engineers infrastructure costs for maintenance and improvements, see Jordon Golson, "It's Time to Fix America's Infrastructure: Here's Where to Start," *WIRED* (January 23, 2015), accessed February 23, 2021, https://www.wired.com/2015/01/time-fix-americas-infrastructure-heres-start/.
8. http://www.reuk.co.uk/wordpress/biomass/biodiesel-from-algae/ and http://inhabitat.com/power-your-car-with-algae-algae-biocrude-by-livefuels/.
9. G. Schellenberg, C. Donnelly, C. Holder, R. Ahsan, "Dealing with Sediment: Effects on Dams and Hydropower Generation," *Hydro Review* 25 no. 1 (2017): 6–13, accessed February 23, 2021, https://www.hydroreview.com/2017/02/22/dealing-with-sediment-effects-on-dams-and-hydropower-generation/#gref.

from the Third Pole to the Nine Dragons

keeping the Water, the Power, & the People within the Mekong River Basin [1]

with Jess Vanecek & Rob Birch

More than 40 million inhabitants embrace the Mekong River Basin in Southeast Asia for its dynamic fluctuations of bountiful water resources.[2] To maintain abundance, the Mekong's namesake and its tributaries pulsate—radically—between wet and dry seasons that enable extreme variations in water levels. Communities not only embrace floods and droughts, they also rely on them for plentiful returns. Seasonal fluctuations provide positive, not negative, feedback loops—a truly unique precedent for adaptation and resiliency. But such dynamism is at risk. Due to past, present, and predicted anthropogenic stressors, the Mekong finds itself at a tipping point for two fundamental reasons. One, climate change will create major fresh water scarcities. Two, dam infrastructure that is designed to supply both energy and irrigation demands will exacerbate fresh water scarcities **[Figure 1]**.

In the past, but primarily in the 20th century, dams were seen as a productive model for an alternative energy source that utilizes a river's force to generate hydropower. However, in time, it has come to light that with dams come unintended consequences.[3] These include adverse alterations to riverine ecologies as well as disruptions to local, oftentimes less-advantaged, communities. These effects potentially outweigh the net gains that normally have been reserved for governments and transnational corporations. In what can be argued is perpetuating a 20th-century model of engineering-based design, the governments of Cambodia, Laos, Thailand, and China have set out on an aggressive campaign to construct many large-scale hydropower dams. Primarily constructed since just the early 2000s, most of these dams are funded by countries with geographies outside of the Mekong river boundaries.[4]

The alterations to the dynamics of the Mekong River Basin caused by climate change and dam infrastructure could decouple the critical link between the source at the Third Pole (Tibetan Plateau) and the mouth of the Nine Dragons (Mekong Delta). "From the Third Pole to the Nine Dragons" is a project that outlines a simple call for action for communities to understand their local futures within broader river-basin-scaled threats and adaptations. Due to the ambitious scope of operating at the scale of an entire river basin, the project must be "transboundary" in its approach. This means interrelated actions must span geopolitical boundaries in an effort to sustainably and resiliently engage complicated water resources through cooperative design and decision-making.[5] Part one of the call for action exposes six adverse threats from climate change and dam infrastructure projects on future fresh water availability. Part two engages with six resilient adaptations that keep the water, the power, and the people within the Mekong River Basin **[Figure 2]**. The recommendations culminate in an integrated and flexible design template mapping for the Watershed Architecture of the Mekong River Basin **[Figure 3]**. Ideally, in the future, the template will enable various Mekong communities to holistically understand the threats and adaptations, and be empowered with a proactive role in determining collective future designs for their river basin **[Figure-4]**.

Fresh Water Scarcities

In the upper reaches within the Tibetan Plateau (the Third Pole), rising temperatures and decreased precipitation lead to decreased snowpack, which results in significantly less snowmelt, a crucial source for the Mekong.[6] Simultaneously, in the Mekong Delta (the Nine Dragons), rising temperatures accelerate sea-level rise and saline intrusion. This stresses the current use of fresh water for agriculture, and contributes to deforestation of coastal mangroves that are crucial to ecologies and storm surge protection.[7]

Furthermore, unfettered urbanization in China and Southeast Asia leads to increased supply-demand for major energy sources, and at great distances. Mega-hydropower dam infrastructure that is already constructed, is under construction, or is in the planning and design phases, along the upper and lower reaches of the Mekong main stem, is the supply to meet portions of demand. **[Figure 5]**. Likewise, demands for agriculture prompt the construction of tributary irrigation dams, and while not affecting fresh water scarcity as much, they in turn prioritize certain regions' fresh water access over others.[8]

Combined, climate change and dam infrastructure threaten to disrupt flood-drought cycles, block fish migrations, and suppress sediments and nutrients. As a result, communities will be displaced, agriculture will be reduced, and power will be exported out of the basin to wealthier, more urbanized areas. Adaptations will be required to counter these threats. **[Figures 6-11]**

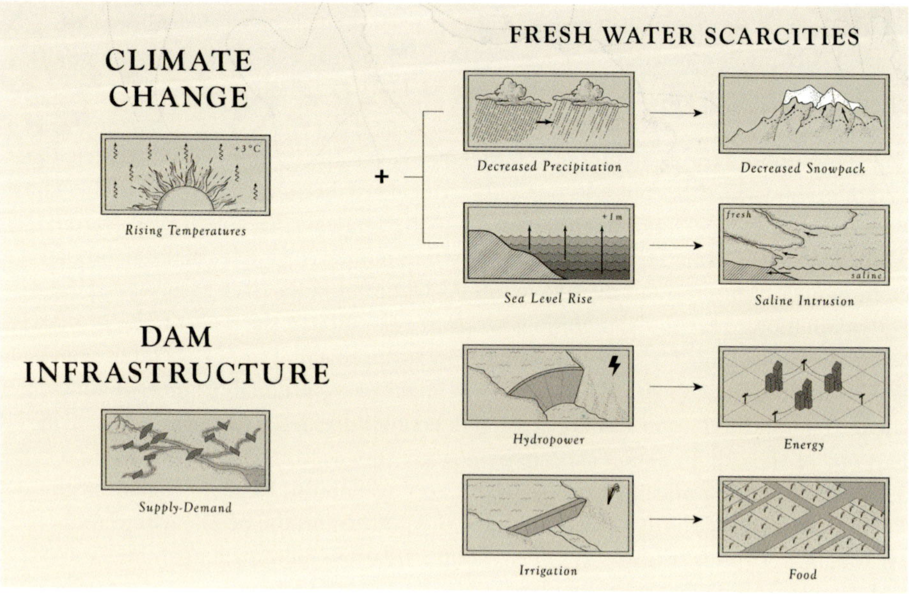

[Figure 1] Mekong River Basin freshwater scarcities as a result of climate change and dam infrastructure projects. (Image credit: Derek Hoeferlin and Rob Birch)

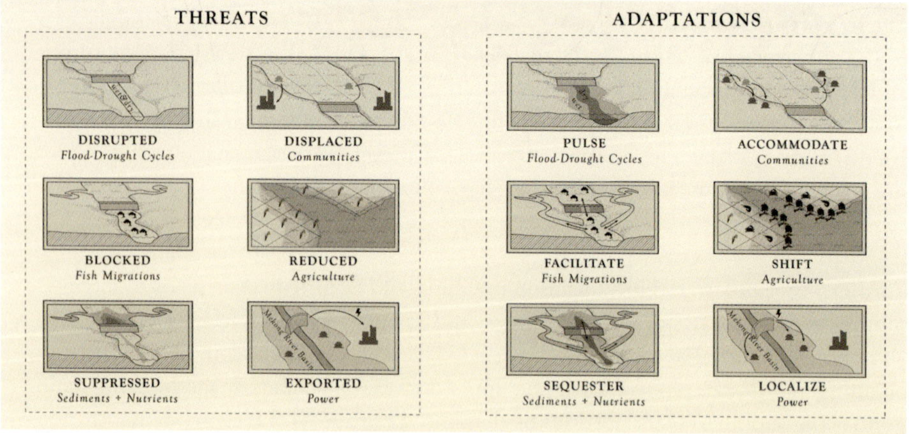

[Figure 2] Transboundary toolkit of the Mekong River Basin (Image credit: Derek Hoeferlin and Rob Birch)

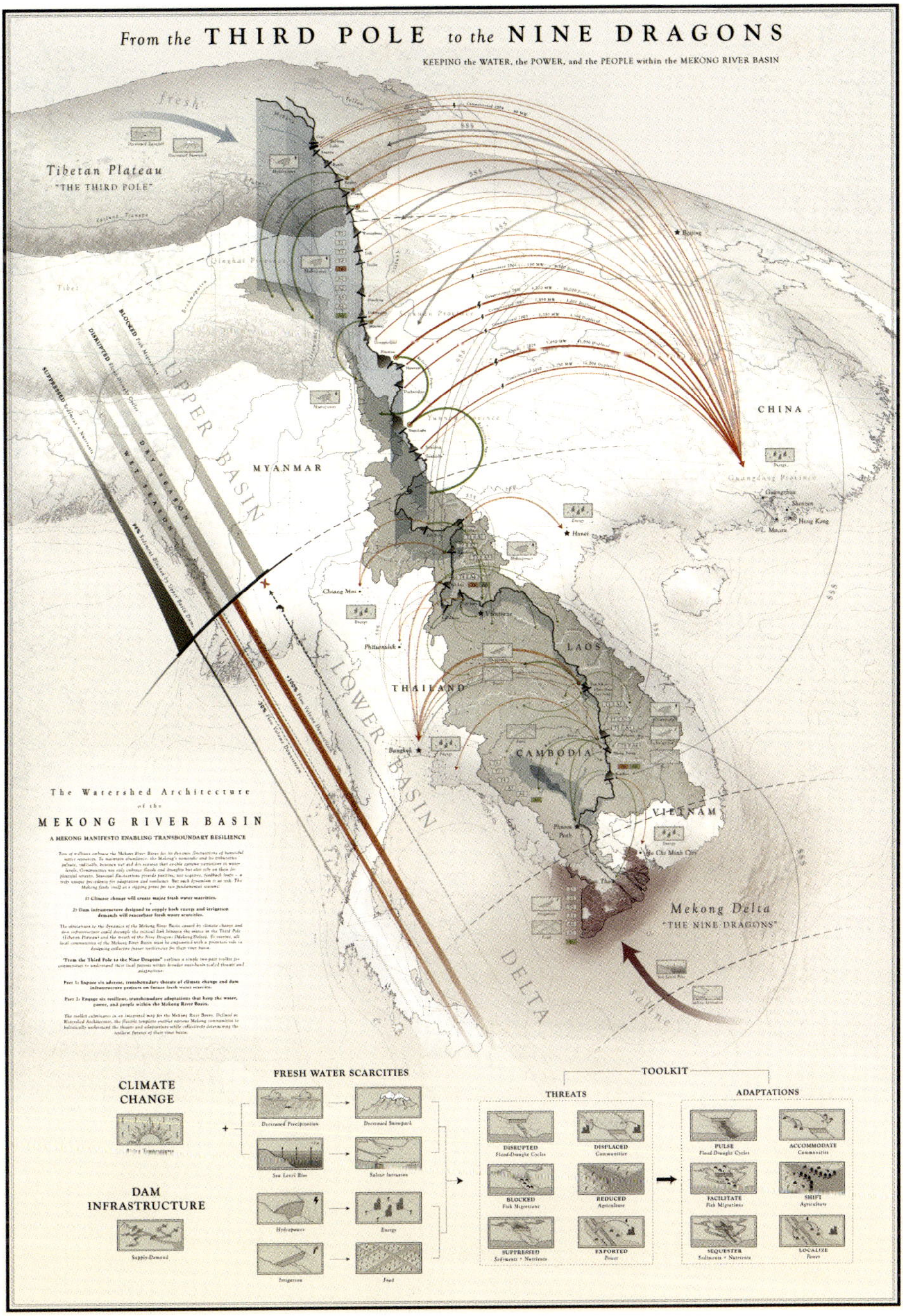

[Figure 3] The Watershed Architecture of the Mekong River Basin (Image credit: Derek Hoeferlin, Jess Vanecek and Rob Birch)

Source

Mouth

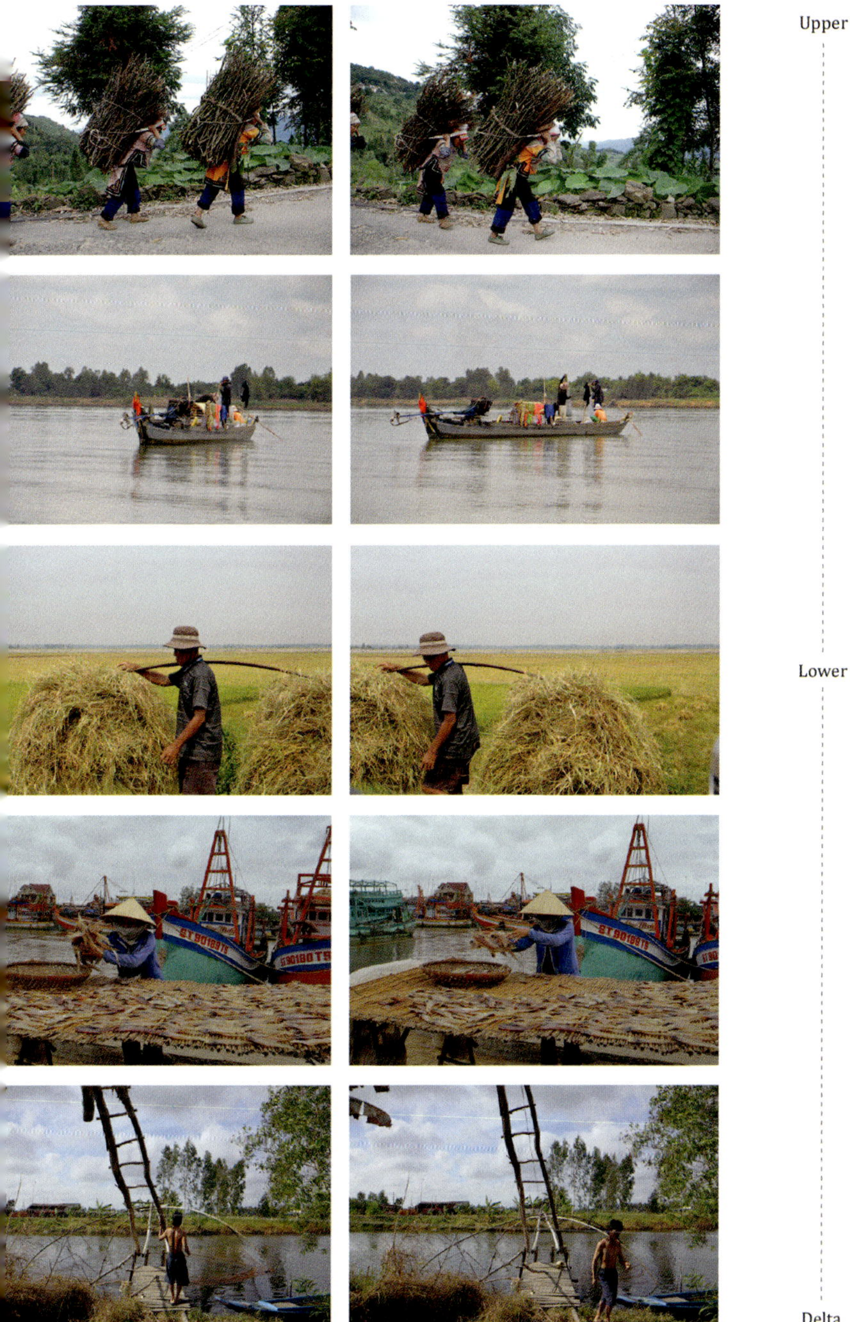

[Figure 4] Upper, lower, and delta communities of the Mekong River Basin and its surroundings, from Yunnan Province, China to the Mekong Delta, Vietnam (Image credit: Derek Hoeferlin)

Threat 1: Disrupted Flood-Drought Cycles

Increased severe weather events alter the historical benefits of flood-drought cycles by delivering more intense floods and sustained droughts, along with shifts from the typically annual fluctuations to multiyear durations that can deliver devastating consequences. Dams tend to regulate more consistent flow between flood and drought cycles, which is antithetical to the natural pulse of the Mekong system.[9] In addition, dams can be regulated by upstream countries such as Laos and China, regardless of corresponding climate stressors such as the most recent sustained droughts of 2019 to 2021, in turn causing uncertainties for the downstream countries of Cambodia, Thailand, and Vietnam.[10] Finally, the Mekong's Tonlé Sap Lake region typically reverses its flow in the wet season due to massive monsoons upriver, which provides a tremendous source for fisheries. If dams continue in their current form and operation, this radical reversal may cease in the near future, resulting in serious issues for the fish migrations in the Mekong.[11] For propagation, fish make seasonal journeys over vast distances up and down the Mekong and its tributaries. Dams block migrations, delivering dire consequences for crucial fishery supplies in the Mekong, and particularly so in the Tonlé Sap Lake region.[12]

Adaptation 1: Pulse Flood-Drought Cycles

The Mekong's future must entail transboundary water management strategies to facilitate the reestablishment of the flood-drought cycles. This may require the removal of dam infrastructure, but more realistically, would mandate the adaptation of existing dams and development of new proactive design standards that require these structures to allow seasonal pulses for various demands downstream. There is a positive transboundary precedent. During the extreme drought of 2016 in the delta, the Chinese government released water from upper basin reservoirs as requested by Vietnam.[13] However, such reactionary solutions to immediate crises are not sustainable. For true sustained transboundary coordination, as well as agreed-upon regulations, it is crucial for China to quickly become a "member state" of the Mekong River Commission for Sustainable Development (MRC), rather than China's current, and nonbinding, "dialogue member" status. This would allow investigating implementation strategies that propose moratoriums on any further dam infrastructure construction until local Mekong communities have adequate input. Although the MRC is greatly improving the monitoring of challenges across the basin, along with international data sharing, more robust, socially engaged methods will need to be coordinated throughout the basin for communities to hold governments and corporations accountable.[14] One option is to advocate for the design disciplines to become much more involved in facilitating such complex decisions. Design-based, multidisciplinary workshops can bring together various interest groups, opinions, academic research, and government agencies, thereby assisting the mission of the MRC.[15] In terms of physical design options that can accommodate important ecological factors, such as fish migrations, for instance, retrofitting existing or proactively designing future dam infrastructure could allow fish migrations during appropriate seasonal cycles. This is a monumental design challenge, as current global technologies of fish ladders and conveyances, designed for other river basins with far less fish, cannot cope with the massive amount

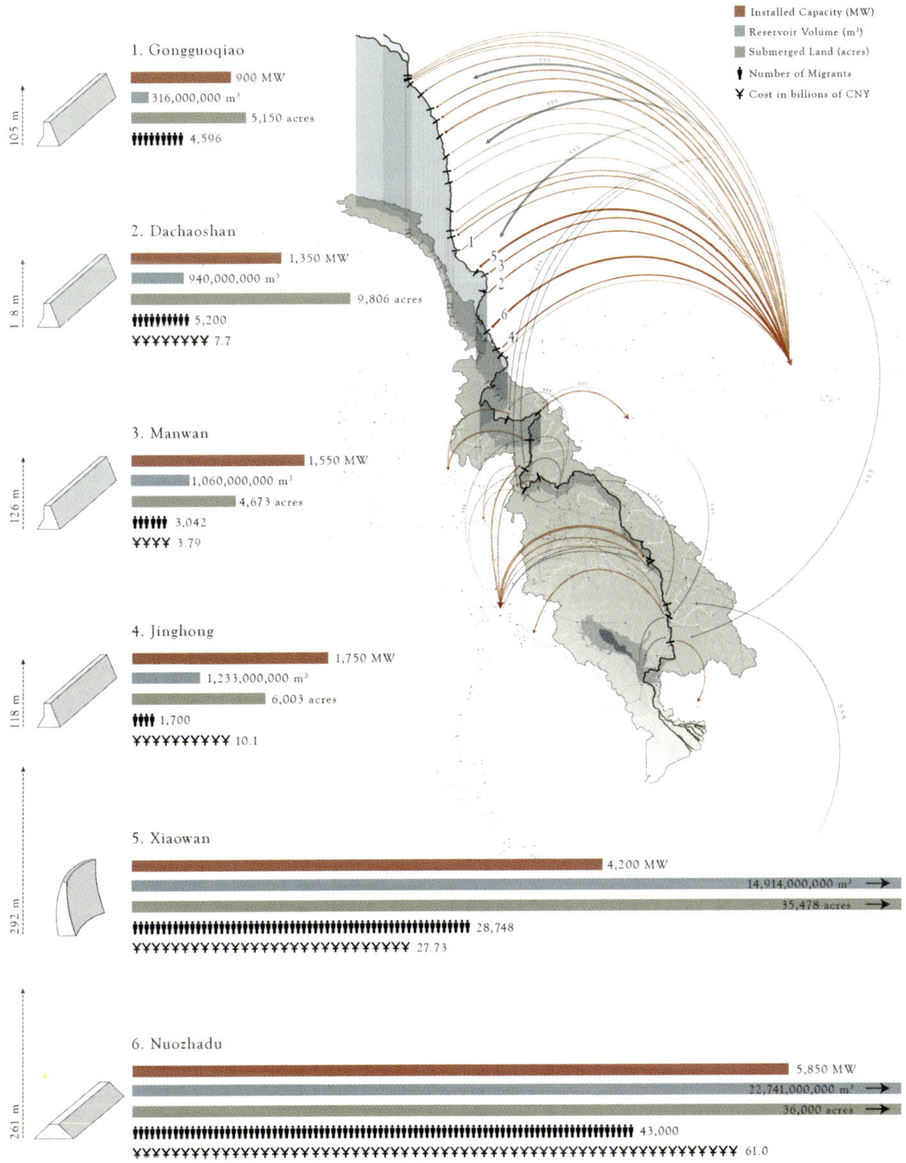

[Figure 5] Dam infrastructure and power distribution of the Mekong River Basin
(Image credit: Derek Hoeferlin, Jess Vanecek and Rob Birch)

[Figure 6] Houses elevated to accommodate natural flood-drought cycle, Tonle Sap region, Cambodia, 2010 (Image credit: Derek Hoeferlin)

[Figure 7] Near the Don Sahong dam site, Si Phan Don, dry season, Cambodia/Laos border, 2011 (Image credit: Derek Hoeferlin)

[Figure 8] Example of soil with high salinity, Mekong Delta, Vietnam, 2011 (Image credit: Derek Hoeferlin)

of fish migrations in the Mekong.[16] Designs will require safe passage of the fish upriver to spawn, and passage of the fish eggs downriver through the dams. In the recently completed Xayaburi Dam in Laos (the first dam on Laos's portion of the Mekong main stem), a fish ladder has been designed and proposed. However, since this ladder is unprecedented in both its scale and complexity, there are continued reservations with the ladder's potential for success, along with the continued perceived lack of transparent process in such adaptive design.[17]

Threat 2: Reduced Agriculture

Counterintuitively, dam infrastructure projects invert downstream agriculture effects. To deliver continuous hydropower during the wet seasons, upstream dams hold water, and during dry seasons, water is released as evidenced by the reservoirs behind them. Less water reaches floodplains during wet seasons and more water inundates areas needed for cultivation during dry seasons.[18] The pulse moves from dynamic to consistent, destroying river-edged agriculture in many areas. Rice cultivation radically diminishes too, since less fresh water reaches the Tonlé Sap and Delta. Increased periods of floods and droughts, due to climate change, exacerbate agricultural conditions, while saltwater intrusion threatens rice cultivation.[19] Additionally, dam infrastructure traps sediments and blocks nutrients from making their way throughout the Mekong, with most consequences on the delta and Tonlé Sap regions of Vietnam and Cambodia. Sediments and nutrients are critical for agricultural areas in the Lower Mekong, especially for rice cultivation. Lack of sediment also causes more riverbank

[Figure 9] Mangrove polyculture farm, Mekong Delta, Vietnam, 2011 (Image credit: Derek Hoeferlin)

erosion downstream.[20] Sediment mining dredge operations for construction and navigation management also threaten bank stability.

Adaptation 2: Shift Agriculture

If future dam infrastructure projects are managed to pulse in service of downstream agriculture, riverine edges and floodplains in Thailand, Laos, and Cambodia's Tonlé Sap region may sustain current practices, with moderate adaptation. Yes, the Mekong Delta will receive more fresh water, sediment, and nutrient supply as well, but this will not be enough to combat the climate change effects of sea-level rise and saltwater intrusion. The Mekong Delta "rice bowl" will need to continue a potentially radical shift. Currently, farmers are beholden to Vietnam's "rice first" policy, requiring three harvests per year.[21] The stresses of meeting such a policy are difficult. Farmers are already shifting from freshwater crops such as rice, to saline crops, such as shrimp and salt flats, but at their own expense. However, some of these adaptations, such as intensive shrimp farming which rely on methods like electroshock, have negative ecological results. Alternate methods, such as "mangrove polyculture farming" sustainably rotate shrimp, crabs, and mud clams, while utilizing replanted mangrove forests.[22]

Threat 3: Exported Power

In this context, most of the power generated from dam infrastructure is planned to be exported outside of the Mekong's less wealthy countries and provinces (Laos, Cambodia, Yunnan Province) to wealthier, urbanized regions (Thailand, Vietnam, and China's

[Figure 10] Urbanized demand for energy via hydropower, Bangkok, Thailand, 2011
(Image credit: Derek Hoeferlin)

Guangdong Province). Arguably, governments working hand in hand with global energy conglomerates will reap financial benefits, while local communities may suffer. During my Xayaburi site visit, I learned that the project is being 75-percent funded by Thai banks, and developed and operated by the Thai-based Xayaburi Power Company, with the remaining 25 percent funded by the Lao government. Ninety-five percent of the power will be exported to Thailand. But this will be the case for the next 30 years, when operation of the dam will be returned completely to Laos. How will local communities benefit during these 30 years? Furthermore, the construction of dam infrastructure displaces communities due to the filling of reservoirs. This has been happening for years in China's Yunnan Province. And recently this is the case in Laos, with the Xayaburi Dam. Left unchanged, this will continue with more planned megadams in Yunnan, Laos, and Cambodia.

Adaptation 3: Localized Power

To sustain transboundary river basin resiliency, communities must strive for localized power. One effective action would be to stop transporting current majorities over large distances, outside of the Mekong River Basin. This may require no more large-scale dam infrastructure projects, but that is unrealistic given current growth projections. Instead, hydropower could be rerouted for local distribution. This is actually a simple task since once hydropower is generated and transmitted into the grid, it can be routed anywhere, which, arguably, is easier to locally distribute than over major distances. The development of decentralized modes of renewables, where efficiently available, including solar, geothermal, biofuels such (e.g., algae) and of course wind, should

[Figure 11] Fishing community, Mekong Delta, Vietnam, 2011 (Image credit: Derek Hoeferlin)

also be considered. The smaller the scale and more local the distribution, the more compatible it will be with local communities. In terms of trade-offs, if funded by areas outside the Mekong, local communities can export crops and goods, for mutual benefit. Social programs must be enabled, along with physical adaptive designs. Although I witnessed well-constructed, relocated communities while at my Xayaburi Dam site visit, it remains unclear if such social programs have been offered. The same holds true for communities affected by climate change, such as altered agriculture or fisheries, potentially leading to climate change refuges. This is a challenging design solution, but it possibly speaks most to the core definition of resiliency.

Conclusion

The need for transboundary cooperation and design solutions are critical in the future of adaptive, water-based design, especially when it comes to a better understanding of coupling the challenges of climate change and dam infrastructure across entire river basins. The threats are clear and the adaptations are feasible. However, these should be carefully, and variably, implemented in different reaches of river basins, understood alongside with multiple interest groups and at multiple scales. The proposed *Watershed Architecture* at the Mekong River is proposed to be variably implemented in the upper, lower, and delta reaches of the basin **[Figures 12-15]**.

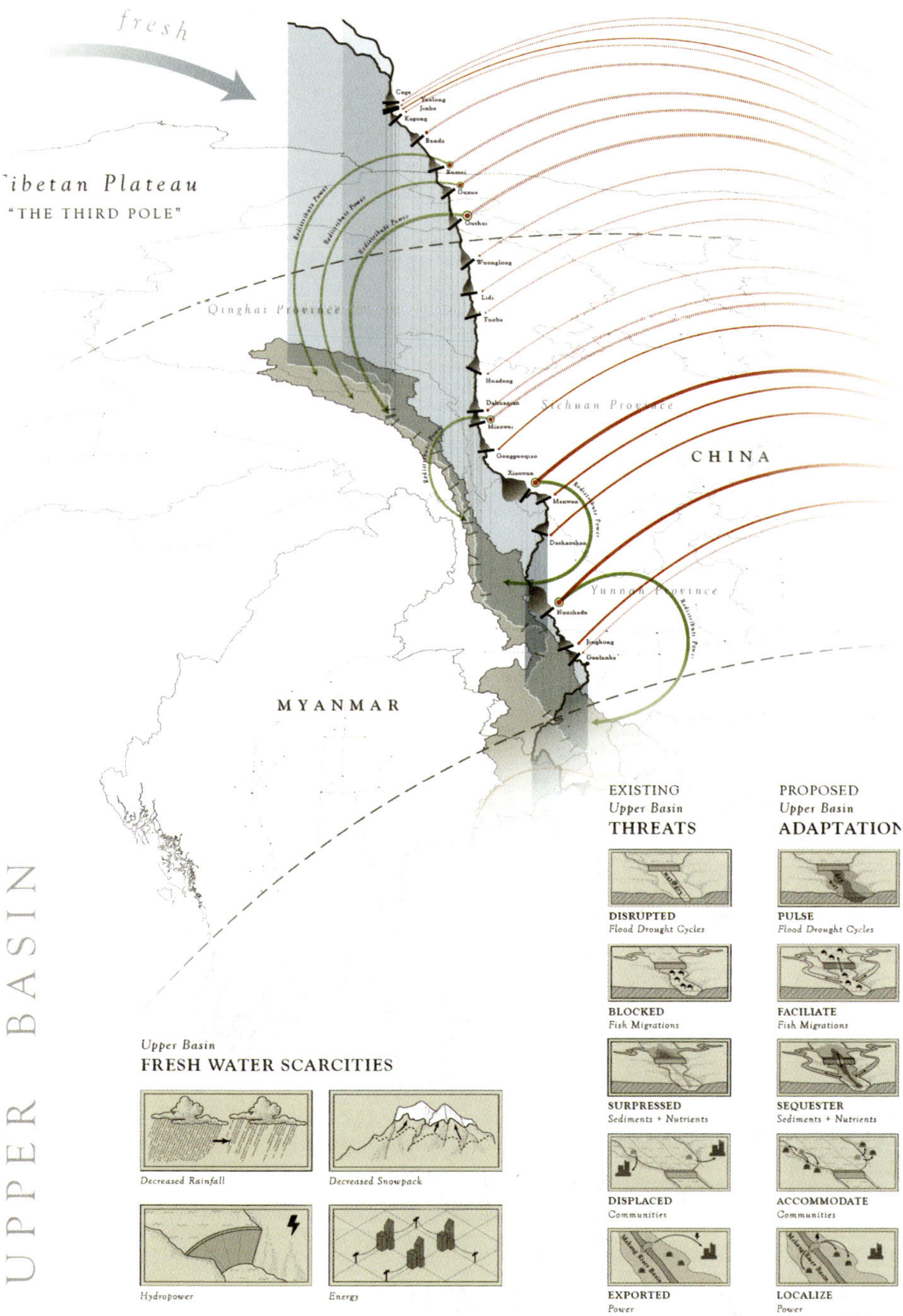

[Figure 12] Proposed toolkit measures in the Upper Mekong River Basin (Image credit: Derek Hoeferlin and Jess Vanecek)

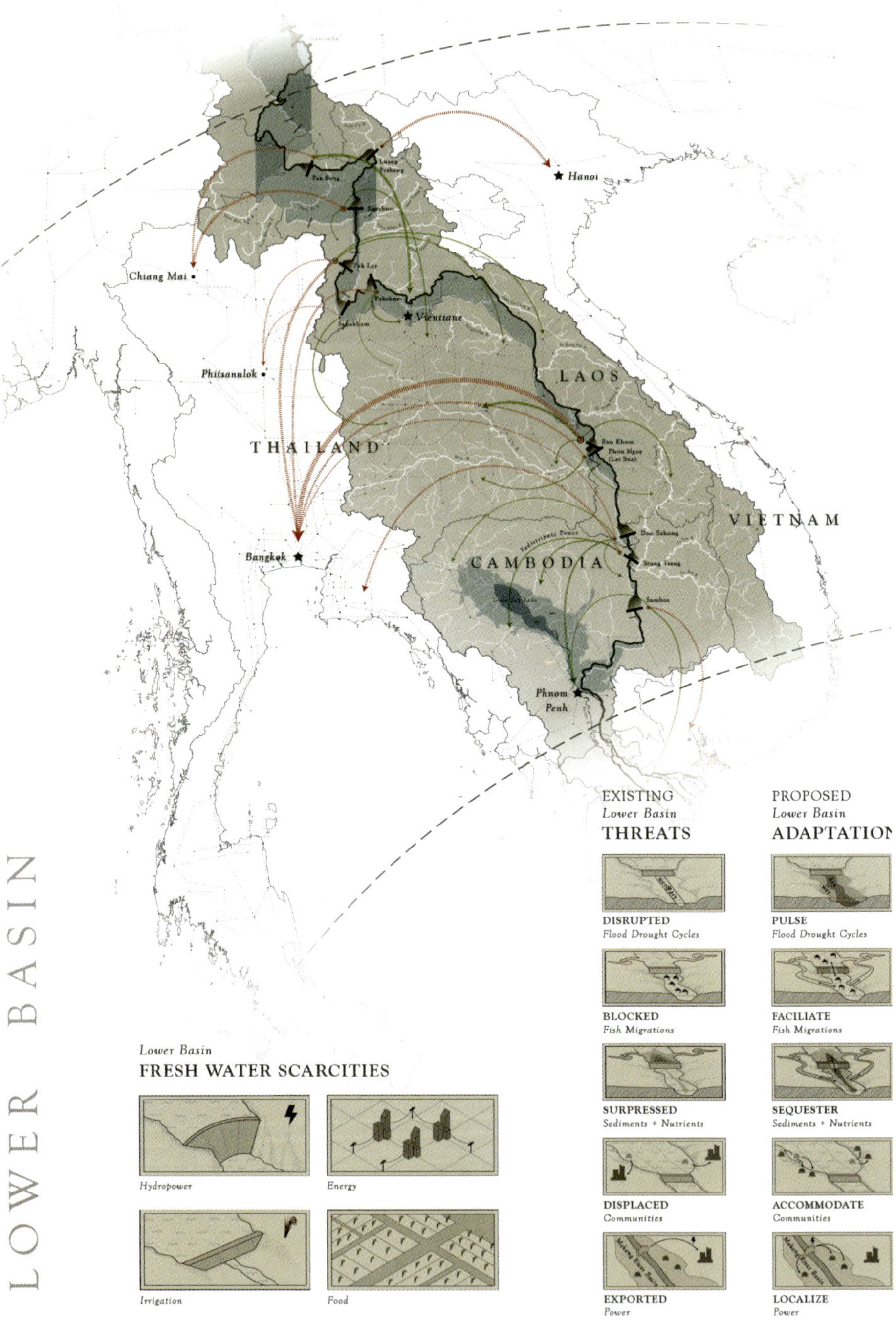

[Figure 13] Proposed toolkit measures in the Lower Mekong River Basin (Image credit: Derek Hoeferlin and Jess Vanecek)

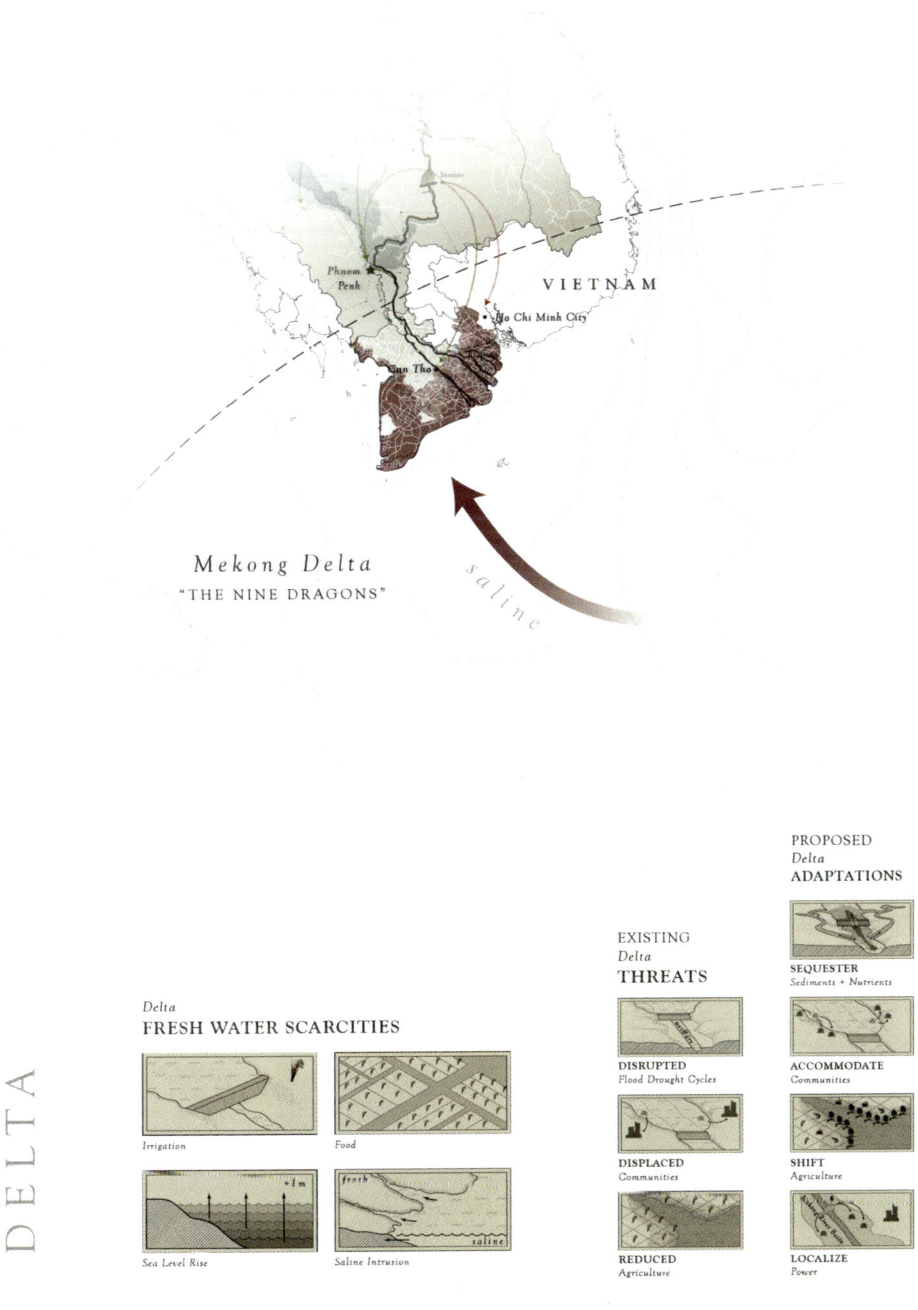

[Figure 14] Proposed toolkit measures in the Mekong Delta (Image credit: Derek Hoeferlin and Jess Vanecek)

Ethnic minority community, Yunnan Province, China (technically in the Red River Basin, immediately adjacent to the Upper Mekong River Basin), 2007 (Image credit: Derek Hoeferlin)

Typical riverbank seasonal agriculture threatened by future dam reservoirs in the Lower Mekong River Basin, Stung Treng, Cambodia, 2011 (Image credit: Derek Hoeferlin)

Fishing net and canal threatened by saline intrusion in the Mekong Delta, Can Tho Vietnam, 2011 (Image credit: Derek Hoeferlin)

[Figure 15]

1. Portions of this chapter previously published in: Derek Hoeferlin, "The Watershed Architecture of the Mekong River Basin," in *Journal of Architectural Education "H20 Issue,"* 74:1, 70–82 (Routledge/Taylor & Francis, 2020).
2. International Rivers, *Lancang River Dams: Threatening the Flow of the Lower Mekong,* PDF file (2013), 1.
3. Yukako Ono, "Mekong River Nations Face the Hidden Costs of China's Dams: Dozens of Projects Threaten Agriculture and Fishing in Southeast Asia," *Asian Review* (9 May 2018), accessed 30 October 2019, https://asia.nikkei.com/Spotlight/Cover-Story/Mekong-River-nations-face-the-hidden-costs-of-China-s-dams.
4. Hannah Beech, "Our River Was Like a God: How Dams and China's Might Imperil the Mekong," *New York Times* (12 October 2019), accessed 15 October 2019, https://www.nytimes.com/2019/10/12/world/asia/mekong-river-dams-china.html.
5. UN Water, *Transboundary Waters,* accessed 15 October 2019, https://www.unwater.org/water-facts/transboundary-waters/.
6. International Rivers, *Lancang River Dams: Threatening the Flow of the Lower Mekong,* 2.
7. Mekong River Commission, *Climate Change,* accessed 30 July 2019, http://www.mrcmekong.org/topics/climate-change/.
8. Mekong River Commission, *Integrated Water Resources Management-based Basin Development Strategy for the Lower Mekong Basin 2016–2020,* PDF file (2016), 18–19.
9. Ibid., 20.
10. Dominic Faulder, "Dams Threaten Way of Life in Mekong Countries: Thailand, Vietnam, Cambodia Blame China and Laos for Drought Conditions," *Nikkei Asian Review,* 30 July 2019, accessed 30 July 2019, https://asia.nikkei.com/Economy/Dams-threaten-way-of-life-in-Mekong-countries.
11. Fred Pearce, "The Damming of the Mekong: Major Blow to an Epic River," *Yale Environment 360,* 16 June 2009, http://e360.yale.edu/features/the_damming_of_the_mekong_major_blow_to_an_epic_river.
12. Bin Kang, Lisa Perret, Yungang Li, Daming He, "Are the Fish of the Upper and Lower Mekong Interconnected?" *Chinese Journal of Oceanology and Limnology* 27, no. 2 (May 2009): 400–407.
13. Mekong River Commission, *The Effects of Chinese Dams on Water Flows in the Lower Mekong Basin* (6 June 2017), accessed 30 July 2019, http://www.mrcmekong.org/news-and-events/news/the-effects-of-chinese-dams-on-water-flows-in-the-lower-mekong-basin/.
14. *Mekong River Commission Strategic Plan 2016–2020,* accessed 15 October 2019, http://www.mrcmekong.org/highlights/strategic-plan-2016-2020/.
15. Mekong River Commission, "About MRC," accessed 30 July 2019, http://www.mrcmekong.org/about-mrc/.
16. Kirk Herbertson, International Rivers, *Sidestepping Science: Review of the Powry Report on the Xayaburi Dam,* PDF file, (2011).
17. Kirk Herbertson, "Dams and the Politicization of Science: A Precautionary Tale of Xayaburi Dam's Fish Passage," *World Rivers Review* 29, no. 4 (December 2014): 6–7.
18. Timo Räsänen, Jorma Koponen, Hannu Lauir, and Matti Kummu, "Downstream Hydrological Impacts of Hydropower Development in the Upper Mekong Basin," *Water Resources Management* 26, no. 12 (September 2012): 3495–3513.
19. Tyson Roberts, "Downstream Ecological Implications of China's Lancang Hydropower and Mekong Navigation Project," *Smithsonian Tropical Research Institute* (2011).
20. International Rivers, *Lancang River Dams: Threatening the Flow of the Lower Mekong,* 3.
21. Jane Perlez, "Drought and 'Rice First' Policy Imperil Vietnamese Farmers," *New York Times* (28 May 2016), accessed 30 July 2019, https://www.nytimes.com/2016/05/29/world/asia/drought-and-rice-first-policy-imperil-vietnamese-farmers.html?_r=0.
22. International Union for Conservation of Nature, "A Model Shrimp Farm in the Mekong Delta" (22 September 2015), accessed 30 July 2019, https://www.iucn.org/content/model-shrimp-farm-mekong-delta.

from the Rheinquelle to the Leo Hollandicus

Integrating the Energies, the Economies, & the Environments in the Rhine River Basin

with Jess Vanecek, Paul Wu, & Han Meyer

Over the last two centuries, the Rhine River has been significantly modified in the process of creating a modern, industrialized society. In its current phase, climate change and existing patterns of industrialization are creating uncertainties regarding the utilization of the Rhine River. The course of development has proven to be unsustainable and is coming to a close for two main reasons. First, the subjection of the natural system has reached its absolute limits, and second, the character and values of industrialized society are changing. As the backbone of the European community, the time has come for radical change in the concepts and implementation strategies within the Rhine River Basin. This sets the stage for a new period of industrialization within the basin, one that integrates methods of energy production, transboundary economics, and natural environments.

Three future opportunities emerge in response to challenges regarding the present utilization of the Rhine River. First, a renegotiation of navigation structures to accommodate and assist in the restoration of a nature-based river system. Second, the reintroduction of historic characteristics and land use patterns from the preindustrial period to strengthen the relationship between rivers, cities, and landscapes. Third, a reengagement with transboundary agreements that have allowed the Rhine to emerge as the urban and economic center of Europe.

Four driving forces of integration enable these future adaptions: energy transition, climate adaptation, the rise of a circular economy, and increased digitalization and robotization in regards to intermodalities. Necessary to facilitate these forces are a set of **eight implementable actions**, a constellation of measures aimed at rehabilitating the natural versatility of the water system and adapting to the changing logistics of energy supply and economies.

Ultimately, the current challenge for the Rhine is to create a fundamentally European story in which a new collective approach to the basin can be regarded as a "Grand Project" of the European community. At present, Europe is struggling with the question of what kind of role it can and should play. **"The Watershed Architecture of the Rhine River Basin"** project can become the framework for Europe's next phase of industrialization, a new European story, one focused on restoring and improving the natural environment through the sustainable combination of urbanization, mobility, environment, and economy. After all, the Rhine River Basin is still a central part of the economy and history of the European community

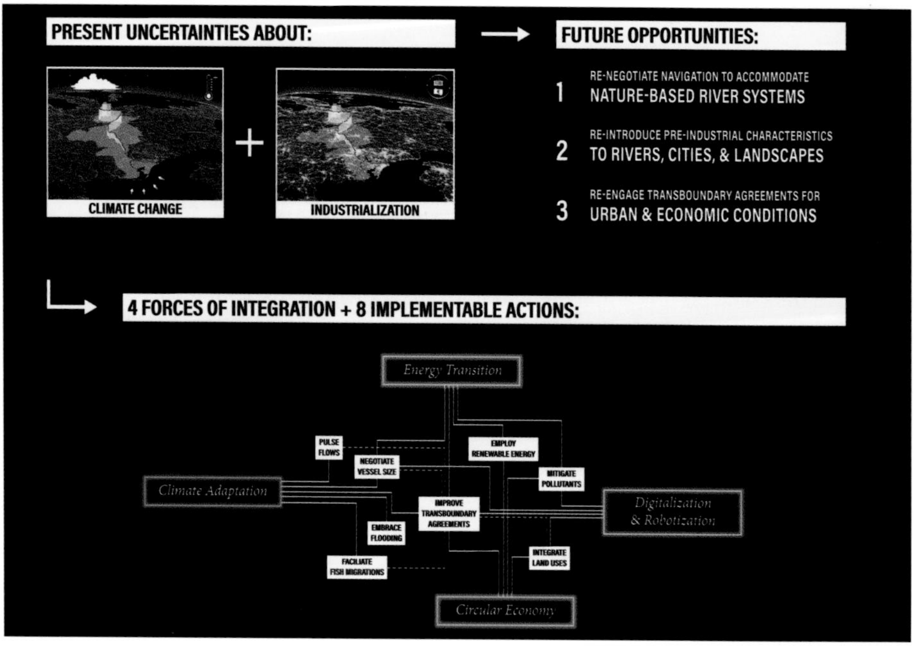

Toolkit for The Watershed Architecture of the Rhine River Basin
(image credit: Derek Hoeferlin, Jess Vanecek, Paul Wu, Han Meyer)

Neuhausen am Rheinfall with fish hatchery in foreground, Switzerland, 2018
(image credit: Derek Hoeferlin)

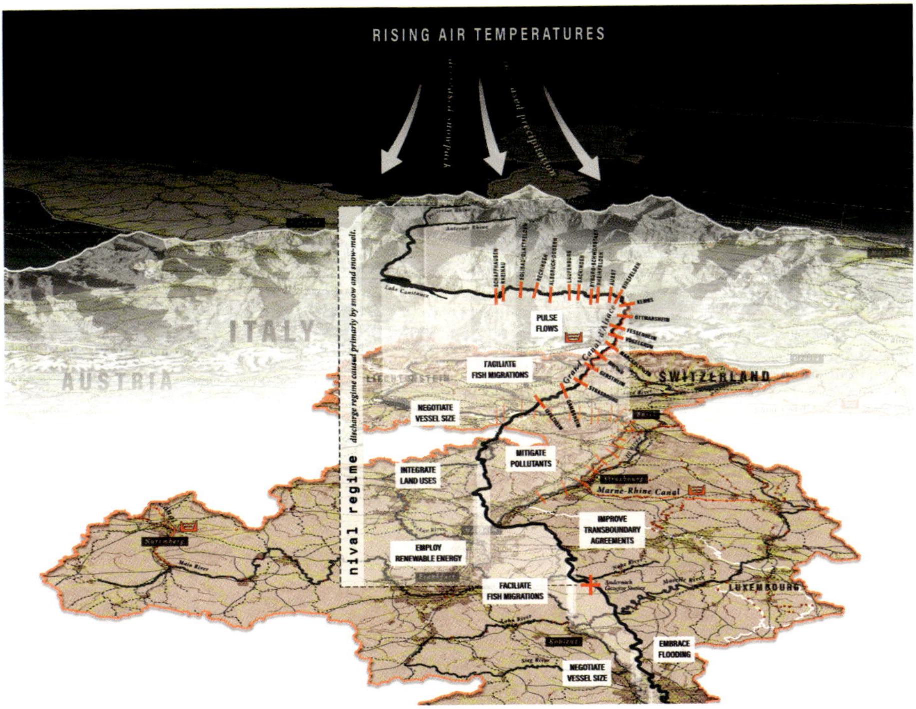

Upper Rhine River Basin actions (image credit: Derek Hoeferlin, Jess Vanecek, Paul Wu, Han Meyer)

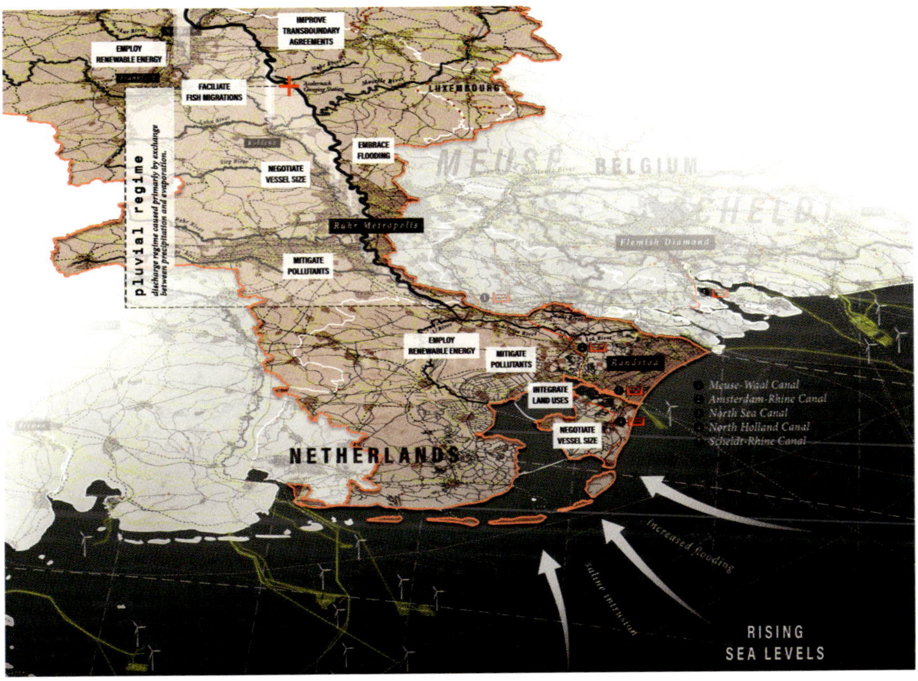

Lower Rhine River Basin actions (image credit: Derek Hoeferlin, Jess Vanecek, Paul Wu, Han Meyer)

The Watershed Architecture of the Rhine River Basin, situated in context within the central European "Blue Banana" economic and urbanization corridor (image credit: Derek Hoeferlin, Jess Vanecek, Paul Wu, Han Meyer)

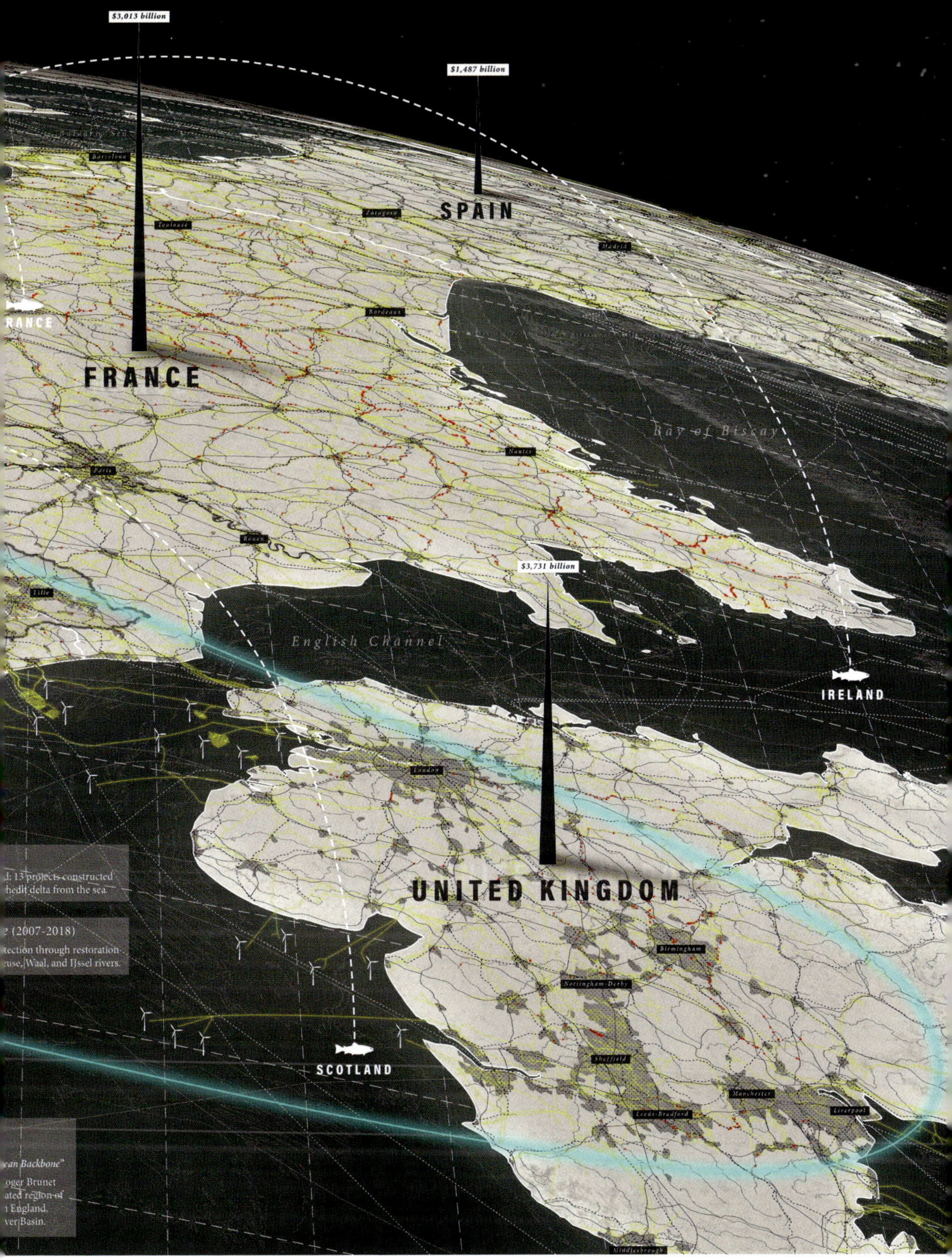
$3,013 billion
$1,487 billion
SPAIN
Barcelona
Toulouse
Zaragoza
Madrid
Bordeaux
FRANCE
Bay of Biscay
Nantes
Paris
Rouen
Lille
English Channel
$3,731 billion
IRELAND
London
UNITED KINGDOM
Birmingham
Nottingham-Derby
Sheffield
Manchester
Liverpool
Leeds-Bradford
SCOTLAND
Middlesbrough

Strasbourg, France, 2018 (image credit: Derek Hoeferlin)

Fort Pannerden, view towards Waal River, Netherlands, 2018 (image credit: Derek Hoeferlin)

Collaborate + Catalyze [C+C]

(or the need for transboundary engagement)

In part three, Collaborate + Catalyze [C+C], after Neeraj Bhatia's introductory essay "Advocacy," I feature four specific efforts in the Midwest region in the Mississippi River Basin. Although I have conducted several other collaborative efforts up and down the Mississippi River, mostly in the New Orleans deltaic region, as well as interdisciplinary workshops and engagements in the Mekong and Rhine, I have made the decision to return to, and feature, where I grew up, practice, teach, and currently live—St. Louis, and more broadly, the Midwest. The four projects constitute what I believe offer alternative forms of "engagement." In other words, the efforts are not driven by your typical community or participatory planning models. Although I believe these existing models are of tremendous use, I truly believe that in order to be able to comprehend the large-scale territorial implications—and the ambitions of "Watershed Architecture"—we will need different, oftentimes messy and creative, models of collaboration and engagement in the future. These include alternative modes of *field documentations, site interventions, and programmatic usages.*

The first effort, "Public Lab River Rat Pack," highlights alternative modes of *field documentations.* Collaborating with the citizen-science nonprofit Public Lab, I led an interdisciplinary seminar at Washington University in St. Louis in the spring term of 2016. Using Public Lab's mapping kits, we deployed big red balloons to take aerial photographs—over 35,000, in fact, over the course of the semester—of various river-edged conditions along the Mississippi River in the St. Louis region. The timing was important, because we were able to document in this short timeframe both one of the highest and one of the lowest river levels on record, all during the course of one semester.

The second effort, "FLOOD—FIGHT—FAIL," highlights alternative modes of *site interventions.* It was part of two exhibitions, first at *Art + Landscape STL*, curated by Gavin Kroeber, at the Granite City Arts and Design District (G-CADD) in Granite City,

Illinois (within the American Bottom floodplain), and then re-presented later at the *Decoys and Depictions* symposium and exhibition at Washington University in St. Louis, curated by Constance Vale. I contributed a didactic piece that marked the "what-if-the-levees-failed" scenario on a storefront in the G-CADD complex.

The third effort, "Territories—Watersheds—Infrastructures," highlights alternate modes of *programmatic usages.* As part of the Haus der Kulteren der Welt (HKW) "Mississippi: An Anthropocene River" project, I led another interdisciplinary seminar at Washington University in St. Louis in the fall of 2019 that collaborated with Continental Cement Company, Big Muddy Adventures, and the Pulitzer Arts Foundation. At Continental Cement Company's industrial site along the Mississippi River, we took over its platform barge for a day, and reprogrammed it as a reconstituted and hybridized series of "platform zones of dialogues and exhibits." The highlight of the event was a dynamic panel discussion that brought together multiple experts and points of view to speculate on the future viability of the Mississippi River Basin. I feature the transcript of this dialogue, as well as selected works from the "pop-up" exhibition.

The fourth effort, "Tracing Our Mississippi," returns to alternative modes of *site interventions.* As part of the *New Middles: From Main Street to Megalopolis, What Is the Future of the Middle City?* exhibition at "Exhibit Columbus" in 2021, co-curated by Iker Gil and Mimi Zeiger, I was honored to be part of the University Design Research Fellows cohort. My contribution was an abstracted model of the Mississippi River Basin, broken up into its six smaller sub-basins, constructed 800,000 times smaller than the actual watershed, and exaggerated 200 times in the vertical dimension. This was a three-dimensional interpretation of my *Mississippi River Basin Atlas*. Sited at the terrace of the Upland Pump House and adjacent to the nearby river, it was designed to encourage a one-to-one human scale interaction. The project culminated with a public program in Columbus to generate collective "Watershed Stories," co-organized with the artists Angie Tillges and Monique Verdin and my research assistants Nathan Stanfield and Paul Wu.

In full disclosure, these alternate forms of engagements are just that—alternatives. They do not offer solutions, and I realize they open themselves up for potential, and possibly fierce, criticism in regards to community engagement. Or even borderline hubris, given the scale of the challenges. The jury is out as to whether they even offer valid forms of "collaboration" or "catalyzation." But I hope they at least crack open new doors to new interactions and possibilities that address, debate, and offer future possibilities for trans-boundary river basin understandings, and ones that are not limited to our status quo. Because let's face it, the status quo quite simply does not work—no matter what the political points of view, or agenda-driven stakes in the game may be.

Advocacy

Engagement with the Territory

Neeraj Bhatia

The dilemma of participation / collaboration implies a closed system in which the options available for choice, and those who present them, cannot be challenged. Seeking to force the subject into compliance, a set of alternatives might thus be posed in such a way that "free-subjects," choosing for their interests in moderating harm, would end up serving the aims of this power.

—Eyal Weizman[1]

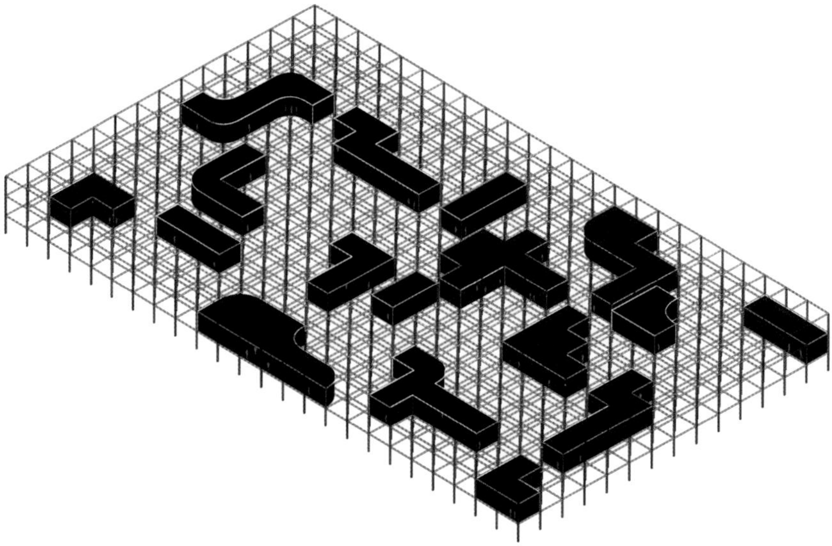

[Figure 1] Ville Spatiale, Yona Friedman (1959–), a collective framework containing individual, flexible and mobile pods (image credit: drawing by The Open Workshop/Alicia Hergenroeder)

As architecture increasingly interfaces with the scale of urbanism, architects are confronted with how to reconcile forms of control, inherent in any act of design, with a pluralistic series of subjects that are, and should remain, incontrollable. If we understand territory as an expression of forms of control between people and environment, when we encounter the scale of territorial design, the ramifications of such control become more invisible, impactful, and potentially dangerous. Participation in the design process has been a key mechanism for citizens to gain a voice and agency in developing the final design, but have these venues yielded meaningful forms of action? My contention is that at the intersection of participation in the design process (collaboration) and catalyzing these designs into material form (action) is the production of advocacy and future stewardship—critical components to having a citizenry engaged with their environment. How we enlist diverse voices into the design of the extra extra large needs to be reconsidered to gain transparency, empathy, and ultimately, have more meaningful impact.

The Emergence of Participation

Every act of design exerts some form of control over the environment and the users that inhabit it. As late modernism's architectural project grew in size to interface with urbanism, it exposed the increasing difficulty that modern architects had in recognizing the diversity of the subjects that would inherit and inhabit their visions. The fissures of social control were notably revealed by Team X in the critique of their CIAM mentors. Their criticism was in part due to Modernism's oversimplification of "the individual" who aggregated into a mass rather than a diverse public. This, coupled with top-down urban renewal and infrastructure projects that decimated cities and communities, incited this postwar generation to question how architecture, the city, and its inhabitants could find productive synergies. With emphasis on relational thinking, Team X's insistence on *habitat*—how dwelling meets landscape and culture—attempted to bring local voices into the conversation. Both the *stem* and *frame* as organizational models of late modernism were expandable and allowed for other components to be added that, in theory, had a specificity related to the subject.[2] Consideration of the individual inspired the "non plan" movement that advocated for "open ends," which enabled individuals to curate life from this kit of parts. Consider, for instance, the invention of the megastructure—a late-modern building type that became a diagram for the non plan goals and the city at large. **[Figure 1]** The megastructure was an attempt to distribute the architect's control to the individual. Consisting of a large frame (or, for the metabolists, a tree trunk) that organizes the diverse and transforming components of the city (or the leaves), the megastructure shifted the control of the architect to the collective frame, and within it, smaller components could be curated, designed, or constructed by the individual. Instead of the architect imposing order on society, they were reconceived as the designers of the infrastructure and systems, leaving the rest openended to enable individual choice and empowerment.[3] Despite the new forms of agency provided to the individual, the unit was subservient to the frame and thereby only as diverse and evolving as the frame permitted. Yona Friedman attempted to overcome this issue in his *Flatwriter Project* (1967–1971), wherein individuals were empowered with a flatwriter keyboard of 53 keys, each printing figures of various housing types. This act of self-planning was to allow nondesigners to understand the consequences of their choices, and by doing so, have the ability to make more informed decisions. Friedman's interest in having design-control transferred to the final user aligned with ideas espoused by Rudofsky's *Architecture without Architects* exhibition at the MoMA (1964–1965), wherein a series of architectures were put on display to show how communities had formed their own specific formal arrangements from reconciling various factors (climate, material, construction knowledge, etc.) related to specific ways of life. Rudofsky viewed these architectures as a source of inspiration and knowledge, overcoming the architect as the sole expert of form, stating, "Part of our troubles results from the tendency to ascribe to architects—or for that matter, to all specialists—exceptional insight into problems of living when, in truth, most of them are concerned with the problems of business and prestige."[4] Late modernism exposed the paradoxical challenges of architects working on the city—seeking both order and openness. With the end of modernism and the formation of countercultural movements in the late 1960s, participation became a key vehicle embedded in the design process as a way to offer agency to the subject. This shifted participation away from having agency within and upon the constructed form and into the design process itself, before form was fully conceived.

The Limits of Participation

From the ashes of modernism emerged a social strain of design that aimed to find more ground to learn from community groups and residents so that design offered a better fit to end users. The inclusion of citizen participation intended to create a form of citizen power, by redistributing power to those presently excluded from the political and economic process to have a voice in the decisions that would impact their future.[5] These forums take many different formats—surveys, educational workshops, engagement discussions, community think tanks, to name just a few. Acting as a microcosm for democracy itself, these initiatives require the participation of an informed citizenry as a way to redistribute power. But just like democracy, a particular framework needs to be put in place for the system to function and flourish, and most importantly to have people take action. Two critical criteria for a functioning democracy are the ability to go beyond necessity and having frameworks for negotiation where people are free and have an equal voice at the table.

The ability to go beyond day-to-day necessity and consider what is best for the collective and for today, tomorrow, and the future is the cornerstone of a functioning democracy. Using ancient Greek civilization—where the first democracy was formed—to model her argument, Hannah Arendt revealed a stark separation between the roles of the private and public realms.[6] For Arendt, the private realm in ancient Greece operated through strict hierarchy and attended to the necessities of life. It ensured the reproduction of life. Only once necessities were attended to, could one be fit for engagement with the political public realm. As one left their private household and entered the public realm, they entered a realm of equality, freedom, and politics. As she states, "The realm of the polis, on the contrary, was the sphere of freedom, and if there was a relationship between these two spheres, it was a matter of course that the mastering of the necessities of life in the household was the condition for freedom of the polis."[7] Freedom was a critical tool to ensure that citizens were able to act. Further, while the private realm operated through a hierarchical framework, in the public realm, citizens existed as equals, albeit each with a unique vantage point that was revealed through action and speech.

If we understand democracy as a form of governance that requires shared responsibility, neoliberal policies are pushing more people into precarious conditions, which requires competition for security and status—transforming a collective responsibility to an individual responsibility.[8] As espoused by governance and political scientists Sofia Näsström and Sara Kalm, "the production of precarity that is operative in many democratic countries fosters a privatization of responsibility that corrupts the public core of democracy. Instead of encouraging commitment to democracy, the emphasis on individual ambition, competition and distinction runs the risk of producing a 'market for monarchy.' "[9] As more people live in precarity and are forced to make decisions through sheer necessity, it poses a direct threat to democratic participatory processes. This is to say, it is unfair to ask residents to put the needs of the collective first, when they are struggling to survive. Moreover, it is impossible to ponder what is best for the future, when immediate needs are not being met. Differences in class have a direct effect on participation, as expressed by Chomsky, "Another feature of a capitalist democracy such as the United States is the inequity in distribution of resources, which translates into vast differences in the ability to participate in a meaningful way even in the narrow margin of decisions that remain with the political system."[10] The increasing precarity we witness around the globe highlights a major issue in citizen participation—how can we create formats for citizens to *understand* and *empathize* with longer-term collective issues despite the inability to tend to individual necessity?

If the subject is both informed and able to go beyond necessity, we must further question the forums and formats for participation, and how much meaningful agency they offer to citizens. Scholar Sherry Arnstein has developed a metaphoric "Ladder of Citizen Participation" to describe the actual transformative gradations in various forms of citizen participation. By analyzing the different formats of participatory processes, Arnstein sheds light on the many hollow participatory processes. As stated, "participation without redistribution of power is an empty and frustrating process for the powerless. It allows the powerholders to claim that all sides were considered but makes it possible for only some of those sides to benefit. It maintains the status quo."[11] The lower rungs on Arnstein's ladder include *manipulation* and *therapy*—forms of nonparticipation wherein powerholders "educate" or "cure" the public. The third rung is composed of *informing*, a one-way flow of information from powerholders to citizens with no mechanisms for feedback or negotiation. This is followed by *consultation*, wherein citizens have "participated in participation" with little outcome, but wherein powerholders have evidence that they have gone through the required motions. The four lower rungs on Arnstein's ladder offer almost no ability for citizens to influence the outcomes of the design process. The fifth rung involves *placation*, which gives citizens a degree of influence that is largely a product of their ability to articulate and press on their priorities. Tokenism is often associated with these forums. The last three rungs—*partnership*, *delegated power*, and *citizen control* all offer forms of negotiation between citizens and powerholders. This occurs through shared decision-making or community control.[12] Arnstein's ladder is a useful tool in evaluating the formats of participation and the actual agency and design influence offered to the citizen. What becomes evident in her analysis is the myriad of false forums that limit and exclude citizen voices, as expanded upon by Myron A. Levine in his book *Urban Politics*, "Yet too often, citizen engagement has proven more illusory than real. Entrenched bureaucracies and privileged interests do not always want new players at the table; in such instances, residents are allowed to participate in the decision-making process without being given any real power to affect outcomes."[13] The deceptive nature of participation is facilitated by romantic notions of inclusion, democracy, and productive negotiation.[14] As design goes from big to "Way Beyond Bigness," implicating many more citizens and stakeholders, how can participatory processes reorient agency to citizens? The aim here is not to find a way out from citizen participation, but rather to find a productive discourse that does not yield a compromise of the lowest common denominator and offers real agency.

Participation Beyond Bigness

> *Bigness is no longer part of any urban tissue. It exists; at most, it coexists. Its subtext is fuck context.*
> —*Rem Koolhaas*[15]

In Koolhaas's manifesto on "Bigness," he reveals a dialectic condition within massive architectural projects—sustaining their autonomy against context, while losing their autonomy to the associated "web of umbilical cords to other disciplines whose performance is as critical as the architect's".[16] But as contemporary design challenges require designers to move beyond the scale of just bigger and bigger buildings, or even beyond scales of landscapes and cities, and approach the scale of the territory, context and collaboration become primary drivers. No longer is the architectural object stable, it is part of the transforming territory, and how it negotiates various (often irreconcilable) factors is key to its value. Simultaneously, the scale of territorial design introduces new challenges to the participatory process. Not only do these projects involve more stakeholders, the sheer complexity of the projects requires a deeper level of information and knowledge-sharing as well as transparency. In addition, the incomprehensible scale of these projects both in space and time, makes them difficult to access and judge, and they are thereby rendered with a degree of abstraction. As a way beyond these challenges, mechanisms to make this abstraction legible have one go beyond individualism, and understanding impacts today and tomorrow becomes key in the participatory process. The following case studies shed light on productive and meaningful ways communities might gain a stronger voice at the table.

Agonism through Game Play

> *To recognize the constitutive role of power relations implies abandoning the misconceived ideal of a reconciled democratic society. Democratic consensus can be envisaged only as a "conflictual consensus." Democratic debate is not a deliberation aimed at reaching "the one" rational solution to be accepted by all, but a confrontation among adversaries.*
> *—Chantal Mouffe*[17]

Board games can be useful tools to deindividualize one's ideology and form empathy. Based in scenarios, games model forms of negotiation and collaboration while questioning resources and value. Board games consist of a *board*, which forms an abstract spatial geography; *players* with individual values and goals; a set of *rules*, which inform the game play; and *game pieces*, which often represent resources, value, or currency, and interface between rules, space, and each other. The relationships between these components are driven through narratives and scenarios, forming a bounded subset of reality. These scenarios abstract reality in a way that fosters new relationships and insights that might have otherwise been overlooked. During game play, decision-making is nonlinear and is part of a web of relationships that are tied together with feedback mechanisms. The decisions that different players/characters play out are both *strategic*, and tied to an overall goal, as well as *tactical*, and immediate. Games importantly require the players to understand the ramifications of their choices, enabling meaningful forms of action. Perhaps most importantly, games highlight conflict rather than presupposing consensus. Games allow oppositional positions to be played out. This agonism between viewpoints both clarifies each position while going beyond the status quo.

The architect and scholar Janette Kim has used games to "model alternate relationships among stakeholders, urban economies, political power, risk and the space of the city."[18] Working specifically on community engagement around climate action, her board game *In It Together* became a powerful tool to bring various stakeholders around the table in the 2018 Resilient by Design Bay Area Challenge.[19] The game acts as a stage for role-playing—East Oakland Residents, the City of Oakland, the City of Alameda, the Airport, Utilities, Developers, and Wildlife—to highlight ideological and value differences among stakeholders. **[Figure 2]** Players use these roles to advocate for different forms of climate adaptation. Game pieces include adaptation infrastructures (levees, pumps, freeway tunnels, etc.) and buildings (housing, tech hubs, etc.), and are positioned on an abstracted version of the San Leandro Bay. Players have limited income to purchase adaptation pieces, which they can pool or use individually. Through different scenarios of sea-level rise, players adjust their strategy—moving between individualism to collective gains. These scenarios in fact are operating at differential timescales, demanding that players look beyond more immediate issues and envision the future that they are contributing to. Kim's game offers a way in for different stakeholders to learn and experience the complex negotiations between evolving territories and design. This not only allows one to comprehend the trade-offs in such negotiation, it evokes a form of "empathy through agonism."[20] This empathy is the key mechanism to go beyond individualism and recognize conflicting and/or collective goals. Moreover, this empathy enables an understanding of incommensurate value systems, and asks how might there be meaningful ways to redistribute power (also explored in Kim's game *Bartertown*). Simultaneously, game play helps actors understand and articulate their values, which for many communities offers a way to push against tokenism. The game models a "provisional kind of consensus" that aligns with the complex and multifaceted actions required for tackling climate change. Instead of consensus of compromise or a singular fix to complex and evolving issues, the game enables a temporary and conflictual consensus,[21] producing more radical yet nuanced forms of change. This positions power not as a zero-sum game, wherein the gain of one player results in the loss for another, but shows how working in complex forms of collaboration allows for a redistribution of power. In some cases, climate change might heighten tensions among players while in others it diffuses it. The negotiation and redistribution of power and resources that the games incite in fact problematize the deeper structural issues around climate adaptation. While games cannot end the increasing precarity and necessity-oriented views of many, games do have the ability to abstract issues as a way to go beyond individualism and envision long-term planning. Being one step removed from oneself allows a productive conflict with adversaries. **[Figure 3]**

Legibility of the Background

> *An inability to cognitively map the gears and contours of the world system is as debilitating for political action as being unable mentally to map a city would prove for the city dweller. The absence of a practice of orientation that would be able to connect the abstractions of capital to the sense-data of everyday perception is identified as an impediment to any socialist project.*
> *—Alberto Toscano & Jeff Kinkle*[22]

If architectural "Bigness" for Koolhaas had the subtext of *fuck* context, as we approach the scale of the territory, design in fact becomes embedded within context. We could say that context subsumes design to the point that it resides in the background. The background refers to the spaces, infrastructures, and protocols that govern many aspects

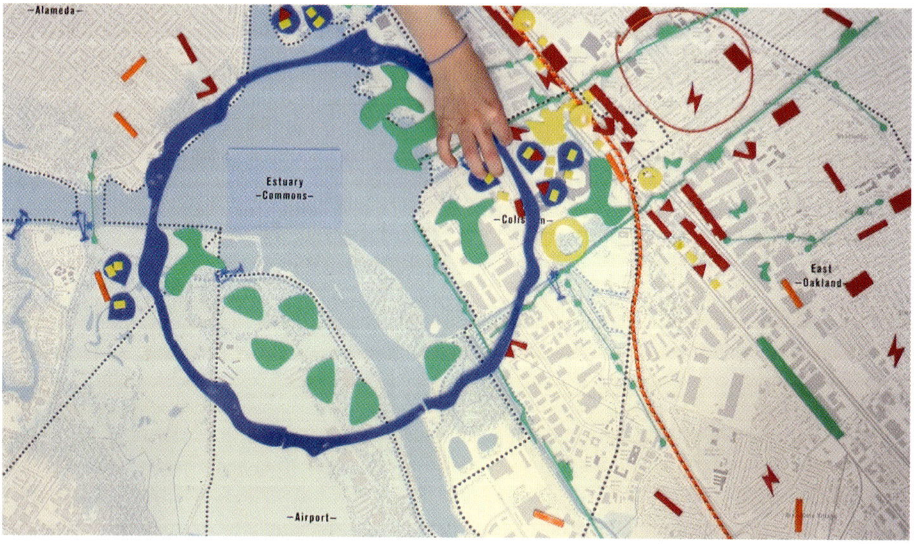

[Figure 2] Living Levee Loop (image credit: Sara Lafleur-Vetter for the All Bay Collective)

of our lives, yet are largely unacknowledged. These systems working at the territorial scale often situate us between layers of mediated abstraction. While I advocated for abstraction of scenarios and roles in game play as a way to go beyond individualism and the immediate, abstraction of the physical environment often renders us incapable of understanding our position against the territory and its associated distribution of power. Many of these "background" infrastructures only become visible when they fail or cause an inconvenience.

Consider for instance, conduit infrastructures—highways, pipelines, electric corridors, etc.—which have enabled the seamless logistical flow of materials across the country and the globe. The conduit was a critical invention in making commodities—energy, water, iPhones, etc.—abstract by separating sites of extraction or production from those of consumption. Beyond other effects, this act of separation makes the environmental or labor costs associated with these commodities highly removed—allowing those who benefited from these resources and products to not confront the consequences. The abstraction fostered by spatial detachment has characterized these conduits as forms of *dissociated technology*.[23] The estrangement between us and how these territorial infrastructures collectively organize our lives and environment is largely due to this abstraction. The simultaneity of being economically integrated yet spatially dissociated makes many large-scale issues such as climate change, the Covid-19 pandemic, shifts in labor regimes, etc., register as something over *there* but not *here* and not *now*. How can we be concerned with the social or ecological collective if we cannot understand our relationship to these broader environments?
It is precisely this background that Derek Hoeferlin's collaborative process engages, and by doing so, acts as a political tool to take action. He has led several fieldwork

[Figure 3] Bartertown, original version in Play (image credit: Janette Kim/Urban Works Agency)

documentary seminars at Washington University in St. Louis's Sam Fox School of Design & Visual Arts where he and his students have worked collaboratively to document the Mississippi River and its tributaries in relation to St. Louis's infrastructure and built environment. **[Figure 4]** The multiscalar field documentations bring an understanding of how what we are seeing on the ground relates to the larger territorial watershed. From canoe trips to aerial photography via balloon and drone mapping,[24] Hoeferlin and his students connect the view from above to the human perspective to bring legibility to territorial systems and reduce their abstraction. Connecting the XXL to the human scale offers a way into understanding and offering scales of measure to the background. The beautiful images and forms of cartography created by the group act as the critical first step in engaging how and where to act. **[Figure 5]**

In 2019, in his "Territories—Watersheds—Infrastructures" project and seminar, partially sponsored by the Haus der Kulturen der Welt's "Mississippi: An Anthropocene Project," Hoeferlin further curated a conversation with a diverse transdisciplinary group including the U.S. Army Corps of Engineers, Big Muddy Adventures, Continental Cement Company, City of St. Louis, Great Rivers Greenway, Missouri Confluence Waterkeeper, Mississippi River Cities and Towns Initiative, National Great Rivers Research and Education Center, and Pulitzer Arts Foundation. In an engagement and dialogue session on a barge adjacent to the industrial site of Continental Cement Company, Hoeferlin assembled the conversation in the normally inaccessible and incomprehensible background geography. The river and its context were no longer abstract in these conversations. They literally formed the ground of the dialogues. Through engaging and inhabiting the background, the ramifications of distant top-down ideas or decisions were immediately connected with the realities on the ground. This offered a way to link the territorial and human scale, bringing understanding to the complex interactions that are occurring in these overlooked spaces. Ultimately, these ways of learning how to see and comprehend the scale and complexity of systems at work allow conversations and design ideas to go beyond the status quo. **[Figure 6]**

Advocacy

These examples offer new insights into how the formats, mediums, and sites of engagement processes might bring about novel ways to engage the abstract scales of time and space while creating vehicles to go beyond individualism and foster empathy. They ask us to grapple with territorial scale, how power is distributed, and the complexity of its systems, as a way of clarifying what one wants to advocate for and how this might be more effectively catalyzed. The history of architecture and urbanism is full of examples wherein a singular vision attempted to "liberate" or condition a population. The disjuncture between social goals and lived reality asks us to reconsider the mechanisms for engaging a more diverse set of voices. At the scale of the territory, having communities advocate for their interests and the project at large, are key to catalyzing change. Moreover, these communities are more likely to steward and maintain their urban environment if they are part of building its vision. While much work still needs to be done to go beyond tokenism and offer meaningful platforms for citizen voices, these case studies offer a departure point to engage the territory. Going "Way Beyond Bigness" has the subtext of the consolidation of power to reify these massive projects. Against this, finding mechanisms to produce citizen power both in the design process and its eventual actualization are critical components to ensuring democracy.

[Figure 4] Derek Hoeferlin and his Washington University in St. Louis students "locking" through Melvin Price Locks & Dam, in canoes, 2019 (image credit: Derek Hoeferlin)

[Figure 5] Example of Derek Hoeferlin's "Territories-Watersheds-Infrastructures" seminar installation on the Continental Cement Company platform barge, St. Louis, 2019 (image credit: Xinyang Chen and Yongdi Li)

[Figure 6] Derek Hoeferlin's "Territories—Watersheds—Infrastructures" platform dialogue on a barge with the Mississippi River and St. Louis as backdrop (image credit: Derek Hoeferlin)

1. Eyal Weizman, "The Paradox of Collaboration," in *The Nightmare of Participation*, Markus Miessen (London: Sternberg Press, 2010), 9.
2. Simon Sadler, "Open Ends: The Social Visions of the 1960s Non-Planning," in *Non-Plan: Essays on Freedom Participation and Change in Modern Architecture and Urbanism*, eds. Jonathan Hughes and Simon Sadler (Oxford: Architectural Press, 2000), 139.
3. Hadas Steiner, "Within the Big Structure," in *Megastructure Reloaded: Visionary Architecture and Urban Planning of the 1960s Reflected by Contemporary Artists*, eds. Sabrina van der Ley and Markus Richter (Berlin: Hatje Cantz, 2008), 148.
4. Bernard Rudofsky, *Architecture without Architects, an introduction to non-pedigreed Architecture* (New York: MoMA, 1964), iv.
5. Sherry R. Arnstein, "A Ladder of Citizen Participation," *Journal of the American Planning Association*, 35, no. 4 (July 1969): 216.
6. While much criticism has surfaced in response to this delineation, particularly in terms of the characterization of the private realm, it is worthwhile outlining Arendt's argument for our purposes, which centers more overtly on how one approaches the public realm.
7. Hannah Arendt, *The Human Condition* (Chicago: University of Chicago Press, 1958), 31.
8. Sofia Näsström and Sara Kalm, "A democratic critique of precarity," *Global Discourse* 5, no. 4 (2014): 1–18.
9. Ibid., 568.
10. Noam Chomsky, *On Power and Ideology* (Chicago: Haymarket Books, 2015), 152.
11. Arnstein, "A Ladder of Citizen Participation," 216.
12. Ibid, 217, 218–223.
13. Myron A. Levine, *Urban Politics: Cities and Suburbs in a Global Age* (New York: Routledge, 2015), 174.
14. Markus Miessen, "What Is at Stake" in *The Nightmare of Participation*, Markus Miessen (London: Sternberg Press, 2010).
15. Rem Koolhaas, "Bigness" in *S,M,L,XL*, eds. Rem Koolhaas, Bruce Mau, Jennifer Sigler (New York: Monacelli Press, 1998), 260.
16. Ibid., 262.
17. Chantal Mouffe, "Introduction" in *The Challenge of Carl Schmitt*, ed. Chantal Mouffe (London: Version, 1999), 4.
18. Janette Kim, "Modelling a Critical Resilience: Board Games and the Agonism of Engagement" in *Games and Play in the Creative, Smart and Ecological City*, eds. Dale Leorke and Markus Owens (New York: Routledge, 2020).
19. The "Resilient by Design Bay Area Challenge" was a yearlong collaborative effort between designers, community groups, and policy makers around questions of sea-level rise. Unlike the New York version of this challenge, which was reactionary to Hurricane Sandy, the Bay Area Challenge was a proactive endeavor. It consisted of six months of research before specific sites were assigned, followed by a collaborative design process.
20. Ibid.
21. For more on this topic, see: Markus Miessen, "Collaboration and the Conflictual" in *The Nightmare of Participation*, Markus Miessen (London: Sternberg Press, 2010).
22. Alberto Toscano and Jeff Kinkle, *Cartographies of the Absolute* (Portland: Zero Books, 2015).
23. Christopher F. Jones, "Pipelines and Power," *Routes of Power* (Cambridge, MA: Harvard University Press, 2014): 143–144.
24. Done in collaboration with Jess Vanecek and Hoeferlin's Washington University in St. Louis seminars "Public Lab River Rat Pack" (2017), "Territories—Watersheds—Infrastructures" (2019) and "Field Work 2.0: Reality + Remote=???" (2020)

Public Lab River Rat Pack

Alternative Modes of Field Documentations (1)

with Washington University in St. Louis & Public Lab River Rat Pack

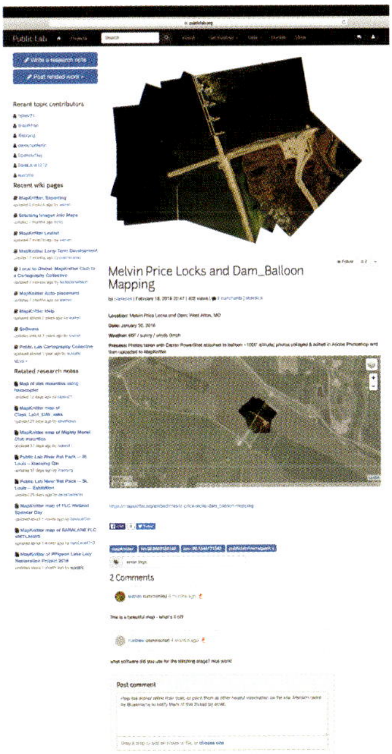

[Figure 1] Screenshot of Public Lab River Rat Pack's uploaded documentation to the publiclab.org open-source website (image credit: Public Lab)

The *Public Lab River Rat Pack* (PLRRP) was a group fieldwork documentation and mapping project to work with students, colleagues, and St. Louis communities and stakeholders about the critical importance of our intertwined, yet complicated, relationship with the Mississippi and Missouri Rivers and their tributaries.[2] The project collaborated with Public Lab (www.publiclab.org), a nonprofit, citizen-science organization that enables communities to have access to inexpensive D.I.Y. scientific mapping techniques to "investigate environmental concerns … [and] seek to change how people see the world in environmental, social, and political terms."[3]

Utilizing Public Lab's DIY Mapping Kits, to date, the PLRRP has taken over 35,000 photographs above sites in the Mississippi River watershed. The efforts are accomplished by attaching camera rigs to big red balloons. The documentation has been curated and distilled into photographic and diagrammatic analyses of each site for comparative purposes, along with being imported into Public Lab's open-source website for dissemination.[4] **[Figure 1]** The work is ongoing, and we will continue our collaboration with others in the St. Louis region, the Mississippi River Basin, and beyond.[5]

By design, the big balloons and documentary rigs require a *team* to operate, unapologetic in their embracing of trial and error, and by extension, promote a hybridized analogue-digital approach to fieldwork. The balloons are expressive, highly visible objects in the sky. People easily see them. People ask questions about them. People tend to trust them, and even ask to participate in the teamwork. **[Figures 2, 3 & 4]**

Various mappings document the difference between high and low river stages; others map the intensity of industrial uses along the rivers; others highlight more ecological or restorative areas; and most question a profound lack of access by the public to the rivers, much that is managed by the U.S. Army Corps of Engineers.

Following are a selection of five sites documented with PLRRP colleagues and my Washington University in St. Louis students from 2014 to 2016.[6] The sites are along the Mississippi River, primarily in the St. Louis region, **[Figure 5]** as well as a coastal restoration site and the Mississippi River Delta. Each attempts to make highly visual, time-specific understandings of sites related to the speculation presented earlier in this book, "*from the Big Six to the Birds Foot.*"

Specifically, documentations include: (1) a locks and dam structure as a potential site for a future algae farm, (2) a large navigation canal to facilitate barge traffic up and down the river, possibly transporting algae and sediment in the future, (3) a deurbanized area along the river with potential for new industrial retrofits such as algae refining, (4) a current staging area for industrial use and transport, and (5) a river crevasse currently being modified as a wetland restoration project.

Each condition highlights the varying conditions of the actual water at each site as well, such as the radical difference between high and low river stages that can occur in short timeframes. To do the latter, the PLRRP quickly mobilized on January 1, 2016,

[Figure 2] The big red balloons take a team to operate, (left to right: Elise Novak, Jonathan Stitelman, Allison Mendez, Natalie Yates), St. Louis, Missouri, 2016 (image credit: Derek Hoeferlin)

at the peak of the (then) third-highest flood stage in recorded history for the Mississippi River in the St. Louis region. Over the span of just four months, the Mississippi River fluctuated up, then down, and then up again within a range of over 30 feet, from major flood stage to normal river stage. (Low river stage would have needed to be another 10 to 20 feet lower.)[7] **[Figure 6]** In other words, the Mississippi River at St. Louis can fluctuate over an astounding 50 feet in height. This not only poses problems for flood and drought management, it also poses significant challenges to river access and the navigation industry.

Site 01: Melvin Price Locks and Dam

This site is on the Missouri side of the Mississippi River, about 17 miles north of St. Louis. Documented conditions include: the intersection of major river infrastructure (Melvin Price Locks and Dam) with ecological restoration (Audubon Center at Riverlands), including pooled and free-flowing river conditions resulting from the dam infrastructure. The U.S. Army Corps of Engineers (USACE) built the Melvin Price Locks and Dam in 1978 as part of the *9-Foot Channel Project*, a large effort by the USACE to maintain navigability along the Upper Mississippi River. South of here, the Mississippi River is free-flowing, unimpeded all the way to the river's mouth at the Gulf of Mexico. Critics of locks and dams have pointed out that these structures, while enabling low-emission transport of materials via barges, harm the river ecologically and exacerbate flood damage in the long term. By constructing a dam, the river moves from being a free-flowing path to an "artificial slack-water reservoir habitat."[8] As a result, the chemical and physical properties of the water change, putting undue stress on the native fauna. The "pooled" water at this point is also high in nutrient content, specifically nitrogen from big-agricultural runoff to the north, as explained in the [S+S] section of this book in the speculation *from the Big Six to the Birds Foot,* which proposes algae farms at such nutrient-rich locations. Additionally, the dams trap sediment, thereby altering the flow of the river. The site of the Melvin Price Locks and Dam is at the intersection of another USACE partnership: the Audubon Center at Riverlands. The surrounding land is a restored prairie marsh and managed wetland network, providing important habitat for birds migrating along the Mississippi Flyway.[9] **[Figure 7]**

Site 02: Chain of Rocks Canal

This site is on the Illinois side of the Mississippi River, at the north confluence of the Mississippi River and Chain of Rocks Canal. Documented conditions include: the 500-year levee with levee road and bike path, a parking pad at the canal's edge, the canal, erosion control along the canal, and the northern tip of Chouteau's Island. In 1953, as part of the *9-Foot Channel Project*, the USACE constructed an 8.4-mile-long canal with a 600-foot lock for ships and barges to bypass a unique natural navigational impediment—an exposed limestone dam that forms the "Chain of Rocks"—that rendered navigation through a stretch of the Mississippi River impossible during low river stages. This project's main aim was to facilitate barge traffic, primarily for petrochemicals and agricultural products up and down the river system. To mitigate erosion, the USACE constructs rock embankments known as "rip-rap," ubiquitously implemented up and down the river system. This infrastructure prevents soil from scouring and ensures that canal depth remains stable. However, a downside to this practice is the lack of a fluctuating riparian-edged habitat for the surrounding fauna and migratory birds, along with an undesirable edge condition for recreation, accessibility, and public amenity. **[Figure 8]**

Site 03: North St. Louis Riverfront

This site is on the Missouri side of the Mississippi River, just north of downtown St. Louis, Laclede's Landing, and the Gateway Arch. Documented conditions include: the 500-year floodwall, high and low water river stages, a bike path along the floodwall, and abandoned land and buildings. This is a large deindustrialized site, with a significant number of abandoned buildings and large open spaces within and surrounding it. The large concrete wall seen at this site is a floodwall—a large structure used to maintain the navigation of the river channel and to constrain floodwaters during high flow conditions. Floodwalls are typically used when levee construction is not possible, most often in cities where space is at a premium or in areas where bank access is necessary for commercial use. The photos were taken just six weeks apart, first during the December 2015–January 2016 flood when the river stage crested at 42.3 feet, the third-highest on record. Six weeks later, the PLRRP documented the river stage more than 30 feet lower. The flood was of particular interest because its duration was much shorter than usual and because floods of this magnitude tend to happen during the spring, and very rarely during the winter months. Another point of interest here is the notion of public access to the river. Of note is the submerged bike path on the river side of the floodwall during the high river stage. **[Figure 9]**

Site 04: South St. Louis Riverfront

This site is on the Missouri side of the Mississippi River, just south of downtown St. Louis, Choteau's Landing, and the Gateway Arch. Documented conditions include: the 500-year floodwall, high and low water river stages, a pumping station, an active staging area for various industrial uses, and a submerged ship. As with the North St. Louis Riverfront, areas south of St. Louis were historically a vibrant industrial district, and home to thousands of immigrants. Today, on first investigation, the site exhibits large areas of abandonment and deindustrialization. But there is more here than meets the eye. The photos were taken on the same days as those of the North St. Louis Riverfront, documenting the river stages varying over 30 feet. The flooded conditions show the river water up against the floodwall, and in fact, higher than the protected city side of the wall. Piles of raw building material, equipment, and industrial byproducts that sat unprotected on the riverside of the floodwall were completely submerged, increasing pollutants in the river. While the floodwall served to protect the St. Louis downtown area from the rising Mississippi, it simultaneously concealed from the public's view the adverse effects happening just on the opposite side. When we documented the site in normal river stage, we found out from workers there that the site served as the staging area for making concrete for the current renovations to the Gateway Arch grounds, just to the north of this site, so it is in fact a very active, working riverfront. Also of note in the documentation is a pumping station, crucially important for stormwater management of the city to the west. Barely noticeable in the bottom-left corner of the normal level photo is a portion of a sunken World War II German U-boat. This boat used to be moored at the base of the Gateway Arch as a tourist site. The great 1993 flood, the highest on record, knocked the boat off its moorings, only to be submerged just south, at this mostly unknown location. Finally, at this particular section of floodwall is a "legal" graffiti wall, where the city-side portion of the floodwall becomes a canvas for a yearly international graffiti art and hip-hop festival known as *Paint Louis*.[10] This section—which has become a destination point for locals and visitors alike—encourages public engagement and acknowledgement of an otherwise solely industrial riverfront. **[Figure 10]**

Site 05: Mississippi River Delta

This site is on the east bank of the Mississippi River in the Louisiana Delta, south of New Orleans, in Plaquemines Parish, near the river's mouth at the Gulf of Mexico. Documented conditions include a crevasse in the Mississippi River and a constructed marsh restoration project. The final site is far south of St. Louis, close to where the Mississippi River's mouth meets the Gulf of Mexico. A crevasse is a breach in a river, usually caused by a flood, when a river in a delta decides to alter its course. At this particular site on the east bank of the Mississippi River there is no levee. There is a levee on the opposite west bank of the river that protects the developed land and assists in maintaining the navigation channel. However, the river has been allowed to spill over at this location. This site was the first one documented with the balloons, and Public Lab and the Gulf Restoration Network, along with a local boat operator, joined and supported the effort, allowing access to the site. The boat operator along

35,000+ aer

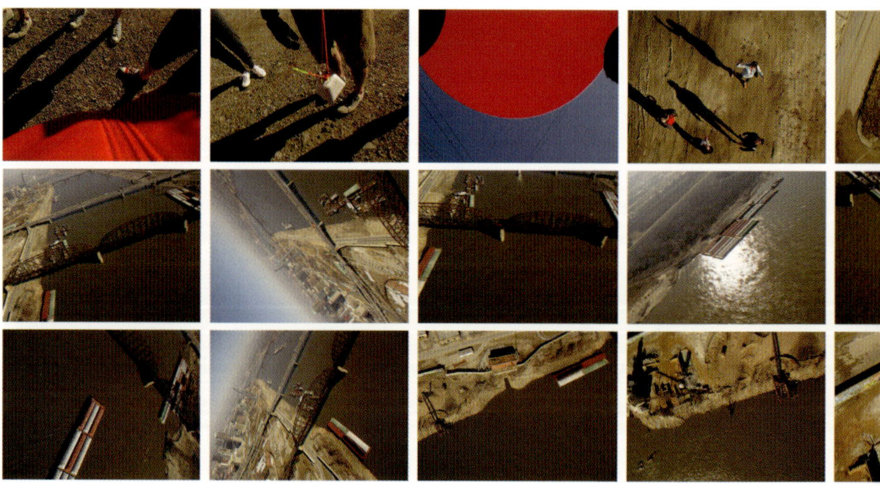

[Figure 3] (ABOVE) Various aspects of the documentation process (BELOW) sampling of photographs taken above the Mississippi River at downtown St. Louis (image credit: Derek Hoeferlin's Public Lab River Rat Pack seminar, Sam Fox School of Design & Visual Arts, Washington University in St. Louis, 2016)

photographs

[Figure 4] Documenting Melvin Price Locks & Dam, West Alton, Missouri, 2016 (image credit: Derek, Max & Jake Hoeferlin)

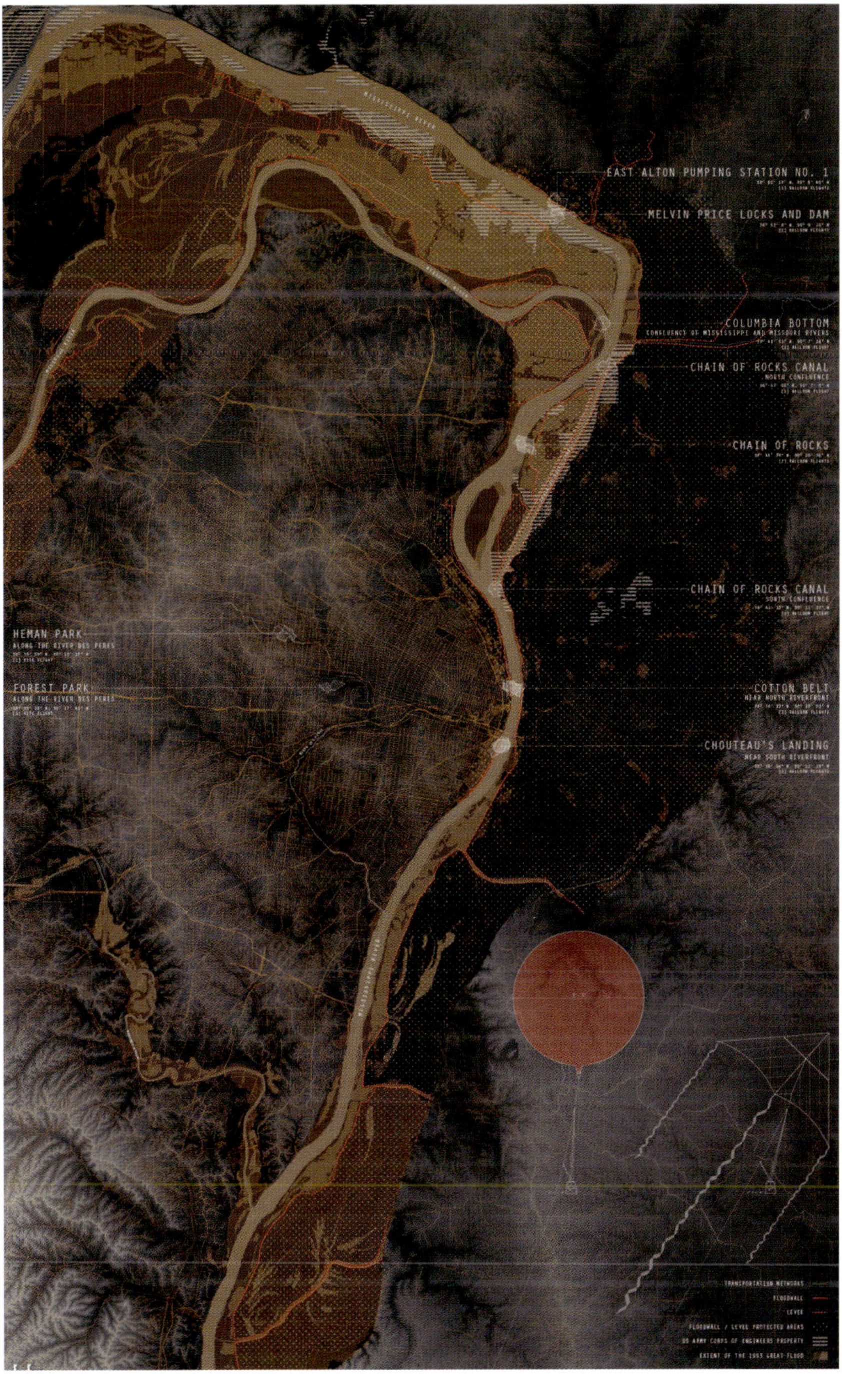

[Figure 5] Map of the St. Louis river region, indicating various sites documented and diagrams of the mapping equipment (image credit: Derek Hoeferlin's Public Lab River Rat Pack seminar, Sam Fox School of Design & Visual Arts, Washington University in St. Louis, 2016)

[Figure 6] Chouteau's Landing, south St. Louis riverfront; main background image during low river stage; smaller image superimposed in upper left during fourth highest river stage on record just six weeks earlier (image credit: Derek Hoeferlin's Public Lab River Rat Pack seminar, Sam Fox School of Design & Visual Arts, Washington University in St. Louis, 2016)

[Figure 7] Site 01: Melvin Price Locks & Dam, West Alton, Missouri (image credit: Derek Hoeferlin's Public Lab River Rat Pack seminar, Sam Fox School of Design & Visual Arts, Washington University in St. Louis, 2016)

[Figure 8] Site 02: Chain of Rocks Canal, Lewis and Clark State Memorial Park, Illinois (image credit: Derek Hoeferlin's Public Lab River Rat Pack seminar, Sam Fox School of Design & Visual Arts, Washington University in St. Louis, 2016)

[Figure 9&10] Site 03: (above) low river stage and (below) high river stage at North St. Louis riverfront (image credit: Derek Hoeferlin's Public Lab River Rat Pack seminar, Sam Fox School of Design & Visual Arts, Washington University in St. Louis, 2016) Site 04: (above) low river stage and (below) high river stage at South St. Louis riverfront (image credit: Derek Hoeferlin's Public Lab River Rat Pack seminar, Sam Fox School of Design & Visual Arts, Washington University in St. Louis, 2016)

[Figure 11] Site 05: Taken from approximately 3,000 feet in the air, highlighted is a stitched-together panorama that documents a marsh restoration project south of New Orleans in Plaquemines Parish, near the "Birds Foot" mouth of the Mississippi River at the Gulf of Mexico, 2014
(image credit: Derek Hoeferlin's MISI-ZIIBI-DISAPPEAR studio, Sam Fox School of Design & Visual Arts, Washington University in St. Louis, Public Lab, Gulf Restoration Network)

with others have taken it upon themselves to construct this marsh restoration project, on their own terms, and without outside support. Locally harnessing what is left of the sediment from the river crevasse represents a grassroots effort by doing one's part to incrementally build land. It is a simple design. Mound up soil from below the water's surface to be just a couple of feet above the water. Construct a gridded network of channels to let the water flow with sediment, and saline-friendly marshes and grasses then naturally grow. Because we were so off the grid, we were able to fly two balloons, one at 1,000 feet and the other at 3,000 feet, the latter represented in this image. **[Figure 11]**

The Public Lab River Rat Pack looks forward to continued partnerships and advocacy efforts for reconnecting the public to our river systems in the future in more resilient and sustainable ways. **[Figure 12]**

[Figure 12] The Public Lab River Rat Pack preparing to document the southern tip of the Chain of Rocks Canal where it reconnects with the Mississippi River, with downtown St. Louis in background, 2016 (image credit: Derek Hoeferlin)

1. Portions of this text previously published in "Chasing #Antidrone," in *Chasing the City,*" eds. Joshua Nason and Jeffrey Nesbit (Abingdon, Oxfordshire: Routledge, 2018).
2. *Public Lab River Rat Pack* members: Derek Hoeferlin (Principal Investigator), with Washington University in St. Louis students: Spring 2016 (St. Louis sites): Xiaoxin Cao, Molly Chaney, Nicholas Gentile, Katheryn Haas, Nina Lang, Rachel LeFevre, Amanda Malone, Xiaoqing Qin, Jinghan Shi, Micah Stanek, Rory Thibault, and Jess Vaneсek; Fall 2014 "MISI-ZIIBI-DISAPPEAR" studio (Mississippi River Delta site): Lex Agnew, Paige Bergmeier, Cristina Clow, Grace Davis, Shira Grosman, Taylor Halamka, Kayla Kroot, Andy Lee, Jennifer Rokoff, and Amy Sun; additional ad hoc members: Michael Allen, Emily Chen, Allison Méndez, Elise Novak, Jonathan Stitelman, Fred Stivers, Tiffin Thompson, and Natalie Yates; partners: Public Lab; support: U.S. Army Corps of Engineers St. Louis District and Audubon Center at Riverlands; funding: Sam Fox School of Design & Visual Arts, Washington University in St. Louis.
3. www.publiclab.org (accessed February 27, 2021).
4. https://publiclab.org/notes/derekhoeferlin/05-09-2016/public-lab-river-rat-pack-st-louis-exhibition (accessed February 27, 2021).
5. Special thanks to: Public Lab (Shannon Dosemagen and Stevie Lewis); a 2015/2016 Washington University Sam Fox School of Design & Visual Arts Creative Activity Research Grant for equipment, exhibition and research assistants; the U.S. Army Corps of Engineers St. Louis District (Charlie Deutsch and Lane Richter) for permission and access to sites; Audubon Center at Riverlands (Julie Watson); Gulf Restoration Network (Scott Eustis); Stan Strembicki for printing access at the Sam Fox School; and others, for their time and support.
6. Portions of text descriptions of documented Sites 1–4 in this chapter are revised versions generated by Washington University in St. Louis students, primarily by Molly Chaney, under the direction of Derek Hoeferlin and his Spring 2016 seminar *Public Lab River Rat Pack.*
7. The record high for the Mississippi River gauge at St. Louis is 49.98 feet (August 1, 1993) and the record low is -6.20 feet (January 16, 1940), a 56.18-foot differential. For river stages, see the National Weather Service Advanced Hydrologic Prediction Service: http://water.weather.gov/ahps2/hydrograph.php?wfo=lsx&gage=EADM7 (accessed February 27, 2021).
8. https://www.internationalrivers.org/environmental-impacts-of-dams (accessed February 27, 2021).
9. http://riverlands.audubon.org/audubon-center-riverlands-0 (accessed February 27, 2021).
10. https://www.stlpaintlouis.com (accessed February 27, 2021).

Flood—Fight—Fail

Alternative Modes of Site Interventions

Derek Hoeferlin

After all, experts say, there are only two types of levees: those that have failed, and those that will fail.(1)

—Alex Prud'homme

A single-line-defense, "500-year" flood protection system of levees and floodwalls cuts the Mississippi River off from the American Bottom floodplain in Illinois, a vast area across the river from St. Louis. Stretching from the confluence of the Mississippi and Missouri rivers to the confluence with the Kaskaskia river, the plain and its native inhabitants, such as those at Cahokia Mounds, welcomed seasonal floods. Today, the anthropogenic plain is designed to resist floods, also known by the U.S. Army Corps of Engineers as "Flood Fighting." The American Bottom encompasses complex, and oftentimes very much contested sites such as East St. Louis, U.S. Steel, America's Central Port, Wood River Refinery, Miles Davis's childhood home, and Sauget (formally Monsanto Town). In other words, if flooded, the American Bottom, and everything south of it downriver to the Gulf of Mexico, could become a terrible toxic cocktail. This installation was my contribution to the *Art + Landscape STL* exhibition at Granite City Art and Design District (G-CADD), curated by Gavin Kroeber in March and April 2019.[2]

Temporary markings horizontally striped on a G-CADD storefront invite subjects to hypothetically occupy scientific datums of water depths in a "what-if-the-levees-failed" scenario. Red electric tape annotates, and curiously does so at an intimate, human-scaled understanding, the two highest Mississippi River stages taken as of February 2019—the 1993 flood (#1) and the 1973 flood (#2), according to the National Weather Service's nearby St. Louis river gauge.

Subsequent to this installation, the Mississippi River radically rose once again and set a "new" #2 height in June 2019, just two months after the exhibition finished. If this new record had been additionally taped to the storefront, it would track about midway between the 1993 and 1973 heights. This absence only reinforces our constant and desperate battle to track, organize, synthesize, and spatially and legibly re-present big data, especially during our accelerating contemporary challenges. And in this case, the accelerating effects of climate extremes in the St. Louis region. Four of the top-ten river stages have occurred since the Great Flood of 1993. This is a no-brainer. We must adapt, collectively.

1. Alex Prud'homme, "There Will be Floods," *New York Times*, February 27, 2008, accessed February 28, 2021, https://www.nytimes.com/2008/02/27/opinion/27prudhomme.html.

2. See http://www.gcadd.org/events/artandlandscapestl (accessed February 28, 2021).

View of storefront from within "In-Out" building at G-CADD, with red markings indicating 1973 and 1993 flood heights (image credit: Derek Hoeferlin)

Detail of red tape adhered to storefront's existing moldings and polycarbonate panels (image credit: Derek Hoeferlin)

Detail of red tape with date (image credit: Derek Hoeferlin)

Just over two months after the exhibition closed, a new record flood occurred (indicated with dashed line), just a few feet below the "Great Flood of 1993" record (image credit: Derek Hoeferlin)aa

View of storefront from street, with red markings indicating 1973 and 1993 flood heights (image credit: Derek Hoeferlin)

Territories—Watersheds—Infrastructures

Alternate Modes of Programmatic Usages

with Washington University in St. Louis

Derek Hoeferlin's "Territories—Watersheds—Infrastructures" Washington University in St. Louis seminar paddling the Mississippi River with Big Muddy Adventures, 2019 (image credit: Derek Hoeferlin)

“Territories—Watersheds—Infrastructures” was a collaborative, community-engaged, multiscalar field documentation and mapping project that positioned the Mississippi River, its tributaries and the St. Louis region within its broader watershed, particularly highlighting the anthropogenic and complicated intersections of recreation, river management, and industry.

In early October 2019, an exhibition and panel discussion occurred at the Continental Cement Company on the North Riverfront in St. Louis, as part of the “Anthropocene Vernacular” field station, within the larger “Mississippi: An Anthropocene River” project, sponsored by the Haus der Kulturen der Welt (HKV) in Berlin.[1] Multiple installations included: photographic field documentations from canoe trips guided by Big Muddy Adventures; 2016 and 2019 aerial photography of various high- and low-water river stages shot via balloons and drones by Derek Hoeferlin, Jess Vanecek, and the Public Lab River Rat Pack; Hoeferlin’s multiscalar Mississippi River Basin drawings and photography from his “Way Beyond Bigness” research; and projects created by Hoeferlin’s students in his fall 2019 seminar at Washington University in St. Louis.[2] The work and industrial context of the site also challenged participants to question the role design plays in such conditions and in turn advocate for future resilient and integrative built environments.

Not only was the work used to represent ideas, but as objects of action for a set of dialogues about responsibility, agency, and possible futures for the Mississippi River Basin. These are especially pointed when weighed in relation to contemporary and future stresses to the Mississippi River system, such as climate change and economic and industrial uncertainties, set within broader social, political, and ecological landscapes.

The fascinating industrial site of the Continental Cement Company straddles the intersections of the Mississippi River, barge traffic, a riverfront bike trail, a “500-year” floodwall, the Stan Musial Veterans Memorial Bridge/Interstate 70, multiple rail lines, and even the site of the erased Mississippian culture’s Big Mound. The collaborative work was scattered across the site in various platform zones for dialogues, including the roof of the cement silo, which has a spectacular panoramic view of the St. Louis region, as well as exhibited on the platform barge that is used for loading cement from barges. The cement is then transported via big tubes to the dueling silos on land, as if going through an enormous vacuum.

These dialogues included local and regional representatives from the U.S. Army Corps of Engineers, Big Muddy Adventures, Continental Cement Company, City of St. Louis, Great Rivers Greenway, Missouri River Waterkeeper Alliance, Mississippi River Cities and Towns Initiative, Pulitzer Arts Foundation, and National Great Rivers Research and Education Center. A follow-up public programming event was held in November 2019, hosted by the Pulitzer Arts Foundation, with a field trip led by Derek Hoeferlin. Titled “Your Mississippi,” it brought “river citizens” back to the barge, complemented by a visit to the Corps of Engineers’ Applied River Engineering Center in South St. Louis.

These events are not meant to propose solutions per se. Rather, the dialogues attempt to bring together various points of view "to the barge" and " to the river" in hopes of advocating for collective and climate-forward actions. Now's the time!

Platform Barge Dialogue

Jesse Vogler: So, we're on a barge. It is a condition and a place that is incredibly distant from our everyday life in St Louis. The entire choreography and geography that we just had to go through to get here in some ways are measures of that distance. The river has, in many ways, been organized to be distanced from our life in the city.

We're here on the first, opening event of a weekend of events that are part of a much larger project than just this experience that we're having right now. We're here at the opening of Field Station 3, which has been organized around the idea of the "Anthropocene Vernacular." This initiative and the work of our Field Station is part of a much larger, Mississippi-wide initiative called "Mississippi: An Anthropocene River" that is being brought together by Haus der Kulturen der Welt (HKW) and the Max Planck Institute (MPI). We are incredibly grateful to be in this session today with colleagues from up and down the river, and would also like to highlight that this set of events is one of five similar Field Stations up and down the river, each taking a focused look at the way we are fundamentally finding ourselves at a point of environmental acceleration and utter transformation. So, this is the kick off for what is going to be a weekend-long set of bus tours, of community engagements, of cookouts… and we welcome you all to join us at all of these events.

Before I hand over the stage to Derek, I want to highlight the fact that we are going to be talking a lot today about the way that the river *works*. We're here at Continental Cement Company, witnessing a sort of industry that's literally contributing to building the city as we speak. But I think it's also a really important time to ask questions about what the river *means*. And it has meant a lot of different things, to a lot of different people, at a lot of different times. I think it's worth acknowledging those changing forms of meaning that have attached themselves to the river, right here, right where we are sitting.

For Native Americans, this might mark a site of incredible displacement and dispossession. Here was the meeting of the Illinois, Missouria, and Osage nations, and the river marked both a center and a boundary for numerous campaigns of Indian displacement. For others, it was the meaning of empires. This was the site where the British, the French, the Spanish, and then a growing American empire really collided, and we'll be addressing many of the issues related to empire and its aftermath throughout the weekend. It is also a very complicated and dark history of slavery for the country. The river in St. Louis marked a dividing line between free and slave states, but even this is troubled by a deep and complicated history between what it meant to be free and enslaved in both Missouri and Illinois. And it remains a site where life and production continue, and the river remains an active part of many people's livelihoods as well.

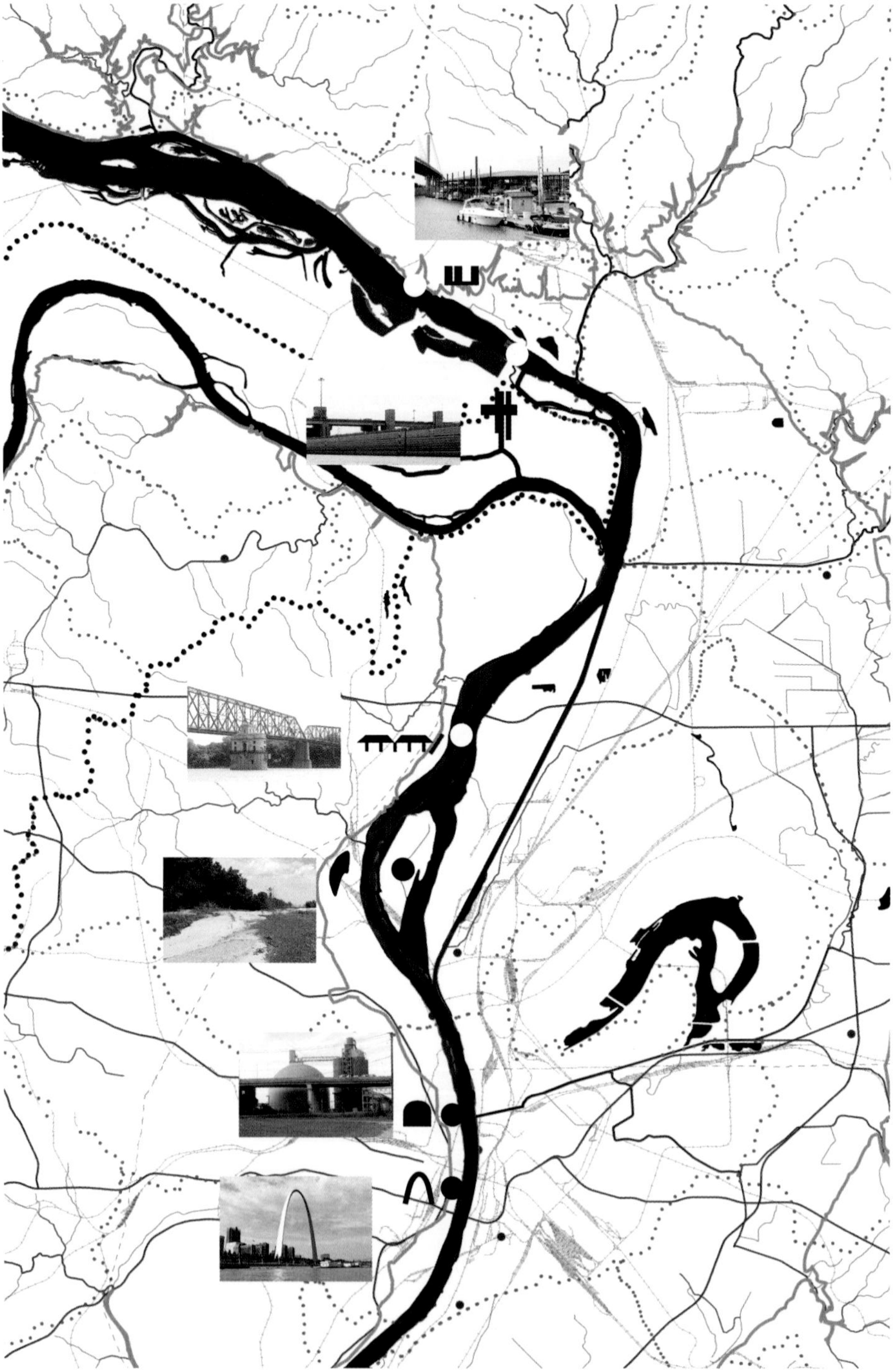

Map of documented St. Louis river sites, 2019
(image credit: Derek Hoeferlin's "Territories—Watersheds—Infrastructures" seminar)

Site photographs of Continental Cement Company, St. Louis, Missouri, 2019 (image credit: Derek Hoeferlin)

Dustin Whited, Operations Manager for Continental Cement Company, welcoming event participants and providing security briefing, St. Louis, Missouri, 2019 (image credit: Derek Hoeferlin)

Atop the Continental Cement Company cement silos, with student project by Samuel Bell-Hart and Natia Kapanadze suspended between guardrails (foreground, bottom right), Interstate 70 below, and downtown in background, St. Louis, Missouri, 2019 (image credit: Derek Hoeferlin)

Student temporary installation by Liz Hambor, Damon Xiang and Makio Yamamoto titled "Industrial Domesticities" on Continental Cement Company platform barge, St. Louis, Missouri, 2019 (image credit: Liz Hambor, Damon Xiang, Makio Yamamoto)

Student temporary installation by Virginia Eckinger and John Whitaker titled "Lo(e)ss Gradiants" on Continental Cement Company platform barge, St. Louis, Missouri, 2019
(image credit: Virginia Eckinger, John Whitaker)

Temporary installation of Derek Hoeferlin's "Mississippi River Basin Atlas" on Continental Cement Company platform barge, St. Louis, Missouri, 2019
(image credit: Derek Hoeferlin)

As we kick off the conversation, I would like to note that all of this would not be happening without the incredible creativity and real spirit of the Anthropocene Vernacular team. So here in the audience we have project leaders including Gavin Kroeber, Lynn Peemoeller, Matthew Fluharty, Jennifer Colten, as well as Derek, and Treasure Shield Redmond who could not join us tonight. We have the incredible organizing and facilitating capacity of James McAnally at the Luminary, and really it is the creativity of this entire team that is allowing this event to happen this week. So, we would welcome you all to the Luminary in a couple of hours where we'll also have the opportunity to introduce you to our team. And you might be wondering—who are all of these people on the barge this afternoon? Many of these people are River Travelers, folks who have been on the river for the past 39 days, travelling from the headwaters up in Minnesota down to St. Louis, and then after here, all the way to New Orleans and the Gulf of Mexico. And so, we welcome you here and we look forward to the chance to meet you all a little bit more personally at the opening this evening, as well as over the course of the coming days. Others joining tonight are from St. Louis and regional communities, and let's not forget to thank Derek's students from Washington University in St. Louis for sharing their installations on the elaborate infrastructure path out here to where we now gather together on this barge. With that, I'll hand over to Derek.

Derek Hoeferlin: Jesse, thank you very much for that introduction. It really sets the stage for both today and our overall field station. We're all honored to be here and have all of you out here on this barge. I'll be brief, so I'll jump right into this and first introduce the guest panelists that I've invited. It's quite a good group, and a good number of people, and also all good friends. I'm going to ask them to first introduce themselves and give a brief overview of their interest in the river and why they're here and speak to a couple of questions I've already prepped them on: One, what do you see as future productive intersections of recreation, river management and industry on the Mississippi River; and, two, what are the pressing issues challenging the future viability of the Mississippi River Basin? And then we'll see how it spins off from there, and end with a Q & A.

So, here we go, from one side of the barge to the other—Dustin Whited, our host, from Continental Cement Company. Kristin Fleischmann-Brewer from the Pulitzer Arts Foundation. Eddie Brauer and Chuck Theiling, both from U.S. Army Corps of Engineers. Eddie works in the Applied River Engineering Center here in the St. Louis District and Chuck is a river rat and he's always kayaking around, and now he's stationed in Vicksburg, Mississippi, but he's spent a lot of time upriver in the pools and backwaters. Colin Wellenkamp, executive director for the Mississippi River Cities and Towns Initiative. Mike Clark and Christine Ingrassia from Big Muddy Adventures. Christine is wearing an important second, political, hat tonight as alderwoman for the City of St Louis representing our 6th Ward. But before I forget, I need to first give a shout out to Christine, because if it wasn't for her and her willingness to put me in touch with Dustin, we literally would not be here today. But even backing up a bit, I need to thank Roo Yawitz, who is not here today. He might be out on the river somewhere. Roo manages Big Muddy Adventures and is the guy that initially

Derek Hoeferlin introducing panelists on Continental Cement Company platform barge, St. Louis, Missouri, 2019 (image credit: Derek Hoeferlin)

Continental Cement Company hopper barge, St. Louis, Missouri, 2019 (image credit: Derek Hoeferlin)

connected me to Christine, so let's just say this all starts, and maybe ends, with Big Muddy Adventures, so I am incredibly grateful for all of those connections. OK, I digress, back to the panelists. Ted Kratschmer from the National Great Rivers Research and Education Center, just upriver in Alton. Todd Antoine from Great Rivers Greenway. And last but not least, Rachel Bartels with the Missouri River Waterkeeper Alliance. Rachel and I like to go up in Cessnas over St. Louis and photograph floods and other complicated things like our region's crazy reliance on the coal-fired power plants, built in our floodplains, and that circumscribe the St. Louis region.

I'd like to make our way down the line, starting with Colin, and for him to set the stage, both bluntly and economically, since I'm not sure the conversation with this project has been framed in that capitalist, globalized context. But first, and to reiterate, the overall theme for this dialogue, which I admit is possibly overly simplistic and probably not too smart, is to get people's varied points of views about the complicated intersections of recreation, industry, and river management, as well as the Mississippi River Basin's future challenges. But I do want people to get deeper into the critical, anthropogenic theme on the overall HKW project. And that's why this panel is up here, because each comes at this with varying views, and I believe that is super important.

Colin Wellenkamp: Good afternoon, thank you so much Derek for the invitation to be here today. I know most of the folks that are my fellow panelists and have worked with many of them, a star-studded group here, much more eloquent and incredible than I am so I'll keep mine brief. I run an association of United States mayors, 95 mayors on the Mississippi River in all ten states. So, geography quiz: the northernmost city on the Mississippi River is…? Bemidji, Minnesota, very good. Bemidji, Minnesota all the way down to New Orleans—2,500 miles of waterway. *It is the world's most important river. In the world's most important river basin.* We produce more food and more commodities than any other basin on earth. And we move more. Forty percent of the world's food supply comes out of the Mississippi River Basin. An additional 40 percent of *all* United States agricultural output from coast to coast moves right by here, up and down this river. One in every twelve human beings on earth ingests commodities made in the Mississippi river basin. If you wanted to destroy or otherwise compromise the globe's food web, shut down the Mississippi River for thirty days in two places and the food web of the planet will collapse. Eighty percent of what is grown in the Mississippi River Basin goes overseas. The rest is used here for different domestic purposes, mostly, almost half now, is for fuel, renewable biofuels. Most of the commodities that leave our basin, destined for other ports around the world, have the majority of it turned into industrial animal feed: pellets. Our largest purchaser is China. They grow 20 percent of the world's food but they eat all of what they grow. Every single piece of food they grow they eat there, and none of it leaves their country. The rest they get from us and places like Brazil. Only one-sixth of China's land is arable. The rest can't grow crops. However, they can graze as many animals as they want, so they buy our commodities, and turn it into industrial feed, and those animals eat the feed, and they eat the animals. So, the bread and butter of our valley is the global commodity supply chain. Our mayors depend on this river for manufacturing (1), tourism (2), and agriculture (3).

Those are the three top economies on the Mississippi River. We just went through the longest, largest flood in United States history. It was a basinwide flood. It took place from November 1, 2018 to July 25, 2019. It was 270 days of consecutive flood fighting. It blew all the previous records away. That flood occurred from Pennsylvania to Oklahoma, and from Minnesota to Louisiana. It was of epic proportions. Our cities had high water for so long, the soil and all the infrastructure inside it actually liquefied and shifted as much as half a mile away in some places underneath our cities. So that type of impact on the infrastructure is considerable. We're now looking at a 3 to 8 percent loss of our economy annually, due to natural disasters. This was an unprecedented event, and it's only four years after the last 200-year event. Which was only four years after the last 500-year event. So, these are stacking up and they're getting very expensive. This flood will be north of $10 billion basinwide in actual losses, for sure. So for our mayors they have something very important to consider. Jesse, I think you talked about the sense of place that the Mississippi River is. For so long, particularly in the last century, our cities have turned their backs on the Mississippi River and considered it a liability—something that is from the past and to be controlled and ignored. And detached from. Now the river is going through a renaissance of sorts, in some places. Now some mayors see this river as their number-one asset, their future, and the reason their cities exist, and the undercurrent and depth of their heritage. So, we're working very hard with very little money and a heck of a lot of disasters to recapture this river and everything it offers us. I'll just end with one of the solutions that we see to counteract these floods as a result from the increasing climate risk, is a deployment of natural infrastructure. These floods would not be so expensive, nor would the droughts be, if we had the wetlands that we used to have, and the marshes and the forests. We have removed 80 percent of the wetlands in the entire Mississippi corridor. Those were natural absorption points for impacts. Hold water in dry periods and absorb water in wet periods. With all that gone, the water has nowhere to go but inside our cities, unfortunately. So, we see deploying new wetlands, new marshes, reconnecting backwater areas and reconnecting floodplains back to the main channel as one of our single most important, most effective ways of dealing with increased climate risk. It doesn't saddle us with expensive infrastructure that we have to maintain and repair, and it has ancillary benefits, creating heatsinks which reduce the heat island effect for our cities, which prolong the life of built infrastructure. And all of that natural infrastructure cleans our water. It also increases our property values, and makes our cities and our regions most resilient and more adaptive to what's happening to the planet at the global scale. And trust me, that scale is critical. Mayors used to treat this river as a problem just in their backyard, and now we treat it as corridor, river-basin scale level. Everything we do as an association operates considering the *entire* river, all the way to the Gulf of Mexico, and all of its assets and all of its needs. I'm going to give you an example and then I'm going to shut up. The flood this year was the worst in Davenport Island. They reached a new flood record. Nine miles of Davenport's riverfront park is designed to flood. That park is their flood control solution. It is a piece of natural infrastructure. It is amazing to see this happen. If Davenport had pushed that water with a floodwall or a levee, back out into the channel, I would lose five to six cities. They would be gone today. They would cease to exist. But if we absorb that risk on site, instead of sending it out to our neighbors and if each of us does that and contributes to that capacity, we create a new thriving corridor, that might have a chance—I say might—in the climate future we're facing. So, thank you for being out here. And Derek, thank you again for putting this together. What a logistical lift, but I'm so glad you're here and connecting all of us to learn about this important river. Thanks.

Mike Clark: I'm the founder, the senior guy at Big Muddy Adventures. So, nineteen years ago I moved here to St. Louis as an educator, as a teacher, and I decided I was very frustrated with a classroom with walls and I went to Lake Itasca, and built a virtual schoolhouse from my canoe and paddled to the Gulf of Mexico. We were connecting students virtually to us long before that become a thing. Along the way I went with my dear friend and he was guiding and I got bit—or as we say, I got the mud in my toes and I couldn't shake it out. I've paddled over 23,000 miles of the great rivers, give or take, one of the great joys is to have people such as yourselves, every one of you, come out there and experience the river in a way that we have been experiencing for over 5,000 years—and that's in a canoe. And to do that, when I first started, that was fairly difficult because when you start a business and your first marketing line is trying to drag people out to a place where they've been told over and over is a dangerous place where they're probably going to die, um, that's a tough sell. But over time, over years, more and more people have gone out and experienced the river, in a canoe, and then kayaks and so on, and we've built up kind of a foundation of basin people and it gets easier and easier to go out here, even here in this industrial part of the river, and find a sense of recreation and a little bit of peace and reconnecting. Which I think is really important for this city in particular, reconnecting people back to the reason why it exists, that in and of itself is I think a good mission.

Eddie Brauer: I'm a river engineer here with the U.S. Army Corps of Engineers and the St Louis district and also Mississippi Valley division. My job—and it's great that I'm speaking after these two guys—is really to balance everything they just talked about. My job is to come up with designs to help us *train* the river to ensure that we can get the navigation that we need to support all the economics that Colin mentioned, but also to make sure that we have a good safe channel for Mike Clark when he's out giving tours and experiencing the river the way that many have for thousands of years. So, what we do with the Corps, is that we design different types of structures to help manage the sediment to move through so that we're able to get the depths that we need for navigation. We use a lot of innovative approaches to not only facilitate the navigation, but also to be able to create some different types of environmental habitat. Unfortunately, we can't really see any of those structures that we have out here because the water is at about flood stage. So, the structures that we have out there are quite a bit lower obviously than the water surface that we currently have. But our regulating works project is what we use to maintain navigation. Within the whole entire Corps portfolio, it's the most economically justified and most environmentally acceptable project that the Corps is doing right now. So that's my spiel and I'll wait for questions.

Chuck Theiling: I am currently with the Corps of Engineer Research and Development Center (ERDC) down in Vicksburg, Mississippi. Previously, I was upriver in Davenport, Iowa, working for the Corps' Rock Island district for a long time, and that's when I met Derek who already was looking at anthropocene issues. With the help of Dale Morris at Royal Netherlands Embassy in Washington DC, Derek and John Hoal and others at Wash. U., along with the advocacy groups American Rivers and Earth Economics, we organized a couple of interdisciplinary workshops that brought Dutch and American experts together here in St. Louis, as well as with communities to sketch out future-forward design scenarios to adapt to flooding and drought issues regionally. And then how could these climate adaptation strategies positively affect us for the next century or so, all the while recognizing that there's all sorts of unforeseen changes that will be coming our way, and not just climate-related. That's why it's so important to get all of these different disciplines together and working together to find interdisciplinary approaches. So, it's unusual to have engineers and ecologists and architects and artists and economists and lawyers and politicians and environmentalists and academics and river rats and community developers all in one place, but this is exactly what it takes to make these systems work together, and so cool to do it out here, with all of you, on a working barge in north St. Louis. From my perspective, I've worked on river ecosystem projects in the space between the bluffs and the river channels themselves and backwaters and showing students and communities the differences in the life forms that live both in the hydraulic channels and also within the drier backwaters. The other aspect of what we do is we look from the bottom of the river up to the watershed and work with good people like Eddie Brauer, who's a geomorphologist working in the river, and there are a lot of other guys like him working in the watershed. They've taught us some really important lessons about how materials move from sources in the headwaters, through these pathways which are rivers and down to the various sinks where the sands and the nutrients and all this stuff settles out. It's really interesting when you're looking at how different materials move through these systems. And that's what the engineers and ecologists and water quality experts are doing together. We are seeing how materials are flowing from the sources through these systems and where can we make operations and interventions more sustainable along the way.

Christine Ingrassia: I serve as the Sixth Ward alderwoman in the City of St Louis. My ward does not touch the river at all but I seem to be one of the only alderpersons who makes the river a priority of the city. When I first got involved with river issues in the winter of 2016, I was pretty shocked by how high the floodwaters were and tracked down something called the Galloway Report which was released subsequent to the 1993 flood, and I figured out pretty quickly that we have not implemented most or any of the recommendations that were set forth in that report. I met up with Mike Clark and his partner Roo Yawitz when we went and did a river cleanup just a couple months prior and I asked if I could take a colleague of mine out on the river, so we could see the flooding from there. And from there I was kind of hooked. I think most people, if you're from St. Louis, know that everyone has a story about how dangerous the river is, but typically it's not an actual connection. It's like "my cousin's sister's boyfriend's dog looked at the river and drowned immediately" and so I started trying to hope to change that narrative. I try to get elected officials out here. We had a group from the new county executive's office, some of his staff members, some new aldermen, some new reps to paddle out here. Our water director of the City of St. Louis should be coming out with us in a couple of weeks just so that we can try and change the narrative. Actually, former mayor Francis Slay was the mayor who actually founded the Mississippi River Cities and Towns initiative that Colin directs, and I think it's really important and one of the first efforts to really comprehensively address river issues from source to sea. We are also completely, and uniquely situated here at the confluence of the two largest moving bodies of water on this side of the planet. And it's freshwater. So if you're paying attention, water politics is one of the new things that people are going to be really mired in, because there's such a lack of fresh water and people who are not paying attention to that issue will be behind. And I think in St. Louis we definitely need to be at the forefront of those conversations since we have a lot of water, mismanaged as it currently may be. Our water plant currently has the capacity to produce much more drinking water than it already does and is set to do some significant infrastructure improvements here soon once we get the legislation on the ballot and passed. So, I'm really appreciative of all of you being here and being interested and I hope that you take away not just something from today in particular, but something that you can do for our great rivers here.

Kristin Fleischmann-Brewer: I'm the director of public engagement at the Pulitzer Arts Foundation in Grand Center here in St. Louis. I guess I could say that my work at the Pulitzer is that I work with artists and community organizations to do different types of projects on topics that are both socially and civically relevant to your lives, but looking at the lens and feeding it through art. So, it's both poetic and practical and building interdisciplinary partnerships to look at things differently and get people involved. So maybe two quick examples because I realize that I'm literally looking at the site of one of our collaborative projects from here on the barge. Directly behind you, just downriver is the old Cotton Belt building where we worked with an artist a few years ago. His name is Chris Kallmyer, and he came in and dug clay from the riverfront and built chimes. I think over there is one of our chime players. But we spent a year with him listening and thinking and getting a group of people together talking about the city and social topics and we used the sediment material to make instruments. Then we had a series of performances and workshops about listening. So that might be a poetic example of a project we would do to build community that directly ties into our ecological and river system. A more practical project that is happening right now is with the landscape artist Chris Carl. Chris is from the region, and a lot of you might have seen his work already at the Granite City Arts and Design District (G-CADD), but he's currently working on bringing an infrastructure project across the street from the Pulitzer Museum as we look at it in relation to our campus in Grand Center. And it's about an acre site and it's all about channelling stormwater runoff into the site through rain gardens and rainscaping techniques to reduce the impact on these combined river overflow systems that we have here, which then once we get too much stormwater, it overflows the system and goes right into this river. And so he has designed this project which I hope you'll all come and see which is both very practical and connects back to the river system, but also the way that he's done it as a designer and as an artist has revealed the archaeology of the site so you can see layers of history and special plants that he's used as well. So that's something that I'm working on now, and I hope you all come and see it.

Rachel Bartels: I'm the cofounder and director of the Missouri Confluence Waterkeeper. We're a grassroots conservation organization focused on advocacy and enforcement of the Clean Water Act here in the St. Louis region and throughout Missouri. I think like many people, growing up in St. Louis I felt massively disconnected from our rivers. They were these muddy looking things you drive across, not living, evolving ecosystems that also provide drinking water, recreation, and respite from city life. I grew up learning about Mark Twain and the economic importance of the Mississippi River, but the closest I got was maybe Boat McDonalds a few times a year. Like Muddy Mike said, we're taught that the river is a dangerous place, so the thought of actually paddling on the Mississippi River was never something I even considered. In 2018, I got out there for the first time, and the experience shifted my entire perspective on our interconnectedness and the responsibility we have to protect this great river. Waterkeepers have been around since the 1960s, when a group of fishermen united to save the Hudson River in New York. Their style of citizen-led advocacy ensured that laws were enforced and that their river, livelihood, and the health of their families were all protected. The Hudson Riverkeeper's success and their tough, grassroots brand of environmental activism that sparked the Hudson River's miraculous recovery was an inspiration to many. So in 1999, the Waterkeeper Alliance was founded to support the growing number of "keepers" organizing to protect local waterways. Today there are over 340 Waterkeepers in 44 countries protecting almost three million square miles of watersheds.

Here in Missouri we work to protect the environmental, recreational, and commercial integrity of the Lower Missouri and Middle Mississippi watersheds. We're out on the rivers monitoring water quality, investigating pollution, and working collaboratively to address issues that impact the people and wildlife that depend on our waterways. On behalf of our community and members, we act as a voice for the rivers. St. Louis is in a unique and important position at the confluence of two of the greatest rivers in the world. We have a responsibility and the great opportunity to have a positive impact on the way we engage with our rivers and prepare for future challenges. Referring back to what Colin said about the unprecedented flooding in 2019 and the increasing frequency of these massive flood events, it's definitely time to rethink our critical infrastructure and floodplain development. As Derek mentioned, we flew around a few times during the flooding to survey damage to our coal energy plants, and the Sioux Energy Center near the Missouri-Mississippi confluence looked like an island. We have these massive coal power plants disposing of toxic waste in unlined pits in the floodplain. We know coal ash is toxic. We're drinking this water. We're fishing, eating fish, and recreating in this water, exposing our bodies to this water and everything in it. In recent years we have also seen a dismantling of clean water protections such as Waters of the U.S. (WOTUS), designed to protect valuable resources like wetlands, which are critical to flood mitigation. At the state level, we are faced with deregulation and lack of enforcement of clean water laws. The problem is that all water is connected, and what someone does upstream impacts everyone. As Alderwoman Ingrassia said about water politics, access to clean, freshwater sources like the Mississippi should not be taken for granted. According to the EPA, in 2019, 318 million pounds of toxins such as nitrates, arsenic, mercury, benzene, and other carcinogens were released into the Mississippi River watershed and ultimately the Gulf of Mexico. Thanks to regulations and laws like the Clean Water Act, our rivers don't catch on fire anymore, but we still dump sewage, industrial waste, and trash into them with little thought of longer term consequences. Things like recreation, river management, and industry can coexist on our rivers but we need to be smart about it. Innovation and creativity are key, and just because something has been done one way for many years doesn't mean it's the right way or the best way. Connecting people to the river is a critical step to engaging people in its protection.

Todd Antoine: I work at Great Rivers Greenway, and for those who aren't from St Louis, we are a regional park district that was created by the voters in St. Louis City, St. Louis County, and St. Charles County back in 2000, so we're a multicounty park district with the mission of building an interconnected system of greenways, parks, and trails. My job at the agency is to work with a team of project managers who are out building the various greenway trail systems. One of the greenways runs right through this site along the Mississippi. It is named the Riverfront Trail and runs twelve miles from where we are up to the historic Chain of Rocks Bridge. And one of the things that I think is always fascinating is that in St. Louis you hear the stories and think "oh the river is dangerous," but actually people are fascinated by the river. We talk to residents all the time that are just out here watching the river, looking at the barges, looking at the birds, just coming down here to experience the river. It is something that more and more people are realizing is such a national treasure for us to have in St. Louis. And to have the confluence right up not too far from us here in the city is really something special. And one of the things that we're hearing more and more, is people are going to have more access to the river, not just looking at it, but to actually be on the water and to get out and engage the river. I think that's something that we're all interested in seeing, and how we can complement that access. This is a great opportunity because I think that people want it. There's a spot just right downriver from here north of the Arch known as Laclede's Landing, which is the one spot basically in the entire 28 miles in the city of St. Louis that doesn't have any flood protection. We're building a park there that's going to be started soon and will overlook the river. It is going to become a neat little spot to just get outside and watch the river, watch the barges go by, watch the sunrise and the sunset.

Ted Kratschmer: I work for the National Great Rivers Research and Education Center, just upstream in Alton, Illinois, by Melvin Price Locks and Dam 26. We do research and education on the Mississippi River. We try to do very applied research to take the data that we collect or have been collected by numerous federal, state, and local agencies and turn that data into knowledge. With the hope that managers and policymakers can make better decisions about river management. Part of our philosophy about being an education center along with a research center, is the research we do without being able educate people, children through to adults, often will live in a vacuum. So, one of the programs we have is to work closely with groups including Big Muddy Adventures, to get kids out on the river through several of our projects. I live here in the City of St. Louis, and I travel about thirty miles to and from my office. You've heard it a lot today but I'm probably between a quarter and a half mile from the river along that whole thirty miles and I see it only twice, once when I get to my office and I can see it out the window, and once when I cross the Poplar Street Bridge and the McKinley Bridges. That's because we've literally walled it off, the entire way. And so, without the actual connection of people in the region to the river, it's hard to get anywhere, literally and philosophically. So, I think making this connection is a very important thing. As an aside, I'm a river rat. I spend a lot of time on the river, both personally and for work, so it's a treat always to be out here. This is a very cool part of the river. Going upstream is much different and also a very cool part of the river. One thing that people aren't familiar with is the great fishery in this river. This part of the river especially was known for trophy catfish, and blue catfish in particular. From downstream all the way up to Mel Price Locks and Dam 26 is a phenomenal catfish route. This part of the river is known for huge catfish up to 100 pounds or more. And they can be caught right in this stretch of river. So even though it is largely industrial, it still remains a very productive river, ecologically, and I think it's up to us to keep it that way.

Dustin Whited: I'm the one that's been yapping at you during the tour all day through the red megaphone with Derek. I am the site manager here; I've been the site manager for about three years at this site. I also work on projects at other sites up and down the river. I guess I'm the de facto corporate America representative here. You can throw eggs at me if you want, but as a private citizen yet corporate American, my goal is always to try and push all the businesspeople towards doing something that actually means something. Something that makes a difference, something that makes an impact. This project is a great opportunity to do that. I hope that everybody walks away from here not just fascinated by what we have out here, but more importantly, fascinated by what potential exists out here on this river and the future that can be if we just make it happen. That's most of my involvement with the river. Again, I've been doing it for three years and up and down the river I see the way different cities have done different things on the riverfronts, and I think St. Louis is way behind even a city like Memphis—and that is saying something. They've invested in their riverfront, both in terms of design and security. It looks beautiful. They have Mud Island, and things like that that bring recreation and people to the river. I am hopeful that in the future that industry and recreation can find a way to coexist together to make that kind of thing happen here because, again, this place is just flooding with potential, and I hope we can harness that.

Derek: Alright, thanks a lot. We've got a lot of really smart, cool people up here that are interested in the river. So, I'd like to detour a bit from the original two questions, to maybe push it a little bit and jump into bigger, bombastic ideas. I'm going to start with you Dustin, because when you first welcomed me out here back in August, I asked you if there was one thing you could do, along this stretch of the river, to make the barges go smoother for the river industry, maybe regardless of other issues like, say, history and culture and ecology and significant works of military infrastructure and the like, what would be the *one* thing that needs to happen to make the barge industry sustain itself? And then I would like the conversation to spin out from there.

Dustin: So, this may sound pretty controversial to this audience, and maybe it's my corporate America side coming out, but one of the biggest limitations that we saw during the flooding this year was getting barges to our facility. Despite those challenges of access, we're completely capable of loading and unloading barges until the water goes over that floodwall just over there, to the west of us. Unfortunately, the harbor closes at about 38 feet, so it's really difficult to get barges here when we reach that river stage. During this recent spring flooding, I had a whole bunch of barges that were south of here, down by the JB Bridge, all fleeted up. And since I couldn't get those barges, a lot of projects around the city came to a screeching halt—homes being built, roads being poured, safer sidewalks being installed … *huge economic projects.* To the point—the biggest limitation that we saw here in St. Louis was the height of the historic Eads Bridge, that you can see from here just in front of the Arch. The steel arches wouldn't allow passage, given the short distance between the high water and famous arches. We could find boats that had enough horsepower but they were too tall to fit underneath the bridge, or vice versa, they could fit under the bridge but the boats didn't have enough horsepower. And so because of that, I think that eventually that historical bridge needs to become a part of history, maybe in a museum somewhere so that we can open up navigation on the river here in situations like that.

Derek: So, to those who are not from here, do people realize the significance of the Eads Bridge? It's one of the most important historical steel-span bridges in the world, since at the time, in the late 1800s, it held the record as the longest rigid span between piers, anywhere in the world. And in engineering terms, arguably it's as important, if not more important, than the Brooklyn Bridge, since it was completed just a few years earlier. And on top of that, during the construction of the Eads Bridge, that's when they started to figure out what "the bends" and "caisson disease" were—all that bad stuff. So, it's pretty historically significant, and beautiful, no less, and Dustin is saying—just get rid of it, right? So that's an example of a simple, bombastic solution.

Dustin: Maybe get rid of it, maybe engineer something around it. Maybe something even bigger, a bigger idea like a canal that goes around. Or if you look at it from here, you can see that the piers that go into the water are misaligned with the other bridges, which makes it really hard for riverboat pilots. That's because the other bridges are designed for rail traffic, and not sure if you know, but rail and barge and truck traffic are in serious competition with each other, so the misalignment is intentional to screw with the barge captains. If you talk to a boat pilot out here on the river, they tell you they don't want to do it. They don't want to go through there. Maybe some of you saw on the internet earlier this year there was viral video of the Eads Bridge, of a towboat losing its cabin and hitting right down there on one of those arches. So as the river goes up, that arch gets lower and closer to the water so you can only fit smaller and smaller, far less efficient, things underneath it.

Ted: I suspect Eddie has something to say about this, but one of the reasons the harbor closes at such a high level is because the weight from the barges put a huge stress on the levees, which is one of the consequences of confining the river in such a way. So, I'll just say that.

Eddie: Sure, but I'm going to go in a totally different direction. But first off, we haven't seen any barges go by since we've been out here, but generally they're about 1,200 feet long by 110 feet wide. When we get into the lock and dam system which is just upstream from here, once we get past the lock that's just right up here in the Chain of Rocks Canal, there are no restrictions on what size they can be. Obviously, they need to be able to control their barges. If they have an accident, that's a big economic impact. But no, like I said, I'm going to go in a different direction and you know we have some restrictions on our bridges, there are also safety issues with our levees and our floodwalls. But the one thing that we do have control over is at low water. So, we have issues here in the harbor—we have high water during floods and we have extreme low water when we don't have enough water. And one of the things that we've done here, particularly in the St. Louis harbor, is come up with different strategies to get additional depth that we need for navigation during low water while also keeping facilities like this one open. So, the strategy we've used for hundreds of years is called "river training," to keep the channel against the city of St Louis because it naturally wants to shift east to Illinois and the American Bottom Floodplain. And by the way, one of the first river training structure projects was here in St. Louis in an effort by Robert E. Lee, yes that Robert E. Lee, to do just such. If not done, it would have made the city look very different if all the industry was on the Illinois side here. But you know the traditional way is that we can essentially restrict the river, right. We make it narrower which then gets additional depth. And if we still applied that engineering solution here for us to get navigation over there, we'd have to cut off over in areas like this when we couldn't access it. So, if the water was lower you could see a series of horseshoe-shaped structures upstream and those are known as "chevrons," and the purpose of those structures is to get the constriction we need in the main channel while also creating a secondary channel for access. So, there's a facility that's just about a mile upstream. In the past, when they had low water they were only able to access their facility for maybe, I'm throwing out a ridiculous number, just maybe 70 percent of the time. Now that we've put in these new structures, they can now access it all year long. And they've been able to have a lot of economic activity as a result of the chevrons.

Derek: If you want to see some drawings of mine of those chevrons, you can see them exhibited on the shipping container wall over here. If I can just go real quick back to Mike, because I want to stay on the topic of bridges for a few minutes, but in a completely different light. I vividly remember earlier this month when we were paddling this stretch and we were talking about the "big one," the big New Madrid fault earthquake coming someday....

Mike: So, I've circumnavigated St. Louis five times. People in St. Louis don't realize it, but we live on an island, surrounded by the Meramec, Mississippi, and Missouri rivers, which is literally the "Great River Ring" of the Great Rivers Greenway initiative, and all of that. There are only seven miles of land, that's highway 47 between Union and Washington, that is not river. In that ring there are 42 bridges, and what I hear from geologists, it's not a question of if a big earthquake hits us, but it's a question of when. And to my knowledge of the bridges circling the ring from Washington to Union, all the way around, the only one that'll stand after "the big one" is this one, the "Stan Span" directly behind us.[3] So, I don't know if I want to be stuck on the island with all of you. So, you just come and see me. I've got a navy. I've got a lot of boats. We can get a bunch of people out of here.

Derek: I didn't mean to take it in an apocalyptic direction. What else? Does anybody else want to talk about some big things that should happen? Or little things?

Colin: So, we're going to have to have a real "coming to Jesus" moment here real soon. Mike and I were talking about this earlier. We're now at $200 billion in actual losses along this corridor from 2005 to 2018. And I'm not counting the floods in 2019. Those numbers should be out later this year or early next year.[4] *Two hundred billion.* That's just actual property loss. I'm not talking about the costs in ripple effects to the supply chain or the displaced populations—none of that. So, if these events are going to keep coming at us fast, furiously, and persistently, and they're getting worse each time. And it's not just floods, it's droughts too. Droughts and intense heat. My mayors are actually more worried about droughts than we are floods. We can't clean mud for drinking water, as our water managers tell us. So, 50 cities, 20 million people drink this surface water right here, including me and my little girl and my wife, and all of you if you're drinking water from the City of St. Louis. Four hundred million gallons per day is pumped out of this river right here and put into people. It is one of the best sources of water in the world and it's actually one of the most secure. As long as we have a functioning EPA that does what it's supposed to do. So, these disasters are exacerbated by the fact that we constrict the river. But, we're going to have to change some things. Levee systems that come all the way up to the water's edge, right here, and are extremely high, dangerously high, too high for the Corps to certify with no setbacks so the Corps won't certify them for that reason either, they create very dangerous situations for our cities. To protect land where no one lives in order to put at risk land where everybody lives. Those "where no one lives" areas are very politically powerful. And I'll let you know, it's a big secret in America. Rural America controls American politics. That's just the way it is. And most of my cities are rural cities. Most of my mayors manage cities of 2,000 people or less. I only have seven cities with populations above 100,000. Everybody else is rural America. Some of my mayors are full-time grain farmers. So, we depend on farmland. We depend on the agricultural economy. But we're going to have to engineer this stuff in order to let water move around a little bit more than it does now, or we're gonna have such an expensive impact from climate risk that you'll see areas let go. We just won't have the money to address it anymore. It's just going to get too expensive, and we're not going to repair it. So, to avoid that, there's a lot of interests that have to come to the table and I would urge all of you to look into, as a possible career path, public administration and elected office like Christine. These are the folks that will end up making the ultimate decisions on what to do with these resources. I'm a policy guy, so I try to engineer policies for our mayors and help them work through policy challenges so we have positive impact on the ground through the law. But it really comes down to what is the direct impact from the way we manage these resources going forward. So those are some of the significant challenges, and real-world challenges that we're facing right now and a lot of times our mayors, when we get together, we talk about how can make regular Americans care about this river instead of just drive over it. We make coffee with it. We make beer with it. And we make wine with it. So you drink it in the morning, drink it in the midday and drink it at night. That's how we can make people care about it. And all the stuff that goes into those drinks is growing here. It moves here. So that kind of kinetic connection is basically where policy meets mainstream. Y'all are the future of that, so hoping you can help.

Chuck: Colin said a couple of things that gave me a couple of ideas. I got into this really because I wanted to help farmers do a better job, and we have farmers all over this watershed in the uplands and in the floodplains. I've worked in the Minnesota River Basin and also I am a planner, by training and by nature in my old job, so what we have learned as planners, and Eddie knows all too well is that as engineers we use models in our design and evaluation phases. And what we've been trying to do in the Corps is to use hydrologic models to track water and materials moving through the system. And that's what we're doing up in Minnesota, and folks in Minnesota really like their water and they're good neighbors and they like people in New Orleans in the Gulf. So they're cleaning up the Minnesota River Basin to address Gulf of Mexico hypoxia as well as local nutrient enrichment and pollutants in the sediment and all that. But the point is that they—we—work as an interdisciplinary team of state agencies and federal agencies to use state water-resource models to track materials moving through the system, and we tested what would the material move through if it was a natural landscape from the 1800s, what would it look like now, what does it look like in the future when Minnesota puts in a 50-foot buffer law? And what does it look like in the future when there's nothing but agriculture, and what does it look like in a future with a lot more water quality treatment best management practices? And there was one more scenario, what does it look like with a major biodiversity emphasis? And we put all of that together and it was very interesting, and it took a long time. And the answer is so interesting and wild. We found that through all the hydrologic modeling, of course what we would love to do is set aside wetlands and stuff like that, but there's really not enough land left to do that. So you look at how much surface area is in soil, and the benefits of healthy soil and cover crops fell out as highly beneficial. You hear about these miracle farmers who can suck up to six inches of water into their cropland which should be a basinwide objective. And those are the kinds of solutions that I think are really integrative, where we can work with the upland people to keep resources up where they fall, rather than running through all our systems creating problems downstream.

Eddie: Real quick, one thing I think is worth noting, one thing that's really interesting about the U.S. and all the things that Colin said is, you know, we're late to the dance on this. I was just in the Netherlands last week, and I got a chance to look at some of their "Room for the River Programme" measures. They're doing a series of levee setbacks and floodways and different measures to lower the water surfaces and to reduce flood impacts and here we did that on the lower Mississippi River, after the 1927 flood. If you read John Barry's *Rising Tide*, you'll read all about a bunch of floodways and levee setbacks and everything else. The Room for the River Programme is actually based off a lot of those measures, although the Netherlands' versions are more multifunctional, so we can certainly learn from that. And then it stopped, right in 1993 we had the big flood, we had the Galloway Report and no one's done anything since. So, it's just really interesting how here in the U.S. we're really late to the dance on this type of policy.

Christine: And to add to that, we give a lot of lip service to being good stewards of the river. Especially, I mean I can speak for the City of St. Louis. We have a sustainability report; we had a grant to find a resiliency offer who came up with a really amazing report and then just upstream here, on the Mississippi, we allowed for the "Lighthouse St. Louis" development project. I don't think it is actually ever going to happen, and the City of St. Louis itself has paid, what I have been able to figure out to date, $500,000, to dump clean fill to have this area come out of the floodplain. This means that the river is now moving water differently than it used to, and flooding North Riverfront Park in different ways. So, we spent a lot of money on our plans for the City of St. Louis than I think other places, but when we have actual legislation come before us, everyone just rubber-stamps it, then a few of us get viewed as obstructionists if we start asking questions. So, back to your point. I think politicians are a huge problem, so please pay attention to that and who you're voting for.

Derek: We've got about a half hour left on the barge, so I think I'd like to open it up to the floor for questions.

Unknown Attendee: Just a general question, out of all the cities and small towns on the Mississippi, who is the most progressive in their policies, and who's doing the best job and what are they doing, specifically?

Colin: I would probably say Minneapolis and Saint Paul. Now the river is a little different in Minneapolis and Saint Paul, as the engineers can tell you. Here it's half a mile wide, up there it's not quite that big. But the Twin Cities have made this overt commitment around managing their river and their riverfront and developing it in a very smart way. You can probably see the renaissance of the riverfront most overtly there, as it winds through Saint Paul and Minneapolis. But again, it's less of a river that they have to manage than other places. On the big river side of things, Memphis was mentioned earlier and we just had our annual meeting in Memphis, where all our mayors came together there two weeks ago. Memphis just celebrated their 200th anniversary this year. They have done a tremendous amount of investment in their riverfront and in the Wolf River, which is a tributary of the Mississippi. It winds through Memphis neighborhoods, not unlike our River DePeres or the Meramec do here, but it's much more dense than River DePeres or the Meramec Valley. And when the Mississippi floods, the Wolf River backs up and that water goes into people's basements and homes. And it wasn't like that when there were natural assets there to absorb that. But now you have communities, neighborhoods, homes. You can't expect those people to move out. They've got nowhere to go and they don't have the finances to do that. So, what do we do? And the city is putting together, and has put together, some very, very progressive plans of holding water, in natural areas, along the Wolf River, and these natural areas in these neighborhoods create property value assets and these green ornaments in the area that attract business. This increases property values and home values, and creates resilience for those neighborhoods. Dubuque, Iowa, is another great example. They had the largest number of disaster declarations per capita in the nation, and that was due to a tributary, rolling off of a mountain, a small mountain, trying to get to the Mississippi River, and they put that tributary underground into pipes. It used to be aboveground, but they piped it, and those pipes were bursting and breaking, especially with increased rain events of the last 25 years. So literally homes were exploding from the pressure in these pipes. That's what was happening. So they dug them all up and they re-daylit the creek. They took out the pipes and they put the creek the way it used to be, just a natural flowing creek. Now, where an area of the city that no one wanted to live, where everyone was running from, is now the most desirable piece of property in Dubuque. It's got bike paths, it's got walking paths, it's got parks, it's got these winding trails next to it, it's got benches. And it winds its way through the city to the Mississippi River and it's where everybody wants to be. And it is a natural solution to a disaster vulnerability, a climate vulnerability. So those are some of the best examples I can come up with, where cities have really chosen to go that way. One of the cities on the opposite end of the spectrum that have some of the most significant challenges and that are going to take years and years and billions of dollars to make resilient, is New Orleans. New Orleans and Baton Rouge too, are both low-lying areas. Downriver from New Orleans they are going to reroute the Mississippi River to accommodate a new navigation canal while rebuilding the Delta. The Delta was a natural buffer to hurricanes, so in order to rebuild that, we've got to push that silt out of the way, the way that the river used to do that, but you can't have your cake and eat it too—if you do that you can't have navigation because you don't have enough of a channel. So, they want to create a navigation canal, and reroute the river alongside it, where it will rebuild the Delta to be a natural buffer. Because we're losing Delta, right? We're losing a football field every 90 minutes to the ocean. So those are some examples.

Mike: So those of you all that are paddling the length of the river, you have the opportunity to stop at various places. It's interesting when you do that, in my experience, paddling from Itasca to the Gulf, has been the cities that built walls, like that (pointing to the floodwall nearby), their downtown dies. Davenport, Iowa, is a thriving downtown area and it just got crushed by the flood. But they'll clean it up and they'll be back eventually. And there's actually stores and stuff like that instead of the old wino bar and a recycle place. Dubuque downtown, not doing so great. Memphis has opened it back up to the river, there are a lot of bluffs of course. But if you go down the river, you see places where they do this, where they wall the city off from the water, and those downtowns die quickly. That and Walmart comes in along the highways and so on, and that condition is ripe for them. So, the more that I think for instance, here, St. Louis, the more we open up access to the river the better, without compromising the high waters. Sure, if the river goes over that wall, forget about it, the downtown goes. But the more you can find ways to open it up, the more thriving the communities will become along the river. And let's not forget about all the small river towns. They just get crushed with the floods. And yet, they're still trying to maintain a connection to the river.

Eddie: Real fast, for people that aren't from around here, I want to throw in just one quick little challenge that we experience here in St. Louis. And that is the fact that between extreme low water and extreme floods, there's about 55 feet of difference in water level here in St. Louis. We get asked very often "you know, why don't you have a downtown like Minneapolis or something else," because those are controlled by dams so they have a consistent water level. And there's things we can do but I guess that's one unique challenge that we have, here on our riverfront is that 55 feet of water-level difference that we have to deal with.

Dustin: Which is why you see most of these structures to get out here have to get above the floodwall, and then you've got to have structures everywhere to actually support this floodwall, *which is not cheap to do.*

Derek: Any other questions or any other thoughts from people on the panel? If not, we can enjoy it out here and walk around all of this.

Emiliano Lopez: Who owns the riverfront? Who and what has legal rights? Is it public? Private? Both?

Christine: It depends, there are private property owners all along the river and then the City of St. Louis itself owns property too.

Mike: And then there's always the question about how far out to the river do you, can you, own? Is it out to the middle of the river, or wherever you call bank stabilization? So, for instance on the Meramec River, that's a big issue. In fact, a guy got shot and killed because an owner of property declared he owned all the way out into the river including the shoals and the sandbar and there was a guy having a beer on his property and the owner came down and blasted him away, declaring his ownership of his part of the river.

Eddie: It depends on what state you are in. Different states have different riverfront property rights.

Chuck: In Illinois, whoever has the bottom of the lake or the river, owns it. Other places have right of servitude, navigation servitude. But there's one really big striking difference. It's the flood control system from about this point all the way down south is maintained by the Corps of Engineers, but if you go north of here, the levee districts all the way up are individual entities, so it's really hard to coordinate floodplain management as you go north. So, it's a big difference.

Colin: We have what's called the MR&T. The Mississippi River Tributaries program is south of here, *and it's wonderful.* We don't have as many problems south of here because the Corps requires that those levees be set back and not above a certain height. But north of here it's the Wild Wild West. Missouri has no statute for levees at all, and Illinois has selective enforcement of its own levee statutes—basically, where Illinois wants to enforce it. And then you have different statutes in Iowa, Minnesota, Wisconsin and so on. So, it's a mismatched patchwork quilt and mayors get sort of caught in the middle of these things and get on the receiving end of levees that do not meet Corps certification. We wish the Corps had more stick. They have a lot of carrot, but not a lot of stick. So, if your levee is illegal, quote unquote, you're taken out of the Corps' program and the Corps won't come out and rebuild it for you if it gets destroyed. But that's about the extent of it. So, folks don't care. They just build what they want to build. As high as they want to build it, wherever they want to build it, and see what happens. And what happens is the water goes in our basements.

Eddie: Yeah, the consequence is, the shorter levee that is the legal height on the other side of the river overtops and their land is flooded. It's an arms race. I'll muddy the water a little more about this and that's with "flood fighting." You've got the wealthier levee districts that can go out and can sandbag more and put out protective measures that effectively raises their levee height. And then what happens to other people around them? Of course, the water is going to go higher and that makes their flood protection even less than they thought.

Derek: So, this might not be a good point to end on, but we're ending with the *law.* Take someone like Mark Davis down in New Orleans. He's a lawyer and friend of the water and the director of the Tulane Bywater Institute. Mark and I were on a panel together last spring about coastal and river urbanism challenges, hosted by Dean Iñaki Alday at Tulane School of Architecture. Mark put up maybe the two most powerful slides at the panel—two simple, text-only slides burned in my brain. The first shows about ten types of water law in the U.S., and I'll miss a few, but they include at the top ones like state, federal, tribal, and then further down ones like treaties, common, statutes, and so forth, and his point was, whether you're a lawyer or not, you better know the various water laws to engage any of these issues of water management. In the next slide, Mark goes as far to provoke, and I think he said something to the effect, "water management is driven by law, not hydrology, ecology, or any science." So therein lies the rub. Here in the United States, if we honestly think we are going to engage these challenges in an interdisciplinary way to propose adaptations to these challenges we're discussing today, it still comes down to one thing—the law that ultimately structures rights and resolves conflicts. Any other thoughts?

Eddie: We don't want to end on law.

Derek: Jesse Vogler, Matt Fluharty, our Field Station 3 hosts—what are your thoughts?

Jesse: Let's not end on something so negative as law and order.

Derek: I don't think it's a negative way to end. It's totally necessary. Take Louisiana for example. The law is huge in terms of the current state of the coast. Because law really puts a different understanding on coastal wetland loss. Again, I would need Mark Davis to correct me if I'm wrong, but it's my understanding people are literally losing their rights to their land when it becomes water. And then take what's happening post-Katrina for instance. Who owns the land in the Lower Ninth Ward when it becomes water? Or on the other side of the Lower Ninth Ward's back-levee where in Bayou Bienvenue, which is now mostly water, but was originally platted to be owned as land since it was a freshwater marsh with land? I guess people had rights to that land? That's why it becomes so raw to people when their land is dispossessed. But then that healthy freshwater marsh was washed away from saline intrusion and sea-level rise, and has now become mostly open water, mostly because of the adjacent Mississippi River Gulf Outlet boondoggle. And then their neighborhood was catastrophically destroyed from the hurricane because of that stupid Mississippi River Gulf Outlet's erosive effects. So, I'm really intrigued by that negotiation of the edge, of the floodwall, the levee, that separates the land from the water. If we need to end on something, it's "the wall" right, that floodwall *right over there*, right? That we as Americans think we need to foolishly defend ourselves with building bigger and more expensive walls? Anyone else have something more optimistic?

Lynn Peemoeller: Are there any shipwrecks around here? Any famous shipwrecking incidents?

Dustin: That's a very interesting question. You're actually sitting above a sunken barge. It sank here back when the bridge, the "Stan Span," was being built. There was a slow leak in the barge. It was on Super Bowl weekend, and by Monday morning the barge was pretty much vertical in the water. They called Marine Resources to come out and help them but by the time they got here the entire barge was underwater. Since then about 95 percent of it has been removed in very small sections and the barge was full of cement so it has made retrieving it very difficult. We also have to have water levels below zero gauge so we can get a crane in here and also have to move this barge out of this position to do the work.

Ted: There are sunken barges all up and down the river. Everywhere. Abandoned. Every once in a while, you'll see a hull poking out of the river. Sediment just covers them. Low water comes and reveals them. They're ephemeral. Sure, they're permanent, but seeing them is ephemeral. There's also a famous shipwreck just downstream along the floodwall at Chouteau's Landing just south of the Arch. It's a World War II minesweeper I think? I don't remember the name of it. It was parked at the riverfront in front of the Arch for many years, but the Great Flood of 1993 took it out. It reappeared in the 2012 record low water. Pretty interesting.

Chuck: In Vicksburg, they dug up and rebuilt an old warship from the Civil War. It's very cool to see the past in the present and then the future.

Derek: On that note, thanks to all of you so much. Let's enjoy the sunset and toast the Mississippi River!

1. Special thanks for funding support to *Mississippi: An Anthropocene River*, a project by Haus der Kulturen der Welt (HKW), Berlin, and the Max Planck Institute for the History of Science (MPIWG), Berlin, in collaboration with numerous international partners, funded by the German Federal Foreign Office as part of the initiative #WunderbarTogether as well as by the Max Planck Society.
2. Students in Derek Hoeferlin's Sam Fox School of Design & Visual Arts, Washington University in St. Louis, fall 2019 seminar: Samuel Bell-Hart, Xinyang Chen, Virginia Eckinger, Liz Hambor, Natia Kapanadze, Yongdi Li, Mason Radford, Erin Socha, Mingjian Suo, Mengru Wang, John Whitaker, Damon Xiang, Makio Yamamoto.
3. "Stan Span" is short for the "Stan Span Veterans Memorial Bridge," partially named after Stan Musial, considered the greatest St. Louis Cardinal to play major league baseball for the team.
4. In 2020, the Mississippi River Cities and Towns Initiative released a report saying there were $20 billion in total direct losses due to the 2019 floods, spread across 19 states. See: https://www.vicksburgpost.com/2020/03/09/2019-flood-caused-negative-economic-impact-of-more-than-20-billion/ (accessed June 06, 2020).

Tracing Our Mississippi

Alternative Modes of Site Interventions

with Washington University in St. Louis

In 2021, I was invited to participate as a University Design Research Fellow in the third iteration of Exhibit Columbus, co-curated by Iker Gil and Mimi Zeiger and titled *New Middles: From Main Street to Megalopolis, What is the Future of the Middle City?* Given that the site was in Columbus, Indiana, a central aspect to Gil's and Zeiger's vision was to situate Columbus, which is in the Ohio sub-basin of the Mississippi River Basin, and the installations within a renewed potential connectivity across the Mississippi Watershed. Given my research focus, I was invited to contribute *Tracing Our Mississippi*, an interactive installation with public programming components at the site of the Columbus Pump House, on a terrace adjacent to the Flatrock River.[1] **[Figure 1]** By representing the Mississippi Watershed as a large-scale, abstracted model, composed as a set of moveable pieces, the installation emphasized the relentless infrastructures controlling the Mississippi's landscapes, communities, and resources. **[Figure 2]**

Tracing Our Mississippi translated the *Mississippi River Basin Atlas*, previously presented in the Appreciate + Analyze portion of this book, into three dimensions.[2] Moving to the third dimension has always been a desire of mine while creating the 2D atlas, and this venue provided the perfect opportunity to do so. Intentionally abstracted, the model vertically exaggerated the watershed 200 times and is constructed 800,000 times smaller than the actual size of the Mississippi Watershed. These exaggerations of scale meant to bring a more one-to-one, human-scaled relationship to what are often only understood as abstract and confusing large-scale challenges. **[Figure 3]** Similar to the atlas, the model organized into three portions and was a giant puzzle of sorts: 1)

Missouri River Basin; 2) Arkansas-White-Red and Lower Mississippi River Basins; and, 3) Upper Mississippi, Ohio, and Tennessee River Basins. **[Figure 4]**

Layers of information overlaid on, and embedded within, the exaggerated topographies, levees, and levee-protected areas that were finished in white. Layers included: locks, dams, spillways, and floodways as red monoliths; crude oil pipeline networks as red dashed lines; ancestral tribal lands as curved black dots with black labels; current tribal reservations as solid black lines; state boundaries as black squares; and state names and cities as black labels. **[Figure 5]**

Amplifying methods of control, the installation asked: "Is the Mississippi Watershed really a watershed anymore?" This may be an open-ended, or maybe even a bizarre, question to ask in ending this book. But rather, maybe it is an important jumping-off question for what comes next for **Way Beyond Bigness: The Need for a Watershed Architecture**. In such a context, what does it mean to empower all of us to question our past methods of control and power, with the hope of reestablishing new, collective understandings, and in turn connecting all of us across ecological and cultural geographies? What would it mean to retrace our Mississippi, or the Mekong or the Rhine for that matter, or any global river basin? In an attempt to do so, I organized a public programming event with my research assistants Nathan Stanfield and Paul Wu and the storytelling artists Angie Tillges from St. Paul, Minnesota, and Monique Verdin from New Orleans and the Houma Nation. We put out a call for "Watershed Stories" seeking contributions in the form of stories, songs, poetry, interviews, essays, photographs, and drawings and other images, to help us re-story the Mississippi Watershed in an attempt to create a collectivism formed through the intimacies of our local stories. We all gathered in Columbus, Indiana, on a brisk fall day in October 2021 to share our diverse stories, and maybe more importantly, to be optimistic about the future of our shared watersheds. **[Figure 6]**

1. *Tracing Our Mississippi* installation team: Washington University in St. Louis Sam Fox School of Design & Visual Arts, Derek Hoeferlin (project design lead), Research Assistants: Nathan Stanfield (lead), Joel Leon, Weicong Huang, Qianshan Hu, Lindsey Compeaux, Gregory Cuddihee (shop technician); funding support: Washington University in St. Louis Sam Fox School Creative Activity Research Grant, "The Divided City" Mellon Foundation Graduate Student Summer Research Fellowship, Walter B. Kromm Endowed Intership. See: www.tracingourmississippi.com.

2. Mississippi River Basin Atlas team: Derek Hoeferlin (lead), Jess Vanecek, Paul Wu, Chenyu Zhang, Caroline Amstutz.

[Figure 1] View of "Tracing Our Mississippi" installed on terrace of Columbus Pump House, adjacent to Flatrock River, 2021 (image credit: Hadley Fruits, courtesy Exhibit Columbus)

[Figure 2] View of Lower Mississippi River Basin and Arkansas-White-Red River Basin components of installation; constructed out of CNC-milled foam, painted and attached to polycarbonate and plywood bases, 2021 (image credit: Hadley Fruits, courtesy Exhibit Columbus)

[Figure 3] Public opening of Exhibit Columbus, August, 2021
(image credit: Hadley Fruits, courtesy Exhibit Columbus)

[Figure 4] Aerial view of installation with the six Mississippi River sub-basins, 2021
(image credit: Hadley Fruits, courtesy Exhibit Columbus)

[Figure 5] Detail view of various layers of information, including confluence of crude oil pipelines passing through predominantly tribal reservations in Oklahoma, 2021
(image credit: Hadley Fruits, courtesy Exhibit Columbus)

[Figure 6] The story-telling artists Monique Verdin (pictured presenting) and Angie Tillges sharing their stories at the "Tracing Our Mississippi" public program, October, 2021 (image credit: Derek Hoeferlin)

Afterword "...to Quarantine Island"

"Big Muddy" Mike Clark

The first indication that Derek Hoeferlin's work and style align with my experience and passion occurred at our first meeting. The plan was to introduce his architecture students to the complex and ever-changing landscape of the Mississippi River by taking them on a field trip, or rather, a river trip.

A plan was hatched. We would paddle the whole group in thirty-foot Voyageur canoes from the confluence of the Missouri and Mississippi Rivers to the iconic Gateway Arch in downtown St. Louis. The canoe experience touches the origins of transportation on the waterways. The route would pass through 11 miles of noncommercial river channel, enter the port of St. Louis, pass under five bridges, including the historic Eads Bridge, and take out.

Of note on the credulity of this plan, there is a prevalent hometown myth about the Mississippi and Missouri Rivers. Don't go near them. But I was confident. Derek was bold and assured of the risk and reward. We went for it.

The trip was actually the very first meeting of his studio semester in fall of 2017. Over a dozen students arrived individually or in shared rides at the Kanu House, the original north St. Louis outpost of Big Muddy Adventures. The house is set one block from the river, with Cementland nearby, a 54-acre property infamously formed from a wasteland of industrial decay, and never finished.

Lacking a suitable meeting room to gather, I offered camp chairs under the shade of a tough, barely surviving peach tree in the side yard. Derek had not arrived as his group sat in bewilderment at the setting.

The diversity of the group, the language differences, the worldwide geographic range of cultural and racial and experiential perspectives, and the educational backgrounds, all blended as we introduced ourselves. I began to describe my sense of place, relative to the rivers, and expressed my excitement and my love for the extraordinary experience that they would share. I followed up with some basic guide talk about safety issues and comfort concerns. And then Derek arrived, camera slung over his shoulder.

I contemplated it for a minute. Yes, this is a design course. We shook hands, and he casually joined his group, appearing to me like a Bob Dylan figure. I stood amazed that this first encounter with his students was under a peach tree, in a postindustrial, decaying neighborhood of Riverview, one block from the Mississippi River. And as it turns out, Derek's family is from this neighborhood.

I knew that the perspective our group had at that moment would be dramatically changed by paddling past our location within three hours, a perspective from a canoe, half a mile into the main channel of the largest flowing body of water on our side of Earth. Everyone paddling. Together. Working together not by the passing of digital work, but rather by uniformity and proximity, real time, getting our paddle strokes together. The creative and empirical overwhelmed by the visceral, the tactile, the extrasensory awareness, and the Teamwork. A physical exercise of balance, strength, endurance, and technique with no experience necessary.

Since that first meeting, we have replicated this opening class for his studios or fieldwork seminars every year, and sometimes multiple times a semester—seven or eight times so far. Our explorations have introduced his students to the massive scale of the great rivers and their contested landscapes, and the structures that both purposefully and chaotically define it. The conditions have varied with season and climate effects. The routes have been planned to align with class projects. We have paddled in wind waves, towboat wakes, and over the Chain of Rocks rapids. Most recently, we paddled down the 8.4-mile Chain of Rocks Canal, which basically has no flow since it is a lakelike condition, all the while paddling against brutal 25-mile-per-hour headwinds. We have seen pristine islands with first-level habitats and passed through large locks and alongside towboats and barges.

I think I know a lot about the rivers, and yet I came to realize how much is possible to learn exploring rivers. One of the most profound experiences has been witnessing the end of Derek's projects and his unique methodology of design-research, especially from a "nondesign" point of view. They are magnificent in insight and technical calculation. Yet, better than the expertise, is the creativity and outside-the-box experience that is shared. From paddle perspective and waterline image, to drone- and eagle-view video, from floodplain to waterfall, to adventure and fun, this work is valuable. In digital form, it is timeless. But the perspective is rivertime.

Of note, this writing has occurred at a time of pandemic and social upheaval. At the outset of the Covid-19 outbreak, I took advantage of a mandated quarantine and took refuge on a Mississippi River island, solo with dog. I called it Quarantine Island. It is the very one, the one Derek and colleagues and I explored on our very first "field trip."

It is also the one that his father and family used to water-ski past decades ago, and where they got stuck in its willow trees and reeds.

For thirty days I lived roughly, if not skillfully, in a pristine setting of sand, willows, and cottonwoods, and amid the dawning of spring. Didn't quite make it to 40 (quaranta) days for other reasons. I was at one with my sense of place. I abided by the local directive to quarantine and protect us all by staying away from each other. And I contemplated how misunderstood our connection to the very essence of our survival here is. I lived disconnected from the chaos and threats of the pandemic to our community and I lived connected in an essential way to the Mississippi Watershed. It is the one essential thing we all share.

****

Personal note....

Derek's curiosity is infectious. He is as courageous as he is innovative. His collegial style, blended with a great knowledge of the rivers, are ingredients for the uniqueness of the river experience we share. Most of all, his projects are so fun!

"Big Muddy" Mike Clark on the Mississippi, St. Louis, Missouri, 2019 (image credit: Derek Hoeferlin)

Mississippi River during low stage at Mosenthein Island, St. Louis, Missouri, 2020 (image credit: Derek Hoeferlin's "Field Work 2.0: Reality + Remote = ???" seminar; drone photograph by Yiqi Jiang)

Chain of Rocks Low Water Dam, Mississippi River, north of St. Louis, Missouri, 2020. (image credit: Derek Hoeferlin's "Field Work 2.0: Reality + Remote = ???" seminar; drone photograph by Yiqi Jiang)